Time Out

Brussels Guide

Antwerp, Ghent & Bruges

Penguin Books

PENGUIN BOOKS

Published by the Penguin Group
Penguin Books Ltd., 27 Wright's Lane, London W8 5TZ, England
Penguin Books USA Inc., 375 Hudson Street, New York, New York 10014, USA
Penguin Books Australia Ltd., Ringwood, Victoria, Australia
Penguin Books Canada Ltd., 10 Alcorn Avenue, Toronto, Ontario, Canada M4V 3B2
Penguin Books (NZ) Ltd., 183–190 Wairau Road, Auckland 10, New Zealand

Penguin Books Ltd., Registered offices: Harmondsworth, Middlesex, England

First published 1996
10 9 8 7 6 5 4 3 2 1

Colour reprographics by Precise Litho, 34–35 Great Sutton Street, London EC1
Mono reprographics, printed and bound by William Clowes Ltd, Beccles, Suffolk NR34 9QE

Edited and designed by
Time Out Magazine Limited
Universal House
251 Tottenham Court Road
London W1P 0AB
Tel: 0171 813 3000
Fax: 0171 813 6001
E-mail: net@timeout.co.uk
http://www.timeout.co.uk

Editorial
Managing Editor Peter Fiennes
Editor Nicholas Royle
Consultant Editor Sarah Burnett
Copy Editor Kei Kikuchi
Researcher Jane Evans
Indexer Dorothy Frame

Design
Art Director Warren Beeby
Art Editor John Oakey
Designers Paul Tansley, Mandy Martin
Picture Editor Catherine Hardcastle

Advertising
Group Advertisement Director Lesley Gill
Sales Director Mark Phillips
Advertisement Sales (Brussels) Aneta Robinson

Administration
Publisher Tony Elliott
Managing Director Mike Hardwick
Financial Director Kevin Ellis
Marketing Director Gillian Auld
Production Manager Mark Lamond

Features in this Guide were written and researched by:
Introduction Sarah Burnett. **Essential Information** Joanne Fowler. **Getting Around** Jane Evans. **Accommodation** Steven Tate. **Brussels by Season** Joanne Fowler. **Sightseeing** Bridget Hourican (*Eyes wide shut* JG Ballard). **Architecture** Bridget Hourican. **History** Sarah Burnett (*Altered images* George Melly). **Brussels Today** Sarah Burnett. **Brussels by Area** Bridget Hourican. **Restaurants** Sarah Burnett. **Cafés & Bars** Sarah Burnett. **Shopping & Services** Steven Tate. **Museums** Elisabeth Unna. **Art Galleries** Bridget Hourican. **Media** Steven Tate. **Clubs** Steven Tate (*Andale, ándale, ándale...* Jane Evans). **Film** Sarah Burnett. **Music: Classical & Opera** Julius Stenzel. **Music: Rock, Folk & Jazz** Michael Leahy. **Sport & Fitness** Simon Read. **Theatre & Dance** Bridget Hourican. **Business** Joanne Fowler. **Children** Bridget Hourican. **Gay & Lesbian** Steven Tate. **Students** Elisabeth Unna. **Women's Brussels** Elisabeth Unna. **Trips Out of Town** Steven Tate. **Survival** Joanne Fowler. **Further Reading** Sarah Burnett, Nicholas Royle.

The editor would like to thank the following: Edouard Angelucci, JG Ballard, Belgo Centraal, Books for Cooks, Michael Booth, Sabine Buseyne, Sheila Chellun, Jonathan Coe, Feico Deutekom, Julie Emery, Peter Fiennes, The Harvill Press, Hotel Galia, Simon Ings, Maxim Jakubowski, Kei Kikuchi, Fraser McIlwraith, George Melly, Cécile Neyret, Jon Perugia, Brian Radcliffe, Simon Read, Kate Ryan, Steven Tate, Charles Van Deun.
In memoriam Paul Delvaux, John Van Der Griend.

Maps by Mapworld.

Photography by Jon Perugia except for pages 35 **Tate Gallery, London/Bridgeman Art Library**; 49 **Moulinsart, Belgium**; 65, 225, 228, 235, 241, 239 **Belgian Tourist Office**; 71, 79 **Hulton Getty**; 74 **Giraudon/Bridgeman Art Library**; 115 **Mark Guthrie**. Pictures on pages 31, 73, 178, 179, 196 supplied by featured establishments.

Contents

About the Guide **vi**
Introduction **1**
Essential Information **3**
Getting Around **9**
Accommodation **15**
Brussels by Season **29**
Sightseeing **33**
Architecture **52**

History

Key Events 58
Romans to the Spanish 59
Catholic Turmoil to National Unity 65
Independence to the Postwar Era 72
Brussels Today 80

Brussels by Area

Brussels by Area 84

Eating & Drinking

Restaurants 102
Cafés & Bars 117

Shopping & Services

Shopping & Services 132

Galleries & Museums

Museums 155
Art Galleries 162

Arts & Entertainment

Media 168
Clubs 171
Film 177
Music: Classical & Opera 180
Music: Rock, Folk & Jazz 184
Sport & Fitness 189
Theatre & Dance 193

In Focus

Business 200
Children 205
Gay & Lesbian 209

Students 213
Women's Brussels 217

Trips Out of Town

Trips Out of Town 222

Survival

Survival 259

Further Reading **266**
Index **267**
Advertisers Index **273**
Maps **276**

About the Guide

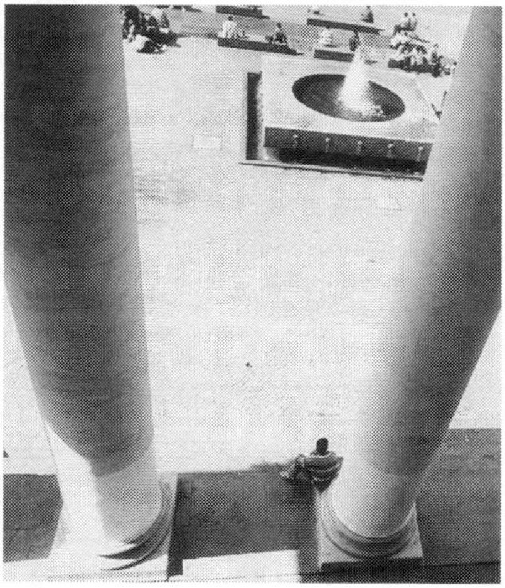

This is the first edition of the *Time Out Brussels Guide*, one in a series of 12 city guides that includes London, Berlin, New York, Madrid, Rome, San Francisco, Budapest, Amsterdam, Prague, Paris and Barcelona. It paints a complete and detailed picture of the *carrefour de l'Europe*, the crossroads of Europe; in addition to which, our writers have sampled the cream of the rest of Belgium, with particular emphasis on the cities of Antwerp, Ghent and Bruges. Selected listings are included in relevant sections, and the **Trips Out of Town** chapter is the longest and most detailed yet in the series.

Present & correct

All information was thoroughly checked and correct at press time, but please bear in mind that, even in the home of EU bureaucracy and red tape (or should that be particularly in the home of EU bureaucracy and red tape), listings details are liable to be complex and by no means set in stone. It is always wise to check opening times, dates of exhibitions, admission prices and other key details.

Names & addresses

Brussels is divided into districts known as *communes*, although these do not feature in addresses in our listings. Postcodes are written in four figures: 1000 in the city centre, 1050 is Ixelles, and so on. Although Brussels is officially a bilingual city, it is in fact about 80 per cent francophone and at the risk of upsetting Flemish speakers and Flemish nationalists who campaign for Brussels to become an entirely Flemish-speaking city, we have listed most names and addresses in French only. When something is located in a Flemish *commune*, we list it in Flemish. Given that it is impossible to please all of the people all of the time, we have taken a view on this infinitely complex problem and therefore can only apologise to anyone who feels we have got it wrong.

Prices

The prices listed should be used as guidelines. Because of inflation and fluctuating exchange rates, prices in shops and restaurants are always subject to change. All are quoted in Belgian Francs (BF). If prices and services vary wildly from those quoted, you might ask if there's a good reason. If there's not, take your custom elsewhere and then, please, let us know. We endeavour to give the best and most up-to-date advice, so we always want to hear if you have been ripped off or given the runaround.

Credit cards

The following abbreviations have been used for credit cards: AmEx – American Express; DC – Diners Club; JCB – Japanese credit cards; MC – Mastercard/Access; V – Visa.

Right to reply

The information we give is impartial. No organisation or enterprise has been included in this guide because its owner or manager has advertised in our publications. Impartiality is the reason our guides are so successful and well respected. We trust you will enjoy the *Time Out Brussels Guide* and that it helps you make the most of your stay. But if you disagree with any of our assessments, let us know; your comments on places you have visited are always welcome. You'll find a reader's reply card at the back of this book.

There's an on-line version of this guide, as well as weekly events listings for several international cities, at http://www.timeout.co.uk.

Introduction

When a friend moved to Brussels a few years ago, his reasons were unconvincing: it's close to Paris and Amsterdam, he said, and the restaurants are good. This inspired few of his friends to visit his new Belgian home, but those who did were pleasantly surprised by the city. Most have returned several times since then.

It's easy to be dismissive of Brussels. It's quiet. It's small. And it's populated by lawyers and civil servants. The city itself seems to have trouble marketing its attractions, its tourism posters concentrating on the Manneken Pis, and mussels and chips. In fact, it can offer far more than that, and its bland image is misleading. Any city with a football team called Racing White Daring Molenbeek cannot be entirely dull.

Perhaps it's because the city has been occupied by just about every other European power, or perhaps it's the weather, but either way, Brussels can be reticent with its attractions. Streets which are deserted in the daytime come alive with bars and clubs after midnight. Buildings which appear dowdy on the outside have wonderful art nouveau interiors. Famous restaurants hide away in gloomy parts of the city. And some of the best architecture and museums are found outside the centre (although they are easily reached because Brussels is so small).

What this all means is that the uninitiated visitor may find Brussels disappointing. After visiting Grand Place and a couple of chocolate shops, the day tripper thinks there is nothing left to see. You see them standing by the Manneken Pis disconsolately checking their watches to see if it is time to return to their coach.

If only they had done a little more homework. They could have sat in art deco bars and considered a choice of hundreds of beers. They could have gorged themselves in countless pavement cafés or restaurants with shady walled gardens. They could have wandered around the flea market at the Jeu du Balle or the more upmarket version in the Sablon. They could have taken a wonderful tram ride through the forest to the African Museum at Tervuren. Or walked around Ixelles and St Gilles, looking for art nouveau houses. They could have visited bars with live jazz at teatime or later in the evening, or visited excellent clubs without having to worry about falling victim to an overly rigorous door policy. Or they could have gone to the Comic Strip Museum or walked through the sewers of Anderlecht.

Even those who find nothing to please them in Brussels should pause before hastening back to the international train terminal and pushing on towards Paris, Amsterdam or London. Belgium being tiny and its transport systems excellent, Brussels is an excellent base for day trips. You can visit Antwerp, Bruges, Ghent, Waterloo, or the World War I cemeteries and still be back in time for an evening's drinking.

The only problem with all of this is money. Cash seems to disappear very quickly in Brussels. The problem is not just high prices or the low sterling exchange rate, it's also that there are so many bars to visit and things to consume. In fact, much of Brussels is good value. Prices are usually comparable to those in Paris and Amsterdam, and portions of food and measures of alcohol can be dauntingly generous.

At the end of a visit to Brussels, you will probably find yourself fatter, poorer, and possibly hungover as well. But you should also be surprised by what you found there. It's almost inevitable that on your return someone will ask you that tired old question, 'So can you name ten interesting Belgians?' If you can be bothered to reply, the answer should be fairly simple, with the names encompassing sport, fashion, art, architecture, literature and music. Brussels and its inhabitants, as you will discover, are the subject of a joke which is wearing very thin. *Sarah Burnett*

Essential Information

Sorting out money matters, getting tourist info and insuring your health, plus the weather and how to talk about it in bilingual Brussels.

Visas

All EU and Swiss citizens need to show a national identity card or passport when they enter Belgium. Americans, Canadians, Australians, New Zealanders and Japanese need a valid passport; no visa is required to enter as a tourist (*see chapter* **Survival** for more information).

Customs

For non-EU citizens and anyone bringing in duty-free goods, the following customs allowances apply when entering Belgium:

- 200 cigarettes **or** 100 cigarillos **or** 50 cigars **or** 250g (8.82 ounces) tobacco;
- 2l still table wine **and** either 1l spirits/strong liqueurs (over 22% alcohol) **or** 2l fortified wine (under 22% alcohol)/ sparkling wine/other liqueurs;
- 50g perfume;
- 250ml toilet water;
- 500g coffee **or** 200g coffee extracts/coffee essences;
- 100g tea **or** 40g tea extracts/essences;
- other goods for non-commercial use up to a maximum value of 7,300BF.

Since the EU member countries became one big happy family with the Single Market in early 1993, EU citizens over the age of 17 aren't required to make a customs declaration. That means you can bring as much duty-paid beer or wine as you can carry. There's also no limit to the amount of foreign currency that can be brought in or out of Belgium. For more information, call the Belgian Administration of Customs & Excise on 210 30 11 (9am-5pm Mon-Fri).

Insurance

As members of the European Union, both the UK and Ireland have reciprocal health agreements with Belgium. You'll need to apply for the necessary E111 form back home first. British citizens can get this by filling in the application form in leaflet SA30, available in Department of Social Security (DSS) offices or at post offices. Try to get the E111 at least two weeks before you leave. Make sure you read the small print on the back of the form so you know how to obtain medical or dental treatment at a reduced charge.

The E111 doesn't cover all medical costs – for example, dental treatment – so it's wise to take out private insurance before heading off to Belgium. Non-EU citizens should take out full private insurance before they visit. In the United States, STA and Council Travel and most other travel agencies offer short- and long-term coverage policies.

Remember to keep all receipts for medicine or treatment that you have paid for. You'll need it to claim reimbursement from your insurance company once back home. For more information on Belgian doctors, *see chapter* **Survival: Health**.

Lastly, before shelling out money on health insurance, college students should check whether their university's medical plan already provides coverage. A homeowner's policy may similarly cover vacations.

In the case of long-term visitors to Belgium, after six months of residence you are eligible for coverage under Belgium's basic health insurance system, the *mutuelle*. It allows you to recover a large chunk of doctors' and dentists' bills, and other costs. Regular payments are automatically deducted from your salary. For contact telephone numbers look in the *Yellow Pages* under Mutualités/Ziekenfondsen.

Discount travel

Acotra World Travel Agency
51 rue de la Madeleine, 1000 (512 55 40/fax 512 39 74). Métro Gare Centrale. **Open** 10am-5.30pm Mon-Fri. **Credit** AmEx, DC, MC, V.
This agency across from Gare Centrale offers discounts on plane tickets, and can make train and room bookings. It also sells international student travel cards for 350BF.

Money

The unit of Belgian currency is the franc, abbreviated to BF or FB. And it's worth bearing in mind that a Belgian franc is worth much less than a French franc. Exchange rates at the time of writing were: £1 = 47BF/US$1 = 31BF. It comes in 1, 5, 20 and 50 coins. There is also a 50-centime coin (half a franc). Banknotes come in 100, 200, 500, 1,000, 2,000, 5,000 and 10,000 denominations.

Try to keep a few 5BF and 20BF coins handy. They are constantly needed, whether for a public phone, supermarket trolley deposit, toilet fee or a tip. Also be on the lookout for Luxembourg coins slipped into your change. They are on a parity with the Belgian franc and are accepted in Belgium, but are not very popular and can be a pain to dump.

Belgians tend to use cash for petty transactions, and debit cards (such as Bancontact or Mister Cash) for more expensive purchases. Although not as widely used, credit cards are fairly common, especially in restaurants, shops and hotels.

The use of Eurocheques is avoided, since most Belgian banks charge customers a whopping 450BF fee for each cheque written.

Banks & foreign exchange

Banks are the best places to exchange money. Generally they open from about 9am to between 3.30pm and 5pm on weekdays. A few have half-days on Saturdays. It's wise to call and check opening times beforehand as hours vary, even between branches of the same bank.

After banking hours you can change money and traveller's cheques at offices in Gare du Nord, Gare du Midi (7am-11pm daily) and Gare Centrale (8am-9pm daily), although they don't give advances on credit cards. However, several banks at the airport give cash advances on MasterCard (called EuroCard in Belgium) or VISA, as well as convert currency. Most open early and close around 10pm. Banque Bruxelles Lambert (BBL), for example, opens daily from 7am to 9.45pm. Kredietbank also has a branch at the airport.

American Express has two branches in Brussels, which issue traveller's cheques, replace lost or stolen cards, offer cash advances and even book flights for various fees.

American Express Gold Card Travel Service

2 place Louise, 1050 (676 27 33). Métro Louise. **Open** 9am-5pm Mon-Fri; 9.30am-noon Sat.

American Express Travel & Financial Services

100 boulevard du Souverain, 1170 (676 26 26/24-hour Customer Service 676 21 21). Métro Hermann Debroux. **Open** 9am-1pm, 2-5pm Mon-Fri.

Report lost or stolen credit cards to the police and the 24-hour services listed below.

Diners Club

36 rue Ravenstein, 1000 (515 95 11/fax 513 52 66). Métro Gare Centrale. **Open** 9am-5pm Mon-Fri.
After hours, the above telephone number handles calls 24 hours a day.

MasterCard (EuroCard)

(24-hour toll free 0800 150 96).

Visa International

(24-hour toll free 0800 187 56).

Tourist information

As the tourist information office at the airport has closed, travellers must go to the main tourist office in the Grand Place in the city centre.

TIB

Hôtel de Ville, Grand Place, 1000 (513 89 40/fax 514 45 38). Métro Bourse, De Brouckère or Gare Centrale. **Open** *31 Mar-30 May, 1 Oct-31 Oct* 9am-6pm Mon-Fri; 9am-1pm, 2-6pm, Sat, Sun. *1 June-30 Sep* 9am-7pm Mon-Fri; 9am-1pm, 2-7pm, Sat, Sun. *1 Nov-30 Mar* 9am-6pm Mon-Fri; 9am-1pm, 2-6pm Sat; 1-5pm Sun.
This cramped little office is conveniently located on the Grand Place. The English-speaking staff can offer tips on what to see in Brussels and how to go about it. They can also book rooms. For 80BF you can buy the *Brussels Guide and Map*, which provides complete information on sights within walking distance of the city centre. Eurocheques and traveller's cheques are accepted.

Belgian Tourist Information Office

63 rue du Marché aux Herbes, 1000 (504 03 90/fax 504 02 70). Métro Bourse, De Brouckère or Gare Centrale. **Open** *1 Jun-30 Sep* 9am-7pm Mon-Fri; 9am-1pm, 2-7pm Sat, Sun. *1-31 Oct* 9am-6pm Mon-Fri; 9am-1pm, 2-6pm, Sat, Sun. *1 Nov-30 Mar* 9am-6pm Mon-Fri; 9am-1pm, 2-6pm, Sat; 1-5pm Sun. *1-31 May* 9am-6pm Mon-Fri; 9am-1pm, 2-6pm, Sat, Sun.
If you plan to make an excursion out of the city, this is the place to contact. The national tourist service, located in a handsome old building, provides information about the whole of Belgium. One of the most useful books they offer is the annual *Tourist Attractions Guide*, which covers the whole country. The office is broken down into Flemish and French sections. If you're planning a trip to the romantic town of Bruges or a weekend on the coast, ask for the Flanders Tourist Office. They sell a useful brochure, *Le Pays Flamand de Vos Vacances* (95BF), which lists over 200 quick trip ideas in Flanders. For information about the French-speaking region, including the Ardennes, ask for the Walloon Tourist Office. They can advise on tourist attractions and have loads of info on accommodation from hotels to B&Bs. You can book a room through BelsudReservation (504 02 80/fax 514 53 35).

Waterloo Tourist Information Centre

149 chaussée de Bruxelles, 1410 (354 99 10/fax 354 22 23). Phone for directions. **Open** *1 Nov-31 Mar* 10.30am-5pm daily; *1 Apr-31 Oct* 9.30am-6.30pm daily.
For war buffs who want to visit the site that made the name Waterloo synonymous with Napoleon, call this centre first. They can direct you to all the key places involved in the great battle, including the little Frenchman's former headquarters. A nearby location hosts a panorama and videos about the battle. Both are informative but lack historical context.

Maps

If your visit to Brussels is brief and you'd rather not fork out a lot for a map, pick up the *Brussels Guide and Map* at **TIB** (*see above*). If you plan to stay longer, the only way you will be able to navigate the city's labyrinth of crooked thoroughfares is by investing in one of several booklike street maps that are on the market. **De Rouck** sells one for about 300BF. **Girault-Gilbert** offers a similar map (270BF) that is a bit easier to use. The German company **Falk** offers a more compact version (100BF) – if you're in the mood for lots of folding and unfolding – though it only covers the city centre.

WH Smith
71-75 boulevard Adolphe Max, 1000, (219 27 08/fax 217 86 63). Métro De Brouckère or Rogier. **Open** 9am-6.30pm Mon, Wed-Sat; 10am-6.30pm Tue. **Credit** AmEx, MC, V.
This downtown bookstore is bit of an institution in Brussels. Here you can find not only a generous selection of maps, but also a wide variety of English-language publications from guide books to trashy paperback novels.

Street names

When addressing an envelope, write the house number after the street name and place the postcode before the city, as in the following example: Monsieur Ledoux, avenue Louise 100, 1050 Bruxelles. To avoid confusion between the numbers 7 and 1, get into the habit of crossing your 7s.

Numbers

Dates are written in the following order: day, month, year.

When writing figures, Belgians use commas where Americans and the British would use decimal points and vice versa. For example, two thousand five hundred Belgian francs is written as 2.500,00 BF.

Times are written in a 24-hour military style. For example, 4pm is 16:00.

Public holidays

New Year's Day; Easter Monday; Labour Day (1 May); Ascension Day (sixth Thursday after Easter); Pentecostal Whit Monday (seventh Monday after Easter); Belgian National Day (21 July); Assumption (15 August); All Saints' Day (1 November); Armistice Day (11 November); Christmas Day (25 December).

Although it is not an official holiday, banks and government offices usually close on 15 November for King's Day.

And as if the country didn't have enough holidays, the Belgians make a habit of tacking on more free days to make long weekends even longer. If a holiday falls on a Tuesday or Thursday, most offices, by tradition, will 'make the bridge' (*faire le pont/de brug maken*) and observe a four-day weekend. The longest of these 'bridges' is Easter, when many Belgians embark on short trips across Europe.

As with everything in Belgium, the French and Flemish communities celebrate separate regional holidays. A day off on 11 July marks the anniversary of the Battle of the Golden Spurs in 1302 for the Flemish region of Flanders, while a holiday on

Post offices are generally open from 9am to 5pm – post boxes stay open 24 hours daily.

27 September commemorates the end of French-speaking Wallonia's revolution for independence from Holland in 1830.

Time & the seasons

Belgium is one hour ahead of British time. The Belgian climate is mild. Winters are very cold and damp, without much snow; summers are warm and often hot. Rain, however, is a force to be reckoned with all year round. The best line of defence in dealing with Brussels' fickle weather is to always bring an extra jumper or two and a collapsible umbrella.

The biggest drawback to **winter** in Brussels is the shortness of the days. Much of the city stays at home or in cosy pubs in the evening, since daylight only lasts from 8am to 4pm in December and January. The city starts to shake off the winter blues at Easter.

Spring is officially welcomed as attractions open and activities, dormant during winter, start up again. In April and May, average temperatures range between 4C (40F) and 16C (60F).

The heat picks up in June and July, reaching the mid-twenties (seventies) and occasionally hitting the high twenties (eighties). The flip side to depressingly short, dark winter days is the seemingly endless days of **summer** in Brussels. It's not uncommon to sit out on a café terrace at 10pm with the sky still light.

Autumn is often a rainy season, with temperatures usually around 10C-16C (50F-60F) throughout October.

Street crime

In crowded areas such as the Grand Place, pickpockets and purse-snatchers are always on the prowl, so never leave your handbag on the back of a chair or out of your reach. The same goes for mobile phones. Never leave them lying on your car seat. They'll be gone in a flash.

Weights & measurements

Food items are priced by the kilogram, or kilo. There are 1000g (or 2.2lbs) in a kilo. *Une livre*, literally a pound, is a half-kilo or 500g. Distances are measured with the metric system. To work out miles, multiply kilometres by 0.6. To convert centimetres to inches, divide by 2.54.

Electricity

The current used in Belgium is 220V AC. It works fine with British appliances (which run on 240V), but you'll need to change the plug or buy an adapter. Both are available at most electrical goods shops. American appliances run on 110V. To use an American hair dryer in Belgium, you'll need to buy a converter, which can be pricey. Don't bother if you're staying at a good hotel. They are often equipped with hair dryers, as well as adapter plugs to fit appliances from most countries.

Opening times

Banks

Most banks are open at 9am and close between 3.30pm and 5pm. Some also close for lunch.

Museums

Most museums are open 9am to 4pm Tuesday to Saturday, and sometimes on Sunday. They close on Mondays. Several are only open from Easter Sunday to September. It's wise to call the museum before visiting.

Offices

Many close early on Friday, although this is an unofficial policy.

Post offices

Generally, post offices are open 9am to 5pm; some remain open until 5.30pm or 6pm (*see chapter* **Survival** for more details).

Shops

Although there is no official closing time, most shops open from 9am to 6pm. Some grocery stores and supermarkets stay open till 9pm. Big department stores open till 9pm on one day a week, usually Friday. There is also a chain of (mostly) 24-hour grocer-tobacconists called White Night.

Smoking

Smoking in confined public places is banned by law. This amounts to no smoking in railway stations (except on open-air platforms) and public buildings such as town halls and theatres.

The law has had little effect on restaurants, though. Very few have non-smoking sections. Recently, some of the top hotels have initiated no-smoking rooms and floors.

Telephones

To phone Brussels from outside Belgium, first dial the international code (00 from Britain), followed by 32 (the code for Belgium), then 2 (the code for Brussels), and finally the seven-digit number.

For calls from Brussels using a payphone, you'll need 5BF and 20BF coins. If you're making an international call, buy a phonecard. It's simply more convenient (*see chapter* **Survival**).

Tipping

Most restaurants, hotels and taxis include a service charge in their bill. People throw in a few extra francs when service has been exceptional. At cinemas and theatres, tipping the attendant 20BF for a programme is expected. Although there's no charge for a public lavatory, it's customary to leave between 5BF and 20BF for the attendant.

Water

It's safe to drink the water in Belgium. In restaurants, Belgians normally order bottled water.

Forked tongues

The Belgians are an adaptable group of people. Unlike their French-speaking neighbours to the south – who turn up their noses at the sound of English – Belgians will eagerly speak English. In fact, it's the language many francophone Belgians use to communicate with their Flemish countrymen and vice versa. (There's a small German population near the border with Germany, but that language is not widely spoken in Belgium.)

In general, it's easier to find someone who speaks English in a Flemish region than in a French area. If you speak French in some of the Flemish areas, the locals may take offence, so English tends to be the more diplomatic option, even though Flemish Belgians more often than not speak all three.

In a French-speaking area, it's considered polite to greet shopkeepers with 'Bonjour, Madame' or 'Bonjour, Monsieur'.

Useful words & phrases

yes/no – *oui/non* – ja/nee
please – *s'il vous plaît* – alstublieft
thank you – *merci* – dank u
hello – *bonjour* – dag
good morning – *bonjour* – goede morgen
good night – *bonne nuit* – goede nacht
goodbye – *au revoir* – tot ziens
excuse me – *excusez-moi*– verontschuldig mij

I understand – *je comprends* – dat begrijp ik
I don't understand – *je ne comprends pas* – ik begrijp het niet

where's the toilet? – *où sont les toilettes?* – war is het toilet?
how far... ? – *à quelle distance... ?* – hoe var... ?

avenue – *avenue* – laan
street – *rue* – straat
square – *place/square* – plein

turn – *tournez* – raaien
left/right – *gauche/droite* – links/rechts
straight ahead – *tout droit* – rechtuit

open/closed – *ouvert/fermé* – open/gesloten
how much is... ? – *combien coûte... ?* – hoeveel kost... ?

I'd like the bill, please – *l'addition, s'il vous plaît* – ik wil graag ober, mag ik afrekenen
service included – *service compris* – bediening inbegrepen

how long... ? – *combien de temps... ?* – hoe lang... ?

cheap/expensive – *bon marché/cher (chère)* – goedkoop/duur
good/bad – *bon(ne)/mauvais(e)* – goed/slecht
big/small – *grand(e)/petit(e)* – groot/klein
far/near– *loin/près* – ver/dichtbij

Numbers

0 *zero* – nul; **1** *un(e)* – een; **2** *deux* – twee; **3** *trois* – drie; **4** *quatre* – vier; **5** *cinq* – vijf; **6** *six* – zes; **7** *sept* – zeven; **8** *huit* – acht; **9** *neuf* – negen; **10** *dix* – tien; **11** *onze* – elf; **12** *douze* – twaalf; **13** *treize* – dertien; **14** *quatorze* – veertien; **15** *quinze* – vijftien; **16** *seize* – zestien; **17** *dix-sept* – zeventien; **18** *dix-huit* – achttien; **19** *dix-neuf* – negentien; **20** *vingt* – twintig; **30** *trente* – dertig; **40** *quarante* – veertig; **50** *cinquante* – vijftig; **60** *soixante* – zestig; **70** **septante* – zeventig; **80** *quatre-vingt* – tachtig; **90** **nonante* – negentig; **100** *cent* – hondred; **1000** *mille* – duizend; **1,000,000** *un million* – een miljoen.
*The numbers 70 and 90 are said differently in Belgium and France. Belgians say *septante* for 70, the French call it *soixante-dix* and the Belgian 90 is *nonante*, while the French call it *quatre-vingt-dix*.

Food

See chapter **Restaurants**.

Place names

Belgium's bilingual divide can be quite confusing – and downright frightening when you're on the motorway. If you're traveling to Liège, you may think you've gone mad when all you can find are signs to a place called Liuk. In fact, Liuk is the Flemish name for Liège. It's best to familiarise yourself with the French and Flemish versions of place names before setting off.

Belgian towns: Anvers/Antwerpen; Mons/Bergen; Tournai/Doornik; Gand/Gent; Louvain/Leuven; Liège/Luik; Bruges/Brugge; Ypres/Ieper.

Brussels *communes*: Bruxelles/Brussel; Forest/Vorst; Ixelles/Elsene; Uccle/Ukkel; Auderghem/Oudergem.

Getting Around

Getting from A to B is as easy as ABC with public transport. Getting behind the wheel and living to tell the tale is another story.

Brussels has a modern, comprehensive, integrated and cheap public transport system. A combination of Métro, rail, bus and tram facilitates access to all parts of the Eurocapital, with the particular attraction of timed tickets that let you hop on and off as many times as you like for up to one hour. If you prefer to walk – the town is so compact that it's possible to do most sightseeing on foot – remember to take some flat shoes, as many roads and pavements in the centre are cobbled.

Arriving in Brussels

By air

Brussels' international airport is located at Zaventem, 14km north-east of the capital, with good road and rail connections to the city centre. The new airport terminal building, inaugurated in June 1994, boasts an impressive selection of shops and restaurants. Part of the old terminal is used for arrivals from and departures to Schengen countries (Belgium, Holland, Luxembourg, France, Germany, Portugal and Spain) and the new terminal serves non-Schengen countries.

The aiport information desk (7am-10pm daily) is in the check-in area of the new terminal. This terminal no longer has a tourist information desk. Instead, there's a board in the arrivals section, by the meeting point, which displays hotel information and is equipped with a telephone link for reservations. Hotel shuttle buses run from level 0. For flight information call 753 39 13 (7am-10pm daily).

If you lose something on the plane, contact the airline via their handling agent. **Belgavia** and **Sabena** represent most of the major airlines. For property lost in the airport, try the **Belgian Police**, **Airport Police** or **Airport Authorities** (*see chapter* **Survival**).

AIRPORT PARKING

Airport Park International, next to the new terminal, charges 295BF a day. There are also monitored car parks, such as **LockPark** *(720 41 91/720 63 25)* and **Car Hotel Airport Parking** *(753 53 53)*.

CONNECTIONS TO THE CITY

There is a frequent shuttle **train** service – Airport City Express (753 24 40) – from Zaventem to Gare du Nord, Gare Centrale and Gare du Midi. Tickets cost 85BF for a second class single and 120BF for a second class weekend return. The train runs three times an hour and the journey takes about 20 minutes (first train 5.25am, last train 11.46pm). If you are a woman travelling alone at night and planning to use public transport for your onward journey, it's safest to disembark at Gare Centrale.

An hourly **bus** service to Gare du Nord operates from the ground-floor level of the new terminal. The journey time is about 35 minutes and a single ticket costs 70BF.

Taxis wait directly outside the arrivals building and should display a yellow-and-blue licence emblem. The fare from Zaventem to central Brussels should cost 1000BF-1300BF. Many taxis accept credit cards. If in doubt, check the fare with the driver first. Some firms, such as Autolux, offer 25 per cent off for a return journey (see cabs with an orange-and-white aeroplane sticker). Brussels taxis have a rooftop tariff indicator system, showing 1 or 2 for single or double tariff in operation. Strictly speaking, the double tariff is only applicable outside the limits of the 19 Brussels *communes*. In practice, most drivers switch to double as soon as they're on a motorway. *See below* for more details.

By rail

EUROSTAR

The high-speed passenger train connection, which began service in November 1994, has revolutionised travel between London and Brussels. With a city-to-city journey time of 3 hours and 15 minutes (passing through the tunnel takes less than 25 minutes), it provides a reasonably priced and relaxing way of visiting Brussels. There are usually seven departures a day from Brussels Gare du Midi and London Waterloo. Check in at least 20 minutes before departure. In the UK, Eurostar information and reservations are available from appointed travel agents and selected BR stations. In Belgium, Eurostar tickets are available at travel agents and international ticket desks in mainline stations.

Waterloo International Terminal

(01233 617575/local rate charges for callers within the UK 0345 881881). **Open** 7am-10pm Mon-Fri; 7am-9pm Sat; 9am-5pm Sun. **Credit** AmEx, DC, MC, V.
Prices from London to Brussels start at £69 for a special non-exhangeable deal and rise to £220 for an all-the-works first-class return trip.

Gare du Midi

(203 36 40/telephone sales 224 88 56). **Open** 8.15am-7pm Mon-Fri; 9.15am-4.30pm Sat, Sun, public holidays. **Credit** MC, V.
Adult prices from Brussels to London start at 3200BF for a Supersaver or Saturday day return. A second-class tourist return costs 5940BF and an Apex return is 4500BF (book at least 14 days in advance).

LE SHUTTLE

If you're driving to Brussels, Le Shuttle can transport you and your vehicle from Cheriton Park on the M20 near Folkestone to Coquelles near Calais in 35 minutes. There are good motorway connections to Brussels from there. Le Shuttle is a 24-hour service with up to four shuttles an hour departing from Folkestone. There are also facilities for the disabled. Tickets can be bought from a travel agent, Le Shuttle or (with the exception of Apex or promotional offers) on arrival at the tolls. Hertz and Le Shuttle have a Le Swap rental system so that you can drive a left-hand- and right-hand-drive car in France and the UK respectively.

Le Shuttle

(UK 0990 353535). **Open** 8.30am-6.15pm daily. **Credit** AmEx, DC, MC, V.
Five-day returns cost £70, £115, 147, or £169. Single tickets can cost £63, £109, £133 and £164.

By sea

Ostend Lines

5 Natienkaai, Ostend 8400 (059 55 99 55). **Credit** AmEx, DC, MC, V.
The ferry crossing takes 3 hours and 45 minutes. An Ostend-Ramsgate standard return for one foot passenger costs 1600BF. Crossing by jetfoil is faster (1 hour and 35 minutes), but carries a supplementary charge of 200BF each way.

Hoverspeed

Central Reservations, International Hoverport, Marine Parade, Dover, Kent CT17 9TG, England (01304 240241/fax 01304 240088). **Credit** AmEx, DC, MC, V.
Dover to Calais by hovercraft takes a mere 35 minutes. Return fares (including the coach from London Victoria to Dover and from Calais to central Brussels) are: £44 for an adult; £39 for under-26s; and £33 for under-16s.

By coach

Eurolines (Brussels)

(ticket sales only) 50 place de Brouckère, 1000 (217 00 25). Métro De Brouckère. **Open** 9am-6pm Mon-Fri. **No credit cards.**
Eurolines buses depart from CCN Gare du Nord (80 rue de Progrès, 1210). It also has an office for ticket sales (203 07 07).

Eurolines/National Express (Luton)

(01582 40 45 11). **Open** 8am-8pm Mon-Sat; 10am-3pm Sun; answerphone service after hours.
An adult return from London's Victoria to Brussels between 1 Sept-30 June costs £44 (1 Jul-31 Aug £49). There are reductions for youths and over-60s.

Belgian rail

In 1835, Belgium's King Léopold I inaugurated the first railway in mainland Europe. **Société Nationale des Chemins de Fer Belges (SNCB)** now has 4,000 kilometres of track, connecting Brussels to other major European cities. Its three mainline stations – Gare Centrale (a kilometre from the Grand Place), Gare du Midi (in a zone under reconstruction and home to a popular Sunday market) and Gare du Nord (in the red-light district) – are directly linked. Two additional rail stations, Schuman and Quartier Léopold, serve the European institutions.

Belgium is a small country and most of its tourist spots are less than an hour away by rail from Brussels. The majority of trains, although basic in terms of design, are clean and efficient. Rail travel is good value with a variety of special offers available. These include the **Eurodomino** pass, which provides: unlimited travel for periods of five or ten days in the European country of your choice; reductions for over-60s, under-26s and groups of two or more; and substantial savings during school holidays for day trippers. Tickets are generally not sold on trains, so inform the guard beforehand if boarding without a ticket (a supplement will be charged if you buy the ticket on the train). For information about Belgian railways call 0891 516 444 in the UK or 203 28 80/203 36 40 in Belgium.

There is also an excellent local rail network serving Brussels and the outlying areas. Further details and train timetables can be obtained from the stations.

Baggage facilities are available at mainline railway stations. Gare du Midi's left luggage office is next to the Eurostar terminal and charges 60BF per item of luggage per day.

TGV

The TGV (Train à Grande Vitesse) to Paris departs at least five times daily from Gare du Midi and the journey takes two-and-a-half hours. A second-class return costs 2780BF plus the TGV supplement of 120BF-360BF. There is also a TGV service to Nice. For further information call 203 3640.

Maps

Street names are marked in both French and Flemish. A-Z plans and maps of Brussels can be obtained from kiosks, newsagents and bookshops throughout the city, and tourist information offices (*see chapter* **Essential Information**).

Transport maps and timetables are available free of charge from the main STIB office and the STIB information centres at Gare du Midi, Porte de Namur and Rogier.

Métro, trams & buses

The efficient public transport network in the capital is run by STIB (Société des Transports Intercommunaux de Bruxelles).

As well as the Métro, STIB has maintained and developed a tram system, providing Brussels with a non-polluting and picturesque mode of transport. The T2000 model, introduced in 1994, with gliding electric doors and low-level passenger gangways, has taken Brussels' public transport system some way into the future.

In addition to the STIB buses that serve the capital, two other bus services meet the requirements of commuters from the provinces.

De Lijn (Flanders Public Transport Service) *(526 28 11).* **Open** *phone enquiries* 8.15am-4pm Mon-Fri. Call the above number for information on services leaving from Brussels.

L'Epervier *50 place de Brouckère, 1000 (217 00 25/fax 217 31 92).* Contact this office for reservations on Europabus and Eurolines buses.

Time flies by when you're the driver of a tram.

STIB *6th floor, 20 Galeries de la Toison d'Or, 1060 (general enquiries 515 20 00/bus information 515 30 64). Métro Louise or Porte de Namur.* **Open** 7.30am-5.30pm Mon-Fri; 8am-4pm Sat. Some bus routes that take in the sights are no.71 (De Brouckère – Delta), which passes through place Royale, and no.48 (Bourse – Stalle Station), which meanders around the Sablon area.
TEC (Wallonia Public Transport Service) (010 48 04 04). **Open** 6.30am-7pm Mon-Fri; 8am-noon Sat.

Tickets & travel passes

Tickets can be bought at Métro and rail stations, on buses and trams, at a kiosk next to the Bourse, at STIB information centres, and at many newsagents. A one-day **Tourist Passport** is available for 220BF from the tourist information office in the Grand Place and includes reductions on admission to museums. Points of sale for monthly passes are Métro Porte de Namur, Gare du Midi, the kiosk by the Bourse, SNCB stations and approved outlets. A ticket (*trajet*) entitles the user to travel on the Métro, buses and trams for one hour. Tickets must be electronically stamped by the machines at Métro stations and on trams and buses at the beginning of the journey. Controllers run random checks and can enforce a penalty of 2000BF for being without a validated ticket. The fine increases dramatically for subsequent infractions.

The most economical way of travelling for a few days is to buy a batch of ten tickets (***une carte de dix trajets***) for 320BF. Five tickets cost 230BF, one costs 50BF and a **one-day unlimited travel pass** is 125BF. A **monthly pass** costs 1325BF. There is also a **Brussels Business Pass**, valid for one year of unlimited travel on the STIB network (for details call 515 20 54). Children under six can travel free if accompanied by an adult with a valid ticket. Public transport in the city generally operates from 5.30am to midnight.

Signs & lines

Métro stations are indicated by a white letter 'M' on a blue background, while red-and-white signs mark tram and bus stops.

The first Métro started operation in 1976. Brussels is now well served by three lines and Pre-Métro trams, which run through various underground sections. Métro Line 1 is divided into Lines 1A and 1B. 1A runs from Heysel (home of the Atomium) to Hermann Debroux. 1B goes from Bizet to Stockel. Line 2 is a ring that links Simonis to Clemenceau and mirrors the inner-city ring of *boulevards* above. The main Pre-Métro line links Gare du Nord to the new station Albert in St Gilles via Gare du Midi.

The Métro system is efficient, clean and well signposted. On Line 2, you can track the progress of the train you are waiting for with computerised information boards. At night the Métro does not generally carry the same volume of passengers as the London Underground, and certain sections after 10pm can be intimidating for lone women passengers (for example, alighting at fairly deserted stations such as Yser and Porte de Hal).

Disabled travel

Public transport is not specially adapted for disabled passengers, though the latest trams with a low-level platform improve access slightly. A low-cost STIB minibus service (515 23 65) with vehicles equipped for wheelchairs is available to transport disabled travellers door-to-door. STIB has also installed facilities for blind passengers, such as Braille information panels, in at least 12 of its Métro stations.

For those travelling outside Brussels by train or on certain bus services, the disabled passenger pays and any accompanying person travels free. There are also reductions for the blind (call SNCB on 224 64 00 for details).

Taxis

Taxi ranks are situated outside mainline railway stations and at strategic locations such as Porte de Namur, the Bourse and De Brouckère. They are seldom hailed on the street. If you have a complaint

Bodeghem
Tram
18
T2000
INFO 515 2000

The price per kilometre is 38BF or 76BF, depending upon whether the journey is inside or outside Brussels' 19 *communes*. Minimum fare is 95BF (plus 75BF at night). A few taxi comapnies are listed below.
Taxis Verts *54 rue des Carburants, 1190 (349 46 46).*
Autolux *1 rue du Maroquin, 1080 (411 41 42).*
Taxi Orange *37 place du Nouveau Marché aux Grains, 1000 (511 22 88).*

Bicycles

Cycling in the centre of Brussels remains a daunting prospect despite many cycle lanes and tracks. However, cycling out of town – eg along the route to Tervuren – is a scenic and relatively safe method of exploring the city's environs. Cycle lanes are designated by two broken white lines and are less secure than the cycle tracks, which are separated from the traffic.

Bike-In

18 rue Kelle, 1200 (763 13 78). Phone for details.
If you want to explore further afield, SNCB operates a scheme whereby you can purchase a combined ticket for train journey and bike hire. A bike will be reserved for your collection on arrival at one of the 31 participating stations.

Car hire

To hire a car, you must have a full current driving licence (normally with a minimum of one year's experience) and a passport or ID card. Car rental is pricey, starting at 13500BF per week with unlimited mileage. The major car hire companies are in the airport arrivals hall and are open from 6.30am to 11pm. Hire rates at the airport are higher than in town. Special all-inclusive weekend rates (Fri pm to Mon am) are available from around 3000BF.
Avis *107 rue Colonel Bourg, 1140 (730 62 11/airport 720 09 44). Métro Diamant.* **Open** 8am-6pm Mon-Fri. **Age requirement** over 23. **Credit** AmEx, DC, MC, V.
Budget *327 avenue Louise, 1050 (646 51 30/airport 720 80 50). Tram 93, 94.* **Open** 8.30am-6pm Mon-Fri; 9am-noon Sat. **Age requirement** over 23. **Credit** AmEx, DC, EC, V.
Hertz *8 boulevard M Lemonnier, 1000 (513 2886/airport 720 60 44). Métro Anneessens.* **Open** 7.30am-7pm Mon-Fri; 8am-2pm Sat; 8am-noon Sun. **Age requirement** over 25. **Credit** AmEx, DC, MC, V.

Driving – essential tips

It's not easy driving around Brussels. Firstly, there's the 'priority to the right' rule. Second is the aggressive behaviour of drivers, especially in tunnels. Then there's the rush hour to contend with. The cacophony of car horns and radio traffic warnings builds early on Friday afternoons when Belgians and Eurocrats alike begin their mass exodus. If you've survived all this, there are still the potholes. In contrast to the sleek motorways, the roads in town are riddled with flaws. (*See also chapter* **Survival**.)

Crossing the road – as safe as snake-tickling.

A comprehensive tunnel system links major points in the city, making it possible to traverse Brussels without seeing the light of day. The inner ring is a pentagon of boulevards (marked with signs showing a blue ring on which the yellow dot is your current location). The secondary city ring was never completed and the outer ring has ended up as an elongated pear shape with a missing base, divided into an East and West Motorway ring.

Motorists must give way to the right even on a major road, except when marked otherwise – eg a white sign with a yellow diamond on your road means cars from the right must stop for you. Priority must also be given to vehicles on rails.

The speed limit on motorways is 120kph, on main roads 90kph and in residential areas it's 50kph. The drinking and driving limit is 0.2g/l (that is no more than two small beers or two glasses of wine). Seat belts are compulsory at the front and rear of the car.

Walking – essential tips

Be wary at zebra crossings. Drivers do not automatically stop. If a car hurtles in your direction mid-crossing, techniques to avoid certain death include looking the driver straight in the eye (this often doesn't work) or looking away (suicidal body language that can rile the driver into accelerating).

Accommodation

From the spectacular to the sterile to the downright dodgy... Brussels has rooms for just about everyone.

Brussels has more hotels per capita than most major cities, which makes it definitely a renter's market. The majority, alas, are targeted for the travelling business client as one out of every two visitors to the city is here for work. This means a high ratio of chain hotels and accommodation that emphasises efficiency and the practicality of the rooms over individual charm.

Listed below are peak rates for hotels, but you can save 50 per cent or more by going through the Belgian Tourist Reservations office (513 74 84/ fax 513 92 77). This free service has a list of over 800 hotels in Belgium, which often turn to BTR to unload during off-peak times.

As Brussels is a city that works more than it plays, these tend to be weekends and during the summer holidays – when hotels in most other tourist destinations are heavily booked. The drawback is that normally you can't reserve too far in advance, as the hotels often wait until the last minute to offer cut rates. But the prices are well worth the wait.

STAR RATINGS

Star ratings are given to hotels by the government, largely relying on Michelin for assistance. These ratings are as much about the quantity of services offered as about the quality. Hence a good hotel offering many services will exceed in star ratings an excellent hotel that offers a more modest number of services, even if those offered are actually better than the hotel with the higher star rating. This is not to say that five-star hotels are bad – merely to say that a lower star-rating does not necessarily mean a worse hotel.

Although some of the hotels at the lower end of the price scale listed here have communal toilets and showers, we have listed only prices of rooms including private bath and WC. If you are going the bargain route, make sure that you specify if you want your own facilities when reserving.

Also, there is always someone on the staff who speaks English at most mid- and up-market hotels, but as you drift further down the scale in price, the ability to speak French becomes much more useful.

Most hotels, residences and hostels, even the ones which have no wheelchair access or accommodation for the disabled, allow animals – much to the displeasure of those with allergies. If you are sensitive to animal hairs and the like, do ask about the hotel's animal policy and whether there are allergy-free rooms available when reserving.

HOTEL CAVEAT

The more elaborate a hotel's name, often the dodgier its accommodation. A snazzy name is often employed as a cheap way to jazz up a lustreless hotel's image. With the exception of chain hotels, beware especially of hotels in one city christened the same as a prestigious name of a hotel in another city. Whether it's a Dorchester in Marbella or a Le Crillon in London, chances are it will be a stay to remember – for all the wrong reasons.

Hotels

Very expensive

Conrad Brussels

72 avenue Louise, 1050 (542 42 42/fax 542 42 00). Tram 93, 94. **Rates** *single* 13,000BF; *double* 14,000BF; *suite* 27,000BF-73,000BF; *extra bed* 1,500BF; *breakfast* 650BF-950BF. **Credit** AmEx, DC, JCB, MC, TC, V.

The Conrad has the distinction of being one of the largest hotels in Brussels that aspires to luxury and elegance as much as efficiency. From the vast chandeliered ground-floor lounge furnished with tapestried wing-back chairs, chintz sofas, polished maple tables and marble floors, to the well-appointed rooms that live up to the lobby's promise, the Conrad's old-style restrained opulence almost makes you forget it has only been open since April 1993. If there is one thing to fault the hotel with, it is that the studied, ultra-professional approach of its staff can leave you a bit cold: cosy it ain't. But otherwise some find it Brussels' finest.

Hotel services *Air-conditioning. Babysitting. Bar. Car park. Conference facilities. Currency exchange. Fax. Gift shop. Laundry. Lifts. Multi-lingual staff. Non-smoking floor/rooms. Sauna. Sport/fitness facilities. Restaurants. Wheelchair: access; rooms for disabled.* **Room services** *Hair-dryer. Mini-bar. Radio. Refrigerator. Room service. Safe. Telephone. TV/VCR.*

Hilton Brussels

38 boulevard de Waterloo, 1000 (504 11 11/fax 504 21 11). Metro Louise or Porte de Namur/bus 34. **Rates** *single* or *double* 10,900BF-13,000BF; *suite* 23,000BF-46,000BF; *extra bed* 1,000BF; *breakfast* 600BF. **Credit** AmEx, DC, JCB, MC, TC, V.

To slag off a Hilton for its lack of individual character is to miss the point: this is the hotel for the frequent traveller who wants the feeling of instant familiarity, whether in Abu Dhabi or Albuquerque. And let's face it: they do excel at providing comfort. The Sunday brunch has become a Brussels institution with the city's ex-pat community.

Hotel services *Air-conditioning. Babysitting. Business centre. Car park. Conference facilities. Currency exchange. Fax. Garage. Gift shop. Gym. Laundry. Lifts. Multi-lingual*

staff. Non-smoking floors. Piano bar. Restaurants. Sauna. Wheelchair: access; room for disabled (1). **Room services** *Hair-dryer. Mini-bar. Radio. Refrigerator. Room service. Safe. Telephone. TV.*

Le Meridien

3 carrefour de l'Europe, 1000 (548 42 11/fax 548 40 80). Métro Gare Centrale/bus 29, 38, 63, 65, 66, 71. **Rates** *single* 11,000BF; *double* 12,000BF; *suite* 15,000BF-17,500BF. **Credit** AmEx, DC, JCB, MC, TC, V.

Another hotel to cash in on Brussels' longcoming business boom, which means a feeling of déjà vu hits you upon entering... but that's the point for any hotel where frequent travellers stay: instant familiarity. The cavernous colonial-style lobby features a giant brass chandelier suspended spider-like from the ceiling, while a pianist tinkles nightly for guests. The rooms are spacious and warmly decorated – in English Victorian repro style. Ultra-convenient and efficient.

Do it yourself...

There are a number of establishments catering to travellers often in Brussels on business for long-term stays, but not so long-term that they need to rent an apartment here, especially as most apartments in Brussels have a minimum three-year lease. Below are just a few of the residence hotels, or self-catering apartments, whose rooms come with kitchenettes and bathrooms.

Cassiopée

15-17E rue Capouillet, 1060 (233 32 11/fax 533 35 55). Métro Louise/tram 91, 92. **Rates** *double* 10,050BF a week; *suite* 54,000BF a month. **Credit** DC, MC, TC, V.

The building looks like what the 1950s thought the future would look like: streamlined and a hair's breadth away from ugly. There are 50 spacious apartments, near avenue Louise.

Services *Car park. Lifts. Multi-lingual staff. Parking. Hair-dryer. Radio. Refrigerator. Telephone. TV.*

New Yorker Résidence

403 avenue Louise, 1050 (649 90 05/fax 640 30 76). Tram 93, 94/bus 38, 60. **Rates** *suite* 11,200BF-19,600BF a week; *breakfast* 200BF. **Credit** AmEx, MC, V.

The swank location is an ideal address if you're in town on business for a long stay. The most complete of residence hotel services offered in Brussels.

Services *Meeting rooms. Garage. Lifts. Restaurant.*

Résidence Corelli

53 avenue de la Renaissance, 1040 (734 67 99/fax 735 80 77). Metro Schuman or Merode/bus 20. **Rates** *double* 18,000BF-22,000BF a week. **Credit** AmEx, V.

Right across from the scenic Parc Cinquantenaire, among the largest and most majestic parks in the city, the Corelli is a favourite of the EC, which is just a stone's throw away.

Services *Lifts. Multi-lingual staff. Parking. Refrigerator. Telephone. TV.*

Hotel services *Air-conditioning. Babysitting. Business centre. Bars (2). Business centre. Conference facilities. Currency exchange. Fax. Fitness machines. Gift shop. Ice-machines on each floor. Laundry. Lifts. Multi-lingual staff. Non-smoking floors (2). Restaurants (2). Wheelchair: access; rooms for disabled (2).* **Room services** *Hair-dryer. Mini-bar. Modem. Radio. Room service. Safe. Telephone. TV (pay & cable).*

Radisson SAS Hotel

47 rue Fossé-aux-Loups, 1000 (219 28 28/fax 219 62 62). Bus 29, 63, 65, 66, 71. **Rates** *single* 11,590BF; *double* 13,180BF; *suite* 15,000BF-48,000BF; *extra bed* 1,000BF; *breakfast* 590BF. **Credit** AmEx, DC, JCB, MC, TC, V.

Finished in 1991, the Radisson SAS is a joint venture of the American and Scandinavian companies which form its name – and it exemplifies an ultra-professional (if a tad too programmed) approach that you'd expect from these two countries. Crisp, clean, efficient: the perfect hotel to stay if you're in town on business. With glass lifts travelling up the atrium and a seven floor-high skylight with a lounge and goldfish pond below, the Rad SAS feels like the swankiest mall you've ever been in. Each room is decorated in one of four styles – Italian, Scandinavian, Oriental or World Club – which is apparent mostly in the carpeting, curtain and bedspread selection (if you're expecting a futon or tatami mat in the oriental room, sorry: the only Asian touches are the gingko leaf patterned rug and vaguely Japanese-styled lamps and cupboards). The Scandinavian room does feature teakwood floors, which combat allergies because, unlike carpeting, they don't hold dust. The World Club rooms are finer versions of the single and double rooms, with art deco-esque furniture and a more intimate atmosphere. The Radisson has rooms which are among the most spacious in Brussels, and it is just a five-minute walk to Gare Centrale.

Hotel services *Air-conditioning. Babysitting. Business centre. Bars (2). Car park. Conference facilities. Currency exchange. Fax. Gym. Hairdryer. Ice-machine on each floor. Laundry. Lifts. Massage. Multi-lingual staff. Non-smoking rooms. Sauna. Shoe shine. Restaurants (2). Wheelchair: access; rooms for disabled.* **Room services** *Fax. Hair-dryer. Mini-bar. Modem. Trouserpress. Radio. Refrigerator. Room service (24 hours). Safe. Telephone with voicemail. TV (pay & cable).*

Expensive

Amigo

1-3 rue de l'Amigo, 1000 (547 47 47). Tram 23, 52, 55, 56, 81/bus 34, 48, 95. **Rates** *single* 6,200BF-7,300BF; *double* 6,950BF-9,000BF; *suite* 12,450BF-20,500BF; *extra bed* 1,200BF. **Credit** AmEx, DC, JCB, MC, TC, V.

If your first impression upon walking into the Amigo is that it has been around for ages, you're half right: the hotel was built for Brussels' 1958 World's Fair, but much of the materials and furnishings used were taken from buildings as old as sixteenth century – flagstones and tiling from medieval abbeys, Aubusson tapestries, Empire and colonial-styled armoires and chairs, and Flemish paintings from such artists as Courtens and Bastien. For many the Amigo is the most Belgian of the city's larger hotels (only the Métropole comes close in catching the city's character). Built on the site of an old jail (another jail still sits across the way), the Spanish Renaissance-style 'mansion' hotel is a favourite of opera singers, French stars and starlets, and ministers. A two-minute walk from the Grand Place.

Hotel services *Air-conditioning. Babysitting. Bar. Car park. Conference facilities. Currency exchange. Laundry. Multi-lingual staff. Non-smoking rooms. Restaurant. Wheelchair: access; rooms for disabled.* **Room services** *Hair-dryer. Radio. Refrigerator. Room service. Safe. Telephone. TV/VCR.*

Auberge de Jeunesse Jacques Brel – *one of the cleanest youth hostels in town.* *See p28.*

Carrefour de l'Europe

110 rue Marche aux Herbes, 1000 (504 94 00/504 95 00). Métro Gare Centrale. **Rates** *single* 8,500BF-11,500BF; *double* 9,500BF-12,500BF; *suite* 18,000BF. **Credit** AmEx, DC, JCB, MC, TC, V.

One of the four hotels which sprawl connected to each other across from the Gare Centrale like a theme park. Borderline swanky, in a pre-fab way.

Hotel services *Air-conditioning. Babysitting. Bar. Beauty salon. Conference facilities. Currency exchange. Laundry. Lifts. Multi-lingual staff. Non-smoking floor/rooms. Restaurant.* **Room services** *Hair-dryer. Mini-bar. Radio. Refrigerator. Room service. Safe. Telephone. TV/VCR.*

Chateau du Lac

87 Chateau du Lac, 1332 Genval (654 11 22). Train to Genval. **Rates** *single* 5,200BF-8,950BF; *double* 6,150BF-9,900BF; *suite* 19,950BF-23,000BF. **Credit** AmEx, DC, JCB, MC, TC, V.

Just south of Brussels in the upscale community of Genval, this hotel is worth noting as a place to get away from it all. On a small lake, this four-star deluxe pile has all the regal charm you would expect from its name, but its 98 spacious rooms have all modern creature comforts. The fitness centre housed in the building's newer addition is a separate entity from the hotel, but is used by many guests.

Hotel services *Air-conditioning. Babysitting. Bar. Conference facilities. Currency exchange. Gym. Laundry. Lifts. Massage. Multi-lingual staff. Sauna. Non-smoking floor/rooms. Restaurants. Wheelchair: access; rooms for disabled.* **Room services** *Hair-dryer. Mini-bar. Radio. Refrigerator. Room service. Safe. Telephone. TV/VCR.*

Hotel Bristol Stephanie

91-93 avenue Louise, 1050 (543 33 11/fax 538 03 07). Tram 93, 94. **Rates** *single* 7,950BF-8,950BF; *double* 8,950BF-9,950BF; *suite* 15,000BF-35,800BF; *extra bed* 1,000BF; *breakfast* 540BF. **Credit** AmEx, DC, JCB, MC, TC, V.

Though this four-star hotel was bought four years ago by a Norwegian group, it has retained an English name evoking its original owners. The anglo-inspiration remains in its décor, in the airy but intimate lobby of tapestry-upholstered armchairs and blue-and-gold curtains. The rooms have an efficient but spartanly elegant feel, while the suites on the tenth floor are more personable: each is individually decorated in the style of a Scandinavian chalet, with features such as a seashell-shaped bath and a sauna. Cute. Right on avenue Louise, which is the closest thing Brussels gets to New York's Fifth Avenue.

Hotel services *Air-conditioning. Babysitting. Bar. Car park. Conference facilities. Currency exchange. Garage. Laundry. Lifts. Multi-lingual staff. Non-smoking floor/rooms. Swimming pool. Restaurants (2). Wheelchair: access; rooms for disabled.* **Room services** *Free tea & coffee. Hair-dryer. Kitchenette (in 17 rooms). Radio. Refrigerator. Room service. Safe. Telephone. Trouserpress. TV (satellite & cable).*

Métropole

31 place De Brouckère, 1000 (217 23 00/fax 218 02 20). Métro De Brouckere/tram 23, 52, 55, 56, 81. **Rates** *single* 6,850BF-9,850BF; *double* 8,400BF-11,400BF; *suite* 12,500BF-31,000BF; *extra bed* 1,000BF. **Credit** AmEx, DC, JCB, MC, TC, V.

Opened in 1895, the Métropole Hotel was actually an afterthought when it was built: it's still owned by the brewery family that originally added it on to the café it had opened to promote its range of beers. Today, it stands as one of the grandest hotel interiors in Brussels. The main entrance is all French Renaissance flourish, leading to an Empire-style reception hall replete with gold stained-glass windows characteristic of the city's art nouveau heritage. The rooms mix art deco, art nouveau and modern style with a subtle flourish – some bathrooms still have the original tiling from the turn of the century, preserved to perfection. The restaurant downstairs offers opulence and value-for-money meals, and the piano bar lounge even attracts locals, which is a ringing endorsement for any hotel bar.

Hotel services *Air-conditioning. Babysitting. Lifts. Conference facilities. Currency exchange. Laundry. Lifts. Multi-lingual staff. Fitness facilities. Massage. Non-smoking rooms. Piano bar. Restaurant. Sauna. Wheelchair: access; rooms for disabled.* **Room services** *Hair-dryer. Mini-bar. Radio. Room service. Safe. Telephone with voicemail. TV/VCR.*

The **Galia** *– in place du Jeu de Balle. See p21.*

President World Trade Centre

180 boulevard Emile Jacqmain, 1000 (203 20 20/fax 203 24 40). Métro Rogier/tram 23, 52, 55, 56, 81, 90. **Rates** *single* 7,500BF; *double* 8,000BF; *suite* 10,500BF. **Credit** AmEx, DC, JCB, MC, TC, V.

This hotel stands as a testament to the property speculation from the late 1960s to the '80s which led to the destruction of many of the city's most beautiful buildings to make way for the business boom that is only now beginning to happen. Taking its name from Brussels' version of the famed New York twin towers (the Belgian WTC made it to 27 stories before the builders ran out of money), the President World Trade Centre stands across from a barren, weedy lot and amid glass and steel office buildings – just about the worst place you could imagine building a hotel. Which makes the fact that it is actually a quite good hotel all the more strange. Like a second-string Hilton, the WTC has a mildly Las Vegas gleam in its spacious lobby and rooms. WTC's one standout is their garden, arguably the largest in Brussels.

Hotel services *Babysitting. Conference facilities. Currency exchange. Fax. Garden. Gym. Laundry. Lifts. Multi-lingual staff. Non-smoking rooms. Piano bar. Safe.*

Sauna. Sunbed. Restaurant. Wheelchair: access. **Room services** *Hair-dryer. Mini-bar. Radio. Room service. Mini-bar. Trouserpress. TV (cable)/VCR.*

Royal Crown Hotel Mercure

250 rue Royale, 1210 (220 66 11). Métro Botanique/tram 92, 93, 94. **Rates** *single or double* 8,000BF; *suite* 12,000BF-32,000BF; *breakfast* 650BF. **Credit** AmEx, DC, JCB, MC, TC, V.
What used to be the Scandic Crown Hotel has merged with the Hotel Mercure to create one of the most predictable good hotels in Brussels. Not the top of the heap, but the service and accommodation are professional enough.
Hotel services *Air-conditioning. Babysitting. Beauty salon. Car park. Conference facilities. Currency exchange. Fax. Laundry. Lifts. Multi-lingual staff. Non-smoking floor/rooms. Piano bar. Sauna. Sport/fitness facilities. Restaurants. Wheelchair: access; rooms for disabled.* **Room services** *Hair-dryer. Mini-bar. Radio. Refrigerator. Room service. Safe. Telephone. TV.*

Sheraton Brussels Airport

Brussels National Airport, 1930 Zaventem (725 10 00). Train from Gare Centrale to Zaventem. **Rates** *single* 4,050BF-9,900 BF; *double* 5,100-10,900BF; *suite* 18,200BF-26,000BF; *extra bed* 1,000BF; *breakfast* 575BF. **Credit** AmEx, DC, JCB, MC, TC, V.
The sister hotel of the larger city centre location.
Hotel services *Air-conditioning. Babysitting. Business centre. Bars (2). Car park. Conference facilities. Currency exchange. Garage. Laundry. Lifts. Multi-lingual staff. Non-smoking rooms. Restaurant. Sport/fitness facilities. Wheelchair: access; rooms for disabled.* **Room services** *Hair-dryer. Mini-bar. Radio. Refrigerator. Room service. Safe. Telephone. TV/VCR.*

Sheraton Brussels Hotel & Towers

3 place Rogier, 1210 (224 31 11/fax 224 34 56). Métro Rogier/tram 23, 52, 55, 56, 81, 90. **Rates** *single or double* 7,500BF-9,900BF; *suite* 11,950BF-16,950BF; *extra bed* free; *breakfast* 570BF. **Credit** AmEx, DC, JCB, MC, TC, V.
The biggest hotel in Brussels and, as with the Hilton, if you've seen one Sheraton, you have seen them all. But that's the hotel's strength: you know exactly what you're getting yourself into when you book at one. Thirty floors of standardised comfort, with what are among the largest rooms in Brussels. A great view of the city from most floors. Close but not too close to the city's red light district, for those so inclined.
Hotel services *Air-conditioning. Business centre. Babysitting. Car park. Conference facilities. Currency exchange. Fax. Fitness facilities. Laundry. Lifts. Multi-lingual staff. Non-smoking floors (5). Piano bar. Restaurants (2). Sauna. Swimming pool. Wheelchair: access; room for disabled (1).* **Room services** *Hair-dryer. Radio. Mini-bar. Room service. Safe. Trouserpress. TV (pay & cable). Telephone with voicemail.*

Stanhope Hotel

9 rue du Commerce, 1000 (506 91 11/fax 512 17 08). Métro Trone. **Rates** *single* 9,500BF; *double* 12,500BF; *suite* 22,000BF-35,000BF; *extra bed* 1,000BF. **Credit** AmEx, DC, JCB, MC, TC, V.
Three turn-of-the-century townhouses were converted into this intimate hotel five years ago, retaining much of its original architectural splendour while providing thoroughly modern comfort. No two rooms are exactly the same, but the décor is mostly late nineteenth century English – all the rage in Brussels hotels these days. The lobby evokes the country home salon that most wish we had, while the basement bar is pure gentlemen's club. If you're willing to spend, check into a junior suite: the layout is duplex, with a small sitting room with TV on the first level and bedroom on the second. Off the beaten path, but still very accessible to the centre.
Hotel services *Air-conditioning. Babysitting. Bar. Car park. Conference facilities. Currency exchange. Garage. Garden. Laundry. Lifts. Multi-lingual staff. Restaurant. Sports facilities (limited). Wheelchair: access; rooms for disabled.* **Room services** *Hair-dryer. Mini-bar. Radio. Room service. Safe. Telephone. TV (satellite & cable)/VCR.*

Medium range

Alfa Sablon

2-8 rue de la Paille, 1000 (513 60 40). Tram 91, 92, 93, 94. **Rates** *single* 5,300BF; *double* 7,100BF; *suite* 12,000BF. **Credit** AmEx, DC, JCB, MC, TC, V.
Efficient if unexceptional hotel whose principal attraction is its proximity to the Sablon, where Brussels' old and new money change hands over antiques, art and over-priced espressos.
Hotel services *Air-conditioning. Babysitting. Bar. Currency exchange. Laundry. Lifts. Multi-lingual staff. Non-smoking rooms. Wheelchair: access; rooms for disabled.* **Room services** *Hair-dryer. Radio. Refrigerator. Room service. Safe. Telephone. TV.*

Arenberg

15 rue d'Assaut, 1000 (511 07 70/fax 514 19 76). Bus 29, 60, 63, 65, 66, 71. **Rates** *single* 5,800BF; *double* 6,800BF; *suite* 8,000BF-9,000BF. **Credit** AmEx, DC, JCB, MC, TC, V.
At this price, you could do with better service. The 1980s disco lobby leads to less garish but unexceptional rooms. Stay here only if everything else in Brussels is booked.
Hotel services *Bar. Car park. Conference facilities. Lifts. Parking. Restaurant.* **Room services** *Mini-bar. TV (cable).*

Aris

78-80 rue Marche aux Herbes, 1000 (514 43 00/fax 514 01 19). Tram 23, 52, 55, 56, 81. **Rates** *single* 3,500BF-5,000BF; *double* 4,000BF-6,000BF. **Credit** AmEx, DC, JCB, TC, V.
The bleached-out salmon-coloured lobby welcomes you to the mass-produced, sterile charm of this decent hotel. Here again is a hotel whose location is its basic attraction: the rooms are spotless and the furniture new (the hotel opened in June 1995), but there is an overall lack of character: Aris is the kind of hotel that McDonald's would open. The beds are a bit smallish, if firm.
Hotel services *Air-conditioning. Breakfast room. Currency exchange. Lifts.* **Room services** *Hairdryer. Telephone. TV (cable).*

Diplomat

32 rue Jean Stas, 1060 (537 42 50). Métro Louise/tram 91, 92, 93, 94. **Rates** *single* 3,600BF; *double* 4,200BF. **Credit** AmEx, DC, JCB, MC, TC, V.
Uninspiring but practical hotel for visitors doing business in the area. Clean, comfortable – but nondescript.
Hotel services *Lifts. Room services.* **Room services** *Hair-dryer. Mini-bar. Radio. Telephone. TV (cable).*

Le Dixseptieme

25 rue de la Madeleine, 1000 (502 57 44/fax 502 64 24). Métro Gare Centrale. **Rates** *single* 6,500BF; *double* 7,300BF. **Credit** AmEx, DC, JCB, MC, TC, V.
In a word: gorgeous. This 23-room hotel is housed in a seventeenth-century building that once served as the residence of the Spanish ambassador to Belgium, and the current proprietor has taken care to retain the building's former grandeur while providing comfortable accommodation. When the building was bought in the late 1980s by a Swedish consortium, the plan was to turn the building into apartments – which is the reason why the majority of the rooms feature fully fitted kitchens. Now owned by a Belgian

family, the conveniently located hotel (a scenic five-minute walk from Gare Centrale) features a burnished, listed staircase leading up to the individually decorated rooms, which are mostly decorated in Louis XVI or French Renaissance style. Alabaster white walls create an airiness, while antique furnishings (a four-poster bed in one room, an ornate oak dining table in another) create an instant feeling of home. Ultra-comfortable. Highly recommended.
Hotel services *Bar. Conference facilities. Garden. Lift. Kitchenette.* **Room services** *Mini-bar. TV (cable).*

Le Dome

12-13 boulevard du Jardin Botanique (218 06 80/218 41 12). Métro Rogier/tram 23, 52, 55, 56, 81, 90. **Rates** *single* 6,800BF; *double* 7,650BF; *suite* 7,000BF-8,600BF. **Credit** AmEx, DC, JCB, MC, TC, V.
There are actually two parts to this hotel: the original Dome, on the corner of the major thoroughfare boulevard Adolphe Max and boulevard du Jardin Botanique, dates back to 1902, with the original façade of the ten-floor building maintained, while Le Dome II, added on 20 years ago, is a few doors down. The rooms are basically identical, functional and with small flourishes (framed Gustav Klimt posters, faux art deco furnishings) to diminish the overall sterile atmosphere. The newer Dome II attracts a mostly American, business clientèle, who appreciate its air-conditioning.
Hotel services *Babysitting. Bar. Lifts. Conference facilities. Currency exchange. Laundry. Trouserpress. Multi-lingual staff. Non-smoking rooms. Restaurant. Wheelchair: access; rooms for disabled.* **Room services** *Free tea & coffee. Hair-dryer. Mini-bar. Radio. Room service. Safe. Telephone. TV (cable).*

Galia

16 place du Jeu de Balle, 1000 (502 42 43). Bus 20, 48. **Rates** *single* 1,500BF-3,000BF; *double* 1,600BF-3,000BF; *suite* 4,000BF; *breakfast* 160BF. **Credit** AmEx, JCB, MC, TC, V.
Standard hotel with spartan amenities for the person who needs a clean, safe room as a base while in Brussels. The restaurant downstairs is filled in the mornings not only with backpacking travellers but also with local bargain-hunters and merchants from the daily fleamarket, just a few steps out the front door.
Hotel services *Bar. Lifts. Restaurant. Currency exchange.* **Room services** *TV.*

Hotel Ibis

100 rue Marché aux Herbes, 1000 (514 40 40/fax 514 50 67). Métro Gare Centrale. **Rates** *single* 4,000BF; *double* 4,300BF. **Credit** AmEx, DC, JCB, MC, TC.
Efficiency overrules aesthetics at the Ibis. From the spacious salmon and mint-green lobby with plastic plants and brass accents to the efficient if a tad institutional rooms, the Ibis is an experience in familiarity to anyone who has stayed in an Ibis anywhere in the world. One of the most appealing features about the hotel is its 15-minute contracts, whereby if there is a problem with your room and it has not been seen to in 15 minutes, your stay is free.
Hotel services *Currency exchange. Lifts. Meeting room. Restaurant. Parking. Wheelchair: access.* **Room services** *Mini-bar. Telephone. TV (cable).*

New Hotel Siru

1 place Rogier, 1000 (203 35 80/fax 203 33 03). Métro Rogier/tram 23, 52, 55, 56, 81, 90. **Rates** *single* 5,200BF; *double* 5,900BF. **Credit** AmEx, DC, JCB, MC, TC, V.
Although it's been around since 1935, the Siru got a new lease of life in the 1980s when it decided to model itself on New York's famed Chelsea Hotel and feature works by local artists in every room. The rooms themselves are compact but well-laid-out – think neat student room at the beginning of the school term, and you've got the picture. An excellent view of Brussels is available from the higher floors. The hotel is located a few metres away from Gare du Nord and the red light district – but the area is safe.
Hotel services *Bar. Car park. Conference facilities. Currency exchange. Laundry. Lifts. Multi-lingual staff. Non-smoking rooms. Restaurant.* **Room services** *Hair-dryer. Radio. Telephone. TV (cable).*

Palace

3 rue Gineste, 1210 (203 51 51/203 44 44). Métro Rogier/tram 23, 52, 55, 56, 81, 90. **Rates** *single* 6,500BF, *double* 7,500BF; *suite* 9,000BF-18,000BF. **Credit** AmEx, DC, JCB, MC, TC, V.
Another major hotel near the Place Rogier (the Sheraton is just across the way). The elegance here looks a little shop-worn, but the rooms are moderately good-value for money.
Hotel services *Bar. Conference facilities. Laundry. Lifts. Multi-lingual staff. Restaurant. Wheelchair: access.* **Room services** *Hair-dryer. Radio. Telephone. TV.*

Inexpensive

L'Agenda

6 rue de Florence, 1050 (539 00 31/fax 539 00 63). Métro Louise/tram 91, 92. **Rates** *single* 3,500BF; *double* 3,800BF; *suite* 4,500BF; *extra bed* 500BF. **Credit** AmEx, DC, JCB, MC, TC, V.
This 15-year-old hotel was renovated in June 1995, giving the set of apartment-like rooms a fresh feel. Clean and comfortable with a personable desk staff, this is a great place for a couple who are planning to stay a few days. Near the fashionable avenue Louise.
Hotel services *Babysitting. Currency exchange. Fax. Multi-lingual staff. Non-smoking rooms.* **Room services** *Free tea & coffee. Hair-dryer. Kitchenette. Trouserpress. Telephone. TV (cable).*

Auberge St Michel – *good value* – *see p23.*

Argus

6 rue Capitaine Crespel, 1050 (514 07 70/fax 514 12 22). Métro Porte de Namur or Louise. **Rates** *single* 3,200BF; *double* 3,500BF. **Credit** AmEx, DC, JCB, MC, V.
The practically but not lavishly sized rooms resemble motel rather than hotel accommodation, with inoffensive modern furniture and a cosy feel. A few steps away from the Toison d'Or, a popular promenade of mid-range clothing stores, and the more upmarket boulevard de Waterloo.
Hotel services *Babysitting. Bar. Lift. Parking (limited).* **Room services** *Hair-dryer. TV (cable).*

Arlequin

17-19 rue de la Fourche, 1000 (514 16 15/fax 514 22 02). Métro De Brouckère/tram 23, 52, 55, 56, 81. **Rates** *single* 2,400BF; *double* 3,200BF-3,400BF; *suite* 3,600BF-5,200BF. **Credit** AmEx, DC, MC, V.
Don't let the graffiti-covered corridor leading to the hotel entrance scare you off – this is a fine place to stay if your needs are modest. The student-sized rooms have just enough space to pack and unpack, with the décor being nondescript enough not to annoy.
Hotel services *Lift. Meeting room.* **Room services** *TV (cable).*

Armorial

101 boulevard Brand Whitlock, 1200 (734 56 36/fax 734 50 05). Tram 23, 90. **Rates** *single* 1,900BF-2,800BF; *double* 2,300BF-3,100BF. **Credit** AmEx, DC, MC, V.
Another hotel whose principal attraction is its location. This one is on a tree-lined boulevard leading to square Montgomery which has an Arc de Triomphe arch and one of the most dangerous intersections in the city – much like Paris's place de la Concorde.
Room services *TV (cable).*

Ascot

1 place Loix, 1050 (tel/fax 538 88 35). Tram 91, 92. **Rates** *single* 2,300BF-2,700BF; *double* 3,000BF. **Credit** AmEx, DC, MC, V.
Charmless service unfortunately diminishes an otherwise charming hotel's appeal. Unless you are a masochist on holiday, you could do better.
Hotel services *Airport shuttle. Bar. Lift. Meeting room. Parking.* **Room services** *Mini-bar. TV (cable).*

Auberge Saint Michel

15 Grand Place, 1000 (511 09 56/fax 511 46 00). Métro Gare Centrale/tram 23, 52, 55, 56, 81. **Rates** *single* 2,100BF-3,500BF; *double* 2,800BF-3,500BF; *suite* 3,900BF-4,200BF. **Credit** AmEx, MC, V.
When visiting the city, you can't get a much better location in Brussels for sightseeing than this… and the price is dead cheap for the neighbourhood. The catch? Windows are not double-glazed, which means that light sleepers might have problems with traffic and rowdy carryings-on outside, but to be able to open floor-to-ceiling double windows on to the Grand Place at these prices is quite something. The hotel itself? A mixed bag: booking here is a crapshoot, with attractive low-rent versions of Louis XV furniture in some rooms containing the bare necessities, and other rooms resembling something from a halfway house – garage-sale sofas, saggy matresses and threadbare carpets. Housed in the sixteenth-century home of the Duke of Brabant, which makes it sound a lot grander than it is today: the façade is massive and impressive, with inlaid gold and all that, but the hotel only takes up a minuscule portion of the building. Near everything you want to see in Brussels.
Hotel services *Lift.* **Room services** *Mini-bar. TV.*

Balladins

600 avenue Houba de Strooper, 1020 (476 15 14/fax 476 13 96). Tram 18. **Rates** *single or double* 3,200BF. **Credit** AmEx, DC, MC, V.

Basic, no frills **La Madeleine** *– see page 24.*

If you want to see one of the most attractive residential districts in Brussels with tree-lined avenues and friendly shops then the Balladins is a good choice. It's near the Atomium and Mini-Europe, popular tourist attractions.
Hotel services *Bar. Lift. Meeting room. Parking. Wheelchair: access.* **Room services** *Mini-bar. TV (cable).*

De Boeck's

40 rue Veydt, 1050 (537 40 33/fax 534 40 37). Tram 91, 92, 93, 94. **Rates** *single* 2,100BF-2,800BF; *double* 2,300BF-3,200BF. **Credit** AmEx, DC, MC, V.
Quiet, airy, intimate, this renovated townhouse has charm.
Hotel services *Airport shuttle. Garden. Meeting room. Lift. Parking.* **Room services** *TV (cable).*

Du Congrès

40-44 rue du Congrès, 1000 (217 18 90/fax 217 18 97). Métro Madou. **Rates** *single* 2,600BF; *double* 3,000BF. **Credit** AmEx, DC, MC, V.
The lobby is clean but nondescript, just like the inoffensive-borderline-bland 512 rooms of this hotel near place Madou.
Hotel services *Parking.* **Room services** *TV (cable).*

La Grande Cloche

10-12 place Rouppe, 1000 (512 61 40/fax 512 65 91). Tram 23, 52, 55, 56, 81. **Rates** *single* 1,700BF-2,900BF *double* 2,100BF-2,900BF. **Credit** MC, V.
La Grande Cloche is situated on the charming place Rouppe, which gives on to the wide avenue Stalingrad leading to Gare du Midi, where you can take advantage of the city's best-known flea market every morning. It's only a two-minute walk away from your hotel room.
Hotel services *Bar. Lift. Parking.* **Room services** *TV (cable).*

Hotel Sema

6/8 rue des Harengs, 1000 (548 90 30/fax 548 90 39). Tram 23, 52, 55, 56, 81. **Rates** *single* 3,000BF; *double* 3,500BF. **Credit** MC, TC, V.

Intimacy is the operative word for this converted private home opened in April 1995 and boasting 11 cosy, wood-beamed ceiling rooms so quiet it's easy to forget that you're in the centre. You have to pass two doors to enter each room: an outer, more soundproofed one followed by an ornate, older version. At press time, the chalet-styled breakfast room was in the midst of becoming a crêpe restaurant .

Hotel services *Currency exchange.* **Room services** *Hair-dryer. Radio. TV (cable).*

Lambeau

150 avenue Lambeau, 1200 (732 51 70/fax 732 54 90). Métro Georges Henri. **Rates** *single* 2,100BF-2,600BF; *double* 2,900BF-3,100BF. **Credit** AmEx, MC, V.

This is as suburban as you can get without a picket fence. Quiet and with rooms a little on the smallish side – but with more facilities than most establishments in this price range.

Hotel services *Airport shuttle. Bar. Lift. Parking.* **Room services** *Mini-bar. TV (cable)/VCR.*

La Légende

35 rue du Lombard, 1000 (512 82 90/fax 512 34 93). Tram 23, 52, 55, 56, 81. **Rates** *single* 1,800BF; *double* 2,500BF. **Credit** AmEx, DC, MC, V.

If you want to be in the centre of Brussels nightlife, this place is ideal: salsa clubs, most of the city's gay bars, and bistros for thirtysomethings are all within spitting distance. There are 45 rooms, only half of which have bath or shower and WC, so specify when booking.

Hotel services *Lift.*

Lloyd George

12 avenue Lloyd George, 1050 (648 30 72/fax 646 53 61). Tram 23, 90, 93, 94. **Rates** *single* 1,900BF-2,400BF; *double* 2,200BF-2,800BF; *suite* 2,800-3,600BF. **Credit** AmEx, DC, MC, V.

Away from the hubbub of the city centre, this small hotel is good value for money. Near the lush Bois de la Cambre.

Hotel services *Bar. Garden. Lift. Restaurant.* **Room services** *TV (cable).*

La Madeleine

22-24 rue de la Montagne, 1000 (513 29 73/fax 502 13 50). Métro Gare Centrale. **Rates** *single* 1,900BF-3,000BF; *double* 2,800BF-3,300BF. **Credit** AmEx, DC, MC, V.

Don't expect much, that way you won't be disappointed: all the basic necessities in a no-frills hotel that's less attractive for what it is than for where it is. Five minutes on foot from Gare Centrale, with the architecturally impressive Galeries Royales St-Hubert and the bustling restaurant street rue des Bouchers even closer. Clean enough.

Hotel services *Breakfast room. Lift.* **Room services** *Telephone. TV (cable).*

Maison du Dragon

158-160 boulevard Adolphe Max, 1000 (218 82 15/fax 218 81 25). Métro Rogier/tram 23, 52, 55, 56, 81, 90. **Rates** *single* 2,200BF; *double* 2,600BF-2,800BF; *breakfast* 180BF. **Credit** DC, MC, V.

So-so smallish hotel on one of the city's main strips, which can be noisy at night. Near WH Smith so at least you can pick up something to read for nights without sleep.

Hotel services *Bar. Lift. Restaurant.* **Room services** *TV (cable).*

Mozart

15A rue du Marché aux Fromages, 1000 (502 66 61/fax 502 77 58). Bus 34, 48. **Rates** *single* 1,895BF-2,495BF; *double* 2,795BF-3,295BF. **Credit** AmEx, DC, MC, TC, V.

Not as scary as the name would lead you to believe – in fact, quite nice. A speckled grey marble staircase leads you up to the first-floor reception of this tiny hotel squeezed in between two of the many pitta shops on this street. The rooms are mostly duplexes, with a small sitting room and bathroom on a different level than the bedroom. As you would expect, classical music emanates throughout the lobby and hallways, but the room furnishings are mostly Ikea – good Ikea, but Ikea nonetheless. The street outside is a bustling area of activity at night, so it might be wise to get a room at the back.

Hotel services *Lift. Currency exchange. Multi-lingual staff.* **Room services** *Radio. Hair-dryer. Refrigerator. Telephone. TV.*

Opera

53 rue Gretry, 1000 (219 43 43/fax 219 17 20). Métro De Brouckère/tram 23, 52, 55, 56, 81/bus 29, 63, 65, 66, 71. **Rates** *single* 1,950BF; *double* 2,350BF-2,500BF; *suite* 2,950BF-3,150BF. **Credit** AmEx, JCB, MC, TC, V.

With a black and bordello-red lobby, the Opera does follow the rule of thumb that the posher the name, the more modest the accommodation is likely to be. Utilitarian painted plywood closets and sepia-toned bathrooms with horrid lighting are the drawbacks to this very basic hotel. Thinking of how much money you're saving by staying here makes your visit more endurable.

Hotel services *Lift.* **Room services** *Telephone. TV (cable).*

Les Tourelles

135 avenue Winston Churchill, 1180 (344 02 84). Tram 23, 90/bus 38. **Rates** *single* 2,300BF-3,000BF; *double* 3,500BF-3,800BF; *suite* 3,900BF-4,600BF. **Credit** AmEx, MC, TC, V.

Ultra-comfortable inn where the feel is more that of a country home than a hotel. In the elegant Uccle quarter of town on a tree-lined street where many in the city aspire to reside. Child-friendly.

Hotel services *Babysitting. Bar. Meeting room. Restaurant.* **Room services** *Hair-dryer. Radio. Telephone. TV.*

Van Belle

39 chaussée de Mons, 1070 (521 35 16/fax 527 00 02). Bus 47. **Rates** *single* 2,000BF-2,200BF; *double* 2,300BF-2,600BF. **Credit** AmEx, DC, MC, V.

Near Brussels' garment district, this is another hotel built in anticipation of Brussels' business boom. There are 126 rooms here in an area of town that you'd only want to stay in if you had business there.

Hotel services *Bar. Car park. Lift. Meeting room. Restaurant.* **Room services** *TV (cable).*

Windsor

13 place Rouppe, 1000 (511 20 14/fax 514 09 42). Tram 23, 52, 55, 56, 81. **Rates** *single* 2,000BF; *double* 2,400BF. **Credit** AmEx, DC, MC, V.

Another hotel on the lovely place Rouppe with 24 rooms but only ten have bath and toilets, so specify when reserving.

Hotel services *Bar. Parking. Lift.* **Room services** *TV (cable).*

Cheap

Accueil Stéphanie

11 rue de la Grosse Tour, 1000 (511 82 26/fax 513 82 16). Tram 93, 94. **Rates** *single* 1,000BF-2,500BF; *double* 1,200BF-2,900BF. **Credit** AmEx, MC, V.

Child-friendly ***Les Tourelles*** *– on a tree-lined street in the elegant Uccle quarter of Brussels.*

Another inn-type establishment that is always booked due both to its intimate atmosphere and calm-within-a-storm setting: a few blocks away is the bustling Toison d'Or shopping district. The garden, a rarity in Brussels, is a delight.
Hotel services *Bar. Garden.* **Room services** *Mini-bar. TV (cable).*

Les Bluets

124 rue Berckmans, 1060 (tel/fax 534 39 83).Métro Hôtel des Monnaies. **Rates** *single* 1,400BF-2,000BF; *double* 1,600BF-2,500BF. **Credit** AmEx,MC, V.
The geraniums spilling out of flower boxes outside the windows of this converted townhouse give you an idea of the personal touch given here. Run by a lovely couple, the atmosphere is more that of a country house than a hotel. Popular with Belgians.
Hotel services *Garden.*

De France

21 boulevard Jamar, 1060 (522 79 35/fax 522 11 11). Métro Gare du Midi/tram 23, 52, 55, 56, 81, 90. **Rates** *single* 1,400BF-1,600BF; *double* 1,600BF-2,600BF. **Credit** AmEx, DC, MC, V.
The kind of hotel that you'd expect to rent by the hour, if you know what we mean. But it's cheap and close to the Gare du Midi, so handy for the Eurostar.
Hotel services *Bar. Lift.*

Duke of Windsor

4 rue Capouillet, 1060 (539 18 19). Tram 91, 92. **Rates** *single* 1,300BF; *double* 2,000BF. **Credit** AmEx, DC, MC, V.
A minimum two-night stay is required to lodge at this private home converted to a five-room inn. A charming corner lounge accompanies each room. Reserve well in advance by phone and confirm by letter. Speaking French helps a lot.

Fouquets

6 rue de la Bourse, 1000 (512 00 20/fax 511 93 57). Tram 23, 52, 55, 56, 81. **Rates** *single* 1,350BF-1,650BF; *double* 1,850BF-2,250BF; *suite* 2,300BF; *breakfast* 150BF. **Credit** AmEx, DC, MC, V.
Given the location, if this eight-room joint was really top notch, it would be hellishly expensive. Although they do have a modest bar and restaurant, do yourself a favour and

Put up with the tacky décor and save yourself some cash at the ***Opera*** *near De Brouckère.*

take advantage of the many restaurants and bars literally minutes outside your hotel room.
Hotel services *Bar. Fax. Lift. Restaurant.* **Room services** *Mini-bar.*

George V

23 rue 't Kint, 1000 (513 50 93/fax 513 44 93). Tram 18. **Rates** *single* 2,000BF; *double* 2,450BF. **Credit** MC, V.
Modest 17-room hotel that is in one of the few areas of the centre that actually has the feeling of a neighbourhood: a mix of long-time city residents, immigrant families and artists. A good selection of bars and cafés within walking distance.
Hotel services *Bar. Lift. Parking.* **Room services** *TV (cable).*

Hôtel des Eperonniers

1 rue des Eperonniers, 1000 (513 53 66/511 32 30). Métro De Brouckère/tram 23, 52, 55, 56, 81. **Rates** *single* 1,800BF; *double* 2,500BF. **Credit** AmEx, MC, V.
The kind of hotel that fugitives from justice would stay in. Most of the furnishings look as if they came from someone's attic, and the building itself, situated conveniently near Gare Centrale and the Galeries Royales St-Hubert, is squeezed in between other buildings that make it easy to miss. If you do stay here, specify that you would like a room with a bath and a toilet – those lodging in rooms without facilities can take advantage of the communal showers and WCs, which can be an interesting way to get to know people.
Hotel services *Lift.*

Madou

45 rue du Congrès, 1000 (218 83 75/fax 217 32 74). Bus 63. **Rates** *single* 1,500BF; *double* 1,800BF-1,900BF. **Credit** MC, V.
This old townhouse has been converted into nine rooms that offer a homely atmosphere. Often booked, which is the best indication of a hotel's popularity.

New Galaxy

7A rue du Progrés, 1210 (203 47 76/fax 203 45 54). Tram 23, 52, 55, 56, 81, 90. **Rates** *single* 1,400BF-1,500BF; *double* 1,600BF-1,900BF. **Credit** DC, MC, V.
The name alone should give you pause, but if you really want to be a stone's throw from Gare du Nord, then pitch your tent here. Only two-thirds of the hotel's rooms have bath or shower and WC, so specify when booking.
Hotel services *Lift. Parking.* **Room services** *TV (cable).*

Rembrandt

42 rue de la Concorde, 1050 (512 71 39/fax 511 71 36). Tram 93, 94. **Rates** *single* 1,400BF-1,900BF; *double* 1,900BF-2,500BF; *suite* 2,300BF-2,900BF. **No credit cards.**
Pension-type accommodation near avenue Louise, which means that there is a chi-chi factor at work. Décor borders on cutesy-quaint and kitschily twee: lots of blond wood and frills. Check out the lobby of antique bric-à-brac, lace doilies and antique lamps, and one word comes to mind: grandma.
Hotel services *Lift.*

Royotel Brussels

312 rue Royale, 1210 (218 30 34/fax 219 93 79). Tram 91, 92, 93, 94. **Rates** *single* 1,800BF-2,100BF; *double* 2,400BF-2,500BF. **Credit** AmEx, DC, MC, V.
Chain hotel with very reasonable prices and good enough service. Out-of-the-way location in an area that has not yet been fully gentrified.
Hotel services *Bar. Lift. Meeting room.* **Room services** *TV (cable).*

La Tasse d'Argent

48 rue du Congrès, 1000 (217 83 75/fax 217 32 74). Métro Madou. **Rates** *single* 1,500BF; *double* 1,750BF-1,900BF. **Credit** MC, V.
Seventeen rooms in a slightly tacky style reminiscent of the 1950s, which only adds to its charm. Popular at weekends, which is a rarity for a hotel in Brussels.
Hotel services *Bar.*

Youth hostels

Auberge de Jeunesse Bruegel

2 rue de Saint-Esprit, 1000 (511 04 36/fax 512 07 11). Métro Gare Centrale. **Open** 7.30am-1am daily. **Rates** *double* 650BF per person; *quad* 550BF per person.
More central than the other hostels, which makes it more suitable for those who like to enjoy a little nightlife before turning in. Not the most attractive in this range, but that's all the more reason to get out and see Brussels.
Hostel services *Currency exchange.*

Auberge de Jeunesse Jacques Brel

30 rue de la Sablonniere, 1000 (218 01 87/fax 217 20 05). Métro Botanique/tram 91, 92, 93, 94. **Open** 8am-1am daily. **Rates** *double* 550BF per person; *quad* 450BF per person.
Near the Botanique but accessible by foot from the centre, this hostel has 140 beds and ranks as one of the cleanest.
Hostel services *Currency exchange. Laundry.*

CHAB – Hôtel des Jeunes

8 rue Traversiere, 1030 (217 01 58/fax 219 79 95) Métro Botanique/tram 91, 92, 93, 94. **Open** 7.30am-2am daily. **Rates** *double* 510BF per person; *quad* 430BF per person; 10 per cent discount YMCA or ISIC holders.
Divided into two sections, this trendy hostel has 220 beds, spread out in quirky spaces such as a former concert hall, where there are even beds on the stage. Rooms for two to four people with dormitories taking from six up to 16, with bigger savings to be had the more you share. There's a fountain, patio and a garden. Out of the way but accessible.
Hostel services *Bed linen rental. Phone booth. Washing machine.*

La Fonderie – Auberge de Jeunesse Jean-Nihon

4 rue de l'Eléphant, 1080 (410 38 58/fax 410 39 05). Métro Comte-de-Flandre. **Open** *reception* 7am-noon, 2pm-1am, daily. **Rates** *double* 550BF per person; *quad* 450BF per person.
The name translates as foundry – former incarnation of this hostel. What it lacks in character it makes up for in comfort.
Hostel services *Bed linen rental. Dining room. Garden. Laundry room. Parking.*

Sleep Well Youth Hostel

23 rue du Daimier, 1000 (218 50 50/fax 219 13 13). Métro Botanique/tram 91, 92, 93, 94. **Open** 10am-1pm (later entry 50BF) daily. **Rates** *double* 640BF per person; *quad* 510BF per person.
If you want hotel-style accommodation but still to pay hostel rates, then this former YMCA is the place for you.
Hostel services *Bar. Bed linen rental. Currency exchange. Guided tours. TV (cable, in lobby).*

Bed & breakfast

Bed & Brussels

58 rue Victor Greyson, 1050 (646 07 37/fax 644 01 14). Tram 93, 94. **Reservations** 9am-6pm Mon-Fri.
B&Bs both in Brussels and throughout Belgium can be booked through this agency. If you phone and get their answering service, then just leave your name, telephone number and a time that you can be contacted, and they'll get back to you. They also publish a guide of bed & breakfasts, imaginatively titled *Bed & Breakfast*.

Brussels by Season

Brussels, boring? Read on for the fest life of the Belgians and other round-the-year cultural frolics.

Despite Brussels' reputation as a boring town full of Eurocrats, the city dishes up a full plate of activities for its residents – from the highbrow to the offbeat and funky.

After months of grey skies, the city most noticeably comes alive during spring and summer with a stream of rock, pop, and jazz concerts and cultural festivals. Among the activities not to be missed are the many quirky, folkloric events held in Brussels and the provinces. You'll soon discover that Belgians never turn down a chance to dress up. *See also chapters* **Music: Rock, Folk & Jazz** and **Trips Out of Town**.

For information about upcoming events in the city contact **TIB** (513 89 40/fax 514 45 38), which publishes an annual brochure filled with colourful photographs and information about the year's festivals and happenings. Copies can be picked up at the office or received by post free of charge. For activities beyond Brussels, the helpful and multilingual **Belgian Tourist Office** (504 03 90/fax 504 02 70) can give tips on offbeat outings such as kayaking down the River Semois in the Ardennes or riding a hot-air balloon in west Flanders. *See chapter* **Essential Information** for addresses and opening times of tourist information offices.

Public holidays

New Year's Day (1 Jan); **Easter Monday**; **Labour Day** (1 May); **Ascension Day** (May); **Whit Monday**; **National Day** (21 July); **Assumption Day** (August); **All Saints' Day** (1 Nov); **Armistice Day** (11 Nov); **Christmas Day**.

You need to get your timing right for the **Serres Royales** *or Royal Hothouses – see p30.*

Spring

Serres Royales (Royal Hothouses)

61 avenue du Parc Royal (Domaine Royal), 1020 (513 89 40). Métro Heysel/tram 52, 92/bus 53. **Open** 9.30am-4pm Wed, Thur; 9-11pm Fri; 9.30am-4pm, 9-11pm Sat, Sun. NB: only open two weeks around end April to early May, when the flowers are in bloom. Dates vary annually but are given out by the tourist office from Jan. **Admission** free during day; 100BF at night.

For a few weeks at the end of April and in early May Belgians get to peek into King Albert and Queen Paola's private world, when the royal hothouses are opened to the public. The elegant complex known as 'the city of glass' was designed by nineteenth-century architect Alphonse Balat, commissioned by King Léopold II who wanted it to be a showcase for the tropical plants he found in the Belgian Congo. The king later became so fond of the serene atmosphere within that he moved into one pavilion shortly before his death.

Foire Internationale du Livre (International Book Fair)

Date late April to early May. **Admission** 200BF; 100BF students; 50BF groups. **Information** *Foire Internationale du Livre, 72 rue A Campenhout, 1050 (646 38 90/fax 646 5285).* **Open** 9am-5pm Mon-Fri.

Although not on par with Frankfurt's famed book fair, the Brussels five-day event does attract a significant crowd of readers. About 80,000 visitors passed through in 1996. Don't expect to find many goodies in English as the fair focuses on European languages – French, Spanish, German as well as Hungarian and Albanian.

Heilig-Bloedprocessie (Procession of the Holy Blood)

Bruges. **Date** Ascension Day in May. **Information** *Bruges Tourist Information Office, 11 Burg, 8000 Bruges (050 448 686/fax 050 448 600).*

Religion buffs will not want to miss the Procession of the Holy Blood, when the town of Bruges turns out to venerate a few drops of liquid thought to be blood from Christ's crucified body. Thousands of actors dressed in medieval garb parade through the streets, re-enacting how the vial arrived in Bruges in the twelfth century. Floats, banners, musical instruments and choirs add to the atmosphere. Reserved grandstand tickets can be bought from the tourist office after 1 Feb. Bruges is an hour away from Brussels by train.

Concours Musical International Reine Elisabeth de Belgique (Queen Elisabeth International Music Competition)

Palais des Beaux Arts & Conservatoire Royal de Musique (see chapter **Music: Classical & Opera***).* **Date** May-mid-June. **Tickets** 500BF-2500BF. **Information** *Palais des Beaux Arts, 23 rue Ravenstein, 1000 (507 82 00).* **Open** 9am-6pm Mon-Sat; *box office* 11am-6pm Mon-Sat.

Founded over 40 years ago by Belgium's former Queen Elisabeth, an avid violinist, this prestigious month-long competition is a must for classical music aficionados. Young musicians from around the world compete in the rotating categories of voice, violin and piano. Voice was the category for 1996 and violin is the theme in 1997. Concerts are held at the Royal Music Conservatory and Palais des Beaux Arts, and for the most part tickets are available to the public. The 12 musicians who make it to the final have a chance to hobnob with King Albert and Queen Paola. Lesser mortals can catch a piece of the action on Belgian television.

Brussels 20-kilometre Run

Start & finish Esplanade du Cinquantenaire. Métro Merode or Schuman. **Date** last Sunday in May. **Admission** 350BF participants; free spectators. **Information** *Syndicat d'Initiative – Bruxelles Promotion 1886, 17 rue de la Chapelle, 1000 (511 90 00/fax 511 37 15).* **Open** 9am-6pm Mon-Fri, 9am-4pm Sat.

Belgium's biggest track and field event attracts about 20,000 amateur and professional runners every year, the vast majority being Belgian. Competitors start at the Parc du Cinquantenaire and are led past many of Brussels' finer landmarks, including the Palais Royal, the Palais de Justice, avenue Louise and the Bois de la Cambre. If there's no rain, about 100,000 Bruxellois usually turn out to cheer on participants, especially those last panting stragglers. Winners receive a trophy, a medal and a certificate, but no cash.

Jazz Marathon

venues throughout Brussels and nearby towns. **Date** late May to early June. **Information** *Jazz Marathon, 34 rue Africaine, 1060 (concert details 534 22 00).* **Admission** three-day pass to all events 400BF in advance, 450BF on the day. Tickets also available at Fnac, TIB and participating venues.

In late May, music lovers can enjoy non-stop jazz for three days straight. The somewhat unknown bands – nearly all Belgian – play at cafés and small clubs throughout Brussels and in nearby towns. To sample sounds at the 50 or so clubs in the city, buy a three-day pass. A special jazz bus will be on hand to shuttle you around at no extra cost. Marathon-goers also get the added bonus of reduced beer prices at participating venues. Several concerts held at the Grand Place are free to the public and feature such luminaries as Maceo Parker.

Summer

Battle of Waterloo

Date mid-June. **Information** *Waterloo Tourist Information Centre, 149 chaussée de Bruxelles, 1410 (354 99 10/fax 354 22 23). Phone for directions.* **Open** *1 Nov-31 Mar* 10.30am-5pm daily; *1 Apr-31 Oct* 9.30am-6.30pm daily.

War buffs will have to wait until the year 2000 to see the 1815 Battle of Waterloo re-enacted in this Brussels suburb. About 2,000 men get together every five years in June, don period uniforms, wield vintage guns and play war – with some representing the troops of England's Duke of Wellington and Prussia's Marshall Blucher, while others act as French soldiers fighting under Napoleon's leadership.

Ommegang

place du Grand Sablon to the Grand Place. **Date** first Tue & Thur in July. **Information** *TIB (see chapter* **Essential Information***).* **Admission** *tickets for Grand Place perf* 935BF-1335BF.

The Ommegang, which is Flemish for 'Walkabout', is a medieval-style procession from place du Grand Sablon to the Grand Place. The colourful parade originated in the fourteenth century as a religious event to celebrate the safe arrival of a statue of the Virgin Mary by boat from Antwerp. Over the years, the Ommegang became more secular and grew in stature when, in 1549, Charles V and his family watched the procession. Today's re-enactment ends in a dance (9pm-midnight) at the illuminated Grand Place. Tickets are expensive and are available from late May. Buy in advance as it always sells out. Those reluctant to fork out for the finale can watch from the streets along the way.

Brosella Jazz & Folk Festival

Groen Theatre, Parc d'Osseghem, 1020 (269 69 56). Métro Heysel. **Date** second weekend in July. **Admission** free.

Organised by a group of unpaid music lovers, the Brosella festival has been going strong for over 20 years, despite a shoestring budget. A sampling of jazz and folk from Belgian and international musicians is served up all weekend long at the Parc d'Osseghem near the Atomium. Cartoons are also shown to keep the kiddies happy.

Actor-director Tim Robbins – guest of honour at the 1996 **Brussels Film Festival**. *See p32.*

Festival d'Ete de Bruxelles (Brussels Summer Festival)

Selected venues. **Date** early July to early September. **Admission** prices vary. **Information** *108 avenue de Tervuren, 1040 (735 06 13/fax 735 47 99).*

Lovers of Mozart, Schubert and Beethoven have a chance to listen to more than a dozen concerts over a two-month period. The performances are held at some of Brussels' finer halls and feature the Orchestre National de Belgique among others.

Foire du Midi (Brussels Annual Fair)

boulevard du Midi. Métro Gare du Midi. **Date** mid-July to mid-Aug.

Every summer since 1885, Bruxellois have thronged to the annual fair held near Gare du Midi. The family-oriented fair is one of the largest in Europe, spanning two kilometres with Ferris wheels, shooting galleries, dodgems, roller-coasters and fortune-tellers. Plenty of food stalls are on hand with traditional Belgian fare – from *moules et frites* to grilled *boudin* (sausages) and *caricolles* (a poor man's escargot).

National Day

Parc de Bruxelles and other city parks. **Date** 21 July.

Belgium celebrates its independence and the accession of the first king of Belgium with festivities throughout the city. The biggest party takes place in the Parc de Bruxelles – across from the Palais Royal – with a military parade topped off by fireworks. On the outskirts of the city, Bruparck runs family-oriented activities, including many concerts geared to the easy-listening crowd.

Palais Royal Open Days

2 rue Ducale, 1000 (551 20 20/fax 512 56 85). Métro Trône or Parc. **Date** last week of July to second weekend in September. **Open** 10am-4pm Tue-Sun. **Admission** free.

Every year, just after Belgium's National Day, the king and queen open up their home to the public for nearly six weeks. You won't catch a glimpse of the royal boudoir or any other rooms that the couple actually inhabit, though – they're strictly off limits.

Meiboom (Raising of the Maypole)

place du Grand Sablon to the Grand Place. **Date** 9 August. **Admission** free. **Information** *TIB (see chapter* **Essential Information***).*

For a truly folksy experience of Belgian culture, stick around for the Raising of the Maypole, or *Meiboom*. This involves a festive procession of giant puppet-like and cartoon-style characters that winds through the streets from the Sablon to the Grand Place. Legend has it that in 1213 a wedding party was celebrating outside the city when they were attacked by a gang from Leuven. The gang was chased out of town, and as a token of appreciation, the local duke allowed the victorious wedding party to plant a maypole on the eve of their patron saint's feast day.

Floral Carpet (Tapis des Fleurs)

Grand Place, 1000. Métro Bourse or Gare Centrale. **Date** mid-August. **Information** *TIB (see chapter* **Essential Information***).*
Every other year (1996 and 1998) Brussels' main landmark, the Grand Place, is showcased even more than usual for three days when hundreds of thousands of cut begonias are carefully laid in a giant 1,860-square-metre floral carpet. The flowers of every hue imaginable are arranged to form significant symbols and pictures including a scene of Brussels' patron saint, St Michael, slaying a dragon. This gorgeous display is not to be missed.

Autumn

100 Years of Comic Strips

Date mid-Sept 1996 to first week in Jan 1997. *Centre Belge de la Bande Dessinée, 20 rue des Sables, 1000 (219 19 80). Métro Botanique, De Brouckère or Rogier/tram 55, 58, 81, 90/bus 38, 61, 71.* **Open** 10am-6pm Tue-Sun. **Admission** 180BF; 120BF groups (of 15 or more); 60BF under-12s. **No credit cards**.
As part of Belgium's celebration of 100 years of comics, the capital is hosting an array of exhibitions, tours and festivals throughout 1996 and into the start of 1997. In addition to permanent exhibitions on such superstars as Tintin, the Centre Belge de la Bande Dessinée (CBBD) hosts an exhibit on the cartoon character Lucky Luke (16 Sept-15 Dec 1996). The fiftieth anniversary of the Blake & Mortimer cartoon character is also marked with a display (8 Oct 1996-5 Jan 1997). Walking tours of buildings that have comics on their exteriors are also planned. Call the CBBD for information on outdoor festivals during spring and summer.

Journées du Patrimoine (Heritage Days)

Date first or second weekend in September.
Admission free. **Information** Brussels *Heritage Days Brussels, CCN, 80 rue de Progrès, 1030, (204 24 49/fax 204 15 22).* Flanders and Wallonia *Fondation Roi Baudouin, 21 rue Bréderode, 1000 (511 18 40/fax 512 00 35).*
Belgium, along with several other European countries, has a tradition of opening up several buildings – normally off-limits to the public – for one weekend of the year. Based around a different theme each year, these two days are meant to give ordinary citizens a rare glimpse into life on the farm, inside an abbey, or even in a château. In Brussels, the event takes place during the second weekend in September. In the countryside it's a week earlier.

Europalia

Palais des Beaux Arts, 23 rue Ravenstein, 1000 (507 84 86). Métro Gare Centrale. **Date** 4 October 1996 to 5 January 1997. **Open** 10am-6pm Tue-Sun. **Admission** 250BF; 200BF over-60s; 150BF students.
The Europalia festival focuses on a different theme or person each year and Europalia '96 is Victor Horta's turn under the spotlight. One can't live long in Brussels without hearing Horta's name – the renowned architect designed many of the city's art nouveau buildings. A prime example is the Palais des Beaux Arts, which will host a retrospective of Horta's work, including photographs, sketches, models and furniture. Visitors can get a closer look at his architectural finesse with a guided tour in English of his buildings throughout the city, including Gare Centrale. Concerts, lectures and films about the Palais des Beaux Arts are also planned.

Audi Jazz Festival

Venues throughout Belgium. **Date** mid-Oct to mid-Nov. **Information** *Jazztronaut, 55 Boechtlaan, Grimbergen 1853 (534 22 00/fax 460 01 36).* **Open** 9am-7pm Mon-Fri.
This month-long musical jamboree offers a mixed bag of artists, both obscure and well-known. In its ten years of existence, the Audi Jazz Festival has featured the likes of Ray Charles and Herbie Hancock. Philip Glass was slated to perform in 1996. Around 60 concerts are scattered throughout the country with the big names appearing at the Palais des Beaux Arts in Brussels and the lesser-knowns at smaller venues in the capital and in the provinces.

Winter

Le Marché de Noël

Grand Place. **Date** three days in mid-December.
Information *TIB (see chapter* **Essential Information***).*
Admission free.
Brussels holds a European Christmas market every year at the Grand Place, at which stalls representing various EU countries display their finest yuletide wares. If you're not in the mood for shopping, tuck into the multitude of ethnic food and booze. If you hate getting jostled in a crowd, avoid going midday. Concerts featuring music from EU countries are held each night from 7.30-8pm.

Brussels Film Festival

Palais des Congrès de Bruxelles (513 41 30) and Actors Studio (218 10 55). **Date** mid- to late January. **Tickets** from 250BF; from 200BF students. **Information** *Brussels Film Festival, 50 chaussée de Louvain, 1210 (218 53 33/fax 218 18 60).* **Open** 9:30am-6pm Mon-Fri.
One of the lesser known international movie fests, the Brussels Film Festival has gained more recognition in recent years by featuring first screenings and bringing in big-name stars. For example, in 1996 American actor-director Tim Robbins appeared as guest of honour. A competition for the best European feature film has also been initiated. Contact the festival's organisers at the above address for a catalogue of films to be shown. For listings, check with the TIB or look in the weekly *Bulletin*.

Festival du Dessin Animé (Animation Festival)

Auditorium du Passage, 44 boulevard du Jardin Botanique, 1000 (218 27 35) and Centre Culturel du Botanique, 236 rue Royale, 1210 (226 12 11). **Date** 5-16 February 1997. **Admission** 200BF single ticket; 2000BF pass for all shows; 900BF pass for five shows.
Information *Folioscope, 19 rue de la Rhétorique, 1060 (534 41 25/fax 534 22 79).*
This non-competitive festival aims to promote animation among professionals as well as among a general audience of students, families and film lovers. Over 100 short films and features are shown, along with retrospectives of and tributes to famous animators. Members of the public are invited to submit their films for review before 10 January. Call before 5 November for an application form.

Binche Carnival

Binche. **Date** mid-Feb (including Shrove Tuesday).
Admission free. **Information** *Belgian Tourist Office in Brussels (504 03 90/fax 504 02 70).*
Just over an hour's drive from Brussels, the town of Binche hosts Belgium's largest and wildest carnival. The highlight of the event takes place on Mardi Gras, or Shrove Tuesday, when the traditional 'Gilles' – dressed in clogs and embroidered costumes – don masks and dance in the Grand Place carrying bundles of sticks to ward off evil spirits. They reappear later in the day, toting enormous head-dresses made from ostrich feathers, and toss oranges at the crowd as they pass through town – so look out.

Sightseeing

Opening hours are tricky and the best things are often hidden, but there's a lot more to Brussels than a little boy pissing and nine metal balls.

Brussels always seems vaguely mistrustful of visitors. It has about five famous sights to which everyone flocks, and after that you may draw a blank. In fact there's a great deal to see, but you get the impression that it doesn't quite want to be seen. Brussels doesn't court visitors like other cities. In particular, opening hours can be infuriating, as you will see below. For too many places, you have to be in a group and book a month in advance, which involves the kind of preparation most people don't have time for.

The Belgian capital is a city of fine churches, monuments, parks and museums, and most of these are accommodating, but you are denied access to too many of the really intriguing palaces and houses. No one can prevent you walking round to admire the façades, and some of the tours mentioned below will actually get you inside, notably **ARAU** (*see below* **Trips & tours**). Otherwise, just hope you have the good fortune to be around on the second Sunday of September. This is the Jour de Patrimoine, when almost everything is munificently thrown open to the populace. Suddenly you can see the hidden treasures – in the company of the whole city, of course, but don't let that put you off.

Focal points

Arc de Triomphe

Parc du Cinquantenaire, 1000. Métro Merode.

Obviously inspired by the great Arc de Triomphe in Paris, this imposing structure was built by Girault in 1905. It is in Brussels' most famous park and stands like a gateway from the peripheries into the centre. Avenue de Tervuren rushes from the suburbs to meet it and the long, narrow, gloomy rue de la Loi takes over to bring you in a straight line to the centre of town. Most of the EU buildings are to be found grouped at the town end of the park on Rond Point Robert Schuman.

Grand Place/Grote Markt

1000. Métro Bourse or Gare Centrale.

If Brussels is the 'crossroads of Europe' and the Grand Place is the crossroads of Brussels, then presumably there

Brussels' **Arc de Triomphe**, *located in Parc du Cinquantenaire, was built by Girault in 1905.*

is nowhere more central in Europe. But a crossroads does not sound like a place to linger and this is undoubtedly one of the most beautiful squares in the world. It is daily engulfed by swarms of tourists who, if they see nothing else in Brussels, will carry away the impression of baroque splendour, gilded façades (now stripped of grime) and firm cobbles. Almost totally destroyed by the French bombardment of 1695, the Grand Place was triumphantly rebuilt by the guilds of Brussels in less than five years and emerged even more distinctive than ever. It is the pivotal centre of the city: from here you could strike out on foot to almost all of Brussels' major sights. The Grand Place undergoes seasonal transformation, with a great carpet of flowers in the summer and a Norwegian tree (twin of the one in Trafalgar Square) together with a crib of live animals at Christmas, plus various pageants and parades throughout the year.

Guildhouses of the Grand Place

Some of the Grand Place has been taken up for administrative purposes over the centuries, but the guildhouses remain the heart of it. Each guild left individual markings on its house and gave it a distinctive name, deriving from the façade. Looking at the array of ornate splendour, it is well to reflect that its origins are neither royal nor aristocratic, but firmly and proudly mercantile. The grandly named 'Maison du Roi' (now the Musée de la Ville de Bruxelles) is known in Flemish as the Broodhuis, which is a more

Eyes wide shut

JG Ballard on Paul Delvaux's landscapes of nostalgia and desire.

Each of Delvaux's paintings is a doorway into a unique and enchanting dream, one of the most mysterious realms in twentieth-century art. Under an evening or late afternoon sky, the temples and palaces of a Renaissance city stand in their own shadows, the stage-sets for a drama of the unconscious that has yet to begin or may have ended decades beforehand. The perspectives are exact, and every cornice and column is strictly in place. Only time is absent, banished from the unearthly light and replaced by memory and a pervading nostalgia.

Almost without exception, this is a city of women. Calm and bare-breasted, they stand or recline in the posture of mannequins, but each has the dormant power of a sleeping goddess. The few men who enter this realm are timid, uneasy figures, like toddlers who have strayed into their mothers' boudoirs and glimpsed a fearful but fascinating beauty. The women guard each other, but now and then a violent panic seems to threaten them. They signal wildly to the dark air, as if the sleeper whose mind encloses them has stirred uncomfortably in his dream.

For the most part, though, a deep and reassuring calm presides over this twilit space. It emanates from the broad hips and heavy breasts of these stately women, and from their placid contemplation of some inner world glimpsed within their large and unflinching eyes. As we observe them we feel an intense yearning for a richer and more real domain that may have existed on the far side of the womb. Our memories of the oedipal conflicts of our childhoods are assuaged by these impassive beings, and our deepest passion for womanhood seems sanctioned by their welcoming gaze.

Delvaux is generally considered to be a surrealist, but he had little in common with other members of that restless and international movement. Unlike Dalí, Ernst and Tanguy who travelled ceaselessly, he rarely left his native city, took almost no part in the surrealists' group activities and spent his life working quietly in his studio, content to embark each day on his solo voyage into his imagination.

He was born in 1897, the son of a Brussels lawyer, and seems to have been dominated by his strong-willed mother. It was only after her death, when he was in his mid-thirties, that the heavy curtains across his mind drew back and he saw clearly for the first time the luminous world he was to make his own. As a young artist he painted in a loosely expressionist way, but after a trip to Italy he was deeply impressed by its classical architecture and by the poetic perspectives in the works he had seen on show by de Chirico.

From then on Delvaux's art scarcely varied for more than half a century. A childhood fascination with trains sometimes revealed itself, and he meticulously painted the stationary carriages pausing at a quiet suburban station before setting off to some destination we will never know, that terminus at the dream's end. During World War II his painting became populated by skeletons, sinister visitors who stand beside his placid nudes, male intruders from the fields of death that the horrors of wartime Europe had driven into the dreamer's mind.

For the most part, Delvaux remained true to his vision of a twilight paradise, in many ways an Edenic image that only a male imagination could evoke. As a result, accusations of voyeurism have made Delvaux less familiar to British gallery-goers than to those on the Continent. But his unselfconscious and consoling women, immersed in their tribal solidarity, in many ways meet all the demands for a nurturing and

accurate title since it was owned by the bakers' guild and never by a king.
Nos.1-2 'Au Roi d'Espagne' – also the bakers' guild.
No.3 'La Brouette' (the wheelbarrow) – the grocers' guild.
No.4 'Le Sac' – the joiners' and coopers' guild.
No.5 'La Louve' (the she-wolf) – the archers' guild.
No.6 'Le Cornet' (the horn) – the bargees' guild.
No.7 'Le Renard' (the fox) – the haberdashers' guild.
No.9 'Le Cygne' (the swan) – the butchers' guild.
No.10 'L'Arbre d'Or' (the golden tree) – the brewers' guild.
No.24-25 'La Chaloupe d'Or' (the golden galleon) – the tailors' guild.
No.26 'Le Pigeon' – the artists' guild, where Victor Hugo stayed in 1852.

Major sights

Atomium

boulevard du Centenaire, 1020 (477 09 04/477 09 77). Métro Heysel/tram 81. **Open** *Sept-Mar* 10am-6pm daily; *Apr-Aug* 9am-8pm daily. **Admission** 200BF; 150BF groups (minimum 20); 120BF children. **Credit** AmEx, MC, V.
Probably the second most famous monument in Brussels, the Atomium is Brussels' equivalent of the Eiffel Tower, but it has aged less well and was never as impressive anyway. It's a 102-metre representation of the nine atoms of a molecule, done in steel and aluminium. It was designed by Andre Waterkeyn for the 1958 World Fair and has a dated feel. You

Paul Delvaux*'s 'Vénus Endormie', 1944, Tate Gallery, London.*

self-sufficient feminist collective, a world of women content to be without men.

During a century dominated by formalist experiment in the arts, surrealism has been almost alone in its dedication to the poetic imagination, a faculty that may have atrophied among the British audience brought up on concept and installation art. Delvaux's world is as far removed as possible from those of Duchamp and Damien Hirst (where no one ever feels an emotion or has an erection), but his appeal lies in that realm of memory, eroticism and desire that has its roots far beyond the retina and the frontal lobes in the archaic deeps of the brain.

To mark the centenary of Delvaux's birth a major retrospective of his work will be held at the Musée d'Art Moderne (see chapter **Museums***) from 21 March-7 July 1997.*

can go inside and view the *Biogénium* exhibition about human life, which is not that remarkable. The best thing about the visit is travelling to the spheres by long escalators and the view of the city from the top, which is one of those indisputably modern phenomena like New York from the Empire State Building and Paris from the Eiffel Tower.

Hôtel de Ville

Grand Place, 1000 (tourist information 513 89 40). Métro Bourse or Gare Centrale. **Guided tours** *Apr-Sept* 11.30am, 3.15pm Tue; 3.15pm Wed; 12.15pm Sun. *Oct-Mar* closed Sun. **Admission** 75BF. **No credit cards.**
The only building to survive the 1695 French bombardment, this magnificent Gothic structure adorned with numerous sculptures was begun in 1402, taken up again in 1444 and completed in four years. The architect, Jan van Ruysbroeck, then added the splendid 100-metre tower, which upon its completion seemed to decentre the rest of the building and legend has it that the architect, in true Renaissance despair, climbed to the top of his masterpiece and threw himself off it. There are guided tours inside, which take in the elegant official rooms hung with famous tapestries and the gallery of the Spanish kings with portraits executed after the monarchs were dead.
Wheelchair: access.

Manneken Pis

corner of rue de l'Etuve & rue du Chêne, 1000. Métro Bourse or Gare Centrale.
Famous both as a national symbol and for the disappointment it causes visitors. 'But it's so small' is the inevitable cry. The tiny bronze statuette perched on a stone façade pissing cheerfully down is certainly miniature, but if you go prepared for his diminutiveness, you might find him amusing. The idea is worth more than the execution. It says something for the irreverence of the Bruxellois that they chose this to

Don Quijote and Sancho in place d'Espagne.

embody their *esprit*. There are numerous legends (he was the son of a count, he extinguished a fire), but nothing much is known about his origins. The present statue was executed in the seventeenth century by Jerome Duquesnoy, it was stolen in 1745 by the British, in 1777 by the French and in 1817 it was taken and smashed by a French convict. The convict got a lifetime of hard labour and the little fellow was moulded together again. At the last count he had 518 costumes (kept in the **Musée de la Ville de Bruxelles** in the Grand Place), but don't expect him to stop there.

Palais de Justice

place Poelaert, 1000 (508 64 10/508 65 78). Métro Louise/tram 92, 93, 94. **Open** *Aug-Sept* 9.30am-noon, 1.30-3pm, Mon-Sat. **Admission** free.
This mammoth building – bigger than St Peter's in Rome – was purposefully situated on the Galenburg hill so that it could loom threateningly over the populace. One of

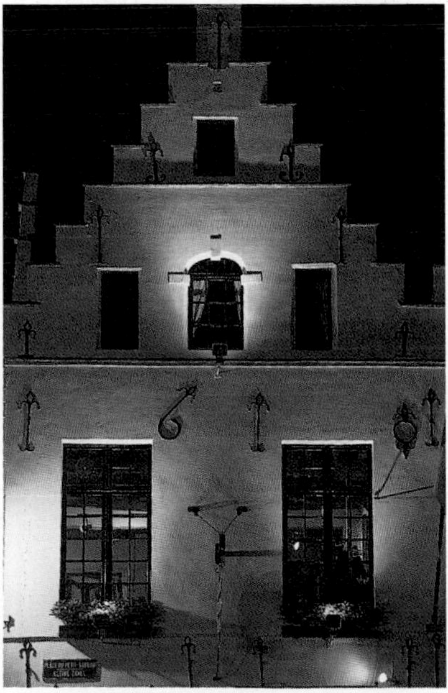

Sablon *comprises Notre Dame du Sablon (left) and place du Petit Sablon (right).* *See page 39.*

Palais de Charles de Lorraine – *see page 40.*

Léopold II's key projects, it is frequently referred to by those who wish to denigrate his grandiose notions. It is has a strong imperial air, deliberately modelled along the lines of the ancient Egyptian temples, and was so exhausting a project that the architect, Poelaert, collapsed and died mid-construction in 1879. The interior is equally imposing and equally good at overawing luckless criminals, with giant magisterial statues of Demosthenes and Cicero, and the echoing Salle des Pas Perdus (waiting room). You get a fine view of northern Brussels from the terrace at the front – try the telescopes.
Wheelchair: access.

Sablon

1000. Bus 20, 34.
Sablon – or Zavel in Flemish – is the elegant area comprising place du Grand Sablon, the church of Notre Dame du Sablon and place du Petit Sablon. Grand Sablon has flamboyant bars, numerous antique shops and a pricey flea market every Saturday. Notre Dame du Sablon is probably the loveliest Gothic church in Brussels. It was built in the fifteenth and sixteenth centuries; the interior, with exquisite stained glass, is especially stunning (open 9am-5pm daily, entrance on rue de la Régence). Just across the road is Petit Sablon, a small park designed in 1890 by Henri Beyaert. Its railings were designed by the art nouveau architect, Paul Hankar, and are divided by 48 columns, each with a statuette representing one of the ancient guilds of Brussels. Inside are statues of humanists and of the martyrs Egmont and Hornes.

Palaces & castles

In Brussels any important building can be called a 'palais' – you will even find the European Commission building referred to as the Palais Berlaymont (though not very often). Those included here either have royal origins or were built as private homes. (For the administrative 'palaces' *see below* **Notable buildings**.)

Château Malou

45 chaussée de Stockel, 1200 (761 27 66/762 21 05 gallery). Bus 28. **Open** when gallery has exhibition, phone to check.
Now an art gallery and cultural centre, this is a fine eighteenth-century castle set by a lake in the elegant Parc Malou.

Palais Stocklet – *closed to visitors after treasures had started to disappear. See page 40.*

It was built in 1776 by Baron Lambert, but then passed to the Malou family who lived in it until 1951. The stables have been turned into an art exhibition centre.

Palais de Charles de Lorraine

1 place du Musée, 1000 (519 53 71). Métro Gare Centrale. **Open** group visits by prior arrangement only.
Beautiful eighteenth-century palace whose interior has been remarkably well restored. The staircase is huge and has an imposing statue of Hercules. The state room has a star with 28 points on the floor, each one made of a different Belgian marble.

Palais d'Egmont

off place du Petit Sablon, 1000. Tram 20, 48/bus 34, 95. **Not open to the public.**
Begun in the sixteenth century by the mother of the Count of Egmont, it was enlarged in the eighteenth century and had to be rebuilt at the beginning of this century after a fire. It is now used for receptions by the Minister for Foreign Affairs. It was here that Great Britain, Ireland and Denmark signed the Treaty of Accession to the EEC in 1972. The rooms are magnificent, with rich tapestries and carpets, but only the gardens are open to the public. These are lovely, if overshadowed by the Hilton Hotel in a typical piece of bad town planning. There are statues, including one of Peter Pan by Sir George Frampton, and a beautiful octagonal fifteenth-century well.

Palais Royal

place des Palais, 1000 (551 20 20). Métro Parc/tram 92, 94. **Open** *25 Jul-8 Sept* 10.30am-4.30pm Tue-Sun. **Admission** free.
The old seat of the dukes of Brabant, this was destroyed by fire in 1731 and rebuilt until it was given its final form in 1904 by Balat and Maquet at the request of the indefatigable Léopold II, who is largely responsible for the imperial feel of Brussels. Now it's the official residence rather than the home of the royal family. Only in late summer can you see inside the great state rooms and view the tapestries designed by Goya, but it's in a fine square with a broad sweep of cobbled road, overlooking Parc de Bruxelles and the Horta-designed Palais des Beaux Arts. Changing of the guard, which is not the great ceremonious occasion it is in London, occurs daily at about 2.30pm.
Wheelchair: access.

Atomium – *go for the view –* *see page 35.*

Palais Stocklet

281 avenue de Tervuren, 1150. Tram 39, 44. **Not open to the public.**
Brussels' most interesting palace is now unfortunately closed to the public after it was discovered that visitors had been making off with the smaller treasures. It's a marvellous geometric building designed by the Austrian Josef Hoffmann, and is in deliberate opposition to the lavishness of art nouveau. It is, in its sparseness and purity, entirely modern. Only old black-and-white photos give a tantalising clue to the interior, with the Klimts in the dining room. The palace is laid out back to front with the main entrance facing the garden. Legend has it that the industrialist Stocklet, who built the palace, wanted the avenue to be named after him, so when it wasn't, he turned his back to it and sulked.

Churches & abbeys

Abbaye de la Cambre

avenue E Duray, 1050 (648 11 21). Tram 23, 90, 94. **Open** 9am-noon, 3-6pm, Mon-Fri; 3-6pm Sat; 8am-12.30pm, 3-6pm, Sun; 9am-noon Catholic feast days.
Founded in the twelfth century by a noblewoman called Gisèle for the Cîteaux Order, the abbey was badly damaged during the wars of Religion and was rebuilt in the sixteenth and eighteenth centuries. There is also a fourteenth-century church attached to the abbey. The buildings are set in elegant French gardens and now house the National Geographical Institution and an art exhibition centre.

Basilique Nationale du Sacré Coeur

1 parvis de la Basilique, 1083 (425 88 22). Métro Simonis then bus 87. **Open** *Apr-Sept* 8am-6pm Mon-Sat; Oct-Mar 8am-5pm Mon-Sat. **Guided tours** by appointment. **Services** 9am Mon-Fri; *Flemish* 5.30pm, *French* 6.30pm Sat; *Flemish* 9am, *with Gregorian choir* 10am Sun.
This twentieth-century basilica (not actually completed until around 1970) is impressive for its commanding position and its size – 167m by 89m. It's a national monument dedicated to the memory of patriots, but the dull red-brick style is heavy and it fails to move the beholder. The interior is rather better, though, with its chapels, large choir and statue of Our Lady by Goosens.

Cathédrale des Sts Michel et Gudule

place Ste Gudule, 1000 (217 83 45). Métro Gare Centrale or Parc. **Open** *Nov-Mar* 7am-6pm Mon-Fri; 7.30am-6pm Sat; 8am-6pm Sun; *April-Oct* 7am-7pm Mon-Fri; 7.30am-7pm Sat; 8am-7pm Sun. **Services** *Flemish* 4pm, *French* 5.30pm, Sat; 10am, 11.30am, 12.30pm Sun. **Admission** *crypt* 40BF; 30BF groups.
This magnificent cathedral, tactfully dedicated to the male *and* female patron saints of Brussels, would probably enjoy greater prominence were it not the victim of bad planning, which has left it hemmed in on three sides by ugly modern buildings. The scaffolding was recently removed from most of the exterior after countless years of work and it emerged from its chrysalis gleaming. It was completed by the end of the fifteenth century in the Brabant Gothic style, but was damaged by the French shelling of 1695. The interior is splendidly proportioned and stuffed with treasures, chiefly

Hidden churches

Scattered around the Grand Place are some of Brussels' oldest and most beautiful churches. The *commune* has been quite good about preserving them – the seventeenth-century Eglise de la Madeleine was transported stone by stone to another site when the construction of Gare Centrale on its former site threatened it with demolition. However, the churches' surroundings have been less well preserved: none of them has its own square and the area has been wholly given over to the demands of tourism and shopping, so walking amid the glitz, you are taken by surprise by these ancient buildings.

Eglise de la Madeleine

rue de la Madeleine, 1000 (511 28 45). Métro Gare Centrale. **Open** 7am-noon, 2-5pm, Mon-Fri; 7am-noon, 3-7pm, Sat; 7am-noon, 5-7pm, Sun. **Services** 7am, 7.30am, noon, 7pm, Mon-Fri; noon, 7pm, Sat; 7am, 9.30am, 10.30am, 7pm, Sun.

A slightly bleak seventeenth-century church built in dark-brown brick. Transported to make room for Gare Centrale, it looks rather sad and isolated in its new upbeat surroundings. A chapel to St Rita was added in 1958.

Eglise Notre Dame de la Chapelle

place de la Chapelle, 1000 (512 07 37). Métro Gare Centrale/bus 20, 48. **Open** *Oct-May* 1-4pm daily; *Jun-Sept* 9am-4pm daily. **Services** 4pm Sat; 11.30am Sun.

A little way from the Grand Place, this is the burial place of Pieter Bruegel the Elder. Although there is no tomb, there is a memorial erected by his son Jan. This fine, large church stands at the beginning of rue Haute – where the painter was born – flanked on all sides by graceless, high-rise buildings. It boasts a wealth of styles: part of the chapel is twelfth-century; the transepts are seventeenth-century Romanesque; the nave is fifteenth-century Gothic. Most of the paintings date from the nineteenth-century, though there are some seventeenth-century de Clerks.

Eglise Notre Dame du Finistère

rue Neuve, 1000 (217 52 52). Métro De Brouckère. **Open** 8am-6pm Mon-Sat; 8am-noon Sun. **Services** 9.15am, 12.10pm, 5pm, Mon-Fri; 9.15am, *Flemish* 4.30pm, *French* 6pm, Sat; *Flemish* 9am, *French* 11am, Sun.

This eighteenth-century church has found itself in probably the most incongruous setting of all: in the middle of the most famous and busiest of the downmarket high streets. Its very doors are splattered with graffiti. Within a metre of its porch, fluorescent sweets are sold and buskers strum their erratic tunes. Like the other churches, it has an air of long-suffering sanctity. The interior is ornate with a great carved pulpit and baroque paintings.

Eglise Notre Dame aux Riches Claires

21 rue des Riches Claires, 1000 (511 09 37/511 50 99). Métro Bourse. **Closed** for renovation except 9.30am-12.30pm Sun. **Services** *French* 11.15 am Sun; *Spanish* 10am Sun.

Tucked away down a small street, this is attached to buildings on every side. It is a charming, ruddy, asymmetrical building – also part of the Flemish Renaissance. Unusually, it has a jutting gable, which is more common in a town house than a church, and is probably the work of Rubens' pupil, Luc Fayd'herbe.

Eglise St Nicolas – *Brussels' oldest church.*

Eglise St Nicolas

1 rue au Beurre, 1000 (513 80 22). Métro Bourse or De Brouckère. **Open** 7.45am-6.30pm daily. **Services** *French* 8am, 11.30am, 5pm, Sun; *English* 10am Sun; *Flemish* 6.30pm Sun.

The oldest church in Brussels is almost lost in the area's tourist and boutique glitz. Founded in the eleventh century, the oldest part of it dates from the twelfth; it managed to survive the 1695 bombardment, preserving a cannon ball in its wall. St Nicolas is – appropriately, in the light of the church's proximity to the Grand Place – the patron saint of merchants. A calm model of medieval sanctity, its slightly curved shape follows the old line of the River Senne. The interior is invitingly dark and twisting with small, bluish stained-glass windows.

Notre-Dame du Bon Secours

rue du Marché au Charbon, 1000 (514 31 13). Métro Bourse or De Brouckère. **Open** 9am-5pm daily. **Service** *Flemish* 11am Sun.

A strange little seventeenth-century baroque church behind boulevard Anspach, Notre Dame du Bon Secours is attached to a bar on one side. It was designed by Willem de Bruyn, who was also the architect of the Chaloupe d'Or and the Maison des Brasseurs on the Grand Place. Like them it's a fine example of the Flemish Renaissance style. The interior contains a fourteenth-century wooden statue of Our Lady of Perpetual Succour.

Wheelchair: access.

Eurocrats' Brussels

Looming in the background – **Berlaymont.**

To most of Europe, and indeed to most of its English-speaking inhabitants, Brussels means the EU. One in four people in the city is a foreigner. It's home to the Commission, the Council of Ministers and part of the Parliament. The European buildings are to be found all round the end of rue de la Loi, near the renamed Rond Point Schuman. At the moment the Commission buildings are in a state of flux and the workers are displaced since asbestos was discovered five years ago in their royal palace, the Berlaymont. This has now been totally evacuated and new buildings hastily erected, chief among them, the Breydel (*see chapter* **Brussels by Area**). It's difficult to visit, though, because for all of them you have to request in writing six weeks in advance and it's for groups only – but, of course, if you happen to know anyone working there, they can take you round.

Berlaymont

Rond Point Schuman, 1040. Métro Schuman. **Closed** for refurbishment.

Long despised as the epitome of heavy-handed 1970s architecture, this impossible-to-miss building has now achieved something approaching cult status. Riddled with asbestos, it has been closed for five years. The first plan was to knock down the reviled structure and commission a *chef-d'oeuvre* of modern elegance. It was then discovered that it had become too powerful a symbol to tear down and so it is being allowed to remain. The four-pointed star form is at the moment encased in white plastic, rather like a Christo creation. It looms over the area and looks, as everyone agrees, better than ever.

Council of Ministers

175 rue de la Loi, 1040 (285 61 11). Métro Schuman. **Closed** to the public except on open day, 11 May.

In contrast to the looming Berlaymont opposite, this sprawling building – finished in polished peach-coloured stone – is immense but long and low; more of a ground-grazer than a skyscraper.

Wheelchair: access; toilets.

European Parliament

43 rue Wiertz, 1047 (284 21 11). Métro Maalbeek.

This huge construction, glittering blue-green above the Quartier Léopold, undulates around a great area, going off into rounded corners and pausing for massive archways. It's like a small covered city rather than a mere building, run through with long corridors of abstract art.

Breydel

rue de Breydel, 1040. Métro Schuman.

Overlooking the Parc du Cinquantenaire, this is a modern building, not at all ungracefully executed and with a geometric façade.

the wonderful pictorial stained-glass windows by Bernard van Orley and the thirteenth-century choir. The altar is surprisingly cool and modern; the great Flemish painter Roger van der Weyden is buried nearby.

Collégiale des Sts Pierre et Guidon

place de la Vaillance, 1070 (521 84 15). Métro St Guidon. **Open** 9am-noon, 2.30-6pm Mon-Fri (closed holidays and Sun during services).

A fine example of the Brabant Gothic style, it was built between the fourteenth and sixteenth centuries but has a crypt dating from the eleventh, which is one of the oldest in Belgium. However, the spire is a youthful nineteenth-century addition. Inside the crypt is a Celtic stone called the tombstone of St Guidon. There are other ancient tombs in the church as well as medieval wall paintings. To the left of the church, in rue de Chapelain, is the thirteenth-century Béguinage of Anderlecht, whose surviving seventeenth-century buildings have been turned into a museum.

Eglise Notre-Dame de Laeken

parvis Notre-Dame, 1020 (479 96 61). Tram 81/bus 53. **Open** for guided visits 2-6pm Sun. **Services** 5pm first Fri of month; 5pm Sat; 9.15am, 10.15am, 11.30am, Sun.

This is the burial place of Belgium's kings and queens and opening times are firmly restricted to days of national significance (those dates you don't recognise above are probably those of royal deaths). But the huge, neo-Gothic exterior, designed by Poelaert in 1851, is well worth a look. In the cemetery behind are tombs of important Belgians – including Poelaert himself – and a cast of Rodin's sculpture *The Thinker*. There are also a couple of incongruities: a mosque and an Egyptian temple. If you do get in, make sure to look out for the wonderful thirteenth-century Madonna on the altar.

Eglise Ste Cathérine

place Ste Cathérine, 1000 (513 34 81). Métro Ste Cathérine. **Open** 8.30am-5pm (summer until 6pm) Mon-Sat; 9am-noon Sun. **Services** *chapel* 8am, *church* 10am, Sun.

Looming over its own square, Eglise Ste Cathérine is as unkempt-looking as its surroundings. It was designed in 1854 by Poelaert, architect of the Palais de Justice. Fortunately, the interior looks better – it's arched and graceful, with pretty blue-and-yellow glass windows and a fifteenth-century Black Madonna statue.

Eglise St Jacques-sur-Coudenberg

place Royale, 1000 (511 78 36/502 18 25). Métro Parc. **Open** 10am-6pm Tue-Sat; 9am-noon Sun; 3-6pm Mon. **Services** *French* 5.15pm Sun.

The most important of the lovely neoclassical buildings in this exceptionally gracious square. It was built in 1775 to resemble a Roman temple and has none of the Gothic piety exuded by most of Brussels' churches. The interior is just as imposing as the outside and one can easily imagine that it served perfectly as a Temple of Reason and then as a Temple of Law under the French Revolution, before being returned to Catholicism in 1802.

Eglise St Jean-Baptiste

place du Béguinage, 1000 (217 87 42). Métro Ste Cathérine. **Open** 10am-5pm Tue; 9am-5pm Wed-Fri; 10am-5pm Sat (first, third & fifth of the month); 9.30am-noon Sun. **Services** *French* 5pm Sat; *Flemish* 10am; *French* 8pm Sun.

One of the best examples of Flemish baroque in Belgium, this large church was designed by Luc Fayd'herbe, a pupil of Rubens. It has a honey-coloured, vertical and symmetrical façade. Inside there is a beautiful pulpit and paintings by the seventeenth-century Brussels painter van Loon.

Attractions

The Clock

mont des Arts, 1000. Métro Gare Centrale.

A rather uninspiring title for this landmark, but there appears to be no proper name for this giant timepiece set into the wall at the lower end of mont des Arts. It consists of 12 figures, each representing a historical personage. On the striking of the hour, the relevant figure emerges from his cubby hole and performs a mechanical action. If you're not there on the hour, it just looks like an ornate façade.

Mini-Europe

Bruparck, 20 boulevard du Centenaire, 1020 (478 05 50). Métro Heysel/tram 18, 19, 81, 91. **Open** *1 Apr-30 Jun* 9.30am-6pm daily; *1-19 Jul & 20-31 Aug* 9.30am-8pm daily; *20 Jul-19 Aug* 9.30am-midnight daily; *1 Sep-6 Jan* 10am-6pm daily (closed 6 Jan-31 Mar). **Admission** 380BF; 340BF groups (minimum 20); 290BF children. **Credit** V.

Lying at the foot of the Atomium is the kitsch manifestation of Brussels' Europhilia. The whole of Europe is laid out here over 2.5 hectares. The models are exact copies, on a scale of 1:25, of the major European monuments including Athens' Acropolis, Berlin's Brandenburg Gate and London's Big Ben. Similarly shrunk cars, buses and trains speed along the roads and under the tunnels. At the last count there were about 300 monuments, but the number has to keep growing to keep up with the ever-expanding EU.

Wheelchair: access; toilets.

Planétarium National

10 avenue de Bouchot, 1020. Métro Heysel/tram18, 19 81. **Open** 9am-4pm Mon-Fri. **Shows** 1.30pm Tue; 9.45am, 3.30pm, Wed; 11am Thur; 9.45am, 2.30pm, Fri; 3.45pm first & third Sun. **Admission** 120BF; 80BF groups.

Like so many other attractions, this is right beside the Atomium. Besides the telescope trained on the sky, there is a huge cupola – 24m in diameter – on which is projected the movements of the planets and stars.

Wheelchair: access; toilets.

The **Serres Royales** *or Royal Hothouses, also known as 'the City of Glass' –* *see page 44.*

Janneken Pis – *whatever next, we wonder?*

Serres Royales (Royal Hothouses)

61 avenue du Parc Royal (Domaine Royal), 1020 (513 89 40 tourist info). Métro Heysel/tram 52, 92/bus 53. **Open** 9.30am-4pm Wed, Thur; 9-11pm Fri; 9.30am-4pm, 9-11pm Sat, Sun. NB: only open two weeks around end Apr-begin May, when flowers are in bloom. Dates vary annually but are given out by the tourist office from Jan. **Admission** free during day; 100BF at night.

Magnificent sequence of 11 linked greenhouses built on the orders of Léopold II by Balat and the young Horta. Sometimes called 'the City of Glass', they rise up from the royal grounds like the Emerald City in *The Wizard of Oz*. The largest is 60m long and 30m high. Exotic plants bloom within, but like so much else in Brussels, their opening days are strictly limited. However, the exterior can be viewed from Parc de Laeken – for the best aspect, turn left at the main exit on avenue du Parc Royal and look down on them from the left-hand pavement.

Théâtre de Toone

6 impasse Schuddeveld, petite rue des Bouchers, 1000 (511 71 37). Métro De Brouckère. **Open** noon-midnight Tue-Sat. **Box office** tickets available 8pm, just before perf. **Tickets** 400BF; 250BF under-12s, students (Tue-Thur only). **No credit cards**.

This puppet theatre is one of the best sights in Brussels and deservedly famous. The building is old and small and winding. Now in the hands of the seventh generation of the Toone family, there are performances about four times a week in *Bruxellois*, the regional dialect. There is also a charming café, a puppet museum – which includes the ancient collection of Marcel Wolfers – and a workshop where you can buy marionettes.

Walibi

Wavre, 1300 (010 414 466). **Getting there** *by train* Ottignies-Louvain-la-Neuve line from Schuman to Gare de Bierges (the station is 300m from Walibi); *by car* take the E411 Bxl-Namur motorway to exit 7. **Open** *27 Apr-1 Sept* 10am-6pm daily; *2-29 Sept* 10am-6pm Sat, Sun. **Admission** 730BF; 680BF children under 1.5m tall; free children under 1m. **Credit** V.

Before Disneyland Paris brought America right into the heart of a reluctant France, this was the biggest theme park in mainland Europe. It has the usual assortment of stomach-churning rollercoasters, gentle carousels, elaborate river rides. It also boasts an enormous slide and splash complex, Aqualibi, which is open all year round and costs 480BF when Walibi is closed (*see chapter* **Children**).

Wheelchair: access; toilets.

Monuments & statues

Butte de Lion (Lion Hill)

252-254 route du Lion, 1420 Braine-l'Alleud (tourist information 354 99 10). **Open** *15 Oct-31 Mar* 10.30am-4.30pm daily; *1 Apr-14 Oct* 9.30am-6.30pm daily. **Admission** 40BF; 20BF children.

Just outside Brussels, the site of Waterloo is an essential pilgrimage for British visitors. It's one of the most impressive battle commemorations around. The Lion is set on an 45-metre long slope and weighs 28 tonnes. It was built by van Geel ten years after the battle and stands on the spot where the Prince of Orange fell. It's a good climb to the top – 230 steps – but when you do go for it, you get a fine view of the surrounding fields, which have fortunately been left much as they were, so you can mentally reconstruct the battle. If you have problems doing that, there are audiovisuals in the museum at the foot of the hill to do it for you.

Colonne du Congrès

place du Congrès, 1000. Métro Madou.

Another Poelaert piece, this was built in 1850 to commemorate the National Congress of 1831 that proclaimed the Belgian Constitution. A statue of Léopold I tops the column, which has that heaviness associated with so much of Poelaert's work. At the foot burns the eternal flame, a homage to the Unknown Soldier of the two World Wars.

Janneken Pis

impasse de la Fidelité, 1000. Métro Bourse or De Brouckère.

Squatting, grinning and vulgar – if you didn't take to the Manneken, don't distress yourself by going to see his female counterpart. She was erected in 1985 in response to feminist demands or in shameless exploitation of an existing famous site – it's hard to know. Either way, she fails to inspire any national pride, and the official tourist office-approved guide doesn't even mention her.

Monument aux Martyrs Juifs

rue E Carpentier, 1070. Bus 47, 103.

On the walls of this moving monument are imprinted the names of 23,838 men, women and children who were taken from Malines, between August 1942 and July 1944, and sent to Nazi concentration camps. Not one of them survived.

Monument aux Martyrs de 1830

place des Martyrs, 1000. Métro De Brouckère.

Erected to commemorate the 445 rebels who died in the 1830 revolution, this ought be a key national monument pertaining to the very foundation of the Belgian state. In fact, the monument is unremarkable-looking and has been terribly neglected. Underground there is a shrine containing the names of the patriots. Place des Martyrs is completely derelict – its neoclassical buildings empty – and has become haunt for the city's homeless.

Famous residences

Maison de Bruegel

132 rue Haute, 1000. Bus 20, 48. **Open** *May-Oct* groups by prior arrangement only (with written request).

This sixteenth-century house has now been restored as authentically as possible. It does not, however, contain any precious prints or old letters, so it is better as an illustration of what the painter's living quarters would have been like than as a museum.

Maison d'Erasmus

31 rue de Chapitre, 1070 (521 13 83). Métro St Guidon/tram 56/bus 49. **Open** 10am-noon, 2-5pm, Mon, Wed, Thur, Sat, Sun. **Admission** 20BF. **No credit cards**.

The great humanist only spent five months here in 1521, but there is an impressive collection of documents, including first editions of *In Praise of Folly* and *Adages*, and letters from Charles V and Francis I. The house itself, with its Renaissance furnishings, is well worth seeing. There are portraits of Erasmus by Dürer and Holbein, and a medal by Cellini.

Notable buildings

Pre-sixteenth century

Hôtel Ravenstein

1 rue Ravenstein, 1000 (restaurant 512 77 68). Métro Gare Centrale. **Open** *restaurant* 11.45am-1.30pm, 6.45-8.30pm, Mon-Sat. **Credit** AmEx, DC, MC, V.

The last surviving building from the fifteenth-century Burgundy period is in what used to be the Jewish district, and is now occupied by science associations and a restaurant.

Moulin de Lindekamaele

6 avenue JF Debecker, 1200 (770 90 57). Métro Roodebeek. **Open** *visits* 9am-noon, 3-6.30pm, Mon-Fri; *restaurant* noon-3pm, 6.30-9.30pm, Mon-Fri.

This fifteenth-century mill was originally owned by the Hannecart family and was first a paper then a flour mill. Bought by the *commune* in 1932, it is now a restaurant and conference centre.

Porte de Hal

boulevard du Midi, 1000 (534 15 18). Métro Porte de Hal. **Open** 10am-5pm Tue-Sun. **Admission** 120BF; 80BF group; 50BF children; free disabled. **No credit cards**.

This fourteenth-century tower, embellished in the nineteenth century, has something of a fairytale appearance. It has been a prison, a toll house, a grain store, a repository for archives and is now the museum of folklore. It houses a rather hazy collection of popular images and documentation of the area's history.

Wheelchair: access.

Eighteenth century

Palais de la Nation

place de la Nation, 1008 (519 81 36 Parliament; 515 82 11 Senate; 515 83 55 visits). Métro Arts-Loi. **Entrance** *Senate* 7b rue de Louvain; *Chamber* 11 rue de Louvain. **Open** 10-11am, 2-3pm, Mon-Sat. **Admission** free.

To visit the seat of the Belgian Parliament you have to ensure it is in session, and guided tours need to be arranged in writing at least two months in advance. The palace has a lovely eighteenth-century façade by Guimard, but the exchanges within make Britain's House of Commons sound like Plato's academy.

Nineteenth century

Botanique

236 rue Royale, 1210. (226 12 11). Métro Botanique. **Open** 9am-6pm daily.

This long and beautiful neoclassical building was built in 1826 as a botanical garden. Now the cultural heart of the French community, it's also a centre for theatre, films (especially cartoons) and exhibitions. It also retains a hothouse atmosphere and has some impressively fleshy plants.

La Bourse

Palais de la Bourse, 1000 (509 12 11). Métro Bourse. **Open** by prior arrangement for visits by school parties, business people etc. **Admission** free.

The Belgian Stock Exchange is set in a neoclassical building with a decorative frieze sculpted by Carrier-Belleuse. If you go inside, you discover that business is as methodical and unemotional here as elsewhere in Brussels – it's a long way from Wall Street. Perhaps when WH Auden was here the brokers were 'roaring like beasts on the floor of the Bourse' but they're not, unfortunately, any longer.

Halles de Schaerbeek

22 rue Royale Ste Marie, 1030. Tram 90, 92, 93, 94. **Closed** for restoration, possibly reopening autumn 1996.

One of the last examples of Brussels' nineteenth-century industrial architecture, this is now a very good cultural centre with numerous specialised programmes of events.

Wheelchair: access.

Hôtel Solvay

224 avenue Louise, 1050 (647 37 33). Métro Louise. **Open** request in writing giving your phone number.

This is one of art nouveau architect Victor Horta's masterpieces and was built in 1894 for the industrialist Solvay.

The eternal flame at the **Colonne du Congrès**.

Van Geel's 28-tonne lion at the **Butte de Lion**, *where the Prince of Orange fell. See page 44.*

Marché St Géry

place St Géry, 1000. Métro Bourse.

Built by Dubois in 1881, this used to be a meat hall. The red-brick building is best seen from a distance to appreciate its glass roof. Due to be knocked down in 1982, it was saved by local protest and has been turned into a shopping centre.

Théâtre de la Monnaie

place de la Monnaie, 1000 (229 12 11). Métro De Brouckère.

The ornate interior of the opera house – built in 1819 to replace a fifteenth-century Brabant building – is splendid, but the exterior is unremarkable, nor is it helped by the awful Anspach centre that dwarfs it. Here it was, in 1830, that the Belgian Revolution began. During a performance of Auber's *La Muette de Portici*, the *Marseillaise*-style words of the duet, *Sacred Love of the Fatherland*, so electrified the audience that they rushed headlong into the streets.

Twentieth century

Palais du Centenaire

Parc des Expositions, place de Belgique, 1020 (477 02 11). Métro Heysel.

Eleven palais were built here, the first in 1935 to commemorate a century of Belgian independence. They allow Brussels to offer a unique European venue for trade fairs. They cover 120,000m² and have parking space for 15,000 cars. The largest of them, the Grand Palais built by van Neck, is a triangular composition with ever-decreasing pavilions flanking the imposing, four-columned centre building.

Wheelchair: access.

Pavillon Chinois

44 avenue van Praet, 1020 (268 16 08). Tram 23, 52, 92. **Open** 10am-4.40pm **Tue-Sun. Admission** 80BF (120BF tour of Pavillon Chinois and Tour Japonaise; 80BF groups).

Inspired by the 1900 Paris Exhibition, Léopold II had this delicate house built from plans by French architect Marcel. The ornamented façade was made in Shanghai. It stands incongruously but graciously between solid Belgian trees. Fortunately, it has the Japanese Tower across the road to keep it company. Inside there is a fine porcelain collection.

Résidence Palace

155 rue de la Loi, 1040 (231 03 05). Métro Schuman.

This is the most stunning art deco building in a city where art nouveau reigns and many art deco examples are – like the Palais des Beaux Arts and Gare Centrale – heavy and

Monument aux Martyrs Juifs – *see page 44.*

unimaginative. The 11-storey Résidence Palace has a theatre and an incomparable indoor swimming pool. It's not exactly open to the public and there are no guided tours, but if there happens to be a spectacle showing, you pays your money and you're in. Unfortunately, you'll only get to see a limited area.

Tour Japonaise

44 avenue van Praet, 1020 (268 16 08). Tram 23, 52, 92. **Open** 10am-4.40pm Tue-Sun. **Admission** 80BF (120BF tour of Pavillon Chinois and Tour Japonaise; 80BF groups).

Across the road from the Chinese Pavilion, this fanciful red tower also rises up from between sturdy Belgian trees and it too was designed by Marcel. But the details were executed in Yokohama this time. Closed for 50 years, it is now run by the Musées Royaux d'Art et d'Histoire and exhibits Japanese art.

Parks, gardens & woods

A huge amount of space – about 15 per cent – is given over to parks in Brussels. The built-up business and residential areas are scrupulously broken up by frequent patches of green, which probably help to account for the city's sedate, unfrenzied atmosphere. Around the city centre are congregated many small, carefully laid out parks that provide settings for statues and national monuments. Many of these are now neglected and a little dispiriting, so you're often better off going just outside the centre to the larger, more attractive parks and woods. All parks tend to be quiet until the weekend. They are generally open from dawn to dusk, which means 6pm in winter and 8.30pm in summer.

Central parks

Bois de la Cambre

main entrance on avenue Louise, 1050. Tram 93, 94.

This used to be part of the old Forêt de Soignes and was the favoured strolling spot of the well-to-do. Set at the southern end of avenue Louise, it retains some of that atmosphere with its restaurants, tea-rooms and boating on the lake. The peripheries tend to be merely used as through roads, so you have to penetrate quite far in for tranquillity. It's a good size at 124 hectares, and has plenty of handsome old trees – the beeches are especially beautiful. The avant-garde Théâtre de Poche is situated just inside its borders.

Parc de Bruxelles

entrances on rue de la Loi & place Royale, 1000. Métro Parc or Arts-Loi.

This is an old park – designed in 1717 by Joachin Zimmer – and enjoys one of the best positions in town, in front of the Palais Royal, so it ought to be a small gem. Unfortunately, it's dirty and depressing, chiefly due to the ruthlessly trellised trees with branches tortured into geometric shapes. It's packed with bronze-green statues and none of these is remarkable. The park's most distinctive feature is its set of avenues, laid out in the masonic form of a compass. But that can be admired from a map and is little comfort when you find yourself trundling along the bleak, sandy paths.

Parc du Cinquantenaire

main entrances on avenue de Tervuren & rue de la Loi, 1000. Métro Merode or Schuman.

The largest, most impressive and most famous of the city parks was commissioned by Léopold II, who had 300 labourers working day and night to finish it in time for Belgium's fiftieth anniversary in 1880. It has all the trappings of an imperial park. The Arc de Triomphe is flanked on either side by the Royal Museums of Art, History and Military History as well as Autoworld (*see chapter*

Escape the bustle of Brussels in the ***Bois de la Cambre*** *at the south end of avenue Louise.*

Comic reliefs

One of Brussels' great claims to twentieth-century fame is comics or *bandes dessinées*. These represent a modern outlet for Belgian artistic genius and an obsession with absurdities and miniatures, which in earlier centuries gave us Bruegel, gargoyles and puppets.

Tintin is now a national symbol, almost overtaking that other diminutive figure, Manneken Pis. He is joined by a host of others such as Lucky Luke, the Smurfs and Gaston Lagaffe. Comics are still big business with the major publisher, Dupuis, bringing out about ten million volumes a year.

You could certainly embark on a comic book trail, starting with the glorious art nouveau **Centre Belge de la Bande Dessinée** off rue Neuve (*see chapter* **Museums**). Murals are on the rise with a growing number appearing around the city: on rue de la Buanderie is Lucky Luke; rue de Chevreuil has Boule and Bill; and boulevard du Midi sports Le Chat. You can also visit the comics shops and archive stores, chief among them **Schlirf Book** at 752 chaussée de Waterloo, specialising in American comics, and **Brüsel** at 100 boulevard Anspach (*see chapter* **Shopping & Services**).

Traces of Tintin are inescapable: at 17 rue des Collines, you can buy figures and T-shirts; in the Centre Culturel et Artistique d'Uccle you'll find the famous statue of the tufty-haired boy-hero and his faithful canine pal Snowy.

Museums). There are sculptures, a fairytale tower and, most interesting of all, Horta's Pavilion, which houses Lambeaux's *Haut-Relief des Passions Humaines*. This is kept permanently locked out of respect for the nearby mosque, but a tantalising peephole will allow you a glimpse of a thigh or a breast on a carved fresco. Beside the pavilion is a monument to the Belgian soldiers who 'freed' the Congo: it shows black people in attitudes of ecstatic gratitude to the soldiers and is being allowed quietly to decay. Aside from all these sights, the park itself is quite pleasant to walk in, if rather unkempt, with long avenues and a great cobbled centre. Typically, there's now a tunnel running through it, which makes the whole park feel somehow impermanent. The park has a bad reputation for muggings around dusk, so take care.

Café (in museum), running track, sandpit, tennis.

Parc Duden

entrances on square Lainé & chaussée de Bruxelles, 1190. Bus 48, 54.

An elegant city space, though it has become somewhat ramshackle. It too used to be part of the Forêt de Soignes, and was where Emperor Charles V went hunting. It has tall trees and is set on a slope from which you get a good city view. A

Parc du Cinquantenaire – *see page 48.*

bit out of the way, the park is imbued with the atmosphere of the *quartier*, which can either be a good or a bad thing.

Parc Josaphat

entrances on avenue des Azalées & avenue Louis Bertrand, 1030. Tram 23.

The main park in the huge *commune* of Schaerbeek has lots of bonuses, such as a small animal reserve (with deers, goats and lambs), sporting facilities, a sculpture museum and free concerts on Sundays in July and August.

Archery, café, mini-golf.

Parc Léopold

entrance on chaussée de Wavre, 1040. Métro Schuman.

On the side of a steep hill, the Parc Léopold has more character and less grandeur than its near neighbour the Parc du Cinquantenaire. It also conatins a small lake and a museum of natural history (*see chapter* **Museums**).

Outside town

Forêt de Soignes

Boitsfort, 1170. Tram 44.

This huge beech woodland stretched over 12,000 hectares in 1822. Now it's been reduced to 4,000, which is still impressive for such a built-up capital. In summer, old trams from the **Musée de Transport Urbain Bruxellois** make their way through the trees. The forest includes the Tervuren Arboretum (769 20 81), which is full of old and new forest flora; the Groenendaal Arboretum (657 03 86), which has about 500 exotic species as well as a forest museum and a high-class restaurant in what used to be an abbey; and the Jean Massart Experimental Garden (673 84 06), a research centre holding 5,600 species.

Parc de Laeken

entrance on boulevard de Smet de Naeyer, 1020. Métro Heysel.

A visit to this park is inevitable whatever your interests, and there is enough here to keep you amused all day. In the adjacent Bruparck is the **Atomium**, **Mini-Europe**, cinema complex **Kinepolis** and water-slide complex **Océade** (*see chapter* **Children**). If none of these twentieth-century amusements suits your mood, stroll along the attractive footpaths, keeping a look out for glimpses of the Château Royal and the hothouses in the adjacent Domaine Royal.

Parc de Tervuren

entrance on chaussée de Louvain, 1380. Tram 44.

Notable mainly for the African Museum, which was built by Girault to house Léopold II's Congo booty. Even if you don't venture in, the building itself and the huge statue of the elephant give you a lift. The museum is surrounded by formal gardens, but the park around these is large and attractive with a series of canals and woods. The grounds originally belonged to a palace and there are still remains of eighteenth-century stables and the Renaissance Chapelle St Hubert.

Parc de Woluwe

entrance on avenue de Tervuren, 1160. Tram 39, 44.

This is one of the most attractive parks close to the city. Like so many others, it was commissioned by Léopold II, but was renovated after 1945. It has an easy grace, is well-tended and clean, and has none of the stuffy flowerbeds and tortured arrangements of the formal parks. It's large with woods, lakes and slopes, and if it snows, you can skate and sledge.

Boats, café, fishing, mini-golf.

Parc de Wolvendael

entrances on avenue Wolvendael & rue Rouge, 1180. Tram 92/bus 41.

A small, beautiful park in the elegant *commune* of Uccle, it was owned by successive members of royalty through the centuries. There is a restaurant in an enchanting seventeenth-century Louis XV-style pavilion.

Mini-golf.

Trips & tours

ARAU

55 boulevard Adolphe Max, 1000 (219 33 45/fax 219 86 75). Métro De Brouckère or Rogier. **Duration** 3hrs. **Departures** *Mar-Nov Eng* 9.45am first, second, fifth Sat of month. **Pick-up** place de Brouckère, Hôtel Métropole. **Tickets** 500BF (booking advised). **No credit cards.**

This bus tour takes in the art nouveau buildings and is probably the best of such tours. It is recommended as Arau has the whole thing sewn up and is the only way into some of the loveliest of the private houses. Also on offer on the third Saturday of the month is a tour of art deco buildings.

Arcadia

17 rue Wafelaerts, 1060 (534 38 19/fax 534 60 73). **Duration** 3hrs. **Departures** 9.45am Sun. **Pick-up** depends on tour.

Arcadia organises nine different tours including art nouveau, baroque and classic, and nineteenth-century Brussels.

De Boeck's Sightseeing Tours

8 rue de la Colline, 1000 (513 77 44/fax 502 58 69). Métro Gare Centrale. **Duration** 3hrs. **Departures** *Apr-Oct* 10am, 11am, 2pm, 3pm, daily; *Nov-Mar* 10am, 2pm, daily. **Tickets** 780BF; 630BF students; 380BF children.

Take your pick of daily tours, in most European languages and Japanese, which start at the Grand Place and go on to all the major sights. De Boeck's also does trips to Waterloo, Bruges and Antwerp.

Guides TIB-GBB

Hôtel de Ville, Grand Place, 1000 (513 89 40/fax 514 45 38). Métro Gare Centrale.

Tours include a comic book trail, a tour of Jewish Brussels and an underground tour of the archaeological sites. Reserve in groups by fax or writing two weeks in advance.

*The **Grand Place** or Grote Markt – one of the world's most beautiful squares.* *See page 33.*

Architecture

Today's cocktail of styles has been shaken and stirred through the centuries by rousing Gothic, imperial pomp, industrial verve and EU modernity with a dash of art nouveau lunacy.

It is easy to make two immediate observations about architecture in Brussels. The first is that there is no such thing as homogeneity. That uniformity found in the terraces of other European cities does not exist here. On any one street the houses will be of various heights and widths and built with different stone; one will have a wrought-iron balcony, the next will not; one will have fanciful round windows, its neighbour will have discreetly rectangular ones. This came about partly because Brussels was built more by private citizens, who had their own ideas, than by town councils or large building companies. Another factor was the late nineteenth-century practice of opening house façades to competitions which meant architects were more concerned with showing off their flamboyant talents than developing conformity. This eclecticism has been described as akin to attending a concert in which the chords refuse to harmonise. But it can also be regarded as invigorating: the eye does not grow tired at ceaseless repetition as it might elsewhere. The best way to take in this peculiarity of Brussels is simply to walk around the different *communes*, Ixelles, St Gilles and Uccle being particularly pleasant. Almost all the buildings date from the last 150 years, but within this limitation there are seemingly endless combinations.

The other immediately striking point is the richness of the interiors. The blandest of façades will often turn out to contain the most sumptuous décor within. Mirrors, gilt edgings, *trompe-l'oeil*, stained glass, ornamented ceilings, all are found in what appear to be the most ordinary-looking of homes. It is typically Bruxellois, keeping this lavishness and eccentricity inside. It is the same spirit that leads to those clubs where you can dance till midday on Sunday while normal life goes on in the street above you. To get the full feel of the interiors you really have to know some inhabitants, preferably Belgians since they have a habit of keeping beautiful things in the family and so are generally better able to adorn their houses than blow-in foreigners. Failing that, cafés and bars such as **La Chaloupe d'Or**, **A La Mort Subite**, **Le Falstaff** and **De Ultieme Hallucinatie** (*see chapter* **Cafés & Bars**) or public buildings such as the **Théâtre de la Monnaie** and **Centre Belge de la Bande Dessinée** give a good idea of the city's interiors through the ages.

Brussels, having swayed between the French, Spanish, Dutch and Austrians, reflects these different influences in its buildings. Most of the best examples of Dutch baroque and Renaissance architecture are to be found in other Belgian cities, but they survive in Brussels' churches and the **Grand Place**. Meanwhile French neoclassicism leaves its mark all around the **Royal Quarter**. From 1830, the two key styles in the city are Léopold II's imperial grandeur and the hallucinogenic swirlings of art nouveau at the end of the nineteenth century.

Gothic

Under the fifteenth-century Burgundians, Brussels must have looked rousingly Gothic, but very few of the buildings remain. Churches are the main preserve of Gothic and baroque in Brussels. Large-scale, arched, graceful and turreted, the two finest examples of Brabant Gothic architecture are the fifteenth-century **Notre Dame du Sablon** and **Cathédrale des Sts Michel et Gudule**. These, like St Peter's and St Guido's in Anderlecht and Bruegel's burial place (Notre Dame de la Chapelle), are faithful to the Brussels custom of superior interiors: all are beautifully proportioned inside, with tapestries, statues and breathtaking stained glass.

The **Hôtel de Ville** (Town Hall) is Brussels' sole secular example of this period, the only building in the Grand Place to withstand the 1695 French bombardment. It stands among the later ornate buildings, with its arches and its numerous sculptures, clearly harking from an earlier era. But, like the churches, it juxtaposes great size with surprising grace and sombre piety – though the latter impression could be due to the more recent venerable city grime. Cathédrale des Sts Michel et Gudule has now been cleaned, removing the association between Gothic and darkness, but the Hôtel de Ville retains its black exterior.

Flemish Renaissance

This is a loose term applied to the Italo-Flemish rococo baroque style of the seventeenth century (no wonder some shorthand label was needed),

Cathédrale des Sts Michel et Gudule – *one of the finest examples of Brabant Gothic.*

though the term Renaissance is misleading for such a late period. It's a style the Belgians are proud of because it's home-grown rather than imported from their powerful neighbours. **Luc Fayd'herbe** is the key name connected with this style in churches, though again his best work is outside the capital. His Brussels masterpiece is the vigorous, honey-coloured **Eglise St Jean-Baptiste** (*see chapter* **Sightseeing: Churches & Abbeys**) which, along with his other church **Notre Dame aux Riches Claires** (*see chapter* **Sightseeing: Hidden Churches**), has some of the features of a private house.

The gems in this style are, of course, the guild-houses of the Grand Place – ornate and fanciful, each with the distinctive markings of its guild. Remarkably, almost all of them were built in the four years following the 1695 bombardment and they are in impeccable condition. Also remarkable is the fact that the effect of all those decorative façades manages to be harmonious.

Italo-Flemish baroque influenced the sculpture of this period, the chief example being **Manneken Pis**, whom it should be noted has been as much admired for the grace of his design as vilified for his vulgarity.

Neoclassicism

The eighteenth century steadily gave way to a clean, creamy and symmetrical neoclassicism. This was at Austrian and French prompting and it coincided with the transformation of Brussels into a city for the aristocracy. The **Palais de Charles de Lorraine**, former residence of the governor of the Austrian Netherlands, is an early example of this style, though with its numerous statues, pillars and mouldings, it is more elaborate than those buildings that came at the end of the century. The great architect of these was **Barnabé Guimard**, who designed the **Palais de la Nation** (now the Belgian Parliament) and that carefully symmetrical group of stark white buildings around place Royale.

Charles of Lorraine wanted to make Brussels look like Vienna, but it was overtaken first by Napoleon and then briefly by the Dutch before finally gaining independence, so neoclassicism only left its cold mark on the Upper Town. Consequently, the old distinction between the Upper Town (French and aristocratic) and the Lower Town (Flemish and mercantile) is still immediately apparent.

Nineteenth century

The nineteenth century was a time of rapid and widespread construction, not least because of the huge population growth. The River Senne was efficiently buried and boulevards raised on its banks, leaving Brussels as one of the only European capitals without a river. Until the explosion of art nouveau, it was a great century for reworking old styles. Everything can be described as 'neo': the prison of St Gilles imitates English Gothic; the town hall in Schaerbeek is neo-

Art nouveau *may have originated in Britain but Brussels seized upon it with enthusiasm.*

Renaissance. Private houses of the period are a cheerful mixture of styles with Dutch, German and French influences visible everywhere.

The industrial age was felt in Brussels in a profusion of iron and glass as materials in municipal buildings. Europe's first glass-covered shopping arcade, **Jean Pierre Cluysenaer**'s **Galeries St Hubert**, appeared here in 1847; **Charles Girault** used iron and glass to give a feeling of space to his **Musées Royaux d'Art et d'Histoire** and the **Musée Royale de l'Armée et d'Histoire Militaire** in the Parc du Cinquantenaire; and **Alphonse Balat** was the most triumphant of all in his creation of the **Serres Royales** (Royal Hothouses) at Laeken.

Léopold II

If Brussels has some of the imperial feel of Paris and London, it is thanks to this man, who acceded the throne in 1865. Having the Congo as his personal playroom, he used the millions accrued there to endow Brussels with heroic dimensions. Everything monumental and imposing can be credited to him. The enormous **Palais de Justice** is wholly emblematic of his style: heavy and imperial. Léopold gave the city the great **avenues de Tervuren** and **Louise**, the **Arc de Triomphe** and the museums in the Parc du Cinquantenaire, and the **Museum voor Midden-Afrika** in Parc de Tervuren. His style is not much admired as it smacks of imperial arrogance and one can't help thinking of the atrocities committed in the Congo under his reign. His style is held to be un-Belgian: many extol the charms of the Flemish districts and condemn Léopold for giganticism in a city of miniatures. Certainly the style associated with him lacks Flemish wit and delicacy, but it cannot be denied that he opened up the city, giving it breadth and efficiently connecting the centre to the suburbs and parks.

Art nouveau

At the end of the nineteenth century there was a sudden dam-burst of talent and Brussels for the first time was at the centre of a new architectural style. Brussels is full of handsome buildings, but most of them are designed on borrowed lines, using styles evolved in other countries. Art nouveau originated in Britain in the 1880s, but it was Brussels that wholeheartedly seized upon it when architects such as **Paul Hankar**, **Henri van de Velde**, **Paul Cauchie** and, above all, **Victor Horta** made it their own.

Art nouveau was inspired by the shapes of flowers and plants. It is about what Horta called 'maximum fluidity': the intertwining of all elements into a trembling whole. The effect is flowing and hallucinogenic, though nothing in Brussels attains the madness of Gaudí's houses in Barcelona. The hallmarks of art nouveau are sinuous lines, round windows, frescoes and *sgraffiti* (a mural design technique in which the top layer of glaze, plaster etc is incised to reveal parts of the material underneath).

The new style hit Brussels in 1893 with the house that Horta built for industrialist Emile Tassel at 6 rue Paul Emile Janson. This bears all the hallmarks of a Horta house. The bold exterior stands out from the propriety of its neighbours, but doesn't go too far, maintaining a certain rectitude, while madness is given freer reign inside. In this way Horta was in the Belgian tradition and firmly avoided the showy flamboyance of his contemporary in Barcelona. The best way to experience this is to visit Horta's own house in rue Américaine (*see chapter* **Museums**). Or you could go on one of the **ARAU** trips, which get you inside some of the private art nouveau houses (*see chapter* **Sightseeing: Trips & tours**).

The large number of art nouveau houses in Brussels is due to a lucky conjunction of the architects' talent and the wealth and enlightenment of the city's patrons. Men such as **Armand Solvay** and **Edmond van Eetvelde**, industrialists and engineers who built the Congo Free State, commissioned these great houses with no regard for expense, for at the time Brussels was richer than ever before or since. Art nouveau suited the individualistic temperament of wealthy Belgians. Their houses all appear in isolated pockets and there was no coordinated city planning. Only **Ernest Blérot** brought about a whole neighbourhood, building 25 art nouveau houses around the Ixelles lakes.

The architects took the money and followed their visions, but many of them were themselves committed socialists, and more interested in building for the people than the élite. The Belgian Workers Party gave its considered approval of the new style, which cut through the old static forms; such buildings were a concrete illustration of the new ideology. Art nouveau was the preferred medium of freethinkers and socialists, while Catholics condemned it as godless extravagance and turned to neo-Renaissance for their houses. Art nouveau was gradually brought to bear on municipal buildings too. Louis Bertrand, mayor of Schaerbeek, the fastest growing *commune* in Brussels, decreed that all public buildings should be in the new style.

Hankar designed numerous shop fronts, of which only the florist in rue Royale survives. The most famous and daring of the municipal designs was Horta's **Maison du Peuple**, a bold and uneven, glass-covered building which was to house entertainment for the people. However, the people were not to be entertained for long. Having fallen into disuse the Maison was pulled down in 1964. **Alban Chaubon**'s theatres were similarly demolished, as were Hankar's shops and Blérot's personal house. In the scramble towards modernity and becoming one of the foremost conference cities in the world, Brussels held its art nouveau inheritance cheaply. Only architectural action groups such as ARAU managed to raise public awareness and preserve what is left.

Art nouveau was a short-lived phenomenon. Some of the most daring houses were built at the beginning of this century, such as Cauchie's *sgraffiti*-covered house in rue des Francs and the extraordinary **Maison de St Cyr** in square Ambiorix, built by the 22-year-old **Gustave Strauven** with quicksilver confidence. But by 1905, it was fading fast. The rich began to move out to the country and the homes that were built for the mercantile classes had begun to betray the original spirit of art nouveau with their extravagant exteriors and bland interiors. Such ostentation was too much for Horta, who abandoned art nouveau for art deco, heralding the end of the great creative period. It was said that in just ten years, art nouveau had entirely changed the face of the city. Had all the buildings been allowed to remain, perhaps Brussels would now have a fully flowing, narcotic feel instead of just the odd flashback.

Between the wars

Brussels developed tidily between the wars – it was neat if uninspired. The two main innovations were apartment blocks and *cité-jardins*, which were linked. Blocks of rather stolid, geometrical buildings were designed to flank a small garden square and this became a feature of the city. The Tintin books from the period reflect this development: well-brushed paving stones, straight buildings and a certain calm. The reigning style was art deco and this is seen in a number of municipal buildings such as **Gare Centrale** and the **Palais des Beaux Arts**. Both of these were designed by Horta, but their rather static gloom encourages only regret that he gave up on his earlier style. Even worse, the beauty of the Palais des Beaux Arts was obscured by bad 1970s renovations. But from October 1996 it is being restored to its former Horta appearance and perhaps will gain in grace. The great monument to art deco, for which one can forgive all the bad examples, is the **Résidence Palace** (*see chapter* **Sightseeing**). This was very avant-garde when it appeared, pre-dating New York's Rockefeller Centre, which it closely resembles. It was built as an apartment block for the *haute bourgeoisie* and included within its 11 storeys a theatre, shops, Turkish baths, a dreamy green swimming pool and a roof garden. Presumably its inhabitants had no need to leave except to go to work. Now it is surrounded on all sides by EU buildings and has itself ceased to be residential – terrible waste of that swimming pool.

Horta's art deco **Palais des Beaux Arts.**

Postwar

The postwar tale is a sorry one. Dual carriageways sliced through the *communes*. Useful no doubt, but paying scant regard to the calm layout of the city. Brussels might be the crossroads of Europe and delighted to invite Europe in, but it seems unnecessary to have turned the city into an criss-cross of roads. Postwar reconstruction had no coherence. Functional skyscrapers were erected. The areas round Gares du Midi and Nord were demolished and the awful **Tour du Midi** put up. It is frustrating because Belgium was not short on good architects, but Antwerp and Ghent fared better. Van Reeth's house in Antwerp and van Impe's strange, curving, frankly sexual house in Ghent are more interesting than anything from the postwar period in Brussels.

More recently, the picture looks hopeful, despite the prevalence of demolition and building sites. The ludicrous *faux* baroque houses being built around Gare Centrale in supposed harmony with the older buildings are an example of the worst type of empty nostalgia, but the **Council of Ministers** and **European Parliament** buildings are gleaming and definite while the **Conrad Hotel** on avenue Louise has an opulent boldness. This century, much like the last one, is going out with a certain amount of style.

History

Key Events	**58**
Romans to the Spanish	**59**
Catholic Turmoil to National Unity	**65**
Independence to the Postwar Era	**72**
Brussels Today	**80**

Key Events

Early and medieval history

57-51 BC Julius Caesar fights Gallic Wars.
15 BC Establishment of the Roman province Gallia Belgica.
c5 AD Collapse of Roman rule in Northern Europe.
814 Death of Charlemagne.
843 Charlemagne's kingdom split into three.
979 Official founding of Brussels (Bruocsella).
1041 Dukes of Brabant build palace at Coudenburg.
1302 Flemish army beats French armies in the Battle of Golden Spurs.
1337 Outbreak of Hundred Years War between England and France.
1338 Jacob van Artevelde leads pro-English revolution in Ghent.
1348-49 Black Death in Flanders.

Dukes of Burgundy

1369 Margaret of Male marries Philip the Bold, Duke of Burgundy.
1384 Philip and Margaret inherit Flanders, and it becomes part of Duchy of Burgundy.
1459 Philip the Good's court based in Brussels.
1467 Death of Philip the Good.
1477 Death of Charles the Bold.
1482 Mary of Burgundy dies and her husband Maximilian becomes regent.

The Spanish Netherlands

1500 Future Charles V born in Ghent.
1515 Charles declared of age by Netherlands Estates General.
1516 Charles inherits the Spanish throne and so becomes Charles I.
1519 Charles becomes Emperor Charles V, and inherits Hapsburg empire.
1555 Abdication of Charles V in favour of his son Philip.
1565 Nobles in the Netherlands form the League of Nobles opposing Spanish rule.
1566 Iconoclastic Riots in Antwerp and elsewhere.
1567 Appointment of Duke of Alva as governor.
1568 Execution of Count Egmont and Count Horne and outbreak of the Revolt of the Netherlands.
1576 Spanish Fury in Antwerp.
1579 Southern provinces form Union of Arras, in support of Philip II and Catholicism.
1581 Northern provinces form Union of Utrecht and declare they no longer recognise Philip or the Spanish.

Counter-Reformation

1598 Philip hands over the Netherlands to Archduke Albert, who married his daughter Isabella.
1609-21 Twelve Year Truce between the Dutch and the Spanish Netherlands.
1621 The Netherlands revert to Spain after death of Albert.
1648 Spain recognises Dutch independence in the Treaty of Munster.
1695 The French bomb Brussels during the War of the Grand Alliance.

The Austrian Netherlands

1700 Charles II dies and leaves the Spanish throne to Philip Duke of Anjou.
1702-13 War of Spanish Succession. Spanish Netherlands ruled by English and French.
1713 Spanish Netherlands pass to Austria in the Treaty of Utrecht and become the Austrian Netherlands.
1715 Barrier Treaty gives Dutch the right to build forts in Austrian Netherlands.
1740-48 War of Austrian Succession. French troops occupy Austrian Netherlands 1744-48.
1780 Joseph II becomes Emperor of Austria.
1789-90 Brabançon Revolution against Joseph II.
1790 Austrian authority restored.
1792 France occupies Austrian Netherlands.
1795 Austrian Netherlands annexed into France and old provincial boundaries abolished.
1798 French bring in conscription and Belgian peasants riot.
1814 Napoleon defeated and 1814-15 Congress of Vienna redraws European boundaries. Belgium and Netherlands merged into the United Kingdom of the Netherlands.

Unity and revolution

1815 Napoleon defeated at Battle of Waterloo. William Prince of Orange declared King William I.
1830 Start of the Belgian Revolution.
1831 Great Powers recognise Belgium as an independent state and Leopold of Saxe-Coburg-Gotha is invited to be king.
1839 The Dutch recognise Belgian independence.

Independent Belgium

1848 First Liberal government, after initial political domination by Catholics.
1885 Belgian Workers Party founded.
1885 Berlin Declaration recognises Léopold II as head of state of the Congo.
1893 Introduction of universal male suffrage with system of multiple voting.
1898 Flemish language given official equality with French.
1908 Léopold forced to hand Congo over to Belgium.

Belgium in the wars

1914 Germany invades Belgium.
1918 Belgium liberated by Allies.
1919 Universal male suffrage.
1930 University of Ghent becomes Flemish-speaking.
1940 Germany invades Belgium and Léopold III surrenders.
1944 Belgium liberated by Allies and sets up War Tribunals.

Postwar Belgium

1948 Benelux Customs Union comes into force.
1949 Women given the right to vote.
1950 Léopold III returns to Belgium and stands down because of national unease about his behaviour in the war.
1957 Brussels becomes headquarters of the EEC.
1962 Creation of the French-Flemish language frontier.
1967 Brussels becomes headquarters of NATO.
1970-94 Constitutional reforms change Belgium from a centralised state to a federal one.
1993 Death of Baudouin I.

Romans to the Spanish

From Julius Caesar – he found 'the Belgae' tough – to the fifteenth-century Dukes of Burgundy and their Catholic successors, who faced revolting Dutch nobles and a religious bloodbath.

Early & medieval history

When Julius Caesar embarked on the Gallic Wars in 57 BC, most of the tribes in what is now Belgium were Celtic. The Romans called them the Belgae and Caesar complained that of all the peoples in Gaul, they were the toughest. He attributed this to the fact they were the tribes furthest from the Mediterranean and had missed out on the civilising effects of visits by merchants. Nevertheless, they were not too tough to cook: the Flemish coast had become famous for fish sauces, which it exported.

Despite the toughness of the Belgae, Caesar's armies conquered the region. It became a Roman province called Gallia Belgica in 15 BC, and was later divided into administrative districts called *civitates*. The area was thinly populated, backward and does not seem to have had as much economic importance for the Romans as other towns in Gaul. Even so, the districts paid taxes, provided troops to the Romans and a network of roads and army camps was built. Tournai (then called Turnacum), in south-west Belgium, became an important quarrying town, as well as an early centre of Christianity. Salt was refined from sea water along the coast and there was an iron works near Ghent. Wool was also produced. There are no records relating to Brussels itself.

The Roman empire in the north began to founder in the third century when Germanic tribes attacked the northern borders of Gallia Belgica. Excavations of Roman camps show that massive destruction took place at the time. Severe flooding, a problem that recurs throughout the history of the Low Countries, also weakened the empire, and Roman Gaul collapsed in the fifth century.

The Germanic invasions of the third to fifth centuries were the first stage in the process leading to the linguistic division of present-day Belgium. The northern areas slowly became German-speaking, while the southern part of the country continued to speak Latin-based languages. The division was by no means crystallised at this time, and to refer to a clear split before the tenth century is premature, but the roots of the split do stretch back to here.

The Romans' successors were the Merovingian kings, and Gallia Belgica formed the northern border of their authority. They were succeeded by the Carolingian kings, whose empire extended further east and north. Belgium had little strategic or economic importance and was merely a marshy backwater.

Charlemagne died in 814 and his three grandsons went to war over their inheritance. Eventually his kingdom was split into three in 843: East Francia approximately corresponds to Germany; West Francia roughly equates to France plus Flanders and it went to Charles the Bald; and Middle Francia, or the Middle Kingdom, went to Lothair. In the north it comprised the land between the River Scheldt and Germany, and this narrow strip continued down to the Mediterranean.

Charles the Bald and Lothair were not the only ones fighting over the region. Throughout the ninth and tenth centuries, it was subject to regular invasions by the Vikings, who took advantage of the power vacuum. There was a gradual disintegration of central power and a rise of feudal domains. Flanders became the most powerful of them, and although it was in theory subject to the kings of France, the Flemish counts were virtually autonomous. Other principalities to emerge in the ninth, tenth and eleventh centuries were Liège, Hainaut, Namur, Luxembourg and Brabant.

The first mention of Brussels – which was in Brabant – dates from 695, at which time it was a stopping point on the trade route from Cologne to Bruges and Ghent. It was then known as Brocsella or Bruocsella, meaning 'village in the marshes'. However, the city was not officially founded until 979, when Charles of France built a fortress on the island of Saint-Géry.

The history of these principalities and their relations with each other is a complex series of wars, shifting boundaries, trade disputes and intermarriages. And these stretched well beyond the borders of the domains themselves. One of the

Flemish counts, for instance, married the daughter of England's King Alfred the Great, while William the Conqueror was married to a daughter of another. Flanders was already exporting cloth to England in the tenth century and there is also evidence of a slave trade between the two. By the twelfth century, Flemish cloth was being sold in France, Italy, England and the Baltic.

Much of Flanders' economic health depended on the state of its relations with England, or on the state of Anglo-French relations, since Flanders often suffered from reprisals against the French. Despite the fact that the Flemish counts were vassals of the French kings, the Flanders were often hostile to the French and they were dependent upon English wool imports.

Throughout much of the twelfth century, the Flemish towns resisted French influence, murdering French soldiers and Francophile noblemen until a French army was sent to quell resistance in 1302. Surprisingly, on 11 July an army of Flemish peasants and craftsmen defeated the aristocratic French army in the Battle of Golden Spurs at Courtrai. Modern Flanders still has a national holiday on this date.

The balance of the English-French-Flanders triangle became even more fragile when the Hundred Years War between France and England broke out in 1337. At the time of the outbreak, a Flemish landowner called Jacob van Artevelde led a rebellion in Ghent against the pro-French counts of Flanders, who fled to France. Flanders had until then been officially neutral, but van Artevelde actively allied it with the English until his murder in 1346. After that, it became neutral once again.

Further problems arose in the thirteenth and fourteenth centuries because of unrest in the other towns of Flanders, Brabant and Liège. Townspeople and merchants demanded new powers from their rulers, and the rulers were forced to cede them in order to raise money and avoid full-scale rebellions. The power of the guilds increased and the towns gained a share of government. The new rights given to townspeople and the growth of trade caused cultural and economic disparities between the towns and the surrounding countryside. Ghent, Bruges, Ypres, Brussels, Louvain (Leuven), Antwerp and Mechlin (Mechelen) all became wealthier and more powerful at this time. In 1340 Ghent was the largest city in Europe after Paris. Meanwhile, regions such as Hainaut, Namur and Luxembourg in the south remained predominantly agricultural.

The growth of Brussels (still called Bruocsella) had started in the eleventh century when it spread out from the marshy valley of the river Senne into the hills and plateaus around it. The forests surrounding the town provided materials for construction and fuel. They also provided hunting grounds for the dukes of Brabant, who built a palace in 1041 on higher ground at Coudenburg. Wool was the most important trade from the thirteenth to the fifteenth centuries, along with metalwork.

Other problems afflicting Belgium in the Middle Ages were a succession of natural disasters. There were two major famines in the twelfth century and the counts of Flanders were feeding up to 100 paupers a day in Bruges alone. Plague was the major hazard in the fourteenth century.

About a third of Antwerp's population died in the outbreak of 1316 and a chronicler recorded: 'Dancing, games, song, all revels were done away with in those days.' Three decades later, in 1348-49, the Black Death wiped out roughly a quarter of the population of Flanders, although the area's high population density meant that the consequences were less severe than in England and France. In between such catastrophes, there were frequent and severe floods, causing many villages to be deserted.

Dukes of Burgundy

A process of great change began in the 1360s when Margaret of Male, daughter of the Count of Flanders, married Philip the Bold, Duke of Burgundy. When Margaret's father died in 1384, Flanders and subsequently other provinces came together in a loose union under the authority of the Dukes of Burgundy. Before then there had been no particular political groupings among the different domains. The Dukes of Burgundy's rule was also a period of great cultural change.

A key figure in the process was Philip the Good, grandson of Margaret and Philip the Bold. Having inherited Flanders, Burgundy, Artois and other provinces, he added Brabant, Holland, Hainaut, Namur and Luxembourg through a combination of politics, purchase and military action. The only part of the Netherlands remaining outside their realm was the prince-bishopric of Liège. Nevertheless, the Low Countries were by no means a country, merely a group of territories under the control of one family.

Although the Dukes of Burgundy ruled for less than a century, the cultural changes during that period were huge. The Dukes spent more time in the Netherlands than in Burgundy itself. From 1459, Philip the Good and the court, which had previously been itinerant, were based mainly in Brussels, while Lille – now in France – was home to the exchequer. Keen to be viewed as equals of the French court, the Dukes of Burgundy initiated their own court culture in the Netherlands, and were active patrons of the arts.

There are many examples of the cultural flowering under the Dukes of Burgundy. The first university in the Low Countries was founded in

The guilds

The importance of the guilds in Belgium is most evident in the Grand Place in Brussels. The scale of the guildhouses belonging to the haberdashers, boatmen, archers, tallow merchants and hosierymakers leaves little doubt about their wealth.

From the thirteenth century the guilds were far more than organisations of tradesmen. Guild militias took part in the Battle of Golden Spurs in 1302. They had also developed social and charitable roles. In Ghent, six guilds had almshouses, and most others gave charity to members who needed it. Although the textile guilds were the most important and the most frequent instigators of urban unrest, the smiths, brewers, butchers and carpenters were also powerful.

The merchant and artisan guilds had started as occupational organisations, set up to help people trading outside their home town. Later, guild statutes generally regulated hours and conditions of work, inspections, conditions of mastership, entry fees and the length of apprenticeships (from two to eight years, depending on the trade). Some also had courts that levied fines for breach of the statutes. Most guilds were rigorous about restricting entry. The majority started excluding women in the fourteenth century, although some still allowed them to work as journeymen.

In some guilds, entry was based on heredity, and it was also controlled by fees, which were often higher for 'external' candidates. The differences became exaggerated over time, so that in Bruges in 1441, the sons of master carpenters paid the equivalent of 5.2 days' work to join the guild, while applicants from outside Flanders paid the equivalent of 149 days' worth. Not content with that, the guild raised it to 244 days in 1479.

As the textile industry declined, some guilds became more political than occupational. Thus, men were often masters in more than one guild, or changed guild affiliations from one year to the next. From the sixteenth century, the number of guilds multiplied while their power declined, so that by the eighteenth century they were chiefly occupied with lawsuits and disputes among themselves, helplessly watching the rise of new non-guild industries such as cotton and coal.

Leuven (Louvain), Brabant, in 1425. Brussels Town Hall in Grand Place was started in 1402 and completed in 1455, and the awesome tower of Mechelen (Mechlin) cathedral was begun in 1452.

But the best known evidence of the Dukes' patronage is the art of the fifteenth century. The painter Jan van Eyck was born in Brabant and worked in Ghent then Bruges. Rogier van der Weyden was born in Tournai and worked in Brussels as the city's official painter. Hans Memling, having been born in Germany, settled in Bruges in 1465. Although the Dukes were the most prolific patrons, works were also commissioned by city governments such as Bruges and Ghent, and by Italian merchants living in Bruges. Memling was also commissioned to paint portraits by some of the native merchants in Bruges.

Painters had to enrol in guilds in the city where they worked and were regarded as craftsmen. In Bruges, sculptors belonged to the carpenters' guild. Many painters also did banners and decorations for parades and festivals.

Parades were a major part of city life under the Dukes, partly because such festivities were a way of displaying their power and wealth. But also there seems for have been a general taste for pageants and bingeing. When Philip the Bold visited Bruges in April 1398, the festivities lasted a month, during which time the churches provided food for the poor every day. In Chaucer's 'Canterbury Tales', written in the late fourteenth century, the 'Pardoner's Tale' begins with the story of a band of youths who lived in Flanders and led a sinful life of music, bad language, gambling, fornication, honouring the devil and gluttony.

The textile industries may have been declining in the fourteenth and fifteenth centuries – due mainly to cheaper English competition – but other industries were replacing them. Brussels was producing tapestries, Ghent had a growing leather industry, mainly producing gloves and purses, the Flanders coastal towns were exporting pickled herring, and in the countryside new agricultural techniques such as the single-handed plough were boosting production. Nevertheless, the fifteenth century was not entirely smooth in economic and, consequently, political terms. Floods and plagues continued to afflict the Low Countries and poverty persisted in rural parishes.

There were also repeated uprisings and rebellions in Ghent between 1400 and 1450, primarily because economic power had shifted from Flanders to Brabant. Not only were Brussels' industries more prosperous than Ghent's, but Bruges's access to the sea had silted up, causing it to be superseded by Antwerp as a port and trade centre.

Construction of Brussels' **Town Hall** *in Grand Place was started in 1402, completed in 1455.*

The Spanish Netherlands

The end of the rule of the Dukes of Burgundy came with the death of Philip the Good in 1467. He was succeeded by his son Charles the Bold, whose attempts at modernisation were resented and there was no great grief when he was killed at the Battle of Nancy in 1477, fighting the Lotharingians. He was succeeded by his daughter Mary who died five years later, leaving the Netherlands in dynastic disarray. Mary had married Maximilian of Austria, son of the Hapsburg German emperor Frederick III. Their son Philip was only four when she died so the Low Countries were effectively ruled by Maximilian for the next ten years and were thus part of the Hapsburg empire. They were also under attack by Louis XI of France, who had already returned Burgundy to the French crown. Maximilian was unpopular in the Netherlands and unrest in the provinces developed into civil wars in Holland and Utrecht before he restored order.

His son Philip married Juana (Joanna) the Mad, daughter of Catholic Spain's King Ferdinand and Queen Isabella. Their son Charles was born in Ghent in 1500, and over the next 20 years, after an extraordinary series of premature deaths and childless marriages, he inherited most of Europe.

He became lord of the Netherlands in 1506 (although his aunt Margaret of Austria was regent until 1515), king of Spain in 1516 and then Emperor Charles V of Germany in 1519 when his grandfather Maximilian died. One man, born in the Netherlands, became ruler of Austria, the Tyrol, Spain, Mexico, Peru, the Caribbean, Sicily, Naples and the German empire, as well as the Netherlands themselves.

Between 1506 and 1555, Charles enlarged the Netherlands, adding Tournai, Friesland and Utrecht, and he severed the ties between the count of Flanders and the French throne. He spent much of his earlier reign in Brussels, although in the later years he moved to Spain.

When Charles inherited the Low Countries, the province of Brabant had eclipsed Flanders. Brussels had a splendid new town hall with a 295ft steeple, and the Dukes of Brabant and other nobles had built palaces on the higher ground. The Netherlands were still booming culturally – among Charles' advisers, when he was in his late teens, was the theologian and humanist Erasmus. Much of the court's leisure time seems to have been spent hunting wild boar and stags in the nearby Forêt de Soignies. The first regular international mail service was set up in Brussels in 1520 by Jean-Baptiste de Tour et Taxis.

Antwerp, also in Brabant, was even more prosperous than Brussels because it was the crossroads of trading routes between Spain, Portugal, Russia and the Baltic. Each day, as many as 5,000 merchants gathered in the exchange, while up to 500 ships came and went from the port. So euphoric is one Victorian historian about all this that he describes the population of the Netherlands as 'three millions of people, the most industrious, the most prosperous, perhaps the most intelligent under the sun'.

But Charles' rule over the Netherlands was far from trouble-free. Outside Brabant, many provinces were drifting into poverty because of flooding, high taxes and racing inflation. Consequently, Charles had to crush a rebellion in Ghent in 1540. But far more serious was the start of the Reformation, which had devastating consequences for the whole of Europe. Lutherans from Germany quickly extended their influence westwards into the Netherlands and, later, the more radical Calvinism spread northwards from Geneva and was immediately attractive to the poor of the southern Netherlands. It would eventually lead to a full-scale revolt.

Charles abdicated in 1555, in a lachrymose ceremony in Brussels, and handed over the reins to his son Philip. He had already abdicated in Austria in 1521 in favour of his brother Ferdinand, and three months after the Brussels ceremony he abdicated in Spain.

Like his father, Philip inherited a collection of provinces in the Low Countries, rather than a nation. Whereas he was king of Spain, he had no such title in the Netherlands and was never crowned. Instead, he was duke of Brabant, count of Flanders, lord of Utrecht and Groningen and so on. There was no common ancestry or language among the 17 provinces: the French and Germanic language split was already evident. However, there was some administrative unity: provincial assemblies, called the States, sent delegates to the central States General and the rulers had personal representatives called *stadt*holders in each state or group of states.

Some of the problems faced during Philip's rule were similar to those suffered under Charles: heavy taxation and the spread of Protestantism. But whereas Charles had remained popular – partly because his roots and temperament belonged in the Netherlands – Philip was never liked. He was born in Spain, lived there and barely visited the Spanish Netherlands. He had little affection for them and repeatedly misjudged his subjects. He was also more hardline than his father in his defence of Catholicism.

Philip's troubles soon began. He appointed his half-sister Margaret of Parma as regent, and she was reasonably popular, but power remained mainly in the hands of two pro-Spanish councillors, Cardinal Granvelle and Count Berlaymont. The former was hated in the Netherlands. Equally hated was Philip's attempts to reorganise the bishoprics, especially by the clerics and nobles who saw a threat to their power and wealth. Leading the opposition to Philip was Prince William of Orange, also known as William the Silent or Taciturn (although this is probably a mistranslation of a Dutch word for 'sly'). The counts of Egmont and Horne were also powerful opponents and all three demanded the removal of Granvelle.

In 1565 a group of nobles opposed to Philip formed the League of Nobles. Berlaymont referred to them as *ces gueux* (those beggars) and '*Vivent les gueux*' became their rallying cry. In the background to the opposition was the growing popularity of Protestantism, the presence of Spanish troops in the Netherlands, Philip's attempt to centralise power and the heavy taxes imposed on the provinces. The spread of Protestantism was not confined to the League of Nobles. It had burgeoned among the poor in the towns of Flanders, Brabant, Holland and Zeeland. In the 1560s, Calvinist 'field preachers' attracted huge crowds – about 14,000 people gathered outside the walls of Antwerp to listen to one preacher, while another at Tournai had an audience of about 20,000. Part of the attraction was that Calvinist preachers railed against the wealth of the Catholic church. They also criticised the imagery and art in Catholic churches. In 1566, in the Iconoclastic Riots, Calvinist mobs seized and destroyed Catholic churches throughout the Netherlands (*see below* **Blind faith**).

DUTCH REVOLT

In 1567 Philip appointed a new governor in the 17 Provinces, who arrived with an army of 10,000. The Duke of Alva was a man of iron, vindictive, ruthless and a successful army commander. He referred to the Netherlanders as 'men of butter' and said he had come to tame them.

One of his first acts was to set up the 'Council of Blood' (officially called the Council of Troubles). On 4 January 1568 alone he had 84 people executed on the scaffold. In March of that year there were 1500 arrests, 800 of them on one day. In June he had Count Egmont and Count Horn beheaded in the Grand Place in Brussels. Their deaths marked the start of full-scale revolt in the Netherlands, which lasted 80 years.

A major turning point in the Revolt of the Netherlands happened in 1576, when Spanish troops sacked Antwerp. A financial crisis in Spain meant that the troops had not been paid for three years. Soldiers in the Antwerp garrison went on the rampage, setting fire to almost 1,000 buildings in the wealthiest quarter, including the Town Hall. Known as the Spanish Fury, it settled the resolve of any rebels who had been hesitating and solidified their support, particularly in the north.

But from 1578, when Philip sent Alexander Farnese (future Duke of Parma) to govern in the Netherlands, the Spanish began to regain their grip on the southern part of the Netherlands. Although Calvinism had first taken hold in the south, the southern provinces were now feeling the effects of the Counter-Reformation, and in 1579 the Southern Provinces formed the Union of Arras, accepting the authority of Philip and Catholicism.

The north's response was the Union of Utrecht, formed in 1581, which was basically a declaration that they no longer recognised the king's authority. This was the end of the 17 Provinces. By the end of the century, the northern provinces constituted the Republic of the United Netherlands, also known as the United Provinces, while what was left was known as the Spanish Netherlands.

The boundaries were not yet fixed and Parma would reconquer Bruges, Ghent and, later, Antwerp after blockading the River Scheldt. It is possible that Parma could have regained more territory in the north, but Philip II was occupied with the Spanish Armada and the war against France, so Parma was forced to divert his troops to those campaigns.

The original aim of the Dutch Revolt was not to split the provinces into two, and does not even seem to have been independence from Spain. The rebels were anti-Spain and many of them were anti-Catholic, but the general intention was merely to gain greater autonomy and religious freedom and to get Spanish troops out of the Low Countries. But the split, once started, became irreversible, particularly as continuing revolt was a unifying factor in the north.

Blind faith

The death and injury toll of the Reformation was enormous and its effects in the Spanish Netherlands were as bloody and destructive as they were elsewhere.

Charles V was readier than his successor, Philip II, to negotiate with the Lutherans, but he still stamped hard on Protestantism (or heresy as the Spanish preferred to label it). In 1523 the first Lutheran martyrs were burnt in Brussels. In 1550 Charles passed the Edict of Blood, which decreed the death penalty for those convicted of heresy. Protestant propagandists claimed that 30,000 people died as a result of the Edict, although this is probably hugely inflated.

Charles and Philip were helped in their efforts by the Inquisition – although it is the Spanish Inquisition that has come to be most infamous, its colleagues in northern Europe were hardly fops. Most notorious was the Inquisitor of Bruges, Peter Tibelman. If a man trampled on a consecrated wafer, his hand and foot were wrenched off with red-hot irons, his tongue was ripped out and he was then swung by chains over a fire and slowly roasted.

But the violence was not one-sided. In the Iconoclastic Riots of 1566, Calvinist mobs proved how much destruction they could wreak, particularly on property. In Antwerp, crowds ransacked the cathedral with axes and sledgehammers: they hacked up the Madonna, pulled down the statue of Christ at the altar (leaving the statues of the thieves on either side of him), destroyed the chapels, drank the Communion wine, burned manuscripts and rubbed the sacred oil on their shoes. They then did the same to 30 other churches in Antwerp.

Catholic Turmoil to National Unity

Apart from a breather under Austrian 'enlightened despotism' in the eighteenth century, the road to Belgian unity and self-rule was strewn with religious friction, economic dereliction and insurrection.

Counter-Reformation

In 1598 Philip handed over the Netherlands as a 'fief of Spain' to Archduke Albert of Austria, who married Philip's daughter Isabella. The idea was that the removal of Spain might make reconciliation between north and south possible. However, Albert and Isabella's marriage was childless and when Albert died in 1621, the provinces reverted to Spanish rule, although Isabella remained as governor until her death in 1633.

The Dutch Revolt lasted until 1648, although Albert and Isabella negotiated the Twelve Year Truce from 1609-21. Little changed in the last half-century of the war. The religious gap between the two sides became more entrenched, with the United Provinces becoming more firmly Calvinist and the Spanish Netherlands in the grip of the Catholic Counter-Reformation. The Dutch developed a gruesome literature and art of martyrology, portraying the sufferings of the people at the hands of the Spanish and the Catholics. This and the reams of propaganda and treatises issuing from both sides cemented the differences.

The force behind the Counter-Reformation in the Spanish Netherlands was the Jesuits. Although they were a strong influence throughout Europe, their power in the Spanish Netherlands – where

The Ommegang parade in Grand Place commemorates Charles Vth's 1549 visit to Brussels.

Pieter Paul Rubens

The political and military history of the Spanish Netherlands in the seventeenth century may be pitiful, but its cultural achievements were not. Isabella and Albert maintained an ostentatious court, and chief among its claims to glory is the painter Pieter Paul Rubens. The artistic centre, however, was Antwerp rather than Brussels.

Rubens lived from 1577-1640 and studied in Italy from 1600-09. He worked in England (painting the ceiling of the Banqueting Hall at Whitehall), France and Spain as well as Antwerp. In addition to being court painter to Archduke Albert and his wife Isabella, he acted as the ambassador of Philip IV of Spain. He negotiated a peace treaty between Spain and England in 1629 and was knighted by Charles I of England the following year.

Rubens was closely connected with the Catholic Counter-Reformation, and his work fused Italian and Flemish influences. There are plentiful examples of his work (and the work of his studio) in Belgium: in the museums of Brussels, Antwerp and Mechelen, in Antwerp cathedral and his Antwerp house.

Rubens was not by any means working in isolation in Antwerp. Among his contemporaries and students were Jacob Jordaens and Antony van Dyke, who became court painter to Charles I of England. Their works also are abundant in Brussels and Antwerp.

Rubens' House *in Antwerp, which was the artistic centre of the Spanish Netherlands.*

they controlled, for example, secondary education – was particularly great. The influence of Spain itself was minimal at this time. There were still plenty of Spanish officials in Brussels, but the Spanish government and monarchy was too weak to exert much authority, and the Spanish Netherlands were largely autonomous throughout the seventeenth century.

The war ended in 1648 with the Treaty of Münster in which Spain recognised the independence of the north's United Provinces. The borders drawn then coincide with the present-day Belgian-Dutch border. One of the terms of the treaty was that Antwerp's access to the sea was cut by a Dutch blockade of the River Scheldt, rendering it redundant as a port. In the 1660s, Antwerp was allowed a sea outlet via a canal, but this was hardly a substitute. The Scheldt would remain closed for nearly one-and-a-half centuries.

The aftermath of the war was by no means similar in the two halves of the former 17 Provinces. During the war, a flood of Calvinist and anti-Spanish merchants, workers and bankers emigrated from the south to the north, taking their skills, contacts and wealth with them. The result was that the north – Amsterdam in particular – flourished, becoming an affluent maritime and trading power. The south did not. Antwerp was especially hard hit, first by catastrophes such as the Spanish Fury, and later by the Dutch blockade. Its population fell from around 100,000 in 1560 to 42,000 in 1589.

Things became even worse for the Spanish Netherlands in the second half of the seventeenth century. There were two basic reasons for this: Louis XIV of France harboured ambitions to dominate Europe at the expense of the Dutch, English and the Hapsburgs, and Spain's power had dwindled to such an extent that it was pathetically unable to defend its territory. The late seventeenth century brought a succession of different wars – the War of Devolution, the Dutch War, the War of the Grand Alliance (or League of Augsburg) – all involving France and all involving the Spanish Netherlands being attacked, occupied or invaded. The ensuing peace treaties led to the Spanish Netherlands' territory being whittled away – for example, France gained Artois and Ypres. Ironically, almost the only protection given to the southern Netherlands at this time came from the Dutch, who wanted a barrier between themselves and the French.

The semi-permanent war in the Spanish Netherlands caused serious economic decline in the late seventeenth and early eighteenth centuries. The only sector to prosper during those years was agriculture, and there was a shift of population away from the towns to the country. However, the cities were not totally bereft of economic activity. Brussels, for example, was still producing a variety of luxury goods including lace, tapestries and porcelain – both for export and for the wealthy nobles and merchants still living in the Spanish Netherlands.

The low point of the seventeenth century for Brussels came towards the end of the War of the Grand Alliance in 1695. The French suffered a major defeat in the Netherlands and were forced to pull back from the coast. To divert the Alliance's resources, they bombarded Brussels for 36 hours, destroying 3,830 houses. The principal target of the attack was the Town Hall in the Grand Place, which amazingly, given the fact that the steeple was nearly 300ft high, the French missed. Even so, the guns did hit most of the other buildings in the Grand Place, and in 1696-97 there was extensive rebuilding and restoration work in the square. There are several pictures of the bombardment and the devastation in the Musée Communal in the Grand Place.

The Austrian Netherlands

When Philip IV of Spain died in 1665, the Spanish throne passed to his sickly and feeble-minded four-year-old son Charles II. Despite two marriages, Charles was childless and he was the last of the Spanish Hapsburg line.

For most of the 1690s, Charles II seemed to be on the verge of death – there were several false alarms. The great powers of Europe (France, England, Holland and Austria) spent the decade manoeuvring over who would succeed him. By the time Charles finally died in 1700, there were two possibilities: Archduke Charles of Austria and Philip Duke of Anjou, grandson of Louis XIV of France. Charles favoured the Frenchman, partly, it is said, out of dislike for his own German wife, so in 1701 the Duke of Anjou entered Madrid as King of Spain. The English and the Dutch then declared war on France.

The War of Spanish Succession lasted from 1702 to 1713 and during that time the French and English governed the Spanish Netherlands. The dispute was settled at the Treaty of Utrecht in 1713, from which the Austrians came away with the Spanish Netherlands – henceforth known as the Austrian Netherlands – and Spain's possessions in Italy. England gained Gibraltar and Minorca.

Two years later, the Barrier Treaty gave the Dutch the right to keep a line of defensive forts in the Austrian Netherlands, with the cost borne by the Austrian emperors and indirectly by taxes from the inhabitants.

The main effect felt by the Austrian Netherlands during the first years of the eighteenth century was peace, for the country was no longer the prey of French armies. Only once during Austrian rule, which lasted until 1794, were the

Netherlands invaded by the French. Otherwise, there was little change, for the Austrians allowed their new subjects a high degree of autonomy.

This state of affairs changed in the 1740s. Emperor Charles VI of Austria wanted his daughter Maria Theresa to inherit his empire when he died, but the rest of Europe refused to accept this. France invaded again in 1744 and occupied the Austrian Netherlands until the Treaty of Aix-La-Chapelle (Aachen) restored Austrian rule in 1748.

Maria Theresa's style of government is known as 'enlightened despotism'. During the last half of the century there was considerable economic renewal, partly as a result of peace, partly as a result of the efforts of her governor, Charles of Lorraine, to modernise the Austrian Netherlands by building new roads and waterways. There were also improvements in agricultural techniques, so that the late eighteenth century was the only time in Belgium's history when it was self-sufficient in grain. A rural textile industry had grown up, with about half the rural population of Flanders making their living spinning flax and weaving linen. There were also new glass, coal and cotton industries which, unlike the trades before them, did not revolve around the power of the guilds. Smaller industries such as paper mills, sugar refineries and silk factories also developed.

There was less censorship: French books circulated freely and bookshops were opened in the towns. There was also a growing printing industry engaged in reprinting French books. However, the Austrian Netherlands were scarcely at the fore of the Enlightenment and rural culture was still traditional, with companies travelling around the countryside performing medieval mystery plays.

Brussels itself also changed under the Austrians. In 1731 the Coudenburg Palace burnt down. Since this had been the residence of the Dukes of Burgundy and the scene of Charles V's abdication, the loss was emotive. In 1740 work began on a new palace, the Palais du Roi, which is now the town residence of the Belgian royal family. The neoclassical Place Royale and the Palais de la Nation, in which the Belgian parliament now meets, were built in the 1770s and 1780s.

Maria Theresa was succeeded by her son Joseph II in 1780 and his approach to being an enlightened despot was more zealous and radical. He immediately tried to modernise the country, closing monasteries and seminaries, and reforming the judicial system and the administration of government. In 1781 he passed the Edict of Toleration, which recognised religious freedoms. He also tried to unblock Antwerp's access to the sea, but failed.

All of that was hateful to the conservative Belgians, who saw their traditional privileges and vested interests being threatened. The result was the Brabançon Revolution of 1789-90, which involved all the provinces except Luxembourg. The rebels, led by a Brussels lawyer, wrote a new constitution inspired by the US Articles of Confederation and formed the Confederation of the United Belgian States. But the revolution then collapsed into chaos, with a widening split between conservative and progressive rebels. Around 100,000 peasants marched through Brussels, led by priests protesting against the progressives, who were forced to flee to France. In 1790 Austrian authority was restored and when Joseph II died, he was succeeded by the liberal Leopold II who had less enthusiasm for reform.

Liège, which was still an independent prince-bishopric at this time, had its own uprising in 1789, although this was a more radical one, emulating France rather than the USA. This revolt also petered out.

FRENCH OCCUPATION

In 1792, France went to war with Austria, quickly occupying the Austrian Netherlands and Liège. The French armies were initially greeted as liberators, but the welcome soon faltered: when the French temporarily withdrew from Brussels after a defeat in 1793, the people of Brussels ransacked houses of pro-French families. And when France reoccupied the Austrian Netherlands in 1794, tens of thousands of Belgians emigrated.

The French exacted war levies and military requisitions, and they set up an *agence de commerce* to take anything from cattle to art back to France. Among the art was Jan van Eyck's *Adoration of the Mystic Lamb*.

But in 1795, France changed its policy towards the former Austrian Netherlands, annexing them into France itself and setting up a new centralised administration. They abolished the old provinces and created nine new *départements*, based around the old capitals. Brussels became a mere departmental capital answering to Paris, rather than the capital of a nation. Liège and the Netherlands were united for the first time, and the region was increasingly referred to by the French as Belgique.

The French passed laws suppressing feudalism and the guilds. From 1796 French law in its entirety was applied to Belgium. The Belgians accepted the occupation and annexation passively but unenthusiastically, and the French leaders complained of their apathy and slowness. Such protests as occurred were aroused by measures taken against the Catholic church. In 1796 the French confiscated the property of the monasteries, making about 10,000 people homeless. In 1797 they closed the Catholic University of Louvain (Leuven). And in 1798, 585 priests were given the death sentence for refusing to swear their allegiance to France (in the end most of them escaped death).

Brussels' **Théâtre de la Monnaie** *– where the Belgian Revolution began on 25 August 1830.*

The main opposition to French rule came in 1798 after the French introduced conscription. There were riots in East and West Flanders and about 10,000 peasants formed an army in Brabant. The uprising was crushed brutally and hundreds were executed despite the fact that the peasants had been relatively restrained – they had burnt down pro-French houses and destroyed lists of taxpayers, but had not undertaken any murdering or pillaging.

The last five years of the century saw industry in decline, the depopulation of towns, new taxes, economic hardship and organised robber gangs roaming the highways. But from 1800, there was an economic resurgence. The French encouraged the growth of industries such as coal and cotton in the south, and these benefited from the new markets in France. Ghent became an important industrial centre, and the number of people employed in the cotton industry there rose from 1,300 in 1806 to 12,000 in 1816. The new industries were capitalist, largely funded by entrepreneurial nobles and traders who had bought up former monastery lands cheaply.

One of the chief beneficiaries of French rule was Antwerp, for they unblocked its access to the sea and, under Napoleon, constructed a new harbour and port there. He described it as 'a pistol aimed at the heart of England'. France also had an impact on the Brussels landscape: when Napoleon visited in 1803, he ordered the city's old walls to be demolished and replaced with open boulevards.

French rule of the Netherlands came to an end in 1814 when Napoleon was forced to abdicate as Emperor of France, following his defeat at the Battle of Leipzig the year before. The allies (England, Prussia, Russia and Austria) recaptured Brussels in February 1814 and immediately appointed a council of conservatives, whose initial desire was for Belgium to return to Austrian rule. The Austrians, however, had little interest in reclaiming the Netherlands. The Congress of Vienna, which redrew the map of Europe in 1814-15, therefore had to find the country a new identity.

Unity & revolution

In 1814-15 the Congress of Vienna set about redrawing the map of Europe in the wake of Napoleon's military exploits, and one of the dilemmas facing it was the future of the Netherlands and Belgium. Whereas the north had been an independent state since 1648 (and effectively before then), Belgium had no tradition of independence and the Congress was reluctant to create one. Austria had no desire to recover the Netherlands and there was no question of them going to France. The Congress opted to unite the Netherlands and Belgium in the United Kingdom of the Netherlands, which would create a buffer between France and Prussia. It was a solution that few Netherlanders had hoped for, with the exception of Belgian entrepreneurs who saw that union with the Dutch might compensate for the loss of markets in France.

The new kingdom was born as a constitutional monarchy ruled by William Prince of Orange, who was installed as sovereign prince on 31 July 1814 and declared king in 1815. The United Kingdom of the Netherlands had 17 provinces and two capitals, the Hague and Brussels, between which the government alternated. William I was eager to promote prosperity and unity in his new kingdom. He succeeded in the former and failed in the latter.

The Belgians found many reasons to resent the new state. The south of the country was already industrialised and had become wealthy as a result. Although Brussels was joint capital, the new country was governed by a Dutch king, Dutch ministers and Dutch civil servants. Despite being more numerous and more prosperous, the Belgians had little political power, nor did they gain any more over time – even by 1830, only 18 out of the 119 generals and staff officers in the army were Belgian. Many Belgians took refuge in memories of the earlier grandeur of Antwerp and Brussels, regarding the Hague, Amsterdam and the Dutch as upstarts.

There was also fury at the government's attempts to introduce Dutch as the standard language, even in the south. This anger was not confined to French speakers, since those who spoke Flemish dialects also protested against the use of Dutch. Belgium's Catholics were opposed to the new kingdom because it had declared religious freedom. Decrees in 1815 removed the Catholic bias in the education system, which was put under state control, and William I founded three new state universities in Ghent and Leuven.

Finally, Belgian liberals wanted freedom of the press and a less autocratic style of government. As a result, Catholics and liberals formed an alliance in 1828, demanding that Belgium be the dominant force in the Netherlands. The government made concessions, repealing the language decrees in the south and giving freedom of education, but it would not accept Belgian supremacy or freedom of the press.

BELGIAN REVOLUTION

The winter of 1829-30 was severe, and farmers and farm workers suffered accordingly. In addition, overproduction in the industries of the south had caused wage cuts, bankruptcies and unemployment. Workers in both sectors began feeling mutinous, and some regularly protested and demonstrated in Brussels.

On 25 August 1830, an opera called *La Muette de Portici*, written by Daniel Auber, was performed at the Théâtre de la Monnaie in Brussels. It was about the Naples rebellion of 1647 and had been banned since 1828, when it was written. During an aria called 'L'Amour Sacré de la Patrie' ('Sacred Love of the Fatherland'), liberals inside the theatre started rioting and then joined workers protesting in the square outside. Thus began the Belgian Revolution.

The Dutch government negotiated with the leaders of the revolution and there seemed a possibility of administrative separation. But William I prevaricated and the impatient, disillusioned rebels decided to go for secession. William sent 10,000 troops into Brussels at the end of September, and while the numbers were insufficient to crush the uprising, they were enough to inflame the southern provinces into joining the revolution. Belgian soldiers deserted their regiments and the troops were driven out of Brussels.

The new government was assembled rapidly. On 4 October 1830, the rebels declared an independent state and provisional government. On 3 November they held elections for a National Congress. This met for the first time on 10 November and was composed of 200 members, most of whom were intellectuals, lawyers, and journalists. There were few men from industry or finance. On 22 November the new Congress decided on a constitution. Belgium was to be a parliamentary monarchy and unitary state of nine provinces with freedom of religion, education, assembly, press and language, and a separation of church and state. On 3 March 1831, it passed an electoral law defining the electorate, which consisted of about 46,000 men of the bourgeoisie. This meant that one out of every 95 inhabitants had the vote, a relatively high proportion at the time (in France only one in 160 people could vote).

There was fairly rapid recognition of the new nation by the rest of the world, and in January 1831 the Great Powers met in London to discuss the issue. England's Palmerston was in favour of a Belgian state, and France and Germany agreed, thus it was recognised as an independent and neutral state. The choice of a new king was less harmonious. The Belgians initially wanted Louis of Orléans, second son of the French king, but Palmerston resisted and said he was willing to go to war to prevent that choice. Louis's father then forbade him to accept the throne. The Belgians instead chose Léopold of Saxe-Coburg-Gotha who had already been asked by the Greeks to be their king in February 1830 and had turned them down. Léopold, a Lutheran German conservative, took an oath to the constitution on 21 July 1831, which date is now Belgium's National Day.

Shortly afterwards, the Dutch invaded Belgium, and this helped prolong a sense of unity among the Catholics and liberals. The Dutch fought and beat the Belgian rebels at Leuven and Hasselt, but then retreated on hearing reports of an approaching French army of 50,000 troops. The Dutch kept Maastricht and for a short time hung on to Antwerp as well, only surrendering it to the Belgians in December 1832. They did not recognise the new country until 1839.

The Battle of Waterloo 1815

When Napoleon's empire collapsed in 1814, he was given sovereignty of the island of Elba. In 1815, however, he returned to France, landing at Cannes with a force of 800. He landed on 1 March, on 10 March he entered Lyons with 7,000 men, and on 20 March he triumphantly entered the capital. Meanwhile, the Great Powers were thrashing out the future of Europe at the Congress of Vienna. Condemning the landing, they said that Napoleon had made himself liable to public vengeance. Europe prepared for war and the combined armies of the Great Powers numbered over one million men, while Napoleon gathered about 375,000.

The main Austrian armies gathered along the Upper Rhine, the Spaniards were approaching the Pyrenees, the Prussians were in the Netherlands and the Duke of Wellington – commander-in-chief of the British, Hanoverians and Belgians – established his headquarters at Brussels. Napoleon resolved to attack the Prussians (commanded by Blucher) and Wellington's forces, convinced he had the secret goodwill of the Belgians. The English and the Prussians were apprehensive about the loyalty of the 17,000 Belgian and Dutch troops.

Napoleon entered the Netherlands on 15 June. That evening a ball was due to take place in Brussels at the Duchess of Richmond's hotel. Anxious to keep the population of Brussels in ignorance of Napoleon's presence a few kilometres away, Wellington commanded his officers to attend the ball until ten o'clock then slip away to join their divisions. He himself stayed until midnight and left the city the next morning. By the following evening, he had assembled 70,000 troops at Quatre Bras, 20km south of Brussels.

On 16 June, Napoleon fought Blucher's troops at Ligny, and the Battle of Waterloo took place on 18 June on ground which was sodden after heavy rain. Napoleon's troops had marched to Waterloo during the preceding night.

The clash lasted ten hours, during which time almost 50,000 soldiers died. The French broke ranks and fled, pursued by Prussian troops. The Musée Wellington at Waterloo and Ferme du Caillou, where Napoleon stayed, both contain maps and plans of how the battle was fought.

Napoleon fled by coach to Paris, where he eventually abdicated and surrendered to the British. He was banished to the island of St Helena where he died on 5 May 1821.

Independence to the Postwar Era

The taste of freedom turned sour as neutrality failed to keep Belgium out of the wars. Postwar peace allowed deeper Flemish-Walloon strife and left the problem of Nazi collaborators.

Independent Belgium

Inevitably, the coalition between liberals and Catholics in the new state of Belgium was neither harmonious nor long-lived. The political history of Belgium in the nineteenth century consisted of a tug of war between the two sides, and the main battlefield was the education system. Added to the troubled political brew was the Flemish-French language split.

Belgium's history began with the Catholics and the Francophones in the ascendant. The new constitution allowed people to use their language of preference, but French was the language of the dominant class, and it was spoken in the courts, the education system (apart from some primary schools) and government administration. Among the people, Flemish was more widely spoken, with around 2.4 million Flemish speakers to 1.8 million French speakers. Therefore the majority of the population was governed in an alien language.

Intellectuals in Antwerp and Ghent began to resent the prevalence of French. In 1840 they organised a petition demanding the use of Flemish in the administration and law courts of Flemish-speaking provinces. However, it did not generate much popular support, for at this stage the Catholic-liberal split was a far more serious issue.

Initially, the Catholics were dominant at most levels of society. Membership of monasteries and convents more than doubled during the 1830s and 1840s, and in 1834 a new Catholic university was

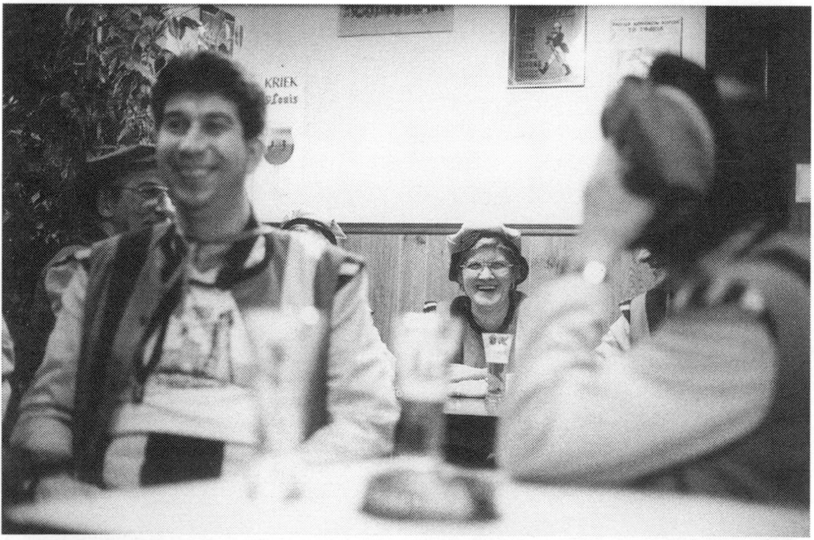

Strife between **Flemish-speakers** *and Francophones was no laughing matter in the 1800s.*

founded at Mechlin (Mechelen), moving to Louvain (Leuven) in 1835. The Catholic church also controlled much of secondary education. It was not until the 1840s that the Belgian liberals gained any impetus. In 1846 they held a congress in Brussels to clarify a political programme and plan an election strategy. Their consequent sense of focus and organisation gave them the upper hand over the Catholics who did not organise themselves in the same way until the 1860s. Consequently, Charles Rogier formed a liberal government in 1848 and the liberals governed, with few gaps, until 1884.

A piece of cake

The second king of Belgium was the ambitious Léopold II, who succeeded his father in 1855. While still heir to the throne, he wrote in a letter to England's Prince Albert that Belgium might be small, but Rome, Carthage, Austria, Russia and Prussia had all started as small states and look what happened to them.

So it is little surprise that Léopold II wanted to accumulate an empire, even though the Belgians themselves showed little appetite for imperialism or exploration. As crown prince, he looked around for suitable territories and considered British Borneo, the Philippines, South Africa and Mozambique. Finally, he decided to grab a piece of the 'magnificent African cake', as he described it. Much of central Africa was still unexplored and in 1876 Léopold set up the Association Internationale Africaine with the help of the English explorer Henry Stanley. Although other European governments and the US expressed qualms about Léopold's activities in Africa, he dismissed them sufficiently for the Berlin Declaration of 1885 to recognise the independent state of the Congo, with Léopold as head of state. He referred to himself as its proprietor. His new territory was 80 times the size of Belgium and he had absolute power.

Until 1895, the Congo was a money pit for Léopold and he was forced to borrow 32 million francs from the Belgian government to bail himself out. But from 1895 – when he started exporting wild rubber – it generated substantial revenue, much of which he passed back to Belgium in the form of public works such as the African Museum at Tervuren.

By the early twentieth century, Léopold's policy of extracting maximum profit from the Congo, regardless of ecological and human cost, was exposing Belgium to international criticism, particularly from Britain. In 1908, the Belgian government forced him to hand it over to the nation.

With the revenue from the Congo, Léopold II set up the **Museum voor Midden-Afrika**.

© ADAGP, Paris and DACS, London 1996

René Magritte's *'L'Empire des Lumières', 1954, Musée d'Art Moderne, Brussels.*

Although Belgium lost the valuable Dutch East Indies markets when it split from the Netherlands, there was considerable industrial expansion in the 1830s, at a time when much of Europe had falling industrial prices. With its major programme of railway construction and large-scale investment in the coal, iron and banking industries, Belgium was the first country in continental Europe to undergo the Industrial Revolution. Nevertheless, there were still occasional economic problems and disasters, such as a banking crisis in 1838.

There were also crises in the countryside. The rural linen and flax industries of Flanders were unable to compete with cheaper, more industrialised competitors in England, added to which there was a potato famine in 1847. That year, 28

Altered images

George Melly on Magritte's multiple magic.

Apart from that silhouette of a great dove, its plumage a summer sky, soaring up from a dark sea in threatening weather, René Magritte's *The Dominion of Light* is the great Belgian master's most popular image. It is a close relation to the dove in its contrast of a day sky with darkness, and as to the dual popularity of these two works, I believe it has to do with the optimistic and universal symbolism of blue skies.

Magritte himself would have angrily rejected this supposition, as he contemptuously resisted the notion that his work was symbolic. His aim was to test reality, to sabotage common sense, to 'solve' the problem of things we take for granted. For example, Magritte's 'solution' of the door? A depiction of a door containing evidence that someone has calmly walked through it rather than opened it. The mirror? Magritte's mirror reflects the back of the head of someone staring into it. Woman? A woman's face, framed by her hair, but whose breasts replace her eyes, her navel her nose, her vagina her mouth.

All these and many other 'solutions' have intrigued the public, but that doesn't mean they would wish to 'live' with them. The dove and the suburb are exceptional. They seduce and charm.

It was after the war that Magritte began to produce more acceptable images. The first version of *The Dominion of Light* is dated 1949. Version? Yes. There are in fact 17 oils and ten gouaches that share this title and image. Why? Well, it may surprise people today – when artists fresh out of art school can become instant millionaires – but until the 1960s you could be world famous and still find it impossible to earn even a modest living from painting.

Magritte became rich only at the end of his life when his creative powers were fading. Until then, he had been forced to design wallpaper, practise commercial art and accept in part living on his wife's earnings. However, in 1947 he acquired an American dealer, an ex-ballet dancer called Iolas who, despite rows over money, gradually nursed Magritte towards success. But at a price. If an image pleased the American collectors, Iolas would demand multiple versions. Magritte, complaining bitterly, became to an extent an image factory.

This cloning of images was not entirely new. Even before the war, Magritte had painted several versions of images on request. Nor, in the case of *The Dominion of Light*, was the exceptional number entirely Iolas's doing. It was the eighth version, the first to be taller than it was wide, which was responsible. Magritte got in a muddle, sold it to Peggy Guggenheim for her museum in Venice, and then discovered he had already half-promised it to three other collectors. So he set to and painted three more, this version being the second.

The upright versions have always proved the more popular, largely, I believe, because the format allows a taller tree (by night) to invade the day sky more dramatically. In the squat pictures the lower half, sometimes a single building, sometimes a whole suburb, can look like a cut-out placed in front of another canvas. As always with Magritte's multiples, there are slight variations. In the three post-Guggenheim versions he introduces a pond reflecting the lamp-lit house with its lighted windows; a device which I believe adds to their nostalgic appeal and deepens the perspective.

Yet even if *The Dominion of Light* is an easy entrance into the work of this great but uneven painter, does it matter? Certainly no more than an initiation into opera via a well-known aria. Some initiates may go no further. Others will persist. Nor is it the only picture by him on show in Brussels. And anyway, beyond its reassuring cosiness, it remains an authentic poetic idea.

Magritte himself put it best: 'I have always felt the greatest interest in night and day, yet without having ever preferred one or the other. This great personal interest in night and day is a feeling of admiration and astonishment.'

per cent of the East Flanders population received poor relief. As in the rest of Europe, a growing proletariat nurtured the rise of socialism. The Belgian Workers Party was founded in 1885, and there were extensive strikes and protests by workers in 1886. Universal male suffrage was introduced in 1893 (although multiple votes biased the system in favour of the bourgeoisie) and in 1894 the socialists gained their first parliamentary seats. But the 1880s also saw the Catholics regain power in Belgium, with the bulk of their support in Flanders. They remained in office until 1917.

By the time the Catholics came to power in 1884, concessions to Flemish speakers had already been made, and the Catholics accelerated the process. In the 1870s and '80s there had been legislation introducing bilingualism in Flanders and strengthening the Dutch position in law and education, but the Flemish were still basically governed and tried in French. In 1898 Flemish was given official equality with French, so that the Dutch versions of laws attained equality with the French versions.

The main focus of the Flemish movement after 1900 was a push for the University of Ghent to become Flemish-speaking. Ignored by Parliament, the issue built up massive momentum so that, in 1912, one meeting on the subject attracted 15,000 people. About 100,000 signed a petition to the government on the subject. When the Flemish finally got their university in Ghent, it was delivered to them by the German occupation in 1916.

Belgium in the wars

At the time of Belgium's creation in 1830-31, the new state was declared to be perpetually neutral. But on 2 August 1914 Kaiser Wilhelm of Germany demanded that Belgium give German troops free passage through the country on their way to invading France. It had 12 hours to respond to the ultimatum, which it rejected. On 4 August German troops entered Belgium and seven hours later Britain declared war on Germany. By midnight, five different empires were involved, and they all thought the war would be over by Christmas.

Belgium suffered horribly in World War I. Snipers – known as *franc-tireurs* – shot at the Germans from ditches and outbuildings, and the Germans retaliated brutally. When snipers struck in the village of Hervé, the Germans decided to make an example of it. Within a few days, only 19 of the 500 houses were still standing, the church was in ruins, and the shattered village was littered with corpses. Massacres occurred elsewhere: 110 were shot at Andenne, 384 at Tamines, and 612 (including a three-week-old baby) at Dinant. Meanwhile the German newspapers were full of stories about the torture and sadistic acts committed by the Belgian *franc-tireurs* against German troops.

Belgium fell quickly despite the *franc-tireurs*, and the Belgian government took refuge in Antwerp. The Germans entered Brussels on 20 August and held a military parade to celebrate. The English nurse Edith Cavell, who stayed on in Brussels, said that conversations with the Germans revealed they were surprised to find themselves there, having believed they were marching on Paris.

By the end of September, Antwerp was under siege and it fell on 10 October, despite the arrival of British troops, among them Rupert Brooke, in a fleet of London buses. About 500,000 refugees left Antwerp, among them thousands of people who had fled there from elsewhere in Belgium. Around 1.5 million people left Belgium in 1914, although many of them later returned. The government moved to Le Havre in France, while the king, Albert I, took up position with the small Belgian army in the northwest of the country between Nieuwport and Ypres. There they fought in the deadly Ypres trenches alongside the French and English. Albert I was known by the Belgians as *le Roi chevalier* (the soldier king) and his bravery achieved legendary status.

The four-year German occupation of Belgium had terrible consequences for the country. Its total war dead, at 44,000, was hundreds of thousands less than that of nations such as Russia and France. But, there were other kinds of suffering. Around 700,000 Belgians were forcibly deported to Germany to work on farms and in factories, so that the economy was devastated. Belgium had depended on other countries for its raw materials

Brussels sprouts

Independence and patriotism led to a massive building spree in Brussels in the nineteenth century. Among the earliest additions were the Galeries Saint Hubert in the centre of Brussels, which were built in the 1840s. These were followed by a spate of commemorative and official buildings as Belgium celebrated its own existence, culminating in the construction of the formal Parc du Cinquantenaire for the fiftieth anniversary exhibition. The vast and monstrous Palais de Justice was completed in 1883.

The main town planning feat of the nineteenth century was the covering of the River Senne. At first sight, Brussels appears to be an urban oddity in that it did not grow up around or near a river. In fact, it did.

The course of the Senne ran past Gare du Midi and the Porte d'Anderlecht, past the Bourse and De Brouckère, to place Rogier and then to the Porte d'Antwerp, with streams branching off to the Sablon and the Palais du Roi. But it was slow-flowing, navigable only by small boats, and frequently caused flooding in low areas such as place St Géry. It was also seen as a source of disease and ill health. So, in 1870, it was covered up and thereafter Brussels' shipping traffic used the Canal de Willebroeck, which joins Brussels to the River Scheldt.

and for export markets – it lost both. Much of its rail system was destroyed in an attempt to halt the German invasion. Agricultural production fell, and there was widespread poverty and hunger.

But the situation was prevented from becoming even worse by the early organisation of committees to provide food and relief. The National Assistance and Nutrition Committee (NHVC) was set up by the Belgians, while Herbert Hoover in the USA helped to set up the Commission for the Relief of Belgium. Belgium was liberated in 1918 and, until 1921, the main consideration of the postwar governments was rebuilding. It is estimated that war losses represented about one-fifth of its national assets in 1914, and it did not recover all of them in reparations.

The war had also stagnated the issues that occupied the country before 1914. The Flemish cause suffered a sizeable setback, partly because a small group of Flemish politicians had collaborated enthusiastically with the Germans, partly because the Germans had been pro-Flemish. In 1916, the Germans made the University of Ghent Flemish-speaking, which had been the chief goal of the Flemish lobby since the turn of the century. Not surprisingly, the university reverted to French when the Germans were defeated, and did not become Flemish again until 1930.

Throughout the 1930s, the Flemish made a series of language gains, having recovered the support they lost in the aftermath of the war. In 1932 Flanders was made monolingual (as opposed to French and Flemish having equality).

The period immediately after the war was marked by political unity: Catholics, liberals and socialists worked together to rebuild the country. The unity quickly dissipated, however, hastened by the introduction of proportional representation. The first universal male suffrage elections without multiple votes for the bourgeoisie were held in 1919, and they resulted in a series of coalition governments. Between 1918 and 1940, Belgium had 18 different administrations.

There was some economic recovery in the late 1920s, with Belgium's workers enjoying a standard of living much higher than before the war. But in the 1930s, Belgium slumped into depression and its politics followed much the same pattern as elsewhere in Europe. There was severe unemployment, social unrest and a move to the right. In the 1936 elections, Flemish nationalist and right-wing parties in Wallonia and Brussels made big gains, blaming a weak parliament, a lack of strong leadership and the unions for the depression.

Just after World War I, the Belgian government tempered its perpetual neutrality with an alliance with France. But towards the end of the 1930s, as Germany flexed its muscles, Belgium returned to its former position, reasserting its neutrality after Germany invaded Poland in 1939.

Brussels' WWI **Monument du Pigeon Soldat**.

WORLD WAR II

But once again neutrality did it little good, and on 10 May 1940, Hitler attacked Belgium. The Belgian response was different the second time round. Whereas Belgium's stance in 1914 had led to international sympathy and admiration for the 'plucky' Belgians, this time there were raised eyebrows. Unlike Albert I, his son Léopold III surrendered to the Germans after 18 days. Much of the population supported his action, but the government did not. Believing that Belgium should commit itself to France and England, it became a government-in-exile in Le Havre and then London.

Despite initially espousing a policy of normalisation in Belgium, the Germans became more authoritarian during the course of war. Slowly, as the people became aware of this, there was greater resistance to the occupation. And in the end, Belgium suffered many of the same problems as it had in World War I: deportations, forced labour, poverty and food shortages. Even so, there were both Walloons and Flemish who were deeply pro-German.

Belgium was liberated by the Allies in September 1944 and one of the leaders' earliest tasks was to tackle the issue of collaboration. During 1944-49, the War Tribunals considered 405,000 cases and reached 58,000 guilty verdicts, of which 33,000 were in Flanders. But most importantly, the

Nazi pieces of work

In the 1990s, Belgium is still struggling with its memories of World War II and the problem of collaborators. In February 1996, a military court in Brussels reconsidered the case of Irma Laplasse, a Flemish farmer's wife who betrayed resistance fighters to the Nazis in 1944. She was executed by firing squad in 1948.

The court upheld her conviction, but ruled that she should have been given a life sentence rather than execution. The judgment was met by protests from both sides. Survivors of concentration camps, and former members of the resistance demonstrated outside the Palais de Justice, in protest at any moves to rehabilitate collaborators. Members of the nationalist Flemish Vlaams Blok party are campaigning for an amnesty for all those accused of collaborating because, it insists, the War Tribunals were an attempt to victimise and repress the Flemish.

Up to 15,000 Belgians, who were convicted of collaboration, still receive reduced pension and property rights.

country had to deal with the behaviour of the king himself. The debate lasted five years and eventually, in 1950, the government held a non-binding referendum on whether the king should return. Only 57 per cent voted in his favour (72 per cent in Flanders and 42 per cent in Wallonia), and when he did come back there were serious disturbances. Léopold then stepped aside in favour of his son Baudouin, who was crowned in 1951.

Postwar Belgium

World War II had made it clear that Belgium's neutrality had failed it, and even before the war was over, the government-in-exile set about rejecting neutrality in favour of international alliances. It signed the Benelux Customs Union with Luxembourg and the Netherlands in 1944 (it came into force on 1 January 1948), abolishing all customs tariffs between the three countries and setting a common external tariff.

The country was also an enthusiastic participant in postwar international relations. This came partly from the desire to avoid a repeat of the two German occupations and partly from the realisation that, as an export-driven economy, it needed to belong to the growing international relations superstructure. Belgium was one of the first signatories of the UN Charter in June 1945, it participated in the Marshall Plan and it joined the Organisation for European Economic Cooperation in 1948. It joined the Council of Europe and the European Coal and Steel Community, and became the headquarters of the European Economic Community when it was set up in 1957 (*see chapter* **Brussels Today**). In 1960, the Benelux countries abolished their internal borders. In 1967 Belgium became the headquarters of NATO.

The other important aspect of the postwar years was the continuation and worsening of Flemish-Walloon strife. As in 1918, the debate was initially dampened after the war by the awkward question of Flemish-German collaboration, but from 1960 onwards the split over language and community deepened. The language barrier between French-speaking Wallonia and Flemish-speaking Flanders was formally created in 1962 (Brussels is officially bilingual). In 1965 the political parties split into Flemish and Walloon wings. With the language question settled, the debate focused more on the constitution and treatment of the Flemish and French communities.

The split between Flanders and Wallonia was exacerbated by economic developments. In the nineteenth and early twentieth centuries, Wallonia was the economic stronghold of Belgium because of its coal and steel industries. But these went into decline between the wars and failed after World War II, and unemployment rose. Meanwhile, Flanders developed new industries, such as telecommunications, and prospered. Flanders then complained that its wealth was being drained in order to prop up Wallonia, while the Walloons accused the government of showing economic favouritism towards the Flemish. In the 1971 elections, language-based parties such as Volksunie, Front des Francophones and Rassemblement Wallon achieved nearly a quarter of the vote.

Since 1970, the Belgian government has made a series of constitutional reforms granting greater autonomy to the two communities and changing Belgium from a centralised to a federal state. There were many prophesies of doom in 1993 when King Baudouin died, for he had been credited with holding the country together with his mixture of pragmatism and idealism.

However, so far the country has not fallen apart and a new constitution was introduced in 1994, creating a system of elected assemblies and governments representing the three regions of Flanders, Wallonia, and Brussels, and the Dutch, Flemish and German language communities.

King Baudouin, *who was credited with holding Belgium together with his mixture of pragmatism and idealism, died in 1993.*

Brussels Today

Euro melting pot and EU gravy train stop, Brussels epitomises cosmopolitan affluence. But the city has more than its fair share of scandals, demos and motor mania.

Walk into one of the many expense account restaurants in Brussels, and you'll immediately hear several European languages being spoken. But glance around, and all the men look the same. If it's summer, they'll be wearing Madras check linen jackets; if it's winter, they will have changed into autumn shades of cashmere. The conversation will also be uniform: business, Euro-business, expat tax breaks and international schools.

When you first come to Brussels, you may expect a mixture of different cultures, with the best of Europe all crammed into a small space. What you first notice is that all those cultures seem to have been melded into a bland whole. Although the different nationalities might stick firmly together, they still end up looking the same and talking about the same things. But if you step outside the Michelin-starred restaurants and look around a bit harder, you notice the diversity in Brussels. You see Turkish coffee shops, African clothes shops, halal butchers and Latin American bars. You hear people speaking Russian and various eastern European languages, and you start to notice the contrasts and anomalies among the Belgians themselves.

Life in Brussels has been pretty fine for many of the Belgians since 1945. Having suffered two German occupations this century, Brussels made a rapid recovery after World War II. The establishment of the EC and NATO headquarters, and the service industries that grew up in their wake, helped create widespread affluence. The city and suburbs are packed with excellent restaurants; designers such as Versace and Gucci have large branches despite Brussels being relatively small; the streets are jammed with BMWs and Saabs; and there is an excellent infrastructure of healthcare, schools and motorways.

So affluent is the image of the Belgians that whole investment industries exist in tax havens such as Luxembourg to cater for the financial needs of the 'Belgian dentist', epitome of the wealthy European professional with large reserves of cash to stash away from the taxman.

But not all of Brussels is the preserve of the well-fed professional. The area around Gare du Midi is depressed, if colourful, while Gare du Nord is in a grimy red-light district. In the very centre of Brussels, the Marolles district around rue Haute is poor, with high infant mortality rates and several homeless hostels. Symbolically speaking, you could say that something seems to be rotten in the heart of Belgium itself. And generally, life in Brussels has become less easy of late, so the inhabitants have had to shed some of their complacency.

Belgium is suffering from rising unemployment and a huge national debt, and the government is struggling to tighten its belt – an activity that does not come naturally to a Belgian. At the beginning of 1996, it raised VAT, taxes on investment and water taxes, but far more serious are plans to cut back Belgium's generous social security system. As a result, opinion polls carried out at Christmas 1995 showed that 50 per cent of Belgians had no confidence in their government. An international poll of people in 47 countries found that the Belgians were one of the most pessimistic nations about their prospects for the year ahead.

All that dismay and resentment is evident in Brussels. Go near any government or European offices, and you have a fairly high chance of witnessing a demonstration. Some of the protests are not specifically Belgian – French farmers occasionally flood the streets around the European Commission buildings with milk or block them with vegetables as a way of pointing out that they receive so little money for their produce that they might as well throw it away.

But most of the protests are domestic and consist of students, teachers, striking transport workers, the unemployed or pensioners demonstrating about redundancies, pension reductions or social security cuts. On days without demonstrations, you can still observe the Brussels riot police sitting around with their shields and barbed-wire blockades, reading the paper and eating crisps while they wait for the next protest.

Elsewhere in Brussels, there are other signs of recession – empty shops, more homeless people, racist graffiti. The extreme right-wing political parties are gaining popularity in Belgium, though the problem of racism is far more serious in Antwerp than in Brussels. The right-wing Flemish nationalist party, Vlaams Blok, attracted more support than any other Flemish party in Brussels in the last elections, and the French-speaking National Front party also gained ground. There have been racially motivated attacks in some of the working class districts, such as Schaerbeek, while the Brussels police attract occasional accusations of racism.

Disillusionment with the government is not just a result of cutbacks. It also stems from a stream of corruption scandals, involving politicians at all levels. The most conspicuous casualty was Willy Claes, who was forced to resign from his job as NATO Secretary-General. The subjects of such scandals have been diverse, ranging from illegal immigrants to military helicopters, while other non-political scandals – such as the child pornography ring centred on a car park by the Grand Place – force the people of Brussels to navel-gaze.

Tougher to crack is the question of the future of Belgium and Brussels. Following the constitutional reforms of 1980-94, Belgium is a federalist monarchy with three regional governments in Flanders, Wallonia and Brussels. Flanders is Flemish-speaking, Wallonia is Francophone and the Brussels region is a bilingual (in practice, mainly Francophone) enclave within the Flemish-speaking area. What happens next is the subject of immense disagreement.

On the one hand, there is a desire, particularly in Flanders, for further separation and an end to the federal state. The Flemish see Wallonia, with its dying coal and steel industries, as a burden on their healthier economy, and resent paying high taxes to cover social security benefits doled out to the Walloons. On the other hand, many Belgians regret the end of a unitary state, and the big show of patriotic mourning that followed King Baudouin's death in 1993 was seen by many as a protest against the dismantling of the Belgian state. Taxpayers also complain about the cost of supporting three regional governments in addition to the central government.

Regionalism contributes to the fragility of the Belgian government. Coalitions of Walloon and Flemish political parties are regularly riven when minor regional problems – such as TV programming in Brabant and bus contracts in Wallonia – blow up into major national issues. Disagreement over how to reform the social security system and meet the economic criteria for European monetary union means that as much energy goes into politicking as into tackling the issues themselves.

Despite being a bilingual enclave, Brussels is by no means untouched by the Flemish-Walloon split. For example, there is anger at Flemish proposals that Belgium be organised into just two regions – Flanders and Wallonia – with Brussels losing its status as a separate political region and being absorbed into Flanders instead.

Nor are the problems confined to politics. In central Brussels, most people speak Flemish and French (although French is dominant), but in many of the Brussels suburbs the visitor's French skills are virtually redundant. One British woman, who has lived many years in Tervuren, says that when talking to her neighbours there, she would naturally talk in French because although Flemish is their first language, they are content to speak French. But in dealings with officials, such as the police or even the staff in the local post office, her French is met with a show of incomprehension. Lacking Flemish, she uses English in these situations, and the officials are happier with that.

None of the above should lead one to see Brussels as a collapsing city of the unemployed, the far right and the corrupt. However much people here complain about rising crime, the fact remains that crime rates are much lower than in cities such as London or Amsterdam. As one inhabitant admits: 'Everyone knows someone who has been burgled or had their car broken into, but they may not know anyone who's been mugged or robbed.'

Furthermore, the large number of expats in Brussels and the suburbs means that recession has barely touched many parts of the capital. Restaurants continue to flourish, new bars keep opening and a fair number of the demonstrators wear furs as they march through the streets. Most noticeably, the Belgians continue to speed through the city in their BMWs, and this may be one of Brussels' main problems, though many would never admit it. But the fact is, Belgium stands out from other Western European countries in its high number of car accidents. The aggression of Brussels drivers makes motoring a nerve-jangling experience at times, but if you really want an enervating journey, a taxi ride should provide all the terror you could want.

Brussels is enclosed by a huge network of excellent motorways (it is said that the lights of the Belgian motorway system are one of the few man-made structures that can be seen from space), which lead right into the centre of the city. Combine high-speed roads with a tradition of low driving standards (there was no practical driving test until 1977), aggression and a climate of regular rain, fog and snow, and it is not hard to imagine the results.

The motorways create another dichotomy. The efficient road network means that many expats (and Belgians) who work in Brussels do not live there. Instead, they roar off down the motorway to prosperous suburbs and towns. You can walk down street after street in European districts such as the Quartier Léopold at the weekend and see nobody except a few old women walking their poodles.

When asked if she was proud to come from Brussels, one resident was surprised. 'Proud? Well, it's nice, but it's like a village compared to London or Paris,' she shrugged. At the same time, Brussels proclaims itself the capital of Europe. Much of the Brussels population seems unsure about which one they want their city to be.

The heart of the chatter

For many years, few British government ministers ever said the word 'Brussels' without sneering. Never mind that on their last visit, they probably had an excellent meal, drank plenty of Belgian beer or fine Burgundy, and generally had a good time – Brussels has come to epitomise bureaucracy and the wasting of British taxpayers' money by the European Union.

Brussels is very much the fulcrum of the EU, and therefore likes to think of itself as the capital of Europe. It is home to the European Commission, which is basically the EU civil service, and it is the primary base for the Council of Ministers, the EU's main decision-making body.

Most of the European institutions are based around the Rond Point Schuman, near the Parc du Cinquantenaire. Until 1991, the European Commission was housed in the star-shaped Berlaymont, but when it became clear that asbestos in the 1960s building was a severe health threat, the staff were moved out. Many are now housed in the nearby Breydel building while others are scattered across the city. The Berlaymont's glass front, which used to represent open government, is now tightly sheathed in plastic while the asbestos is being stripped out. The fact that a building which used to act as pictorial shorthand for the EU is now deserted and dangerous, is a convenient metaphor for Eurosceptics.

Although British politicians and journalists often portray the European Commission as a vast machinery of bureaucrats taking a leisurely ride on the European gravy train, there are only about 15,000 staff, not many compared to most domestic civil services. Of that number, about a third are interpreters and translators.

The Commission itself may be relatively small, but well over 100,000 non-Belgians work in jobs that have some connection with the EU. There are vast armies of diplomats, lawyers, lobbyists, interpreters and journalists working in Brussels. The city is also the international or European headquarters for many multinationals and other organisations. So numerous are the associations and federations in Brussels that there are even associations of associations, such as the Federation of International Associations.

All these organisations support networks of caterers (the cocktail party circuit is huge), cleaning companies, relocation experts, recruitment agencies and so on. This leads to high rents and prices in certain *quartiers*, but most Belgians say they do not resent this because of the employment opportunities created by the EU.

Not surprisingly, there is keen competition among other EU member states for a slice of the pie, and not all the European institutions are based in Brussels. Luxembourg houses the European Court of Justice, the Court of Auditors and the European Investment Bank. It also plays host to Council of Ministers meetings in April, June and October. The European Parliament is based in Strasbourg, France. Many people have pointed out that these divisions lead to vast amounts of time and money wasted on travel between the three bases but, of course, France and Luxembourg are adamant they will not cede their institutions to Belgium, or anywhere else.

As well as housing EU institutions, Brussels is home to the headquarters of NATO and the secretariat of the defence organisation, the Western European Union, but these have a relatively low profile. You don't see people with car stickers bearing their logos, or old *quartiers* being destroyed to make way for their buildings. Nor do you hear Brussels proclaiming itself the capital of the West's defences. But then again, given that the Belgian secretary-general had to resign because of a corruption scandal, NATO may not be a subject Belgians care to boast about.

European Parliament, *Quartier Léopold.*

Brussels by Area

Brussels by Area

Uptown or downtown – from the grandeur of the Royal Quarter to the Ilôt Sacré's glitzy tourism – where there's splendour you'll find sleaze just around the corner.

Eglise Ste Cathérine, *which has a light a graceful interior, dominates place Ste Cathérine.*

Brussels has an Upper and Lower Town, which gives it a large, imperial-sounding ring, conjuring up important buildings and long avenues lording it over small, dark streets. In fact, the two areas are within metres of each other and the city's greatest landmark, the Grand Place, is in the Lower Town – though the streets are broader and royalty resides in the Upper Town. The Belgian capital is not large and you could walk round most of its centre in a day. The *communes* slot neatly into each other, converging round the main *commune* of Brussels, so you can generally keep major sights in view. Some *communes*, such as Anderlecht, are visibly poorer than others, Uccle for example, but often splendour and seediness reside cheek by jowl – Saint Gilles looks elegant till you get near Gare du Midi, while the glitzy tourism of the Ilôt Sacré swiftly turns into the sleaze of rue de Laeken.

Much of Brussels is handsome, if run-down, and it's a good city to walk in, but if you want adventures, you'll have to keep stopping to venture inside. Everything here happens indoors. Only isolated pockets are visibly kicking. Most places look sedate and sleepy or downbeat and seedy. Belgians are not given to demonstrativeness and you don't get any of the fast exchanges of London, New York or Rome. This attitude has affected everyone. The North African *communes* of Schaerbeek and Saint Josse are hardly more lively. Only a few places – such as the unashamedly touristic Ilôt Sacré and Matonge, and the University area by night – have street energy. Yet Brussels has

Fruit and veg stalls and a weekly fish market conduct business in the shadow of the great church in **place Ste Cathérine**.

Holland

Fishy displays in Petite rue des Bouchers in the **Ilôt Sacré** *– their days may be numbered.*

some of the latest opening hours in Europe, a contingency of dedicated clubbers and, in the most unlikely-looking places, plenty of bizarre happenings. Just go indoors.

The Lower Town

The Ilôt Sacré

The Lower Town begins magnificently with the Grand Place (*see chapter* **Sightseeing**) and ends in dereliction and depression at place des Martyrs. Along the way it takes in some of the most interesting and least known parts of inner-city Brussels.

Just off the Grand Place, to the east, is the Ilôt Sacré (Holy Isle), which was restored by the *commune* in 1960. Now one of the liveliest areas, it's a medieval cross-section of small streets almost entirely devoted to food. Fish restaurants display their wares tantalisingly out on the street, with great ruddy lobsters and handfuls of shellfish reclining on mounds of ice. There is talk of the EU prohibiting this on hygiene grounds; something that might turn the EU's most loyal city against it.

Even the street names are appetising, with the likes of rue des Harengs and rue du Marché aux Herbes. Seeing these it is easy to imagine the busy market trading of medieval times, and the present agglomeration of restaurants is in keeping with tradition. In the lovely glass-covered **Galeries St Hubert** – Europe's oldest glass arcade – shops glitter with jewellery, the **Arenberg Galeries** cinema shows erudite films and in the **Taverne du Passage** you can seat yourself at the long central table in the cream-coloured room for good honest Belgian food, and plenty of it.

The other side of the Grand Place is quieter, confirming the tendency of tourists to hunt in packs and go where they're told. Only at the corner of rue de l'Etuve will you find a crowd: camera-clickers throng around the famous bronze boy statue, the **Manneken Pis**. Perhaps it's because this area is less about food than slightly gloomy clothes shops and odd vendors of strange plastic figures. (The streets towards boulevard Anspach, rue Marché au Charbon for example, are livelier, particularly late on.) Opposite the police station is **Le Belgica**, one of the best bars in town, small, packed, eccentric, proudly *Bruxellois* and serving its own lethal juniper-berry drink. Le Belgica is gay, but straights are made to feel welcome. Around the corner is the lively **Au Soleil**. Or there's the lugubrious DNA, where you can play arcade games all night.

Sainte Cathérine

The Ilôt Sacré ends at **La Bourse**, the nineteenth-century stock exchange that faces a huge McDonald's across boulevard Anspach. Venture behind McDonald's and you come across a rather quiet area of large, beautiful buildings in decline. But there is a certain buzz; it is emerging as the place to be. The old, covered meat market, Marché St Géry, has been converted into a shopping centre. Studded discreetly along boulevard Antoine Dansaert are some of the best designer shops in town;

check out the shoe stores and Stilj which has two shops here, one selling designer clothes and the other underwear.

The streets around here are a bewildering tangle, though wider and longer than those of the Ilôt Sacré. Evocative names abound, with place du Nouveau Marché aux Grains and quai au Bois à Brûler. The latter is a reminder that the River Senne once flowed right through this area before being buried in the nineteenth century. At place Ste Cathérine there is still a weekly fish market and the restaurants that line the dilapidated square specialise in seafood. **Eglise Ste Cathérine**, dominating the square, is a heavy Poelaert creation, though the interior is surprisingly light and graceful. Around the corner from Ste Cathérine is the beautiful and unusual **Eglise St Jean-Baptiste**. Churches aside, anything goes around the Ste Cathérine area, so you will also see run-down hotels whose rooms can be rented by the hour.

This is a good area for interesting late-night bars, though you won't get carousing on the streets because, as usual, everything takes place indoors. The bars are an unusual mix. **L'Acrobate**, just down from Marché St Gery, is a fancifully painted bar, complete with dance floor and beautiful people, while the Tuum is a gem of peculiarly Belgian seediness – it looks like a standard *taverne* with small tables and pinball, but stay a while and you'll see the living dead, stay longer and you'll see tempers reach for their knives. At **Le Greenwich** customers compulsively play chess all day.

De Brouckère

Walking back down boulevard Anspach, you reach the unabashedly Americanised high-street area of De Brouckère where advertising billboards reign. This used to be a more upmarket area and distinguished vestiges remain. **Café Métropole** is a magnificent turn-of-the-century bar with *Casablanca*-style pianist. The opera house, **Théâtre de la Monnaie**, is in place de la Monnaie and appears to have given in to the surrounding tack, though this impression is dispelled once inside. It is horribly overshadowed by the awful Anspach Centre, which dominates the skyline and dictates the business of the area. The centre is home to all manner of garish clothes shops, and this gaudy tone continues down the rue Neuve. Pedestrianised it may be, but it is now infamous for its ugliness. Every conceivable brand name (except the more upmarket ones) is present and all the shops along its unrelenting red expanse begin to feel the same. It was not always so. On the site of the concrete shopping complex, **Inno**, there was once 'A sound of revelry by night/And Belgium's capital had gathered then/Her beauty and her chivalry' for the Duchess of Richmond's famous ball on the eve of Waterloo, at which Wellington danced gallantly all night until 'Nearer, clearer, deadlier than before!/Arm! Arm! It is – it is – the cannon's opening roar!' (Byron's 'Childe Harold' Canto III, stanzas XXI and XXII).

Rue Neuve ends, as it began, in a claustrophobic shopping centre, **City 2**. Yet there is an energy to the street that you don't find elsewhere in Brussels. It is always packed, there are numerous stands and buskers, and in summer the hair-wrappers come out. It is a place to walk through rather than linger in, as the crowds and the glitz soon rankle. At night it empties somewhat, though **Le Corbeau**, off rue Neuve, is a lively enough pub.

All around rue Neuve is seediness. Yet Brussels' often mixes sleaze with the sublime. The Flemish theatre on rue de Laeken is a triumphant, flamboyant mock-baroque building surrounded by sex shops and peepshows. Place des Martyrs, with its monument dedicated to the 1830 revolutionaries who gave their lives for the *patrimoine*, is bordered by fine neoclassical buildings. The square has been forgotten and is now dilapidated.

The Upper Town

Royal Quarter

This is one of the most elegant areas in Brussels, the crowning glory of its eighteenth-century neoclassical period and mercifully well preserved. It

Rue Ravenstein – *majestic by any standards.*

is the best approach to the centre of town: driving down the narrow, traffic-choked rue de la Loi, you suddenly hit the Royal Quarter's great cobbled expanse and sweep magnificently around the place Royale, down the curve of rue Ravenstein, into the heart of Brussels. This area was constructed in the eighteenth century, designed mostly by Guimard, to make Brussels a suitable city for royalty. Look out especially for the Old England department store in rue Mont de la Cour near place Royale; it's no longer open, but its art nouveau features can be admired from the outside.

Parc de Bruxelles, around which the palaces are spread, is the only disappointment in the area. It's a dingy and badly kept place. Numerous statues and the avenues in the shape of a compass are testimony to the fact that it was once well-considered, although surely never beautiful. Thackeray wrote of it: 'Numbers of statues decorate the place, the very worst I ever saw. These cupids must have been erected in the time of the Dutch dynasty, as I judge from the immense posterior developments.' The park saw great activity just before the Battle of Waterloo. Again according to Thackeray: 'The greatest folks in England walked in the Park – there was a perpetual military festival.' Fifteen years later, in the 1830 Belgian Revolution, its avenues ran with blood. There are neither festivals nor bloodshed now – the park is sleepy after being the scene of so much upheaval.

The square of palaces (in Brussels 'palace' can mean any important building) here comprises the Palais des Académies, the **Palais de la Nation** (the parliament) and the Horta-designed **Palais des Beaux Arts**. The latter was built in the 1920s, which should sound a warning bell: the great architect was never as good after he entered his art deco period. Most impressive of all is the king's official residence, the **Palais du Roi**, where the guards stand impassively and the flag flies on the rare occasions when the monarch is home. Directly behind the palace grounds is the narrow rue Brederode, where Joseph Conrad visited the Congo Trading Company in 1889, and which still accords with his memorable description in his most famous novel (*see* **Heart of Darkness**).

West of the King's Palace lies place Royale, an even lovelier square because instead of the dreary Parc de Bruxelles, only Simonis's vigorous and triumphant figure of Godfrey of Bouillon ornaments the centre. The square was symmetrically designed by Guimard and its main building is **Eglise St Jacques-sur-Coudenberg**, which looks more like a Roman temple than a cradle of Christian piety.

The Royal Quarter is home to Brussels' great museums, palaces and libraries. The **Musées des Beaux Arts**, which house both the old and modern art collections, are the most impressive with many Renaissance and seventeenth-century Flemish painters, and later Belgian surrealists. On the Mont des Arts, created between 1956-58, are the modern **Musée de la Dynastie** and the **Palais du Congrès** as well as the Alfred I Library, which incorporates several manuscript museums.

Around the corner, off rue de la Régence, are the **Sablon** squares. These are unanimously celebrated, which might make you suspicious, but in fact they have an easy grace and the praise is well deserved. You can walk right around place du Petit Sablon's Paul Hankar-designed railings with their figures of the proud Belgian guilds or sit within them gazing at the elaborate fountain. Behind the little square, Notre Dame du Sablon is one of the

Heart of Darkness

'A narrow and deserted street in deep shadow, high houses, innumerable windows with Venetian blinds, a dead silence, grass sprouting between the stones, imposing carriage archways right and left, immense double doors standing ponderously ajar.'
Joseph Conrad, *Heart of Darkness*

Place du Jeu de Balle is the spiritual centre of the ***Marolles*** *(see page 90) and its early morning flea market is good for bargains.*

Poelaert's masterpiece, the **Palais de Justice**.

finest Gothic churches in the city. Place du Grand Sablon has an expensive antiques market on Saturdays and its shops overflow with ancient *objets*. It also has interesting, if pricey, bars so it's one of Brussels' livelier areas at night. In **Chez Richard**, one of the better Irish bars, Belgians are encouraged to dance on the tables till dawn. In **Le Pitt's Bar**, the studiously hip knock back drinks along the counter. Off the square, leading down towards the Grand Place is the cobbled, pedestrianised rue Rollebeek, which in summer becomes positively Mediterranean, its tables out on the street.

Rue de la Régence leads up to the largest site in the city, the monumental **Palais de Justice**: the biggest nineteenth-century building in Europe, Poelaert's masterpiece, which was literally the death of him, was built appropriately atop Galenburg Hill, where the medieval gallows used to stand. Its heaviness of style does not seem to be much admired, but by sheer dint of size, it cannot fail to impress. Beneath its huge shadow is spread the Marolles, a poor area celebrated for its earthiness, lawlessness and *Bruxellois* patois. It is customary to see the Marolles as cowed by the Palais de Justice – indeed many thousands of tiny homes were demolished to make way for the great building – and it does seem that way if you look down from the Palais, but if you go into the Marolles, the Palais appears more like a beached whale.

The Marolles

This is a district of great poverty and fierce pride, such as you tend to find when an area has managed to retain its age-old local spirit against all the odds of urban expansion and standardisation. It stretches rather haphazardly from the Palais de Justice to Gare du Midi and avenue de Stalingrad. It is a place of short, meandering streets, drying clothes and often, unfortunately, an air of depression. This is said not to deny its unique character, but as a counterbalance to the inverse snobbery that celebrates its very gloom.

The Marolles is not what it used to be. In the seventeenth and eighteenth centuries, it was a thriving, artisanal area for those who were building the upper quarters. Earlier, Pieter Bruegel, who was born around 1525 and lived at 132 rue Haute,

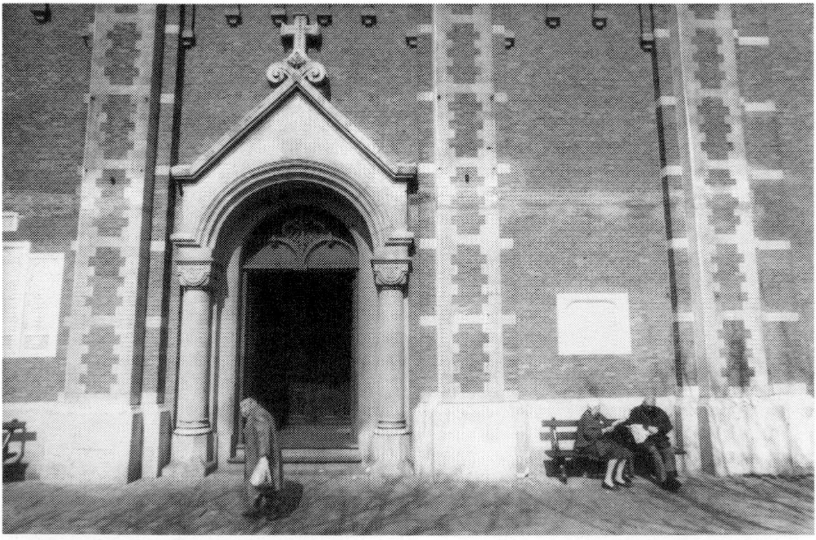

The **Marolles**, *a district of great poverty and yet greater pride, even has its own dialect.*

Away from the glamour of Avenue Louise, **Ixelles** *has pockets of energy and a rambling charm.*

must have drawn inspiration for his great peasant feasts and skating crowds from the energy around him. But since the River Senne was buried in 1870, the district has been in steady decline. Since the Middle Ages it has been a refuge for the persecuted – a leprosy centre was founded here in the twelfth century and today it is a haven for illegal immigrants. Apparently, it is now acquiring a chic charm rather like New York's East Village – one of the forbidden places that yuppies want to get into – so there is an uneasy mixture of pine shops and fashionable boutiques rubbing shoulders with out-and-out poverty. Its future poses a real dilemma since the 'genuine' inhabitants – that ever-decreasing number of locals who still speak the dialect or indeed those illegal immigrants who are part of Marolles tradition – are in no position to save the crumbling buildings or revive the once-thriving trade. There are numerous concerned action groups, but their well-meaning presence is in itself a portent of inevitable doom.

The Marolles is threatened on one side by property and development sharks, and on the other by chi-chi shops, spuriously proclaiming their local flavour. In the meantime, the corner bars still serve their chips and beer while the early hours are peopled by the nightshifters and those who are still up for it after a night at the **Demence** or the **Fuse**. The latter, effortless crowd-attracter of Karl Cox and Derrick May, is among Brussels' best clubs.

The place du Jeu de Balle is the district's spiritual centre, and the easiest way to soak up the atmosphere is to head for the flea market held there early in the morning. An exciting confusion of people and wares, it's highly recommended for genuine bargains.

Ixelles & Avenue Louise

Ixelles, stretching from the uptown glamour of Porte de Namur to the student bars around the university, has pockets of energy and a rambling charm. It also has some of Brussels' best examples of art nouveau houses, particularly on the borders with St Gilles. Avenue Louise, which provides a straight boundary to Ixelles, hardly belongs to its twisting streets and, in fact, is technically in the *commune* of Brussels. In 1864, land was sliced from Ixelles and St Gilles so that a suitably magnificent avenue could tie the centre of town to the pleasant grounds of the **Bois de la Cambre**. Yes, it's Léopold II again. You soon get to know his imperial feel and this avenue, named after his eldest daughter, begins beside his Palais de Justice (not on the Marolles side, of course), the great building sheltering the bourgeoisie from the irreverence of the poor.

Gucci, Versace and Chanel have boutiques on avenue Louise, clashing somewhat with Häagen-Dazs, Hamburger Quick and other fast-food joints. But the start of avenue Louise is quite pretty. From place Louise you can see the dome of the Palais de Justice, then as you go down the avenue there are small pedestrianised streets sloping off to the right, where cafés put out tables, giving it a relaxed Mediterranean feel. However, as soon as you hit

One of the many top-of-the-range boutiques that line **Avenue Louise**, *boundary of Ixelles.*

place Stéphanie, you are into avenue Louise proper and you understand why it generally fails to arouse enthusiasm (apart from in well-heeled sex-shoppers who target a small and rather expensive red-light area around, and just behind, this part of avenue Louise). It seems to be an exercise in how to make pedestrians feel small: the avenue is very long and wide (six lanes of traffic), the buildings very tall (the shortest about ten storeys), the shops out of any decent price range. The only people about are young executives in a hurry and squat, middle-aged wives of the rich, every one of them with dyed blond hair, two inches of make-up and floor-length mink.

The avenue has been parcelled up between travel agencies, large companies, hotels, *haute couturiers* and interior decorators. It's the interior decorators who have the edge – you can get to see some extremely beautiful furniture. The clothes shops offer little temptation; there's something unremittingly bourgeois about them all. Only the **Olivier Strelli** window display is witty enough to be admired. The rest, with their soft suits and low-heeled shoes, you may choose to pass swiftly by. Of the hotels, only the Conrad, resembling an inspired New York apartment block, is interesting. The avenue has few bars or restaurants, so there's not a great deal to detain you except for the Horta-designed **Hôtel Solvay** at no.224; peer through the glass in the front door to get a glimpse of the delights within.

If you persist to the very end (and trams 93 and 94, which run the length of the avenue, will whisk you quickly past the most soulless parts), the **Bois de la Cambre** is a treat. A large and charming park of beautiful trees, it is especially pleasant around the lake and is bordered by the magnificent, embassy-lined avenue Franklin Roosevelt.

Chaussée d'Ixelles is separated from avenue Louise by the lavishly named Galeries de la Toison d'Or, which has a good mixture of shopping opportunities: some of the Louise-style designer shops, but also some of Ixelles' more downmarket brand names such as Ici Paris. No.15 does good, though expensive, club clothes. Here also is the **UGC Acropole** (*see chapter* **Film**), pioneer of Sunday-morning cinema where you can enjoy coffee and croissants with your film.

Lively Porte de Namur, at which the chaussée begins, is where Africans arriving from the Congo were housed, and the tradition has continued. Here and especially further on, around chaussée de Wavre, is the African area known as Matonge.

Matonge

This area is just a stone's throw from avenue Louise, but could hardly be more different; further proof of Brussels' constantly changing cityscape. The population here is predominantly Zairean (most are students), but you also have Indians and North Africans. The shops – mostly selling food, clothes and cosmetics – are wholly exotic. Great bunches of tiny bananas spill on to the street alongside mangos and guavas. Hanging in windows and clothing passers-by are richly patterned dresses and *abacosts*, traditional Zairean menswear. Scattered about are hairdressing salons advertising dreadlocks and displaying additional tresses. In the galerie d'Ixelles is **Musicanova**, a record shop which has its own label and helps to promote new African artists.

Matonge really comes to life at night. On wintry days the area's distinctive colours can seem sad under grey skies, but at night the bars fill up with regulars from all over and clubs such as Mambo go on all night. The area has its problems too: rents are very high so that many students have to move to cheaper Schaerbeek; work permits are difficult to come by and the Belgian police are notoriously unsympathetic to those without proper papers.

Chaussée d'Ixelles itself really has little to recommend it other than its pleasantly undulating shape, representative of the rest of Ixelles, which weaves and ducks, disappears up hills and round corners. The chaussée has all the ubiquitous middle- and low-range names, the likes of C&A and Nopri. It is narrow and uneven, but the streets running off it are more charming.

On rue St Boniface is a spacious and lively café, **L'Ultime Atome**. Round the corner from this is the blackened, sinister, turreted Eglise St Boniface, which has the peculiarity of being attached to the houses on either side of it. Halfway down chaussée d'Ixelles is place Fernand Cocq, an uneven square that seems to have appeared without design. However, the **Maison Communale** set in a garden at the end of the square is a large, pleasant building, which formerly belonged to the violinist Bériot and his Spanish wife, the famous singer La Malibran – they bought the house as an inspired monument to their newly wed love.

By night the square is home to some interesting bars including cybercafé **L'Amour Fou** and, on rue des Tulipes, jazz bar **Sounds** (*see chapter* **Music: Rock, Folk & Jazz**). As the chaussée goes on, it becomes drearier and the shops fizzle out. Near the end, up the steep rue Van Volsem, is Ixelles' art gallery, the **Musée Communal d'Ixelles** (*see chapter* **Museums**), which can boast Belgian Impressionists, Toulouse-Lautrec posters and frequently remarkable exhibitions. The chaussée ends at the Ixelles ponds, which are pretty in spring and summer when there are ducks and fishermen. The long avenue Général de Gaulle has some art nouveau houses, but they are not as remarkable as the ones in St Gilles.

Further down and to the east of chaussée d'Ixelles is the bilingual university (*see chapter* **Students**), the French side being the ULB and the Flemish the VUB. They are both enclosed by boulevard de Triomphe within a pleasant campus. This is a very lively area, though it can be quiet at weekends when the students retreat home. Along chaussée de Boondael by place de la Petite Suisse there are some good, reasonably priced Vietnamese restaurants, and L'**Atelier**, a bar serving about 300 types of beer, is around the corner. The area opposite the Ixelles cemetery is a hub of activity with small bars and bistros such as **Le Campus**, which serve good, cheap Belgian food late into the night.

Saint Gilles

Parts of St Gilles merit its inclusion on any list of Brussels' most beautiful spaces. A small *commune* – running from Porte de Hal, touching avenue Louise, continuing down to Uccle and across to Gare du Midi – its less alluring side is often forgotten. Unsurprisingly, the avenue Louise-Uccle end is very beautiful and the Gare du Midi side is run-down.

It is an area of uneven squares and gentle angles: the short, wide streets lead to small squares or charming crossroads. It is as if the *commune* were designed around the principle of 'pause and contemplate'. Everything is brought to a considered conclusion, whether it is the Barrière de St Gilles at the centre where the main avenues converge and slope off down exciting-looking hills, or a smaller square such as parvis de la Trinité, where elegant houses face the lovely church, which looks as if it might belong in Latin America. Nothing has been allowed to spring up haphazardly. If you avoid the main thoroughfares (chaussées de

Lively **Matonge** *is predominantly Zairean.*

Waterloo and de Charleroi), you can remain among quiet, composed streets where almost every corner has a bar and the small shops are discreetly interesting and expensive.

St Gilles is largely residential and the main reason why people visit is its unequalled number of art nouveau houses (*see also chapter* **Architecture**). It has always been a rich *commune* and all the houses are elegant, but at the turn of the century a few wealthy men commissioned fabulous art nouveau residences which have mercifully escaped destruction. Most of these are to be found in the area between rue Defacqz and the prison. Victor Horta's house, the only one fully open to the public and known as **Musée Horta**, is at the centre of it all in rue Américaine. With their swirling, daring lines and elaborate friezes, the houses appear flamboyant and insouciant beside their more stalwart neighbours.

The art nouveau houses often come in pairs and, peculiarly, one is always more brilliant and lavish then the other. Perhaps the architects worked on the principle of foils or, more probably, one industrialist could afford to pay more than the other. In rue Defacqz, at nos.48 and 50, are the Hankar-designed **Hôtels Ciambarlani** and **Janssens**: no.48 has a marvellous frieze and a beautiful row of dormer windows; no.50 has only an interesting arrangement of brick to proclaim its architect.

The same is true of nos.83 and 85 rue Faider: the first is a marvellously bold design with a curving trapeze balcony; the second only has a few twirls to its railings. All of the houses are now fortunately protected and most are used as embassies or for functions, but a few are rented to the public. Recently available was 92 rue Africaine, which has great round windows, grilled railings in the shape of compasses and looks out on the delightful **Eglise de la Trinité**.

There are more such houses further down towards the prison. The prison itself seems to have been carefully integrated to avoid disturbing the harmony around it. The walls are fairly low and the complex is divided into two, intersected by the pleasant rue de la Jonction so that you don't get a huge walled mass. Softening a prison is a strange exercise, but it is perhaps better to face up to its existence in this elegant *commune* than to stick it in the darkest corner where the bourgeoisie could ignore it. At the beginning of rue de la Jonction is the only other art nouveau house you can get into, the **Hôtel Hannon**, built by Brunfaut in 1902 and now open as a photography gallery. The great breadth of the interior hints at what we are missing in the other houses.

Around the corner from the Hôtel Hannon is the charming square Larousse. Here, for those sick of the lavishness of art nouveau, are houses by Dewin (nos.12, 20 and 22). These are simpler, paler, flatter and more calming to look at.

Straight up from the prison towards the Barrière is St Gilles's Hôtel de Ville, an impressive nineteenth-century building in the French Renaissance style. To the west of the prison are the **Parcs de Forest** and **Duden** (*see chapter* **Sightseeing**). The second of these is the more attractive, but both are now rather ramshackle. You are now in the *commune* of Forest or Vorst and you can feel the difference. The houses are less graceful and the shops cheaper. There is a good local atmosphere, but as an outsider you are likely to feel something of an intruder, which is also true of the parks.

Back in St Gilles, towards Gare du Midi, you are also away from the wealthy district in a part of the *commune* that tourists don't visit. Here the shops cease to display delicate ornamental goods and become more humdrum, the restaurants – mostly Spanish, Greek, Portuguese and North African – are cheaper.

Off the depressing place Bethlehem, on rue Vanderschrick, are more art nouveau houses, but these too have given in to their surroundings: they are not as well tended as their counterparts on the other side. The last of them has been turned into a charming café, the **Porteuse d'Eau**. At Porte de Hal, you are back into open territory. There is a tower here, like something out of a Grimm fairytale, which houses the folklore museum.

Anderlecht

Above St Gilles and over to the south-west of the city, Anderlecht is a poor *commune* but unusual in having only poor Belgians and almost no immigrant population. It's also a large *commune* with a lot of space and small, haphazardly arranged houses – there are no high-risers. It doesn't look appealing, yet it is frequently invaded by visitors drawn by a happy juxtaposition of high and low-brow culture. The name 'Anderlecht' roughly means 'love of Erasmus' and the house where the great humanist lived in 1521 is situated here. But this district is also home to the best football team in the country, **RSC Anderlecht**.

Most of the interesting bits are around Métro St Guidon. On emerging from the station, the first thing you see, standing gracefully aloof from the standard shopping arcade, is the beautiful church of St Pierre and Guidon. The architecture is late fifteenth-century Gothic and inside is a long altar illuminated by light filtering through the stained glass above. Behind it is the seventeenth-century *béguinage*, now a museum. (*Béguinages* were lay sisterhoods whose members lived in religious communities but were not bound by nuns' vows. Often widows or spinsters, they did charity work and existed in large numbers in Belgium and the Netherlands. There are still some *béguinages* in Flanders.) The atmosphere of quiet sanctity is also present in the **Maison d'Erasmus** (*see chapter*

The **Halles de Schaerbeek** *– renovation was due to have been completed in autumn 1996.*

Sightseeing) around the corner, a small, well-preserved, red-brick seat of learning set in a shady garden. Up from the church is a charming lane, rue Porselein, which has cottage-style houses, climbing plants and Jacques Prévert poems written on the wall beside Miro drawings. It ends at a good local bar, the high-windowed Le Porcelain.

Five minutes' walk from the church, in the pleasant and hilly Parc Astrid, announced by its proud purple-and-white flag, is the Anderlecht stadium (*see chapter* **Sport & Fitness**). The stands are regularly packed with enthusiastic supporters singing strange versions of English football songs. The stadium used to have what was known as the 'O-Side', a standing-room only area the heavies used to pack out, but it's now fully seated and quieter.

Moving towards the town side of Anderlecht and the seedy Gare du Midi area, you get other pockets of interest. There is a sliver of canal on which boat excursions were due to start running in summer/autumn 1996 – they had better call them 'urban excursions' to forewarn anyone expecting long grass and dragonflies. On quai de Mariemont you can find food and entertainment at the Fool Moon Café, which hosts an upbeat line-up of music and theatre. Below this, are spread the industrial-looking nineteenth-century abattoirs and markets designed by Tirou. Finally, Anderlecht boasts some key museums. On rue Gheude is the great **Musée de la Gueuze**, last brewer of the naturally fermented beer and more than just a stop on the culture trail. On rue Van Lint you'll find the small and incomplete Musée de la Résistance, which tells some of the important and hidden tales of Belgium's World War II experience.

Schaerbeek & Saint Josse

Schaerbeek is a huge *commune*, running from the Gare du Nord up to Laeken and across to avenue de Woluwé-St Lambert. It has three stations: Gare du Nord, Schaerbeek and Josaphat. Schaerbeek's image ranges from the seediness of its downtown area to the sedateness of its houses near the EU area. Being so large, there is no strong feeling of identity about its streets, but generally speaking, Schaerbeek is mostly residential and fairly impoverished. The latter characteristic is apparent from the poor street lighting, erratic refuse collection and an absence of glitz. It is a *commune* that grew with the new Belgian state: at independence in 1830 there were 1,600 people living here; by 1900 there were 65,000. Schaerbeek's population is now mainly North African and Turkish. The women tend to sport the full yashmak, while the men are more Europeanised. On the streets you will hear strange combinations of Moroccan/Flemish and Turkish/Flemish being spoken (Schaerbeek is a Flemish *commune*).

The heart of Schaerbeek – the area around its Hôtel Communal (town hall) – is most impressive. It is all built on a grandiose scale with long avenues sweeping down to monumental buildings and churches overlook the city. The Hôtel Communal is a mighty work, inaugurated in 1887 by

Léopold II, who is sure to have approved of its massive dimensions. Badly burnt at the beginning of the century and twice occupied by the Germans, the Flemish Renaissance-style building is constructed of red brick, with numerous towers and windows. Inside, it maintains a stately air, hiding dull bureaucracy behind heavy doors.

Place Colignon was constructed around the Hôtel and a contest was held in 1896 for the design of the house façades lining the square. These complement the town hall well with their substantial proportions and preponderance of turrets and gables. Many have flagpoles and just the right degree of solemnity for flags. Just around the corner from the Hôtel Communal is **Eglise Saint Servais**, a large and beautiful, though decaying, church that holds services in Spanish and Italian and has a commanding view over avenue Louis Bertrand. Facing the Hôtel Communal, across lengthy rue Royale Ste Marie, is the neo-Byzantine **Eglise Ste Marie**. This mosque-like building is curvaceous and arched with an octagonal dome, and set up high so that it looks over Schaerbeek and down rue Royale, which runs in a straight line to the Royal Palace.

On one side of rue Royale, nearest the Hôtel Communal, are the **Halles de Schaerbeek** (*see chapter* **Sightseeing: Notable buildings**). A rare example of nineteenth-century industrial architecture, the Halles these days are used as a cultural centre but are currently undergoing renovation. At the city centre end of rue Royale is one of the loveliest of Brussels' myriad cafés, the art-nouveau **De Ultieme Hallucinatie**. The exterior is peeling badly and a glum notice warns you not to leave anything in your car, but inside, the floating lines are indeed hallucinatory. It has a long and fierce Flemish tradition, so don't ever call it by its French name.

Further towards town is the Gare du Nord, which used to have great pull when it was the red-light district. Girls sat in the windows of dark houses; small bars had jukeboxes and more girls. It was unequivocally sleazy, but had a certain downbeat energy. A few years ago, that all ended. Everything was closed down and many of the buildings were razed to the ground to make way for high-rise office blocks.

Now a few sad peepshows with bleak neon lights nestle in the ruins around the station and sex shops are tucked into odd corners. However, it has retained its seedy connotations so you're unlikely to see any women around, for the good reason that hopeful men still hang about. Don't these guys realise the glory days are over? Soon you will alight from the train at Gare du Nord and see nothing but respectably ugly and cheap examples of late twentieth-century offices.

The rest of Schaerbeek is residential and offers little of interest to the visitor, though it's a good place for markets. Lying not far from the town hall is **Parc Josaphat** (*see chapter* **Sightseeing: Parks, gardens & woods**), a reasonably pretty space with ponds, an animal reserve and various sporting facilities.

Saint Josse is a tiny *commune* into which Schaerbeek seems to melt. This is true of certain Brussels *communes*. Only a small neat sign tells you that you have officially crossed into another area. Saint Josse is now almost completely North African and Turkish, though as the cheapest area near the European Commission and Parliament, it has its share of shrewd EU officials. Its trademark seems to be fruit shops. These are everywhere, especially along rue Verbist, where the shop-fronts are decked out in identical lavish displays of seasonal fruit and vegetables.

Saint Josse is bounded by chaussée de Louvain, a long, narrow, ugly and energetic road whose shops are shabby but do throw up great bargains. The clothes store DOD has expanded to at least five branches here. It deals in factory-reject designer clothes, but the stock is erratic: sometimes offering great Italian designers, at other times, pushing lines of boring Bally shoes. The charming baroque **Eglise St Josse** stands on this chaussée, looking bewildered by the bustle and rubble around it. Inside is a beautiful altar with a round ornate roof.

Most of Saint Josse seems rather sleepy. It has some pretty houses and some elegant squares, such as tree-lined place Bosquet, but much of it is now run-down. At place Madou, Saint Josse borders on the city centre. A few minutes' walk along from here you have the **Colonne du Congrès** (*see chapter* **Sightseeing**), with the eternal flame burning at its foot. If you head up boulevard Bischoffsheim, you reach the wonderful-looking **Centre Botanique**, an inspired mixture of neo-classicism, glass and iron. Formerly the city's greenhouse, it is now a cultural centre – with a cinema, theatre and exhibition halls – that maintains a hothouse atmosphere.

EU area – Schuman & environs

Formerly a lively *quartier* with plentiful local bars and beautiful houses, this area is now an administrative centre with Irish bars and blockbuster buildings. Three long, narrow roads cut through it: rue de la Loi, rue Joseph II and rue Belliard. All of them are utterly without merit except for an odd, covered, geometric bridge on Belliard by which EU officials walk from one building to another. These three roads are riddled with the buildings of the European institutions. Chief among them are: the **Berlaymont** – now ghostly white and plastic-covered like Berlin's Reichstag; the sprawling, peachy **Council of Ministers**; and the undulating **European Parliament**, shining blue-green in the Quartier Léopold. Most of the other EU buildings

All the models at **Mini-Europe** *in Laeken's Bruparck are constructed on a scale of 1:25.*

are less startlingly modern and many are dull concrete blocks. Walking along these three traffic-heavy thoroughfares is no pleasure, so it is good that there are three Métro stops on rue de la Loi.

It's still an area in flux, as can be discerned by the wasteland of deserted buildings, cranes and rubble all around the Parliament and the top of rue Belliard. The final picture has not emerged yet, but it seems certain that all will eventually glitter, judging by the liberal use of glass, marble and mirrored windows in recently constructed buildings.

The area has a quiet sense of mighty work going on behind concrete blocks and expansive panes of glass. Only at lunchtime and between 6pm and 8pm could it be described as bustling. (At weekends it becomes a ghost town, the only people on view being a few security guards.) Yet it is not purely a business area. Pressing in on it are the remnants of the demolished *quartier*. This is best appreciated from a height, so try to get up to the top of one of the buildings to look down on the mosaic of rooftops and small gardens struggling on in the midst of encroaching bureaucracy.

The open-air platform of Schuman railway station gives a great view of the incongruous juxtaposition of the Berlaymont, the Parliament and the exquisite honey-coloured art deco **Résidence Palace** (*see chapters* **Architecture** *and* **Sightseeing**). As soon as you move away from the three main streets, you are almost immediately back in the familiar cobbled enclaves of central Brussels. On one side, at the end of rue Archimède, are the twin squares of Ambiorix and Marie-Louise, both of them small and graceful, if unfortunately victim to the national mania for trellised trees. These are squares of beautiful, listed houses. Don't miss no.11 place Ambiorix (*see chapter* **Architecture**), although a reminder is probably unnecessary. Long and thin, with its spidery balconies and bronzed, rounded façade, it stands out like a fairy-tale home of a captive princess. Just behind the square is the sloping rue des Confédérés. Here, in a red-brick house at no.83, WH Auden spent five months in the late 1930s, 'bathing and café-crawling' and visiting the Musée des Beaux Arts, thereby giving us his great poem by that name.

On the other side of rue de la Loi, dominated by the Parliament, is place de Luxembourg, a square of great charm where the numerous bars have Stella and Jupiler signs rather than Guinness and Murphy's. Quartier Léopold train station is here, small and dirty with open-air platforms, evoking the atmosphere of a black-and-white film, while clinging to it still is the age-old, oily, excited smell of departure and arrival.

Behind the Parliament on the other side, lies **Parc Léopold**, a somewhat bedraggled bit of green with a bleak lake and basketball court. This and the monumental **Parc Cinquantenaire** at the end of rue de la Loi are proof that although Brussels might recklessly destroy houses to make way for Europe, it has no intention of losing its parks. At the end of Parc Léopold is the **Muséum de l'Institut Royal des Sciences Naturelles**, through the gates of which you can see the huge canvases in the **Musée d'Antoine Wiertz**, twisted into what Thomas Hardy would call their 'staring and ghastly attitudes'.

Restaurants and cafés around this area reflect the priorities of EU member states – Italian pizzerias, Greek tavernas and five Irish bars, their number ever increasing. They are always packed and it is weird to see so many Belgians forsaking their own beautiful cafés for the *craic* in these standardised bars. Presumably the relaxed warmth draws them in and allows them to forget the banality of the décor. Amid all this European extravagance, the best place to eat is still firmly Belgian: **La Bonne Humeur** does the best *moules et frites* in town. Despite its fame, it has resisted the urge to expand, so you still eat at long tables in a small room and booking is a necessity.

Outside the centre

Laeken

There is far too much in Laeken not to mention it, but it always seems like an unreal city hovering outside Brussels. Its giant amusement park, brimming with treasures that are constantly updated and expanded, efficiently streamlines the populace's leisure time. But it's like a bland spaceman's idea of what humans require for time out. Not our idea. One resents the efficiency of the **Kinepolis**'s endless screens and faultless Dolby stereo that so quickly sucked audiences from the city auditoria, until tiny cinemas such as the Marivaux finally had to close. It's hard to rejoice in that latest Brussels obsession with miniatures, **Mini-Europe**, which is a very poor cousin to the Manneken Pis and marionettes.

There are far too many attractions to list them all here. *See chapter* **Sightseeing** for the **Pavillon Chinois**, **Tour Japonaise**, **Planétarium National**, **Serres Royales** and the wholly artificial 'Village'. The **Atomium** is worth a drive up from the city centre, especially if you go very early in the morning. The exposition park beside the trade mart is something to wonder at – a powerful reminder that Brussels is the fourth largest conference city in the world. The king lives up in Laeken, but in a palace you do not get to see. So also do other wealthy Belgians, in the streets that fan out behind the park.

You can now take the Métro right to the centre of this leisure realm. The station is called Heysel, like the nearby stadium which was the scene of terrible tragedy in 1985 – still the most shocking football hooliganism ever witnessed – and is a sober reminder of real life in the midst of Laeken's careful construction of fun.

From Montgomery to Tervuren

There are a number of compelling reasons to visit Tervuren. The first is that you get to take the 44 tram from Montgomery all the way down the avenue de Tervuren, through the **Forêt de Soignes** to the final destination. It's a great ride. You start off at Montgomery, which is one of the busiest traffic junctions in Brussels, with three lanes of traffic whizzing recklessly round the grass roundabout. A jaunty statue of Monty stands just above the tunnel facing the Cinquantenaire, reminding motorists that the British commander marched along here from France, rolling up the German right flank.

The tram emerges from the underground and trundles down the wide and beautifully tree-lined avenue de Tervuren. It's best to sit on the right-hand side of the tram since then you get a good view of the brilliantly geometric **Palais Stocklet**, eternally sulking with its back to the avenue. You also see the lovely hills and lakes of **Parc de Woluwe** and, further on, catch glimpses of the embassy houses through the trees.

On the left-hand side you get the consolation of the wide windows of the **Musée de Transport Urbain Bruxellois**, which in summer months sends its old trams trundling through the forest. In autumn, the chestnut trees along the avenue rain conkers down on the tram roof. Once in the Forêt de Soignes, you are sheltered by tall, spindly trees and get to cross through Quatre Bras, where the elegant Hussar regiment met Napoleon's troops in 1815 and fled precipitately back to town.

On reaching the final stop of Tervuren, you see Léopold II's **Museum voor Midden-Afrika** immediately before you, announced by a large stone statue of an elephant atop a roundabout in the road. Everyone condemns the idea and practice by which this museum came about, while simultaneously praising the treasures and booty. Proudly displayed are the art, minerals and wildlife of the Congo. The park around the museum has formal gardens and, further down, a sequence of canals. Below the park is an arboretum with old trees and delicate-looking Japanese plants.

Past the boathouse, where you can hire paddling boats, is the small village of **Tervuren**. The cobbled main square has been recently renovated and traffic has been restricted in order to encourage people to linger. The square's focus is provided by the eighteenth-century church of St Jan, and you can pause for excellent ice-creams in the glacerie Mont Blanc. All around the village are fine big houses, which help make this the choice of residence for many British and Irish Eurocrats.

Tervuren is quiet and charming, and a good way to escape the city for a healthy dose of greenery. When you've had your fill, take the 44 tram back to the metropolis, heading for the magnificent **Arc de Triomphe** lighting up the sky.

Take the 44 tram through the Forêt de Soignes to ***Tervuren*** *where you can visit Léopold II's Museum voor Midden-Afrika.*

44

Eating & Drinking

Restaurants **102**
Cafés & Bars **117**

Restaurants

Whether you plump for Flemish* waterzooi, *borscht and blinis or oriental titbits, it pays to boldly go beyond* moules frites *and death by chocolate.

A glance at any street map of Brussels will show how much importance the Belgians attach to food. Around the Grand Place, you'll find rue du Marché aux Fromages, rue des Bouchers, rue du Marché aux Porcs, and rue au Beurre. Surprisingly, there is no rue des Moules, but there is an impasse des Huîtres (Oyster Street) and a rue des Harengs (Herring Street) – pickled herrings were once a major export.

Most people who visit Brussels expect to subsist on mussels, chips and chocolates. This they can do very happily, but the city has far more to offer. Belgian food is similar to French cooking, although it has its own regional specialities and the portions are often more generous. There are countless restaurants in Brussels serving traditional fish, steak, mussels and Flemish stews. There are also numerous bistros serving more modern European cooking, with Italian and Asian influences.

In addition, the European Union and NATO have brought in their wake dozens of international restaurants. The European district in Etterbeek, which is centred around the Rond Point Schuman, is one of the best places for good Italian, Spanish, and Greek restaurants. At lunchtime, they tend to be crowded with journalists, lawyers, lobbyists and diplomats, but they are usually quieter in the evening. If you want very cheap Mediterranean food, the grimy streets around Gare du Midi have plenty of Portuguese and North African cafés and bars, although they are scarcely picturesque.

Like every other major city, Brussels has a growing number of Asian restaurants, and these are particularly useful if your money is running low or you are looking for vegetarian food. They are not concentrated in any particular area, but Ixelles has a fair number.

Decent fish is available in most restaurants, but the specialist fish restaurants are to be found mainly in the north of the city around the fish market at place Ste Cathérine. Most offer good-value set menus, and if you want to eat lobster and oysters, these sets are usually hundreds or thousands of francs cheaper than ordering à la carte. Place Ste Cathérine is slightly touristy, but far less so than the streets around the Grand Place. The likes of rue des Bouchers are lined with restaurants with displays of fish and tanks of lobsters outside. As a very general rule, these restaurants are usually mediocre, so having gawped at the specimens of grim-faced catfish and other marine monsters, it probably pays to eat elsewhere.

Eating out in Brussels is by no means cheap, and UK visitors will find the restaurants more expensive than at home. However, many of them offer excellent value, whatever the prices. The ingredients are usually of a high quality and the portions are large. The average prices given for restaurants listed below are based on one person eating three courses – starter, main and dessert – and do not include drink or coffee. But much of the time, you'll find that you don't even want a dessert, since the first two courses will be ample. 'Very expensive' means an average of 2000BF or more; 'expensive' means 1500BF and upwards; 'moderate' means 1000BF plus; and 'inexpensive' means less than 1000BF. Many restaurants, particularly those in more residential areas such as Ixelles, offer cheap set lunches, with two or three courses for under 500BF.

As for understanding what you're ordering, in Brussels virtually all menus are written in French. Some restaurants in the centre have versions in Flemish and English.

French & Belgian

Very expensive

Comme Chez Soi

23 place Rouppe, 1000 (512 29 21). Métro Anneessens. **Open** noon-2.30pm, 7-11pm, Tue-Sat. **Average** 4000BF. **Menu** 1975BF (minimum four people). **Credit** AmEx, DC, MC, V.

It is universally agreed that this is the best restaurant in Brussels. Chef Pierre Wynants may not have his own BBC show yet, but he's a star of European cooking all the same. The place is often booked out weeks ahead, so advance planning is required if you want to go there and eat such delights as artichoke and asparagus salad with white truffle oil, fillets of sole with a mousseline of riesling and prawns or sweetbreads with hop shoots.

La Maison du Cygne

9 Grand Place, 1000 (511 82 44). Métro Gare Centrale. **Open** noon-2.30pm, 7-10.30pm, Mon-Fri; 7-10.30pm Sat. **Average** 3500BF. **Menu** 1400BF, 1700BF (both lunch); 2200BF, 2600BF. **Credit** AmEx, DC, MC, V.

It's not just the location on the Grand Place that makes this a place for a special treat. The food is also luxurious, from a menu dotted with ingredients such as foie gras and truffles. The cooking (not just the ingredients) is excellent and rich, and it's not the place to go if you're on a diet. But then again, if you do eat here, you probably won't be able to afford to eat anything else for several days afterwards.

Expensive

Le Fils de Jules

35-37 rue du Page, 1050 (534 00 57). Tram 81, 82/bus 54. **Open** noon-2.30pm, 7-11pm, Mon-Thur; noon-2.30pm, 7pm-midnight, Fri, Sat. **Average** 1500BF. **Menu** 395BF (lunch). **Credit** AmEx, DC, MC, V.

An Ixelles brasserie which opened at the beginning of 1996, and immediately became popular. The cooking is based on the Basque country and south-west France, along with modern French items such as *magret de canard* with ginger and blackcurrant. The décor is fairly standard for this part of Brussels, with art deco touches and plenty of space.

La Manufacture

12 rue Notre-Dame du Sommeil, 1000 (502 25 25). Métro Bourse. **Open** noon-2pm, 7-11pm, Mon-Fri; 7pm-midnight Sat. **Average** 1000BF. **Credit** AmEx, DC, MC, V.

Well-known restaurant housed in an old leather factory (hence the name). The food is modern European with Japanese influences, and it's all wonderful. The colour scheme is navy and dark orange, the light is flattering, and the customers are sleek and middle-class. There is a good selection of New World wines, which is unusual in Brussels, and there are tables in the courtyard in summer.

L'Ogenblik

1 galerie des Princes, 1000 (511 61 51). Métro Gare Centrale. **Open** noon-2.30pm, 7pm-midnight, Mon-Thur; noon-2.30pm, 7pm-12.30am, Fri, Sat. **Average** 1800BF. **Credit** AmEx, DC, MC, V.

Grown-up but informal bistro which has been popular for over 20 years. There are old-fashioned, rough-and-ready tins of Cerebos salt on the tables, but the food is sophisticated and ingredients include lobster, turbot and wild mushrooms. The atmosphere feels as if you could go there on the spur of the moment, when the fridge is empty, but you'll probably have to empty your wallet to do so. Excellent if you want a gastronomic treat without having to be too starched about the whole thing.

La Quincaillerie

45 rue du Page, 1050 (538 25 53). Tram 81, 82/bus 54. **Open** noon-2.30pm, 7pm-midnight, Mon-Fri; 7pm-midnight Sat, Sun. **Average** 1300BF. **Credit** AmEx, DC, MC, V.

Of the numerous restaurants around place du Châtelain in Ixelles, La Quincaillerie is the best known and perhaps the most stylish. It is housed in a former hardware shop and attracts affluent customers from all over the city and beyond. Food is mainly traditional and modern French, such as goat's cheese salad, guinea fowl with braised endive and sautéed scallops with basil. The fish is particularly good.

Moderate

L'Amadeus

13 rue Veydt, 1050 (538 34 27). Tram 91, 92. **Open** 6.30pm-2am Mon; noon-1am Tue-Sun. **Average** 1000BF. **Menu** 595BF (lunch). **Credit** AmEx, DC, MC, V.

Popular restaurant with a separate wine bar housed in Rodin's studio. The menu is divided into two sections: *petite faim* and *grande faim*. The cooking is a mixture of traditional choices – such as *waterzooi* and steak tartare – and modern alternatives – scampi and white truffle casserole, and a couple of vegetarian options. There's also a delicious eat-as-much-as-you-want Sunday brunch from 10am to 2pm. This includes cold meats, smoked fish, croissants, *pain au chocolat*, cheese and *tartes* (670BF adults; 390BF children).

La Boule Bleue

176 chaussée de Forest, 1060 (537 90 57). Tram 48. **Open** 7pm-midnight Mon-Sat. **Average** 900BF. **Credit** AmEx, DC, MC, V.

French bistro in the former costume workshops of the Brussels opera. There's no written sign outside, just a large blue ball marks its presence on a grimy, urban street in a Portuguese and North African neighbourhood of St Gilles. Inside, the surroundings are very different, with ornate, brocaded costumes on display. Service can be a touch arrogant.

La Serre – *one of the best, and certainly the friendliest, Ixelles restaurants.* *See page 105.*

Café Camille

559 chausseé de Waterloo, 1050 (345 96 43). Bus 37, 38, 60. **Open** noon-2.30pm, 7pm-midnight, Mon-Fri; 7pm-midnight Sat. **Average** 1200BF. **Credit** AmEx, DC, MC, V.

This café has never grabbed any headlines, but it produces classic French cooking with a twist and is well away from the tourist circuit. At lunchtime, the chattering classes indulge in their expense accounts; in the evening there is a more local feel. Starters include seafood brioche, and goat's cheese with pine nuts; mains include *magret de canard* with mango and sole with saffron. There's a small gravel garden at the back.

L'Idiot du Village

19 rue Notre Seigneur, 1000 (502 55 82). Bus 20, 48. **Open** noon-2pm, 7.30-11pm, Mon-Fri. **Average** 1200BF. **Credit** AmEx, DC, MC, V.

Small and very popular bistro hidden away down a side-street off rue Blaes. The walls are midnight blue and the tables are the type of furniture you hope to find in the near-by Jeu de Balle flea market (but never do). There are dried herbs and roses around the place and the chandelier looks like a leftover Christmas decoration. It sounds faintly clichéd, but works perfectly, and the same can be said about some of the food. The Breton chef's chicken with tarragon bears little resemblance to the tired versions produced in wine bars around Britain. Booking is essential.

Lola

33 place du Grand Sablon, 1000 (514 24 60). Tram 92, 93, 94/bus 34, 95, 96. **Open** noon-3pm, 6.30-11.30pm, daily. **Credit** AmEx, MC, V. **Average** 1300BF.

A long and narrow restaurant with a modern design and classic French cooking with some innovations. Starters include red mullet salad, and foie gras with an apple and Sauternes sauce. There are a couple of vegetarian starters and main courses, and the house aperitif is very good. Customers are mainly thirtysomethings – the Brussels version of the chattering and designing classes.

Mieux Vaut Boire qu'Enface

40 rue Alphonse de Witte, 1050 (644 30 31). Tram 81/bus 71. **Open** noon-2pm, 7pm-10.30pm, Tue-Sat. **Average** 1100BF. **Credit** AmEx, MC, V.

Better known by some as Chez Marie, this good-value Ixelles restaurant has a slightly self-conscious air of rusticity in its design. A choice of three starters and three main courses means this is not a place for those with pernickety tastes, nor is it great for vegetarians. But the food is very fresh, the menu changes daily, and it's particularly strong on fish and vegetables. It also runs a good German bakery from 9am-3pm on Saturdays.

La Meilleure Jeunesse

58 rue de l'Aurore, 1000 (640 23 94). Tram 94. **Open** noon-2.30pm, 7pm-12.30am, Mon-Wed; noon-2.30pm, 7pm-1am, Thur, Fri; 7pm-1am Sat. **Average** 1100BF. **Credit** AmEx, DC, MC, V.

Fashionable restaurant and bar just off avenue Louise with comfortable sofas at the entrance and art on the walls. The food is French bistro cooking with exotic touches, and is mostly good. The service is slow, possibly because the waitresses are more concerned with their putative modelling or acting careers. There's a pleasant terrace at the back with a wonderful view of the Abbaye de la Cambre.

Les Salons de l'Atlantide

89 chaussée de Charleroi, 1060 (537 21 54). Tram 91, 92. **Open** 11am-midnight Mon-Thur, Sun; 11am-2am Fri, Sat; *food served* noon-3pm, 7pm-midnight, daily. **Average** 1000BF. **Menu** 340BF (lunch), 540BF (lunch Sat, Sun). **Credit** AmEx, MC, V.

A former auction house has been turned into a baroque restaurant with drapes, shell-encrusted mirrors and candles. It was opened by the man behind Café Malte, and one of the less positive similarities is the sometimes sluggish

Chez Léon – *dishing out humungous portions of molluscs for over a century.* *See page 111.*

service. Nevertheless, it's popular both at lunchtime and in the evening. The bistro cooking includes *navarin* of lamb and seafood salad.

La Serre

43 rue du Conseil, 1050 (514 31 98). Métro Porte de Namur/bus 54, 71. **Open** noon-2pm, 7-10pm, Tue-Fri; 7-10pm Sat. **Average** 900BF. **Menu** 375BF (plat du jour). **Credit** AmEx, MC, V.

Given the strength in depth of moderately priced restaurants in Ixelles, it is difficult to pick a winner from the runners, but La Serre is certainly up there. The interior of this small, family-run restaurant is immediately soothing – soft light and discreet classical music make for an elegant, unpretentious atmosphere. The décor is simple but impressive and above all the welcome is warm and the food unforgettable. The menu, which is not extensive, but evolves slowly, offers deliciously refined French/Belgian cuisine which strikes a good balance between fish and meat dishes at a cost which compares very favourably with many more ordinary venues.

Inexpensive

Aux Bons Enfants

49 place du Grand Sablon, 1000 (512 40 95). Tram 92, 93, 94/bus 34, 95, 96. **Open** noon-2.45pm, 6.30-10.30pm, Mon, Tue, Thur-Sun. **Average** 600BF-800BF. **No credit cards**.

Basic restaurant which is unusually good value for this part of Brussels. The style is heritage and rustic, with heavy wood tables and a beamed roof, so it's warm and comforting on a cold or rainy evening. It's particularly useful on Sunday evenings, when many Brussels eateries are closed. The menu is mainly steak, pizza and pasta.

Big Sur

11-13 rue du Page, 1050 (538 76 18). Tram 81, 82/bus 54. **Open** 7-10pm Tue-Sat. **Average** 800BF. **No credit cards**.

Small restaurant near place du Châtelain with a short but eclectic Mediterranean menu. It is best known for its *tajine* (a North African stew), but also has interesting salads, couscous, stuffed vine leaves and several roast meats. The cream walls are adorned with large abstract canvases.

Bistro Marilou

104 avenue Adolphe Buyl, 1050 (647 80 99). Tram 93, 94/bus 71. **Open** noon-3pm, 6-11pm, Mon-Thur; noon-2.30pm, 6pm-midnight, Fri; 6pm-midnight Sat. **Average** 900BF. **Menu** 395BF (lunch), 595BF (695BF Sat, Sun). **Credit** AmEx, DC, MC, V.

A small bistro near the university, which is popular with students and lecturers. The menu is simple bistro-style, with the likes of carpaccio, tomatoes stuffed with prawns, salads, and steak. It's all very charming and French with small tables and candlelight.

Le Campus

437 avenue de la Couronne, 1050 (648 53 80). Bus 71, 95, 96. **Open** 9am-5am daily. **Average** 800BF. **Credit** AmEx, DC, MC, V.

As the name suggests, Le Campus is close to the university in Ixelles, and it's a perennial favourite with students. On offer is pretty standard fare – spaghetti, steak and the like – but it is excellent value and open almost all hours, serving as a useful filling station.

Au Charlot

1 rue Froissart, 1040 (230 33 28). Métro Schuman. **Open** 11am-9pm Sat, Sun. **Average** 700BF-900BF. **Credit** AmEx, DC, MC, V.

This brasserie on a corner of place Jourdan has a Charlie Chaplin motif, but fortunately it's not too obtrusive. It's good for lunch and, despite the area, the customers are not exclusively workers from the EU institutions. The menu is limited – substantial salads, steaks and omelettes – but it does cater for vegetarians.

De Ultieme Hallucinatie – *see page 106.*

Au Chat Perché

20 rue de la Samaritaine, 1000 (513 52 13). Tram 92, 93, 94/bus 34, 95, 96. **Open** noon-2.30pm, 7-11pm, Tue-Fri; 7-11pm Sat. **Average** 700BF. **No credit cards**.

Newish restaurant specialising in crêpes, in a cobbled street near place du Grand Sablon. Savoury pancake fillings include chicken and chili con carne, which you can accompany with a salad and there is plenty of choice for vegetarians. The pleasant ambience is aided by good service, sponge-painted walls, wooden tables, mirrors and candles.

En Face de Parachute

578 chaussée de Waterloo, 1050 (346 47 41). Bus 60. **Open** noon-2pm, 7.30-11pm, Tue-Sat. **Average** 900BF. **No credit cards**.

Small bistro in a former shop, which still has the original wooden shelving. The seats are old tram seats, and it's all very cosy. The food is fairly standard for Brussels: goat's cheese with thyme and honey, bruschetta, *stoemp*, spinach ravioli and scampi *à la provençale*.

Le Jardin de Nicolas

137 avenue de Tervuren, 1150 (732 24 49). Métro Montgomery. **Open** 11am-1am daily. **Average** 800BF. **No credit cards.**

A popular restaurant for lunch or an evening snack. The salads are good, the pasta respectable and there are well-priced *plats du jour.* Customers can sit at tables out in the front garden in summer, but being on one of the busiest roads out of Brussels means a certain amount of carbon monoxide inhalation. It's popular with ladies who lunch and their trust-funded offspring, but also some office workers and journos.

Martens

28 rue Antoine Dansaert, 1000 (511 06 31). Métro Bourse. **Open** noon-3pm, 7-11pm, Tue-Sat. **Average** 700BF-800BF. **Menu** 450BF (lunch), 595BF. **Credit** AmEx, DC, MC, V.

Over the last couple of years, rue Antoine Dansaert has become a chic street for eating out, with a growing array of good, stylish restaurants. Martens is no exception, with its light colours, bare brickwork and modern French cooking. The set menus are imaginative and there are some excellent vegetarian options.

Raconte-Moi des Salades

19 place du Châtelain, 1050 (534 27 27). Tram 81, 82/bus 54. **Open** 7.30am-10pm Mon-Sat. **Average** 800BF. **Credit** MC, V.

As the name suggests, it specialises in salads but it has plenty to offer both vegetarians and carnivores. In addition to an imaginative list of substantial salads, there are omelettes, patsa, sandwiches, several types of carpaccio and a few meat meat and fish dishes. There are tables outside on the square and a very pleasant garden at the back.

La Table Gourmande

80 rue des Deux Eglises, 1210 (230 66 56). Métro Arts-Loi. **Open** noon-3pm Mon-Thur; noon-3pm, 7-11pm, Fri; 7-11pm Sat. **Average** 695BF. **Menu** 625BF, 695BF, 725BF. **Credit** AmEx, DC, MC, V.

Set in a large townhouse with parquet flooring, high ceilings and a garden, this restaurant centres around an eat-as-much-as-you-want buffet. This includes cold salmon, terrines and pâtés, smoked fish, cold meats and numerous salads, all of which are excellent. You can have the buffet food as a starter or main course, and there are also hot mains. It's popular with EU officials, lawyers, lobbyists and journalists.

Traditional

Expensive

La Belle Maraîchère

11 place Ste Cathérine, 1000 (512 97 59). Métro Ste Catherine. **Open** noon-2.30pm, 6-10pm, Tue, Fri-Sun. **Average** 2000BF. **Menu** 900BF, 1100BF, 1600BF. **Credit** AmEx, DC, MC, V.

Small and famous fish restaurant by the fish market on place Ste Cathérine. The cooking is traditional French, as is the mood, and there are few surprises. It sounds dull, but it isn't. With excellent fish and great-value set menus, if the customers aren't particularly young or chic, who cares?

Les Brasseries Georges

259 avenue Winston Churchill, 1180 (347 21 00). Tram 23, 90. **Open** noon-12.30am Mon-Thur, Sun; noon-1am Fri, Sat. **Average** 1500BF. **Credit** AmEx, DC, MC, V.

A Parisian-style brasserie on the borders of Ixelles and Uccle with gleaming brass and brisk but impeccable service. The menu comprises classics such as steak, seafood, game, oysters and cassoulet, and although none of it is cheap, it is all good value, as is the house wine. Customers include old people with small dogs, affluent families with scrubbed children and people out to lunch with their parents. It makes for an excellent Sunday lunch treat.

La Marie-Joseph

47-49 quai au Bois à Brûler, 1000 (218 05 96). Métro Ste Cathérine. **Open** noon-3pm, 6.30-11pm, Tue-Sun. **Average** 1500BF. **Credit** AmEx, DC, MC, V.

Fish restaurant near the Ste Cathérine fish market, which belongs to the same people as Le Canterbury. It's bright and comfortable with leather chairs, and everything you'd expect from a Brussels fish restaurant is here: oysters, lobster, sole, turbot, mussels, crevettes etc. There's nothing earth-shattering, but the ingredients are of a high quality and the cooking is reliable.

Ristorante Parigino

12 rue de la Vierge Noire, 1000 (502 36 77). Métro De Brouckère. **Open** noon-3pm, 7pm-midnight, Mon-Thur; noon-3pm, 7pm-1am Fri-Sun. **Average** 1600BF. **Menu** 395BF (lunch). **Credit** AmEx, DC, MC, V.

This used to be called Café de Paris, and the name said it all. It was a Parisian-style brasserie with stained glass and shiny brass, and an impressive counter of seafood. Now it's Italian, and while it still serves the usual oysters, lobsters and other *fruits de mer*, you can also eat *osso bucco*, minestrone and pasta. There is a choice of seafood platters, ranging in price from 1020BF to 2820BF.

La Sirène d'Or

1a place Ste Cathérine, 1000 (513 51 98). Métro Ste Cathérine. **Open** 11.45am-2.30pm, 6.30-11pm, Tue-Sat. **Average** 1900BF. **Menu** 1300BF, 1700BF. **Credit** AmEx, DC, MC, V.

Famous and plush fish restaurant, decorated with ships' prows and busts of mermaids. None of the dishes on offer are particularly original, but if you want perfectly cooked fish and seafood with rich, classic French sauces – and you have plenty of money to spend – this is a good place to come. The 1700BF menu includes an aperitif and wine.

De Ultieme Hallucinatie

316 rue Royale, 1210 (217 06 14). Métro Botanique. **Open** 11am-2am Mon-Fri; 5pm-3am Sat, Sun; *food served* 11am-2.30pm, 6pm-midnight, daily. **Average** 1500BF. **Credit** AmEx, DC, MC, V.

Smart restaurant in an amazingly well preserved art nouveau house in a dingy and slightly threatening area of north Brussels. All the art nouveau details are there – curving wood and iron, mirrors and stained glass. The cooking is sophisticated and French, and it's also expensive, so most people confine themselves to the cheaper and more relaxed café section.

Moderate

Aux Armes de Bruxelles

13 rue des Bouchers, 1000 (511 55 50). Métro Bourse. **Open** noon-11.15pm Tue-Thur; noon-11.30pm Fri Sat; noon-10.45pm Sun. **Average** 1200BF. **Menu** 495BF (lunch), 995BF, 1695BF. **Credit** AmEx, DC, MC, V.

Many of the fish restaurants in the streets around the Grand Place are lacklustre and overpriced, but Aux Armes de Bruxelles is a notable exception. It's a stickler for tradition with starched white tablecloths, good service and a menu of Belgian classics such as *waterzooi*, steak and, best of all, vast buckets of mussels complete with chips and mayonnaise.

There's a good selection of New World wines, unusual in Brussels, at **La Manufacture** – *see page 103.*

Visit **La Quincaillerie** *for an overview of Belgian and modern French cuisine. See page 103.*

The mussels come in several versions including the perennial favourites, *provençale* and *marinière*.

Le Canterbury

2 avenue de l'Hippodrome, 1050 (646 83 93). Bus 71. **Open** 9am-midnight Mon-Sat. **Average** 1300BF. **Credit** MC, V.
Comfortable brasserie with a shaded terrace overlooking the Ixelles lakes. It specialises in chicken and although the food is not adventurous, it is all of excellent quality. In addition to the fowl selection, there are sundry items such as *salade niçoise*, salmon, steak, club sandwiches and very good chips.

In 't Spinnekopke

1 place du Jardin aux Fleurs, 1000 (511 86 95). Métro Bourse. **Open** noon-3pm, 6-11pm, Mon-Thur; noon-3pm, 6pm-midnight Fri; 6pm-midnight Sat. **Average** 1000BF. **Credit** AmEx, DC, MC, V.
It looks like a little old house, but the numerous rooms 'at the sign of the spider' make it surprisingly capacious. The building dates from 1762, and it's cosy with log fires, red flagstones, low ceilings and checked tablecloths. The food is very Belgian: *waterzooi, lapin à la kriek* and steaks. Not surprisingly, it's quite touristy.

La Roue d'Or

26 rue des Chapeliers, 1000 (514 25 54). Métro Bourse. **Open** noon-12.30am daily. **Average** 1200BF. **Credit** AmEx, DC, MC, V.
A mini-brasserie in the centre which has managed to survive mass tourism. It's in one of the streets leading off the Grand Place and has the usual ingredients: brass fittings, a long polished wooden bar and traditional Bruxellois food – although the surrealist murals are a slight break with tradition. As well as fine mussels and chips, the menu includes *waterzooi*, stewed eels, rabbit and steak.

Le Volle Gas

21 place Fernand Cocq, 1050 (502 89 17). Bus 54, 71. **Open** noon-midnight Mon-Thur, Sun; noon-1am Fri, Sat; *kitchen closed* 3-6pm daily. **Average** 850BF. **Credit** AmEx, DC, MC, V.
Traditional Belgian food in what used to be a well-known jazz bar called the Bièrodrome. The menu is fairly short but dependable, with half a dozen classic Belgian starters such as *salade aux lardons, salade au roquefort* and about ten classic main courses, including *stoemp*, cassoulet, *lapin à la kriek* and steak. There's seating on a terrace in front in spring and summer.

Cheap

L'Achepot

1 place Ste Cathérine, 1000 (511 62 21). Métro Ste Cathérine. **Open** 11am-midnight Mon-Sat; *food served* noon-3pm, 6.30-10.30pm, Mon-Fri; noon-3pm, 7-11pm, Sat. **Average** 800BF. **No credit cards**.
Small and basic family-run *estaminet* or tavern, which looks as though it hasn't changed for several generations of said family. The food is traditional Belgian and French, with dishes such as *stoemp* and goat's cheese salad and plenty of offal, including kidneys, brain, tripe and liver.

Au Stekerlaplatte

4 rue des Prêtres, 1000 (512 86 81). Métro Hôtel des Monnaies. **Open** 7pm-1am Tue-Sun. **Average** 800BF. **Credit** V.
The street outside is run-down and the façade is unassuming to say the least, but this traditional bistro is always full. The inside is labyrinthine and dark, the atmosphere convivial. There's a long menu, most of it traditional Belgian food and all of it good value.

Au Vieux Bruxelles

35 rue St Boniface, 1050 (513 01 81). Bus 54, 71. **Open** 6-9.30pm Tue-Sat. **Average** 900F.
A popular restaurant for mussels, which looks as if it has been around for ever. Peeling old signs proclaim the vast number of mussels dishes (over 20) on offer, and this is very much red-and-white gingham territory. Portions are substantial and in addition to mussels, there are steaks, omelettes and snails.

La Bonne Humeur

244 chaussée de Louvain, 1000 (230 71 69). Bus 29. **Open** noon-2pm, 6-9pm, Mon, Thur, Fri; noon-2pm, 3.30-9pm, Sat, Sun. **Average** 900BF. **Credit** MC, V.

A traditional family-run restaurant in St Josse, which produces wonderful mussels and chips, as well as a few other Belgian classics such as shrimp croquettes. If you want *moules frites* and are fed up with the hordes of tourists around the Grand Place, this is a welcome relief. It's also cheaper than the more central restaurants.

Chez Léon

18 rue des Bouchers, 1000 (511 14 15). Métro Bourse. **Open** noon-11pm daily. **Average** 800BF. **Menu** 395BF, 765BF. **Credit** AmEx, DC, MC, V.

One of Belgium's most successful culinary exports – though Belgo nabbed the London market – Chez Léon works to a simple formula: big portions of mussels and chips, paper tablecloths, brisk (sometimes impatient) service and rapid turnover. The Belgians themselves sneer at it, and it's not the place for a romantic tryst, but it's cheap and popular with every other nationality.

Branch: Bruparck, Heysel.

Italian

Clair Obscur

68 rue Mercelis, 1050 (644 06 97). Métro Louise/tram 93, 94. **Open** noon-2.30pm, 7pm-late, Tue-Sat. **Average** 600BF-800BF. **Credit** MC, V.

A small, modern pasta restaurant just off avenue Louise. The menu is short and simple: seven fresh pastas, for example, with smoked salmon or pesto, costing between 250BF and 350BF; two starters and three desserts. The décor is also uncomplicated: brick walls, marble tables and candles.

Cosi

95 rue Américaine, 1050 (534 85 86). Tram 81, 82/bus 54. **Open** noon-2.30pm, 7pm-midnight, Mon-Fri; 7pm-midnight Sat. **Average** 900BF. **Menu** 395BF (lunch). **Credit** MC, V.

Another modern Italian restaurant in Ixelles, with good fresh pasta and starters such as bruschetta, or Parma ham with pears. The lighting is low, there is an assortment of classy bric-à-brac for furniture – plus old radios and clocks around the walls – and the service is engaging.

Da Maria

153 chaussée de Vleurgat, 1050 (649 55 23). Bus 38. **Open** noon-3pm, 6.30-11pm, Mon-Sat. **Average** 750BF. **Credit** AmEx, DC, MC, V.

A good pizzeria, which is not worth the trip if you're on the other side of Brussels, but is useful if you happen to be in the area, especially as it is more down-to-earth than many of its neighbours. There is a long list of pizzas, costing 250BF-300BF (beware – they are occasionally somewhat heavy on the anchovies), while other options include pasta and meat dishes.

Fellini

32 place du Châtelain, 1050 (534 47 49). Tram 81, 82/bus 54. **Open** noon-2.30pm, 7-11pm, Mon-Fri; 7-11pm Sat, Sun. **Average** 1000BF. **Credit** AmEx, DC, MC, V.

The streets around place du Châtelain are packed with restaurants, and this modern Italian is always brimming with the Ixelles bourgeoisie, both young and middle-aged. It's slightly frenetic at times and the staff are rather pleased with themselves, but the food is great, particularly the pasta with smoked salmon and vodka. Pastas are available as starters or mains, and there are several vegetarian sauces. Other food includes carpaccio of salmon and beef.

La Fin de Siècle

3 avenue de l'Armée, 1040 (732 74 34). Métro Montgomery. **Open** noon-2.30pm, 7-10.30pm, Mon-Fri; 7-10.30pm Sat. **Average** 800BF-1000BF.

Not to be confused with the bar of the same name near the Bourse. The food is Italian and not exclusively traditional, with pastas such as tagliatelle with white truffle oil. The décor leans towards kitsch, with *trompe-l'œil* paintings and chandeliers.

Rosticceria Fiorentina

43 rue Archimède, 1000 (734 92 36). Métro Schuman. **Open** noon-2.30pm, 6.30-10pm, Mon-Fri, Sun. **Average** 900BF. **Credit** AmEx, MC, V.

A very good-value, family-run restaurant which has been in the European district far longer than most of the Europeans who work there. The food is simple and tasty: home-made pasta and daily specials such as saltimbocca and *osso bucco*. At lunchtime, it's always full of Italians, from the loftiest bureaucrat down to his lowliest photocopier operator.

Spain

Las Castanuelas

132 rue Stévin, 1000 (280 00 81). Métro Schuman. **Open** noon-2.30pm, 7-10.30pm, Mon-Fri. **Average** 600BF-800BF. **No credit cards.**

A tapas restaurant in the EU district which is always crowded at lunchtime, but less so in the evening. The tortillas are wonderful, and all the usual tapas are on the menu: calamares, octopus, meatballs, chorizo, prawns with garlic and so on, plus some more substantial Spanish cuisine. The house Rioja is good value

La Grillange

7 avenue Eudore Pirmez, 1040 (649 26 85). Tram 81, 82. **Open** noon-2.30pm, 7-9.30pm, Tue-Sat. **Credit** AmEx, DC, MC, V. **Average** 1500BF. **Menu** 1200BF.

A pleasant Spanish restaurant in a somewhat nondescript part of Etterbeek. It's mainly frequented by well-heeled Spaniards, the food is ultra-traditional and the four-course set menu is based around a different Spanish region each month. If you don't opt for the set menu – it's often a good idea to ignore the set – let the owner tell you what's good that day.

Russia & Eastern Europe

Les Ateliers de la Grande Ile

33 rue de la Grande Ile, 1000 (512 81 90). Métro Anneessens or Bourse. **Open** 8pm-2am Tue-Sun. **Average** 1100BF. **Credit** AmEx, DC, MC, V.

Noisy Russian and Slav restaurant in an old foundry, with lots of small, ramshackle rooms leading off each other, candles and gypsy violinists. The food is hearty – blinis, roast meat accompanied by lashings of vodka – and not for someone who likes to pick at a Caesar salad.

Comme Chez Moi

140 rue Haute, 1000 (502 52 09). Bus 20, 48. **Open** noon-3pm, 7pm-midnight, Tue-Sun. **Average** 700 BF. **Menu** 490BF (lunch), 890BF. **Credit** AmEx, DC, MC, V.

Not to be confused with the famous Comme Chez Soi. This place concentrates on Russian and Romanian cooking. It's right in the centre of Brussels, in the scruffy Marolles district, which is cobbled and picturesque in parts but can feel slightly threatening at night. Comme Chez Moi is best at serving up traditional specialities such as blinis, caviar and stuffed cabbage, all of which can be washed down with vodka or Russian, Crimean and Romanian wine.

Greek

L'Atlantide

73 rue Franklin, 1000 (736 20 02). Métro Schuman. **Open** noon-2.30pm, 7-11pm, Mon-Fri. **Average** 800BF. **Menu** 350BF, 450BF (lunch). **Credit** V.

A straightforward place popular with the Greeks who work in the European district. There is no Greek dancing or plate-smashing, just white-and-blue walls, hearty meze and more substantial food, plus retsina and sickly Greek desserts.

Middle Eastern

Al Barmaki

67 rue des Eperonniers, 1000 (513 08 34). Métro Gare Centrale. **Open** 7pm-midnight Mon-Sat. **Average** 800BF. **Menu** 1800BF (two people). **Credit** AmEx, DC, MC, V.

Lebanese restaurant near the Grand Place offering good-value hot and cold meze. The usual Middle Eastern staples are available: felafel, hummus, aubergine salad, tabbouleh, chick peas and so on, and it's a useful place for vegetarians.

Chip tricks

Without doubt, Belgium has the best chips in Europe. British northerners may insist that chips fried in beef dripping are superior to the Belgian version, but few would agree with them. The secret of Belgian *frites* is that they are cut fairly thin (but not too thin) and fried twice.

This may not actually be very healthy, but it makes the chips much crisper than those in other countries.

The other touch of genius that Belgians bring to their chip-making is mayonnaise. Anyone who sneers at the idea of mayonnaise and chips will quickly recant once they try it. The only problem is how to ensure the mayonnaise is evenly distributed over the chips, avoiding those at the top of the cone being swamped and those at the bottom remaining bereft.

But mayonnaise is not the only sauce. Most chip shops offer a bewildering choice: américaine, andalouse, banzai, cocktail, curry, hawaii, hili-pili, mustard, tartare – to name but a few. Most of them taste like mayonnaise with a few E numbers added in. Américaine and andalouse both contain tomatoes, herbs and spices (in theory). Cocktail has a touch of whisky. Alternatively (or additionally), you can go for a dollop of pickles or a mound of mussels on top.

Opinions differ as to the best chip emporia in Brussels, but there are two main contenders: **Maison Antoine** on place Jourdan; and **Homage à Mafrite** on place du Jeu de Balle. Neither is particularly central, so if you're near the Grand Place and can't face a walk, try **Friteland** on rue Henri Maus by the Bourse.

La Fleur d'Oranger

21 rue de Rollebeek, 1000 (511 24 37). Bus 20, 34, 95, 96. **Open** noon-2.30pm, 6.30-11pm, Mon, Tue, Thur-Sun. **Average** 900BF. **Menu** 690BF. **Credit** AmEx, DC, MC, V.

Moroccan restaurant on a picturesque cobbled street just off place du Grand Sablon. There are good tajines and couscous, which can be a welcome change from the traditional and heavy Belgian food that prevails in central Brussels. Service is smooth, but the orange blossom theme is slightly cloying.

L'Ottomanie

97 rue des Alexiens, 1000 (512 08 90/513 29 41). Métro Gare Centrale/bus 34, 48, 95, 96. **Open** 6pm-1am Mon; 11am-3am Tue-Sun. **Average** 250BF (brunch Sat, Sun), 395BF (lunch), 650BF. **Credit** AmEx, DC, MC, V.

A modern Turkish restaurant, with good-value meze and surprisingly drinkable Turkish and Middle Eastern wine. It caters for young Europeans, rather than Turks, and the decoration is odd in places: stencil-painted walls and lights that resemble the teats of milking machines. Some accuse it of pretension, but it remains cheap, popular and relaxed.

Indian

Au Palais des Indes

263 avenue Louise, 1050 (646 09 41). Tram 93, 94. **Open** noon-2.30pm, 6-11.30pm, Mon-Sat; 6-11.30pm Sun. **Average** 1200BF. **Menu** 695BF (lunch). **Credit** AmEx, DC, MC, V.

Upmarket Indian that is definitely not the place to go after you've had 12 pints of lambic. It produces upmarket versions of all the old favourites and specialises in tandoori. All dishes can be tailored to varying degrees of hotness, and the set menu comes in vegetarian and meat versions.

La Porte des Indes

455 avenue Louise, 1050 (647 86 51). Tram 93, 94. **Open** noon-2.30pm, 7-10.30pm, Mon-Sat; 7-10.30pm Sun. **Average** 1500BF. **Menu** 650BF (lunch), 1850BF. **Credit** AmEx, DC, MC, V.

Part of the same international chain as the Blue Elephant Thai restaurant, this sophisticated Indian eatery is also not somewhere to eat when you're 'tired and emotional'. Rather, it's a place where you might be given lemon sorbet between courses. The food involves dishes such as prawns with saffron rather than vindaloos and onion bhajis.

Le Shimla

67 place Jourdan, 1040 (230 71 58). Métro Schuman/bus 34, 80. **Open** 11.30am-3pm, 6.30pm-midnight, Mon-Fri; 6.30pm-midnight Sat, Sun. **Average** 800BF. **Credit** AmEx, DC, MC, V.

Cheap curry house, complete with flock wallpaper, that is much more down to earth than the above establishments. All the usual curries are available – vindaloo, biryani, korma – and there are plenty of vegetarian options, all served with well-mannered patience.

South-East Asian

Apocalypse

20 avenue Adolphe Buyl, 1050 (647 07 18). Tram 93, 94. **Open** noon-3pm, 6-9pm, Mon-Fri; 6-9pm Sat, Sun. **Average** 650BF. **Menu** 350BF, 425BF, 525BF. **No credit cards.**

Cheap Vietnamese restaurant near the university and popular with students. The turnover is rapid and the food is straightforwardly good value, so go elsewhere if it's a long, romantic dinner you're after.

Da Kao

38 rue Antoine Dansaert, 1000 (512 67 16). Métro Bourse. **Open** noon-3pm, 6.30pm-midnight, daily. **Average** 500BF. **No credit cards.**

This no-frills Vietnamese eatery in the centre of Brussels has a fast turnover, brusque service and unflattering lighting. But the food is excellent value by Brussels standards, and Da Kao is justifiably popular. You can accompany your meal with Tsingtao beer, and in addition to the Vietnamese cuisine there are dishes such as tempura and dim sum.

My-Tai

110 chaussée de Malines, 1970 (731 27 26). Bus 30, 39. **Open** noon-2pm, 7-10.30pm, Tue-Sat; 7-11pm Sun. **Average** 900BF. **Credit** AmEx, DC, MC, V.

Thai restaurant well out of the way in suburban Wezembeek-Oppem, but well worth a visit if you have a car, and particularly with children. Provision of a playroom in the basement means you can park the kids downstairs and eat Thai classics such as chicken red curry in peace. The staff are helpful and the chef will cool down dishes on request.

Takesushi

21 boulevard Charlemagne, 1000 (230 56 27). Métro Schuman. **Open** noon-2.30pm, 7-10.30pm, Mon-Fri; 6-10.30pm Sun. **Average** 800BF. **Menu** 850BF-1950BF. **Credit** AmEx, DC, MC, V.

The exterior looks inauspicious, with fading photographs of dishes, but this is one of the most popular Japanese restaurants in Brussels. Japanese customers plus a good smattering of Eurocrats come here to choose between sashimi, teriyaki, sukiyaki, sushi and tempura – either eat in or take away.

Yamato

11 rue Francart, 1050 (502 28 93). Métro Porte de Namur/bus 54, 71. **Open** noon-2pm, 7-10pm, Tue-Fri; noon-2pm, 6.30-9.30pm, Sat. **Average** 450BF. **Menu** 250BF, 340BF. **Credit** AmEx.

A simple Japanese noodle bar just off chaussée d'Ixelles. The noodles are served at a plain wooden counter and the turnover is speedy. It's not somewhere to linger, but it's good value and popular with Japanese living in Brussels.

Caribbean

La Canne à Sucre

12 rue des Pigeons, 1000 (513 03 72). Trams 92, 93, 94/bus 34, 95, 96. **Open** 11.30am-2pm, 7.30pm-midnight, Tue-Thur; 11.30am-2pm, 7.30pm-1.30am, Fri, Sat. **Average** 1200BF. **Credit** AmEx, MC, V.

Caribbean restaurant near place du Grand Sablon dishing up Antilles and Creole cooking plus hundreds of rum-based cocktails. Most of the mains involve seafood or chicken, and much of it with spices or coconut. On Thursday, Friday and Saturday there is live music.

Vegetarian

Le Paradoxe

329 chaussée d'Ixelles, 1050 (649 89 91). Tram 81/bus 71. **Open** noon-2pm, 7-10pm, Tue-Sat. **Average** 800BF. **Menu** 350BF, 390BF (both lunch); 735BF (menu du jour). **Credit** AmEx, DC, MC, V.

Owned by the same people as Tsampa (*see below*), Le Paradoxe's food is vegetarian with Tibetan, Vietnamese and Japanese influences as well as straightforward quiches and *tartes*. It puts on occasional exhibitions, has live music every Friday and Saturday (when it closes half an hour later), and has an adjoining healthfood shop.

Meat, meat & more meat…

and some chicory.

Travelling around Belgium as a vegetarian can be a demoralising experience. Virtually all the country's specialities involve meat or fish, and the vegetarian option in most traditional restaurants tends to be omelette and chips. Only one vegetable features heavily in the country's national cuisine, and that is chicory, which the Walloons call *chicon* and the Flemish call *witloof*.

Chicory, or Belgian endive, was 'discovered' by a farmer in Schaerbeek in the 1830s. He put some chicory lettuce roots in a bag and left them in a dark corner of his granary for the winter. When he went back several months later, he found what looked like a white carrot growing from the root. The Belgians now cook that white carrot in many ways. Another Belgian discovery is red cabbage, which probably originated in Flanders, but this does not enjoy the status of chicory.

Meat and fish eaters are well catered for in Belgium. Mussels feature prominently on most traditional menus in various permutations. A main course of *moules* usually involves around 1kg of the shellfish and some chips. The most common versions are: *provençales* (tomato, garlic and herbs); *marinières* (shallot, carrot, parsley and celery); white wine; white wine and cream; and *gratinées* (with cheese on top). You can also have them in breadcrumbs or batter.

Other seafood is also popular. Ostend is renowned for its oysters (*huîtres*), which are offered by most fish restaurants. Pink or grey shrimps (*crevettes roses/grises*) are ubiquitous, appearing in salads, croquettes, stuffed tomatoes, sauces and so on.

Eels in green sauce (*anguilles au vert*) is a national dish. *Waterzooi* is a popular stew of fish, chicken or scallops cooked in a broth enriched with cream and egg yolks.

On the meat side, rich casseroles and stews abound in traditional Belgian restaurants. *Carbonnade flamande* is beef braised with beer, onions, carrots and thyme, while *lapin à la gueuze* is a casserole of rabbit, beer, onion and spices, and sometimes prunes. A variation on this is *lapin à la kriek*, in which cherry beer is used instead of gueuze.

Faisan à la bruxelloise or *à la brabançonne* is pheasant cooked with butter, white wine and chicory. Dishes cooked *à la liégeois* usually include strips of bacon, while *à l'ardennaise* involves bits of Ardennes ham.

The most basic speciality is *stoemp*, which is mashed potato mixed with different vegetables and occasionally meat. It is usually served with sausages, a combination you can often buy in bars and taverns, along with *tête pressée* (brawn), *kipkap* (jellied bits of meat), *croque monsieur* (cheese and ham on toast) and *toast cannibale* (raw minced beef on toast). And don't expect to get a hamburger if you ask for *américaine* or *steak à l'américaine* – instead you'll be given a large plate of raw minced steak, perhaps with some raw onion, capers, black pepper and Tabasco to help it down.

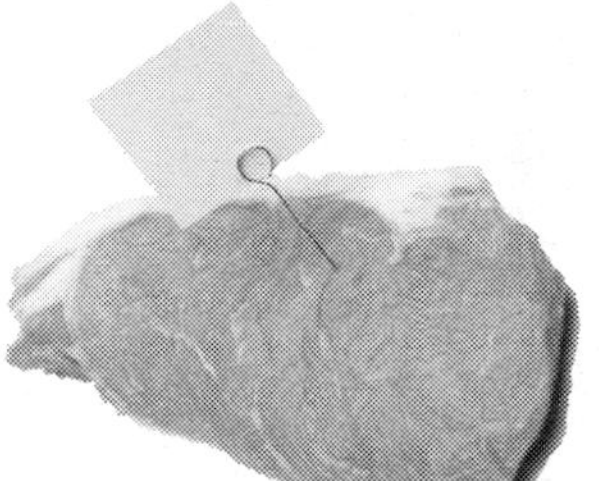

Shanti

68 avenue Adolphe Buyl, 1050 (649 40 96). Tram 93, 94/bus 71. **Open** noon-2pm, 6.30-10pm, Tue-Sat. **Average** 1000BF. **Menu** 400BF (lunch), 600BF, 1000BF. **Credit** AmEx, DC, MC, V.

A mainly vegetarian restaurant above a healthfood shop. It's near the university, so it's popular with affluent students, but the customers also include Ixelles and Uccle thirtysomethings. The food is a relief for vegetarians weary of having to eat omelette after omelette in Brussels' more traditional restaurants. Instead, they can have meat-free pleasure here with the likes of grilled tofu and staples such as vegetarian curry.

Tsampa

109 rue de Livourne, 1050 (647 03 67). Tram 93, 94. **Open** noon-2pm, 7-10pm, Mon-Fri; noon-2pm Sat. **Average** 800BF. **Menu** 350BF (lunch), 430BF. **Credit** AmEx, DC, MC, V.

An unusually imaginative vegetarian restaurant, with a garden at the back, situated just behind avenue Louise. To reach it, you have to make your way through the health food shop (of the same name) at the front. The menu reflects an eclectic range of eastern influences, with curries and Tibetan and Japanese flavours all on offer at any one time. There is plenty of seitan and quorn, and the wines are organic.

Glossary

Meat

viande (f)	meat
gibier (m)	game
agneau (m)	lamb
boeuf (m)	beef
caille (f)	quail
canard (m)	duck
cheval (m)	horse
chevreuil (m)	roe deer
cerf (m)	stag
venaison (f)	venison
dinde (f)	turkey
escargot (m)	snail
faisan	pheasant
jambon (m)	ham
lapin (m)	rabbit
porc (m)	pork
poulet (m)	chicken
veau (m)	veal
boudin (m)	black pudding
boudin blanc (m)	white pudding
cervelle (f)	brain
foie (m)	liver
magret de canard	breast of duck
osso bucco	knuckle of veal
ris (m)	sweetbreads
rognon (m)	kidney
saignant	rare (ie steak)
à point	medium rare
bien cuit	well done

Fish

poisson (m)	fish
anguille (f)	eel
brochet (m)	pike
cabillaud (m)	cod
dorade (f)	sea bream
espadon (m)	swordfish
lotte (f)	monkfish
plie (f)	plaice
raie (f)	skate
rouget (m)	red mullet
saumon (m)	salmon
thon (m)	tuna
truite (f)	trout
waterzooi	Belgian bouillabaisse or fish and eel stew

Shellfish & crustacea

coquille St Jacques (f)	scallop
crevette (f)	shrimp
écrevisse (f)	crayfish (freshwater)
homard (m)	lobster
huître (f)	oyster
moule (f)	mussel

Vegetables & herbs

légume (f)	vegetable
herbes (f)	herbs
artichaut (m)	globe artichoke
asperge (f)	asparagus
champignon (m)	mushroom
chicon (m)	chicory (Belgian endive)
chou (m)	cabbage
échalote (f)	shallot
épinard (m)	spinach
fève (f)	broad bean
haricot (m)	bean
haricot vert (m)	French bean
oignon (m)	onion
poireau (m)	leek
poivron vert/rouge (m)	green/red pepper
pomme (de terre) (f)	potato
truffe (f)	truffle
ail (m)	garlic
aneth (m)	dill
basilic (m)	basil
cerfeuil (m)	chervil
ciboulette (f)	chive
estragon (m)	tarragon
fenouil (m)	fennel
persil (m)	parsley
romarin (m)	rosemary
sauge (f)	sage
thym (m)	thyme

Fruit

fruit (m)	fruit
ananas (m)	pineapple
banane (f)	banana
cassis (m)	blackcurrant
cerise (f)	cherry
fraise (f)	strawberry
framboise (f)	raspberry
groseille (f)	redcurrant
kriek	cherry
marron (m)	chestnut
pamplemousse (m)	grapefruit
pêche (f)	peach
poire (f)	pear
pomme (f)	apple
prune (f)	plum
raisin (m)	grape

General

gaufre (f)	waffle
beurre (m)	butter
fromage (m)	cheese
pâtes (f)	pasta
sel (m)	salt
poivre (m)	pepper
sucre (m)	sugar
oeuf (m)	egg
stoemp	mashed potato Belgian style

Cafés & Bars

No, you haven't died and gone to beer heaven, but it's the next best thing. And if you're no ale fan, take your pick of tipples from posing with a* pressé *to tequila till dawn.

Prime posing territory around the pavement cafés of the **Sablon** *– nothing personal, guys.*

The bars and cafés of Brussels are by far the liveliest part of the city. Anyone who has spent a day wandering around almost deserted streets, bemused by the lack of sightseeing opportunities, might wonder why they have come to Belgium. But as soon as they start visiting the bars, everything becomes clear.

You can sit amid art nouveau splendour and drink coffee or Champagne in the company of the Brussels bourgeoisie and their poodles. You can sample dozens of different beers in bizarrely shaped glasses in comfortable, old bars with wooden booths, surly old men and leather benches. You can sup Guinness in Irish pubs or bottles of Budweiser in all-American bars. You can play the Parisian and pose with a *citron pressé* and a novel at one of the pavement tables in the Sablon. You can salsa in Latin American joints, bop to Europop, and be chic to a backdrop of drapes, candles and distressed paintwork. And you can do all these things from breakfast till dawn.

The first watering holes you are likely to visit are the large, touristy bars and cafés on all sides of the Grand Place. They offer an excellent view of the square and their interiors hint at the wealth and power of the medieval guild houses, but high prices and a distinct lack of Belgians mean it's worth looking further afield. A few paces to the north bring you to the streets around the Bourse, which are good for turn-of-the-century cafés such as **Le Cirio** and **Le Falstaff**. Be warned that if you go to the toilet in any of the larger, more touristy bars around here, you will find an ancient woman attendant demanding 10BF or 20BF, who will screech shrilly until you pay up.

Also just beyond the Grand Place are important drinking streets, such as the meandering rue du Marché au Charbon, which are virtually deserted during the day, but come alive late in the evening. At weekends, the likes of rue du Marché au Charbon, rue Antoine Dansaert and place St Géry are packed until well past 3am, with many of the bars virtually empty until after midnight.

Another fruitful area, to the south, is Ixelles, which stretches out on either side of avenue Louise. Spots around the university are studenty, while closer to the centre you find chic cafés and bars for twenty and thirtysomethings. Food on offer includes French staples such as *croque monsieurs*, and you also get open sandwiches, delicious

After the flea market, enjoy a beer at one of the numerous bars lining **place du Jeu de Balle.**

patisserie and occasionally more substantial salads and steaks.

The average Belgian bar or café sells around 20 types of beer, but a few of the traditional establishments sell over 100 kinds. If beer is not to your taste, there is a good choice of wine by the bottle or glass. Most of the wine on offer is French, and Brussels is very good for white and red Burgundy, but New World and Mediterranean wine is scarce. Cocktails are widely available and flavoured vodkas are popular, particularly in the younger bars.

Opening times for many Brussels bars and cafés are purely theoretical. In practice they may close much earlier or later, depending on the state of their relations with the police and the *commune* authorities, and on how many customers there are that night.

Bars

L'Acrobate

14 rue Borgval, 1000 (513 73 08). Métro Bourse. **Open** 9pm-dawn Fri, Sat. **No credit cards.**
The style of this bar is Central American kitsch, with primary colours, fairy lights, shrines, lanterns and plastic flowers. Open on Friday and Saturday only, it's usually empty until well past midnight, and then quickly fills up. There's a small dance floor at the back.

L'Amadeus

13 rue Veydt, 1050 (538 34 27). Métro Louise/tram 91, 92. **Open** *wine bar* 6pm-2am Tue-Sat. **Credit** AmEx, DC, MC, V.
Wine bar and restaurant (*see chapter* **Restaurants**) housed in the former studio of the sculptor Rodin. Built around a courtyard, with dark colours, exposed brick and tall candles, it is popular with all ages. There's a good wine list – many available by the glass – and oysters when they're in season.

L'Amour Fou

185 chaussée d'Ixelles (on place Fernand Cocq), 1050 (514 27 09). Métro Porte de Namur/bus 54, 71. **Open** 9am-3am Mon-Fri; 10am-3am Sat, Sun. **Credit** AmEx, DC, MC, V.
This long, narrow, modern bar in Ixelles – with an Internet room at the back – gets crowded in the evenings, but it's more relaxed during the day. Various French and Flemish newspapers on wooden sticks are provided on the tables.

L'Archiduc

6 rue Antoine Dansaert, 1000 (512 06 52). Métro Bourse. **Open** 4pm-4am daily. **Credit** AmEx, DC, MC, V.
Elegant and chic, decorated in 1930s ocean liner style, this is many people's favourite bar in Brussels. Mellow without being sedate, it occasionally has a piano player or jazz, sometimes in the late afternoon. Being close to the centre, it is a good place to start or, even better, finish the evening.

L'Atelier

77 rue Elise, 1050 (649 19 53). Tram 93, 94/bus 71. **Open** 4pm-3am Mon-Thur; 6pm-4am Fri, Sat; 6pm-3am Sun. **No credit cards.**
Don't even think about going here if you want peace or sophistication because L'Atelier is right by the university in Ixelles. It's packed with beery students, talking about life or their alcohol intake or playing pinball, and occasionally bands play. Since there are over 200 beers available here at reasonable prices, it also attracts plenty of beer tourists.

Au Soleil

86 rue du Marché au Charbon, 1000 (513 34 30). Métro Bourse. **Open** 10am-2am daily. **No credit cards.**
Formerly a men's clothing shop, this bar still sports the original signs outside and old wooden fittings inside, although some of the fading ads on the walls are recent additions. It gets quite crowded in the evenings, with a fair number of stubbly artist types. There's a good choice of beer and some food, plus tables outside in the summer.

Le Belgica

32 rue du Marché au Charbon, 1000 (no phone). Métro Bourse. **Open** 10am-3am Thur-Sat. **No credit cards.**
The Belgian flag flies outside, and there's a bust of the king inside, but this is no traditional bar for patriotic old Belgians.

It's predominantly gay, but if you go late at weekends, it's by no means wholly so. The music is loud, it's comfortable and crowded, and it's popular as a pre-club bar.

Beursschouwburg

22-28 rue Auguste Orts, 1000 (513 82 90). Métro Bourse. **Open** 7.30pm-dawn Thur-Sat. **No credit cards.**
This huge, cavernous, post-industrial bar next to a theatre and ballroom is near L'Archiduc, but very different in character. Slightly arty and predominantly Flemish, it is usually empty until about 11pm, and then becomes packed. Music is mostly acid jazz and funk, with occasional live bands.

Le Bois sans Soif

60 avenue Adolphe Buyl, 1050 (649 44 73). Tram 93, 94/bus 71. **Open** noon-late Mon-Fri; 4pm-late Sat, Sun. **No credit cards.**
In this pleasant Ixelles bar, near the university and popular with students, you can indulge in the likes of Scrabble, Pictionary, Perudo, Liar Dice and Rummikub. The interior has distressed, tangerine paintwork allied with beech tables and counter, a style which seems popular in this part of Brussels (*see below* **CyberAccess**). There's a garden at the back.

Le Cercueil

10-12 rue des Harengs, 1000 (512 30 77). Métro Bourse or Gare Centrale. **Open** 11am-3am Mon-Thur, Sun; 11am-5am Fri, Sat. **No credit cards.**
Just off the Grand Place, Le Cercueil (which means 'coffin') looks like an undertaker's from the outside. Inside it has coffins for tables, ultraviolet lighting to bring out customers' pallor, and a background music mix of Gregorian chanting and funeral marches. Customers are mainly tourists, students, Goths and horror fans.

Chez Richard

2 rue des Minimes, 1000 (513 70 87). Tram 92, 93, 94/bus 34, 95, 96. **Open** 7am-late daily. **No credit cards.**
Bar and café near Sablon, whose character changes as the day progresses. Lawyers and businessmen prevail at weekday lunchtimes, while visitors drawn by the Sablon antique shops and stalls fill the place at weekends. In the evening, the average age drops by several years, even decades, and customers happily drink and dance to Europop and 1980s hits.

Le Corbeau

18 rue St Michel, 1000 (219 52 46). Métro De Brouckère. **Open** 10am-1.30am Mon-Thur; 10am-2am Fri, Sat; 12.30am Sun. **No credit cards.**
This bar's main claim to fame is its variety of glasses. The 'chevalier' is a glass about 50cm high, so a certain degree of dexterity is required if you want to avoid a faceful of beer. Le Corbeau is close to place des Martyrs, so it can be a good stop-off on a sightseeing tour. The music gets louder and the customers rowdier as the evening wears on. If you want to stand on tables and sing Belgian and English pop songs with young Belgians, then Le Corbeau late on a Saturday night may present the desired opportunity.

CyberAccess

27 avenue Adolphe Buyl, 1050 (640 71 58). Tram 93, 94/bus 71. **Open** noon-midnight Mon-Sat; 2-7pm Sun. **Credit** MC, V.
You can buy magazines, books, games, online time and Net training at this Internet tearoom. The style will seem familiar if you have just been to the nearby Le Bois sans Soif, ie wooden tables and tangerine walls. And as with Le Bois, it's popular with students, being close to the university.

L'Entrée des Artistes

42 place du Grand Sablon, 1000 (502 31 61). Tram 92, 93, 94/bus 34, 95, 96. **Open** 8am-dawn daily. **Credit** AmEx, DC, MC, V.
One of the bars that line the Sablon, where you can while away pleasant hours at the counter or one of tables outside. It's convenient for people-watching, particularly during the Sablon antiques market at the weekend, and it's a good place to start with a coffee, and then move on to something a little stronger as lunchtime approaches. Prices are reasonable considering the location.

Fin de Siècle

9 rue des Chartreux, 1000 (513 51 23). Métro Bourse. **Open** 11.30am-3am Mon-Thur; 11.30am-4am Fri; 4pm-4am Sat; 4pm-3am Sun. **Credit** AmEx, MC, V.
A long, old bar in the centre which has been given a make-over of distressed paint and plasterwork, lanterns on the tables and changing exhibitions of art (for sale). The music is classical and there is a small stage at the back used for occasional performances, such as flamenco shows. Though crowded at the weekend, it's quiet and civilised on weekdays.

Goupil Le Fol

22 rue de la Violette, 1000 (511 13 96). Métro Bourse or Gare Centrale. **Open** 8pm-dawn daily. **No credit cards.**
This eccentric bar near the Manneken Pis looks like a junk shop from the outside. This is also true of the inside – every surface, including the ceiling, is covered in old books, pictures and LPs. The general style is flea market crossed with the early 1970s. As well as standard Belgian beers, there are fruit-based house cocktails.

Le Greenwich

7 rue des Chartreux, 1000 (511 41 67). Métro Bourse. **Open** 10.30am-1.30am daily. **No credit cards.**
Big, bright, old-fashioned bar in the centre of town with marble tables and wood-panelling. What distinguishes it from all the other bars of this type is the lack of talking and the intense games of chess played at the tables by old and young.

H_2O

27 rue du Marché au Charbon, 1000 (512 38 43). Métro Bourse. **Open** 7pm-2am daily. **No credit cards.**
Fairly sophisticated bar in an excellent street for drinking. With candles, drapes and ambient or classical music, it is quieter and has an older clientèle than many of its neighbours – no doubt the scene of many a thirtysomething seduction.

Le Java

14 rue St Géry, 1000 (512 37 16). Métro Bourse. **Open** 8pm-3am Mon-Sat; noon-3am Sun; *summer* noon-3am daily. **No credit cards.**
Small wedge-shaped bar with red marbled walls, huge windows and an almost Gaudí-esque bar top encrusted with old bottletops. It's noisy, crowded, interesting and right in the heart of an area that is excellent for bars. On Sunday afternoons (2-6pm) there is a children's show downstairs.

La Kartchma

17 place du Grand Sablon, 1000 (512 49 64). Tram 92, 93, 94/bus 34, 95, 96. **Open** 10am-2am daily. **Credit** AmEx, DC, MC, V.
Some people think this is the most pleasant of the bars and cafés with tables outside that line one side of place du Grand Sablon, although in summer it is hard to distinguish which tables belong to which establishment. It's a good place to sit in your shades on summer lunchtimes or evenings and observe passers-by.

Le Maldoror

91 rue Américaine, 1050 (539 22 26). Tram 81, 82. 91, 92, 93, 94/bus 54. **Open** 9pm-dawn daily. **Credit** AmEx, V.
This calls itself a 'night bar', and the hours it keeps have led to occasional run-ins with the Ixelles authorities and the police. The music is loud and it's popular as a place to drink pre- or mid-clubbing.

Here for the beer

Roughly three quarters of the beer sold in Belgium is lager, but it's not for this that beer tourists come flocking to Brussels. Estimates of the number of beers brewed in Belgium vary, ranging between 400 and 600, and although not all of them are available in Brussels, a visit to the Belgian capital is probably the next best thing to a holiday in paradise for a real ale fanatic.

Until recently, Belgian beer was fairly obscure, but the opening of restaurants such as Belgo in London has raised its profile substantially. You may already be familiar with brands such as Chimay and Hoegaarden, but there is still plenty to discover in Brussels. Alongside the intriguing – Verboden Vrucht (Forbidden Fruit), Delirium Tremens, Guillotine, Judas, Mariage Parfait and Mort Subite (Sudden Death) – you will find the unpronounceable – Bokrijks Kruikenbier, Breda's Begijntje, Couckelaerschen Doedel and Huyghe. Many beers come with their own glasses, and it is anathema to most Belgian barmen to serve a beer in a glass that pertains to a different brew.

Belgian beer divides into three main categories: bottom fermented; top fermented; and spontaneously fermented – descriptions that reveal little to the uninitiated. The bottom fermented beers are **lagers** such as Stella, Jupiler and Maes, which are fermented at relatively low temperatures, so that the yeast falls to the bottom. Top fermented beers are **ales**, fermented at higher temperatures than lager, so that the yeast rises to the surface.

Belgium's unique **lambic beers** are spontaneously fermented and have no yeast added to them at all. Instead the yeast comes from the microbes and micro-organisms found in the air as the wheat, barley and hops are left to cool. The Cantillon brewery, for example, has hundreds of vents in the roof to let in the necessary microbes.

The most famous ales in Belgium are the **Trappist beers**, made by monks and 'lay brothers'. There are five Trappist breweries in Belgium: Chimay, Orval, Rochefort, Westmalle and Westvleteren. In addition to these, there are **'abbey' beers** (*abbaye* in French and *abdibj* in Flemish), which are modelled on the Trappist beers. They are produced by brewers, rather than monks, although the quaint pictures on the labels suggest otherwise. The quality of 'abbey' beers is variable Some are considered excellent, others are simply cashing in on the popularity of the Trappist brews.

Monastic beers fall into two main categories: *doubel* (double) and *tripel* (triple). *Doubels* usually contain 6 or 7 per cent alcohol by volume, and are dark and sweet, while *tripels* are stronger, at

8 or 9 per cent. Other types are stronger still, for example, the black and heavy Rochefort 10°, and Westvleteren 12°, which taste similar to barley wine. The most famous of the monastery beers is probably Chimay, which comes in three types: Chimay red has 7 per cent alcohol, Chimay white is 8 per cent, and Chimay blue is 9 per cent.

Some of the most popular beers with visitors to Brussels are **fruit beers**. The best known and most traditional flavours are cherry (*kriek*) and raspberry (*framboise*). In recent years, breweries have experimented with other fruits. Damson and peach are fairly successful, while it is also possible – if you've the stomach for it – to buy banana and mint flavour. Most fruit beers are lambic, but you may also come across cherry and raspberry gueuze, as the terms *kriek* and *framboise* cover both types.

Gueuze can be the best or the worst of Belgian beers, depending on your taste and its quality. It is made by mixing old lambic with young lambic and then putting the blend into Champagne bottles.

There is some refermentation and the resulting beer is fizzy and dry with a sourish taste. Sediment remains at the bottom of the bottle, so pour it carefully, although some people prefer the sediment mixed in. You can also buy partially filtered gueuze, some of which is sweeter than the traditional sort.

A much more refreshing beer is *witbier* or *bière blanche*, which means **white beer**. This is made from wheat and looks milky when unfiltered. The most famous brand is Hoegaarden. It is delicious on a hot summer afternoon or evening, and often comes with a slice of lemon, but beware – it can cause dreadful hangovers.

If you are visiting Brussels during the winter, some of the **seasonal and Christmas ales** may be more appropriate. Many of them are spiced with, for example, coriander, cinnamon or ginger and there are honeyed versions. Scotch ale is also good for Brussels' rainy autumns and icy winters. It is brewed in Scotland, but is rarely available in the UK because it is considered too dark and strong for the British palate, so instead, it's exported to Belgium. Some of it is then re-exported to Britain's real ale drinkers. The best known brands are Gordon's and Douglas's – both made in Scotland – and Campbell's, which is brewed in Belgium.

If you want to learn more about Belgian beer, the best places to visit in Brussels – apart from numerous bars – are the beer museums on the Grand Place and the Cantillon brewery's **Musée Bruxellois de la Gueuze** in Anderlecht (*see chapter* **Museums**).

Le Pantin

355 chaussée d'Ixelles, 1050 (640 80 91). Bus 71. **Open** 11am-3am Mon-Sat; 7pm-3am Sun. **No credit cards.**
Slightly scruffy bar right at the bottom of the chaussée d'Ixelles near the lakes, where old and young Belgians play chess on weekdays, and chess and *go* at weekends.

Le Pitt's Bar

53 rue des Minimes, 1000 (514 41 74). Tram 92, 93, 94/bus 34, 95, 96. **Open** 8pm-2am Mon-Sat. **Credit** MC, V.
Small bar near the Sablon with *trompe-l'œil* décor. At weekends DJs play garage music and men pose as if waiting to be spotted by a model agent. Weekdays it's quieter.

Planet Claire

29 rue de l'Hôpital, 1000 (513 89 78). Métro Bourse. **Open** 11pm-5am Thur-Sat. **No credit cards.**
This bar functions more like a club, since many people go there to dance, but there is no membership or entry fee. You go down a long corridor, past bouncers (who have never been seen to throw anyone out) and a staircase that leads nowhere, into a one-room bar. The interior is welded steel, the music loud, and if you go there after midnight it will be packed.

Poechenellekelder

5 rue du Chêne, 1000 (511 92 62). Métro Bourse. **Open** 11am-midnight Mon-Thur, Sun; 11am-2am Fri, Sat. **No credit cards.**
The theme is Brussels in general and puppets in particular. There are puppets all over the place, along with postcards and other objects relating to Brussels folklore, and the snacks include specialities such as *tête pressée* (a type of brawn).

Sounds

28 rue de la Tulipe, 1050 (512 92 50). Métro Porte de Namur/bus 54, 71. **Open** 11.30am-late Mon-Fri; 7pm-late Sat. **No credit cards.**
Comfortable bar just behind place Fernand Cocq which has jazz four or five nights a week. There's a small supplement on drinks during the jazz, but otherwise it's free.

Tierra del Fuego

ground floor, Maison de l'Amérique Latine, 14 rue Berckmans, 1060 (537 42 72). Métro Louise. **Open** noon-dawn Mon-Fri; 7pm-dawn Sat, Sun. **Credit** MC, V.
Situated in a Latin American cultural centre just off avenue Louise, this bar and café's décor is baroque, with drapes, candles, glittery embroidered chairs and murals. Take your pick of tipples from a *caipirinha* (based on cane-sugar spirit) or generous shots of Dominican, Haitian and Cuban rum to coffee from Costa Rica, Mexico, Jamaica, Honduras, Haiti and Brazil, or more standard beers and spirits.

Traditional bars

A la Bécasse

11 rue de Tabora, 1000 (511 00 06). Métro Bourse or De Brouckère. **Open** 10am-1am Mon-Thur; 10am-2am Fri, Sat; 11am-midnight Sun. **Credit** MC, V.
Ancient drinking hall hidden away down a narrow alley. Customers squeeze together on long tables and aproned waiters serve lambic *doux* and gueuze beer in earthenware jugs.

A la Mort Subite

7 rue Montagne aux Herbes Potagères, 1000 (512 86 64/513 13 18). Métro De Brouckère. **Open** 10.30am-1am Mon-Fri; 11am-1am Sat; 12.30pm-1am Sun.
Famous traditional Brussels bar with surly waiters, noisy customers, mirrors and yellowed walls – passive smoking hell (or heaven, depending on how you look at it). The beer list is somewhat short for a traditional Belgian bar, but it does have its own brew, Mort Subite ('Sudden Death').

L'Albertine

53 rue de la Madeleine, 1000 (513 56 71). Métro Gare Centrale. **Open** 7am-7pm Mon-Wed, Fri, Sat; 7am-10pm Thur. **No credit cards.**
An unspectacular but pleasant bar near Mont des Arts, L'Albertine is warm, comfortable and central, and avoids the touristy or desolate air that some Brussels bars take on

Art nouveau and art deco converge at **Le Falstaff** *which has a dazzling list of Belgian beers.*

during the day. The beer is good, there's a decent wine list and it also does some snacks and spaghetti throughout the day. On Thursdays there is jazz until 10pm.

Black Bottom

1 rue du Lombard, 1000 (511 06 08). Métro Bourse. **Open** 9pm-2am Mon-Sat. **No credit cards.**
An old cabaret bar near the Bourse that considers itself to be Parisian. The windows are emblazoned with publicity shots of the owner in his youth, and with acts that include crooners and comedy, it's good for novelty value.

La Chaloupe d'Or

24-25 Grand Place, 1000 (511 41 61). Métro Bourse or Gare Centrale. **Open** 9am-2am daily. **No credit cards.**
One of the famous Grand Place bars/restaurants, opposite the Town Hall, with a fine view from the upper rooms, and tables outside in spring and summer. The building used to be the tailors' guildhouse.

L'Espérance

1-3 rue du Finistère, 1000 (217 32 47). Métro De Brouckère. **Open** 10am-1am Mon-Fri. **Credit** AmEx, DC, MC, V.
Authentic art deco bar to the north of the centre, with wood-panelling, some chrome fittings and a cosseting, comfortable atmosphere. After a dodgy start in the 1930s – there were bedrooms upstairs for the bargirls and their customers – L'Espérance is now highly respectable, and it's a fine place to sip a glass of *half-en-half* (a mixture of Champagne and white wine).

La Fleur en Papier Doré

53 rue des Alexiens, 1000 (511 16 59). Bus 34, 48, 95, 96. **Open** 11am-2am Mon-Thur, Sun; 11am-2am Fri, Sat. **No credit cards.**
This dark old bar in a seventeenth-century building was the local of Magritte and the Belgian surrealists and Dadaists in the 1920s. The walls are covered with pictures, clippings, writings and graffiti by them. Customers are a mixture of gnarled old men and would-be intellectuals.

L'Imaige Nostre-Dame

3 impasse des Cadeaux, 8 rue du Marché aux Herbes, 1000 (219 42 49). Métro Bourse. **Open** noon-midnight Tue-Sat; 4pm-midnight Sun. **No credit cards.**
Under the same ownership as A la Bécasse, this old inn is similar in style. It too is hidden down an alleyway and has a heritage feel, with old wooden tables, stained glass and leather benches. The beers are good and there is some traditional food. It's good for cold days or gloomy Sunday evenings.

Kafka

6 rue de la Vierge Noire, 1000 (513 54 89). Métro Bourse or De Brouckère. **Open** 4pm-3am daily. **No credit cards.**
Smoky old bar with brown walls and a bare tiled floor, selling 18 types of vodka, a fairly long list of Belgian beer and – not so alluring – cups of hot Oxo. Customers are mainly Flemish, with a strong contingent of barflies and eccentrics. Scruffy and relaxed, Kafka can be a welcome antidote to the numerous more style-conscious bars around the Bourse.

La Lunette

3 place de la Monnaie, 1000 (218 03 78). Métro De Brouckère. **Open** 8am-1am Mon-Thur; 8am-2am Fri, Sat; 10am-1am Sun. **No credit cards.**
The Belgian revolution of 1830 started in this square, when opera-goers were inflamed with patriotic fervour. This traditional bar (and café) with mirrors and wooden panels is a pleasant place to sit and read your history books or watch the world go by. Watch out, however, if you order a 'lunette' of beer – it's a litre glass.

Métro Valdi

7 rue des Poissonniers, 1000 (511 66 96). Métro Bourse. **Open** 8pm-late Wed, Fri-Sun. **No credit cards.**
Traditional dingy Belgian bar – of which there are hundreds in Brussels – that becomes a *café dansant* at the weekend, when middle-aged, working-class Belgians dance to an electric organ played by ancient cabaret performers.

Chez Moeder Lambic

68 rue de Savoie, 1060 (539 14 19). Métro Horta. **Open** 4pm-3.30am daily. **No credit cards.**
Moeder Lambic, which means Mother Lambic, is beer heaven – it claims to offer over 1,000 different types, although not all will be in stock at any one time. Given the length of the beer menu, the bar is surprisingly small (perhaps the storerooms are very large), but it's pleasant enough, particularly at quieter times. The neighbourhood is not especially picturesque, but if you're only here for the beer, that won't be a problem.

La Rose Blanche

11 Grand Place, 1000 (513 64 79). Métro Bourse or Gare Centrale. **Open** 10am-1am daily; *food served* 11.30am-3pm, 6-11pm, daily. **Credit** AmEx, DC, MC, V.
A famous Grand Place bar-restaurant with a terrace in front. There's a long list of beers, which might prove tempting if you've just worked up a thirst in the beer museum next door.

Le Roy d'Espagne

1 Grand Place, 1000 (513 08 07). Métro Bourse or Gare Centrale. **Open** 10am-1am daily. **Credit** AmEx, DC, MC, V.
Another famous Grand Place bar, which is housed in one of the grandest guildhouses (that of the bakers). Waiters wear traditional aprons, pigs' bladders hang from the ceiling and the tourists flock. But it's still worth a look, and there is an excellent view of the Grand Place from the upper rooms.

Le Schievelavabo

20 rue Egide Van Ophem, 1180 (332 20 91). Tram 55. **Open** noon-2pm, 7pm-1am, Mon-Fri; 7pm-1am Sat, Sun. **No credit cards.**
Housed in an ancient building in the southern suburb of Uccle, this is not somewhere you'll stumble across in your peregrinations around the main sights, but it is worthwhile if you are staying around here. Youngish customers sit on old wooden settles and choose from a sizeable list of beers, and the atmosphere is convivial. Schievelavabo means 'toilet seat' in Bruxellois, but also translates as 'idiot'.

En Stoemelings

7 place de Londres, 1050 (512 43 74). Métro Trône. **Open** 11am-2am Mon-Fri; 5pm-2am Sat, Sun.
Cosy and traditional bar, whose position on the borders of Ixelles and the EU district makes for a varied atmosphere. There are some lawyers and lobbyists around in the daytime, but it usually has a more local feel in the evening. In addition to some unusual beers, there are snacks such as *croque monsieur*.

La Terrasse

11 avenue de Tervuren, 1040 (733 22 96). Métro Merode. **Open** 10am-11pm daily. **No credit cards.**
Old-fashioned and comfortable bar-café, with leather banquettes and wood-panelling, which has a large, vine-covered terrace in front, although its location on a busy junction means it can be noisy. It sells dozens of Belgian beers and specialises in savoury *tartes* – tuna, salmon, chicken, leek, artichoke and roquefort etc – costing around 175BF-250BF.

Le Pain Quotidien – *a growing chain of bakery-cafés that serve what may be the best chocolate brownies on the Continent.*

Toone

6 impasse Schuddeveld, petite rue des Bouchers, 1000 (513 54 86). Métro De Brouckère or Bourse. **Open** noon-midnight daily. **No credit cards.**

Bar of Théâtre de Toone, where puppets perform plays in the incomprehensible Brussels dialect. The road, which is just off the Grand Place, is packed with (mostly mediocre) fish restaurants, so you have to keep your eyes open to spot it. Inside puppets hang from the ceiling, and it's warm and cosy, but not a bar to visit if you want to avoid tourists.

Anglophone bars & pubs

Big Al's/Conway's

10 avenue de la Toison d'Or, 1050 (511 26 68). Métro Porte de Namur. **Open** noon-2am Mon-Wed; noon-4am Thur-Sat; 6pm-2am Sun. **Credit** AmEx, MC, V.

Noisy New York-style Irish bar with Kilkenny's and Guinness on tap and a big selection of whisky and bourbon. The upstairs sports bar is a popular place to watch rugby internationals, Superbowl and so on. Happy hour is 6- 9pm daily, and women get half-price cocktails and spirits on Thursdays. Food on offer includes burgers and Cajun cooking.

James Joyce

34 rue Archimède, 1040 (230 98 94). Métro Schuman. **Open** 11am-2am Mon-Fri; 11.30am-2am Sat, Sun. **No credit cards.**

Irish pub in the EU quarter which is usually quieter (some call it miserable) than the other Irish joints, but possibly the most Irish. There is Irish folk music on Tuesday evenings. The food is nothing to write home about, except for the Sunday brunch.

Kitty O'Shea's

42 boulevard Charlemagne, 1040 (230 78 75). Métro Schuman. **Open** noon-3am Mon-Sat; noon-3pm Sun. **Credit** AmEx, DC, MC, V.

Another Irish pub in the EU district, which is very popular with Eurocrats, lawyers and journalists. It has a snug at the back, a separate restaurant section serving the likes of Irish stew, and it does a good Sunday brunch fry-up.

Pablo's

51 rue de Namur, 1000 (502 41 35). Métro Porte de Namur. **Open** noon-1am Mon-Thur; noon-2am Fri, Sat; 6pm-1am Sun; *food served* noon-3pm, 6pm-midnight, Mon-Sat; 6pm-midnight Sun. **Credit** AmEx, DC, MC, V.

Cocktail bar serving good Tex-Mex food. Several types of tequila are available, and there are pitchers of margaritas (small 800BF; large 1700BF). The ambience is more suited to groups than couples wanting an intimate evening. There are cheaper cocktails for women on Saturdays 6-11pm.

Rick's

344 avenue Louise, 1050 (647 75 30). Métro Louise/tram 93, 94. **Open** 11am-1am daily. **Credit** AmEx, DC, MC, V.

American bar that seems to exert a magnetic force over every US businessman and frat boy in Brussels. Not the place to go if you want somewhere quiet or continental, but it does a good Sunday brunch, and the garden is pleasant in summer.

The Wild Geese

2-4 avenue Livingstone, 1000 (230 19 90). Métro Maelbeek. **Open** 11am-1am Mon-Wed, Sun; 11am-2am Thur; 11am-3.30am Fri, Sat. **Credit** V.

This Irish pub in the EU district opened on St Patrick's Day 1995. It is packed most evenings with Eurocrats, secretaries, lawyers and students, and has the air of a pick-up joint, especially on Friday nights. There are tables outside in spring and summer.

Cafés & tearooms

A Malte

30 rue Berckmans, 1060 (537 09 91). Métro Louise. **Open** 10am-dawn daily. **Credit** AmEx, DC, MC, V.

Stylish and whimsically decorated café selling delicious sandwiches and *tartes*, plus more substantial brasserie fare. It's good for whiling away rainy afternoons, particularly if you can get the table in the harem-like gallery at the back. There are also tables in the back garden in the summer.

Café Métropole

31 place de Brouckère, 1000 (219 23 84). Métro De Brouckère. **Open** 9am-1am daily. **No credit cards.**

The café of the five-star Hotel Métropole is sophisticated and elegant, with *fin-de-siècle* high ceilings, stucco, tinted mirrors and plush upholstery. Definitely not somewhere to go and drink umpteen pints of traditional Belgian beer; more the place to sip Champagne and nibble at patisserie – and to try star-spotting during the Brussels Film Festival.

Branch: 61 boulevard de Waterloo, 1000 (511 11 27).

Le Cirio

18 rue de la Bourse, 1000 (512 13 95). Métro Bourse. **Open** 10am-1am daily. **No credit cards.**

Large, dark, turn-of-the-century café near the Bourse, which attracts a good cross-section of Brussels life: tourists, Eurocrats and old women with poodles. There's a big choice of beers and it is well known as a place to drink *half-en-half*, a mixture of Champagne and white wine.

Le Falstaff

19-25 rue Henri Maus, 1000 (511 87 89/511 98 77/fax 511 51 25). Métro Bourse. **Open** 10.30am-3am Mon-Fri; 10.30am-5am Sat, Sun. **Credit** AmEx, DC, MC, V.

Vast and famous art nouveau and art deco café spread across several rooms, with a covered terrace in front. The customers are a mixture of young and old, tourists, fur-coated Brussels bourgeoisie, businessmen and expats. There is a dazzling choice of Belgian beers and a lengthy menu, and although the food is not particularly exciting, the long opening hours make it worth remembering.

Le Fiacre

40 rue de la Bourse, 1000 (514 27 51). Métro Bourse. **Open** 9am-4am Mon-Thur; 9am-8am Fri-Sun. **Credit** AmEx, DC, MC, V.

A traditional, dark café near the Bourse, with beer mats covering walls and ceiling. Until recently, it was open 24 hours for food and drink, but it has reduced its opening hours. So if it's 5am and someone says they know a place near the Bourse where you can get spaghetti, don't hold your breath.

Le Frime Out

109 rue Blaes, 1000 (511 13 12). Bus 20, 48. **Open** 11.30am-2.30pm, 7.30pm-2am, Mon-Wed; 11.30am-2.30pm, 7.30pm-4am, Thur-Sat; *food served* 7.30-11.30pm Mon-Sat. **Credit** AmEx, MC, V.

Small bar and restaurant in the Marolles district, just to the west of Sablon, and a youthful antidote to some of the more middle-aged and Anglophone bars there. It's very dark, with midnight-blue walls, velvet drapes and candles.

Gallery

7 rue du Grand-Cerf, 1000 (511 80 35). Métro Louise. **Open** noon-3pm, 6pm-midnight, Mon-Thur; noon-3pm, 6pm-1am, Fri, Sat; 6.30pm-midnight Sun. **Credit** AmEx, DC, MC, V.

Resto-bar ***Le Perroquet****, just off place du Grand Sablon, is popular with young British and Irish expats.*

LE PERRO

Large, halogen-lit cocktail bar and Vietnamese restaurant with sophisticated, slightly 1980s décor. It serves good dim sum and Vietnamese food costing around 350BF per portion. The art and photographs on the walls are for sale.

Hallowe'en

10 rue des Grands Carmes, 1000 (514 12 56). Métro Bourse. **Open** noon-1am Mon-Thur; noon-3am Fri; 4pm-3am Sat.
A central café with a horror theme. On the wall opposite as you enter is a huge sculpture of a devilish monster, and there are candles in skulls. The café also hosts events such as screenings of horror films and magic performances. The menu sticks to the theme with references to the Loch Ness Monster, young virgins and black widows, although the food itself is innocuous enough: smoked salmon, endive salad etc.

Indigo

160 rue Blaes, 1000 (511 38 97). Bus 20, 48. **Open** 10am-2.30pm Tue-Fri; 9.30am-4pm Sat, Sun. **No credit cards**.
Quirky tearoom very close to the Jeu de Balle flea market and furnished with junk – rickety tables and fold-up chairs which the flea market itself might have rejected as too precarious. It serves home-made cakes, breakfast, brunch, salads, quiches and so on, and is useful for vegetarians.

La Librairie des Etangs

319 chaussée d'Ixelles, 1050 (646 97 86). Bus 71. **Open** 10am-7pm Mon-Sat; 10am-5pm Sun. **Credit** MC, V.
Small tearoom at the back of an 'international' bookshop near the Ixelles lakes. There are regular exhibitions of art, which is for sale, as well as occasional events such as poetry readings in French or English.

The Lunch Company

16 rue de Namur, 1000 (502 09 76). Métro Porte de Namur. **Open** 11am-6.30pm Mon-Sat. **No credit cards**.
A 'tearoom' that serves breakfast and good salads and quiches, as well as sandwiches, cakes and flavoured teas. The atmosphere is slightly effete and possibly someone's idea of English style, with comfortable wicker chairs, slightly precarious tables and a little garden at the back.

Le Pain Quotidien

11 rue des Sablons, 1000 (513 51 54). Métro Louise. **Open** 7.30am-7pm Mon-Fri; 8am-7pm Sat, Sun. **Credit** MC, V.
One of a growing chain of bakery-cafés that has spawned several imitators. All branches have a common design: simple rooms with large wooden tables and wooden dressers containing jams, chocolates and coffee to buy. Other food sold includes delicious bread and jam, *tartines* with carpaccio or cheese, *tartes aux pommes* or *aux poires*, ice cream, and probably the best chocolate brownies in Europe.

Le Perroquet

31 rue Watteau, 1000 (512 99 22). Tram 92, 93, 94/bus 34, 95, 96. **Open** 10.30am-1am daily; *food served* noon-1am daily. **No credit cards**.
Authentic art nouveau bar just off place du Grand Sablon, with mirrors, stained glass, serpentine wood, a black-and-white tiled floor and tables outside in summer. Describing itself as a '*resto-bar*', Le Perroquet serves dozens of different stuffed pitta breads (150BF-200BF) and various salads (200BF-350BF). It's quite popular with young British and Irish expats.

La Porteuse d'Eau

48a avenue Jean Volders, 1060 (538 83 54). Métro Porte de Hal. **Open** 10am-1am daily. **Credit** AmEx, V.
Renovated art nouveau café in a grimy, unassuming street in the *commune* of St Gilles. It's light and airy with stained glass, wooden flooring, spiral staircase and a slightly shiny feel. Customers are a mixture of ages, and smarter than at most bars in the neighbourhood. It's a pleasant place to have a drink or some patisserie if you happen to be in the area.

SiSiSi

174 chaussée de Charleroi, 1060 (534 12 72). Tram 81, 90, 91. **Open** 10am-2am Mon-Fri; noon-1am Sat, Sun; *food served* noon-3pm, 6pm-1am, Mon-Fri; noon-1am Sat, Sun. **No credit cards**.
Once very fashionable, this bar and café has now taken on more of a neighbourhood feel, although the nature of the neighbourhood means that customers are still young, chic and reasonably affluent. Large windows and a site on a road junction mean it is a good spot for people-watching. A new chef has raised the profile of the cooking, and it is popular for lunch.

De Skieven Architek

50 place du Jeu de Balle, 1000 (514 43 69). Bus 20, 48. **Open** 6am-1am daily. **Credit** MC, V.
Café overlooking the Jeu de Balle flea market, which does breakfast, croissants, sandwiches, ice cream and oysters. It also sells magazines and newspapers by the front door. There's a garden at the back, and it's all very civilised, but you may prefer the more rough and ready bars around the square.

Le Soleil du Midi

36 rue du Page, 1050 (537 67 36). Tram 91, 92, 93, 94/bus 54. **Open** 10am-6pm Mon-Fri. **Credit** AmEx, DC, MC, V.
A Provençal-style café in Ixelles with yellow walls, tiled tables and dried flowers and herbs. Brussels is not quite the Côte d'Azure, but the café is cheering all the same. It serves various fish soups (150BF-250BF), *salade niçoise* and sandwiches to eat in (100BF-120BF) or take away (70BF-90BF) with staple fillings such as ham or interesting alternatives such as ham mousse and tzatziki.

De Ultieme Hallucinatie

316 rue Royale, 1210 (217 06 14). Métro Botanique. **Open** 11am-2am Mon-Fri; 5pm-3am Sat, Sun; *food served* 11am-2.30pm, 6pm-midnight, daily. **Credit** AmEx, DC, MC, V.
Famous café (and separate restaurant) with a dingy, inconspicuous exterior and an ornate art nouveau interior of rich wood and pale green ironwork. There is a lengthy beer list and the café menu comprises delicious Belgian staples such as prawn croquettes. A slight drawback is the area, which is notorious for thefts, particularly car break-ins.

L'Ultime Atome

14 rue St Boniface, 1050 (511 13 67). Métro Porte de Namur/bus 54, 71, 34, 80. **Open** 9am-1am Mon-Fri; 10am-1am Sat, Sun.
Airy and popular café with wooden tables and very yellow walls. The relaxed atmosphere makes it an acceptable place to have a drink or wait for someone on your own, but it is equally suited to groups. The food – salads and some more substantial meals – is good and the vegetarian options more extensive than many places in Brussels.

Vert de Gris

63 rue des Alexiens, 1000 (514 21 68). Bus 34, 48, 95, 96. **Open** noon-2.30pm, 7.30pm-midnight, Mon-Thur; noon-2.30pm, 7.30pm-12.30am, Fri; 7.30pm-12.30am Sat; 7.30pm-midnight Sun. **Credit** AmEx, MC, V.
Bar, restaurant and deli that has no sign outside but is conspicuous enough. The light and airy front room has a modern iron chandelier and large wooden tables, while at the rear the style changes, with a working humidor (cigar-storer), stuffed animals, ancient and modern sofas, and palm trees. The food – mainly pasta – gets mixed reviews.

A variety of mood and décor awaits you at bar-restaurant-deli **Vert de Gris** *– as long as you can find it.*

Shopping & Services

Shopping & Services

Insatiable consumers will find a lot of ground to cover with money-traps scattered all over Brussels. Alternatively, why not surrender your francs to the shopper's dream that is Antwerp?

Compared to other major cities, Brussels' shopping areas are quite dispersed. There are some areas with a high concentration of stores, but most of the capital's spending temptations are spread throughout the *communes*, making shopping a good way to discover hidden corners of the city. The following is just a sample of what Brussels has to offer.

Only 40 minutes away by train, Antwerp attracts many Brussels residents with its wealth of shops within easy walking distance of Centraal Station. The world centre of the diamond market, Antwerp's affluence is evinced by the range of upmarket international names, such as DKNY and Escada, which have opened there rather than in Brussels. *See page 144* **Shopping in Antwerp**.

The sales periods run just after Christmas and in July/August, but watch for bargains on certain merchandise around relevant holidays. For example, discounts on perfume for St Valentine's Day.

Shopping districts

Uptown

Boulevard de Waterloo and **avenue Louise** are as close to London's Knightsbridge or New York's Fifth Avenue as Brussels gets. The boutiques of Armani, Gucci, Yves Saint Laurent, Hermès and Guy Laroche dot the boulevard, while Louis Vuitton, MaxMara, Gianfranco Ferre, Cartier and Cacharel are some of the avenue's big names. Avenue de la Toison d'Or, running alongside boulevard de Waterloo, is where many mid-range to upmarket toy, clothing, shoe and accessory shops reside. Adjacent to this area, **Galeries de la Toison d'Or** and **Louise**, are worth a look.

Centre

City 2, at the end of rue Neuve (Métro Rogier) is the major inner city mall, catering mostly to the youth market. Its three levels of shops include a Levi's store, along with many other jeans sellers, a Hennes & Mauritz, optical shops including the Sunglass Hut, and record stores, the largest of which is Fnac. **Rue Neuve** itself is a bustling stretch of low- to moderately priced stores. Esprit, men's clothier Celio and department stores C&A, Marks & Spencer and the Belgian chain Inno have branches here. The odd moneychanger, waffle stand and busker can be found here, as well as a bargain CD outlet, pharmacy, perfume store and other inexpensive clothing chains, including the German Pimkie and French Morgan.

Matonge, around **chaussée d'Ixelles** (Métro Porte de Namur), is an enclave of grocers, fabric stores and hair salons catering to the Zairean community. **Galerie d'Ixelles** contains the above, along with a travel agent, record shop and several vendors of home-perm kits and hair extensions.

North African foods, wines and cooking essentials can be found along **boulevard d'Ypres** (Métro Yser), which is not usually frequented by tourists – it's best to have someone familiar with Brussels take you there for safety's sake.

Dating back to 1846, **Galeries St Hubert** (Métro Gare Centrale) is said to be the first of its kind, with other grand, European, glass-covered shopping arcades modelled on it. Don't miss this, more for the architecture than for the shops. The Galerie de la Reine section features upmarket furniture and design shops such as the modernist Ligne (no.12), the quaint lace shop Manufacture Belge de Dentelles (nos.6 & 8) and chocolate-maker Neuhaus's most extravagant location (no.25), comprising a lavish window display, silver trays laden and glass cabinets filled with some of the best chocolates in Belgium.

In the Galerie du Roi there is the Librairie des Galeries (no.2), which has an excellent selection of art books for both the coffee table and the craftsman, in English and French. A small boutique across the Galerie, at no.11, is one of two outlets in

You'll find coffee table books, luxury leather goods, Church's shoes and furnishing fabrics in the Galerie du Roi.

town selling Church's shoes. The luxury leather goods maker Longchamp has a store at no.21 and A La Tentation – two floors of home furnishing fabrics – sits at the end of Galerie du Roi at no.27.

A short walk away, the **Agora** arcade provides a plebeian counterpoint to Galeries St Hubert's refinement – streetwear stores, patchouli and incense vendors, and shops selling leather jackets, cowboy boots and clogs predominate.

Department stores

C&A

27-29 rue Neuve, 1000 (219 02 90). Métro De Brouckère/tram 23, 52, 55, 56, 81. **Open** 9.30am-6pm Mon-Thur, Sat; 9.30am-8pm Fri. **Credit** MC, V.

The inexpensive department store carries mostly clothing on its three floors.

Branch: 69-73 chaussée d'Ixelles, 1050 (511 22 65).

Inno

111 rue Neuve, 1000 (211 21 11). Métro Rogier/tram 23, 52, 55, 56, 81. **Open** 9.30am-7pm Mon-Thur, Sat; 9.30am-8pm Fri. **Credit** AmEx, DC, MC, TC, V.

The largest of Brussels' department stores. Merchandise on Inno's four floors ranges from chic to cheap. The inevitable maze of perfume and cosmetics counters, featuring well-known brands such as Chanel and Lancôme, is on the ground floor, along with baggage and men's and women's apparel. Bed linen and bath towels occupy the cellar, alongside fine crystal, silver and lower-priced ceramics and glassware. On the upper floors are sections devoted to lingerie, children's clothes, home furnishings and a hairdresser. Esprit, In-Wear and French Connection are some of the more casual names on offer, while shoes by Bally represent the pricier side.

Café. Money-changing service.

Branch: 41 chaussée d'Ixelles, 1050 (512 78 00).

Marks & Spencer

17-21 rue Neuve, 1000 (218 50 55). Métro De Brouckère/tram 23, 52, 55, 56, 81. **Open** 9.30am-6pm Mon-Thur; 9.30am-8pm Fri; 9.30am-6.30pm Sat. **Credit** MC, TC, V.

Popular with British expats and locals, the Brussels branch of M&S is so-so compared to branches in the UK, but sufficient for foodstuffs and the good-quality, inexpensive clothing for which the chain is known. Sandwiches, prepared meals and whiskies popular in Britain are stocked in the basement grocery section, while men's, women's and children's clothing are displayed on the other three levels.

Export tax scheme. Moneychanging service.

Branch: 89 Meir, Antwerp 2000 (03 233 32 87).

Fashion

Designer

Bouvy

52 avenue de la Toison d'Or, 1060 (513 07 48). Métro Louise/tram 91, 92, 93, 94/bus 34. **Open**10am-6.30pm Mon-Sat. **Credit** AmEx, DC, MC, V.

Ralph Lauren, Calvin Klein, Alden and Barbour are just a few of the names sold in this expansive, expensive shop. The men's section features sportswear and more formal attire. The latter is displayed on two floors that evoke an English gentlemen's tailor, complete with shelves of shirts and knitwear, glass display cases of shoes and discreet racks of suits. The women's section is almost exclusively mid-range to upmarket fashion shown in a minimalist, slate grey environment. The sales staff could do with less attitude.

Chris Mestdagh

39 place du Grand Sablon, 1000 (513 44 18). Bus 48. **Open** 11am-6pm Mon-Sat; 11am-3pm Sun. **Credit** AmEx, DC, MC, V.

Belgium's answer to Paul Smith does men's and women's wear that is functional but fashionable. The collections are complemented by sleek red wood and softly lit surroundings. Underwear, socks and accessories are also sold.

Branch: 2 Orgelstraat, Antwerp 2000 (03 233 53 26); 18 Jan Breydelstraat, Ghent 9000 (09 225 53 46).

Francis Ferent

443-445 galeries de la Toison d'Or, 1050 (513 12 49). Métro Louise or Porte de Namur. **Open** 10am-7pm Mon-Sat. **Credit** AmEx, DC, MC, V.

The best selection of womenswear designer diffusion (less expensive) labels: DKNY, Giorgio Armani's Mani, and D&G are just a few lines that they carry. The sales staff are friendly but not overly so.

Gerald Watelet

268 avenue Louise, 1050 (647 35 50). Tram 93, 94/bus 38, 60. **Open** 10am-noon, 1.30-6pm, Mon-Sat (appointment recommended). **Credit** AmEx, DC, MC, V.

Belgium's only *haute couturier* to show in Paris, Watelet has cultivated a client list that includes Paola, Queen of Belgium. More of a stylist than an innovator, Watelet works in a studio above his showroom and receives important (ie loaded) customers personally.

Gianni Versace

64 boulevard de Waterloo, 1000 (511 85 59). Métro Louise/tram 91, 92, 93, 94/bus 34. **Open** 1-6.30pm Mon; 10am-6.30pm Tue-Sat. **Credit** AmEx, DC, MC, V.

Two floors (both marble-tiled), a sweeping white staircase and an opulent but airy atmosphere greet you here. The ground floor holds mostly womenswear and leather goods featuring Versace's trademark Medusa emblem. Menswear is upstairs.

Branch: 3 De Keyserlei, Antwerp 2018 (03 232 03 03).

Kaat Tilley

4 galerie du Roi, 1000 (514 07 63). Bus 29, 63, 66, 71. **Open** 10am-6pm Mon-Fri; 10.30am-6.30pm Sat. **Credit** AmEx, DC, MC, V.

The faerie-like décor and display of this store might make Tilley's whimsical womenswear seem twee, but taken away from this context, the knitwear, fur and ingeniously structured work. She also sells in New York and Japan, but this is her flagship boutique.

Natan

158 avenue Louise, 1050 (647 10 01). Tram 93, 94. **Open** 10am-6pm Mon-Sat. **Credit** AmEx, DC, MC, V.

A cross-pollenation of Armani's minimalist refinement and Saint Laurent's glamour best describes the creations of Edouard Vermeulen, the designing force behind Natan. On offer is high-end-of-the-market ready-to-wear for women with cash to spare. Belgium's Queen Paola is a fan.

Branch: 5 Schuttershofstraat, Antwerp 2000 (03 225 17 72).

Olivier Strelli

72 avenue Louise, 1050 (512 56 07). Tram 93, 94. **Open** 10am-6.30pm Mon-Sat. **Credit** AmEx, DC, MC, V.

If Chris Mestdagh evokes Paul Smith, Olivier Strelli is more Calvin Kleinish: classic suits and separates for men and women, rendered with a twist to bring the look up to the minute. There is also a lower-cost line called 22 Octobre.

Creations by top Belgian designers are available at **Stijl Men/Women** *on rue Antoine Dansaert – see page 137.*

Ganesh & Co *can ring your bell – Indian bicycles for riding round Antwerp.* *See page 145.*

Branches: 14 galerie Louise, 1050 (511 43 83); 62 Frankrijklei, Antwerp 2000 (03 233 51 36); Huidevetterstraat, 24 Nieuwe Gaanderij, Antwerp 2000 (03 231 81 41).

Stijl Men/Women

74 rue Antoine Dansaert, 1000 (512 03 13). Metro Bourse/bus 63. **Open** 10.30am-6.30pm Mon-Sat. **Credit** AmEx, MC, V.

Downtown Mecca for trendy professionals. The industrial slate and steel interior under cold lighting shows off the collections of Dries van Noten, Dirk Bikkembergs and Ann Demeulemeester, designers who put Belgium on the fashion map. This is avant-garde fashion made accessible.

Thierry Mugler

80 avenue Louise, 1050 (502 64 22). Tram 93, 94. **Open** 10am-6.30pm Mon-Sat. **Credit** AmEx, DC, MC, V.

Bearing the trademark Mugler powder-blue, streamlined interior, this exclusive shop sells womenswear for hourglass figures and menswear for the perfect V-torso. A whiff of Mugler's fragrance Angel permeates the air, and the service ranges from imperious (older staff) to obsequious (younger).

Via della Spiga

42 rue Antoine Dansaert, 1000 (502 20 97). Metro Bourse/bus 63. **Open** 10.30am-6.30pm Mon-Sat. **Credit** AmEx, DC, MC, V.

Another slate-grey and bare-brick wall joint,Via della Spiga sells high-priced casual wear for men and women by Dolce & Gabbana, Romeo Gigli and various other trendy Italian designers.

Mid-range

Privé Joke

8 rue des Riches Claires, 1000 (502 73 68). Métro Bourse or Anneessens. **Open** 11am-7pm Mon-Sat. **No credit cards.**

Kangol, Hang Ten and Daniel Poole are some of the trendy labels sold at this hot spot for club kids. You can catch the latest info on raves around Belgium, and a DJ comes in regularly to spin house, techno and other dance sounds.

Ranch Market

117 rue Neuve, 1000 (217 42 01). Métro Rogier. **Open** 10am-6pm Mon-Sat. **Credit** MC, V.

Decorated with Americana and Canadiana (weathered licence plates, old Coca-Cola posters, hunting trophies and flags), Ranch Market stocks style staples such as Levi's and Oxbow sportswear as well as more daring T-shirts by Belgian madman designer Walter van Beirendonck. Baseball caps, hiking boots and leather jackets are also sold.

rue blanche

9 rue Antoine Dansaert, 1000 (512 03 14). Métro Bourse/bus 63. **Open** 1-6.30pm Mon; 11am-6.30pm Tue-Sat. **Credit** AmEx, DC, MC, V.

Comfortable sportswear for the everywoman with the accent on simple silhouettes in quality fabrics. The collection, including knits and some outerwear, is designed by Belgian Marie-Chantal Regout. It's all a bit androgynous, but the accessories on sale add a feminine touch.

The Western Shop

77-79 boulevard Adolphe Max, 1000 (219 55 17). Métro Rogier. **Open** 10am-7pm Mon-Sat. **Credit** AmEx, DC, MC, TC, V.

The faux-barn interior and the country music warbling in the background create the right ambience for browsing round cowboy boots, fringed leather jackets, silver belt buckles and other western wear. Alterations and repairs can be ordered on items bought in the store.

Zara

8-10 avenue Louise, 1050 (511 37 60). Metro Louise/tram 93, 94. **Open** 10am-6.30pm Mon-Thur; 9.30am-7pm Fri, Sat. **Credit** AmEx, DC, MC, V.

A sort of upmarket Hennes & Mauritz for the whole family. The attraction of this polished redwood and cream store is the ever-changing stock, which means every two weeks or so the shopper can choose from a whole new variety of clothing. The Spanish chain has an even more luxuriously appointed store in Antwerp that belies their relatively cheap prices.
Branches: 48-50 rue Neuve, 1000 (219 87 47); 58 Meir, Antwerp 2000 (03 226 44 25).

Budget

Hennes & Mauritz

123 rue Neuve (City 2), 1000 (223 23 31). Métro Rogier. **Open** 9.30am-6.30pm Mon-Thur; 9.30am-7pm Fri, Sat. **Credit** AmEx, DC, MC, V.

Trendiest of the three H&M shops in Brussels, with a garage-like, MTV-friendly atmosphere. The large floor space crammed with merchandise makes for manic shopping.
Branches: 36 rue Neuve, 1000 (218 38 37); 80 rue Neuve, 1000 (219 03 40).

Mango

148 rue Neuve, 1000 (219 09 74). Métro Rogier. **Open** 10am-7pm Mon-Sat. **Credit** AmEx, DC, MC, TC, V.

Adolescent trendy to street-smart casual womenswear is sold in this Brussels branch of the Spanish chain. It wins no points for its bland, nondescript atmosphere, but bargain-hunters can't be choosers.
Branches: 7-9 chaussée d'Ixelles, 1050 (502 32 32); 66 Turnhoutsbaan, Wijnegem 2110 (03 354 28 54).

Second-hand

Les Enfants d'Edouard

175-179 avenue Louise, 1050 (640 42 45). Tram 81, 93, 94. **Open** *men's* 10am-7pm Mon-Sat; *women's/children's* 9.30am-6pm Mon-Sat. **Credit** AmEx, MC, V.

A swanky location, the good condition of its clothing and an excellent window display make it easy to forget that this is a second-hand store. Clothes by designers from Armani to Yamamoto are sold here.

L'Homme Chrétien

1 rue Marché au Charbon, 1000 (502 01 28) Tram 23, 52, 55, 56, 81. **Open** 11am-7pm Mon-Sat. **Credit** MC, V.

A lot of style, both good and bad, has been crammed into this tiny boutique that sells refashioned vintage clothes. Blazers and bell-bottoms from the 1970s are restructured for the 1990s, evening dresses going back to the 1930s are altered along with other garments to suit today's tastes. Technically new shoes – never worn before, but definitely from years gone by – are also sold. It's an ideal wardrobe trove for club-goers and willing fashion victims.

Idiz Bogam

162 rue Blaes, 1000 (502 83 37). Bus 20, 48. **Open** 10.30am-6.30pm daily. **Credit** DC, MC, V.

Edith Piaf warbling in the background, sepia walls and subdued lighting transport the customer to 1940s Paris in this cubbyhole of a shop. Vintage clothing – some preserved, some updated in-house – is sold.
Branch: 58 rue Aqueduc, 1050 (534 85 27).

Kalamazoo

38 rue du Midi, 1000 (502 72 81). Métro Bourse/tram 23, 52, 55, 56, 81. **Open** 10.30am-6.30pm Mon-Sat. **Credit** V.

Second-hand jeans, motorcycle boots and American football varsity jackets are all available in this hole-in-the-wall shop.

Look 50

10 rue de la Paix, 1050 (512 24 18). Métro Porte de Namur. **Open** 10am-6.30pm Mon-Sat. **No credit cards.**
Retro rules at Look 50, where the evening wear ranges from 1930s ballgowns to 1970s tuxedos.

Shoes

Daniel's Doc Shop

736 chaussée de Waterloo, 1180 (648 38 50). Tram 23, 90/bus 38. **Open** 10am-7pm Mon-Sat. **Credit** MC, V.
Ridiculously expensive in comparison to UK prices, but if you desperately need a pair of Doctor Martens, this store has the best selection in town.

Docksteps

28 avenue Louise, 1050 (514 59 93). Metro Louise/tram 91, 92, 93, 94. **Open** 10am-6.30pm Mon-Sat. **Credit** AmEx, DC, MC, V.
Selling their own brand ranging from men's hiking boots and deck shoes to women's dainty loafers, Docksteps also carries Harley Davidson motorcycle boots and accessories. It's situated at the start of chic avenue Louise, where most tourists find themselves at some point.

Hatshoe

83 rue Antoine Dansaert, 1000 (512 41 52). Métro Bourse/tram 23, 52, 55, 56, 81/bus 63. **Open** 10.30am-6.30pm Mon-Sat. **Credit** AmEx, DC, MC, V.
The name is misleading, as only footwear is sold here. The boots, mules, loafers, pumps and sandals (from makers such as Patrick Cox and Robert Clergerie) on sale walk a fine line between trendy and traditional.

Lilly's

52 rue Antoine Dansaert, 1000 (513 80 90). Tram 23, 52, 55, 56, 81/bus 63. **Open** 11am-7pm Mon-Sat. **Credit** AmEx, MC, TC, V.
Mid-priced (for Belgium) trendy Italian and French footwear for women is sold in this sun-yellow, petite boutique. The occasional thigh-high boot does feature, but clunky platforms, strappy heels and more sensible but stylish shoes are the norm. A small selection of knitwear is also sold.

Preiser

78 chaussée de Wavre, 1050 (511 27 19). Bus 71. **Open** 9am-6pm Mon-Sat. **Credit** AmEx, MC, V.
Most Belgian shoe stores carry only standard sizes, which makes Preiser special: men's sizes go from a European 36 to 52, women's from 31 to 44. The brands range from affordable to expensive, with Bally, Church's and Clarks sold alongside Timberland and Camel.
Branch: 59 rue du Midi, 1000 (511 26 02).

Underwear

Patricia Shop

158 rue Blaes, 1000 (513 36 48). Bus 20, 48. **Open** 9.30am-5.30pm Tue-Sat. **No credit cards.**
Most lingerie in Belgium is overpriced when compared to other countries, so bargain-hunting women make this shop a stop to catch deals on end-of-lines. The selection – crammed into the small, narrow store – runs from leopard-print and lace to no-nonsense cotton. Swimwear is also sold.

Stijl Underwear

47 rue Antoine Dansaert, 1000 (514 27 31). Tram 23, 52, 55, 56, 81/bus 63. **Open** 10.30am-6.30pm Mon-Sat. **Credit** AmEx, MC, V.
From the lacy garters and corsets of Chantal Thomass to the streamlined singlets of Calvin Klein and Crummay, Stijl Underwear is where fashion victims indulge in intimate apparel. It's all a bit pricey, but that's part of the fun.

Entertaining

Picard

75 rue Lombard, 1000 (513 07 90). Bus 34, 48, 95, 96. **Open** 9am-6.30pm Mon-Sat. **Credit** AmEx, DC, MC, V.
Masks, make-up and other festive wear are sold in this candy-coloured store. The stock spills over like Mardi Gras, with something for everyone. The jumbled and jam-packed window display makes this shop hard to miss.

Tailors

Maison de Gand

415 avenue Louise, 1050 (649 00 73). Tram 93, 94. **Open** 10am-7pm Mon-Sat. **Credit** AmEx, DC, JCB, MC, TC, V.
Housed in an early twentieth-century private house with most of its original interior preserved, Maison de Gand has created luxury apparel for men and women since 1981. Cufflinks in semiprecious and precious stones, quality cravats and other accessories are also on offer.

Fashion accessories

Christa Reniers

28 rue du Vieux Marché aux Grains, 1000 (514 17 73). Tram 23, 52, 55, 56, 81/bus 63. **Open** noon-7pm Thur-Sat. **Credit** AmEx, DC, MC, V.
Selling in Paris and New York, jeweller Reniers uses each new collection as an extension of the old: models are never deleted, which gives her mostly silver cufflinks, rings, bracelets and keyrings a sense of continuity. Her popcorn starbursts, melting teardrops and chain-combinations mix austerity with extravagance.

Delvaux

27 boulevard de Waterloo, 1000 (513 05 02). Métro Louise or Porte de Namur/tram 91, 92, 93, 94/bus 34. **Open** 10am-6.30pm Mon-Sat. **Credit** AmEx, DC, MC, V.
Belgium's answer to Louis Vuitton creates bags that are distinctive without being flashy. The telltale 'D' lets people know it's a Delvaux.
Branches: 22 boulevard Adolphe Max, 1000 (217 42 34); 31 galerie de la Reine, 1000 (512 71 98).

Elvis Pompilio

10 rue du Midi, 1000 (511 11 88). Tram 23, 52, 55, 56, 81/bus 34, 48. **Open** 10.30am-6.30pm Mon-Sat. **Credit** AmEx, DC, MC, TC, V.
The interior of this hat shop is *Aladdin*-meets-*Alice in Wonderland*: vivid-coloured bands adorn the walls, while kitsch bric-à-brac (a Barbie doll here, a velvet stuffed poodle there) peek out from certain areas in the spacious one-floor shop. Lavish is the word for the *chapeaux*: the Liège-born Elvis (yes, the name is real) almost singlehandedly brought headgear back into fashion in Belgium. A mingling of high drama with street-smart wearability characterises his collection of men's, women's and children's titfers, alongside which are sold parasols, handbags and other accessories.
Branch: 18 rue Lombard (511 11 88).

Ici Paris XL

63 rue Neuve, 1000 (219 22 07). Métro De Brouckère or Rogier. **Open** 9.30am-6.30pm Mon-Sat. **Credit** AmEx, DC, MC, V.
One of the largest stores of the chain, carrying the best selection of men's and women's fragrances in Belgium. Cosmetics

Brussels-based Liège-born ***Elvis Pompilio*** *has made headgear fashionable again in Belgium – chapeau bas, monsieur.*

Vanrijk '94

and toiletries are also available, with prices for designer products lower here than at the designer boutiques around town, making this something of a fragrance supermarket. *Giftwrapping. Tax free for exports worth 7000BF or more.*
Branches: 51 throughout Belgium. Call 511 33 06.

Kipling

111 rue Neuve, 1000 (223 08 62). Metro Rogier/tram 23, 52, 55, 56, 81, 90. **Open** 10.30am-6pm Mon-Thur, Sat; 10.30am-7pm Fri. **Credit** AmEx, DC, MC, TC, V.
This young, fresh and affordable Belgian leather goods label was one of the first to capitalise on backpack-street chic. Most of the models are in canvas and parachute fabric, but there are a few in leather.
Branch: 36a galerie Louise, 1050 (511 72 41).

Lorenzo Lebon

200 chaussée d'Ixelles, 1050 (646 35 01). Bus 71. **Open** 11am-7pm Thur-Sat (and by appointment). **No credit cards.**
Ostend native Lebon creates backpacks and handbags that have a no-nonsense utility despite their whimsical shapes (accordion or violin case, for example). His silver-walled boutique is downstairs from his showroom-cum-studio.

Swatch – Boutique de la Montre

34 boulevard de Waterloo, 1000 (511 36 86). Métro Louise or Porte de Namur/tram 91, 92, 93, 94/bus 34. **Open** 10am-5.30pm Mon-Fri. **Credit** AmEx, DC, MC, V.
Timepieces for the faddish are sold on this swanky street (Ralph, Giorgio and Gianni are just a stone's throw away).

Children

Fashion

Dujardin

82-84 avenue Louise, 1050 (512 75 75). Tram 93, 94. **Open** 10am-6.30pm Mon-Sat. **Credit** AmEx, DC, MC, V.
The BCBG (*bon chic bon genre*) set – the Belgian equivalent of Sloane rangers – come here to kit out their offspring, from newborns to pre-teens. The ground floor is devoted to infant and toddler sleepwear, playwear and quasi-formal attire, while the first floor holds school uniforms, macs and other clothing for children aged five and upwards.

Peau d'Zebre

40 rue du Midi, 1000 (513 05 28). Métro Bourse/tram 23, 52, 55, 56, 81. **Open** 10.30am-1pm, 2-6pm, Mon-Sat. **Credit** MC, V.
For the trendier child, Peau d'Zebre sells toddler and infant-sized versions of whatever's popular on the street and in the clubs at the moment. Moderately priced, the store is small, but very accessible, so it's worth a peep in.

Toys

Serneels

69 avenue Louise, 1050 (538 30 66). Tram 93, 94. **Open** 9.30am-6.30pm Mon-Sat. **Credit** AmEx, DC, MC, TC, V.
Expensive toys for kids of all ages are sold in this spacious shop, from baby dolls to roulette wheels. The stuffed animal and gambling game sections, with items imported from all over Europe and the US, are the most impressive.

Gifts

Aga

14 rue Plétinckx, 1000 (513 86 72). Tram 23, 52, 55, 56, 81. **Open** noon-6.30pm Mon-Fri; 10.30am-6.30pm Sat. **No credit cards.**
The earthenware and stoneware created by Belgian and Dutch craftspeople run from the raw to the refined: cow-print coffee cups with gold-horned trophy head handles, delicate art deco-esque teapots and tinted Japanese *raku* pottery. Aga also sells handmade and hand-dyed paper.

Au Grand Rasoir – Maison Jamart

7 rue de l'Hôpital, 1000 (512 49 62). Bus 34, 48, 95, 96. **Open** 9.30am-6.30pm Mon-Sat. **Credit** AmEx, MC, V.
Supplier to the Royal Court of Belgium, AGR has an exquisite selection of straight razors (with handles in mother of pearl, ebony and bone), high-quality kitchen cutlery and Swiss Army knives. The old-style service (the shop has been around since 1821) alone makes a visit worthwhile.

Candar

164 rue Blaes, 1000 (514 58 77). Bus 20, 48. **Open** 10am-6pm Tue-Sat; 10am-3pm Sun. **Credit** AmEx, DC, MC, TC, V.
A variety of scented candles, ceramics, dried flowers and spices are sold in this fashionably rough-hewn store. Ingredients to make your own candles are also sold.

Collector's Gallery

17 rue Lebeau, 1000 (511 46 13). Bus 34, 48, 95. **Open** 11.30am-1pm, 2.30-6pm, Tue-Sat; 11.30am-1.30pm Sun. **Credit** MC, V.
If vintage perfume bottles and Barbie dolls are up your alley, this shop is a must. Model trains and other toys round out the selection.

Courrier Sud

34 rue du Marché au Charbon, 1000 (514 57 09). Tram 23, 52, 55, 56, 81/bus 48. **Open** 10.30am-7pm Tue-Sat. **No credit cards.**
Moroccan and Egyptian lanterns hang above this bazaar-like mix of Asian, African and Latin American bags, jewellery and accessories. The jewellery, a main attraction, is mostly silver from Indonesia, which employs semiprecious stones such as lapis lazuli, amethyst and onyx.

Dans la Presse ce-Jour-là

126 rue Antoine Dansaert, 1000 (511 43 89). Bus 63. **Open** 11.30am-6.30pm Mon-Fri; 11.30am-5pm Sat. **Credit** V.
Looking for a birthday gift? What about an original copy of a French, Belgian, Swiss or even English newspaper printed on the date of the recipient's birth? This quaint little shop also does gift packages that include wine, port or Armagnac from the relevant year.

Histoire d'Eau

646 chaussée de Waterloo, 1050 (343 63 27). Bus 38. **Open** 11am-7pm Mon-Sat. **Credit** MC, V.
Luxury toiletries on sale here include almond shaving soap, originally produced in the 1930s, French and Italian shampoos in medicinal-looking retro bottles, and other potions and lotions to pamper yourself with. Histoire d'Eau could be described as an upscale Body Shop – less politically correct, but much more refined.

La Maison d'Art G Arekens

15 rue du Midi, 1000 (511 48 08). Tram 23, 52, 55, 56, 81. **Open** 10am-1pm, 2-6pm, Mon-Sat. **No credit cards.**
The reproductions and replicas of great works of art (Lempicka, Magritte and Memling are a few) sold here take a back seat to the religious icons on offer. Shiva, Vishnu and Buddha strike various poses among the crucifixes and ankhs in plaster, brass and other materials. Prices are reasonable, as most of the objects are decorative rather than authentic.

La Maison du Bridge

61 rue du Bailli, 1050 (537 43 85). Tram 81. **Open** 10am-1pm, 1.30-6.30pm, Tue-Sat. **No credit cards.**

The name's a bit misleading because every board game imaginable is sold here, along with larger table games. Gaming paraphernalia such as card mats and gambling chips are also sold, plus de luxe chess and backgammon sets. It's a fun place to browse around, even if you're not buying.

Ma Maison du Papier

6 galerie de la rue de Ruysbroek, 1000 (512 22 49). Bus 34, 48, 95. **Open** 1-7pm Wed-Fri; 3-7pm Sat (and by appointment). **No credit cards.**

Of interest for collectors, Ma Maison feels like a store of treasures waiting to be unearthed, with its drawers of prints, plaques and posters of art exhibits and adverts from the late 1800s to the present.

Nature Gallery

3 rue de la Reinette, 1000 (502 67 66). Métro Porte de Namur. **Open** 10am-6.30pm Mon-Sat. **Credit** MC, V.

An eco-friendly treasure trove of trinkets with a nature theme. Items sold range from botanical prints and aboriginal art to children's games and birdsong whistles. An in-store travel agency can even help you book a holiday tracking wolves in Quebec or swimming with dolphins.

Rêves d'Art et de l'Orient

146 rue Blaes, 1000 (514 31 40). Bus 20, 48. **Open** 9am-6pm Tue-Sat; 9am-2pm Sun. **Credit** AmEx, DC, MC, V.

An outpost of Far and Middle Eastern decorative objects, from Persian carpets to Indian carvings. Enriched with figurines in silver, bone and jade, totems and tapestries, the selection on display here is definitely worth a look.

Rosalie Pompon

65 rue Lebeau, 1000 (512 35 93). Bus 34, 48, 95, 96. **Open** 11am-6pm Mon; 10.30am-6pm Tue-Sat; 11am-4pm Sun. **Credit** AmEx, V.

An imperial toy-chest of home and fashion accessories, trinkets and cards for those with a juvenile style. The gold-leaf walls make the mobiles, circus wagons, ladybird paperweights and cartoon keyrings seem like *objets d'art*.

La Vie en Soie

433 chaussée de Waterloo, 1060 (347 04 97). Tram 92. **Open** 1.30-6.30pm Tue-Sat. **Credit** AmEx, DC, V.

It's worth going out of your way for the Indian silk sold here, which is dyed in a rainbow of colours and plethora of patterns, fashioned as blouses, neckties, scarves and other garments. The quality is higher than standard, which is reflected in the prices. Jewellery and games are also sold.

Flowers

Het Witte Gras

7 rue Plétinckx, 1000 (502 02 59). Tram 23, 52, 55, 56, 81. **Open** 9am-6pm Mon-Sat. **No credit cards.**

Fresh flowers spilling from terracotta pots and reed baskets or dried flowers hanging overhead offer a more artistic alternative to traditional twee arrangements. The prices are competitive too.

Stationery

Nias

2-4 rue Capitaine Cespel, 1050 (512 12 17). Métro Louise or Porte de Namur/bus 34. **Open** 9.30am-6pm Mon-Sat. **Credit** V.

Though seriously lacking in the customer service department, this store does sells a pretty good selection of quality stationery as well as photograph albums, schoolkids' backpacks, diaries and office supplies. But it's pricey – as befits this area of Brussels.

Hobbies, arts & crafts

Crafts

45 avenue Louis Lepoutre, 1060 (343 86 66). Bus 60. **Open** 10am-6pm Mon-Fri; 10am-5pm Sat; **No credit cards.**

Baubles and beads in metal, clay, wood and semiprecious stones to make your own jewellery are on offer here, with cord and clasps to get it all together.

L'Estampe

71 rue Blaes, 1000 (512 87 27). Bus 20, 48. **Open** 10am-12.15pm, 2-4pm, Tue, Thur-Sun. **No credit cards.**

Fashion sketches, hunting and historical scenes, and nature prints of animals, insects and fruit are arranged in a carefully calculated clutter to give the shopper the impression of sifting through rubble.

La Fiancée du Pirate

118 rue Blaes, 1000 (502 11 93). Bus 20, 48. **Open** 10am-2pm Tue, Thur, Sat, Sun (and by appointment). **Credit** AmEx, MC.

The smell of the sea hits you upon entering The Pirate's Fiancée, so to speak. Old chests and antique lanterns, aged maps and portholes from old wrecks are just some of the nautically themed items on display. There is also a selection of vintage postcards on sale.

Historic Marine

23 rue du Lombard, 1000 (513 81 55). Métro Bourse/bus 34, 48, 95, 96. **Open** 10.30am-7pm Mon-Sat. **Credit** AmEx, DC, MC, TC, V.

Blond-wood floors and white walls show off the boat-lover's paraphernalia (clocks, compasses, weather vanes) to good effect. HM's models come from the Maritime Museum in Paris, so they aren't exactly a bargain-hunter's dream.

Kasoeri

20 rue de la Paix, 1050 (514 22 51). Métro Porte de Namur. **Open** 10.30am-6.30pm. **Credit** AmEx, DC, MC, V.

The shelves of Indian cottons, wools, silks and linen range from subdued naturals to richly hued patterns. Run by Belgian Danielle Vanden Driessche, Kasoeri is a favourite of professionals. It also sells buttons of coral, coconut and shell.

Branch: 3 Wijngaardstraat, Antwerp 2000 (03 231 02 52).

La Maison du Timbre – Belgasafe

24 rue du Midi, 1000 (512 63 49). Métro Bourse/bus 34, 48, 95, 96. **Open** 9.30-11.30am, 1-5.30pm, Mon-Fri; 9.30am-12.30pm Sat. **No credit cards.**

This is just one of many stores specialising in stamps along rue du Midi, near the Grand Place. La Maison du Timbre sells not only the stamps of countries ranging from Austria to Zaire, but also philatelists' aids such as cutters and display books.

Sougné

33 rue Antoine Dansaert, 1000 (511 03 07). Tram 23, 52, 55, 56, 81/bus 63. **Open** 8.30am-6.30pm Mon-Sat. **No credit cards.**

Since 1929, Sougné has been selling a fine selection of fishing gear and outerwear. The art deco interior has a timeless charm and the service, sometimes glacially slow, is more personal than in the larger stores.

Les Tissus de Chien Vert

2 rue de Chien Vert, 1080 (411 54 39). Tram 18. **Open** 10am-6pm Mon-Sat. **No credit cards.**

A pool table on which to cut fabric, a boat to store it and a punching bag (just for customer amusement) make up just some of the quirky décor of this shop, which is a warehouse-cum-rec-room. There are two whole floors of fabrics, covering both the unique and the utilitarian, and the place itself is worth a few pictures.

Les Tissus du Sablon

34 rue Joseph Stevens, 1000 (502 48 60). **Open** 10.30am-12.30pm, 1.30-6.30pm, Tue-Sat. **Credit** V.
Former Miss Belgium Ilsa De Meulemeester opened this shop selling discounted exclusive, luxurious fabrics for home decorating in 1995. Cosy and quaint, Les Tissus du Sablon also offers consultations.

Auctions

Galerie Moderne

3 rue du Parnasse, 1040 (511 54 15). Métro Trône/bus 38, 54, 60, 95, 96. **Sales** twice monthly. **Viewing** preceding Fri-Sun.
One of the largest auction venues in Brussels, Galerie Moderne's first sale of the month features high-end-of-the-market arts and antiques. The second sells bric-à-brac and household odds and ends, often obtained through the owners' having gone bankrupt or owing back taxes.

Galerie Vanderkindere

512 rue Vanderkindere, 1180 (344 54 46). Tram 23, 90/bus 38. **Open** 9am-noon, 2-5pm, Mon-Fri. **Sales** phone for schedule and catalogue.
If seventeenth- and eighteenth-century art and *objets* are your cup of tea, this auction house is a must. Items coming under the hammer here include museum-quality collectibles.

Palais des Beaux Arts

10 rue Royale, 1000 (513 60 80). Métro Gare Centrale/ bus 29, 63, 66, 71. **Open** 10am-9pm Wed; 10am-6pm Thur-Sun. **Sales** every two months (phone for schedule).
The three-day sales held here have the largest selection of fine art and antiques elegantly displayed in huge exhibition rooms. These auctions also rank as some of the most expensive, so be prepared to spend.

Food

Bakeries & pâtisseries

Dandoy

31 rue au Beurre, 1000 (511 03 26). Tram 23, 52, 55, 56, 81. **Open** 8am-6.30pm Mon-Sat; 10.30am-6.30pm Sun. **No credit cards**.
Simply the best *speculoos* (traditional Belgian cinnamon biscuits) and frangipanes (small, almond-flavoured cakes) in Brussels are sold here. Belgian waffles can either be eaten in-store or taken away.
Branch: 24 rue Houblon, 1000 (513 48 48).

Le Pain Quotidien

16 rue Antoine Dansaert, 1000 (502 23 61). Tram 23, 52, 55, 56, 81/bus 63. **Open** 7.30am-7.30pm daily. **Credit** V.
Haute paysanne best describes this café-bakery, which sells and serves upmarket renditions of traditional French baked goods. Diners take their croissants and *café au lait* at a common dining table that is LPQ's effort to create instant intimacy. Light lunches and rich desserts are also sold.
Branches: are too numerous to list here.

La Parisienne

47 rue Washington, 1050 (648 29 69). Tram 81/bus 54. **Open** 7.30am-1pm, 2-7pm, Mon-Sat. **No credit cards**.
La Parisienne sells what are arguably the best croissants in Brussels: lighter yet richer than those from most of the city's bakeries. This is a dearer than average corner croissant shop, but definitely worth it.

Chocolate

Godiva

22 Grand Place, 1000 (511 25 37). Métro Bourse or De Brouckère. **Open** 9am-10pm Mon-Sat; 10am-10pm Sun. **Credit** AmEx, DC, MC, V.
Name-recognition and pretty packaging mean higher prices, but locals sniff that Godiva is average when it comes to Belgian chocolate (Neuhaus and Corné are deemed superior). Godiva's smaller shops mean more personalised service.
Branches: are too numerous to list here.

Leonidas

46 boulevard Anspach, 1000 (218 03 63). Métro De Brouckère. **Open** 9am-7pm daily. **No credit cards**.
This is the Mars bar of Belgian chocolates, which is not to disparage it at all: only the snootiest of Belgians would turn up their nose at Leonidas. Unlike the more expensive brands, Leonidas chocs (or pralines, to be more accurate) keep longer – probably because the others use fresh cream and butter. Service in the shops is assembly-line style.
Branches: are too numerous to list here.

Planète Chocolat

57 rue du Midi, 1000 (511 07 55). Métro Bourse. **Open** 9am-6.30pm Mon-Thur; 11am-6.30pm Sat; 1-6.30pm Sun. **Credit** MC, V.
While other chocolate shops just sell the finished product, here customers can get a look at how the bonbons are done. Confectioner Frank Duval tends two vats of constantly churning chocolate (one milk, one plain) and fashions bite-sized candies, bars and tablets out of various decorative moulds. A tearoom upstairs serves continental breakfasts.

Wittamer

12-13 place du Grand Sablon, 1000 (512 37 42). Tram 92, 93, 94/bus 34, 48, 95, 96. **Open** 8am-6pm Mon; 7am-7pm Tue-Sat; 7am-6pm Sun. **Credit** AmEx, DC, MC, V.
Although this is the most chic of Belgium's chocolate-makers, that doesn't exactly mean it's the best – just one of the priciest. The packaging is the most beautiful, though, which means a Wittamer box of chocs makes a more impressive gift. In one of the poshest parts of town, it also serves breakfast.

Delicatessens

L'Atelier Gourmand

470 rue Vanderkindere, 1180 (344 51 90). Tram 23, 90. **Open** 8.30am-7pm Mon-Sat. **No credit cards**.
A little out of the way, but worth the visit: Chef Richard Kopp prepares almost everything himself, from the breads used for the sandwiches to the gleaming white platters of French, Greek and other European specialities. It's all quite expensive, but the breakfast pastries are exceptional. Wines, oils and other upmarket cooking staples sold.

Au Suisse

73-75 boulevard Anspach, 1000 (512 95 89). Tram 23, 52, 55, 56, 81. **Open** 10am-8pm Mon, Thur, Fri; 10am-7.30pm Tue; 10am-9pm Sat; 5-9pm Sun. **No credit cards**.
A Brussels institution for nearly 130 years, this is the place where most people stop for a quick bite or a sandwich. The restaurant has a limited but delicious selection of cheeses, salads (such as tuna and herring) and veggies served from a counter on one side. The adjacent store sells pretty much the same sandwich fixings, including *filet américain* (a steak tartare-like concoction). Prices throughout are reasonable.

Health food

Den Teepot

66 rue des Chartreux, 1000 (511 94 02). Bus 47. **Open** 11.30am-7pm Mon-Sat. **No credit cards**.

Markets

Each of the 19 *communes* in Brussels has a market. The markets are usually one of two types: *brocante* (*rommelmarkten* in Flemish), which sells exclusively new and used goods, or markets that include food, plants and other items along with *brocante*. The following are the most popular markets in the city (plus a couple in Antwerp). Unless stated, no markets accept credit.

Sablon

The area around place du Grand Sablon (*tram 91, 92, 93, 94/bus 48*) is where old money (or discreet new money) shops for antiques, art and home furnishings. A small market featuring mostly collectibles (coins, china, stamps etc) takes place at weekends (10am-6pm Sat; 10am-2pm Sun). Acceptance of credit varies.

Grand Place

Brussels' Grand Place (*Métro Bourse/tram 23, 52, 55, 56, 81*) is the site of two markets. A medium-sized flower market takes place daily (8am-6pm) and there is a bird market on Sundays (7am-2pm) where you can browse around budgies, parakeets and other feathered friends.

Gare du Midi

The Marché du Midi (*Métro Gare du Midi/tram 23, 52, 55, 56, 81, 82, 90*) is reputed to be the second largest market in Europe, attracting throngs of residents and out-of-towners every Sunday morning. From 7am, stalls selling veg, fruit, fish and meat set up on disused train racks, under flyovers and in parking lots adjacent to the train station. There's a heavy Mediterranean flavour, with a maze of stands selling a wide variety of olives, cheese and fresh herbs and spices. Cheap clothing, cassettes of North African music, plants and flowers are also sold, the latter going for next to nothing as the market draws to a close, normally around 1pm.

Marolles

The flea market held on the cobblestoned Marolles square, place du Jeu de Balle (*bus 48*), takes place every day (7am-early pm, depending on the weather) and, quite frankly, features a lot of junk. But real finds are always lurking within the jumbled piles and boxes of the unattractive and the useless. Old vinyl records, costume jewellery, army coats and assorted furniture and home accessories make up the bulk of goods on offer. It's worth popping along to seek out diamonds in the rough.

Sjacherbeurs

The Sjacherbeurs in Antwerp (*9 Henri Van Heurckstraat, 2000*) is either loved or loathed. Held in an old auction hall, it feels like the garage sale from hell. The atmosphere wins no points, what with cigarette smoke clouding the fluorescent-lit air and a mishmash of junk that passes for merchandise. But, again, there are treasures amid the trash – depending on your taste – which includes videos, used bicycles, CDs, ceramics, hardware and odd items such as bubble-gum-flavoured condoms with an expiry date that urges you to have sex pretty soon.

Antwerp

The Antwerp Sunday market, located near the Bourla Theatre, is a decidedly more northern affair, with live poultry and pets for sale as well as food, toys and other new and used items.

Reputedly the second largest market in Europe, Sunday morning's **Marché du Midi**.

Shopping in Antwerp

Fashion

Coccodrillo

9A/B Schuttershofstraat, Antwerp 2000 (03 233 20 93). **Open** 10am-6pm Mon-Sat. **Credit** AmEx, DC, MC, V.

The collections of Prada, Dirk Bikkembergs, Patrick Cox and Joan & David are well represented at this mecca of fashion footwear.

Dany-May

36 Frankrijklei, Antwerp 2000 (03 233 97 35). **Open** 10am-6.30pm Mon-Sat. **Credit** AmEx, DC, MC, TC, V.

Showcasing the younger, trendier (but still traditionally chic) lines of Calvin Klein, Byblos and Iceberg, as well as other designers. It's located on the Meir, a main shopping street in Antwerp.

De Puzzel

43 Kammenstraat, Antwerp 2000 (03 233 90 69). **Open** noon-6.30pm Mon; 10am-6pm Tue-Sat. **Credit** AmEx, DC, MC, V.

Postcards and women's shoes are sold in De Puzzel, which takes advantage of its colonial décor by providing a café and lounge area for weary shoppers. Thigh-high leather and utilitarian work boots, platform trainers and sensible brogues are stocked. The postcard styles include art deco and Roy Lichtenstein.

Dierckx

108 Frankrijklei, Antwerp 2000 (03 233 23 93). **Open** 9.30am-6.30pm Mon-Fri; 9.30am-6pm Sat. **Credit** AmEx, DC, MC, TC, V.

For over a century, Dierckx has been the pre-eminent name in Belgian bespoke tailoring. Men's and women's suits are sold in this finely appointed shop.

Dries van Noten

16 Nationalestraat, Antwerp 2000 (03 233 94 37). **Open** 10am-6.30pm Mon-Sat. **Credit** AmEx, DC, JCB, MC, V.

One of the designers who helped launch world interest in Flemish fashion, van Noten sells his own collections and selected items from Paul Smith in this landmark building dating from 1886. The men's and the women's floors are decorated with late nineteenth-century furniture, complemented by contemporary lighting and furnishings. Jewellery by Belgian duo Wouters & Hendrickx is also on sale.

Esprit

52 Meir, Antwerp 2000 (03 233 60 20). **Open** 10am-6pm Mon-Fri; 10am-6.30pm Sat. **Credit** AmEx, DC, MC, V.

A bargain-priced store that has spent on its interior: three floors of steel tubing and grating give the Antwerp branch an industrial feel. The Brussels stores are blander, with blond wood that lets the clothes grab your attention. **Branches**: 40 avenue de la Toison d'Or, 1050 (512 32 67); 4-6 rue Neuve, 1000 (219 57 68).

SN3

48 Frankrijklei, Antwerp 2000 (03 231 08 20). **Open** 10am-6.30pm Mon-Sat. **Credit** AmEx, DC, MC, V.

Called 'Snoopy 3' with something less than affection by some locals, this designer boutique carries the principal collections by the likes of Chanel, Prada, Lacroix and Claude Montana. Despite a tradition of being snobbish and a touch sterile (two floors of streamlined plate glass and flattering soft lighting), SN3 is still worth a visit.

XSO

13-17 Eiermarkt, Antwerp 2000 (03 231 87 49). **Open** 10am-6pm Mon-Fri; 10am-6.30pm Sat. **Credit** AmEx, DC, MC, V.

The décor is a mix of Japanese purity (white walls, slate floors) and Italian flourishes (lanterns), which is appropriate with two sections, one dedicated to Issey Miyake and the other to Romeo Gigli. The lower-priced G Gigli collection is housed in a boutique within XSO.

Jewellery & watches

Ginotti

3 Appelmansstraat, Antwerp 2018 (03 231 56 92). **Open** 2-6pm Mon; 10am-12.30pm, 2-6.30pm, Tue-Sat. **Credit** AmEx, DC, MC, TC, V.

These days it's hard to impress anyone with a Rolex, Cartier or Breitling – with so many good counterfeits around, it's difficult to tell who's wearing the genuine article. That's why Ginotti sells the really exclusive names in watches – Blancpain, Audemars Piguet and relative newcomers Daniel Roth and Franck Muller – that start at about £3,000 a pop.

Nadine Wijnants

26 Kloosterstraat, Antwerp 2000 (03 226 45 69). **Open** 11am-6pm Tue-Sat. **Credit** MC, V.

One of the top young jewellery designers in Belgium, Wijnants creates charming trinkets with semiprecious stones and oxidised or sterling silver, bronze and gold plate. Incorporating influences that run from India to street style, Wijnants always aims to make her collections affordable. She does customised jewellery too.

Health & beauty

Optometrix

43 De Nieuwe Gaanderihji, Antwerp 2000 (03 231 93 21). **Open** 10am-6pm Mon-Sat. **Credit** AmEx, DC, V.

High-fashion spectacle frames such as Calvin Klein, Matsuda, Alain Mikli and Beausoleil are sold at this Antwerp branch of a Belgian chain.

Sirenzo

61 Leopoldstraat, Antwerp 2000 (03 231 29 68). **Open** noon-6pm Mon; 11am-6pm Tue-Sat. **Credit** MC.

A recent addition to the New Age scene, Sirenzo sells crystals and Tarot cards in addition to herbs and vitamins. Books are also sold, but almost exclusively in Dutch.

Soap

13 Plantinkaai, Antwerp 2000 (03 232 73 72). **Open** 9am-8pm Tue-Fri; 9am-5pm Sat (booking advisable). **No credit cards.**

The salon in Belgium where the ultra-stylish get their hair dyed, fried or laid to the side. The interior features large paintings of Japanese superhero art and milky fluorescent colours, and it has been the backdrop for more than a few fashion shoots. Unlike Brussels salons, everyone speaks fluent English – a must if you're trying to get your hairdresser to understand what look you're striving for.

Interiors

HaZorFim

20 Schupstraat, Antwerp 2018 (03 227 16 66). **Open** 10am-6pm Mon-Fri; 10.30am-2pm Sat. **Credit** AmEx, DC, MC, V.
This is a factory outlet of the 43-year-old Israeli manufacturer, which explains the reasonable prices for high-quality silver pieces. Platters, gondola-shaped bowls, picture-frames, champagne buckets and jewellery boxes are just some of the merchandise on offer.

Jos Hofmans

42&53 Kloosterstraat, Antwerp 2000 (03 233 89 29). **Open** 11am-6pm daily. **No credit cards.**
The chances of getting a bargain here are increased by the fact that there is so much junk on offer: you have to dig deep through these two depots of bric-à-brac to reach something of value, but it's also worth a stop just to have a peek in.

Nine D

9B Schuttershofstraat, Antwerp 2000 (03 232 42 99). **Open** noon-6.30pm Mon; 10.30am-6.30pm Tue-Sat. **Credit** MC, V.
Natural fabrics, comfortable wooden furniture and wholesome food in a soft-hued setting as cosy as your own living room. Most of the furniture is designed by proprietor Nathalie van Reeth, but French tableware is also on offer.

N Vrouyr

6-8 Komedieplaats, Antwerp 2000 (03 232 36 87). **Open** 2-6pm Mon; 9.30am-12.30pm, 2-6pm, Tue-Fri; 10am-12.30pm, 2-6pm, Sat. **Credit** AmEx, MC, V.
Since 1920, this spacious Antwerp store has been selling luxury carpets from the Near, Middle and Far East. N Vrouyr is a member of the prestigious Belgian Chambre des Antiquaires.

Oude Bureaus, Oude Spiegels

68 & 79 Kloosterstraat, Antwerp 2000 (03 238 73 62). **Open** noon-6pm Mon-Sat; 2-6pm Sun. **No credit cards.**
The name translates as 'Old desks, old mirrors', which pretty much sums up the late nineteenth- and early twentieth-century English and German office furniture and French ornate mirrors on sale.

Scapa of Scotland

16 Huidevetterstraat, Antwerp 2000 (03 227 38 54). **Open** 10am-6.30pm Mon-Sat. **Credit** AmEx, DC, MC, V.
Ralph Lauren is the name that immediately springs to mind upon entering this two-floor store: Turkish, Irish and Austrian are a few of the cultures influencing the clothes and home furnishings on display. The ground floor is mostly British-inspired apparel, while upstairs you find patchwork cushion and duvet covers, Indian brass statuettes and teak and walnut cupboards arranged in the perfect home setting.
Branch: 9A boulevard de Waterloo, 1000 (514 26 98).

't Koetshuis (Chelsea)

62 Kloosterstraat, Antwerp 2000 (03 231 36 43). **Open** noon-6pm Tue-Fri; 1-6pm Sat, Sun. **No credit cards.**
This store's official name is Chelsea, but 't Koetshuis (literally 'the carriage') is what you'll find written in large letters over the front door. The art deco and art nouveau furnishings – large and small – are chosen and displayed with care, which means the proprietor clearly knows the value of the pieces, therefore bargain-hunters beware. On the first floor there is a cosy, rustic café-bar that serves soup and drinks.

Leisure

Ganesh & Co

19 St Katelijnevest, Antwerp 2000 (03 226 95 59). **Open** 10am-6pm Tue-Sat. **No credit cards.**
Started by Johan Declerck and Peter Auwrex as a green alternative to city travel, Ganesh & Co provides Indian bicycles for rent and for sale. Indian jewellery and trinkets are also on sale here, with proceeds going to a variety of relief projects in India.

USA Import

75 St Jacobsmarkt, Antwerp 2000 (03 232 04 29). **Open** 10am-6.30pm Mon-Sat. **No credit cards.**
A favourite of DJs, USA Import sells mostly vinyl dance music, including house, techno, garage, jungle and ambient. For the most part, prices are surprisingly competitive with those in New York and London, the cities from which most of USA Import's stock originates.

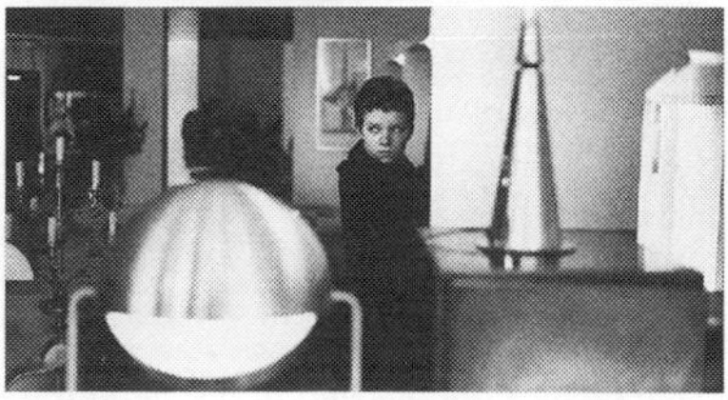

The **Galerie du Prince** *– part of the beautiful Galeries St Hubert which date back to 1846.*

It may be off the beaten track, but Den Teepot has a good selection of healthy snacks and more substantial food, frozen or fresh. Health and beauty products from ginseng shampoo to eastern massage oils are also available.

International cuisine

African Asian Foods

25 chaussée de Wavre, 1050 (514 03 86). Métro Porte de Namur. **Open** 9am-8pm Mon-Sat. **No credit cards.**
In the heart of Matonge – the Zairean quarter of Brussels – AAF is one of many grocers selling African produce. Foodstuffs stocked here include salted fish, oils, fruits and vegetables such as yams and African peppers that make *jalapeños* seem mild.

La Ferme Landaise

41 place Ste Catherine, 1000 (512 95 39). Metro De Brouckère/tram 23, 52, 55, 56, 81. **Open** 8.30am-6pm Mon-Sat. **Credit** AmEx, DC, MC, V.
Duck liver pâté, Sauternes and prepared specialities of the South of France. Special orders are also made up for gifts.

Magasin Tagawa

119 chaussée de Vleurgat, 1050 (648 59 11). Tram 81, 93, 94/bus 38, 60. **Open** 9.30am-7pm Mon-Sat. **No credit cards.**
The place to go for Japanophiles, though prices are distinctly upmarket. At the front are Japanese publications and videos, while the back and upstairs hold drinks and a wide selection of food, including fresh and frozen fish. Prepared dishes are also sold, as well as Japanese beer and over 40 different brands of saké.

MTM

25-27 boulevard d'Ypres, 1000 (219 88 91). Métro Yser/tram 18. **Open** 9am-6pm Tue-Sat. **No credit cards.**
The warehouse for the former 'morning market' of the area, MTM sells a variety of north African fresh herbs, spices and other ingredients from coriander to couscous. Henna, tea services and other non-food items are also sold.

Sun Wa Chinese Supermarket

1 rue de la Vierge Noire, 1000 (512 58 33). Tram 23, 52, 55, 56, 81. **Open** 9am-7pm Mon-Sat. **No credit cards.**
A favourite of expats. Despite the name, Sun Wa sells a variety of British and American hard-to-find (in Belgium, at least) food items, such as ginger beer, allspice and HP sauce, as well as Asian staples such as basmati rice, ginseng and a whole range of spices. Next door is smaller Thai store, which has keyrings, parasols and other souvenirs as well.

Drink

Beer, wine & spirits

Alexopoulos Frères

17 boulevard d'Ypres, 1000 (219 73 07). Métro Ste Catherine/tram 18. **Open** 8.30am-6pm Mon-Sat. **No credit cards.**
If you've a taste for retsina or ouzo, the brothers Alexopoulos is worth a visit. Other Greek wines and spirits are also sold, but there is a catch: most are sold in quantities of at least 6 or 12 bottles.

Bière Artisinale

174 chaussée de Wavre, 1050 (512 17 88). Métro Porte de Namur. **Open** 11am-7pm Mon-Sat. **Credit** AmEx,DC, MC, V.
With over 400 Belgian beers to choose from, you're bound to find something to satisfy your thirst. Most beers have a particular glass in which they should be served, and BA carries them. Gift packages are also sold.

Coffee & tea

De Boe

36 rue de Flandre, 1000 (511 13 73). Métro Ste Catherine. **Open** 9am-1pm, 2-6pm, Tue-Sat. **Credit** AmEx, V.
For over 100 years, De Boe has been selling coffee (both new mixes and traditional flavours such as arabica) and teas from around the world. Fine wines and chocolate are also sold, along with a good selection of dried fruits.

La Maison du Thé

11 rue Plattesten, 1000 (512 32 26). Tram 23, 52, 55, 56, 81/bus 48. **Open** 9am-6pm Tue-Sat. **Credit** V.
Choose from the 50 teas on offer and displayed in large tins. Ceramic and china teapots are also sold.

Home furnishings

Carpets

Au Tapis Volant

7 place du Jeu de Balle, 1000 (511 01 63). **Open** 9.30am-6pm Tue-Sat; 9.30am-1.30pm Sun. **Credit** AmEx, V.
This hole-in-the-wall shop has a good selection of carpets from north Africa, the Middle East and parts of Asia, but you do have to sort through the lot – especially because many so-called north African carpets are actually produced in Belgium, a leading textile centre. Haggling can get you a

VAT facts

Visitors living outside the European Union (EU), who stay no longer than three months, can claim back value-added tax – TVA in French, BTW in Flemish. In Belgium, this currently stands at 21 per cent. The catch is that you'll probably have to spend over 7000BF or 10000BF, depending on the shop, to benefit from this rebate. However, the procedure is simple: take along your passport when shopping, fill in a form after your purchase (which the salesperson will stamp) and hand the document to the customs official at the airport or port (officials may want to see the goods). There is normally a six to nine-week wait for the VAT refund, and payment is made by cheque or accreditation to your credit card. Not all shops offer this scheme (usually, the more expensive the shop, the more likely it is to have this set-up), so it's best to check before spending any money. If you are having goods shipped directly from the shop to somewhere outside the EU, you can often persuade the seller to deduct the VAT prior to payment. But bear in mind that not all shop assistants are as well-informed about this system as they should be.

better price, but you are at a disadvantage if they hear a foreign (that means non-French-speaking) accent.

Didden

66 rue Blaes, 1000 (512 72 85). Bus 20, 48. **Open** 9am-6pm Mon-Fri; 9am-6pm Sat; 10.30am-2.30pm Sun. **Credit** MC, V.
The huge sign outside reads 'Tapis Brettar', Didden's former incarnation. It carries a wide variety of carpets, from the offbeat American flag pattern to an Afghan model.

Crystal

Cristallerie Anspach

123 boulevard Anspach, 1000 (512 76 96). Tram 23, 52, 55, 56, 81/bus 48, 95, 96. **Open** 9am-6.30pm Mon-Sat. **Credit** AmEx, DC, MC, V.
Baccarat, Waterford, Val Saint Lambert and Lalique are all well represented in this shop. The décor wins no prizes, but the pieces are actually better served by being displayed in such an austere environment.

Furniture

Dominique Rigo

154 avenue Louise, 1050 (649 95 94). Tram 93, 94. **Open** 10am-6.30pm Mon-Sat. **No credit cards.**
Upmarket store selling reproductions of classic furniture design from masters such as Corbusier and Mackintosh. High-gloss, streamlined Italian and Scandinavian furniture for the home and office is Rigo's speciality.

Max

90 rue Antoine Dansaert, 1000 (514 23 27). Tram 23, 52, 55, 56, 81/bus 63. **Open** 10.30am-6.30pm Tue-Fri; 11am-6pm Sat. **Credit** AmEx, V.
1950s-inspired furniture with 1990s whimsy: think kidney-shaped coffee tables and high-backed *Jetsons*-style chairs, and you get the picture. Lamps, vases and other smaller home furnishings are more affordable.

Silverware

Coutellerie du Roi

27 passage du Nord, 1000 (217 54 94). Métro Rogier/tram 23, 52, 55, 56, 81. **Open** 9.30am-6.30pm Mon-Sat. **Credit** AmEx, MC, V.
If it's got a blade, you'll find it at the Coutellerie du Roi: cigar- and sugarcube-cutters, along with more traditional knives and scissors.

Antiques

Ars Islamica

33 rue Blaes, 1000 (512 80 60). Bus 20, 48. **Open** 2.30-6pm Tue, Wed; 2-6pm Thur, Fri; 10am-1pm, 2.15-5pm, Sat; 10am-1pm Sun. **No credit cards.**
Turkish cigarette cases, Moroccan teapots, Egyptian prints and various other Middle Eastern and North African objects make up the sparsely displayed stock of this tiny but quite fascinating store.

Espace

38 & 63 rue Blaes, 1000 (512 10 52). Bus 20, 48. **Open** 11am-5pm Tue-Thur, Sat, Sun; 1-5pm Mon, Fri. **No credit cards.**
Less polished than most antique shops, but not as grungy as a garage sale. Espace specialises in eighteenth- and nineteenth-century European furniture, including grandfather clocks and wardrobes – most of it suitable for a colonial home. Restorations are done too.

Collectibles

L'Ame des Rues

49 boulevard Anspach, 1000 (217 59 67). Mètro De Brouckère/tram 23, 52, 55, 56, 81. **Open** noon-6pm Mon-Sat. **No credit cards.**
Film memorabilia is stocked here, including posters, soundtracks and T-shirts. A special section is devoted to *Star Trek*.

Style & Kezoen

124 rue Blaes, 1000 (387 01 22). Bus 20, 48. **Open** 9am-2pm Tue, Thur-Sat. **No credit cards.**
Vintage fountain pens from famous makers such as Parker, Mont Blanc and Sheaffer are bought and sold here. The shop also does repairs.

Records, tapes & CDs

Fnac

City 2, rue Neuve, 1000 (209 22 11). Métro Rogier/tram 23, 52, 55, 56, 81, 90. **Open** 10am-7pm Mon-Thur, Sat; 10am-8pm Fri. **Credit** MC, V.
This Brussels branch of the French chain carries stereo and video equipment, CDs and cassettes (video and audio), and books and maps. The music section is a good mix of English and French-language recordings (Dutch is underrepresented), while the book department on the first floor features fiction, self-help, business and computer-related texts.

Free Record Shop

rue Fossé aux Loups, 1000 (217 88 99). Métro De Brouckère/tram 23, 52, 55, 56, 81. **Open** 10am-7pm Mon-Sat; noon-6pm Sun. **Credit** AmEx, DC, MC, TC, V.
Situated in a former concert hall, this is the only serious competitor to Brussels' Virgin Megastore. It has a good selection of Europop, soul, techno and disco, and 15 listening stations at which you can check out CDs before buying. A modest selection of videos is also available.
Branches: 147 rue Wayez (523 49 18); 42 chaussée d'Ixelles, 1050 (512 13 54).

Mélopée

12 rue Plattesten, 1000 (502 33 83). Tram 23, 52, 55, 56, 81. **Open** 10.30am-7pm daily. **Credit** MC, V.
This is a goldmine for film soundtrack fans. The selection runs from classic (*La Dolce Vita*) to kitsch (Mr Spock's *Music From Outer Space*). Prices are good too.

Musicanova

24 galerie d'Ixelles, 1050 (511 66 94). Métro Porte de Namur. **Open** 10am-6pm Mon-Sat. **No credit cards.**
Small in shop size, but boasting a fine selection of African music, particularly from Zaire, a former Belgian colony.

Music Mania

4 rue de la Fourche, 1000 (217 53 69). Métro De Brouckère/tram 23, 52, 55, 56, 81. **Open** 11am-6.30pm Mon-Fri; 11am-6pm Sat. **Credit** TC, V.
The best shop in town for rock and dance alternative CDs. Some vinyl is sold and the first floor has an eclectic choice of blues, country, rock and soul CDs going back to the 1950s.

Top 30

50 rue du Marché aux Poulets, 1000 (218 76 41). Métro De Brouckère/tram 23, 52, 55, 56, 81. **Open** noon-7pm Mon-Sat. **Credit** V.
The import store for American R&B in Brussels.

P Genicot – *see page 151 – and other second-hand booksellers enjoy beautiful surroundings in galerie Bortier.*

Virgin Megastore

Anspach Shopping Centre, 1000 (219 90 04). Métro De Brouckère/tram 23, 52, 55, 56, 81. **Open** 10am-7pm Mon-Sat; noon-6pm Sun. **Credit** AmEx, MC, V.

A letdown compared to other branches in the Virgin chain. It has only one floor, sells a smaller selection and is severely understaffed. Otherwise, it's as good as Brussels gets for pop, rock and classical, plus it has a fine selection of videos.

Second-hand

Arlequin

5 rue des Teinturiers, 1000 (512 42 59). Métro Bourse. **Open** 11am-7pm Mon-Sat. **No credit cards.**

This is one of the last stands for vinyl in Brussels, although a limited selection of CDs is also sold. This branch is better for punk, pop and older disco, while the branch listed below is exceptional for its reggae, soul and jazz funk sections. Most people end up leaving with something that they had forgotten they were looking for.

Branch: 7-8 rue Athênée, 1050 (512 15 86).

DiscoSold

97 boulevard Adolphe Max, 1000 (217 61 13). Métro Rogier/tram 23, 52, 55, 56, 81, 90. **Open** 10.30am-6.30pm Mon-Sat. **No credit cards.**

Eclectic selection of CDs, mostly American and British soul, pop and jazz with some classical thrown in. A small section at the back carries second-hand videos.

Branches: 110 rue de Stassart, 1050 (502 10 28); 644 chaussée d'Alsemberg, 1180 (345 15 90).

Newsagents & bookshops

City Press

67 boulevard Anspach, 1000 (511 11 22). Tram 23, 52, 55, 56, 81. **Open** 8am-7.30pm Mon-Sat. **Credit** AmEx, MC, V.

The most central newsagent in Brussels, with a good stock of English, German, French, Spanish, American and even Belgian periodicals.

Grande Muraille

5 galerie de la rue de Ruysbroek, 1000 (512 14 56). Bus 34, 48, 95. **Open** 2-6pm Mon; 10am-6pm Tue-Sat. **Credit** AmEx, V.

For wealth of choice, this is essentially the best store in Brussels for books, videos and brochures on traditional Chinese medicine, philosophy and cooking.

Librairie de Rome

50 avenue Louise, 1050 (511 79 37). Tram 91, 92, 93, 94. **Open** 7.30am-9pm daily. **Credit** AmEx, DC, MC, V.

The Librairie de Rome is the best place to get fashion mags and newspapers, English and non-English (they keep the *Sunday Times* – difficult to find in most shops – a few days longer for those who forget to pick it up). The store is narrow, so be ready to manoeuvre your way among the stacks. LR also sells books and mags on boating, bodybuilding, music and other interests.

Maxi-Livres

3-5 rue des Fripiers, 1000 (218 70 17). Métro De Brouckère/tram 23, 52, 55, 56, 81. **Open** 10am-11pm daily. **Credit** AmEx, DC, MC, V.

A branch of the inexpensive bookstore chain selling cookery, children's and photography tomes

The key to success – personalised service from the saviour of soles, **Francesco**. *See page 153.*

Branches: 15 avenue de la Toison d'Or, 1060 (502 03 55); City 2, level 1, 1000 (219 63 74).

Tropismes

galerie des Princes, 1000 (512 88 52). Métro Gare Centrale. **Open** 1.30-6.30pm Mon, Sun; 10am-6.30pm Tue-Thur; 10am-8pm Fri; 10.30am-6.30am Sat. **Credit** AmEx, MC, V.

The most Parisian of Brussels bookstores, with works on philosophy, architecture, fine arts and other topics. There is a small but good English-language section.

L'Univers Particulier

194 chaussée de Charleroi, 1060 (538 17 77). Tram 81, 91, 92. **Open** 10am-7pm Mon-Sat. **Credit** AmEx, MC, V.

The place for occult and New Age books in French, as well as tarot cards and other spiritual/psychic aids – though it's more for dabblers than devotees.

WH Smith

71-75 boulevard Adolphe Max, 1000 (219 27 08). Métro Rogier/tram 23, 52, 55, 56, 81. **Open** 9am-6.30pm Mon, Wed-Sat; 10am-6.30pm Tue. **Credit** AmEx, MC, V.

The place where folk in Brussels get most of their English-language reading matter. The magazine selection is better than the average Brussels newsagent and the staff do allow you to skim through (and sometimes even read) articles.

Second-hand books

De Slegte Bookshop

17 rue des Grands Carmes, 1000 (511 61 40). Métro Rogier/tram 23, 52, 55, 56, 81, 90. **Open** 9.30am-6pm Mon-Sat. **Credit** AmEx, MC, V.

In addition to four floors of discounted new books, De Slegte claims to have the largest selection of second-hand books in Belgium. Titles (in English, Dutch, German and French) cover mostly academia, esoterica and the classics, but sifting through the stock often yields treasures.

P Genicot

6 galerie Bortier, 1000 (514 10 17). Métro Gare Centrale. **Open** noon-7pm Mon-Sat. **Credit** AmEx, DC, MC, V.

Housed in a gorgeous gallery that is one of the city's best known secrets, this booklover's treasure trove sells books from the seventeenth century to the present, covering literature, art, science and more. A good 90 per cent of the stock is in French, with the remainder in English.

Pêle Mêle

55 boulevard Lemonnier, 1000 (513 49 12). Tram 23, 52, 55, 56, 81. **Open** 10am-6.30pm Mon-Sat. **No credit cards.**

The cheapest second-hand bookstore in Brussels, carrying a wide variety of French-language periodicals, comic books, novels and cookery volumes. Dutch, as usual, gets short shrift, but there is also a CD department.

Comics

Brüsel

100 boulevard Anspach, 1000 (502 35 52). Tram 23, 52, 55, 56, 81/bus 34, 48, 95, 96. **Open** 10.30am-6.30pm Mon-Sat. **Credit** AmEx, MC, V.

Expect nothing from Disney here. In Belgium, Tintin is the animated icon, and Brüsel has not only comic books, but also tea sets, posters and other collector's items. Brüsel also sells comics and souvenirs from English-language favourites, such as Calvin & Hobbes and The Far Side, but most books are in French, with Dutch, Italian, German and Spanish-language titles rounding out the stock.

Postcards

C'arts

25 rue Neuve, 1000 (217 58 99). Métro De Brouckère/tram 23, 52, 55, 56, 81. **Open** 10am-6pm Mon-Sat. **Credit** AmEx, DC, MC, V.

For wealth of selection, this gallery of cards is hard to beat: pop stars, supermodels, classic photographs and well-known artworks pop up on cards and a limited range of posters. Greeting cards in French and Flemish are also sold.

Health & beauty

Condoms

Condomi

37 rue des Pierres, 1000 (513 59 83). Tram 23, 52, 55, 56, 81. **Open** noon-6.30pm Mon-Sat. **No credit cards.**

A large and varied array of rubbers, from the utilitarian to the unique. Although many customers go for the novelty items, the shop more importantly sells condoms for those with special needs such as unusual size or allergies.

Opticians

Optic Nº1

25 avenue de la Toison d'Or, 1050 (514 53 34). Métro Louise or Porte de Namur. **Open** 10am-6.30pm Mon-Sat. **Credit** AmEx, DC, MC, V.

More of an eyeglass supermarket, despite the swanky names sold: Versace, Burberry and Karl Lagerfeld are just a few. You can also buy contact lenses and products for their care.

Saunas

Bio Etna Centre

31 place de Brouckère, 1000 (219 24 68). Métro De Brouckère/tram 23, 52, 55, 56, 81. **Open** 10am-10pm daily. **No credit cards.**

Billed as a relaxation centre where visitors can avail themselves of a sauna, Turkish steam bath and other facilities. Massage, shiatsu, reflexology, facials and peelings are other comforts that you can pamper yourself with. The swanky setting attracts a high-rolling clientèle and it's advisable to book an appointment.

Tattooists

European Tattoo Academy

23 boulevard Lemonnier, 1000 (502 43 52). Tram 23, 52, 55, 56, 81. **Open** 2-10pm Mon-Sat. **No credit cards.**

The environment is reassuringly antiseptic, with off-white walls and dentist-like chairs. Tattooist Michel takes on most jobs, large and small. Piercing is also done here.

Ethnic goods

Bali – Africa

154-156 rue Blaes, 1000 (514 47 92). Bus 20, 48. **Open** 9am-6pm Mon-Sat; 9am-3pm Sun. **No credit cards.**

Two stores have been merged into one here. The first floor and basement stock art, fabrics and jewellery from Africa and Asia. Kalimbas (buffalo-skin-covered drums) and other musical instruments take up most of one of the stores with prices ranging from inexpensive to exorbitant. Tiger balm, sandals and silver rings are the most affordable items. According to the owner, all proceeds go to help developing countries of the merchandise's origin.

Terres Nomades

152 rue Blaes, 1000 (502 38 90). Bus 20, 48. **Open** by appointment. **No credit cards.**

Proprietor Nouria Bajat travels to Morocco to gather her stock of handmade tiling. The fruits of her journeys are sold here, and consultations are given.

Sporting goods

Heaven

58 rue des Minimes, 1000 (502 45 60). Bus 34, 48. **Open** noon-6.30pm Tue-Sat. **Credit** MC, V.

Multicoloured kites, frisbees, boomerangs and other flying objects are sold for beginners and seasoned fanatics. Models include decorative cow and butterfly designs to more aerodynamic Cayman sport kites.

LocaBike

4 avenue Geo Bernier, 1050 (646 40 07). Bus 71. **Open** 10am-5pm Mon-Fri, Sun (and by appointment). **Credit** AmEx, DC, TC.

This company does bike rentals from four Brussels locations. Call the above number for details.

Ride All Day

39 rue St Jean, 1000 (512 89 22). Bus 20, 48. **Open** noon-6pm Mon-Wed, Fri, Sat. **No credit cards.**

Called RAD by most customers, this joint is as much a hangout for local skateboard junkies as it is a retailer of the 'boards themselves – the shop is located near a youth hostel, which explains a lot.

Pets

Royal Dog Shop

7 place de la Justice, 1000 (513 32 61). Bus 34, 48, 95. **Open** 9am-6pm Mon, Wed-Sat. **Credit** AmEx, DC, MC, V.

The name says it all. Come here for canine grooming products and doggie accessories from the luxurious to the naff, depending on your opinion of jumpers and jumpsuits for man's best friend.

Services

Dry cleaning

De Geest

41 rue de l'Hôpital, 1000 (512 59 78). Bus 34, 48, 95. **Open** 8am-7pm Mon-Fri; 8am-6.30pm Sat. **No credit cards.**

The official dry cleaners to the Belgian Court, De Geest cleans fur, leather and suede garments, carpets, curtains and upholstery. It also provides a pick-up and delivery service.

Shoe repairs

Francesco

13 rue Stassart, 1050 (no phone). Métro Porte de Namur. **Open** 9.30am-6pm Mon-Sat. **No credit cards.**

Francesco offers a more personalised shoe-mending and key-cutting service than you will get at most chains.

Mister Minit

City 2, 1000 (223 34 70). Métro Rogier. **Open** 10am-7pm Mon-Sat. **No credit cards.**

The fastest – if not exactly the best – shoe-menders in the city. You can also get keys cut here.

Branches: are too numerous to list here.

Museums & Galleries

Museums **155**
Art Galleries **162**

Museums

Brussels' laid-back museums are about diversity, charm and quality rather than quantity.

Chances are you weren't drawn to Brussels for its museums – there is no Louvre, no Hermitage, no MOMA here. Scoff if you will, but take note: beautiful plants have been known to sprout when towering trees don't steal all the light. In museum terms, this means that what Brussels lacks in size and reputation, it more than makes up for in diversity and charm. There is no shortage of smaller-scale museums with well-presented permanent displays, excellent temporary exhibitions and uncrowded spaces. Unlike other capital cities, there is no museum mob scene here, and when a good exhibit comes to Brussels, it is always possible to see it without endless queuing and bruised ribs. And if it doesn't come to town, bypassing Brussels for Paris or London (as happened with the 1995-96 Cézanne exhibition), it is more often than not only a three-hour journey away.

The main museums in Brussels are the two **Musées des Beaux Arts** (**Musée d'Art Ancien** and **Musée d'Art Moderne**) and the **Musées Royaux d'Art et d'Histoire** (*see below*). The first two, connected by an underground passage and situated by place Royale, contain mostly Belgian and Dutch works by the early masters, in addition to works by Bruegel, Rubens, Magritte, Ensor and Delvaux. The latter, situated in the Parc Cinquantenaire, houses one of the largest collections of artefacts from around the world and is best known for its antiquity collections. The museum has recently added several new rooms to its already vast collection, including *Eighteenth-Century Carriages* and *Feather Art of the Amazon Indians*.

The nearby **Palais des Beaux Arts** (*see chapters* **Art Galleries** *and* **Music: Classical & Opera**), on rue Ravenstein, has no permanent exhibition, but holds regular art exhibitions and is at the centre of the 1996 Europalia festival (*see chapter* **Brussels by Season**). Europalia '96 focuses on the architect Victor Horta and the exhibitions run from 4 October 1996 to 5 January 1997. Horta designed the Palais des Beaux Arts, which opened to the public in 1928, and his drawings,

Hergé meets Horta at the **Centre Belge de la Bande Dessinée**. *See page 156.*

scale models, furniture and photos will be on display. Another good venue for temporary exhibitions is the **Musée Communal d'Ixelles**, which organises strong and often controversial shows. In February 1996, it displayed Pierre Klossowski's work, which was deemed X-rated so the exhibition was open only to adults.

A major problem in the past with Brussels' museum scene has been a serious lack of publicity and recognition. Many museums are hard to find or are simply not advertised at all. Also, many close for the indispensable lunch hour, or are only open at inconvenient times, such as the **Musée David et Alice van Buuren** which opens its beautiful doors on Sunday and Monday afternoons. Try to fit that into your schedule.

Nevertheless, good news is nigh. Sixty of the city's 70 or so museums have recently decided to come together to form the Brussels Museum Council, receiving funds from both the Flemish and the French communities. Their goal is to improve the image of the city's museums and provide visitors with a museum map, better advertising, improved transport links and a museum card. The project was only just getting on its feet at time of writing, so expect no real changes until the end of 1996.

For a full list of the city's museums, contact the **Tourist Information Office** at 61 rue Marché aux Herbes (504 02 70).

Art & Architecture

Centre Belge de la Bande Dessinée

20 rue des Sables, 1000 (219 19 80). Métro Botanique, De Brouckère or Rogier/tram 55, 58, 81, 90/bus 38, 61, 71. **Open** 10am-6pm Tue-Sun. **Admission** 180BF; 120BF groups (of 15 or more); 60BF under-12s. **No credit cards.**

Oh, happy day, when this museum was completed! It masterfully combines two of the city's most appealing traditions, that of art nouveau architecture and the comic strip. An unholy union, some might say – would Horta and Hergé approve? – but the museum is pure joy. The building, a *grand magasin* from the early 1900s, was designed and built by Victor Horta. Despite its architectural importance, it was almost in ruins by the early 1980s. Saved from the wrecking ball, it was restored in 1986 and now triumphantly survives as home to the 'ninth art' (the seventh and eighth are cinema and television). Although *la bande dessinée* was not invented in Belgium, ever since Hergé brought Tintin to the world in 1929, Belgian artists have been at the forefront of the comic strip revolution. Spirou, Lucky Luke, Gaston Lagaffe and the Smurfs are all born of Belgian ink. The museum recreates the worlds of these and other cartoon heroes through photos, original documents and 3-D props in an engaging display called *The Museum of the Imaginary*. In another display, visitors follow the progress of a comic strip from initial conception to finished product. There are also original drawings from hundreds of artists, from Belgium and elsewhere: Hergé, HG Wells, Peyo, Jules Verne… And did you know that 1996 was dubbed The Year of the Comic Strip? For a full guide to the events and exhibitions throughout Belgium, contact the Tourist Information Office (*see above*).

Bookshop. Restaurant. Wheelchair: access.

There's no chance of the crowds getting in the way at **Musée Communal d'Ixelles**.

Musée d'Antoine Wiertz

62 rue Vautier, 1050 (648 17 18). Métro Trône or Maelbeek/bus 20, 34, 38, 60, 80, 95, 96. **Open** 10am-noon, 1-5pm, Tue-Fri (and alternate weekends). **Admission** free.

Antoine Wiertz (1806-1865) liked to think of himself as a bit of a Michelangelo, and his immense, ambitious paintings attest to the Renaissance influence on his work. His subject matters are mostly religious or philosophical, the tone dramatic, lofty, bold and often gruesome. This museum is supported by the royal art museums.

Musée d'Art Ancien

3 rue de la Régence, 1000 (508 32 11). Métro Gare Centrale or Parc/tram 92, 93, 94/bus 38, 60, 71, 95, 96. **Open** 10am-noon, 1-5pm, Tue-Sun. **Admission** free; *maps* 20BF. **Credit** AmEx, DC, MC, V (minimum 500BF).

A fine collection of works dating from the fifteenth century and continuing up to the nineteenth including an important collection of Pieter Bruegel paintings, namely *Landscape with the Fall of Icarus* and *Winter Landscape with Skaters and a Bird Trap*. Don't miss his miniature *Yawner*, which can be found in the hallway beyond the Bruegel room. The focus of the museum is on early Flemish and Dutch masters, but overall the collection is refreshingly diverse and includes several international names such as Gauguin and Seurat. Memling, Rubens and Jordaens are well represented, and other highlights include an astonishing triptych of *St Anthony's Temptation* by Hieronymus Bosch, Jacques-Louis David's depiction of Marat's death plus several of Ensor's macabre masks and skulls. The museum is connected to the Musée d'Art Moderne by an underground passage.

Shop. Wheelchair: access.

Musée d'Art Moderne

1-2 place Royale, 1000 (508 32 11). Métro Gare Centrale or Parc/tram 92, 93, 94/bus 38, 60, 71, 95, 96. **Open** 10am-1pm, 2-5pm, Tue-Sun. **Admission** free (*maps* 20BF). **Credit** AmEx, DC, MC, V (minimum 500BF).

Belgian art of the twentieth century is diverse and dynamic, but too often overshadowed by contemporaries from France, the USA and Germany. Here the Belgians do the overshadowing, even in the midst of Dufy, Chagall and Kokoschka. Surrealists Magritte (*see chapter* **History: Altered images**) and Delvaux (*see chapter* **Sightseeing: Eyes wide shut**) steal the show, but Pol Bury and his moving sculptures, as well as fauvists Spilliaert and Wouters, hold their own too. The museum entrance is closed at weekends, so use the Musée d'Art Ancien entrance on rue de la Régence and follow the signs through the underground tunnel to the twentieth-century collection. A major Delvaux retrospective will be held in 1997, from 21 March to 7 July.

Shop. Wheelchair: access.

Musée Charlier

16 avenue des Arts, 1210 (220 28 19). Métro Arts-Loi or Madou/bus 29, 63, 65, 66. **Open** 1.30-5pm Mon, Wed, Thur; 12.30-5pm Tue; 1.30-4.30pm Fri. **Admission** 100BF. **No credit cards**.

Guillaume Charlier was an active figure in the artistic world of Brussels in the late 1800s. Trained at the Beaux Arts in Brussels, he was taken under the wing of Henri van Cutsem, a collector and patron of the arts. Charlier actually moved into van Cutsem's house, the site of this museum, where he organised concerts and salon discussions for the city's intellectual and artistic circles. The house is crammed with beautiful tapestries (including a Credo tapestry from 1500), paintings by Ensor, Meunier and lesser known Belgian contemporaries of Charlier, and furniture. The guide book, which you'll need, costs 25BF but it exists only in Flemish or French. Concerts still take place in the concert hall (*see chapter* **Music: Classical & Opera**) and you can contact the museum for a full programme.

Legs eleven at the **Musée d'Art Ancien**.

Musée Communal d'Ixelles

71 rue Jean van Volsem, 1050 (511 90 84 ext 1158/reception ext 1459). Bus 38, 60, 71. **Open** 1-7pm Tue-Fri; 10am-5pm Sat, Sun. **Admission** *permanent collection* free; *temporary exhibitions* 200BF; 150BF 12-18s, over-60s, students, groups.

This remarkable little museum, founded in 1892 in a former slaughterhouse, is famed for its frequent temporary exhibitions, but its permanent collection is not half bad. In fact, it's charming. Amid the Toulouse-Lautrec posters, visitors will discover many Belgian artists, such as Magritte, of course, Delvaux, Spilliaert, Gustave de Smet and van Rysselberghe. The museum recently purchased *Portrait d'Albert Devis* by the nineteenth-century Belgian artist Henri Evenpoel, and it has recovered Picasso's *Guitar and Fruit Bowl*, which was stolen from the museum two years ago. A new wing was opened in 1994 and it blends perfectly into the old, creating a large, well-lit space for the paintings. This museum, like many others in Brussels, is slightly off the tourist trail and deserves far more attention than it gets.

Bookshop.

Musée de Constantin Meunier

59 rue de l'Abbaye, 1050 (648 44 49). Tram 93, 94/bus 38, 60. **Open** 10am-noon, 1-5pm, Tue-Fri (and alternate weekends). **Admission** free.

Constantin Meunier (1831-1905) is best known for his sculpture, although he actually began as a painter and only started sculpting at the age of 54. Much of his work is found in this museum, which was his home and studio, though several of his statues are dotted around Brussels, in the Musée d'Art Ancien, for example. The predominant theme in Meunier's work is social realism, portraying the experience of workers, miners and farmers.

Musée David et Alice van Buuren

41 avenue Léo Errera, 1180 (343 48 51). Tram 23, 90. **Open** 2-4pm Mon; 1-6pm Sun; *garden* 2-6pm daily (group visits for 12-30 people any day by appointment only). **Guided tours** *English, French or Flemish* on request. **Admission** 300BF; 200BF students; free under-10s; *garden only* 100BF; 50BF students. **Credit** V.

Have you ever wondered where the other two versions of Bruegel's *Landscape with the Fall of Icarus* were hidden? Well, one of them is here in the private collection of the late David van Buuren, a Dutch banker who struck rich in Belgium. His house, built in 1928 and run as a museum since 1973, is home to an incredible and little-known collection of paintings by, among others, Ensor, van Gogh and seventeenth-century Dutch masters. There are also several remarkable paintings by Gustave van de Woestyne, a close friend of the van Buurens. The house, a delightful art deco creation, is a splendid work of art and the gardens are as immaculate as the interior, enclosing a maze designed by René Péchère, the Belgian landscape architect. Definitely worth a detour.

Bookshop.

Musée Horta

25 rue Américaine, 1060 (537 16 92). Tram 81, 91, 92/bus 54, 60. **Open** 2-5.30pm Tue-Sun. **Admission** 120BF Tue-Fri; 200BF Sat, Sun. **No credit cards.**

Victor Horta founded a new architectural language – one that combined glass, iron and wood to create airy, fluid and rhythmic spaces. He is responsible for much of the art nouveau architecture in Brussels, some of which no longer exists. His Maison du Peuple was torn down in 1965 during Brussels' wrecking-ball period, but this house survived. Horta built it between 1898 and 1901 as his home and atelier. The attention to detail is astonishing and every functional element is transformed into a thing of beauty. The staircase is so rhythmic and light that you will practically float up it.

Musée Royal d'Art et d'Histoire

10 parc du Cinquantenaire, 1000 (741 72 11). Métro Merode or Schuman/tram 81, 82/bus 20, 28, 36, 67, 80. **Open** 9.30am-5pm Tue-Fri; 10am-5pm Sat, Sun. **Admission** 150BF; students 100BF; children 50BF. **No credit cards.**

This vast museum has one of the world's largest antiquity departments, with a huge collection of artefacts from the ancient worlds of Egypt, Rome, Greece and the Near East. Of considerable interest are the Roman Apamea mosaic – discovered in Syria in the 1930s by a team of Belgian architects – and *The Lady of Brussels*, an Egyptian statue dating back to 2650 BC. Other collections include: European art from the Middle Ages through art deco to the present; glass and metal work; and eighteenth-century carriages.

Bookshop. Wheelchair: access.

Science

Muséum de l'Institut Royal des Sciences Naturelles de Belgique

260 chaussée de Wavre, 1050 (627 42 11). Métro Trône or Maelbeek/bus 20, 34, 38, 60, 80, 95, 96. **Open** 9.30am-4.45pm Tue-Sat; 9.30am-6pm Sun. **Admission** 120BF; 90BF students, groups; 50BF disabled. **Credit** AmEx, MC, V.

The recommended first stop at the natural history museum, which is mainly a haven for schoolchildren, is the dinosaur department. There are 30 Iguanadon skeletons that were discovered in a Belgian coal mine plus, thanks to the robotic wonders of 'dinamation', blinking, wiggling and snarling dinosaurs at full and half scale. The insect department is informative and well displayed thanks to a recent facelift, which much of the rest of the museum is in need of. In all fairness, the whale department was, at the time of writing, undergoing renovation and a new wing was being added on.

Bookshop. Wheelchair: access.

Museum voor Midden-Afrika

13 chaussée de Louvain, Tervuren 3080 (769 52 11). Tram 44 (from Montgomery to end of the line). **Open** 10am-5pm Tue-Fri; 10am-6pm Sat, Sun. **Admission** 80BF; 40BF groups; 30BF 6-18s, students, groups; free under-6s. **Credit** AmEx, DC, MC, V.

At its inception in 1897, the Museum voor Midden-Afrika (called by its Flemish name because of its location in the Dutch-speaking *commune* of Tervuren) was devoted to glorifying the Belgian presence in Africa. It is difficult to visit without thinking of its less than noble past. King Léopold II (1865-1909), was named Sovereign King of the Congo Free State in 1885. He employed the British explorer Stanley to help him secure the territory, which the king milked for all it was worth. International outrage at the atrocities – murders, mutilations, the destruction of entire clans – committed against Africans in Léopold's haste to make as much money as possible forced the monarch to hand over the reins to the Belgian state in 1908. It is estimated that between 1896 and 1906 Léopold earned his country US$15 million and cost the territory at least 3 million lives. The permanent display consists of dioramas illustrating the ecological and conditions in central Africa, and rather musty-looking stuffed animals. A great favourite with schoolchildren is the insect and invertebrate section where, among other creepy-crawlies, giant earthworms are preserved for eternity in formaldehyde. In 1995 the museum unearthed 250 stunning pieces, of which half had never been seen by the public, for an exceptional exhibition, *Treasures from the Africa Museum*. The display thrust the somewhat drowsy museum into the public eye again. The beautiful grounds, which once served as summer residence for the Dukes of Brabant, provide popular surroundings within which to spend Sunday afternoon.

Wheelchair: access; toilets.

Horta's home, now one of the essential Brussels sights: the **Musée Horta**.

History

Musée de la Dynastie

7 place des Palais, 1000 (511 55 78). Métro Parc/tram 92, 93, 94/bus 38, 60, 71. **Open** 10am-4pm Tue-Thur, Sat, Sun. **Admission** free.

Dynasty refers, of course, to the beloved Belgian royal family – not, thank God, to the twisted traumas of the Colbys and the Carringtons. Memorabilia, photographs and written documents chronicle the history of Belgian royalty.

Musée Royal de l'Armée et d'Histoire Militaire

3 parc du Cinquantenaire, 1000 (733 44 93/734 52 52). Métro Merode or Schuman/tram 81, 82/bus 20, 28, 36, 67, 80. **Open** 9am-noon, 1-4.30pm, Tue-Sun. **Admission** free. **No credit cards.**

If you like guns, you'll like it here. Guns, swords, cannons grenades, uniforms and artillery are arranged in somewhat haphazard displays with special emphasis on, of course, the Belgian Army. Perhaps of more universal appeal is the aviation section's enormous hangar, housing planes from World War I to the present. There are Russian MIG fighter jets, US Dakotas and Sikorsky helicopters.

Bookshop. Library (Mon-Fri).

Musée de la Ville de Bruxelles

Maison du Roi, Grand Place, 1000 (511 27 42). Métro Bourse, De Brouckère or Gare Centrale/tram 23, 52, 55, 81/bus 29, 34, 47, 48, 60, 63, 66, 71, 95, 96. **Open** *May-Sept* 10am-12.30pm, 1.30-5pm, Mon-Fri; 10am-1pm Sat, Sun. *Oct-Apr* 10am-12.30pm, 1.30-4pm Mon-Fri. **Admission** 80BF. **No credit cards.**

Situated opposite the Town Hall on the Grand Place, the Maison du Roi (King's House) occupies the site of the thirteenth-century 'Bread Hall' where bakers sold their products. The building was torn down and reconstructed in 1887 and has since been a museum chronicling the city's history. For the newcomer to Brussels, this is a good place from which start exploring. The museum's models, paintings and maps successfully convey what the city has been through. This is also where you'll find Manneken Pis's extensive wardrobe.

Transport

Autoworld

11 parc du Cinquantenaire, 1080 (736 41 65). Métro Merode or Schuman/tram 81/bus 20, 28, 36, 67, 80. **Open** *Apr-Oct* 10am-6pm daily; *Nov-Mar* 10am-5pm daily. **Admission** 150BF; 100BF over-60s, students; 80BF 6-12s. **No credit cards.**

Cars, cars and more cars in what is reputed to be the world's most prestigious collection. Starting from 1886, the exhibit traces the development of the automobile through hundreds of its incarnations, including the glamorous 1928 Bentley and the 1930 Bugatti.

Wheelchair: access.

Musée de Transport Urbain Bruxellois

364b avenue de Tervuren, 1150 (515 31 08). Tram 39, 44/bus 36, 42. **Open** *6 Apr-6 Oct* 1.30-7pm Sat, Sun, public holidays. **Admission** 150BF; 75BF 6-11s; free under 6s (for a ride from Woluwe to Tervuren and back). **No credit cards.**

Visitors are taken in antique trams from the depot to Tervuren – where they can visit the African Museum and its parks – and then back again. There are also trips to the Cinquantenaire and, if the pub or restaurant just won't do for that special occasion, you can rent out the trams for private parties.

Wheelchair: access.

Children

Museé des Enfants

15 rue du Bourgmestre, 1050 (640 01 07). Tram 23, 90, 93, 94/bus 71. **Open** 2.30-5pm Wed, Sat. **Admission** 200BF; 1500BF for a group of 10 or more; *family card* 1500BF valid one year for ten admissions. **No credit cards.**

You'll want to be a child again when you accompany one through this wonderful, intelligent museum. The guiding principle here is that 'doing' is everything, and that only by actively participating in exhibits will children discover themselves and the world around them. The exhibit changes every three years and the current one – running from November 1995 to May 1998 – is entitled *The Treasures Within Me*. Children, aged six to 12, interact with displays that encourage the child to think about their feelings, their dreams, their talents and their body. Along the way there are cooking, painting and puppet workshops. The displays are in French and Flemish so bring along a friend to translate if you don't speak either of these languages.

Wheelchair: access.

Lace

Museé du Costume et de la Dentelle

6 rue de la Violette, 1000 (512 77 09). Métro Bourse, De Brouckère or Gare Centrale/tram 23, 52, 55, 56, 81/bus 34, 60, 71, 95, 96. **Open** *Apr-Sept* 10am-12.30pm, 1.30-5pm, Mon, Tue, Thur, Fri; 2-5.30pm Sat, Sun. *Oct-Mar* 10am-12.30pm, 1.30-4pm Mon, Tue, Thur, Fri; 2-4pm Sat, Sun. **Admission** 80BF; 50BF under-15s, groups (of 12 or more). **No credit cards.**

Lace and Brussels are inseparable and have been so since the Middle Ages. This museum has on display fine examples of Belgian lace and traditional costumes which date back to the eighteenth century. There is also an atelier where visitors can see lace being made. It was due to reopen in June 1996.

Beer

Musée Bruxellois de la Gueuze

56 rue Gheude, 1070 (520 28 91). Métro Gare du Midi/tram 18, 52, 55, 56, 81, 82/bus 20, 47. **Open** *Jun-Sep* 8.30am-4.30pm Mon-Fri; 10am-1pm Sat. *Oct-May* 8.30am-4.30pm Mon-Fri; 10am-5pm Sat. **Admission** 70BF. **No credit cards.**

In the 1930s there were at least 50 independent lambic breweries in Brussels. Today all but one, the Cantillon Brewery, have folded amidst increased competition. This sole survivor dates back to 1900 and has been turned into a museum in order to prevent the complete extinction of the characteristically Bruxellois trade. Lambic is a spontaneously fermented beer, meaning fermentation occurs when certain bacteria – found only along the valley of Belgium's River Senne – are present. Gueuze is made by combining lambics of different ages, whereas kriek is made by adding cherries to the lambic. The taste? Well, suffice to say that it is an acquired one – connoisseurs, however, label it 'the champagne of beers'. A visit to the museum consists of a tour through the operational, family-run brewery and a sampling of the product at the end. The brewery is located amongst several near-demolished buildings in a dreary neighbourhood. Take public transport as parking spaces are hard to come by here. (*See chapter* **Cafés & Bars: Here for the Beer**.)

Swords galore at the **Musée Royal de l'Armée et d'Histoire Militaire** *(opposite).*

Art Galleries

***Belgium's rich heritage awaits visiting art lovers in the capital's public galleries, but the modern scene lacks a certain* je ne sais quoi.**

Christine et Isy Brachot – *tough door policy but worth it if you can get in. See page 164.*

Belgium has a long and proud art tradition, evident in Brussels' fine public galleries and permanent collections. For the most important of these, *see chapter* **Museums**. For the art museums of Flanders, *see below*.

On the contemporary side of things, the good news is that some public centres, such as **Atelier 340** and the **Centre d'Art Contemporain**, and the odd commercial gallery, such as **Sabine Wachters Fine Arts**, promote young talent. However, considering Belgium's past glories, the modern art scene in Brussels is disappointingly thin and conservative. The art is there – sometimes it's very good – but there is no impression of movement, which is essential for a vigorous scene.

Most galleries are frankly commercial and offer little encouragement to newcomers. Belgian artists continue doggedly to produce beautiful work, but there just isn't the necessary excitement generated around them. Even opening hours are restricted. Walking round the commercial galleries is for quiet, afternoon excursions as most don't open before lunch. Exhibition centres operate on a more art-lover-friendly basis and make informed, slightly eccentric choices that don't succumb to the lure of big names. These are worth checking out.

There is no particular art area. Ixelles and St Gilles are homes to discreetly good galleries which also handle big international names. Around the **Palais des Beaux Arts** are exhibition centres. There is also a Renaissance-style alliance between banks and art, with major financial institutions owning galleries. The weekly *Bulletin* gives information about all current exhibitions while *Art Brussels*, which can be picked up in most galleries, gives a seasonal list of what's on. Unless otherwise indicated, credit cards are not accepted.

Public galleries & spaces

Atelier 340

340 drève de Rivieren, 1090 (424 24 12). Métro Beekkant/tram 84. **Open** 2-7pm Tue-Sun (when exhibiting). **Admission** 150BF-200BF. **Credit** V.

Non-profit-making, artist-run and assembled in a block of condemned houses, Atelier 340 celebrated its fifteenth anniversary in 1995 and currently looks more secure than at any time in its fraught history. In 1980 Wodek Majewski, a Polish sculptor in search of a space, set up in a house here and has been developing it ever since, emerging triumphant from his run-ins with the demolition squads. It has now been accepted as an established space and plans are ongoing for further development. It is a great forum for sculpture and shows the best Belgian contemporary works, which are then circulated to galleries abroad. Majewski has also acquired a permanent collection through buying directly from his artists.

L'Autre Musée

place des Martyrs, 41 rue St Michel, 1000 (640 84 37). Métro De Brouckère. **Open** 2-6.30pm Tue-Sat (when exhibiting). **Admission** free.

An enthusiastic showplace for contemporary work, l'Autre Musée has two spaces: the one in place des Martyrs is for large sculptures while the rue du Viaduc site is for paintings and engravings. It shows mainly Belgian and northern European artists, and is a welcome forum for young unknowns. The beginning of 1996 saw its fifteenth anniversary exhibition which was a triumphal grouping of 43 artists.
Branch: 22 rue du Viaduc, 1050.

Centre d'Art Contemporain

63 avenue des Nerviens, 1040 (735 05 31). Métro Merode or Schuman. **Open** 9am-1pm, 2-5pm, Mon-Fri; 1-6pm Sat (when exhibiting). **Admission** free.

This is a documentation and information centre for contemporary Walloon art, with a small exhibition space. It organises thematic shows of Belgian and European artists and remains one of the few places where young artists can get a start. Seeing the delicacy and originality of works here is a reminder of the strength of Belgian talent, unfocused at the moment but still following in a great tradition.

Palais des Beaux Arts

23 rue Ravenstein, 1000 (507 84 86). Métro Gare Centrale. **Open** 10am-6pm Tue-Sun. **Admission** 250BF; 200BF over-60s; 150BF students.

Atelier 340 – *watch this space. See p162.*

This huge cultural centre, which groups together theatre, art and music, has the largest exhibition space in the city. Eleven interlinked rooms in hexagonal and circular shapes ensure that there is room for even the largest sculptures and that you can get lost wandering round a show. There is a well-thought-out programme of events ranging from Man Ray's photographs to Christo's conceptual sculptures. The Palais also hosts the regular Europalia festival, which focuses on a different theme each year. The Horta-designed building was badly refurbished in the 1970s, but from October 1996 it is being stripped and restored to its former state.

Photography

Contretype – Hôtel Hannon

1 avenue de la Jonction, 1060 (538 42 20). Tram 90, 92. **Open** 1-6pm Tue-Sun. **Admission** 50BF; 30BF groups.

This is the only art nouveau private house – other than Horta's – that is open to the public. Light and spacious with its alcoves and marble, it was the home of Edouard Hannon,

Brush strokes

If you think of Belgian art and look back any further than this century, you begin to get swamped with names. Here are ten of them, with no cheating – no mention of Bruegel's son or van Eyck's brother.

1. Jan van Eyck (c1390-1441). Had a grasp on perspective long before the Italians. Has a habit of including hidden self-portraits in his paintings, as in the convex mirror in the great *Arnolfini Wedding Portrait*.

2. Rogier van der Weyden (c1400-64). Also stole an effortless march on Italy. Tended towards powerful religious scenes with Flemish towns in the background.

3. Hans Memling (c1435-94). Great Bruges painter. Those pale Flemish faces that stare out from his canvases seem not to have changed in five centuries.

4. Antoine Wiertz (1806-65). Hugely celebrated in his time, now rather out of fashion, but there's still a museum dedicated to him in Brussels, where you can see some of the largest canvases ever painted.

5. Pieter Bruegel the Elder (c1525-69). Famous for *The Fall of Icarus*, crowd scenes and portraying lots of busy people doing busy things. He's also known for his depictions of hell.

6. Pieter Paul Rubens (1577-1640). Huge, lush canvases, flamboyance and fleshy redheads.

7. James Ensor (1860-1949). Ostend painter who in the late nineteenth century shocked even the Impressionists with his lurid imagination; known for wild caricatures.

8. Rik Wouters (1882-1916). Cut down by World War I, Wouters is the gentlest and most attractive of the Belgian Impressionists.

9. René Magritte (1898-1967). Master surrealist (*see chapter* **History: Altered images**).

10. Paul Delvaux (1897-1994). Last of the great Belgian fevered imaginations. Skeletons, naked women and chaos (*see chapter* **Sightseeing: Eyes wide shut**).

Palais des Beaux Arts – *see page 163.*

an amateur photographer, and has been open as a photography gallery since 1989. The choice tends towards artistic, beautiful photographs rather than gritty realism.

Commercial galleries

Christine et Isy Brachot

8 rue Villa Hermosa, 1000 (511 05 25). Métro Gare Centrale. **Open** 2-6pm Tue-Sat.

It's a New York-style set-up: you have to ring the bell and announce your intentions – browsers are not encouraged. Similarly, artists who have not been vetted are not encouraged either, but if you want to buy a Magritte or a Delvaux, there is probably nowhere better to present yourself. The owners, who also have a gallery in Paris, only bat with the big boys. Their other great artist is Panamarenko, whose weird and delicate flight-obsessed sculptures are worth braving that bell for.

Damasquine

62 rue de l'Aurore,1000 (646 31 53). Tram 93, 94. **Open** 1-7pm Thur-Sat; 11.30am-2pm Sun.

This small gallery has been showing mostly contemporary Belgian work since 1981. It has six exhibitions a year and the range is wide, including video and lasers. It is cautiously willing to take on young artists.

Fred Lanzenburg

9 avenue des Klauwaerts, 1050 (647 30 15). Tram 23, 90, bus 71. **Open** 10am-12.30pm, 2-7pm, Tue-Sat.

For 30 years, Lanzenburg has been making careful and erudite choices, presenting artists of international standing in a discreet gallery overlooking the Ixelles lakes. Recent selections include the Japanese Takayoshi Sakabe and the Polish Malgorzata Paszko.

Meert Rihoux

13 rue du Canal, 1000 (219 14 22). Métro Ste Cathérine or Yser. **Open** 2.30-6pm Tue-Sat.

In this spacious third-floor gallery, the speciality is conceptual work, especially German and American artists from the 1970s. Meert Rihoux handles about 16 artists and is good at taking on young Belgians who have cut their teeth elsewhere.

Rodolphe Janssen

35 rue de Livourne, 1050 (538 08 18). Tram 93, 94. **Open** 2-7pm Tue-Sat.

This is one of the galleries at the forefront of strong, original contemporary art. It does about six shows a year, covering all types of art, ranging from photography to sculpture. It's a simple, whitewashed space with a very good collection of art books.

Sabine Wachters Fine Arts

36 rue Bosquet, 1060 (534 14 41). Métro Louise/tram 93, 94. **Open** 11am-7pm Tue-Sat.

One of the few commercial galleries that will show young unknowns, Sabine Wachters has two large, airy galleries with mostly thematic exhibitions. The work here is experimental and therefore erratic, but it has a verve and energy you won't find easily elsewhere.

Branch: 26 avenue de Stalingrad, 1000 (502 39 93).

Xavier Hufkens

8 rue St Georges, 1050 (646 63 30). Tram 23, 90, 93, 94. **Open** noon-6pm Tue-Sat.

Here you'll find an interesting choice of Belgian and international artists in painting, sculpture and photography. The gallery attracts big names, such as Robert Mapplethorpe, as well as those of national repute such as Didier Vermeiren and Geert Verheuren.

Outside Brussels

If you are at all interested in art, you really have to take a short journey north-east of the capital. Flanders has always been the womb of Belgian art, and in St Bavo's cathedral in Ghent hangs one of the country's proudest possessions: Jan van Eyck's *Adoration of the Lamb*. The cities of Bruges and Antwerp remain art capitals, in terms of their collections and the quality of their exhibitions. The selection below is only a brief sample of what there is on offer.

Antwerp

Koninklijk Museum voor Schone Kunsten (Royal Museum of Fine Arts)

1-9 Leopold de Waelplaats, 2000 Antwerp (03 238 78 09). **Open** 10am-5pm Tue-Sun. **Admission** 150BF; 120BF groups (min 15), students; free under-18s.

This museum has an unequalled collection of Flemish Masters, boasting about 2,500 works from the Flemish primitives to the surrealists. Flemish art seems like a standing army with unending resources – so many of the most famous works are scattered around the world, yet this collection is effortlessly large and brilliant. You can move chronologically from the exquisite early work of van Eyck and van der Weyden, through the magic landscapes of Patinir and the great expanses of Rubens, up to Ensor's weird caricatures, Wouters' gentle Impressionism and Delvaux's eccentricity.

Middelheim Open-air Sculpture Museum

61 Middelheimlaan, 2020 Antwerp (03 828 13 50). **Open** *1 Oct-31 Mar* 10am-5pm Tue-Sun; *Apr, Sept*

Brussels' underground art scene...

The Métro stations in Brussels are all built along the same lines: black rubber floor, low ceilings, shiny walls and central ticket desk. But within this formula, huge efforts have been made to make each station a showpiece for some kind of contemporary art – sculptures, tiles, paintings, wall friezes... Some of these are less than impressive, so that you find yourself looking at some coloured tiles and have to be reminded that this is 'Art'. However, more recent stations on the peripheries, such as Porte de Hal and Stockel, are immediately striking and Métro stations remain some of the best public spaces for contemporary Belgian art. Below are listed some notable examples.

Delvaux's **'Nos Vieux Trams Bruxellois'.**

Anneessens *Sept Ecritures* by Alechinsky and Dotremont (ink on wood).
Botanique *Les Voyageurs* by Caille (21 coloured freestanding figures).
Bourse *Nos Vieux Trams Bruxellois* by Paul Delvaux (oil painting); moving ceiling by Pol Bury (steel cylinder).
Comte de Flandre Sixteen suspended figures of Icarus by van Hoeydonck (bronze).
Hankar *Notre Temps* by Somville (acrylic on concrete).
Hermann Debroux *L'Aviateur* by d'Haese (bronze sculpture); *Ode aan een Bergrivier* by Poot (bronze sculpture).
Horta Pieces from the Maison du Peuple and Hôtel Aubecq (demolished Horta buildings).
Josephine-Charlotte *La Fleur Unique ou les Oiseaux Emerveillés* by Vanderkam (coloured wooden relief).
Montgomery *Thema's* by Mara (six oil paintings); *Magic City* by Folon (oil painting on wall); *Rythme Bruxellois* by Delahunt (coloured tiles).
Porte de Hal *Le Passage Inconnu* by François Schuitten (murals composed of red and white tiles); *Hallepoort* by Raoul De Keyser (oil painting on canvas).
Porte de Namur *Het Uiteindelijk Verkeer* by Octave Landuyt (four round ceramic reliefs).
Stockel Tintin figures by the Atelier Hergé.
Vandervelde *La Grande Taupe et le Petit Peintre* by De Gobert (huge wall painting in acrylic).

10am-7pm Tue-Sun; *May, Aug* 10am-8pm Tue-Sun; *Jun, July* 10am-9pm Tue-Sun. **Admission** free.
There are works here by major sculptors from Rodin to the present day, including the Belgians, Panamarenko and Vermeiren. This open-air venue is also well worth visiting for its biennial summer exhibition of international contemporary sculpture.

Provincaal Museum voor Fotografie

47 Waalse Kaai, 2000 Antwerp (03 216 22 11). **Open** 10am-5pm Tue-Sun. **Admission** free.
Opened quite recently in a warehouse, the gallery has a permanent collection of historic photographs, including views of old Antwerp. There are some generally excellent temporary exhibitions of European photographers. Also on show are antique cameras and a turn-of-the-century photographer's studio.
Wheelchair: access; toilets.

Bruges

The city of Bruges is like an extended work of art itself – an intact relic of a gracious age – so it comes as no surprise to find it full of quietly perfect paintings in small museums and galleries, of which we list the following.

Groeninge Museum

12 Dijver, 8000 Bruges (050 44 87 11). **Open** *Apr-Sept* 9.30am-5pm daily; *Oct-Mar* 9.30am-12.30pm, 2-5pm, Mon, Wed-Sun. **Admission** 150BF; free under-18s.
This is a great place to visit because it is full of works by Bruges painters so you get a true sense of the city from its medieval peak to its eighteenth-century leisure period. Here are the pale, stern Flemish faces of van Eyck and the images of Bruges in the paintings of Gérard David. There is also one of Bosch's nightmarish images, and in the last room are the Belgian surrealists, seen here, as in Antwerp, as part of a national tradition rather than an international movement.

Hans Memling Museum

Hospice of St John, Mariastraat, 8000 Bruges (050 448 770). **Open** *Apr-Sept* 9.30am-5pm daily; *Oct-Mar* 9.30am-12.30pm, 2-5pm, Mon, Tue, Thur-Sun. **Admission** 100BF (200BF family ticket); 70BF groups, over-60s, students; 50BF schools; free children.
This museum is housed in the medieval Hospice of St John, whose quiet, religious atmosphere is perfect for Memling's peaceful paintings. There are only six of his works here, all but one religious, all exquisite. The Shrine of St Ursula, a small gilded wooden shrine that holds the saint's relics, is one of Belgium's 'Magnificent Seven'. The only non-religious painting is a portrait, *Sibylla Sambetha* – the expression of this pale woman rivals the *Mona Lisa* for enigma points.

an INTERNATIONAL journal of the fine arts
OUT EVERY QUARTER
MODERN PAINTERS
CEZANNE
PATRICK HERON
MODERN PAINTERS
A QUARTERLY JOURNAL OF THE FINE ARTS
LEON KOSSOFF AT THE TATE
MODERN PAINTERS
VENICE
MODERN PAINTERS
A QUARTERLY JOURNAL OF THE FINE ARTS
CLAES OLDENBURG
by Julian Barnes
FROM EVERY QUARTER
to subscribe +44 181 986 4854 to advertise +44 171 580 5618

Arts & Entertainment

Media	168
Clubs	171
Film	177
Music: Classical & Opera	180
Music: Rock, Folk & Jazz	184
Sport & Fitness	189
Theatre & Dance	193

Media

Couch potatoes will be lost without cable, but otherwise name your lingo and take your pick from the news of the world at the crossroads of Europe.

Pick up an English paper at any newsstand.

You get a picture of just how international a city Brussels is by looking at its media. Even the smallest newsstand carries newspapers, magazines and other periodicals in at least four languages: Dutch, English, French and German – and the larger newsstands sell Spanish, Italian, Greek and Portuguese publications as well. And basic cable, which is necessary to receive television broadcasts, features German, Italian and English channels, in addition to the native French and Flemish stations and their linguistic compatriots in France and Holland. The four different bands receive broadcasts from neighbouring countries, as well as emissions from stations such as the BBC's World Service and Radio 4.

But beware: despite Belgium's small size, a broadcast in Brussels doesn't come in on the same frequency as it does outside the capital. If travelling to Antwerp, Ghent, Bruges or any other city in Belgium, consult the local newspapers to find out where your favourite station falls on the dial.

Newspapers

La Dernière Heure

This is the closest thing Brussels has to a tabloid in French – but lacking in viciousness. Good sports coverage is its main attraction, which even detractors admit is excellent. It's read mostly by kids who want to see their names in print.

European Voice

Published by the usually acerbic *Economist*, this upstart weekly shies away from overly critical analysis of the workings of the EU. It provides an insider's view of Commission policies and politics, manoeuvrings and management – albeit an inoffensive one. Style-wise, *European Voice* looks like a university student newspaper, but if you know how to read between the lines, you might actually learn something.

Het Laaste Nieuws

Once known as the traditionally liberal Flemish daily with both bourgeois and populist leanings. In an effort to lure readers, *Het Laaste Nieuws* has lately entered the tabloid fray, going in for sensationalist coverage of crime stories and star interviews etc. Though nowhere near as repugnant as Britain's *News of the World*, HLN is not the paper it used to be, which is disappointing.

La Libre Belgique

Very Catholic, *La Libre Belgique* has the distinction of being the only francophone paper to have maintained its editorial independence during World War II. If you don't mind wading through an article or two every other day about some aspect of the papacy, this paper is actually a better read than anything else you'll find on the newsstand in French.

De Morgen

Once the staple of socialist workers, *De Morgen* has gradually evolved into a more general Flemish left-wing daily. Covering the arts, fashion and human interest as well as national and international news, it is Belgium's answer to France's *La Libération*.

Le Soir

The quality francophone paper – which is a sad reflection on the state of journalism in Belgium. It's good on Wednesdays for the cultural supplement, *MAD*.

De Standaard

The quality Flemish daily is very Catholic and conservative in its approach to reporting, which means that while its accuracy is usually unimpeachable, the newspaper itself can be a bit boring.

Magazines

Bulletin

The only English-language weekly in Brussels, this is the magazine to read if you're unfortunate enough not to understand French or Flemish but still want to know what's happening around Brussels and the rest of the country. A good portion of each issue is devoted to business and EU-related issues, as well as cultural goings-on about town. Writing style reserved to the point of derision by some, who generally number among the most fervent readers. It contains *What's On*, a supplement of comprehensive cinema, concert and television listings.

Dag Allemaal

If you've ever wondered how *Hello!* magazine would read in Dutch, *Dag Allemaal* is the answer: frothy interviews, entertaining (or inane, depending on your taste) articles and glossy photo spreads – bought from other publications and, in the case of interviews and articles, translated for Flemish readers. This weekly is universally looked down upon, but that doesn't stop it from being the largest-selling magazine in Belgium.

Humo

Originally just a Flemish mag with television listings, *Humo* has become what you would get if you crossed *Rolling Stone* with *Time Out* and threw in healthy doses of satire *à la Private Eye*. Music, film, politics and the arts all get a weekly skewering and/or rave. Irreverent, ironic, intellectual, anarchistic, it's like the lefty student who never grew up.

Kiosk

If you read French, this monthly is a must for finding out what's going on about town. Cafés, bars, art shows, clubs and events are all covered in this thin, paperback-sized mag.

Le Vif-Express/Knack

These sister publications – the former in French, the latter in Flemish – are the only news magazines in Belgium. Given the complexities of Belgium as a country, it makes sense that there is an emphasis on national news (international news is better covered in the dailies). Both publish glossy weekend supplements covering fashion, travel and lifestyle.

Listings

J'Annonce/Koopjeskrant

Less established and substantial than *Vlan* (*see below*), this weekly paper is more interesting for its personal ads than for the apartments, automobiles and appliances for sale or hire. It comes out on Friday.

Vlan

From used cars to new loves, this is the paper to which everyone in Brussels turns to buy or sell, rent or find. Although the French-language *Vlan* is delivered free on Thursdays, most people in the market for something in its listings buy it the Monday before, to beat other would-be nabbers.

Radio

Being at the centre of Europe gives Brussels a wealth of choices when it comes to radio broadcasts. Listed below are only the Belgian stations available. To stave off 'cultural imperialism' – or rather, to give Belgium's domestic recording industry a chance to grow amidst the overwhelming popularity of US and British music – radio stations receiving subsidies must make at least 60 per cent of their broadcasts in the language of the region from which the station is funded.

Most stations sidestep this requirement, but politicians often exploit the language issue to whip up voter support.

Remember, the frequencies will be different in other parts of Belgium.

BRTN – Radio 1

91.7 mhz

The most serious of the three Flemish state-owned radio stations, Radio 1 features political discussions as well as classical music.

BRTN – Radio 2

93.7 mhz

The popular station in the Flemish state-owned BRTN triumvirate, playing oldies and some Top 40 fare.

BRTN – Radio 3

89.5 mhz.

High culture is this Flemish station's forte: profiles of composers; choral, chamber and classical concerts; and opera.

Bruxelles – Capitale

99.3 mhz.

Nostalgia and news format.

La Première

92.5 mhz.

Either charming or naff, depending on your predilections. Game shows, agony aunts, serials and phone-ins take up a good part of La Première's schedule. *Chansons françaises* do give the station a cultural dimension, but otherwise it's a mix of froth, pop psychology and mild sensationalism.

Radio 2

193.2 mhz.

The francophone pop station, often playing music neither new enough to be current nor old enough to be nostalgia. If the stylings of songstress Celine Dion are your thing, this is the station for you.

Radio Contact

102.2 mhz.

The pop station for francophones in Brussels. Loud and fast, this is the best imitation of an American AM station Brussels has to offer. If you've seen the video for a song a million times on MTV this week, then Radio Contact will playing it to death next week.

Radio Cristal

106.5 mhz.

Though not always the easiest frequency to get, extra fiddling with the dial and rearranging of your antenna are worth it if trip hop, trance, house and deep garage are your thing. Cristal is also a good source of information on raves.

Radio Donna

97.0 mhz.

Flemish pop station.

Radio Nostalgia

100 mhz.

As the name implies, oldies but goodies are this station's specialty. French stars such as Johnny Hallyday, Sheila and the late Claude François get played often, as well as lots of American and British rock 'n' roll and soul.

Studio Brussel

100.6 mhz.

The most popular station for those with eclectic and international tastes in music. Studio Brussel lays on slots dedicated to genres ranging from R&B to reggae and rai (North African pop). Jazz (acid, freestyle and old school), hip hop, alternative rock and other sounds all get tossed into the mix. This is as hip as Brussels gets.

Television

Again, Brussels' location in Europe affords it a huge variety of programming. With basic cable (an essential, as you can't receive broadcasts otherwise), viewers have access to not only the national and local stations, but also French, German and Dutch television.

Especially popular are France's **TF1**, **France 2** and **3** stations, film channel **Canal Plus**, the cultural channel **Arte** and **MCM**, the Gallic version of MTV. **Eurosport** is available for sport

Brussels' TV Tower – cable provides access to channels from several European countries.

fans, while **Holland 1**, **2** and **3** provide a wide choice of chat shows, educational programmes and entertainment, often Dutch versions of American programmes. Because of their general fluency in English, the Flemish tune in regularly to **BBC1** and **BBC2**, **NBC Superchannel** and **CNN**.

BRTN, the Flemish state-owned network, was long known for its higher quality programming, until the advent of **VTM**, the popular private channel. Now BRTN is in a quandary. Trying to maintain its ratings while avoiding becoming as frothy as VTM, the station has ended up with rather hit-and-miss programming. Intelligent news programmes alongside bad American soap operas characterise BRTN's state of confusion.

As with all Flemish stations, foreign programming is subtitled, which means at least you can get to see *The Bold and the Beautiful* in its original glory. Technology show *Alle Vijf*, news magazine *Ter Zake* and *Gisteren Gekeken?* – a weekly look through the station's archives – are all well worth watching.

Ka2

A sister station of VTM (*see below*) which shows mostly anglophone series and films made for television. Broadcasts 4.30pm-midnight.

RTBF

The state-run francophone station has retained respectability due to a lack of competition – its Flemish counterpart, BRTN, has sullied its name by trying to best VTM in the ratings. Because of the excellent coverage of international events on stations coming out of France, RTBF is only so-so when it comes to news reporting. The cultural programme *Françoise et les Siens*, the travel show *Télétourisme* and the twice-weekly citizens' advice show *Cartes sur Table* are some of the station's most notable highlights. Broadcasts 6pm-midnight.

RTL

This Luxembourgeois station runs most of its programmes uninterrupted and puts on blocks of French, Luxembourgeois, Swiss and Belgian commercials at designated times between the shows. Unfortunately, the ads are often more interesting than RTL's programming, which consists of dubbed versions of *Baywatch* (*Alerte à Malibu* in French), *Dallas* and the like. Broadcasts 4.30pm-midnight.

Télé-Bruxelles/TV Brussel

This local public access station covers news and happenings from out and about town, doing it with more of a street feel than the state-owned and commercial stations. The programming is obviously produced on a shoestring budget – but that makes it all the more interesting.

VT4

Despite its name, VT4 is not an offshoot of VTM. This independently owned station started out in the early 1990s as a cultural alternative to VTM's populist programming and BRTN's stodgy stance at the time. However, its experimentation with off-the-wall chat shows and would-be innovative series failed to draw the ratings to justify costs. Thus, VT4 has had to resort to cheaper US programming, which has turned it into a lowerbrow VTM. Broadcasts 3pm-1.30am.

VTM

Started up in the early 1990s, privately owned VTM has taken a lot of flak for being the first station to buy up large quantities of middle- and lowbrow foreign programmes (British and US shows make up the bulk) and broadcast them to the Belgian public. But, despite *Rescue 911*, *EastEnders* and *Home and Away*, VTM actually has the best news coverage of Flanders. Flemish shows of note include: *Vanavond Niet, Schat* (*Not Tonight, Dear*), a phone-in show about sex; soap opera *Familie*; and the game show, *Rad van Fortuin* (yes, *Wheel of Fortune*). Broadcasts 5pm-1am.

Clubs

Most musical tastes are catered for and dress codes are laid-back in Brussels, but if you're thinking of blagging, think again.

Clubbing in Brussels and sister city Antwerp is, as in other major cities, appreciated much more by outsiders than by the natives. Bruxellois are infinitely less attitudinal than New Yorkers, Londoners or Parisians, but influenced and impressed by them (make that the first two – Paris is close enough to be considered a pain in the ass). So if you are wily enough to use your non-Belgian status to the max (speaking no more French or Flemish than is necessary to be charming), you can find yourself the flavour of the minute with an instant coterie of *copains* inviting you all over the place. When in doubt, regarding social situations, speak English – not arrogantly, but with enough vulnerability to throw others off balance: it's harder for them to give attitude in a language that's not their own. Nationalities that are at a disco disadvantage in Belgium include the neighbouring Dutch, Germans, and French (again) and, unfortunately, north Africans – xenophobia rears its ugly head even more boldly at night.

Although most clubs open at around 11pm, only the most desperate arrive before midnight. Before then, clubbers congregate at cafés and bars to decide which spots to hit – or whether to hit any at all. If you're out with Belgians, remember that buying rounds is the custom, with everyone taking their turn. The larger the group, the more drinks bought… and the more likely everyone is to end up thoroughly gone before the night's end.

Speaking of getting pissed, about the only time being Anglophone (particularly British or Australian) works against you is when it comes to drinking. Because of limited licensing hours back home, some Brits and Aussies – used to cramming in the pints before 11pm – get rat-assed long before everybody else, giving their countrymen a lousy reputation for being lushes. In fact, the Belgians get just as drunk, but they take their time – allowing ample opportunity to witness everyone else's excesses. Therefore, pace yourself.

Dress codes are laid-back: in a city where jeans and a blazer can almost pass muster for formal, the trend is to be stylish but comfortable. Remember, though, that certain looks which might afford instant *entrée* into certain *soirées* (nose-ring or chartreuse mohican, say) can render you untouchable at other clubs (a yuppy emporium, for example).

If you're thinking of trying to get into a club free, think again. A few Belgian club-goers will still trot out the 'I know the boss' or 'I'm the DJ's girlfriend' line, but Brussels is so small (and Antwerp even smaller) that practically everyone knows the boss and/or has been the DJ's girlfriend at some point. In fact, these are more likely to be reasons not to let you in at all. Unless you are on the guest list or willing to shag someone at the door, pay up. If you're really skint, come back to the club an hour or so before closing, when entrance is usually free. (The drawback is that the only people still inside are normally out of their heads courtesy of booze or certain chemicals…)

Doormen in Belgium generally range from thuggish to scuzzy, the former being prevalent at upmarket venues. The selection process at the wannabe exclusive clubs often defies logic: the same person admitted one Saturday might be turned away by the same doorman the following week. More irritating is the perverse splitting up of groups and couples – allowing a woman in, for example, while deeming her boyfriend unsuitable for entry.

'Club privée', or private club, is the excuse most doormen give when denying someone entry. Although many clubs do have a membership scheme, most people in any given club are not part of it – 'members only' filters out the undesirables. If you look like a club's target public, getting in is a cinch.

Should you wish to come back to a club at a later date, remember it is customary to tip the doorman at least 40BF when you leave. If you don't, be prepared to be refused admission the next time, with the standard '*club privée* – members only' excuse.

Bear in mind that most public transport stops some time around midnight and resumes around 5.30am. Taxis can be hired, but there is a 75BF supplement for all fares beginning between 10pm and 6am.

Clubs

L'Acrobat

14-16 rue Borgval, 1000 (513 73 08). Tram 23, 52, 55, 56, 81. **Open** 9pm-4am Fri, Sat. **Admission** free.

A late-twenties and thirtysomething crowd flock to this unpretentious disco bar that falls neatly between alternative and mainstream – perfect for '80s trendies who have grown up in the last few years. The interior is eclectic kitsch: a little India-inspired gold leaf painting here, mixed with Fabergé-egg-like designs there – it all adds to the slightly decadent ambience. The DJ spins rap, rock, world music, disco and soul in a thoroughly engaging mix.

L'Asile

12 rue du Magasin, 1000 (218 17 04). Metro Yser. **Open** 11pm-late Thur-Sat. **Admission** 300BF.

The music is firmly entrenched in the 1980s, so you'd expect the club to be a tad tacky – and l'Asile does not disappoint, with gold walls, a trapeze in the middle of the dancefloor, thuggish doormen, a python and a pool table. L'Asile aims for James Bond chic but only manages Shirley Bassey. A guilty pleasure if ever there was one, l'Asile also has an art gallery upstairs.

Café d'Anvers

15 Verversrui, Antwerp 2000 (03 226 38 70). **Open** 11pm-6am Fri, Sun; 11pm-7.30am Sat. **Admission** 250BF; free on regular nights before midnight and an hour before closing.

Antwerp is renowned for having a much more approachable club scene than Brussels, and Café d'Anvers is exemplary. Large but surprisingly intimate, this former Protestant church is in the heart of the city's red-light district, an irony observed only by visitors. Friday nights are predominantly techno, while on Saturday and Sunday nights the Café pumps out house and garage grooves. The public ranges from trendies to the occasional tranny, with select everyday folk thrown in. Saturday nights are hottest and the door policy is relaxed.

Café Local

25 Waalsekaai, Antwerp 2000 (no phone). **Open** 11pm-6am Thur-Sun. **Admission** from 200BF.

Gorgeous venue… shame about the punters. If Café Local took as much care over its door policy as it has with décor, the club would be perfect. Modelled on a Cuban market square, the bar area is impressive: stands of fresh fruit and vegetables, shelves of coffee beans, toys and tins of produce and the *cantina*-like bar in the centre seem authentic to anyone who's never been to Havana. The dance area resembles an old-style tango hall, with bead-curtained entrances and softly lit tables around the edge. Music ranges from salsa to world to pop, which reflects the crowd: a little too much of everything to create any real atmosphere.

Factory

4 impasse de la Fidélité, 1000 (514 55 14). Métro De Brouckère or Gare Centrale. **Open** 11pm-late Wed. **Admission** 250BF.

This gay club caters to 'all sex types' on Wednesdays, which is their way of saying that it's mixed midweek. Students and trendies without day jobs turn out in moderate numbers to take in the garage and techno sounds. The décor comprises basic bare brick and steel gratings.

The Fuse

208 rue Blaes, 1000 (511 97 89). Métro Porte de Hal/bus 20, 48. **Open** 11pm-7.30am Sat. **Admission** 300BF.

This self-proclaimed 'first techno club in Brussels' has been around since 1993, and keeps getting better. DJs from Detroit, New York, London and Amsterdam spin regularly for the technoheads who turn out a thousand-strong every Saturday. The Fuse wins few points on décor, though: the former Spanish disco relies on the music and the crowd to attract. A smaller dance floor on the second level takes care of crowd overflow and 'Cosmos', the chill-out room hidden away on the first floor, plays deep garage and ambient music while video monitors show Japanese animation. If techno is your bag, this is the joint.

Le Garage

18 rue Duquesnoy, 1000 (512 66 22). Bus 48. **Open** 11pm-dawn Wed-Sat. **Admission** 100BF Wed, Thur; 300BF Fri-Sun.

After 14 years, one-time hotspot le Garage is at the end of the road, catering mostly to students, out-of-towners and tourists who don't know any better. A somewhat predictable lorry provides the décor in what might pass for a really happenin' disco in the Former Soviet Union. Fun for all the wrong reasons.

Genesia

44 avenue de la Toison d'Or, 1050 (514 33 04). Métro Louise. **Open** 10pm-7am Mon-Thur, Sun; 10pm-10am Fri, Sat. **Admission** 250BF.

A former bordello, Genesia has maintained its very 1970s feel, with red velvet, silk flowers and Hugh Hefneresque booths. But the music is strictly '90s soul – mostly American R&B with heavy doses of hip hop, some African and the occasional reggae tune thrown in for good measure. Dress your best and watch your step, as the scene can get quite heavy, but Genesia is the best of its kind in Brussels.

Mirano Continental

38 chaussée de Louvain, 1030 (218 57 72). Métro Madou/bus 29, 63. **Open** 11pm-late Sat. **Admission** 300BF-500BF midnight-4am (depending on the event); free regular nights before midnight and after 4am.

For years the only disco in town, this former cinema has undergone a rebirth as other clubs have sprung up. With a reduced attitude quotient, the Mirano crowd runs from yuppy to trendy, while the music is mainly house. Door policy is lenient, although it helps not to look like a dealer or a druggy. Monthly advance screenings of films are also shown here.

Pitt's Bar

53 rue des Minimes, 1000 (514 41 74). Bus 34. **Open** 8pm-3am Wed, Thur; 8pm-5am Fri, Sat. **Admission** free.

Party central for house, techno and garage lovers, Pitt's Bar (pronounced 'Pete's bar' by locals) has all the info on what's going down in the ever-changing party scene. The mostly sedentary crowd is made up of university students and early-twentysomethings.

Planet Claire

29 rue de l'Hôpital, 1000 (513 89 78). Bus 34, 48. **Open** 11.30pm-5am Thur-Sat. **Admission** 250BF.

MTV-friendly rap and soul mixed with smart, danceable pop.

Rick's River Boat

quai des Péniches, 1020 (374 69 10). Métro Yser. **Open** 9pm-3.30am one Friday each month (phone for schedule). **Admission** 400BF.

This modest boat docked on the canal plays host to the Brussels Singles Group, an association of unmarrieds in their early thirties and upwards. The music is ultra-nostalgic, ranging from the mid-'60s to the mid-'80s, the romantic heyday of most of these swingers. Although the organisers deny that this is a pick-up joint ('Our 4,000 members are very happy being single!'), a boat full of unattached people can get a little desperate as the night wears on.

The Sound

7 rue des Riches Claires, 1000 (no phone). Tram 23, 52, 55, 56, 81/bus 48, 95, 96. **Open** 11pm-6am Thur-Sat. **Admission** price varies; 300BF annual membership card for unlimited access.

An alternative to the pervasive house and techno that rules most clubs. Trip hop, trance, ambient and deep garage provide the soundtrack to the navel-, nose- and nipple-pierced crowd of dreadlocked and dye-jobbed youth. Housed in a former gay disco, the Sound has a chill-out room upstairs for clubsters who want to take a breather from the small, mirrored dance floor downstairs.

Free expression at laid-back **Mirano Continental**, *where the punters range from yuppy to trendy.*

good i-Deas every month!
i-D
URBAN WARFARE: LONDON'S NEW ECO TERRORISTS
SHAMPOO: RETURN OF THE WASH AND GO-GO GIRLS
WALKING THE LINE: EDINBURGH LIFE AFTER TRAINSPOTTING
TOP GEAR: SUMMER MENSWEAR SPECIAL
.. LOVE BITES
BJÖRK & GOLDIE
GET YOUR TEETH INTO THIS!
KATE MOSS
JARVIS COCKER
PRINCE NASEEM
IRVINE WELSH
NICK CAVE
LOU REED
LL COOL J
LOUISE WENER
EWAN McGREGOR
Primal Scream
Christy Turlington
Jungle!
the truth about drugs
GENERATION ECSTASY
TIME TO STOP TAKING THE PILL?
What are drug-free clubbers on?
super nature
GET UP! GET HAPPY!

Andale, ándale, ándale…

Canoa Quebrada

53 rue du Marché au Charbon, 1000 (511 13 54). Métro Bourse. **Open** 9.30pm-late Tue; 10.30pm-late Wed-Sun. **Admission** free. **Drinks** cocktails approx 250BF.

A buzzing South American night spot with a canoe-shaped bar serving potent *caipirinhas* to the sound of samba. Soft lighting, occasional bands and a mixed South American and European crowd make this a popular alternative to the Cartagena across the street.

Cartagena

70 rue du Marché au Charbon, 1000 (no phone). Métro Bourse. **Open** 9.30pm-late Fri, Sat. **Admission** free. **Drinks** cocktails approx 200BF.

The Cartagena, one of the most traditional and longest running of Brussels' South American clubs, provides a comprehensive selection of salsa and merengue music for the over-25s. Deserted until midnight, by 2am there is barely room to swing an enchilada on the raised central dance floor, flanked on either side by video screens featuring favourite salsa bands. The bar staff are friendly and the décor is simple.

Papagayo

47 rue de l'Ecuyer, 1000 (502 78 02). Métro De Brouckère. **Open** 9pm-dawn Thur-Sun. **Admission** free. **Drinks** cocktails approx 300BF.

The trappings of a 1970s disco – complete with mirrored dance floor, ultraviolet lighting, red carpeted walls and psychedelic globes – combined with a friendly ambience, set the scene for this lively spot. Salsa and merengue rhythms animate the mix of dancers, who range from glamorous Latin couples to groups of petite South American girls, plus the odd Anglo-Saxon interloper.

Tom Tom Club

5 place de la Constitution, 1070 (523 10 55). Métro Gare du Midi. **Open** 11.30pm-late Thur. **Admission** free. **Drinks** cocktails approx 250BF.

For hardcore salsa fanatics and those who just like a drink in a lively atmosphere, Thursday at the Tom Tom Club is a must. This long, high-ceilinged, brightly lit bar provides an excellent blend of South American music. Long benches border a dance floor sticky with spilt Corona and tequila, around which male Latinos and Eurocrats hover, sipping their beer and watching the dancers.

Upside Down

24 rue du Lombard, 1000 (511 00 93). Bus 34, 48, 95, 96. **Open** 7pm-4am daily. **Admission** free.

Technically a café-bar, Upside Down's dance floor at the back makes it the place to go for funk, soul and African music, and not just current MTV faves – DJs here have been known to dip into some Cameo and George Clinton. The décor is sparse, with deep azure walls displaying murals of African tribesmen, slaves and colonial settings. Weekends see the liveliest action, but musicians occasionally drop in for jam sessions during the week.

Zébu

50 rue de Flandre, 1000 (514 44 53). Métro Ste Catherine/bus 63. **Open** 6pm-late Wed-Sat. **Admission** free.

Although serving pretty much as a meeting point for many clubbers, yuppies and others before a night on the town, Zébu is highly recommended for often far outshining its customers' eventual destinations. A mix of African and Asian culture with Euro-kitsch, the constantly evolving interior features animal prints and cherubs, trophies and comfy armchairs, ornate picture frames and various other

The more approachable Antwerp scene is exemplified by the **Café d'Anvers** – *see page 173.*

ultra-tacky furnishings and paraphernalia. The music is mostly world, reggae and Latin, with the odd bit of acid jazz thrown in for good measure.

Party series

Action Girl

Mirano Continental, 38 chaussée de Louvain, 1030 (218 57 72). Métro Madou/bus 29, 63. **Scheduled** phone for details. **Admission** varies, but usually around 500BF.

It's a mixed night, but Action Girl has a heavy drag queen element – as befits the name.

Paradise

Café d'Anvers, 15 Verversrui, Antwerp 2000 (03 226 38 70). **Scheduled** phone for details. **Admission** 800BF.

Café d'Anvers owner Pim and house impresario Patrick Soks' house happening – which takes place roughly every two months – has become a must for trendies, teens and twentysomethings. Past themes include Karma in Paradise, which featured party-goers being showered with rose petals, incense wafting through the air and India-inspired décor to complement the deep garage and heavy house beats.

Who's Who's Follies

The Fuse, 208 rue Blaes, 1000 (511 97 89). Métro Porte de Hal/bus 20, 48. **Scheduled** every three months, phone for details. **Admission** varies.

Organised by Carl de Moncharline, formerly of Mirano Continental, this two-year running event bounces between the Queen discotheque in Paris and the Fuse in Brussels – with buses transporting party-goers to the action. There's plenty of sparkle, smoke and glitter, with over 2,000 attendees tripping to house and deep garage, courtesy of guest DJs from London, Paris, New York and Amsterdam. It may all be a bit gruelling for the disco novice, but it's worth a stop for house aficionados. The flyers themselves are collectibles.

Film

Belgium is big on film festivals and Brussels has cinemas aplenty, but home-grown gems are thin on the ground.

The **Musée du Cinéma** in Brussels recently carried out a survey asking its film audiences for their favourite films of all time. The results contained much the same choices as film surveys all over the world. None of the films was Belgian.

Belgium is big on film festivals, and Brussels is well provided with movie venues, but the country's film-makers are low on international hits and classics. They are low even on national hits – only two of the 100 top-grossing films in Brussels last year were Belgian.

But the country's film-makers are by no means moribund. Every so often they produce something notable, and many of Belgium's exports are refreshingly warped. Rémy Belvaux's *Man Bites Dog (C'est arrivée près de chez vous)* was an excellent addition to the serial killer genre, and *Toto le Héros* was far more biting than the usual childhood reminiscence. *Crazy Love* merged three Charles Bukowski stories involving, among other things, necrophilia and one of the most grotesque cases of acne ever seen on film.

Much of Belgium's output consists of sex comedies and examinations of Belgium's history, whether it be World War II or the decline of the wool trade. The biggest hit of 1995, *La Vie Sexuelle des Belges*, falls firmly into the former category. There was also a comedy called *Manneken Pis* doing the festival circuit and winning prizes in Montreal, Cannes, Brussels and Ghent.

Other than these, Belgium's most famous cinematic exports lie at opposite ends of the spectrum, with minimalist feminist director Chantal Akerman and action man Jean-Claude van Damme, neither of whom have a guaranteed place in cinema history.

The best place to see home-grown films is at the **Brussels Film Festival** in late January, which has sections devoted to Belgian shorts, animation, full-length features and documentaries.

MOVIEGOING IN BRUSSELS

Belgian films may not be high on anyone's list of unmissables, but Brussels' cinemas are more enticing. The language split means that foreign films are rarely dubbed. English and American movies remain in the original version and it only takes a few minutes to get used to the disconcerting sight of French and Flemish subtitles taking up the bottom third of the screen. In most cinemas the seats are comfortable, the legroom extensive and the tickets no more expensive than in London.

What's more, some American and many European films are released here weeks or even months before they appear in the UK, so you can have the added satisfaction of sneering that you saw that film ages ago when it finally opens in Britain. On the other hand, though, some British films and a few American independents come to Brussels months or even years later.

In addition to the main cinemas listed below, there are occasional film screenings at the **Goethe Institut** (230 39 70) – in German – the **Botanique** arts centre (*see chapter* **Sightseeing: Notable Buildings**) and various cultural centres in the suburbs. More tempting are the drive-in films at the **Parc du Cinquantenaire** on weekends in July and August. Carless souls need not feel left out – though they might look a bit odd – as headphones with a chair can be provided.

Five screens at **Vendôme**. *See page 179.*

Many films open in Brussels before the UK.

Rémy Belvaux's **Man Bites Dog** *– packs heat.*

Cinemas

Films change on Wednesdays in Brussels. For details, check listings in the *Bulletin* and a supplement published with *Le Soir* on Wednesdays. There are various abbreviations to look out for: **VO** = *version originale*, ie not dubbed; **V fr** = French version; **V angl** = English version; **EA** = children admitted; **ENA** = children not admitted

It's customary to tip ushers or usherettes 20BF when they take your ticket. Fail to do this and you risk them screeching incomprehensible phrases at you until you cough up. The exception is UGC De Brouckère. Tickets usually cost 240BF-280BF, and some cinemas give reductions on Mondays. None of the cinemas listed below accepts credit cards (except UGC De Brouckère).

Several car parks offer cheap parking if the ticket is validated at the box office. *Le Soir* provides details of participating cinemas and car parks.

Actors Studio

16 petite rue des Bouchers, 1000 (512 16 96/217 94 41). Métro De Brouckère. **Tickets** *season* 720BF four films for one person; 1080BF six films for two people.

Located in a passageway near the Grand Place, this small cinema is one of the venues for the Brussels Film Festival. Two screens show four or five films a day, mostly arthouse movies with a few mainstream foreign films thrown in. A typical day's programme might include *To Die For*, Ken Loach's *Land and Freedom* and a Belgian-Palestinian co-production.

Arenberg Galeries

26 galerie de la Reine, 1000 (512 80 63). Métro Gare Centrale. **Tickets** *loyalty cards* ten films for 200BF each or ten films at full price with the eleventh free.

An elegant cinema in a converted art deco theatre within Galeries St Hubert. It has two air-conditioned auditoria and sells film posters, videos and Häagen-Dazs ice cream.

Aventure

57 galerie du Centre (entrances on rue des Fripiers & rue de la Fourche), 1000 (219 17 48). Métro Bourse or De Brouckère. **Tickets** 200BF.

Three air-conditioned screens each show several films a day. Some are shown daily, some alternate. It's mostly mainstream fare – the likes of *Apollo 13* and *The Madness of King George* – but you do tend to get a fair proportion of non-English films as well.

Kinepolis

Bruparck, 1 avenue du Centenaire, 1020 (bookings 474 26 04; information French 0900 35 241, Flemish 0900 35 240). Métro Heysel. **Tickets** *season (valid eight weeks)* 900BF five films.

Huge multiplex at the end of the Métro line in Heysel, near the Atomium. Bruparck is an odd out-of-town complex containing Mini-Europe, the Planétarium and a mock village of cafés and restaurants. Most of it is packed with noisy kids at weekends. Kinepolis itself has two bars and 25 screens, most of them with excellent sound quality. In total, the multiplex seats around 7,000. One of the auditoria boasts the largest IMAX screen in Europe. Most films start at the same time, so if one is sold out, you have a choice of plenty of others. Most of the films are mainstream Hollywood fodder. *Wheelchair: access.*

Movy Club

21 rue des Moines, 1060 (537 69 54). Tram 18. **Tickets** 200BF.

Arthouse films are shown in this old theatre with a 1934 interior. It's not convenient to get to, but Forest is an interesting *commune* and Movy Club is popular with students.

Musée du Cinéma

9 rue Baron Horta, 1000 (507 83 70). Métro Gare Centrale or Parc. **Tickets** 80BF on the door; 50BF 24 hours in advance. No children under 16, except children's screenings (3pm Sun).

Shows five films a day: two silent films with piano accompaniment and three talkies. Many of the talkies are early cinema classics, but there are more recent offerings too. A look at a typical week's menu revealed Bergman, Polanski, Godard, Russ Meyer, Eisenstein, and Laurel and Hardy.

Styx

72 rue de l'Arbre Bénit, 1050 (512 21 02/217 94 41). Métro Porte de Namur. **Tickets** 160BF.

Slightly chaotic cinema in Ixelles with two tiny screens showing several films each a day. It's manned by a skeleton staff – sometimes just one person is selling tickets, vending cans of drink *and* working the projector – so be patient if the door appears to be locked ten minutes before the film is due to start. With arthouse staples making up the bulk of Styx's programming, anyone interested in seeing *A Clockwork Orange*, *Brazil* or *Ai no Corrida* should look here first.

UGC Acropole

entrances at 17 Galeries de la Toison d'Or & 8 avenue de la Toison d'Or, 1050 (218 59 50/French 0900 29 930/Flemish 0900 29 920). Métro Louise or Porte de Namur. **Tickets** *UGC privilege card (valid two months)* 680BF four films for one person; 1020BF six films for one or two people.

This 11-screen cinema is not quite as glitzy or stylishly

Crazy Love – *Bukowski made celluloid.*

André Delvaux's dreamy **Rendezvous à Bray**.

designed as UGC de Brouckère. Finding the right film and box office is confusing because it has two different entrances: one on the main street, the other in an arcade of shops with neon arrows showing the way. Queues for tickets can be long and chaotic, but it is comfortable inside. The menu is a mix of mainstream Hollywood movies and French blockbusters.

UGC De Brouckère

38 place de Brouckère (French 0900 29 930; Flemish 0900 29 920). Métro De Brouckère. **Tickets** *UGC privilege card (valid two months)* 680BF four films for one person; 1020BF six films for one or two people. **Credit** AmEx.

Right in the city centre, this provides ten good-sized, air-conditioned auditoria ingeniously fitted into a stripped-brick and exposed-metal building. The flagship screen is the super-comfortable and lavish 70mm UGC Gran Eldorado. Films on offer are generally Hollywood mainstream stuff and most start at the same time, allowing a wide choice, but box office queues can be lengthy and the bars inside are overpriced. *Wheelchair: access.*

Vendôme

18 chaussée de Wavre, 1050 (502 37 00/512 65 53). Métro Porte de Namur. **Tickets** Arenberg Galeries loyalty card can be used here; 240BF; 190BF students.

Five comfortable screens show a mix of arthouse and mainstream in a location convenient for Ixelles' bars and cafés.

Cinema Specials

Weary of the cinema? Need more than a blockbuster to tempt you to the big screen? Brussels' cinema-owners have a few extra features up their sleeves, from breakfast at the movies to the *frisson* of a mystery flick. See above for venue details (except **Espace Delvaux**).

Ciné-Apéro

Espace Delvaux, place Keym, 1170 (672 13 01). **Times** 6pm, 8.30pm, Wed. **Tickets** 160BF; 120BF students, over-60s.

Wednesday is film and cocktail night in a venue more often used as a theatre. The movie is a repeat of what was shown at Les Petits Déjeuners du Cinéma (*see below*), so don't make the mistake of going to both.

Ciné-Famille

Espace Delvaux, place Keym, 1170 (672 13 01). **Times** *Oct-Apr* 3pm Sun. **Tickets** 160BF; 120BF under-12s.

Sunday afternoon is reserved for a big family film from the year before. NB: Ciné-Famille only operates outside the summer months, from October to April.

Les Petits Déjeuners du Cinéma

UGC Acropole. **Times** 10am Sun. **Tickets** 240BF.

The ticket price covers coffee, croissant and a film, which is usually a hit from the previous year.

Les Samedis du Cinéma

UGC de Brouckère. **Times** 9.30am Sat. **Tickets** 60BF.

Adults and children each get their own film at these Saturday morning screenings. The children's show is usually animation and their ticket includes a free ice cream.

Sneak Preview

Arenberg Galeries. **Times** 9.30pm Thur. **Tickets** 180BF.

As the title suggests, this involves a surprise film shown pre-release – the main purpose being to gauge audience reaction. The guinea pigs watch mostly mainstream, arthouse and independent films from the UK or US, but there can be obscure exceptions – for example, you might get a long and plotless Iranian feature about an earthquake. It usually fills up so it's best to arrive in decent time. The ticket price often includes a free ice cream or drink. Sneak Preview does not operate between 26 June and 5 September.

Take off

Kinepolis. **Times** 8pm or 10.30pm Tue, depending on schedule (phone to check). **Tickets** 220BF or 250BF, depending on film.

Kinepolis's version of Sneak Preview is more likely to show mainstream Hollywood fare.

Festivals

Cynics say that Belgium produces more film festivals than films, and certainly there are quite a few around. The main event of the year is the **Brussels Film Festival** in January. As well as a competition for Belgian films, there is an award for the best European feature film, with a top prize of 4.5 million Belgian francs.

Brussels' **Animation Festival** takes place in February (*see chapter* **Brussels by Season**), and there is a fantasy, science-fiction and thriller festival in March.

Elsewhere in Belgium, Mons puts on a festival of romantic films that happens, naturally enough, around St Valentine's Day; Namur holds a French-language film festival in late September to early October; and Ghent hosts the Flanders Film Festival in mid-October.

Music: Classical & Opera

Some groups and venues have fallen by the wayside, but after several precarious years the Orchestre National de Belgique is thriving while authentic baroque ensembles are booming.

Brussels may not be on anyone's list of cities with great orchestras. It has nothing like the prestige of Amsterdam, Berlin, London or Vienna. And yet, less than half a century ago, the Belgian capital was something of a musical powerhouse: major works by Bartok, Stravinsky and Prokofiev had their European premières here. The 'Belgian violin school', led first by Vieuxtemps and then Ysaÿe, attracted players from all over the world. The subsequent symphonic decline was perhaps due to a lack of genuinely top-flight home-grown conductors. Apart from André Cluytens (most of whose career was in France anyway), it's hard to name any *chefs* of real stature.

The Brussels classical music scene, like so much of Belgium in general, is marked by the Franco-Flemish linguistic split. Officially bilingual, and thus theoretically neutral, Brussels is nevertheless home to francophones in the main. The language division is mostly a politico-economic problem, but it has its effects on cultural budgets as well. As the whole country is going through a sustained, painful phase of belt-tightening in an attempt to reduce mammoth deficits, this is a financially nerve-racking time for artistic ensembles, especially those who depend on hefty state handouts.

At the same time, audiences continue to flock to concerts, big and small. The choice is vast despite the demise or musical downsizing of several major orchestras and venues. As recently as ten years ago, Brussels was home to La Monnaie (the opera orchestra), several chamber groups and three full-size symphony orchestras: the Orchestre National de Belgique, the Dutch-speaking radio symphony, and the French-speaking radio symphony. The latter folded in 1991; the Dutch-speaking BRT (Belgian radio and television) orchestra is now to be assimilated in part into a varying-sized chamber ensemble. The splendid broadcast hall on place Flagey, which both radio orchestras shared from the 1930s, is now boarded up and abandoned.

The picture is not uniformly bleak. After several precarious years, the Orchestre National de Belgique is thriving under Yuri Simonov (formerly of the Bolshoi Opera). Under the baton of rising star Antonio Pappano, the radically reformed La Monnaie plays symphonic concerts as well.

The shrinking of conventional full-time symphonic formations is partly compensated for by the growing popularity of early music and original-instrument ensembles, an area in which Belgium – halfway between Paris and Amsterdam – has excelled historically. **La Petite Bande**, one of the first authentic baroque ensembles in the world, is still flourishing after over 30 years. Philippe Herreweghe and his **Chapelle Royale** are also regular performers, as are **Anima Eterna** (Jos Van Immerseel), **Il Fondamento** (Paul Dombrecht) and many other fine groups. Such concerts often take place in the many smaller venues found throughout Brussels and outlying areas.

Belgian concert-goers are likely be amateur musicians themselves. Besides its six conservatories, the country has an extensive network of preparatory academies at which anyone can learn an instrument for a modest fee. Graduates unable to find professional work often end up in one of the many amateur orchestras and choirs.

This may explain the excitement generated every May by the world-class **Concours Musical International Reine Elisabeth de Belgique** (Queen Elisabeth International Music Competition), which changes focus each year between violin, piano and voice. Founded by the great Belgian violinist Eugène Ysaÿe in collaboration with the then Queen Elisabeth (herself a keen amateur violinist), the contest's first winner was David Oistrakh in 1937. The level of virtuosity has remained very high. The final-round gala concerts – always sold out – are broadcast live on both French- and Flemish-speaking TV.

Contemporary music fans should check out the annual **Ars Musica** festival, which stages events throughout Brussels, featuring Belgian and international performers. Recent years have seen the creation of several fine local groups specialising in new music, including **Ictus Ensemble**, **Oxalys** and the Liège-based **Musique Nouvelle**.

Théâtre de la Monnaie – *see page 182.*

Details on all concerts can be found in *What's On*, a supplement to the the *Bulletin*, which is also distributed free in many hotels and tourist spots.

Tickets

Ticket prices vary from one event to another, even for the same venue. Philharmonic Society prices range from about 200BF-800BF, with gala concerts such as the Queen Elisabeth finals costing up to double the normal price. At Théâtre de la Monnaie expect to pay at least 400BF and up to 1500BF for orchestra seats. Prices at other venues range from 150BF-400BF, but there are no strict guidelines. Listed below are the two main ticket agencies.

TIB

Hôtel de Ville, Grand Place, 1000 (513 89 40/fax 514 45 38). Métro Bourse or Gare Centrale. (*See chapter* **Essential Information** for opening times.) **Credit** DC.

The Brussels tourist information office can furnish all the necessary information, including addresses and telephone numbers, for most events in the city. Reservations should be made at the Grand Place office. Many tickets (but not all) can be purchased directly from TIB.

Fnac

City 2, rue Neuve, 1000 (reservations 209 22 39). Métro Rogier/tram 23, 52, 55, 56, 81, 90. **Open** 10am-7pm Mon-Thur, Sat; 10am-8pm Fri. **Credit** MC, V.

Like TIB, Fnac can sell tickets to selected events in Brussels, Antwerp, and even France.

Major venues

Palais des Beaux Arts

23 rue Ravenstein, 1000 (box office 507 82 00/ 24-hour information French & Flemish 507 84 44). Métro Parc. **Box office** 11am-6pm Mon-Sat. **Tickets** 300BF-700BF; 300BF students, disabled. **No credit cards.**

Home of the Orchestre National de Belgique, the Palais is also the seat of the Philharmonic Society, which organises and coordinates the bulk of big-name concerts throughout Brussels. The Society puts out a glossy brochure of its events, which include performances by many foreign orchestras, soloists and chamber groups. Acoustics in both the splendid Salle Henri LeBoeuf and the smaller, 400-seat chamber-music hall are excellent. The entire complex, Brussels' most prestigious venue, is a fine example of art nouveau design. The finals of the Concours Musical International Reine Elisabeth de Belgique are held here.

Conservatoire Royal de Musique

30 rue de la Régence, 1000 (box office 507 82 00/24-hour information French & Flemish 507 84 44). Métro Gare Centrale. **Tickets** one hour before perf or ten days in advance from Palais des Beaux Arts (*see above*). **No credit cards.**

Smaller than the Palais des Beaux Arts and slightly shabby, but also with great acoustics, the Conservatoire Royal de Musique was partially designed by the French organ-builder Cavaillé-Coll. The stage is too narrow for symphonic orchestras but it's perfect for chamber formations and voice recitals. It is here that the preliminary rounds of the Concours Musical International Reine Elisabeth de Belgique are held – the most interesting part, according to contest connoisseurs.

DeSingel

25 Desguinlei, Antwerp 2015 (03 248 38 00). **Box office** 10am-7pm Mon-Fri; 4-7pm Sat. **Tickets** 400BF-900BF. **Credit** MC, V.

If you arrive by train, it's better to get off at Berchem, the last station before Antwerp. DeSingel is Antwerp's modern equivalent to Brussels' Palais des Beaux Arts. The huge Blue Hall can accommodate major philharmonic orchestras. The Red Hall is ideal for smaller groups. Acoustics are excellent.

Churches

Cathédrale des Sts Michel et Gudule

place Ste Gudule, 1000 (217 83 45/343 70 40). Métro Gare Centrale or Parc. **Open** *Nov-Mar* 7am-6pm Mon-Fri; 7.30am-6pm Sat; 8am-6pm Sun. *Apr-Oct* 7am-7pm Mon-Fri; 7.30am-7pm Sat; 8am-7pm Sun. **Admission** *crypt* 40BF; 30BF groups. **No credit cards.**

Brussels' largest church – too large, in fact, to be acoustically ideal for music much more complicated than Gregorian chant. Nevertheless, it's the venue for quite a few major events. The interior is just as grandiose as the exterior, and audiences of a thousand or so help absorb some of the ten-second echo. Sunday noon Masses feature special concerts during much of the year.

Chapelle Royale

(Eglise Protestante) 5 Coudenberg, 1000 (673 05 81). Métro Gare Centrale. **Open** varies. **Tickets** varies. **No credit cards.**

The favourite hall of many musicians, and a jewel both acoustically and architecturally. It's too small for anything larger than a baroque chamber orchestra, but ideal for authentic instruments. As maximum audience size is about 150, early booking is advised. It's also Brussels' best-heated church in winter, a fact – literally – not to be sneezed at.

L'Eglise des St Jean et Ste Etienne aux Minimes

62 rue des Minimes, 1000 (511 93 84). Bus 48. **Open** varies. **Admission** varies. **No credit cards.**

This high-baroque church, near the Sablon and Marolles quarter, has medium-quality acoustics but hosts a huge number of concerts. The Philharmonic Society produces most of its early-music recitals here. Throughout most of the summer, the Midi-Minimes concerts attract a mixed crowd of tourists and locals on their lunch hours. One Sunday morning a month during the rest of the year, a 15-year-old mixed amateur and professional ensemble called La Chapelle des Minimes does fine performances of Bach cantatas. The admission fee is voluntary and you get erudite programme notes translated into four languages. It's always advisable to arrive half an hour before the 10.30am starting time for these often standing-room-only events. Wrap up warm during the winter months, as the Minimes is not very well heated, alas.

Occasional venues

Some interesting places – such as museums, *châteaux* or large townhouses – hold concerts sporadically. Catch a summer opera production at Château de la Hulpe (south of Brussels), for example, and try to recognise the setting from the film *The Music Teacher*. Also, many of Brussels' outlying *communes* have their own cultural centres whose halls may be used for concerts (*see chapter* **Theatre & Dance**).

L'Atelier

51 rue du Commerce, 1040 (511 20 65). Métro Trône. **Open** *concerts* 8.30pm. **Tickets** 250BF. **No credit cards.**

Definitely the funkiest recital hall in Brussels. The former workshop of a music-loving painter and his wife, l'Atelier is filled with canvases, old posters and sundry memorabilia. Despite the somewhat down-at-heel aspect, the place has hosted many great musicians, often before they made names for themselves. A venerable coal stove standing in the middle of the room keeps audiences toasty even in the dead of winter.

Hotel Astoria

103 rue Royale, 1000 (513 09 65/217 62 90). Métro Parc. **Open** *concerts* 11am Sun. **Admission** 250BF. **No credit cards.**

Magnificent turn-of-the-century elegance in a working hotel that hosts Sunday brunch concerts. The hotel's small, opulent hall is ideal for chamber music – a suitable ambience is guaranteed.

Hôtel de Ville – Salle Gothique

Grand Place, 1000 (tourist information 279 43 11). Métro Bourse or Gare Centrale. **Open** varies. **Tickets** usually free. **No credit cards.**

Although concerts here are rare, it's worth looking out for a performance, if only to savour the interior of the Grand Place's most grandiose building. The Gothic Hall can accommodate a chamber orchestra and the acoustics are fine, although the ornate décor is almost a distraction.

Lunatheater

20 place Sainctelette, 1000 (201 59 59). Métro Yser. **Box office** 9am-6pm Mon-Fri. **Tickets** 480BF; 300BF students. **Credit** MC, V.

A medium-sized hall with a wide range of programmes, from Renaissance to contemporary.

Wheelchair: access.

Musée Charlier

16 avenue des Arts, 1210 (220 28 19). Métro Arts-Loi or Madou/bus 29, 63, 65, 66. **Open** *museum* 1.30-5pm Mon, Wed, Thur; 12.30-5pm Tue; 1.30-4.30pm Fri. *concerts* 12.30pm, 8pm, Sun. **Admission** *museum* 100BF; *concerts daytime* 150BF; 120BF under-26s; *concerts evening* 300BF-500BF. **No credit cards.**

The modest recital hall is part of an ancient stately home now surrounded by faceless office buildings. Sunday concerts usually begin at 12.30pm. It's too small for anything larger than a chamber-music format.

Musée d'Art Ancien

Auditorium, 3 rue de la Régence, 1000 (508 32 11/512 82 47). Métro Gare Centrale or Parc/tram 92, 93, 94/bus 38, 60, 71, 95, 96. **Open** 10am-noon, 1-5pm, Tue-Sun. **Admission** free; *maps* 20BF. 12.30-1.30pm Weds 100BF. **Credit** AmEx, DC, MC, V (minimum purchase 500BF).

This museum features regular lunchtime concerts on weekdays, which can make a nice break during a tour of the exhibits. The museum guides have been encouraging musical events with themes, such as baroque concerts played on original instruments in the Rubens paintings hall.

Shop. Wheelchair: access.

Opera

Théâtre de la Monnaie

place de la Monnaie, 4 rue Léopold, 1000 (229 12 11). Métro De Brouckère. **Box office** 11am-5.30pm Tue-Sat. **Tickets** 300BF-3000BF. **Credit** AmEx, DC, MC, V.

The national opera house is the jewel in the Brussels cultural crown, and soaks up the lion's share of arts subsidies. Its lavish interior reveals its glorious past; a recent and costly renovation shows confidence in the future. Former director Gerald Mortier, principal architect of its current success, has since moved to Salzburg, but his influence is still felt. Mortier steered the repertoire towards more contemporary works and innovative productions of the classics. He also tried to hire fine singers not yet famous enough for their prices to be out of reach. Current director Bernard Foccroulle, himself a musician, has had notable success with baroque works played by period-instrument ensembles. Perhaps most importantly, he hired Antonio Pappano, a conductor appreciated by audiences, critics and – especially revealing – players. Results are consistently first-class. Unfortunately, this means tickets are almost impossible to get hold of for many productions. Last-minute possibilities exist, but there are always more people than seats.

Wheelchair: access.

Vlaamse Opera

8 Van Ertbornstraat, Antwerp 2080 (03 233 66 85). **Box office** 11am-5.45pm Tue-Sat. **Tickets** 250BF-2500BF. **No credit cards.**

The Flemish Opera has also recently undergone a radical overhaul, especially the orchestra, which is now excellent. Productions are divided between the newly revamped opera house in Ghent (3 Schouwburgstraat, 09 225 24 25) and the old but acoustically splendid Antwerp hall. The latter is a mere 35-minute train ride from central Brussels. From the station in Antwerp, five minutes' walk down the café-lined Frankrijklei brings you there. As with the Brussels opera, the emphasis is on quality rather than big names and productions are usually thoroughly rehearsed. The management encourages orchestra players to participate in weekday lunchtime chamber concerts in the building's foyer.

Perfect for chamber formations and voice recitals – the **Conservatoire Royal de Musique**. *See page 181.*

Music: Rock, Folk & Jazz

Brussels is firmly on the Euro-gig map and has long been fertile ground for top jazz cats. Now its rock clubs seem to herald a new generation of local battling bands.

The **Botanique** *– for rock and world music.*

Good news for gig-going visitors. As Brussels is slap-bang in the middle of the northern European tour trail, bands usually stop off here between Paris and Amsterdam or Cologne. The largest gigs are held in **Forest National**, unless they are mega-events such as the Rolling Stones, Prince or Pink Floyd, which are held out of town but are easy to reach. Medium-sized affairs happen in the **AB**, **Botanique** or **Cirque Royale** theatre.

Rock clubs are a surprisingly recent phenomenon in Brussels. Newer bands such as dEUS, Metal Molly and K's Choice all come from Flanders, where there is a healthy live scene. Apart from Vaya Con Dios, who have achieved near-superstar status in Scandinavia and Central Europe, few groups from Brussels have made it big over the past few years. Bands on the rise include metal-funk outfit PPz30, Belgo-Irish singer Perry Rose, Odex Protocole and Betty Goes Green. The arrival of rock clubs hopefully heralds the emergence of a new generation of bands. If nothing else, they have brightened up the music scene considerably.

Rock venues

AB

114 boulevard Anspach (phone tbc). Métro Bourse/tram 52, 55, 81/bus 48, 95, 96. **Open** tbc. **Admission** 700BF approx. **Credit** tbc.

The best medium-sized venue in town (room for 2,000 people standing) is also the music showcase of the Flemish community in Brussels. The AB (Ancienne Belgique) hosts regular shows every week, with smaller gigs in the club up on the first floor. Major renovation, scheduled to end in December 1996, has transformed the former variety hall (Jacques Brel and Edith Piaf played here) beyond recognition. This is one of the best venues for rock.

Botanique

236 rue Royale, 1210 (226 12 11). Métro Botanique/ tram 92, 94/bus 38, 61. **Open** varies. **Admission** 350BF approx.

The former botanical gardens of Brussels were taken over by the French-speaking community and turned into a pretty cultural centre. The Orangerie hosts an increasing number of rock and world music events, as well as a good selection of quality French acts. However, the size of the hall limits numbers. Don't miss the highly rated Festival de la Chanson – held in the gardens and indoors during September – which bridges the gap between Les Rita Mitsouko and Willy DeVille. One last thing: as the sign on the door proclaims, for tourists, there are no botanical gardens here.

Beursschouwburg

22 rue Auguste Orts, 1000 (513 82 90). Métro Bourse/bus 34, 47, 48, 63, 95, 96. **Open** varies. **Admission** varies.

The tiny theatre of the stock exchange is a pretty leftover from the nineteenth century, now run with considerable flair as a venue for the performing arts. Avant-garde theatre used to predominate, but the organisers have decided to run the place as an experiment in juxtaposition. Fervently devoted to inner-city life, they also programme rap, North African music and jazz. If that sounds too formidable for a Saturday night, try the café on the ground floor, which is a venue for frequently silly parties (including the Tupperware variety). Of particular note, however, is the annual Spoken Tongues festival, featuring much of rock's literary fraternity (we're talking Richard Hell and Gavin Friday here) doing surprising readings.

Cirque Royal

81 rue de l'Enseignement, 1000 (218 20 15). Métro Madou/bus 29, 63. **Open** varies. **Admission** varies.
The former indoor circus is a great seated venue because the circular structure allows the audience to get close to the performer (and vice versa). This is one of the few places that still has usherettes (who expect a tip) and a bell to announce the start of the show. But that didn't stop David Byrne, Vaya Con Dios and Lou Reed from doing memorable gigs here.

Esseghem Blues

329 rue Léopold I, 1090 (427 80 39). Métro Bockstael/ bus 49, 89. **Open** 9am-late. **Admission** 400BF-500BF.
What's in a name? This club prides itself on hosting nothing but American blues artists, says the organiser quite testily. A staple of the Brussels rock scene, it co-hosted (with the AB) the first indoor blues festival in the town at the much larger Lunatheater in 1996.

Ex-Voto

44 rue des Eperonniers, 1000 (502 73 86). Bus 34, 48, 95, 96. **Open** 8pm Thur; 10pm Fri, Sat. **Admission** 200BF approx.
A hastily renovated music venue in a former hairdressing college near the Grand Place. The décor of this small club is garish and sloppily done, which matches the clientèle. Unlike sister venue Magasin 4, the Ex-Voto has a more underground cultural programme, with London's Exploding Cinema being a regular guest.

Flanagan's

55 boulevard de l'Empereur, 1000 (502 52 88). Métro Gare Centrale/bus 29, 60, 63, 71. **Open** *music* from 10pm. **Admission** free.
Popular with young expats at the weekend, this busy café, boasting the largest bay window in town, has a small cellar club for rock bands. They tend towards the blues-pub rock vein, but can often be surprisingly good. Guitarist Charlie Maker has been overseeing weekly jam sessions there for years. Food is served at lunchtime.

Fool Moon

26 quai de Mariemont, 1080 (410 10 03). Bus 63, 89. **Open** *concerts* 10pm. **Admission** 300BF approx.
Another warehouse that has been successfully transformed into a music venue, with a preference for dance-based acts. Expect soul, acid jazz or dub to be high on the agenda. Notable bands that have played here include Odex Protocole, who jammed with producer Mel Gaynor (former drummer with Simple Minds), and the Reggae Twins. The Fool Moon is off the beaten track by a long mile so spare some cash for a taxi home if you plan to hang around after the show.

Forest National

36 avenue du Globe, 1190 (347 03 55). Tram 18, 52/bus 48, 54. **Open** varies. **Admission** varies.
The city's biggest venue also used to have the worst reputation for muddy sound; the Sportpaleis in Ghent is the current titleholder. Recent renovation has improved the acoustics and increased capacity to about 11,000. Parking remains a major problem, however. The local police are notoriously unsympathetic towards badly parked cars. It's advisable to arrive early or take public transport.

KK

VUB campus, boulevard du Triomphe (629 30 56). Tram 23, 90/bus 34. **Open** *concerts Oct-end Apr* 9pm. **Admission** usually free.
A student club at the Flemish university with free weekly gigs, usually from left-field indie bands such as local heroes PPz30 and Wizards of Ooze. Exhibitions and art movies are shown up on the first-floor gallery. The KK (Kultuurkaffee) gets *nil points* for ventilation (bring your own oxygen mask), but ten out of ten for its choice of acts.

A venue with lively jazz, beer, light snacks and meals – **Sounds** *good to us. See page 188.*

Magasin 4

4 rue du Magasin, 1000 (223 34 74). Métro Yser/tram 18. **Open** *when there is a concert* 8pm Mon-Fri; 9pm Sat, Sun. **Admission** 200BF-400BF.

A small rock club on two levels with a good selection of alternative rock bands. Acts performing here are the ones that will break over the next few months (probably moving up to the VK or AB on their next visit). The former warehouse has kept some of its slightly apocalyptic charm, and is the place to catch the new crop of Flemish bands on their first venture into the capital.

Le Sud

43 rue de l'Ecuyer, 1000 (no phone). Métro De Brouckère/bus 29, 63, 65. **Open** varies. **Membership** 100BF.

This labyrinthine, bohemian club started life as a secret venue built in the alleyways between a number of semi-abandoned buildings. Since being raided by the police several times, it has had to clean up its act and comply with fire regulations. The mixture of eastern European and Arabic décor is worth a visit in itself. The choice of bands is also eclectic, but usually good. The Clo-Clo club in the cellar is named after the late French cheapo singing star Claude François (composer of the original 'My Way'), and it revels in the tackier moments of the 1970s – best enjoyed after a few drinks.

Thunderbird Café

48 quai du Commerce, 1000 (219 39 80). Métro Yser/tram 18. **Open** 10.30pm-late Sat. **Admission** usually free.

'Lots of great things about Brussels. Tex-Mex food is not one of them.' The rock historian (and Texan), Ed Ward, said this before the Thunderbird opened, so don't take it as the last word. In addition to commendable grub, the venue boasts gigs twice a week on average. There have been some great moments here: blues guitarist Roland, the equally blue (but considerably more upbeat) Electric Kings and expat Bob Christopher. There aren't that many country fans in Brussels, but this is where they are likely to congregate.

VK

76 Schoolstraat, 1080 (414 29 07). Métro Comte de Flandre/bus 89. **Open** *concerts* 8-11pm Fri. **Admission** 400BF.

Best known for its good selection of international indie acts, the VK (short for Vaartkapoen) is tucked away in a back street of Molenbeek. This is hardly the best location for a music venue, but it makes up for the handicap by laying on the hottest bands and one of the better selections of beer at the bar. A shuttle bus service is sometimes organised from the centre of town (phone for details).

Folk venues

Folk remains a minority interest in Brussels. The influx of English-speaking expats has swelled the ranks of local amateur groups, yet concerts are still very much a word-of-mouth operation. More successful world music artists regularly appear at venues such as the **AB** (*see above*), **Auditorium 44** and the **Salle de la Madeleine**.

Auditorium 44

Passage 44, 44 boulevard du Jardin Botanique, 1000 (218 27 35). Métro Botanique/tram 93, 94/bus 38, 61. **Open** varies. **Admission** varies.

The Auditorium was part of a 1960s utopia: an office block with a shopping gallery, cinema and theatre in the basement. The cinema folded many years ago, but the theatre remains – most notably as venue for the highly recommended annual cartoon and science fiction festivals. More recently, it has become a home of sorts for a number of folk events. Past shows include Finland's Varttina and Ireland's Dervish.

Cancan

95 rue de Jérusalem, 1030. (215 91 30). Bus 59. **Open** 7pm-late Wed-Sat; 5.30pm-late Sun. **Admission** varies.

One of a dying breed, Cancan stages so-called café-concerts.

Alanis Morissette – *one of the big acts to have played to a Brussels audience in 1996.*

Dancing in the streets

For a country which is known for its rain, Belgium has an outstanding number of festivals every year. Many of these are open-air. Brussels has proportionately fewer than the rest of the country, but then the idea is probably to get away from cities rather than bring people into them. Having said that, there is still plenty of music around if you care to check the local press.

Jazz Marathon is the new name for an old idea: hosting up to 400 musicians in cafés, clubs and restaurants around town and setting up a network of vintage buses to ship the audience from one venue to another. It usually happens around May.

Viva Brazil welcomes the greatest stars of said country for a week in June, making it one of very few of its kind in Europe.

Brosella is a jazz and folk festival held every July in the pretty Parc d'Osseghem, practically in the shadow of the Atomium. As the fest is a freebie, don't expect to find big names. But the organisers are very particular about the quality of the acts, while the atmosphere is very relaxed.

World music has always been strong in Belgium, and **Couleur Café** is the best way to catch it. Over a July weekend, a village springs up in the decaying splendour of the former customs depot, Tour et Taxis. The organisers are always anxious to create bridges between styles and generations, finding the missing link between Burundi Black and Zap Mama.

Klinkende Munt – another freebie – features rock and more avant-garde fare in front of the Théâtre de la Monniae (Munt) in July.

Boterhammen in het Park – literally sandwiches in the park – is a lunchtime festival of Dutch-language music held in Parc de Bruxelles, opposite the Palais Royal, in July.

And although July is *the* festival month, there is another major event that attracts some musical big hitters, the **Audi Jazz Festival**, in the autumn (*see chapter* **Brussels by Season**).

Originally intended as a place where anyone could step up and oblige punters with their amateur or semi-pro talents (usually in French), it has now become one of Brussels' few outlets for less commercial acts, hence its inclusion in the folk section.

James Joyce

34 rue Archiméde, 1000 (230 98 94). Métro Schuman/bus 36, 54, 63, 67. **Open** 11am-2am Mon-Fri; noon-2am Sat, Sun; *music* from 9pm Tue. **Admission** free.

An Irish pub in the European quarter with folk music every Tuesday night. Bring your fiddle, and a notebook to catch details of upcoming gigs elsewhere around town.

Movida

3 rue St Géry, 1000 (649 59 14). Métro Bourse/bus 47, 48, 95. 96. **Open** *flamenco* 10pm approx Fri, Sat. **Admission** free.

A Spanish tapas bar which was once wildly popular for its flamenco music (and occasional dancing). It has now been relegated to moderately popular, yet it's still one of the best places to find flamenco.

Le Paradoxe

329 chaussée d'Ixelles, 1050 (649 89 81). Tram 81/bus 71. **Open** *restaurant* noon-2pm, 7-10pm, Mon-Fri; noon-2pm, 7-10.30pm, Sat, Sun; *music* from 8.15pm. **Admission** free. **Credit** AmEx, DC, MC, V.

One of the capital's first vegetarian restaurants, and a good place to catch highbrow world music, jazz and folk acts.

Salle de la Madeleine

14 rue Duquesnoy, 1000 (511 97 32). Métro Gare Centrale/bus 34, 48, 95, 96. **Open** *music* midnight-late. **Admission** varies.

A venue that has never really been popular, despite its central location. In between book and collectibles fairs, there are occasional concerts by African artists such as a seemingly endless number of bands stemming from the Zaiko Langa Langa family.

Jazz venues

'I'm not Caucasian, I'm Belgian.' Toots Thielemans – the best known by far of Belgium's impressive number of jazz musicians – reportedly made the comment to Miles Davis, who was impressed by Toots's playing on an early visit to the States in the 1960s yet could not resist mocking his whiteness. Belgium actually has a jazz tradition that goes back to the 1920s, when big bands turned on to the sounds coming across the Atlantic. Later, guitarist René Thomas and sax-player Jacques Pelzer laid the foundations of what has become one of Europe's most consistent – if not innovative – sources of jazz musicians. The conservatories of Liège, Brussels and Antwerp turn out players who usually go and polish off their technique in the US. They then return home to continue the cycle through teaching and to play in a dizzy number of jazz groups. Top Belgian names include the above-mentioned harmonica-playing Thielemans (whose credits include the theme tunes for *Midnight Cowboy* and, improbably, *Sesame Street*), guitarist Philip Catherine, pianists Michel Herr, Charles Loos and Nathalie Loriers, and drummer Bruno Castellucci. Yet even among the lower ranks, there are names worth catching playing around town.

Sheraton Brussels Airport Hotel

Brussels National Airport, 1930 Zaventem (725 10 00). **Open** noon-2.30pm Sun. **Admission** free. **Brunch** 1200BF.

The idea of listening to some soft, comforting jazz in a sound-proofed atrium as planes literally take off over your head

Stéphane Grappelli – *recently in Brussels.*

might or might not appeal to you. But you can't deny it's an original way to spend a Sunday brunchtime.

L'Archiduc

6 rue Antoine Dansaert, 1000 (512 06 52). Métro Bourse/bus 47, 63. **Open** 5-8pm Sat, Sun. **Admission** 400BF.

Built in the 1930s, this superb little bar was for a long time a secretive after-hours club for jazz fans. The new owner restored the place faithfully to its former glory and now hosts the occasional concert by artists such as Mal Waldron.

Au Travers

11 rue Traversière, 1210 (218 40 86). Métro Botanique/tram 92, 94/bus 38, 61. **Open** *concerts* 9pm Mon-Fri; 10pm Sat. **Admission** 300BF; free Mon.

Au Travers is a venue that has been on the brink of going bust for as long as anyone can remember. Its reputation is built upon music that makes no concessions to commercial considerations. The Monday-night jam sessions are an institution. Au Travers is small, untidy and fiercely proud of its role in jazz.

Exito 13

13 rue Haute, 1000 (511 00 38). Bus 20, 48. **Open** 7pm-late Tue-Sat. **Admission** 100BF Sat.

A South American joint that opened early in 1996, continuing on the success of the wildly popular Do Brasil salsa club. As well as dining on various Latin dishes, punters are regaled by a mix of Brazilian and jazz music. Notable appearances have included Dynamita Salsa and the incredible Irakere.

New York Café Jazz Club

place Stéphanie, 5 chaussée de Charleroi, 1060 (534 85 09). Métro Louise/tram 92, 93, 94. **Open** 10pm-1am Fri, Sat. **Admission** free.

The New York Café is a brasserie-type restaurant. The club behind it is a comfortable venue for catching local acts.

Preservation Hall

4 place de Londres, 1050 (502 15 97). Bus 34, 95, 96. **Open** 9.30pm-12.30pm Tue, Thur; 9.30pm-1.30am Fri, Sat. **Admission** free.

Home to the trad fraternity, this is where Dixieland is still talked about – and played – avidly.

Sounds

28 rue de la Tulipe, 1050 (512 92 50). Métro Porte de Namur/bus 34, 54, 71, 80. **Open** 11.30am-late Mon-Fri; 7pm-late Sat. **Admission** usually free.

The bar at the front resembles a fairground attraction. At the back, a small stage plays host to a healthy assortment of local and touring jazzmen, usually in the modern styles. There is a good selection of beers (a small supplement is charged during the jazz) and a better-than-average choice of snacks and light meals offered by the Italian owners.

Out of town, out of mind?

Out of town is most definitely not out of mind in Belgium, a country whose motorway and rail networks are among the densest in Europe. Beyond Brussels, regular rock shows are also staged at the venues listed below.

Antwerp

Koningin Elisabethzaal *Koningin Astridplein, 2018 (03 233 84 44).* **Box office** noon-6pm Mon-Sat.
Pacific *7-11 Jan Van Gentstraat, 2000 (03 248 28 77).* **Open** *concerts/dancing times vary* Sat, Sun.

Bruges

Cactus Cultuur Café *121 Langestraat, 8000 (050 33 20 14).* **Box office** 9.30am-5.30pm Mon-Fri.

Dour

Rockamadour *10 rue du Marché, 7370 (065 63 10 54).* **Info** 6pm-midnight Wed-Sun. **Concerts** 9.30pm

Ghent

Vooruit *23 Sint-Pietersnieuwstraat, 9000 (09 267 28 20).* **Box office** *phone lines* 10am-6pm Mon-Fri; *in person* 4-6pm Sat.
Flanders Expo *1 Maaltekouter, 9051 (09 241 92 11).* **Box office** 8am-5.30pm Mon-Fri.

Liège

La Zone *27 rue Mean, 4020 (041 41 07 27).* **Information** 10am-6pm Mon-Fri.

Werchter

Near Louvain, this site of an annual festival held on the first weekend in July (info & tickets 09 243 77 77) is twinned with Torhout (near Bruges). The 1996 event featured the Afghan Whigs, Alanis Morissette, Rage at the Machine. Red Hot Chili Peppers, Neil Young & Crazy Horse, Pulp, Massive Attack, Radiohead and Björk in Werchter, and Therapy?, Mazzy Star, David Bowie, Chemical Brothers, Foo Fighters, Underworld and Pridigy in Torhout.

Sport & Fitness

Brussels collects sports almost as fast as its people play them – cricket, anyone?

Sport enlivens what many people still assume is a soulless city, filled with EU bureaucrats. To be fair, that large influx of foreign nationals, drawn here because of the European Parliament, adds part of its own culture to the city. The dozens of overseas sporting clubs, playing games such as cricket, are testament to that. The fact that around 25 per cent of Brussels' population has its origins beyond the Belgian frontiers explains the recent explosion of interest in both watching and taking part in sport.

But it's not just organised sports that are popular. Cycling is part of the national psyche, and many of Brussels' parks and forests are ideal for cyclists, as well as walkers and horse riders. Brussels' natural beauty offers plenty of healthy outdoor exercise, while an increasing number of indoor activities are also springing up.

Regrettably, the Belgian capital is most famous in the world of sport for the Heysel stadium disaster of 1985, when 39 Juventus fans were crushed by a wall after fighting with Liverpool supporters. The city hopes to be remembered more positively after Belgium co-hosts, with Holland, the European Championships in 2000. English football fans, following their teams in Belgium, have already noted the warm welcome they get from locals, although, predictably, policing remains fairly heavy.

The future of sport in Belgium looks positive, whether you are spectating or taking part, as more and better facilities are being planned.

Spectator sports

Athletics

The Ivo Van Damme Memorial athletics meeting is held each August in Brussels and claims to be one of the world's leading athletics events. It certainly attracts some of the world's most famous athletes. It is named after the Gold Medal winner of the 800m at the 1976 Montreal Olympics, who died in a car crash soon after the competition.

The Brussels Marathon is held annually in September. The long-standing Brussels 20km Run, which attracts more than 20,000 runners, is held on the last weekend of May by way of a warm-up.

Brussels 20-kilometre Run

Start & finish: Esplanade du Cinquantenaire. Métro Merode or Schuman. **Date** last Sunday in May. **Admission** 350BF participants; free spectators.

Information *Syndicat d'Initiative – Bruxelles Promotion 1886, 17 rue de la Chapelle, 1000 (511 90 00/fax 511 37 15).* **Open** 9am-6pm Mon-Fri, 9am-4pm Sat.
See also chapter **Brussels by Season**.

Cycling

In recent years the Tour de France has occasionally made a detour through Belgium, and Brussels is one of the stop-off points. The Grand Prix Eddy Merckx, named after Belgium's most famous cyclist, is a race for speed cyclists. It is held annually in Brussels, usually in May or June.

Football

Among sports fans, the Heysel Stadium disaster in 1985 is the chief source of Brussels' fame, or infamy. That year, the European Cup Final was played between Liverpool and Juventus. The score – 1-0 to Juventus – was incidental to the sporadic fighting between the fans. A wall collapsed and 39 Italian spectators died. Since then, international games held in Belgium have been accompanied by a heavy police presence in a bid to prevent any such tragedy happening again.

If you want to see a football match, there is plenty of action in and around Brussels. Rumours of Belgian football being on the slide, after the national team (the Red Devils) failed to qualify for Euro '96, appear to be premature.

In fact Belgium has already qualified for Euro 2000 – the country is going Dutch with Holland for the right to host the European Championships, in 2000. Games will be evenly split between the two countries. The event should help boost the club game, while interest in and around the championships sparks renewed support for local teams.

Keen football fans may like to make the trip north to the famous Belgian club Antwerp. Also not far from Brussels are Standard Liège and Club Bruges. All are easily be reached by public transport; Antwerp is about 40 minutes away while Bruges and Liège take around an hour by train.

RSC Anderlecht

Vanden Stock stadium, 2 avenue Theo Verbeeck, 1070 (522 15 39). Métro St Guidon. **Tickets** 500BF-1000BF; *season tickets* 6,500BF-11,000BF.

Anderlecht is Belgium's most famous club, often doing well in European club competitions. In the 1995-96 season, however, the club crashed out in the preliminary round of the European Champions League to Hungarian champions

Heysel Stadium – home of **Racing Jet de Bruxelles** *and host to annual rugby cup finals.*

Ferencaros; hardly a good performance. Anderlecht has battled with Bruges in recent years for national prominence, losing out in the 1995-96 season while Bruges took a double league and cup triumph.

Racing Jet de Bruxelles

Heysel Stadium, avenue de Marathon, Laeken (262 12 45). Métro Heysel.
The team that actually plays at the infamous Heysel are a lower division club so, while it's relatively easy to get tickets to matches, don't expect to see top European football.

Horse racing

Horse racing has become a popular Belgian pastime comparatively recently. Now there are plenty of opportunities to lose your shirt in and around Brussels. Any of the following can give you details of race times and events.
Boitsfort *chausee de la Hulpe, 1170 (660 28 39).*
Sterrebeek *43 du Roy de Blicquylaan, 1933 Sterrebeek (767 54 75).*
Groenendael *Léopold II, 1560 Hoeilaart (657 03 37).*

Rugby

There are both Flemish and French rugby leagues administered by the Belgian Rugby Union with teams spread all over the country. Annual cup finals are held at the Heysel Stadium in Brussels.

Tennis

The Belgium Tennis Championships are held in Antwerp in February, while the indoor championships take place at the same time in Brussels at the Heysel Exhibition Hall or at Forest National (*see chapter* **Music: Rock, Folk & Jazz**).

Activities

Organisations

You can get information about sporting events and activities in Brussels from the following organisations:
Cellule Information de l'ADEPS (Administration de l'Education Physique, des Sports et de la Vie en Plein Air) *3rd floor, 44 boulevard Léopold II, 1080 (413 28 37).*
Sport For All *Clearinghouse, c/o Espace 27 Septembre, boulevard Léopold II, 1080 (413 28 93).*
Belgian Sports Federation for the Handicapped *4 place Van Gehuchten, 1020 (478 48 50).*

Aerobics

It's fairly easy to track down an aerobics class to keep you trim while you're in Brussels. Classes are organised by many organisations.
British and Commonwealth Women's Club *(772 53 13).*
American Women's Club *(358 47 53).*

Badminton

Brussels British Badminton Club

(380 70 84).
The club holds matches in Brussels (Woluwe-Saint-Lambert) and at nearby Waterloo.

Basketball

Basketball is popular in Belgium which is presumably why the annual NBA European street basketball tour visits Brussels (normally during August). It promises three-on-three tournaments and interactive activities such as a two-ball skills session, and the NBA Jam Session. Also popular in Belgium is korfball, the mixed-sex cross between basketball and netball. The korf, or net, is 11 feet high, eliminating height advantage, which makes it popular with both sexes. Basketball and korfball pitches are dotted around the city.

Bowling

For slightly more indolent sports folk, bowling is ideal, offering the chance to drink and relax while you compete. Not surprisingly, Brussels has its fair share of bowling alleys where you can go for the strike.
Crosly Super Bowling *36 boulevard de l'Empereur, 1000 (512 08 74).* Offers 20 lanes.
Bowlmaster *45 rue Van Zande, 1080 (465 05 10).*

Chess

It is still possible to find the occasional Brussels café which encourages chess on its premises – for example Le Greenwich (*see chapter* **Cafés & Bars**) – but expect an audience, all with their own suggestions or criticisms of your play. There are also more formal clubs for the budding grandmaster, including the following:

Cercle Royal des Echecs de Bruxelles

(215 20 00).
A long-established chess club.

Cricket

Cricket has a long and distinguished history in Brussels: British regiments had a few overs at the Bois de la Cambre on the eve of the Battle of Waterloo as long ago as 1815. These days the Royal Brussels Cricket Club plays host to many visiting sides from the United Kingdom, enabling you to hear the familiar sound of leather against willow on soft summer days.
Royal Brussels Cricket Club *Ground 51, Centre-Obain, 117 Vieux Chemin de Wavre, 1328 Obain-Lasne (764 75 24).*

Cycling

Cycling is something of a national sport in Belgium. Bikes can be hired fairly cheaply from most railway stations, and returned to any station – ask for details of the Train-Plus-Vélo scheme. In town it's wise to keep clear of the roads and some of Brussels' drivers' unexpected habits. Luckily there are plenty of cycle tracks to follow and the Forêt de Soignes offers excellent cycle rides; bikes can be hired from the nearby Vélo Pipette.

Vélo Pipette

(672 16 98).

Ligue Vélocipedique Belge

(349 19 11).
The league provides details of cycling clubs.

Football

Playing football in Brussels is relatively easy, from park pick-up games to amateur leagues. There are two expatriate clubs that are always looking for new players:
British United Football Club *(296 37 74).*
Royal Brussels British Football Club *(352 54 76).*

Golf

With more than 60 golf courses in Belgium, you won't be too far from a game if you want one. In Brussels itself there are no full-size courses but mini-golf can be found in the summer months at Parc de Wolvendael and at the Parc Josaphat (*see chapter* **Sightseeing**).

Federation Royal Belge de Golf

(067 22 04 40)
The federation will supply details of golf courses in Belgium.

Hôtel Le 1815

(387 00 60)
This Waterloo hotel has a gimmicky miniature 18-hole golf course depicting scenes from the famous battle at that site.

Health & fitness

If you want to work out while you're in Brussels, there are plenty of places.
American Gym *144 boulevard General Jacques, 1050 (640 59 92). Bus 71.*
Winners *13 rue Bonneel, 1040 (280 02 70). Métro Madou.*
Hotel Sheraton *3 place Rogier, 1210 (224 31 11). Métro Rogier/tram 23, 52, 55, 56, 81, 90.* The hotel has a rooftop fitness centre which offers panoramic views.
Royal Crown Hotel Mercure *250 rue Royale, 1210 (220 66 11). Métro Botanique/tram 92, 93, 94.* The hotel has a health club.

Martial arts

Centre de la Culture Japonaise

44 rue des Augustines, 1090 (426 50 00). Métro Pannenhuys.
The centre holds English-speaking classes in Judo and Karate and like activities

Rambling

The Forêt de Soignes (*see chapter* **Sightseeing**) offers excellent rambling opportunities, taking the keen walker far beyond the city's boundaries. A map is recommended as the array of paths can be bewildering. The winding *sentiers* are likely to be much more interesting and rewarding than the straight *drèves*. Take a tram out and walk back into the city, but take refreshments, as there are no restaurants or cafés.

Riding

There is a riding path through the Bois de la Cambre (*see chapter* **Sightseeing**), and bridle paths in the sprawling Forêt de Soignes (*see above*) for keen horseriders.

Rollerskating

There is a public outdoor rollerskating rink in the **Bois de la Cambre**.

Rugby

Brussels British Rugby Club *(759 23 78).* Half the members of the Rugby Club are British nationals. The rest come from as far afield as America, South Africa and Australia. Expect the normal level of rugby humour from a club which has the Manneken Pis as its logo.

Running

The annual Brussels 20km Run is popular with keen runners. The Marathon is in September, giving regular 26-milers plenty of time to rest following the London and Paris marathons in the spring. But most joggers are content to pound the alleys in the Parc du Cinquantenaire, or the tree-strewn Parc de Woluwe (*see chapter* **Sightseeing**).

Hash House Harriers *(734 36 77).* The Harriers organise Saturday afternoon and Monday evening runs for fun-runners and more serious types.

Skateboarding

Mont des Arts

north of place Royale.

The main congregation place for skateboarders. Offers a marble surface with stairs of different heights to test even the most experienced boarder. And there's the handy Ride All Day skate shop nearby to pick up any new equipment.

Bois de la Cambre

at the south end of avenue Louise.

There's a public outdoor skating rink here which boasts a small double concrete bowl and ramps, although it tends to be frequented by rollerskaters.

Roller Park

300 Quai Biestebroeckkaai, 1070.

In Anderlecht, the Roller Park's distinguishing features include a pyramid and two volcanoes.

Squash

Numbers of squash courts in Brussels are increasing, as demand from foreign nationals generates interest among Belgians.

Castle Club *16 avenue de la Becasse, 1970 Wezembeek-Oppem (731 68 20).* The club is a favourite among English-speaking squash players.

Flanders Gate Squash Club *17 boulevard Barthelemy, 1000 (512 51 33). Tram 18.*

Fort Jaco *1333 chausée de Waterloo, 1180 (375 26 77). Tram 92.*

Swimming

Océade

Bruparck, 20 boulevard du Centenaire, 1020 (478 43 20). Métro Heysel/tram 18, 19, 81, 91. **Open** *Apr-Aug* 2-10pm Tue-Thur; 2-11pm Fri; 10am-11pm Sat; 10am-10pm Sun. *Sept-Mar* 2-11pm Fri; 10am-11pm Sat; 10am-10pm Sun. **Admission** 450BF; 330BF children 1.25m-1.5m tall; free children under 1.25m tall. **Credit** MC, V.

For families this impressive complex offers everything to keep youngsters happy, including a wave-making machine.

The **Parc de Woluwe** *– popular with runners.*

Poseidon

2 avenue des Vaillants, 1200 (771 66 55). Métro Tomberg. **Open** 8am-7pm Mon-Fri; 8am-7.30pm Sat, Sun. **Admission** *pool* 75BF; 60BF under-14s; *ice-rink* 250BF; 210BF under-13s. **No credit cards**.

The Poseidon has a separate children's pool and a separate ice rink, but it gets quite crowded.

Centre Sportif de Woluwe St Pierre

2 avenue Salome, 1150 (762 12 75). Tram 39. **Open** 8am-7pm Mon-Thur, Sat, Sun; 8am-8pm Fri. **Admission** *pool* 100BF; 90BF under-14s. **No credit cards**.

This massive sports complex offers an Olympic-sized pool and water slide. It also offers squash, volleyball and leisure activities, a solarium and steam baths.

Tennis

There are plenty of tennis courts around town. Most are private, but you can often rent them by the hour.

Association Francophone de Tennis

203 galerie Porte Louise, 1050 (513 29 20). Métro Louise/tram 93, 94.

French-speaking organisation which supplies information on hiring tennis courts.

Theatre & Dance

Belgian theatre offers an inspired mix of French realism and German grotesquerie with no shortage of visiting talent, while terpsichorean Brussels is a thoroughly modern affair.

It doesn't have a Shakespeare or a Sartre, but the festivals are huge, the theatres are beautiful, new talent is on the rise and all touring companies stop by the 'crossroads of Europe'.

Brussels has good-quality, varied theatre and a particularly strong contemporary dance scene, both of which suffer from rather inadequate funding, though Belgium cottoned on to Lotto-funded arts long before Britain did. There's a certain fluidity between dance and theatre: many of the venues are used equally for both and the numerous festivals generally run the gamut of performing arts.

There are often first-class foreign companies in town, but some of the most exciting performances are to be seen outside the capital, especially in Antwerp, which boasts larger theatres than Brussels and seems to be the preferred venue for travelling English companies. It is within easy reach (*see* **Trips Out of Town**) and there are often amazing performances at more affordable prices than those in London.

Belgian theatre is an inspired mixture of French realism and German grotesquerie. In the famous **Théâtre de Toone**, puppets are pulled into performing grotesque antics, gabbling in *Bruxellois* dialect, while at the **Théâtre National**, perfect productions of Racine are classically staged. The Belgian genius for painting and interior design comes out in the stage sets, which are either incredibly surreal – including gargoyles and fairgrounds – or conventionally but stunningly beautiful. They justify a visit even if you don't understand the language.

Despite all the long-running problems of poor arts funding and a tradition of exporting its talent, Belgian theatre has remained buoyant through its 150 years. Except for the brief flowering of Maurice Maeterlinck at the end of the nineteenth century, there have been few national playwrights. Theatres survived on French plays until after World War II, when they turned to translating American and British plays, sustaining themselves through the 1970s on Alan Ayckbourn, Tom Stoppard and Harold Pinter; only returning recently to contemporary continental playwrights. The recent trend is for co-productions, notably with nearby Strasbourg, and this has helped to maintain quality. Most of Brussels' 30 theatres perform in French, though the much smaller Flemish scene is reputed to be more creative.

The curtain rises all over Brussels at 8.30pm. There is no central booking office, so tickets have to be booked from individual venues. Box offices are generally open all day, Tuesday to Saturday. Tickets are generally not expensive and there are always good discounts for students, groups and the over-60s.

To find out what's on, check the French-language daily newspaper, *Le Soir* (28BF), or for complete weekly listings, the English-language *Bulletin* (80BF).

Theatre

Main theatres

Rideau de Bruxelles

Palais des Beaux Arts, 23 rue Ravenstein, 1000 (box office 507 82 00). Métro Parc. **Box office** 11am-6pm Mon-Sat. **Tickets** 300BF-700BF; 300BF students, disabled. **No credit cards.**

Set up in 1953 to promote Belgian talent, it shows a lot of work by young and contemporary writers, and is a good venue for touring Belgian companies. The staple diet is Mamet and Stoppard; generally good, solid fare. It also stages plays in sign language, using deaf actors.

Wheelchair: access.

Théâtre 140

140 avenue Eugène Plasky, 1030 (733 97 08). Tram 23, 90/bus 29, 63. **Box office** noon-6pm Mon-Sat. **Tickets** 520BF-800BF. **No credit cards.**

The brainchild of Jo Deckmine, Théâtre 140's seats are scuffed and the carpet is studded with cigarette butts, but its subscribers are devoted and the entertainment is world-class. Used for theatre, music and dance, it doesn't have a repertory company, but effortlessly attracts the best touring groups. The theme is contemporary art, and within that you get just about everything, from Pink Floyd to New York Living Theatre.

Wheelchair: access.

Théâtre National

Centre Rogier, place Rogier, 1210 (203 53 03). Métro Rogier. **Box office** 11am-6pm Tue-Sat. **Tickets** 325BF-750BF; 325BF students. **Credit** AmEx, DC, MC, V (credit card bookings by telephone after 7pm only).

The 'National' Theatre, which only serves the French community, is very much into co-productions. It recently enticed the great French director Jean-Marie Villégier from Strasbourg, which means that the current standard of productions is exceptional. It is also a host venue for major touring companies such as Britain's RSC.

Wheelchair: access.

At the world-famous **Théâtre de Toone**, *marionettes are put through their paces.*

Théâtre Royal du Parc

3 rue de la Loi, 1000 (512 23 39). Métro Arts-Loi or Parc. **Box office** 11am-6pm daily. **Tickets** 180BF-850BF; 330BF students under 26. **No credit cards**.

One of the most beautiful theatres in western Europe, it puts on fine classical productions but its best feature is the performance of hopelessly dated 1930s comedies or *boulevards*, which are not seen anywhere else. No attempt is made to update them. It's gruesome, riveting and quite unique.

Wheelchair: access.

Théâtre de Poche

chemin de Gymnase, Bois de la Cambre, 1000 (649 17 27). Tram 23, 90. **Box office** 10am-5.30pm Mon-Sat. **Tickets** 350BF-550BF. **No credit cards**.

An avant-garde and erudite menu of Central European playwrights and others at the cutting edge is offered here – including the likes of Bukowski. The theatre often works with English directors and writers, such as John Godber. It hosts the annual Premières Rencontres festival in September, which shows end-of-year work by Belgian and international drama schools.

Wheelchair: access.

Théâtre de Toone

6 impasse Schuddeveld, petite rue des Bouchers, 1000 (511 71 37). Métro De Brouckère. **Open** noon-midnight Tue-Sat. **Box office** tickets available 8pm, just before perf. **Tickets** 400BF; 250BF under-12s, students (Tue-Thur only). **No credit cards**.

Set in the centre of town, this charming theatre, which has been in the Toone family for seven generations, is world famous and a must for any visitor. Marionette productions of works such as *Cyrano de Bergerac* and *Hamlet* are performed in *Bruxellois*, a regional mixture of French and Flemish. Its equally charming café is open all day.

Café. Wheelchair: access.

Théâtre de Vaudeville

15 galerie de la Reine, 1000 (514 16 00). Métro Gare Centrale. **Box office** 1-6pm daily. **Tickets** 400BF-500BF. **No credit cards**.

Those of us who used to dance all night in this beautiful theatre during its brief years as one of Brussels' hottest clubs, rather begrudged its return to its original use. Still, the result has been triumphant – it was chosen by Deborah Warner and Fiona Shaw for the première of *The Wasteland*. No doubt its founders would be relieved.

Outside Brussels

DeSingel

25 Desguinlei, Antwerp 2015 (03 248 38 00). **Box office** 10am-7pm Mon-Fri; 4-7pm Sat. **Tickets** 400BF-900BF. **Credit** MC, V.

This is an international centre for dance and theatre in a huge concrete setting with a consistently intelligent programme of events. Four international companies are chosen per season, with the emphasis very much on innovation and originality. The choice for spring 1996 was *The Tempest* performed by Britain's Nottingham Playhouse with the Romanian director Purcarete – exactly the kind of cultural mix DeSingel aims for.

Wheelchair: access.

Théâtre Jean Vilar

rue du Sablon, Centre Urbain, Louvain-la-Neuve, 1348 (010 450 400). **Box office** 11am-6pm Mon-Sat. **Tickets** up to 900BF; 300BF students. **Credit** AmEx, DC, MC, V.

In the heart of the university town, Jean Vilar has the verve you would expect from playing to student audiences. It puts on a wide variety of plays, both contemporary and classical. Past productions include a play by and with Benoit Poelvoorde of *Man Bites Dog* fame.

Café-Theatre

For more intimate, relaxed theatre over a drink, check out the venues below. Most of them work with young Belgian companies, but they also take in lesser-known touring groups. Box office opening times vary.

Théâtre 'Le Café' *158 rue de la Victoire, 1060 (538 75 24). Métro Porte de Hal.*

Café-Théâtre du Botanique *236 rue Royale, 1210 (226 12 11). Métro Parc.*

Comiqu'Art *1 rue de la Victoire, 1060 (537 69 37). Métro Porte de Hal.*

La Fleur en Papier Doré *53 rue des Alexiens, 1000 (511 16 59). Bus 20, 48.*

Le Fool Moon Théâtre *26 quai de Mariemont, 1080 (410 10 03). Bus 63.*

English-language groups

Brussels has some extremely dedicated amateur theatrical groups, and in a city where they are often the only chance to see English-language theatre, all performances are booked out. They have become a must for the claustrophobic expat community. Groups such as the **English Comedy Club**, the **English Shakespearean Society**, the **Irish Theatre Group** and the **American Theatre Group** were started about 20 years ago and have flourished ever since, unhampered by the funding problems that dog most amateur groups. Productions are generally safe renditions of established plays. The quality is erratic, but there's often a surprising amount of talent evident. Most societies don't have a fixed venue, but listings of plays and dates of society meetings can be found in the *Bulletin*. If you have thespian proclivities and are planning to stay in Brussels for a while, it's worth phoning to see if you can get involved.

Anne Teresa De Keersmaeker – *in town.*

Dance

In the 1960s, if you mentioned Belgium to the outside world, the inevitable response was chocolates and Béjart. Béjart is gone, and he was French anyway, but he brought his Twentieth-Century Dance Company here in 1959 and set up the enormously influential Mudra school, radically and permanently transforming dance in Belgium. Formerly small and firmly classical, the scene is now large and very contemporary. It remains one of the key European capitals of modern dance, with 50 companies in residence, chief among them those of **Anne Teresa De Keersmaeker** and **Wim Vandekeybus**, whose new and violent choreography earned him prestigious awards in America.

Belgium has a strong reputation for dance and a dedicated audience, which ensures frequent visits by major foreign companies. The only drawback is the lack of a good venue large enough to accommodate the faithful. At the moment, only the hideous **Forest National** – built for rock concerts – has the capacity for the really great companies, but the only point in watching dance there is to buy the programme showing you've been. There are, however, a large number of very good smaller venues and at least 15 first-class contemporary dance shows to choose between at any one moment. Other dance is less well represented: the only classical ballet company is in Antwerp, the excellent **Royal Ballet of Flanders**; and South American, Asian and folk dance can be hard to come by. Check the French-language daily newspaper, *Le Soir* (28BF), or the English-language weekly *Bulletin* to find out what's on.

Main venues

Atelier St Anne

75-77 rue des Tanneurs, 1000 (548 02 60). Bus 20, 48.
Box office 2-6pm Mon-Sat. **Tickets** 280BF-480BF. **No credit cards**.

This centre for music, theatre and dance opened in 1973 as a base for young choreographers and directors. The choreographer in residence at the moment is the Béjart-trained Jose Besprosvany, who uses legends from his native Mexico in his innovative dances.

Chapelle des Brigittines

rue des Visitandines, 1000 (511 99 66). Bus 20, 48.
Box office 8.30am-5.30pm Mon-Fri. **Tickets** 400BF; 250BF students. **No credit cards**.

The **Palais des Beaux Arts** *hosts theatre and dance, including an annual programme of modern and classical dance –* *see p198.*

An exquisite chapel set incongruously in the run-down Marolles area, this is a centre for co-productions and for Belgian companies. It co-produces the annual Festival Bellone-Brigittines (Aug-Sept) of dance, theatre and music, in which each year the programme revolves around one particular theme.
Wheelchair: access.

Cirque Royal

81 rue de l'Enseignement, 1000 (218 20 15). Métro Madou. **Box office** 11am-6pm Tue-Sat. **Tickets** price varies. **No credit cards.**
This is the only good large dance venue in Brussels, with a capacity of about 1,700. It's a renovated circus with a pleasing round shape. The exciting programme is a mix of classical and contemporary dance, and the venue is the most common host for touring companies.
Wheelchair: access.

Lunatheater

20 place Sainctelette, 1000 (201 59 59). Métro Yser. **Box office** 9am-6pm Mon-Fri. **Tickets** 480BF; 300BF students. **Credit** MC, V.
It used to be a cinema, but now boasts an upbeat dance programme and is the preferred venue for Wim Vandekeybus and his ferociously energetic company. His *Live Project 1996* had musicians and dancers performing against a backdrop of moving film images and featured the blind dancer Saîd Gharbi.
Wheelchair: access.

La Movida

3 rue St Géry, 1000 (649 59 14). Métro Bourse or Ste Cathérine/bus 47, 48, 95. 96. **Open** *flamenco* 10pm approx. **Admission** free. **Credit** DC, MC, V.
Authentic rather than touristic, this vibrant bar hosts weekly flamenco shows (*see chapter* **Music: Rock, Folk & Jazz: Folk venues**).

Palais des Beaux Arts

23 rue Ravenstein, 1000 (507 82 00). Métro Parc. **Box office** 11am-6pm Mon-Sat. **Tickets** 500BF approx but price varies. **Credit** MC, V.
This large cultural centre, together with the Paleis (the Flemish arm of the Beaux Arts), co-ordinates music, theatre and dance events and is an umbrella for numerous organisations. It runs a strong modern and classical dance programme, called La Série, in September.
Wheelchair: access.

Théâtre de la Balsamine

1 avenue Felix Marchal, 1030 (735 64 68). Bus 29, 54. **Box office** 10am-6pm Mon-Fri. **Tickets** 450BF; 250BF students. **No credit cards.**
A very avant-garde venue covering both theatre and dance, Théâtre de la Balsamine was recently erected on the site of a ruined barracks, and for the first few productions, actors systematically destroyed different parts of the barracks. Enter stage left and a wall would fall in. At dance performances the spectators are invited to choose one of the dance solos and confront the dancer. It also serves as host of the tremendously experimental Danse à la Balsa festival in February.

Théâtre de la Monnaie

place de la Monnaie, 4 rue Léopold, 1000 (229 12 11). Métro De Brouckère. **Box office** 11am-5.30pm Tue-Sat. **Tickets** 300BF-3000BF. **Credit** AmEx, DC, MC, V.
The beautiful centre of opera and ballet where Béjart held sway for 30 years. Anna Teresa de Keersmaeker and her company, Rosas, are now in residence with their contemporary ballet.
Wheelchair: access.

Smaller venues

The cultural centres of the different Brussels *communes* have small dance, theatre and film programmes. The most active are the **Centre Culturel de Woluwe St Pierre** (773 05 88), the **Centre Culturel d'Anderlecht** (522 74 07) and the **Halles de Schaerbeek** (218 00 31).

Outside Brussels

Vlaamse Opera

3 Frankrejklei, Antwerp 2000/postal address 8 Van Ertbornstraat, Antwerp 2080 (03 233 66 85). **Box office** 11am-5.45pm Tue-Sat. **Tickets** 250BF-2500BF. **No credit cards.**
This and the Stadsschouwberg (070 233 244), also in Antwerp, are where to go to see the Royal Ballet of Flanders and other touring classical ballet companies. The Vlaamse Opera also hosts Israeli and Brazilian dance companies.

Festivals

Kunstenfestivaldesarts

Information 219 07 07. **Date** (biennial) May.
A key international festival of tremendous vitality, and virtually unique for including both French and Flemish works. It's held in theatres all round Brussels and is concerned with all the performing arts. It's also exceptionally well-endowed and sponsors special co-productions.

Rencontres D'Octobre

Information 511 04 60. **Date** (annual) Sept-Oct.
Held in Liège and Brussels, this fest is a yearly chance for Belgian artists to interact with outside companies. The theme is modernity.

Classes & information

Centre de Danse Choreart

985 chaussée d'Alsemberg, 1180 (332 13 59). Tram 55.
The city's biggest dance school has its own professional dance company. Classes in classical ballet, jazz and tap-dancing cost 300BF per session.

Ecole de Danse Universelle

277 chaussée de Boondael, 1050 (649 77 40). Tram 90.
Ballroom, rock 'n' roll, tango, samba etc can be learnt here for 3500BF per batch of 15 lessons. There are reductions for students and partners.

Maison du Spectacle – La Bellone

46 rue de Flandre, 1000 (513 33 33). Métro Ste Catherine.
The Maison is a centre for dance and theatre, and has a library with all current periodicals. It also brings out a seasonal magazine, *Nouvelles de Danse*, which is sold in major bookshops.

Rhapsodie

28 rue Defacqz, 1050 (539 12 04). Métro Louise/tram 93.
This is the place for belly-dancing, African and Latin American dance, plus yoga and meditation – all at 300BF a lesson.

Yantra Académie

16B rue de la Cuve, 1050 (646 25 64). Tram 91, 92/bus 38, 59, 60, 71.
With the exception of classical ballet, all classes at the Yantra Académie are for adults only. Jazz (with six ability levels), contemporary dance and a form of African dance are all offered at 300BF per session.

In Focus

Business **200**
Children **205**
Gay & Lesbian **209**
Students **213**
Women's Brussels **217**

Business

Depending on your bureaucracy tolerance level, Brussels can be a networker's paradise or red-tape hell.

Brussels is a businessman's dream. As chief base for the EU, the city receives a stream of visitors from within Europe and the rest of the world. While many come as tourists, the majority of visitors are Eurocrats and businessman connected to the EU. Networking opportunities abound.

The downside, however, is that all businesses – from one-off boutique to multinational conglomerate – must endure endless bureaucracy and high costs to be here. Taxes are among the highest in Europe and appear to be all-pervasive. The government recently promulgated a law taxing companies for every computer screen in their offices.

The high cost of hiring employees – in terms of healthcare contributions and taxes – has prompted an increase in the number of self-employed. Many physicians and professionals in private practice choose to do without receptionists and handle paperwork themselves. As a result, Belgium has a high rate of unemployment, currently over 10 per cent.

Accountants

Need help coping with Belgium's complex tax system? The 'Big Six' have offices in Brussels and can offer help at the individual or corporate level.

Arthur Andersen & Co *56 avenue des Arts, 1000 (510 42 11/fax 510 44 00 or 513 08 62). Métro Trône.* **Open** 8am-6.30pm Mon-Fri.

Coopers & Lybrand *216 avenue Marcel Thiry, 1200 (774 42 11/fax 774 42 99). Métro Roodebeek.* **Open** 8.30am-5pm Mon-Fri.

Deloitte & Touche Consultants NV-SA *6 Berkenlaan, 1831 (718 92 11/fax 718 92 04). Métro Diegem.* **Open** 8am-6pm Mon-Fri.

Ernst & Young *204 avenue Marcel Thiry, 1200 (774 91 11/fax 774 90 90). Métro Roodebeek.* **Open** 8am-6pm Mon-Fri.

KPMG Peat Marwick *Woluwe Office Park, 101 rue Neerveld, 1200 (773 36 11/fax 772 33 05). Métro Roodebeek.* **Open** 8am-6pm Mon-Fri.

Price Waterhouse *62 boulevard de la Woluwe, 1200 (773 14 11/fax 770 32 49). Métro Roodebeek.* **Open** 8am-6pm Mon-Fri.

Banks

You may want to check with your bank back home to see if they have a branch here. Many UK banks have corporate offices in Brussels, but lack personal banking services. Head offices for Belgium's biggest commercial banks are listed below. Telephone the individual branches first for opening hours, since times can vary. It's worth asking about direct debit cards which are available through the banks. The cards – known as Mister Cash and Bancontact – are accepted nearly everywhere, including supermarkets, for a mere 5BF fee per transaction.

Banque Bruxelles Lambert (BBL)

24 avenue Marnix, 1000 (547 21 11/fax customer service 547 8800). Métro Trône. **Open** 9am-4pm Mon-Fri.

CGER Banque et Assurances

48 rue du Fossé aux Loups, 1000 (228 61 11/fax 228 71 99). Métro De Brouckère. **Open** 8.30am-3.30pm Mon-Thur; 8.30am-5.30pm Fri.

This partly state-owned bank focuses mainly on consumer banking. It also handles car, fire, home and life insurance.

Citibank

263g boulevard Général Jacques, 1050 (information & services 24-hour Citiphone 626 50 50/fax 626 56 18 or 626 56 19). Tram 23, 90. **Open** 9am-5pm Mon-Fri.

All the banking services available at your New York or London branch are also on offer here.

Kredietbank

7 rue d'Arenberg, 1000 (546 41 11/fax 546 42 09). Métro De Brouckère. **Open** 9am-4pm Mon-Fri.

Générale de Banque

3 rue Montagne du Parc, 1000 (information toll free 0800 12345/general 565 11 11/fax 565 4222). Métro Gare Centrale. **Open** 9am-4pm Mon-Fri.

Business information

American Chamber of Commerce

50 avenue des Arts, 1000 (513 67 70/fax 513 35 90). Métro Trône. **Open** 9am-noon, 2-5pm, Mon-Fri.

The Chamber has about a thousand members – half of whom are American and the rest European. It offers help with legal and commercial problems (though you should call for an appointment first), and organises events to maximise networking opportunities. An annual directory of all American and member companies in Brussels is free to members and costs 3500BF for non-members.

Bourse des Valeurs Mobilières de Bruxelles (Brussels Stock Exchange)

Palais de la Bourse, 1000 (information 509 12 11/public relations 509 13 48/fax 509 12 12). Métro Bourse. **Open** 9am-5pm Mon-Fri; *tours* by appointment only.

Of Belgium's two stock exchanges – the other is in Antwerp – this is the more important one. Don't expect to see traders gesticulating wildly on the floor, though. All trading is computerised. Visitors can, however, hear a lecture on how the whole process works. Call Vera Moerenhout in public relations to schedule an appointment.

Comings and goings of business in Brussels.

British Chamber of Commerce
15 rue d'Egmont, 1000 (540 90 30/fax 512 83 63). Métro Trône. **Open** 9.30am-noon, 2.30-5pm, Mon-Fri.
If you're with a British company doing business in Belgium, or a Belgium company doing business in the UK, you may want to become a member. It allows you access to the reference library and entitles you to a free copy of the directory of 300-odd members (2500BF for non-members).

Brussels Chamber of Commerce
500 avenue Louise, 1050 (648 50 02/fax 640 93 28). Métro Louise. **Open** 9am-noon, 1.30-4pm, Mon-Thur; 9am-noon, 1-3pm, Fri.
This private club offers legal support to Brussels-based companies and advises on how economic and trade-related government policies may affect certain industries. Between 3,000 and 4,000 Belgian and foreign companies are members. Membership fees are based on company size.

Euro Info Centre – Commerce Extérieur
500 avenue Louise, 1050 (648 58 73/fax 640 93 28). Métro Louise. **Open** 9am-noon, 1-4pm, Mon-Thur; 8.30am-noon, 1-3pm, Fri.
Confused by EU legislation and how it may affect your business? The Euro Info Centre – sponsored by the European Commission – is designed to help small and medium-sized businesses find answers to such questions.

Ministère de la Région de Bruxelles
Services des Investissements Etranger (Foreign Investment Department), 25 rue du Champ de Mars, 1050 (513 97 00/fax 511 52 55). Métro Porte de Namur. **Open** 9am-5pm Mon-Fri.
Foreign investors looking for opportunities in Brussels will be warmly received by this office. Call for an appointment with a representative and ask about their brochures.

Office de la Propriété Industrielle (Patent Office)
Ministère des Affaires Economiques, Administration de la Politique Commerciale, 154 boulevard Emil Jacqmain, 1000 (206 41 56/fax 206 57 01). Métro Rogier or Yser. **Open** *office* 10am-noon, 2-4pm, Mon-Fri; *library* 9am-noon, 1-4pm, Mon-Fri.
For about 50BF a minute the Patent Office can do an online search to see if a patent exists in most parts of the world. After 30 minutes you should have a good idea of what's out there. The library also contains microfilm and microfiche records of patents. It costs 2000BF to file a Belgian patent, valid for six years, and 40000BF for 20 years' protection.

Vlaamse Dienst voor de Buitenlandse Handel (Flemish Foreign Trade Board)
80 rue Royale, 1000 (504 87 11/fax 504 88 99). Métro Parc. **Open** 9am-5pm Mon-Fri.
Foreign companies interested in importing Flemish goods or services will find all the help they need here.

Reference books

EU Committee
American Chamber of Commerce, Box 5, 50 avenue des Arts, 1000 (513 68 92/fax 513 79 28). Métro Trône. **Open** 9am-6pm Mon-Thur; 9am-5pm Fri.
The valuable EU Information Handbook contains current listings of all European Union-related committees, missions and offices. You can buy a copy for 2100BF at the American Chamber of Commerce or order it by mail.

Ernst & Young
204 avenue Marcel Thiry, 1200 (774 91 11/fax 774 90 90). Métro Roodebeek. **Open** 8am-6pm Mon-Fri.
Bogged down with Belgian bureaucracy? At no cost, E&Y will give you a useful 112-page guide, *Doing Business in Belgium*. Copies are available at all their offices worldwide.

European Report
European Information Service, 66 avenue Adolphe Lacomblé, 10306 (737 77 00/fax 732 67 57). Métro Diamant. **Open** 9am-6pm Mon-Fri.
Businessmen, lawyers and anyone else interested in detailed updates on EU activities can receive this French- and English-language publication twice a week for 46200BF a year.

Focus Career Services
23 rue Lesbroussart, 1050 (646 65 30/fax 646 96 02). Tram 81, 82/bus 38, 59 60, 71. **Open** 10am-5pm Tue, Thur, Fri; 10am-8pm Wed.
For 500BF you can get a head start on setting up a business – non-profit centre Focus produce *Getting Started… Legally: The FOCUS Guide to Working in Belgium and Starting a Business*. A reference copy is available for members. Annual membership costs 2400BF (*see chapter* **Women's Brussels**).

Conferences

Looking for an offbeat conference centre? There are several quaint *châteaux* on the outskirts of the city that offer unusual meeting rooms. Check

中國城酒樓

under Salles (Locations) in the *Yellow Pages*. A few of the better-known conference facilities are listed below.

Espace Moselle
40 rue des Drapiers, 1050 (502 65 45/fax 502 66 28). Métro Porte de Namur. **Open** 9am-6pm Mon-Fri. **Credit** AmEx, DC, EC, MC, V.
For a touch of historic Brussels, Espace Moselle offers a renovated late nineteenth-century home with high ceilings and crystal chandeliers as a meeting venue. Food and cocktails can be arranged for up to 250 people. Parking is available, as is a garden – rain permitting.

Management Centre Europe
118 rue de l'Aqueduc, 1050 (543 21 00/fax 543 24 00). Bus 54, 81. **Open** 8.30am-8pm Mon-Fri. **Credit** AmEx, DC, MC, V.
MCE is one of the top business management and training organisations in Europe, hosting a variety of large seminars and conferences. It also sets up training sessions and conferences specific to a client's request.

Palais des Congrès de Bruxelles
3 Coudenberg, 1000 (513 41 30/fax 514 21 12). Métro Gare Centrale. **Open** 8.30am-4.30pm Mon-Fri. **Credit** AmEx, DC, MC, V.
Near the Grand Place, this is one of the most convenient conference centres in Brussels. Its rooms can accommodate groups of ten for small meetings, or over 1,200 for events such as trade exhibitions.

Couriers

BTC Express
287 avenue Brugmann, 1180 (345 85 05/fax 343 63 81). **Open** 8am-7pm Mon-Fri. **No credit cards**.
Packages can be picked up and dropped off anywhere in Brussels within two hours for 325BF plus VAT.

DBXP
Box 3, 95 boulevard Louis Mettewie, 1080 (fax 469 13 71). **Open** 8am-7pm Mon-Fri (pick-ups also arranged Sat). **No credit cards**.
For 250BF, DBXP will pick up your parcel and deliver it anywhere in Brussels within two hours. Packages can also be sent to the UK and the US within a day or two.

DHL
210 Kosterstraat, 1831 (customer service 715 50 50/fax 721 45 88). **Open** customer service agents available 7.30am-midnight Mon-Fri. **No credit cards**.
Pick-ups are handled through late afternoon in most parts of the city. Packages can be dropped off at the airport in Zaventem until 10pm.

FedEx
119 Airport Building, Melsbroek, 1930 (toll free 0800 135 55/fax 752 72 80). **Open** 8am-7pm Mon-Fri. **Credit** AmEx, DC, MC, V.
If you arrange a pick-up before 2.30pm, your package will reach the US the next day. This office, based by Brussels National Airport, doesn't handle deliveries within Europe.

Electronic services

Internet access

At the time of writing, **CompuServe** was the only commercial (novice-friendly) Internet service provider with a Brussels direct-dial number (726 88 30). **AOL** (a joint venture between US Internet titan America Online and German publishing giant Bertelsmann) was expected to be available from mid-1996. Although there are already several companies providing Net access, most are based outside Brussels, but they can provide local dial-in numbers. The following are a few examples (the telephone numbers given are for customer service): **Arcadis** 02 534 0011; **Infoboard** 02 475 2299; **Innet** 03 281 4983; **Ping** 056 615 894; **Tornado** 016 551 621.

The EU offers opportunities for high achievers.

Electronic mail

Journalists or others interested in EU or NATO matters can receive press releases by e-mail. Contact the EU press office on 299 11 11 and the NATO press office on 707 50 41 for instructions on how to get hooked up.

Equipment hire

Buro Square
25 chaussée de Roodebeek, 1200 (772 41 51/fax 770 28 11). Métro Roodebeek. **Open** 9am-12.30pm, 1.30-5.30pm, Mon-Thur; 9am-12.30pm, 1.30-4.30pm, Fri. **Credit** AmEx, V.
A five-minute walk from Woluwe Shopping Centre, Buro Square carries everything from desks to fax paper. For larger equipment, call for a catalogue and to make an appointment for viewing. Buro Square's sister company Computer Square specialises in office computer systems. It has five locations in Brussels, including one in the Woluwe Shopping Centre (770 33 26).

New Telephone (Protel)
312 chaussée de Bruxelles, 1410 (354 60 98/fax 354 26 19). Bus W (Waterloo Centre stop). **Open** 9.30am-12.30pm, 2-6.30pm Mon-Fri. **Credit** AmEx, DC, MC, V.
New Telephone specialises in equipping offices with new phone systems, answerphones, voice mail, faxes and mobile phones. They also rent out photocopiers.

Papeterie IPL
635 chaussée de Waterloo, 1050 (344 89 61/fax 343 17 51). Tram 90, 94. **Open** 10am-1.30pm, 2.30-6pm, Mon-Fri. **Credit** V.
This office supplies store sells stationery ranging from the serious to the silly. It also makes up business cards for rates much lower than at many printing shops.

Estate agents

Richard Ellis

45-46 boulevard du Regent, 1000 (511 25 05/fax 511 56 16). Métro Arts-Loi. **Open** 9am-5.30pm Mon-Fri.

Healey & Baker

14 rue Montoyer, 1000 (514 40 00/fax 512 04 42). Métro Trône. **Open** 8am-7pm Mon-Fri (telephone for an appointment).

Knight Frank & Rutley NV-SA

14a rue du Luxembourg, 1000 (548 05 48/fax 502 71 91). Métro Trône. **Open** 9am-6pm Mon-Thur; 9am-5.40pm Fri.

Government offices

Administration des Douanes et Accises (Customs & Excise)

Ministère des Finances, Tour Finances, 50 boulevard du Jardin Botanique, 1010 (public relations 210 30 11/fax 210 33 13). Métro Botanique. **Open** 9am-5pm Mon-Fri.

Contact Mr Muylaert in public relations, who will refer you to the appropriate department.

Office National de Securité Sociale (National Social Security Office)

76 boulevard de Waterloo, 1000 (509 31 11/fax 509 36 97). Métro Louise. **Open** 8am-5pm Mon-Fri (telephone for an appointment first).

If you hire employees for your company, you are required to register with the ONSS for tax purposes. Translators are provided free of charge.

Office de Taxe à la Valeur Ajoutée (Value Added Tax Office)

Ministère des Finances, Tour Finances, 50 boulevard du Jardin Botanique, 1010 (210 26 11/fax 210 26 35). Métro Botanique. **Open** 9am-noon, 2-4pm, Mon-Fri.

All companies or individuals setting up business in Belgium must register here.

Lawyers

Bugnion NV-SA

43 rue de Namur, 1000 (511 63 78/fax 513 72 41). Métro Louise. **Open** 8.30am-4pm Mon-Fri.

Bugnion has a staff of English-speaking attorneys who specialise in patent and trademark protection within EU borders and beyond.

Ordre National des Avocats de Belgique (Belgian National Order of Lawyers)

Maison de l'Avocat, 65 avenue de la Toison d'Or, 1060 (534 67 73/fax 539 39 20). Métro Louise. **Open** 8.30am-5.15pm Mon-Thur; 8.30am-4.15pm Fri.

This organisation can provide you with a long list of English-speaking lawyers.

Removals

Arthur Pierre

328 chaussée de Bruxelles, 3090 (689 27 11/fax 687 46 86). **Open** 8am-5pm Mon-Fri. **No credit cards.**

Arthur Pierre has been helping families and businesses in Belgium relocate since 1898.

Maertens

5 Culliganlaan, 1831 (751 70 76/fax 751 47 18). **Open** 8am-6pm Mon-Fri. **No credit cards.**

This family-owned removals company can assist in all aspects of moving but specialises in transporting art work.

Trans Euro

2b Budasteenweg, 1830 (253 25 50/fax 253 25 70). **Open** 8.30am-6pm Mon-Fri. **Credit** AmEx, DC, MC, V.

Trans Euro can help you avoid lots of stress by handling the move from start to finish. The full works includes packing your belongings, loading them, getting it all through customs and reassembling the lot at the other end. A pre-move estimate is provided before any box is loaded.

Staff hire

If you don't feel like using an employment agency, you can place an ad in the Situations Vacant section in the *Bulletin*. Reader response rate is high.

Manpower

523 avenue Louise, 1050 (639 10 70/fax 639 10 71). Métro Louise. **Open** 8.30am-6pm Mon-Fri. **No credit cards.**

This agency can match up clients with secretaries who speak two, three or even four languages. Rates vary according to requirements.

Vedior Gregg

Riverside Business Park, 55 boulevard International, 1070 (555 16 11/fax 555 16 16). Bus 78. **Open** 8am-6pm Mon-Fri. **No credit cards.**

With 90 offices throughout Belgium, Vedior Gregg is one of the largest employment agencies in the country. The positions it fills range from technical to administrative. Rates for bilingual secretaries are 790BF-1000BF an hour.

Telecommunications

Telecom Finland International

23 rue Lozenberg, 1930 (714 86 86/fax 714 86 87). **Open** 9am-5pm Mon-Fri.

Small business owners and residents making a lot of calls to Scandinavia can save up to 30 per cent on their phone bills through this Brussels-based company. Reduced rates are also available for bigger companies with a large volume of international calls.

Translators & interpreters

Also check the *Yellow Pages* under Traducteurs.

Abetras

65-67 rue Traversière, 1210 (223 03 83/fax 223 04 15). Métro Madou. **Open** *office* 9am-6pm Mon-Fri; *telephone enquiries* 24-hours a day. **No credit cards.**

Abetras provides simultaneous interpreters for video conferences and rents out microphones, receivers and booths. Interpreters can be hired on an à la carte basis for 18000BF per day and 12500BF per half-day.

BTS World Translations

Blue Tower, 326 avenue Louise, 1050 (645 16 32/fax 646 99 34). Métro Louise then tram 93, 94. **Open** *office* 9am-8pm Mon-Fri. **No credit cards.**

BTS specialises in translating technical documents from one European language to another. For 36BF per line, you can have English documents translated into French or Dutch. Interpreters are also available, starting at 23500BF a day.

Children

There's lashings of child-sized fun to be had in the city of comics, marionettes and miniature moments.

Much of what makes Brussels famous also makes it child-friendly – the likes of comics, puppets, miniatures and parks. Being fairly safe and relaxed, it's easier to manage than most capitals, but be warned: Belgian children are extremely well behaved – no running, shouting or cursing. They even consent to being dressed in tight knee-length shorts and slip-on shoes. This may be partly due to the Belgians' mania for Cub scouting. If you ride the Métro at the weekend, you see hordes of them (some look as old as 16 or 17), come rain or snow, and no one is quite sure what they do except wear tight shorts, ride the Métro and make lots of noise.

As with the rest of the city's populace, kids' activities tend to be indoors and the sight of children playing out on the streets is almost unknown in middle-class *communes*. Even in parks, they're more likely to be walking politely than running wildly. There is, however, plenty of tolerance for less sedate behaviour, so it is perfectly permissible for your children to kick a ball or charge up and down.

Many of Brussels' best child attractions – the zoo, theme parks and slide 'n' splashes – are outside the capital. Within Brussels, there are good museums, puppet shows, cinemas, parks and that inexhaustible child-pleasure zone, **Bruparck**. The choice of activities is seasonally affected so check what's on in the *Bulletin*, which has a children's listings section. At Christmas, there's a crib holding live animals in the Grand Place and Christmas plays performed in English by amateur acting groups such as the excellent **Children's Opera**. In summer, drive-in movies are shown at the **Parc du Cinquantenaire** and there's the **Foire du Midi**, which has ferris wheels and dodgems, held at Gare du Midi and open until midnight. Early spring offers an annual cartoon festival of new and old releases, while autumn brings a fair (*see chapter* **Brussels by Season**) with stalls, rides and games, and food takes up the whole of avenue Georges Henri.

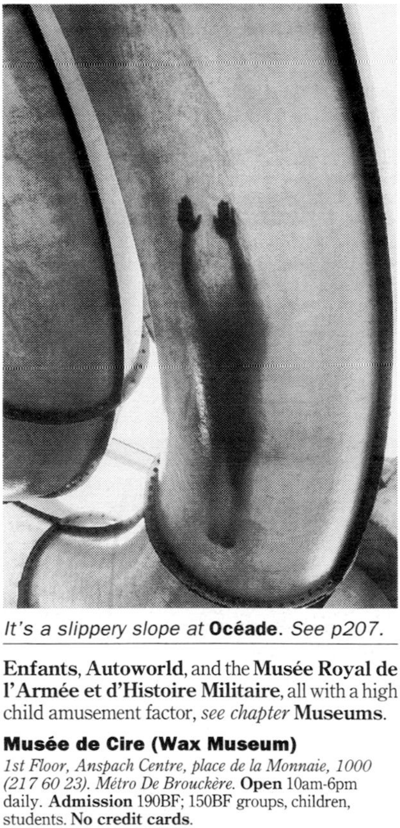

It's a slippery slope at **Océade**. *See p207.*

Museums

Brussels is exceptionally well endowed with good museums for children. Below are three small, interesting museums well worth a visit. For the **Museum voor Midden-Afrika, Muséum de l'Institut Royal des Sciences Naturelles de Belgique (Natural History Museum), Centre Belge de la Bande Dessinée, Musée des Enfants, Autoworld**, and the **Musée Royal de l'Armée et d'Histoire Militaire**, all with a high child amusement factor, *see chapter* **Museums**.

Musée de Cire (Wax Museum)

1st Floor, Anspach Centre, place de la Monnaie, 1000 (217 60 23). Métro De Brouckère. **Open** 10am-6pm daily. **Admission** 190BF; 150BF groups, children, students. **No credit cards**.

If your child has seen Madame Tussaud's, this probably won't impress them. Otherwise, the fascination of lifelike models should work its magic, even if the museum does take itself a little too seriously – what children want to see is Michael Jackson or a chamber of *other* horrors. It goes for the historical trip: 20 scenes are laid out from Roman times to the early twentieth century, or Julius Caesar to Hergé. Still, the models are good and the attention to detail impressive.

Musée du Jouet (Toy Museum)

24 rue de l'Association, 1000 (219 61 68). Métro Botanique or Madou. **Open** 10am-6pm daily. **Admission** 100BF; 60BF groups, 5-12s; free under-5s. **No credit cards**.

Belgium, like Holland, has a worldwide reputation for toy-making, and the examples on display here range from delicate 1850s dolls in glass cases to present-day streamlined and glossy machines. There's a shop selling rather superior toys and the museum will put on birthday parties for 295BF per child.

Scientastic Museum

Level 1, Métro Bourse, 1000 (646 89 15). Métro Bourse. **Open** 2-5.30pm Sat, Sun. **Admission** 150BF; 130BF students; 90BF groups; free under-4s. **No credit cards.**
Located in the Bourse Métro station, this is an interactive museum, all about having a sensual experience of science. There are 36 hands-on exhibits involving optical illusions, making your friend's face disappear and being suspended in mid-air.

Films & TV

Brussels has a good number of cinemas and most films are shown in their original language, so there are generally a few children's films in English to choose from. Films for over-16s are denoted as CNA or ENA, which means children not admitted. At **UGC de Brouckère** on Saturdays at 9.30am, parents can leave their children to watch a suitable film under supervision. However, it's likely to be in French.

With 30 or so channels, finding English television in Brussels is not a problem. The BBC and the numerous Dutch channels are the best bet if you don't have satellite.

Puppets

Théâtre Royal le Peruchet, Musée International des Marionettes

50 avenue de la Forêt, 1050 (673 87 30). Train Petite Gare du Boondael/tram 94. **Open** *Sept-Jun* Wed, Sat, Sun. **Admission** *museum* 30BF; *show & museum* 175BF. **No credit cards.**
This theatre-cum-museum has a good collection of puppets and lively interactive performances, but opening times are erratic so you need to phone beforehand to check.

Théâtre de Toone

6 impasse Schuddeveld, petite rue des Bouchers, 1000 (511 71 37). Métro De Brouckère. **Open** noon-midnight Tue-Sat. **Box office** tickets available 8pm, just before perf. **Tickets** 400BF; 250BF under-12s, students (Tue-Thur only). **No credit cards.**
Despite most of the shows being held in Bruxellois, the regional dialect, this is a gem of a puppet theatre to which all children respond, even if they don't understand a word. There are occasionally some performances in English; check the listings magazine *Bulletin* or phone for details of these. There is also a puppet museum – which you can enter for free during the intermission – and a workshop where you can buy marionettes.

Parks & playgrounds

No area in Brussels is without its regimented patch of green, but many are too small, flat or formal to interest any self-respecting child. The following selection does have some tot appeal, with plentiful games and ice-cream on tap.

Bois de la Cambre

main entrance on avenue Louise, 1050. Tram 93, 94.
This is one of the best inner-city parks for children. It's expansive, with beautiful lakes and woods, there's a skating area and in the centre is the Halle du Bois, a large and tempting games centre complete with bouncy castle. The Halle is open on weekends and holidays 2-6pm and costs 100BF per child per hour.

Parc du Cinquantenaire

main entrances on avenue de Tervuren & rue de la Loi, 1000. Métro Merode or Schuman.
The layout is a little formal, but it has lawns for football, paths for inline skating and a sandpit. Autoworld and the **Musée Royal de l'Armée at d'Histoire Militaire** are guaranteed to impress youngsters for a while, and the small, mock-medieval tower is amusing, though you can no longer climb up it. An ice-cream van can usually be found tinkling in the centre.

Parc de Tervuren

entrance on chaussée de Louvain, 1380. Tram 44.
The **Museum voor Midden-Afrika** is one draw, and those stuffed animals always excite attention, though today's children might find them totally unethical. The park is large and airy and you can hire out boats from the boathouse.

Parc de Woluwe

entrance on avenue de Tervuren, 1160. Tram 39, 44.
This is one of the best parks to take kids simply because it's so attractive. Set on slopes, it engenders an immediate feeling of freedom. It's ideal in winter for skating or tobogganing, and good for kite-flying on a windy day. There are walks and woods, lawns for games, crazy golf and a lake with rowing boats.

Square Ambiorix

entrance on square Ambiorix, 1000. Métro Schuman.
This small, attractive playground – set just beside the EU area – has climbing frames and slides.

Animals & amusement parks

Belgium has a huge number of amusement parks and attractions, most of them situated outside Brussels. A full list can be obtained from the Belgian Tourist Office at 63 rue du Marché aux Herbes (*see chapter* **Essential Information**).

Aqualibi

Wavre, 1300 (010 41 44 66). **Open** *Apr-Sept* 10am-6pm Wed-Thur, Sun; 10am-11pm, Fri, Sat (reserved for Walibi visitors during the day). *Oct-Mar* 2-10pm Wed-Fri; 2am-11pm Sat, Sun. **Admission** 460BF.
Attached to Walibi (*see below*), this most extravagant water attraction offers a wildly wet experience with its array of chutes, huge waves, pools and Jacuzzis plus an adventure trail called Rapido.

Plankendael Animal Park

582 Leuvensesteenweg, Mechelen 2812 (015 414 921). **Open** *summer* 9am-6pmMon-Sat; 9am-6.30pm Sun. *winter* 9am-5pm daily. **Admission** 380BF; 240BF 3-11s, over-60s, disabled (no pets allowed).
This large, attractive farm with over 1000 animals in 40 hectares has a great deal more space and freedom than a zoo. It's children-orientated with cuddly animals in the 'petting farm', a superior playground and an adventure trail. There's also a 'creeps and other horrors' exhibit, which dwells on the scarily fascinating world of spiders, rats and insects – showing an astute awareness of what children want. The farm also caters for birthday parties.

Having a magic-mungous time at the **Scientastic Museum**. *See page 206.*

Walibi

Wavre, 1300 (010 41 44 66). **Getting there** *by train* Ottignies-Louvain-la-Neuve line from Schuman to Gare de Bierges (the station is 300m from Walibi); *by car* take the E411 Bxl-Namur motorway to exit 6. **Open** *27 Apr-1 Sept* 10am-6pm daily; *2-29 Sept* 10am-6pm Sat, Sun. **Admission** 730BF; 680BF children up to 1m 30cm tall; free children under 1m tall. **Credit** MC, V.

It's the nearest theme park to Brussels, and the best. Walibi is constantly expanding, gaining more stomach-churning rides and opportunities to get soaked. It also has roundabouts and slow trains for smaller children. Be warned, though, it is generally overcrowded; during school holidays you can be queuing up to an hour for the most popular rides.

Antwerp Zoo

26 Koningen Astridplein, 2018 Antwerp (03 202 45 40/ fax 03 231 00 18). **Open** *Dec, Jan* 9am-4.45pm daily; *Feb, Oct, Nov* 9am-5pm daily; *Mar-Jun, Sep* 9am-6pm; *July, Aug* 9am-6.30pm daily. **Admission** 425BF; 265BF 3-11s, over-60s, disabled (no pets). **No credit cards**.

Belgium's main zoo is in Antwerp. It's one of Europe's oldest, set right in the city beside the old railway station. The number of animals is most impressive, but the conditions less so, though they are steadily improving. It has that dated and slightly depressing feel of city zoos, where there just isn't the space needed by the animals, and the big cats pace dementedly behind bars. The choice of captive creatures ranges from amphibians to monkeys, and you can catch a show of dolphins leaping through hoops.

Bruparck & Laeken

The whole Atomium area seems to have been created for the 24-hour amusement of your children. They can go up the nine-balled wonder itself for a great view. They can see a film in the **Kinepolis** (*see chapter* **Film**) which, with 30 screens and mostly American films, is almost always showing something suitable. Then there are cafés in the Village. There's the Lilliputian **Mini-Europe**, which has trams that run and boats that sail, and there's **Océade** for slide and splash fun.

Atomium

boulevard du Centenaire, 1020 (477 09 04/477 09 77). Métro Heysel/tram 81. **Open** *Sept-Mar* 10am-6pm daily; *Apr-Aug* 9am-8pm daily. **Admission** 200BF; 150BF groups (minimum 20); 120BF children. **Credit** AmEx, MC, V.

Mini-Europe

Bruparck, 20 boulevard du Centenaire, 1020 (478 05 50). Métro Heysel/tram 18, 19, 81, 91. **Open** *1 Apr-30 Jun* 9.30am-6pm daily; *1-19 Jul & 20-31 Aug* 9.30am-8pm daily; *20 Jul-19 Aug* 9.30am-midnight daily; *1 Sep-6 Jan* 10am-6pm daily (closed 6 Jan-31 Mar). **Admission** 380BF; 340BF groups (minimum 20); 290BF children. **Credit** V.

Océade

Bruparck, 20 boulevard du Centenaire, 1020 (478 43 20). Métro Heysel/tram 18, 19, 81, 91. **Open** *Apr-Aug* 2-10pm Tue-Thur; 2-11pm Fri; 10am-11pm Sat; 10am-10pm Sun. *Sept-Mar* 2-11pm Fri; 10am-11pm Sat; 10am-10pm Sun. **Admission** 450BF; 330BF children 1.25m-1.5m tall; free children under 1.25m tall. **Credit** MC, V.

Sports

For many of Brussels' sports centres, you have to be a member to to use them. Not these.

Centre de Danse Choreart

985 chaussée d'Alsemberg, 1180 (332 13 59). Tram 55.
This is the city's biggest dance school, with classes in modern and classical ballet, jazz, and tap-dancing. It runs classes for children from three-and-a-half upwards.

Poseidon

2 avenue des Vaillants, 1200 (771 66 55). Métro Tomberg. **Open** 8am-7pm Mon-Fri; 8am-7.30pm Sat, Sun. **Admission** *pool* 75BF; 60BF under-14s; *ice-rink* 250BF; 210BF under-13s. **No credit cards**.

Its 25-metre pool and small children's pool can become seriously overcrowded. The same is true of the ice-rink, which should be avoided at peak times, ie weekends and Wednesday afternoons. Otherwise, the ice is well maintained and there are children's skates available for hire.

Centre Sportif de Woluwe St Pierre

2 avenue Salome, 1150 (762 12 75). Tram 39. **Open** 8am-7pm Mon-Thur, Sat, Sun; 8am-8pm Fri. **Admission** *pool* 100BF; 90BF under-14s. **No credit cards**.

The Olympic-size pool has lanes and diving boards. The shallow children's pool has a water chute and inflatable rings. There's also tennis, squash, mini-football and basketball. All can be arranged by the hour except tennis, for which you have to be a member.

Shopping

Christiansen

City 2, rue de la Blanchisserie, 1000 (218 09 28). Métro Rogier. **Open** 10am-6.30pm Mon-Sat. **Credit** AmEx, DC, V.

Belgium's largest toy shop chain has large and all-encompassing stores that run the gamut from Barbie dolls to Nintendo games, but it's all a little mass-produced.

In den Olifant

159 rue de Linthout, 1200 (736 70 68). Métro Merode. **Open** 10am-6.30pm Mon-Sat. **Credit** AmEx, DC, MC, V.

The beautiful wooden toys and Victorian-looking games purveyed here are possibly more parent- than child-friendly.

Maison Picard

71-75 rue du Lombard, 1000 (513 07 90). Métro Gare Centrale. **Open** 9am-6.30pm Mon-Sat. **Credit** AmEx, DC, MC, V.

Maison Picard and **Le Palais des Cotillons** (*see below*) are two great magic and theatrical shops which face each other across rue du Lombard. One sells serious make-up and masks, while the other is full of lurid tricks such as fake flies and whoopee cushions, as well as the best fireworks around and an extensive dressing-up section.

Le Palais des Cotillons

66 rue du Lombard, 1000 (512 23 20). Métro Gare Centrale. **Open** 9.30am-6pm Mon-Sat. **Credit** AmEx, DC, MC, V.

See above **Maison Picard**.

Prémaman

Woluwe Shopping Centre, rue St Lambert, 1020 (770 58 97). Métro Roodebeek. **Open** 9.30am-7.15pm Mon-Sat. **Credit** AmEx, DC, MC, V.

Brussels' answer to Mothercare has all the usual maternity and baby clothes plus simple educational toys.

Child-friendly restaurants

Because Belgian children are so well behaved, there is seldom any difficulty about bringing children into restaurants. However, Brussels seems to be too gastronomically proud to cater much for children and special menus are not generally offered. Listed below are some exceptions, but don't expect to sample great Belgian cooking.

Chi-Chi's

541 Brüsselse Steenweg, 3090 Overijse (657 57 00). **Open** 11.30am-10pm Mon-Thur, Sun; 11.30am-11pm Fri, Sat. **Average** 600BF. **Menu** 250BF (lunch), 695BF, 795BF. **Credit** AmEx, DC, MC, V.

It's a little outside the centre but hugely popular. Children's menus are 140BF and include chicken, burgers or stew. On Sundays this goes down to 99BF with a free drink.

La Maison d'Attila

36-42 avenue Prince du Ligne Nile, 1080 (375 05 70). Bus 60. **Open** noon-midnight daily. **Average** 885BF. **Credit** AmEx, MC, V.

This has a buffet with a wide range of pasta, salads, grills and fondues. An inspired system of payment operates whereby up to the age of 14 you multiply the child's age by 59BF, so for a one-year-old you pay 59BF and for a ten-year-old 590BF. At 15, the adult charge of 850BF operates.

L'Orchidée Bleue

99 boulevard Brand Whitlock, 1200 (734 59 12). Métro Georges Henri/tram 23, 90. **Open** noon-2.30pm, 6-11pm, daily. **Average** 650BF. **Menu** 395BF, 495BF, 695BF. **Credit** AmEx, DC, MC, V.

Good Chinese food at reasonable prices. Its best option is the Sunday brunch (noon-2pm), which offers an enormous choice of dishes at 295BF for under-12s and 495BF for adults.

Childminding

The **Ligue des Familles**, 127 rue du Trône, 1050 (507 72 11), organises daytime childminding services for children aged up to six. They may also provide night-time sitters, or you can phone the local *commune* for a full list of childcarers.

It can be hard to find an English babysitter at short notice. Your best bet is to call Karen Quinworth at **Kids 'n' Carers** (653 39 24), who will do her best to send a suitable, qualified person. For longer-term visitors, there are a number of English-language crèches. The **City International School**, 101-103 boulevard Louis Schmidt, 1040 (734 88 16), runs a full-time weekday crèche.

Health

For emergencies, dial 100 and speak slowly in English. The paediatric emergency number is 535 43 60. There is a 24-hour English-speaking helpline for all problems on 648 40 14.

International schools

British School of Brussels

19 Leuvensesteenweg, 3080 Tervuren (767 47 00). Tram 44.

As the name implies, it's mostly British, but 60 nationalities are represented. Exams offered include GCSE and A levels.

International School of Brussels

19 Kattenburg, 1170 (672 27 88). Bus 95.

Fifty-five nationalities, from nursery age upwards.

St John's International School

146 drève Richelle, 1410 Waterloo (354 11 38).

This ecumenical school has a special services department for children with learning difficulties.

Gay & Lesbian

Gay and lesbian life in Belgium might strike outsiders as strange, being at once far ahead and far behind other countries where the movement for gay rights has a longer history.

The first national lesbian and gay pride event was only held in 1996, more than a quarter of a century after Stonewall in New York, the uprising that led to gay pride events around the world. This might give you the idea of Brussels being a backwater, but the fact is that gays and lesbians enjoy more rights here than in countries such as the US and Britain, simply by virtue of being largely ignored by the law. There is at least one openly gay minister in government, for example, and the Belgian attitude of pragmatism deems his sexuality not an issue for the electorate.

Organisations such as the International Gay and Lesbian Association and Tels Quels, a non-profit Belgian group, have what gays in other countries might consider the luxury of fighting for the same benefits accorded heterosexual couples – as opposed to the more common battle to end discrimination in daily life. Belgium still has a way to go before it becomes the Netherlands, but the current government discussion about recognising same sex relationships as it does traditional marriages is reason for hope.

For women, gay life revolves mostly around bars near the Bourse, and for men in bars around rue des Pierres. Neither mixes with the other all that much – gay awareness being in its infancy here, the male gay scene is touched with more than a little misogyny. But as Brussels mimics London, Amsterdam and New York more and more, this will hopefully soon be a thing of the past.

Bars

Le Belgica

32 rue du Marché au Charbon, 1000 (no phone). Tram 23, 52, 55, 56, 81/bus 34, 48. **Open** 10pm-3am Thur-Sat.
A former favourite of the town's trendy population, Le Belgica has mutated into the most fashionable gay bar in Brussels. Not as prissy or raunchy as most of the competition, Le Belgica features that dilapidated décor that's a hold-over from the 1980s: distressed yellowed peeling walls; functional wood chairs and tables that look as though they were salvaged from a garage sale; and a few kitsch touches behind the bar (a bust of King Léopold). This is the place to find out what's happening on the gay scene as far as parties are concerned. The house drink, a genever cocktail served in shot glasses, is more potent than it looks.

Can-Can

55 rue des Pierres, 1000 (512 74 04). Tram 23, 52, 55, 56, 81/bus 34, 48. **Open** from 9pm daily.

Le Belgica – *trendiest gay bar in Brussels.*

A pick-up joint, plain and simple. Lace curtains hanging in the window obscure the interior from outside, which is just as well: it's strictly no frills. Retro-disco (Laura Branigan, anyone?) mixed with current house provides the backbeat. Borderline hairdresser crowd.

Chez Flo

25 rue au Beurre, 1000 (513 31 52). Tram 23, 52, 55, 56, 81/bus 34, 48, 95, 96. **Dinner show** 8pm Wed-Sun.
A drag show with dinner thrown in, Chez Flo ranks as one of the most touristic places in Brussels, but there's nothing wrong in that.

Le Comptoir

24-25 place de la Vieille Halle-aux-Blés, 1000 (514 05 00). Métro Gare Centrale/bus 34, 48. **Open** from 6pm daily.
In this landmark building, the precious crowd (cravats, kept boys and their keepers, yuppies in dry-cleaned jeans) cruise downstairs with house music providing the soundtrack. Upstairs, the restaurant serves nouvelle cuisine and stylish updates on more traditional European fare in an environment best described as *haut paysan*. Mildly snobby, but that's the attraction.

Le Duquesnoy

12 rue Duquesnoy, 1000 (502 38 83). Métro Gare Centrale. **Open** 8pm-4am Mon-Sat; 6pm-4am Sun.
One of the raunchiest gay bars in Brussels, Le Duquesnoy feels very 1980s, with Tom of Finland posters, a TV playing borderline SM porno, and leather-clad barmen a bit past their prime, but all the less attitudinal because of it. In the back, a staircase leads up to two floors of dark rooms and down to a room with a sling and urinals. The music ranges from generic divas belting out disco versions of familiar tunes to standard Pet Shop Boys and Stock Aitken & Waterman. Every gay man in Brussels denies going here, but the customers must come from somewhere.

Le Feminin

9 rue Borgval (511 17 09). Tram 23, 52, 55, 56, 81/bus 34, 48. **Open** from 10pm Tues, Thur-Sat.

Tels Quels – *a meeting place and documentation centre, it welcomes gay men and lesbians.*

One of only two lesbian bars in Brussels, the other being Sapho (*see below*). Dark, cosy, nondescript bar, where every lesbian in the city who goes out goes.

H_2O

27 rue du Marché au Charbon, 1000 (512 38 43). Tram 23, 52, 55, 56, 81/bus 34, 48. **Open** 7pm-2am daily.
Whether the décor is a stab at Gothic or baroque is hard to say; that it fails on both counts isn't. Still, this cosy dark bar serving a light menu of salds and snacks, as well as a more rounded drinks menu, does have considerable charm. Candelabras dripping with wax are the centrepiece of each table, and there are intimate corners where the clientèle huddle in conversations. It's welcoming to women as well, which is saying a lot for any gay establishment in Brussels.

Het Rijk der Zinnen

14 rue des Pierres, 1000 (511 26 59). Tram 23, 52, 55, 56, 81/bus 34, 48. **Open** 11am-7am Mon-Fri; 3pm-7am Sat, Sun.
The English translation, the Empire of the Senses, is rather grand for this bar: maybe appropriate a long time ago, Het Rijk der Zinnen now has a sort of down-at-heel, loser charm. Definitely not a fashion-type bar, the Rijk is where you end up when everywhere else is closed and you're still trying to get laid. Pasta and other light dishes served.

Incognito

36 rue des Pierres, 1000 (513 37 88). Tram 23, 52, 55, 56, 81/bus 34, 48. **Open** 6pm-2am daily.
Smoked glass windows afford those inside with a view of passers-by on the outside, but peering inside from the street, you can't see the inevitable crowd that packs out Incognito. The clientèle is best described as would-be drag queen, with the music mostly French pop and disco (Celine Dion is a patron saint). Heavy aftershave *de rigueur*. Has rep of being one of the only bars in Brussels to have been firebombed.

Sapho

1 rue St Géry (512 45 52). Tram 23, 52, 55, 56, 81/bus 34, 48. **Open** from 10pm Fri, Sat.
There's a constant boomerang between Le Feminin (*see above*) and here. Men welcome if escorted by a convincing-looking lesbian.

Le Sept

7 Plattesteen, 1000 (513 14 14). Tram 23, 52, 55, 56, 81/bus 34 or 48. **Open** from 9pm daily.
Raunch-ville: the only other bar that competes with Le Sept on the sleazy front is Le Duquesnoy (*see above*). Very 1980s dark interior with monitors playing porn and music videos of the expected divas (Madonna, Barbra and Liza) competting with the machine-gun rhythmed house tapes set the mood on the ground floor. Down below, dark rooms are provided for those who want to get a little more personal.

Shakespeare

24 Oude Koornmarkt, 2000 Antwerp (231 50 58). Tram 23, 52, 55, 56, 81/bus 34, 48. **Open** from 10pm Fri, Sat.
Catering to a largely butch crowd, this small, dark pub is the oldest survivor on the lesbian landscape in Antwerp. Plays a mix of rock, soul, house and disco. Men welcome if accompanied by a woman.

Le Troisième Acte

28 rue des Pierres, 1000 (502 56 49). Tram 23, 52, 55, 56, 81/bus 34, 48, 95, 96. **Open** 6pm-midnight daily.
Unvarnished charm is Le 3ème Acte's appeal: gingham tablecloths, sepia-toned walls and no-nonsense furnishings provide a refreshing change from other rather overdone gay restaurants. The clientèle is mostly downtown and trendy, with some yuppies from uptown making a sojourn every now and then for the traditional Belgian and French cuisine, prepared simply. You can't miss Le 3ème Acte: just follow the smell of grease down the rue des Pierres until you hit it.

Eating & drinking

Big Noise New Generation

44 rue du March au Charbon, 1000 (512 25 25). Tram 23, 52, 55, 56, 81/bus 34 or 48. **Open** from 8pm daily.
This former borderline sleazy men's bar was reconceived in early 1996 to cater also to women. A politically correct vibe reigns over this bare-brick, house-music-playing, hole-in-the-wall of a bar.

L'Orange-Bleu

29 rue Antoine Dansaert, 1000 (513 98 29). Tram 23, 52, 55, 56, 81/bus 63. **Open** 4pm-3am daily.
Greek and Roman statues, art deco prints and burnished oak and redwood turn-of-the-century furnishings make L'O-B an aesthetically fetching bar where you're so entranced by the interior that you almost forget you're paying an arm and a leg for a cocktail that you could have much cheaper just half a block away.

Les Salons de l'Atlantide

89 chaussée de Charleroi, 1050 (537 21 54). Tram 91, 92. **Open** 10am-1am daily; *kitchen* noon-2.30pm, 6-11pm, daily.
This is not strictly a gay restaurant, but it is a favourite of those who appreciate the décor and the artfully served cuisine. Both the menu and the interior take a cue from a variety of cultures. India and Middle Eastern and African mix with baroque and neoclassical, whether it be in dishes such as tangines and pilafs, or the salons, with terra cotta walls, murals and big heavy colonial furniture. There are four different major rooms, with the largest having a hangar-like ceiling that gives it the feeling of a courtyard.

Tels Quels

81 rue du March au Charbon, 1000 (512 32 34). Tram 23, 52, 55, 56, 81/bus 34, 48. **Open** 5pm-2am Mon-Thur, Sun; 5pm-4am Fri, Sat.
This is the most unique meeting place in Brussels, in that it accommodates both lesbians and gay men equally. A Brussels institution, Tels Quels also has a political slant: there's a documentation centre concerning gay rights and history, open Monday and Tuesday evenings, and art exhibits, as well as group discussions. Special evenings catering exclusively to gay men or lesbians are also organised.

Clubs

Bump

208 rue Blaes, 1000 (511 97 89). Métro Porte de Halle/bus 20, 48. **Open** from 11pm first Fri of month. **Admission** 300BF
This offshoot of La Démence (*see below*) is smaller and more casual – while La Démence attracts a crowd of close to 2,000 regularly done up (and overdone up) in their Sunday best, the crowd here is mostly turned out in T-shirts and jeans.

Cercle 52

52 rue des Chartreux, 1000 (514 30 78).Tram 23, 52, 55, 56, 81. **Open** 10pm-6am Thur-Sun. **Admission** 100BF
One of the few discos where there are fewer men on the dance floor than in the toilets – you figure it out. Videos not for the squeamish played on monitors throughout. Strangely, considering the extracurricular activities of the clientèle (popular spot: the dark room), it's amazing how good the music is: the management could just switch the radio on for all the patrons care.

La Démence

208 rue Blaes, 1000 (511 97 89). Bus 20, 48. **Open** from 11pm Sun every three weeks. **Admission** varies.
The largest gay rave in Brussels, attracting disco queens from all around Belgium. Muscleboys, clones, hairdressers and fashion victims mix on the two floors, with more mainstream house dominating the ground floor and deeper garage keeping bodies moving on the upper level. A dark room and chill-out room both available.

D-Light

208 rue Blaes, 1000 (511 97 89). Métro Porte de Halle/bus 20, 48. **Open** from 11pm last Fri of month. **Admission** 300BF
It's ladies' night and the feeling's right for D-Light, the femme alternative to Bump and La Démence. In the same first floor space as Bump, the following here is more devoted and exclusive, with the music being more accessible house than is heard at most venues.

The Factory

4 impasse de la Fidélité, 1000 (514 55 14). Métro Gare Centrale/bus 34, 48. **Open** 11pm-7am Fri, Sat. **Admission** 250BF
Basement party is the atmosphere at this disco playing a groovy mix of house and 1970s and '80s disco (Masters at Work meets Maxine Nightingale) that would reach a wider audience if their door policy was not so hostile to women.

Le Garage

18 rue Duquesnoy, 1000 (512 66 22). Métro Gare Centrale/bus 34, 48. **Open** from 9pm Sun. **Admission** 100BF.
Sunday is gay night in most cities, but the only weekly tea-dance in Brussels happens at Le Garage (La Démence is more sporadic). The music is unexceptional house mixed with some oldies but goodies, the latter also describing the crowd: not as trendy as other clubs, this is more an athletics-socks-with-dress-shoes-and-wearing-enough-eau-de-toilette-to-choke-a-horse crowd. The highlight is the party ritual La Bamba (where people gather in a circle, one person stands in the centre and picks someone to kiss; this person then enters the circle and picks someone else to kiss… and so on).

The Scandal Bar

7 rue Borgval, 1000 (no phone). Tram 23, 52, 55, 56, 81/bus 34, 48. **Open** from 11pm daily. **Admission**
Technically not a lesbian or gay disco, but open enough to make this section of the public comfortable. The music is largely rai, the North African pop that is favoured by a good portion of those in attendance. A bit tacky, but good fun.

Saunas

Le Lagon

86 rue de Livourne, 1050 (534 20 74). Tram 81, 93, 94. **Open** 2pm-midnight Mon-Thur, Sun; 2pm-2am Fri, Sat. **Admission** 450BF
The newest sauna in the city, and the jury is still out: the more established Oasis and Macho have their loyal followings, so it's hard to see if this one will last. Located near the upscale avenue Louise, which would make you think it would attract a chic clientèle. This is not the case: following the 'you don't shit where you eat' maxim, most of Le Lagon's customers are from less swanky neighbourhoods, while the well-to-do sauna clients living nearby prefer to go to somewhere a bit farther away from home.

Macho 2

106-108 rue du Marché au Charbon, 1000 (513 56 67). Tram 23, 52, 55, 56, 81. **Open** noon-2am Mon-Thur; noon-4am Fri, Sat; 2pm-2am Sun. **Admission** 450BF; 300BF under-25s.
Macho 2 offers hygienic facilities for those who might be in

the market for a legitimate sauna. For others, the clientèle is largely more rough trade than elsewhere.

Oasis

10 rue Van Orley, 1000 (218 08 00). Métro Botanique/tram 91, 92, 93, 94. **Open** noon-1am daily. **Admission** 450BF.
Pretty boys and sugar daddies – and aspirants to the status of both – flock to this sauna to work up a sweat. The space is one of the nicest in Brussels – an old converted townhouse that has retained some of its original splendour.

Private clubs

Atthis

7 Volkstraat, 2000 Antwerp (216 37 37). **Open** from 9.30pm Fri, Sat.
A women-only private club that is a little more refined than the majority of lesbian clubs in Belgium. There's a video library with a wide selction for members to choose from. A lesbian centre is also run under the same name.

Boots

22 Van Aerdstraat, 2060 Antwerp (03 233 21 36). **Open** 10.30pm-5am Fri, Sat.
This is without a doubt the raunchiest, sleaziest, most down 'n' dirty bar in Belgium: mention that you are a regular patron here, and you immediately have a reputation to live up to… or live down. Slings, rooms designated for any sexual activity you could imagine (well, almost: no livestock has been used yet) and a crowd that is completely oblivious to anything but their own pleasure.

Hairdressers

Man to Man

9 rue des Riches Claires, 1000 (514 47 53). Tram 23, 52, 55, 56, 81. **Open** 10am-6.30pm Tue-Sat.
The window features an ever-changing display of nipple clamps, handcuffs and other SM hardware, which gives it a more menacing impression than Man to Man really merits. Basic haircutting and styling are done, and there are fetish items on sale.

Sex shops

Erot'X Stars

40 boulevard Maurice Lemonnier, 1000 (513 93 44). Tram 23, 52, 55, 56, 81. **Open** 11am-9pm daily.
Two floors of male videos, with private cabins for in-store viewing, video sales and video rentals. Limited range of poppers, latex and other sex accessories.

Le Classix

13 rue des Riches Claires, 1000 (514 55 62). Tram 23, 52, 55, 56, 81. **Open** 5-11pm Mon-Sat.
Like a sexual supermarket of videos, magazines and other paraphernalia, le Classix is on a more discreet street than Erot'X, which makes entering and leaving the shop less noticeable for those who prefer to keep such things private.

Associations

Education about and action against AIDS are the raison d'être for the organisations Aide Infor Sida (514 29 65/hotline 511 45 29), Act Together (512 05 05) and Act Up (512 05 05). Aide Infor Sida concentrates on combatting ignorance surrounding

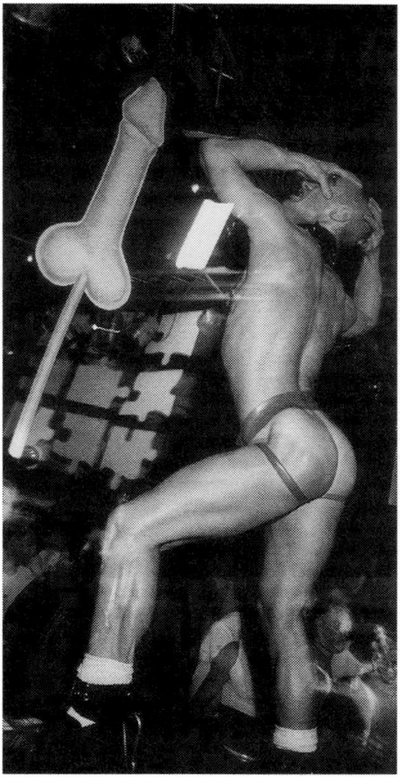

La Démence – *largest gay rave. See p211.*

the disease, while Act Together is more of a support system for those afflicted with it, and for their families and friends. Act Up is motivated to change government policy regarding AIDS, to effect more funding, research and better treatment for the ill.

Egalité

200 rue de la Loi, 1049 (295 98 97). **Lines open** 10am-5pm daily.
This coalition of gays and lesbians working at the European Union institutions aims to fight discrimination in their workplace more than in society as a whole.

International Gay & Lesbian Association

81 rue du Marché au Charbon, 1000 (502 24 71). Tram 23, 52, 55, 56, 81.
Housed in the same building as the Tels Quels Meeting Point, (*see above* **Eating & drinking**) the ILGA has been working for equal rights for lesbians and gay men since 1978.

Tel'Egal

Postbox 1969, 1000 (502 79 38). **Lines open** 8pm-midnight Mon-Fri.
This hotline serves the gay and lesbian community, dispensing legal and social advice.

Students

The language divide complicates matters, but for the student in Brussels opportunity is always knocking, whether it's a chance to make foreign friends or build boozy camaraderie.

Believe it or not, Brussels is a great place for study. It's a great place to live for that matter, so you may find yourself staying on after completing your studies (it has been known to happen). Besides being culturally interesting in its own right, Brussels is blessed with a huge international community that breezes in and out like rainclouds. This huge turnover means that, whether you like it or not, you are constantly meeting new people and expanding your worldview. Isn't that what being a student is all about?

Furthermore, the Belgian capital has a booming nightlife to make up for its less than booming weather – bars, clubs and restaurants stay open till the wee hours and the beer always flows freely. Isn't that, too, what being a student is all about?

The Free University of Brussels is the city's major university. It began as one entity in 1834, but split into independent Flemish (VUB) and French (ULB) schools in 1968, following student demonstrations. In addition to the 20-odd universities and colleges in Brussels, many students gravitate to those elsewhere in Belgium: UCL and KUL, the French and Flemish Catholic universities of Leuven; Louvain-la-Neuve, the new university of Leuven; the Universities of Ghent and Antwerp; and the College of Europe in Bruges for budding Eurocrats (*see chapter* **Trips Out of Town**).

Unlike the American or British systems, admission to Belgian universities is not selective – the selection process occurs throughout the duration of the course, as those who can't hack it drop like flies. The graduating class of most universities will be about a quarter of its initial size. Professor-student contact is minimal and the exams are tough. During the first two years of a course (generally called the *candidature*) most of the exams are oral and take place over June and July. If a student fails these exams, they can resit in September, but failing that, they must repeat the whole year.

Degrees from Belgian institutions are categorised either as legal (*grades légaux/wettelijke graden*), meaning that the curriculum and admisison requirements are set by law, or scientific (*grades scientifiques/wetenschappelijke graden*), in which the university rather than national legislation sets the course. Holders of scientific degrees for legal programmes are not allowed to practice within the field they studied.

The linguistic divide in Belgium has somewhat complicated the education system in the country. The French and the Flemish communities fund their own respective educational institutions, and massive cuts within the French community's education budget have recently led to student demonstrations throughout Wallonia and Brussels. French-speaking universities get the short end of the stick compared to their Flemish counterparts and are seriously underfunded.

Study in Brussels

Universities

Académie Royale des Beaux Arts de Bruxelles

144 rue du Midi, 1000 (511 04 91). Métro Gare Centrale/tram 23, 52, 55.

The Royal Academy of Fine Art has four-year courses in weaving, illustration/comic strip art, advertising and design, but is perhaps best known for painting and sculpture.

Boston University Brussels

8 St Lendriksborre, 1120 (268 00 37). Tram 23 then bus 47.

Boston University set up its campus in Brussels in 1972 and joined with VUB (*see below*) to set up an English-language Masters of Science in Management (MSM) programme. In addition to the MSM course, the university offers an MS in Administrative Studies as well as several specialised graduate certificates.

Ecole Nationale Supérieure des Arts Visuels de la Cambre

21 Abbaye de la Cambre, 1000 (648 96 19). Tram 23, 90, 93, 94/bus 71.

Brussels has two main art schools, this and the Beaux Arts (*see above*), the former being more commercially orientated and perhaps the snootier of the two. Housed in a beautiful thirteenth-century abbey in Ixelles, La Cambre has courses in fine art as well as animation, printmaking and industrial design. But the school's fortes are architecture, graphic design and fashion. Courses are taught in French.

Emerson College

240 avenue Louise, 1050 (648 58 06). Tram 93, 94.

Boston's Emerson College opened its Brussels campus in 1993 and offers a one-year MA in Global Marketing, Communication and Advertising (taught in English).

ICHEC (Institut Catholique des Hautes Etudes Commerciales)

2 boulevard Brand Whitlock, 1150 (739 37 11). Métro Montgomery/tram 23, 44, 81, 90/bus 20, 61, 80.

Founded in 1934, ICHEC is rated as the second best business school in Brussels, after Solvay, and its students tend to be of the BCBG (*bon chic bon genre* – smart set), old money variety. Course work is extremely demanding, with between 30 and 40 class hours per week and, as with ULB, only a quarter of the initial student intake end up bringing home a degree to *maman*. On offer are four-year programmes in *sciences commerciales et financières/consulaires* or a five-year *ingeniorat commerciale*.

Open University

38 avenue Emile Duray, 1050 (644 33 72/73). Tram 23, 90, 93, 94/bus 71.

This caters mostly for working adults who want to get a degree but don't want or can't afford to quit their jobs. Students follow a course book and audiovisual materials at their own pace, and meet regularly with a tutor at study centres either in Brussels or Antwerp. BAs and BScs take anything from four to six years to complete, depending on the student's own study plan. Degrees are offered in the social sciences, technology, computing, mathematics, arts and sciences. There is also an MBA programme.

ULB (Université Libre de Bruxelles)

50 avenue Franklin Roosevelt, 1050 (650 21 11). Tram 93, 94/bus 71.

The Free University of Brussels was founded in 1834 by lawyer Theodore Verhaegen in order to counter the stagnant state of higher education in Brussels. At the time, the Catholic Church had a monopoly over the curricula of the country's three universities, and intellectual advancement proceeded along rigid lines. ULB began as an independent, liberal institution and received strong backing from masonic circles. Today, it is the largest university in Brussels, with over 18,000 students, of whom roughly a third are foreigners. Solbosch, ULB's main campus, is home to most faculties – Philosophy and Letters, Social Sciences, Applied Sciences, Law and European Studies – with the exception of Medicine, which is located at Hôpital Erasme (*see chapter* **Survival**). Solbosch is also home to the city's most prestigious business school, Solvay, which offers a five-year *grade d'ingénieur commercial* and a one-year MBA in English. Courses are tough at ULB. In the first year students find themselves in classrooms with upwards of 600 people, and if they make it to the second year, the numbers will have halved. By the end of the programme, only about 150 will have made it through. Student life is scattered – most students live at home or in apartments around the city – although there are a number of student associations and clubs on the Solbosch Campus.

Vesalius College

2 Pleinlaan, 1050 (629 36 26). Métro Petillon/tram 23, 90/bus 34, 95, 96.

Vesalius was created in 1987 as part of the VUB *(see below)* and in association with Boston University. Although it shares a campus with VUB (which issues Vesalius diplomas), the language of instruction is English and the style of education is decidedly American – selective admission, small classes and close faculty-student relationships, and American-style fees! Vesalius offers Bachelor's degrees in 15 subjects including economics, computer science, engineering (computer and electrical), English literature, business and human resources management. The student body is incredibly diverse, with over 50 nationalities represented, and student life is accordingly interesting.

VUB (Vrije Universiteit Brussel)

2 Pleinlaan, 1050 (629 21 11/library 629 25 05). Métro Petillon/tram 23, 90/bus 95, 96, 34.

In 1970, the Free University of Brussels split into two entities along linguistic lines, the French-speaking ULB and its Flemish-speaking counterpart, VUB. Each is funded by its respective community and educational policies are decided upon separately by the national Parliament and by each of the communities' Cultural Councils. VUB today has an enrolment of roughly 8,000 students. Although most of the courses are taught in Flemish (with the exception of Vesalius College, *see above*), there are a number of English-language postgraduate degrees.

Website: http://www.vub.ac.be

Existentialists squeeze in a little late revision.

Language schools

Brussels is multilingual and it is unfortunately all too easy to spend a significant amount of time there without picking up either of the main languages. Shame, shame on those who don't even try! Most *communes* offer language courses at reasonable prices and can be contacted for more details. The Chamber of Commerce and Industry also offers day and evening classes at VUB (Vrije Universiteit Brussel). The classes, while not free, as the university's name would suggest, are very reasonably priced: a year of two three-hour sessions a week starts at 2700BF. You can contact them on 629 27 61 for more details.

Alliance Française

59 avenue de l'Emeraude, 1030 (732 15 92). Tram 23, 90/bus 29, 63. **Open** 8.30am-noon, 1.30-6.30pm, Mon-Thur; 8.30am-noon, 1.30-5pm, Fri.

Don't want to pick up a Belgian accent? This bastion of French culture has group and private classes in French only. An intensive month-long course, meeting daily from 9am to noon, costs 10,200BF. Alternatively, there are courses that meet twice a week in the evening, which cost 3000BF per month. Classes are no larger than 15 students.

Brussels Language Studies

8 rue du Marteau, 1210 (217 23 73). Métro Arts-Loi or Madou. **Open** 8.30am-8pm Mon-Fri; 8.30am-12.30pm Sat.
This well-reputed school teaches classes in virtually every language imaginable and is extremely flexible about meeting the needs of its students. Group classes number no more than five students and cost 13,500BF for 30 hours of teaching.

CERAN Lingua

Château du Haut-Neubois, 16 avenue du Château, Spa 4900 (087 791 122). Train to Verviers then taxi/or school runs own transport – phone for details.
When the well-heeled want to brush up on a language, they pack their bags and head for this prestigious and beautiful château in the Ardennes. For a period ranging from a weekend to several weeks, students think, eat and breathe in the language of their choice, whether it's French, Italian, Japanese, German, Dutch or Spanish. A week-long stay, including texts and full room and board, starts at 47,000BF. CERAN has other language centres in Spain, France, Ireland and the United States.

Fondation 9

412 avenue Louise, 1050 (640 21 92). Tram 93, 94. **Open** 9am-6pm Mon-Fri.
The '9' refers to the nine languages of the European Union (before Spain and Portugal joined in 1986 – it really should be Fondation 13 by now). Anyway, sponsored by ULB, the Chamber of Commerce and the City of Brussels, Fondation 9 offers group classes of up to eight students in all the official languages of the EU. An eight-week class, which meets for three hours on Saturday mornings, costs 10,500BF. Intensive 'immersion' classes cost 12,950BF per week.

Libraries

It can be tricky finding the book you need in Brussels, unless you have a lot of time to spare, wandering from one library to the next. If you're online, preferably with Netscape, the task is easier – log on to VUB's homepage (http:\www.vub.ac.be). From there you can search several catalogues and find out where any book is located in the country. If you don't have Netscape, you can get direct access through Telnet, an Internet service provider. Once in Telnet, type 'Open' and then the library's electronic address (biblio.vub.ac.be). One of the options is 'Other Catalogues', of which 'Antelope' can hook you in to the main libraries in Belgium. And if you're not online, no problem, VUB's library has computers that are online for you. Call them on 629 25 05.

American Documentation Center

1c square du Bastion, 1050 (512 21 29). Métro Porte de Namur/bus 71. **Open** 2-6pm Mon-Thur.
Part of the United States Information Service, the American Library has over 15,000 texts, most of which specialise in the area of US-Europe economic relations, environment and law. Only students doing research in their final year can take books out on loan, otherwise there is a photocopying machine available to anyone with a copycard. The catalogue is computerised but not on the Internet yet.

Bibliothèque Royale Albert I

4 boulevard de l'Empereur, 1000 (519 53 11). Métro Gare Centrale or Parc/tram 92, 93, 94/bus 20, 34, 38, 60, 71, 95, 96. **Open** 9am-8pm Mon-Fri; 9am-5pm Sat.
This is the state library, holding primarily everything published in Belgium, as well as foreign journals and publications. You need a membership card to consult the vast collection of books here. Bring in a photograph, your identity card and 300BF if you're a student (if you're not a student, the yearly charge is 600BF). As usual, books cannot be taken out. The computerised catalogue lists only books that were printed after 1985. All others are still listed in the card catalogue. To consult the library's catalogue via the Internet, log on to http://www.kbr.be

Center for American Studies

3rd floor, Bibliothèque Royale Albert I, 4 boulevard de l'Empereur, 1000 (519 55 23). Metro Gare Centrale/tram 92, 93, 94/bus 20, 34, 38, 60,71, 95, 96. **Open** 9am-12.30pm, 2-5pm, Mon-Fri.
Although this resource centre does not have very many primary sources, it is well stocked in American books on critical theory, history, sociology and the arts. If the book you need isn't here, staff can tell you where to find it in Belgium and beyond. Again, books cannot be taken out.

Exchanges

Most universities have an office for exchange programmes, or at least their own branches of **Tempus** and **Socrates** on campus. Listed below are the main offices.

AIESEC (Association Internationale d'Etudiants en Sciences Economiques et Sociales)

50 avenue Franklin Roosevelt, 1050 (650 26 21). Tram 93, 94/bus 71.
AIESEC has offices in most universities around the world and helps students in economics or social sciences find internships abroad during their final year. The organisation also contacts companies to set up 'job days'. This address is for ULB's branch of AIESEC.

Commission for Educational Exchange – The Fulbright Program

Bibliothèque Royale, 4 boulevard de l'Empereur, 1000 (519 57 72). Métro Gare Centrale/tram 92, 93, 94/bus 20, 34, 38, 60, 71, 95, 96. **Open** 9am-1pm Mon-Thur; *telephone enquiries* 2-4.30pm Mon-Fri.
Administered by the US Information Agency, the Fulbright Program offers about 50 scholarships a year for nationals of Belgium and Luxemburg to study, teach or conduct research in a US university. This centre has catalogues of almost every college and university in the States, US internship information, youth exchanges, language programmes and study guides for American standardised tests (SATs, TOEFL, GREs etc).

Socrates and Youth

70 rue Montoyer, 1000 (233 01 11). Métro Trône. **Open** 8.30am-6pm Mon-Fri.
Socrates (previously called Erasmus) is the EU agency that sets up student exchanges throughout Europe. The grants are teeny, but the experience is well worth it. If you want to do an exchange with an institution that is not already an Erasmus member, you can set up your own programme.

Tempus (Trans-European Cooperation Scheme for Higher Education)

Ministère de l'Education de la Recherche et de la Formation Generale de l'Enseignement Supérieur et de la

Recherche Scientifique, Cité Administrative de l'Etat, 204 rue Royale, 1010 (210 55 69). Métro Botanique. **Open** 9am-noon, 2-5pm, Mon-Fri.
EU organisation Tempus arranges educational exchanges between European member states and Eastern European countries: Albania, Bulgaria, Czech Republic, Estonia, Hungary, Latvia, Lithuania, Poland, Romania, Slovak Republic, Slovenia. Belgian francophone enquiries only.

Student accommodation

Most universities have some form of student housing, but space is usually limited. Better to rent an apartment – real estate in Brussels never really recovered from the late 1980s dive, so rents are still quite reasonable. One problem to be aware of, when renting in Brussels, is that many bathrooms are fitted with open-flue gas water heaters. These are potentially lethal and indeed cause about 50 deaths a year through carbon monoxide poisoning (it is vital to have sufficient ventilation). Despite increasing awareness, landlords have been slow to address the problem. The *Bulletin* has apartment listings, though *Le Vlan* (*see chapter* **Media**) is much better for cheaper places to rent.

Food & drink

Campus cafeteria food is, without exception, grim. Listed below are a few cheap alternatives, plus some studenty hangouts.

A la Bécasse

11 rue de Tabora, 1000 (511 00 06). Métro Bourse or De Brouckère. **Open** 10am-1am Mon-Thur; 10am-2am Fri, Sat; 11am-midnight Sun. **Credit** MC, V.
Although middle-aged tourists find their way here too, this traditional bar is a late-night haunt for Belgian students.

L'Atelier

77 rue Elise, 1050 (649 19 53). Tram 93, 94/bus 71. **Open** 4pm-3am Mon-Thur; 6pm-4am Fri, Sat; 6pm-3am Sun. **No credit cards.**
A hop, skip and jump away from ULB, this bar has between 150 and 250 beers available for you to get plastered on. Warning: the fruity peach and raspberry varieties come back to haunt the morning after.

Le Belgica

32 rue du Marché au Charbon, 1000 (no phone). Métro Bourse. **Open** 10am-3am Thur-Sat. **No credit cards.**
This has reigned supreme for several years as the trendy, underground, alternative bar in Brussels from which a good night out commences. Many black leather-clad students from the Beaux Arts have made it their home. The bar's speciality is a *sous-marin* – a shot glass of *genièvre* (juniper liquor) and lemon juice submerged in a beer.

Le Campus

437 avenue de la Couronne, 1050 (648 53 80). Bus 71, 95, 96. **Open** 9am-5am daily. **Average** 800BF. **Credit** AmEx, DC, MC, V.
An institution, Le Campus serves cheap decent grub to mainly ULB students. Long opening hours keep it a favourite.

Henry J Bean's

40 rue Montagne aux Herbes Potagères, 1000 (219 28 28). Métro De Brouckère or Gare Centrale/bus 71. **Open** noon-11pm Mon-Fri; noon-3pm Sat; noon-midnight Sun.
A long-time favourite among the young English-speaking community, this meat market is usually packed on weekends. The décor is 1950s and '60s Americana.

Jeux d'Hiver

1a chemin du Croquet, 1000 (647 22 05). Don't even think of taking public transport to get here. **Open** 11pm-2am Wed; 11pm-6am Thur-Sat. **No credit cards.**
You can find students at clubs and venues all over the city, but this one in particular attracts the highest concentration of students from ICHEC and Solvay in the city. It's smack in the middle of the Bois de la Cambre and is a Mecca for *péteux* (loosely defined, this term means 'preppy rich kid with attitude and the keys to daddy's car'). If someone says they want to take you to 'ze games', you know what they mean. Run.

Monkey Business

30 rue Defacqz, 1050 (538 69 34). Tram 93, 94. **Open** 10.30am-3pm, 6pm-late, Mon-Fri; 6pm-late Sat; 11.30am-2am Sun. **No credit cards.**
Tex-Mex food and nightly happy hours from 6-9pm make this popular among English-speaking students. The ground floor is brightly lit and squeaky clean; upstairs, things get a bit grungier, especially on Wednesdays when drinks are half price.

Phil's International Bar

189 rue Haute, 1000 (513 95 88). Bus 20, 48. **Open** 9pm-2am Mon, Tue, Sun; 9pm-4am Wed, Thur; 9pm-6am Fri, Sat.
The atmosphere in Phil's, a major Vesalius hangout, is both comfortable and trendy. Long drinks are its speciality and there is jazz on Wednesdays.

Bookshops

Mark-ups on foreign books are high in Brussels. Belgium is one of the few countries in Europe that does not support its book market and thus books can be quite pricey. If at all possible, you're better off buying abroad. Otherwise you could try the **Galerie Bortier** off of rue St Jean (Métro Gare Centrale), which is full of bookstores, many of them second-hand.

Fnac

City 2, rue Neuve, 1000 (209 22 11). Métro Rogier or De Brouckère/tram 23, 52, 55, 56, 81. **Open** 10am-7pm Mon-Thur, Sat; 10am-8pm Sat. **Credit** MC, V.
Although Fnac's forte is music, it has quite a large selection of books in all the languages of the EU. The English section contains many works put out by lesser known publishers, such as Pandora and Black Swan.

House of Paperbacks

813 chaussée de Waterloo, 1180 (343 11 22). Tram 23, 90/bus R, W. **Open** 10am-6pm Tue-Sat. **Credit** AmEx, DC, MC, V.
Situated on the first floor of a townhouse, this English-language bookstore has a homey feel. The shelves are well-stocked and the staff extremely helpful.

WH Smith

71-75 boulevard Adolphe Max, 1000 (219 27 08). Métro Rogier/tram 23, 52, 55, 56, 81. **Open** 9am-6.30pm Mon, Wed-Sat; 10am-6.30pm Tue. **Credit** AmEx, MC, V.
The English stationery and book chain opened its branch in Brussels in 1920. It is well stocked with fiction, non-fiction and English-language magazines. If you can't find the book you need, it can be ordered within a few weeks.

Women's Brussels

Things are looking up, but right up to the 1990s, conservative and Catholic Belgium had it in for working girls and reluctant mothers.

Belgium is one of the more conservative countries in Europe when it comes to women's issues. Perhaps because of its strong Catholic bent. The language divide may play a part too, for it has kept the women's movement fragmented.

Until only a few years ago, a working woman needed her husband's permission to have her salary deposited directly into her own account. On Belgian official documents, however, married women are referred to by their maiden name and the couple by a hyphenation of both spouses' names. Abortion – legal in all other European countries except Ireland – was only legalised in Belgium in 1990, compared to 1978 in Italy, home of the Pope. Before then, abortion had been entirely illegal since 1867, and was classed under the penal code as a 'crime against the family and public morality', alongside rape and bigamy. This is not to say that abortions were not available before 1990 – they were.

A massive scandal erupted in 1973 when gynaecologist Willy Peers was arrested for performing abortions. The ensuing outrage and protests ultimately led to a tacit agreement between the Justice Minister and the Public Prosecutor, who agreed not to undertake legal proceedings against doctors who performed abortions. The Lallemand-Michielsens Law, legalising abortions up to 12 weeks, was signed in 1990 against the wishes of the then-reigning King Baudouin, so he abdicated for a day while the law was being passed.

An important, high-profile figure in women's issues is Employment Minister Miet Smet, who has been active in the formation of campaigns, from protection against sexual harassment to training the police in how to handle situations in which women have been attacked or raped. Smet was a key player in instituting harsher sentencing for rapists and in widening the definition of the crime to include oral, anal, same-sex and marital rape in the anti-violence law. She was also instrumental in the opening of **Amazone**, a women's centre in Brussels (*see below*).

Anyone who works in Belgium and sees only about half their salary reach their account each month knows that the country possesses a decent, if pricey, social security system. For women, this means 15 weeks' maternity leave at 84 per cent of their salary for the first month and 75 per cent after that, paid by the state. Mothers receive a monthly 'family allocation' for each dependent child and have access to good, even exemplary, childcare facilities, which charge according to income.

Amazone – *keeps Belgian men on their toes.*

SAFETY

Not so long ago in Brussels, it was possible for a woman to hitch-hike her way round the city alone, and to bar-crawl into the early hours in relative safety. The main obstacles would be groups of lads out on the pull, who tended to be annoying in their refusal to piss off, rather than seriously threatening. As Brussels becomes more cosmopolitan and the population grows, it is slowly starting to gain the less desirable attributes of a big city, including increasing levels of street violence. Nowadays, a single woman hitchhiking is a rare sight indeed.

While Brussels may not be as dangerous for women as London or New York, it is important to keep in mind that it is not the innocent city it used to be, and that the rules for going out in other cities also apply to Brussels. Try to avoid being alone late at night downtown, and try to have at least your taxi fare on you in case you lose your ride home. Under Belgian law you are required to have 500BF as well as your ID card on you at all times.

Bookshops & archives

Artemys

8-10 galerie Bortier, rue St Jean, 1000 (512 03 47). Métro Gare Centrale. **Open** noon-6pm Mon; 10am-6pm Tue-Thur; 10am-7pm Fri, Sat.

Artemys is *the* feminist bookstore in Brussels, specialising in lesbian literature in French, Flemish and English. When it opened in 1985 it sold only books, but due to lack of subsidy, it now sells calendars and cards to supplement its income. Belgium does not support its book industry, making competition stiff and specialist bookstores a dying breed. Nevertheless Artemys has quite a following and a reputation among women's circles as a good source of information on women's topics. Upstairs there is a bulletin board advertising housing, rides, workshops and conferences for women.

Centre de Documentation et d'Information (CEDIF)

34 rue de la Tulipe, 1050 (502 68 00). Métro Porte de Namur/bus 60, 71. **Open** 9am-noon Mon, Tue, Thur, Fri; 1-5pm Wed.

Part of the Fédération Francophone Belge pour le Planning Familial et l'Education Sexuelle, this is a good source of information on women's health and feminist issues in French. There are files on ante- and post-natal care, abortion, divorce and equal rights in the workplace.

Centre Léonie La Fontaine (Université des Femmes)

10 rue du Méridien, 1210 (229 38 33). Métro Botanique or Madou/tram 92, 93, 94/bus 61, 65, 66. **Open** 10am-5pm Mon-Fri.

Located within Amazone, a brand new, squeaky-clean centre housing a number of women's groups, this library has a wide selection of research tools and books on feminist issues. There are also dozens of periodicals in several languages: *Feminist Review, Women's Studies International Forum, DonnaWomanFemme, Schoppenvrouw* to name a few. Anyone can use the centre and make photocopies (3BF per A4 page), but only members are allowed to take certain books out (up to three per month). Membership costs 200BF a year.

Rosa

78 & 86 Gallaitstraat, 1030 (216 23 23). Tram 52, 55, 92, 93, 94. **Open** 10am-noon, 1-5pm, Mon-Thur.

Founded in 1978, Rosa was one of the first centres for documentation and research on gender roles and feminist issues in Brussels. Today it is one of the most respected centres because of its track record and tenacity over the years. Available for consultation are documents and periodicals, as well as thematic bibliographies on divorce, lesbian parenting and education, which the centre itself compiles. Although the centre is mostly Flemish-speaking, research materials are also available in French, English and German.

Women's groups & centres

International women's groups abound in Brussels – Canadian, American, South African, Sri Lankan, Swedish, British – you name it, there's one here. These groups organise charity events, excursions, social engagements and courses, and can be a useful way to meet other women in Brussels. The best source of information on the groups' activities is the *Bulletin*, a weekly English-language magazine.

For a more complete list of women's organisations in Brussels, consult the *Repertoire Francophone d'Adresses pour les Femmes*. It can be found at either the Université des Femmes (which compiled the directory) or at Artemys the bookshop (*see above*) and costs 150BF.

Amazone

10 rue du Méridien, 1210 (229 38 00/fax 229 38 01). Métro Botanique or Madou/tram 92, 93, 94/bus 61, 65, 66. **Open** 9am-5pm Mon-Fri.

Amazone opened in May 1995 with the triple goal of supporting women's organisations, providing information on women's issues to the public and offering a '*point de rencontre*' for women in Brussels. The centre is home to the following organisations: Université des Femmes, Sophia, Le Conseil des Femmes Francophones de Belgique, Nederlandstalige Vrouwenraad, Le Comité de Liaison des Femmes, Vrouwen Overleg Komitee, Stichting Vrouwen tegen Mishandeling, La Coordination des Groupes Contre la Violence Faite aux Femmes and finally La Coordination des Groupes Politiques des Femmes pour la Démocratie Paritaire. Described as 'gay friendly' but not exclusively lesbian, Amazone also houses a restaurant (228 38 37) for women and men, open for lunch. The cadre is bourgeois and the food is sandwich/salad fare.

Centre Feminin d'Education Permanente (CFEP)

1a place Quetelet, 1210 (219 28 02). Métro Botanique or Madou/tram 92, 93, 94/bus 29, 61, 63, 65, 66. **Open** 9.30am-4pm Mon-Fri.

CFEP opened in 1956 in response to growing demand among women to be active participants in Brussels' socio-economic life. Today its goal, though evolved, is much the same: to offer women training and support making them better equipped to compete in today's world. Although it may sound patronising, the centre's approach is one of empowerment rather than 'ladies aid'. There are courses available in computing and languages (including French conversation classes), conferences are held on topics ranging from hormone replacement therapy to advertising, and an investment club provides basic information about investing in stocks. Female entrepreneurs looking for funding can find referrals and information here on how best to get their project underway.

Focus Career Services

23 rue Lesbroussart, 1050 (646 65 30/fax 646 96 02). Tram 81, 82/bus 38, 59 60, 71. **Open** 10am-5pm Tue, Thur, Fri; 10am-8pm Wed.

Brussels' finest feminist bookstore, **Artemys** *specialises in lesbian literature in French, Flemish and English.*

Social security provides decent maternity pay, family allowance and exemplary childcare.

While Focus Career Services is open to both women and men, it is predominantly used by women seeking employment in Brussels. It provides career counselling, personal development advice, training and job opportunity information, and job search workshops.

Health

Contraceptive pills cost an average of 200BF per month's supply. Unfortunately, they are not covered by a *mutuelle* (health insurance, which is compulsory under Belgian law). According to some women's centres, this is because the Pill is considered a 'luxury item'.

The quality of healthcare in Brussels is particularly good and there are several women's clinics, many of which operate a sliding scale of payment. Some that specialise in women's healthcare are listed below, but the **Centre de Documentation et d'Information** *(see above)*, part of the Fédération Francophone Belge pour le Planning Familial et l'Education Sexuelle, can refer you to your nearest.

La Famille Heureuse

4 place Quetelet, 1210 (217 44 50). Métro Botanique or Madou/tram 92, 93, 94/bus 29, 61, 63, 65, 66. **Open** 9am-noon, 2-8pm, Mon, Tue, Thur; 9am-5pm Wed; 9am-6pm Fri. **Drop-in visits** 1-3.30pm Wed.

This was one of the first women's clinics to open in Brussels (in 1962) and it is probably one of the most comprehensive. Services provided include contraceptive and psychological counselling, abortion, cervical smear tests and referrals. A visit with a doctor will set you back 580BF.

Branches: St Gilles (Brussels), Mons, Tournai & Verviers.

Aimer à l'ULB

38 avenue Jeanne, 1050 (650 31 31). Bus 71/tram 23, 90, 93, 94. **Open** 9am-7pm Mon-Fri; 9.30am-12.30pm Sat.

Although located on the ULB campus, this bright and cheery clinic is open to all. The cost of medical visits is based on income so if you're on a tight budget, this is a good place to come for a check-up, prescription or cervical smear.

Collectif Contraception (Santé des Femmes)

34 avenue des Celtes, 1040 (736 13 14). Métro Merode/tram 81, 82. **Open** 9.30am-5pm Mon; noon-8pm Tue; 1-5pm Wed; 9.30am-6pm Thur; 9.30am-7pm Fri.

Services provided here include general check-ups and cervical smears, HIV testing, psychological and legal counselling, and abortions. Medical visits operate by appointment only, so call first. A basic visit costs 560BF.

Helplines

Community Help Service Helpline

(648 40 14). **Open** 24 hours daily.

This 24-hour helpline, although not specifically for women, is the only English-speaking one in Brussels. It provides general information, a listening ear and counselling/referral in emergency situations.

Le Refuge (Collectif pour Femmes Battues)

29 rue Blanche, 1060 (647 00 12). Tram 93, 94. **Open** 9am-7pm Mon-Fri; 9.30am-5pm Sat, Sun.

A refuge for victims of domestic violence, which also offers counselling and support.

SOS Harcelement Sexuel

(0800 122 32). **Open** 11am-1pm, 5-7pm, daily.

Counselling and referrals (in French) for victims of sexual harassment.

SOS Viol

29 rue Blanche, 1060 (534 36 36). Tram 93, 94. **Open** 9.30am-5.30pm Mon-Fri.

Telephone assistance for victims of sexual violence, plus psychological counselling and referrals. Volunteers accompany women to the police and to the doctor, if desired.

Trips Out of Town

Trips Out of Town 222

Getting Started

Apart from making sure you don't try to communicate in French in Flanders or chat to the locals in Flemish in Wallonia, there are a few things you should know before venturing outside the capital.

There's an expression, popular among Belgians for describing their own country: 'The little puff of cotton stuffed at the top of the bottle that keeps the aspirin from rattling and breaking.' It is a reference to Belgium's origins as a buffer zone between great European powers... and as the territory for invading forces to audition before taking their raping and pillaging on the road (Caesar, Hitler, the Duke of Elba and Napoleon are just a few who stopped to flex their muscle).

All this mingling of Spanish, Dutch, German, French along with the native Flemish and Walloon has made for a very varied country, even within its cultures. The linguistic confusion common in Brussels becomes even more pronounced (pardon the pun) when you travel outside the city. With French, Dutch and German the three national languages (the last is only spoken by fewer than 100,000 of the country's 10 million citizens), even natives get tongue-tied: it isn't uncommon for a man to chat up a woman in French, take her home and spend the night with her... and find out the next morning that she, like him, is Flemish (first names aren't as telling as you might think). So, if the Belgians aren't all the best with communicating with each other, don't kick yourself for at times being at a loss for words.

This much is clear: when in Wallonia, speak French or, failing that, English. Generations of Walloons never took the time to learn Dutch as it wasn't necessary: for ages French was the dominant language of the country. But the current concentration of economic power in Flanders has meant that the younger generations are beginning to learn Flemish... but just beginning. And any Walloon who speaks good Dutch is bound to speak better English, generally learned from films, TV and pop songs.

What to speak becomes more complicated for the foreigner in Flanders. Depending on the region, speaking French can be considered a political statement, as many Flemings still have bitter memories of the suppression of their language and culture by their francophone compatriots. In other regions, such as Ghent, Knokke-le-Zoute and Antwerp (but only among the upper class in the latter), it is a mark of class. Although most Flemings speak very good to excellent English (again, courtesy of American and British pop culture as much as schooling), it is still a good idea to begin each new encounter with 'Do you speak English' ('Spreekt u engels?' in Dutch) before launching into a monologue.

Rail travel

Belgian railways

Brussels is one of the few cities with three major train stations: the newly renovated Gare du Midi, where the TGV and Eurostar depart and arrive, Gare Centrale and Gare du Nord. Express routes exist between most major cities, with local routes stopping in spots easy to miss on a map. Due to the country's small size (two hours is the longest ride between two connecting stations), the trains are utilitarian in comfort – a notch up from the most basic public transport, but that's it.

Because rail travel is still a major means of transport in Belgium, train tickets are inexpensive. From Monday morning to Friday late afternoon, return tickets cost the same as two one-way tickets and are valid for the day of purchase only. From early Friday evening to Sunday evening, a 40 per cent discount is offered on all return tickets; you have to depart the day you bought the ticket, and the return is valid until Monday evening. Tickets can be purchased at the station.

As for dependability, the SNCB is pretty reliable, if not the most luxurious way to go. And, considering your average Belgian's command of the automobile, rail is often the best way to go.

Train information

Belgium has long had a reputation for Eastern bloc efficiency and bonhomie when it comes to service, but the SNCB is actually showing signs of improving customer service. When you telephone them for schedule and fare information, they actually pick up, though still after a good wait. For information on services in and out of Brussels, telephone 203 28 80/203 36 40.

Coach travel

The importance of train travel means that the bus is the last resort of transportation for the tourist: the schedules seem to be written in hieroglyphics that only the most seasoned commuter can get his head around. And even then, buses are used more for connections to villages and suburbs outside cities than for travel between major points. For further information on buses, TEC (410 21 00) is the bus line for Wallonia, while De Lijn (526 28 28/526 28 11) handles Flanders.

Eurolines *(218 29 93).* For trips outside of Belgium, most people choose this service.

Day trips

Taxistop

28 rue Fosse-aux-Loups, 1000 (223 22 31/fax 223 22 32). **Open** 10.30am-6pm Mon-Fri.

This agency offers a variety of services that save travellers money. The central service is their car service, which goes to destinations throughout Belgium and Europe for a fee of 1.3BF/km, plus 200BF for administration costs. The only catch is that there must be a car already sheduled to depart for your destination when you call to reserve in advance… and there also has to be space. Other services include Airstop and Eurostop, through which airlines and coach companies respectively offer cut-rate tickets on trips as a means to fill otherwise empty seats. Echange des Maisons coordinates holiday home exchanges.

Bed & breakfast

Bed & Brussels

58 rue Victor Greyson, 1050 (646 07 37/fax 644 01 14). Tram 93, 94. **Reservations** 9am-6pm Mon-Fri.

B&Bs throughout Belgium can be booked through this agency. If you phone and get their answering service, leave your name, phone number and a time that you can be contacted, and they'll get back to you. They publish a guide of bed & breakfasts, imaginatively titled *Bed & Breakfast*. *See also chapter* **Accommodation**.

The cavernous hall of Antwerp's **Centraal Station**, *which dwarfs all others in the country.*

Brabant

At one time stretching up past Antwerp into Holland, what is today the most central of the provinces is also the one that best exemplifies Belgium's divided sense of identity.

Contested more hotly than any other province throughout the country's prehistory, Brabant has since 1995 split in two, creating Vlaams Brabant and Brabant Wallon. To mollify the Walloons and the Flemish, the Solomon-like decision was made that Brussels, which falls into the territory of Brabant, would remain autonomous.

Tension between the two cultures still flares up from time to time (the third national culture, German-speaking, is so small as to be almost negligable): there are still stories of the government, in an effort to be fair, having to allocate equal funding to both language communities for similar projects, regardless of need. The results have sometimes been surreal: hospitals and schools have been built in Wallonia to stand empty for no other reason than that Flanders had requested the same done. The separate-but-equal approach seems to be working better than having Brabant be one, but some politicians will still exploit the language problem whenever they lack a scapegoat.

Vlaams Brabant

Leuven

Though in English we often use the French appellation 'Louvain' when referring to this town, it is actually Flemish – defiantly so, as recent history has demonstrated. Up until the 1960s, how the two language communities co-existed depended on which side of the cultural divide you were. The French-speakers had no problem with the status quo, their language being more than well-represented in government, education and cultural life. But the Flemish, like the minorities of the US and Britain, were beginning to assert the importance of their own culture. Before the year was out, the francophones were driven out and forced to set up a sister city, Louvain-la-Neuve (New Leuven), taking the French-speaking half of the Catholic university with them.

While Louvain-la-Neuve (*see below*) is basically a depressingly prefabricated assortment of university and college campuses with homes scattered about, old Leuven has architectural features dating back to the Middle Ages. A major commercial centre from the eleventh century, Leuven still has many buildings dating back to the city's heyday.

The Grote Markt, smaller than those in Antwerp and Brussels, is the site of the late Brabant Gothic fifteenth-century Town Hall, featuring balustrades, pinnacles, detailed tracery and niches with pedestals depicting biblical scenes. Also on the Grote Markt are the Tafelrond (Round Table) – a neo-gothic reconstruction of a row of late-fifteenth-century houses – and St Peter's Church, which is decorated by triptyches of the Last Supper and the Torture of St Erasmus by fifteenth-century painter Dirk Bouts. On nearby Naamsestraat stands the spectacular St Michael's Church, a former Jesuit monastery and a splendid example of seventeenth-century baroque.

If architecture is your passion, the Great Beguinage is not to be missed. A city within a city, it features seventeeth- and eighteenth-century houses and convents in sandstone and brick, which have been modernised into administration departments and classrooms for the Katholieke Universiteit van Leuven, today the largest university in Belgium. The Clothmaker's Hall, a reminder of the city's medieval importance as a textile centre, became the heart of the University in 1432.

Other university monuments and landmarks include the Papal College, a classical building from the eighteenth century, and the Van Dale College, which dates back to the 1500s.

The fine arts on display at the Municipal Museum Vander Kelen-Mertens merit a visit. A converted mansion that was once a university college, the museum houses an impressive number of artworks, many collected from cloisters, churches and municipal institutions. Styles include baroque, rococo, Louis XVI and examples produced in Leuven and Brabant from the fifteenth to eighteenth centuries.

Leuven comes to life in the summer, after the last exams have been taken: this is a university town, remember. 'Beleuvenissen', a series of Friday evening concerts, fills street corners in July, while over three days in midsummer the Marktrock festival features rock, jazz, pop, dance and blues performers from all over the world.

Autumn begins with Leuven's famous annual market, giving way to various cultural events around town in the winter months.

While in Leuven, you should try not to miss the Provincial Recreational Centre in Kessel-Lo (016

25 69 12). Tucked away in the woods, it requires a trek to get to, but if you've got a family to entertain, it is well worth the trip. Beyond the huge pool and many sports fields, there are fishing ponds, skateboarding zones, miniature golf courses and more for all-round athletic fun.

Further information

Getting there *by train* from Gare du Nord, Gare Centrale or Gare du Midi; *by car* N2.
Eating and drinking The gorgeous Grote Markt has various cafés and bars circling it, among which the *Café Gambrinus* is among the most notable. It is one of the grandest in Leuven, with floral-motif windows, gold-leaf wallpaper and frescoes in a pre-art nouveau style dating back to the turn of the century.

Tourist information

30 Leopold Vanderkelenstraat, 3000 Leuven (016 21 15 39/fax 016 21 15 49). **Open** 9am-5pm Mon-Fri; 10am-5pm Sat; *Mar-Oct* also 10am-5pm Sun.

Halle

Lovely but largely unexceptional Halle comes to life during Whitsun, when the procession of the Virgin Mary takes place.

More than six centuries old, this procession originally promised a plenary indulgence to all participants. As with most traditions this old, the original significance has changed over time: today, it's more about the spectacle of the traditionally garbed, flagbearing horsemen and other folkloric touches. It also celebrates Halle's historical peak, which came in the fourteenth century when pilgrims from all over the country journeyed to pay respects to the statue of the Virgin Mary at St Martin's Church.

If you happen to miss this event but find yourself in Halle anyway, a walk through the city reveals some architectural items of interest, such as the Town Hall on the market square, a seventeenth-century Renaissance building. Just outside the city is Halle Woods, which during the spring is covered with bluebells.

Further information

Getting there *by train* from Gare du Nord, Gare Centrale or Gare du Midi; *by car* N6.

Grimbergen

This spot-on-the-map village is within spitting distance of Brussels (even the telephone prefix is the same). It's not exactly the most interesting place in the world, but it does have one worthwhile attraction if you find yourself in the area.

The medieval abbey that used to stand on the square in the centre of Grimbergen is long gone: the seventeenth-century church that used to be attached to it is all that's left. The rough-hewn façade has seen better days, but the look of the church pales next to its history. This was to be the replacement church for the one which had been

Leuven – *Gothic fifteenth-century Town Hall.*

destroyed but the builders started on it before sufficient funds were found to complete the job – a leap of faith, if ever there was one. The proportions inside are more than a little off, which gives even the most religious person a slightly queasy sensation. It genuinely has to be seen to be appreciated.

A short distance from Grimbergen off the A12 between Brussels and Antwerp, are the National Botanical Garden of Belgium (269 39 05). The grounds of the Château de Bouchout are the grand setting for this 92-hectare garden offering one of the most varied collections of plants in Europe – in all, approaching 30,000 dfferent species. Ponds and lawns punctuate the landscape of trees and shrubs, vines and flowering plants. The Palais des Plantes greenhouse contains tropical and subtropical plants.

Further information

Getting there *by car* A14.

Diest

Close to the provincial border with Limburg, Diest is part of the region of Vlaams-Brabant called Hageland, which features many little burgs and towns that all have something unique to offer.

Dating back to the early thirteenth century, Diest is a former textile centre with more than its share of religious monuments, such as the Abbeys of Tongerlo, near the Grote Markt, reserved for the sixteenth century's wretched. Dour, austere and unobtrusive, the Engelenconvent – literally the Convent of Angels – is a museum that doubles as a church. Religious miscellanea are displayed, as you'd expect. The Saint-Sulpice church in Diest was begun in 1321 – and its tower still isn't finished today. Nevertheless, it is a good example of Brabançon architecture – Gothic as re-interpreted in Brabant.

A few kilometres outside Diest on the road to Aarschot, Scherpenheuvel is a must for the holy of heart and heathens alike. This oasis of holiness sprang into existence in the early seventeenth century when it was built in honour of a Catholic cult. Although it was intended to be a very modest monument, it looks like something out of Disney: starting from the ultra-baroque dome and working down, it has a Vegas kind of majesty. The interior features a wood and marble tree. Summer here is full of the faithful, eager to get a gander. On the first Sunday after All Saints Day, there's a procession thanking the Virgin Mary for delivering Belgium from evil.

Further information

Getting there *by train* Gare Centrale or Gare du Midi; *by car* N2 via Leuven.

Tourist information

1 Grote Markt, 3290 Diest (013 31 21 21). **Open** 8.30am-12.30pm, 1.30-5pm, Mon-Fri; 9am-noon Sat.

Hoegaarden

The village that gave the world the white beer (*een blanchke*, in Bruxellois) of the same name is mostly agricultural, but the Vlaamse Toontuinen (016 76 78 43) provides a lush area of serpentine paths through gardens for green-thumbs and other fans of flora. The crown-shaped patch in the back of the garden is dedicated to the memory of King Baudouin.

Further information

Getting there *by car* A3.

Tienen

This is beet country, which explains why Tienen is known as sugar city. It was first destroyed in the seventeenth century, when the French and Dutch were battling with the Spanish. Three centuries of rebuilding were undone in 1944, when World War II destroyed 650 buildings.

The Museum 'Het Toreke' has a variety of tools and decorative objects from Roman times which confirm its former status as a colony of the Holy Roman Empire. That the city enjoyed great wealth in the Middle Ages is still evident in the Grand Place, the second largest in Belgium. The Gothic Onze Lieve Vrouw ten Poelkerk church is grand despite missing its nave. Take a breather on one of the many café terraces here and enjoy the view.

Further information

Getting there *by car* A3.
Events On the huge Grand Place, a *market* takes place every Tuesday morning. In the nearby village of Hakendover, a *horseback procession* takes place after mass on Easter Monday. The theme? The legend of three virgins wanting to build a church who were directed to the site by an angel. With only 12 builders, Saint Sauveur (after whom the church is named) chipped in. *Suikerrock*, one of the largest summer rock festivals in the country, is held every year on the last weekend in July.

Tourist information

4 Grote Markt, 3300 Tienen (016 81 97 85). **Open** *Oct-Apr* 8.30am-12.30pm, 1.30-5pm, Mon-Fri; *Jul, Aug* 8.30am-12.30pm, 1.30-5pm, Mon-Fri; 2-5pm Sat, Sun. *May, Sept* 8.30am-12.30pm, 1.30-5pm, Mon-Fri; 10am-6pm Sat, Sun.

Brabant Wallon

Louvain-la-Neuve

Louvain-la-Neuve is as depressing a town as you might expect of one that had to be built in a hurry. The only sense of history you have here is the reason for its existence: spurred by a rising sense of cultural pride in the 1960s (the same era as the Black is Beautiful movement in the US), the Flemish in Leuven wanted to be rid of their francophone counterparts (at least at their university) and effectively purged them from the city of Leuven (or Louvain, as it is known as in French). The francophones still insist they seceded from what, even after their departure, is still the largest university in Belgium. In any event, the francophones were homeless, and thus the former Université Catholique de Louvain set up house fast in what they christened Louvain-la-Neuve.

There is sort a perverse Eastern bloc beauty about the 'city' (for lack of a better word): builders didn't have the luxury of thinking of style when they fashioned the dormitories, school buildings and the few excuses for private homes that surround the university's campus. It's pre-fab estate houses all the way.

There are, however, a few things Louvain-la-Neuve has going for it. Cars are banned from the city – a car park is provided for people entering LLN – which gives the city a more human scale. Streets – or pathways, rather – are not clearly marked, which means you have to travel around a bit before you figure out exactly where you are. As this is a university town, it is pretty much devoid of activity during holidays periods.

Not far out of town, in the Bois des Rêves, is the Domaine Provincial (010 41 60 72) offering fifty hectares of walks through woods, a fake beach on which to frolic, and a solarium to get that tan that eludes most in Belgium. It's great for families and those who don't mind being around them.

Further information

Getting there *by train* from Gare Centrale or Schuman; *by car* A4 to Louvranges, switch to secondary road.

Nivelles

Nivelles has the distinction of having been founded in the seventh century by a woman, Itte, the wife of Pepin the Elder. Much of the city's original historical beauty was destroyed in World War II. A few sites do remain, though.

Sites include the Collégiale Sainte-Gertrude, which celebrated its 950th year as the largest and most prestigious monument in Brabant Wallon (although some would argue that the lion at Waterloo lays claim to this honour). This distinction isn't entirely correct: what stands now is in fact an exact copy of the original Romanesque building, which was destroyed in World War II. Inside are a fifteenth-century fresco depicting the martyr Saint Laurent, a crypt where mass was held, and archaeological remains of five ancient churches. Named after the first abbess of the city, the Collégiale Sainte-Gertrude makes for a very interesting visit.

The Musée Communal de Nivelles (067 88 20 60) features artefacts from the city's long history in an eighteenth-century building. Glass, gems and tools all figure in the collection, as well as studies of works by the Belgian baroque sculptor Laurent Delvaux.

Further information

Getting there *by train* from Gare Centrale or Schuman; *by car* E19.

Tourist information

place Albert Premier, 1400 Nivelles (067 21 54 13).
Open 9am-noon, 1.30-5pm, Mon-Fri; 10am-noon, 2-4pm, Sat; 2-5pm Sun.

Waterloo

Second only to Bruges as a tourist attraction in Belgium, this village means different things to different people: to those residing outside of the country, historical weight is attached to it, with your version of it dependent on your nationality. To people living in Brussels, it is derided as the place where all the Eurocrats' and other expats' families live. This sneering does carry more than a little envy along with it: as a residential area, it beats Brussels for greenery and a place to raise children.

There are some touristic sites, other than the predictable visit to the lion (*see below*). The Waterloo Wellington Museum (354 59 54/354 78 06) is the perfect school field trip – the particulars of Napoleon's defeat in 1815 are explained by this 18-room exhibit. The expected weaponry, costumes and letters are all there, but some exhibits in particular do stand out. A glass-encased display of a wooden leg of an officer that was found on the battlefield, for example, is especially affecting. Napoleon even gets a room dedicated to him and his officers, in the interest of evenhandedness.

Climbing on the Lion of Waterloo is *the* snap everyone is expected to bring back from a visit to Waterloo and, unlike most tourist attractions that have been drenched in publicity before you ever see them (the Mona Lisa, say), this one doesn't disappoint. Atop a grass-covered pyramid, the Lion marks the space where William of Orange was wounded. Climb the 226 steps to the top.

The Provinicial Museum of Caillou is located on the spot where Napoleon spent his last night before losing the battle. It may not be the best place to see war memorabilia (the Waterloo Wellington Museum is more impressive), but it's still a good enough place to come and gloat over the French dictator's defeat, if that's your bag.

The Musée de Cire (217 60 23) offers a wax-based version of the principals in the battle.

Further information

Getting there *by train* from Gare Centrale; *by car* follow the Brussels ring road.

Wavre

The city has nothing to offer in terms of intellectually stimulating historical blah-blah-blah about Belgium, but there is diversion if you just want to let your hair down.

Two of the biggest attractions here, for Belgians and tourists, are **Walibi** and **Aqulibi**, two theme parks especially popular with families and teens. Walibi (010 41 44 66) is a land-locked park with 47 attractions and shows to provide something for everyone. The rides range from the typical vertigo-and-vomit-inducing horrors (which still pale compared to the American thrill machines, which have to be more frightening than merely living in the US) to the more staid carousels and dodgem cars. The most impressive of the rides, such as the Sirocco which moves at 85 kmph, are normally teeming with the post-pabulum/pre-puberty set. Walibi manages to be more human than Euro-Disney – and it's a darn sight cheaper.

Aqualibi (010 41 44 66) is as tropical a paradise as you're likely to get in Belgium, and it's all courtesy of technology. This sunpark (as they call 'em here) maintains a constant temperature of 29 degrees C inside its huge structure, boasting a huge pool with simulated waves, surrounded by palms to give you that away-on-holiday feel. There are waterslides, Jacuzzis, sunbeds and other thrills for kids and grown-ups. Some of the attractions are purely kitsch for those with a radar for such (its attempt at transporting you to 'the heart of the jungle' comes up a tad tacky, but all the more charming for it). It's best visited if you don't mind loud children.

Both Walibi and Aqualibi are open all year round (*see chapter* **Sightseeing** for full opening times and prices).

Further information

Getting there *by train* direction Ottignies, switch for Wavre; *by car* N4.

Antwerp

Its geographical location has made Antwerp historically one of the most prosperous – if not the most prosperous – province of Belgium. From the diamond district to the thrills and spills of Bobbejaanland, its rich pleasures are there for the taking.

Like Holland, Antwerp's fortune was not (and still is not) made on producing anything: rather, being the most important (or second most important, depending on who's doing the talking) port in Europe has been the province's making. But, unlike Amsterdam, which has become more cosmopolitan as a result of its exposure to the rest of the world through trade, the province of Antwerp has a reputation of being, well, provincial.

Besides Antwerp, only Mechelen can claim city status here: the rest of the province's towns, though not without their positive points, tend to be places people come from rather than go to.

Antwerp

'As Antwerp goes, so goes the rest of Belgium… a few years later,' goes the maxim held as true by many Antwerpers. The grandest city in Belgium (Brussels lost that title years ago, courtesy of overzealous speculators and the government's reckless disregard for many of the city's fine, older buildings), a sort of pint-sized New York, Antwerp has more attitude per square centimetre than any other Belgian city.

The city – which is the capital of the province of the same name – has a long and rich history (both literally and figuratively). Still the diamond capital of the world, its former wealth is evident in the many grand buildings from the Middle Ages up to the present; its present wealth is evident in the number of fashionable shops, the high ratio of flash cars, and the way people go out – much unlike Brussels. Brussels is a city that is a mix of so much – French, Flemish, EU, immigrant – that its identity fails to gel. Antwerp, in its provinciality, has a definite character.

Which is why Antwerp is despised by the rest of Flanders.

The city's initial wealth came from the North Sea, which is connected to it by the River Scheldt. Frisian sailors first established themselves there

Antwerp – *capital of the province of the same name, and the grandest city in Belgium.*

in the second century, and were followed by the Franks, who in turn were followed by the Vikings, who forced the Franks to divide their empire along the river – it was like a grand, millennium-plus-long mini-series.

What is now Antwerp sits on one side of the divide, while Ghent and Bruges sit on the other.

The tenth century saw Antwerp ruled by what would become the Holy Roman Empire, only to become a part of the Duchy of Brabant two centuries later. The Count of Flanders seized Antwerp in the fourteenth century and united Flanders and Brabant through the marriage of his daughter Margaret to the Duke of Burgundy – and so Antwerp's importance began to grow. So much so that merchants left other port cities to do business in Antwerp. By the time of the death of Charles V, the Holy Roman Emperor 1519-56, it had become the trading capital of Europe, as well as an intellectual and cultural capital.

URGE TO PURGE

The city began to decline in the sixteenth century, due to the ruler Philip II. He had to go and spoil a good thing by mixing religion with governing. Of Spanish origin, his Catholicism got the better of him and he began purging the city of Protestants, many of whom had contributed much to the city's economy and cultural life. Religious civil war ensued, resulting in the closing off the Scheldt for an expected four years, until the Catholics hoped there would be no more protestants left in town.

This was suicide for a port city – and Amsterdam was the chief beneficiary, as merchants and artists fled there and contributed to Amsterdam's Golden Age. Antwerp didn't really begin to rebound until the late eighteenth century, when the Scheldt was reopened for navigation.

Just in time for Napoleon to arrive and keep the city hostage for another 12 years. After his defeat, Antwerp became a part of the Netherlands until 1830, when Belgium came into being as a country.

For a port city that owes its wealth to doing business with the outside world, it is ironic that today Antwerp is the stronghold of the extreme right in Belgium, Vlaams Blok. One-third of the populace voted for this Flemish equivalent of the National Front, which makes them definite players in the governing of Antwerp.

This is all the more surprising in light of Antwerp's reputation for embracing and nurturing the avant-garde in the arts: its fashion academy was the training ground for world famous renegade designers Ann Demeulemeester, Martin Margiela, Dries Van Noten and Dirk Bikkembergs; youth culture and streetwear is hotter here than anywhere else in Belgium; and extending marital rights to same sex couples is currently being seriously debated in the Antwerp government, which is an impossibility elsewhere in Belgium.

DESIGN CENTRAAL

Antwerp is a city where people get dressed up, though still not on the level of Paris or London. Still, so important is the city as a fashion force that Donna Karan chose to open the Belgian location of her DKNY franchise here, as did Escada, and not in Brussels. Of the many shopping districts, the teeming Meir promenade is the busiest. With stores that run from C&A cheap to Dolce & Gabbana chic, it's where blue-haired matrons and skateboarding teens cross paths to stock up on the latest fashions.

The tree-lined ring of the city, a single street that changes its name at different points, is home to many of the more exclusive shops such as Dierkcx Tailors, one of the oldest clothiers in Antwerp. And off the Meir, a tangle of streets, including the Huidervetterstraat and the Schuttershofstraat, sell fashion from Calvin Klein to Kookai. For many of the most popular shops *see chapter* **Shopping & Services: Shopping in Antwerp**.

Sites not to be missed include the gothic splendour of Centraal Station. Though the stone of the cavernous hall, which dwarfs any other railway station in the country, has become a sooty grey with time, the gold accents on the clocks and columns remind you of its beauty. Right next to Centraal Station sits the Antwerp Zoo (03 202 45 40), which is the largest in Belgium. Polar bears, dolphins, pelicans and seals are just some of the animals residing there in close to natural settings.

On the Pelikaanstraat running alongside the tracks out of Centraal Station is the diamond district, where shop window after shop window of stones and jewels can make the passerby a little (ahem) jaded. The Jewish quarter is spread around Pelikaanstraat: a community of approximately 20,000, these practitioners of the Hasidim sect are a world unto themselves – living, marrying and socialising largely with their own kind. Most close their shops on the Sabbath (Saturday) and many are then open on Sunday.

OLD, NEW, BORROWED & BLUE

Antwerp's museums are arguably the best in Belgium. The Museum voor Schone Kunsten or Fine Arts Museum (03 238 78 09) was built in 1890, during one of Antwerp's flush periods. Greek Renaissance is the style, with hints of baroque in a building that houses pieces by Van Eyck, Fra Angelico and Van der Weyden, with an extensive collection by Ensor. It was renovated in early 1996 to much fanfair, but the turn-of-the-century atmosphere remains.

The avant-garde MUHKA – the Museum voor Hedendaagse Kunst, whose vast 1920s interior has been divided into a series of sparkling spaces to display the pieces – specialises in art after 1970. As is often the case with experimental work, the permanent and temporary collections are some-

One of the finest Gothic churches in Belgium – Antwerp's **Onze Lieve Vrouwe Cathedral**.

times right on target, other times wildly wide of the mark – but that keeps you guessing. Artists and intellectuals come together in the café on the third floor, to try to make some sense of it all.

Another museum worth visiting is Plantin-Moretus (03 233 02 94), the former home and workshop of Christoffel Plantin, the most important Dutch printer of the sixteenth century. The Ethnographic Museum (03 232 08 82) has an extensive collection of artefacts and objets d'art from around the world. And the Museum and Archives of Flemish Cultural Life (03 232 55 80) documents 200 years of life in Flanders.

No discussion of art in Antwerp would be complete without mention of Rubens, the man who married Italian flourish with Flemish depth to produce some of the world's greatest masterpieces. His house sits as a testament to his life and his art on the Wapper Rubenstraat.

Children love the Miniature City (03 237 03 29), which is Antwerp downscaled to Lilliputian-size. Important monuments of the city, such as the Bourla, the Antwerp Zoo and the Opera house are cut down to size in the exhibit.

More adult pleasures are for sale in the Red Light district (in and around Verversrui), which is unlike most in the world. Only Amsterdam can compare with the scope of prostitution on display… and 'display' is the right word for it: the scantily clad ladies of the night sit in bay windows as would-be clients (and more than a few gawkers) give them the onceover as they walk by, as though they were eyeing a washing machine in a shop window. This area has been commercially sexually active for more than three centuries, as boats docked nearby – with sailors eager to sample what the area had to offer.

Most of the girls today are from Africa, with a few Eastern Europeans and Asians (especially Philippinas) thrown in. Unlike Amsterdam, where some form of worker's protection for hookers is available, in Antwerp there is no such provision: Antwerpers' freewheeling respect for capitalism allows prostitution to go on, but their traditional Catholicism forbids them to acknowledge it. The Red Light district may be interesting to visit once out of curiosity, but any further visits bore… unless you're buying, of course.

LEFT BANK

Antwerpen Linkeroever, the left bank of the Scheldt, offers one of the best views of Antwerp, especially at night. The Sint-Anna beach, popular for its restaurants and cafés, especially in the summer, can be reached by passing through a tunnel under the river or by car.

Further information

Getting there *by train* from Gare du Nord, Gare Centrale or Gare du Midi; *by car* A1 or A12.

Eating and drinking *Ulcke van Zurich* (03 234 04 94) is the happening restaurant of club kids, DJs and fashion victims. The menu is meat and fish prepared and served to stick to your ribs. Where a night on the town begins. *The Pacific* (03 248 28 77) also serves traditional fare, spiced up and presented with more flair than you get at home. But it is more popular as a meeting place for artists and yuppies, and has live music and a DJ spinning reggae, rock and r&b every weekend. Spacious yet warm. *Spaghetti World* (no phone) is the artsy coffee-house/restaurant/meeting place of the city's young, über-trendy types. Acid jazz, trip hop and soul are just of the sounds bubbling from the PA as diners tuck into one of several light pasta dishes. This is where many nights on the town begin. The *Hard Rock Café* (03 227 05 04) – loved and loathed around the world – picked Antwerp as its twentieth location and provides the strange sight of two floors of Flemish people looking and acting more American than Uncle Sam. Have a nice day is their creed. The *Swing Café* (no phone) is popular with yuppies ready to let their hair down. Blues, jazz and soul music punctuate the air in the slightly smoky, two-level bar. Great for scoping out the crowd.

If you want to stay *De Witte Lelie* (03 226 19 66/fax 03 234 00 19) offers modern comfort along with age-old elegance – if you're willing to spend. Opened in 1993, the hotel is composed of three seventeenth-century townhouses. Each room is individually decorated, but all have enough antique charm and subdued five-star luxury. A little further down the price scale, the chain *Ibis* (03 231 88 30/fax 03 234 29 21) has a location that is just as inoffensive and efficient as all its others. Half the price of the least expensive room at De Witte Lelie, so worth a look. And if you're really skint, the *Vlaamse Jeugdherberg op Sinjoorke* (03 238 02 73/fax 03 248 19 32) has dead-cheap rooms for four to eight persons… if you're willing to deal with a 2km hike away from the city centre.

Tourist information

15 Grote Markt, 2000 Antwerp (03 232 01 03/fax 231 79 37). **Open** 9am-6pm Mon-Sat; 9-5pm Sun.

One of the best tourist offices, as far as letting you know about what's going on culturally in the city. Information about where to eat, sleep and amuse yourself. If you're looking for information about the Antwerp province in general, try the tourist office at 11 Karel Oomstraat (03 216 28 10).

Geel

When the Flemish say that you look as if you're from Geel, don't be too impressed with yourself at your talent for assimilation.

Geel is the famous village near Antwerp where the borderline mentally handicapped are welcomed and treated. They are not actually dangerous, but it does make for an eye-opening visit, as they have been completely integrated into society – some are taken in by local families. The twisted legend has it that its patron saint, Dymphne, was trying to flee the come-ons of her father, the king of Ireland. He tracked her down to Geel, where he beheaded her. The church that bears her name, also the museum and hospital attached to it, you'd be crazy to miss.

Likewise Bobbejaanland, a theme park in nearby Lichtaart (45 Olensesteenweg, 014 55 78 11), a quick hop from Geel. Flemish entertainer Bobbejaan Schoepen's penchant for American country & western gear and rock 'n' roll took him to Nashville in the 1950s. He claims to have been on the brink of international stardom when homesickness brought him back. In 1961, when riding his horse across a stretch of Belgian countryside, the rustic charm moved him so much that he thought: I'll destroy it to build a theme park.

Four decades on, the park has become an institution in Belgium, more for nostalgia than for any thrills and chills: for scary rides, try EuroDisney or the Belgian *autoroutes*. The surroundings are more human scale in the family-run park, which caters more to families with young children and groups of teens. The park (open from 10am-5.30pm daily) allows visitors to bring picnic baskets in, so you can avoid buying the overpriced refreshments.

Further information

Getting there *by train* from Gare du Nord, Gare Centrale or Gare du Midi to Berchem, switch for Geel; *by car* N2 to Leuven, then switch to N19.

Tourist information

VVV Geel, Stadhuis, 2440 Geel (014 57 09 52). **Open** 8am-noon, 1-3.30pm Mon-Fri; 10am-3pm Sat, Sun.

Lier

Featuring canals and a Grote Markt that bring to mind the much larger Bruges, this seventh-century city near Antwerp makes for an interesting diversion. Not to be missed is the *beguinage*; constructed in the thirteenth century, it ranks among Belgium's most beautiful. Cycling is one of the best ways to see the town – bikes can be rented at the railway station. Stop at one of the cafés on Grand Place and sample one of their tartelettes, which are renowned throughout Belgium

Further Information

Getting there *by train* from Gare du Nord, Gare Centrale or Gare du Midi to Berchem (direction Antwerp), switch for Lier; *by car* N1 direction Mechelen, switch to N14 direction Lier.

Tourist information

Stadhuis, 2500 Lier (03 488 38 88/fax 488 13 57). **Open** 9am-12.30pm, 3.30pm-5pm, daily.

Mechelen

Although the city of Mechelen has a rich history (it was once the capital of the Netherlands during the Middle Ages), there isn't much to recommend it today, outside of the procession of Hanswijk. Taking place the Sunday before Ascension, this is the oldest historical and religious demonstration of its kind in Belgium.

There are some monuments worth visiting if you ever find yourself in Mechelen, one of which is the Speelgoed Museum (Games Museum), which is as popular with kids as it is with collectors. Puzzles and board games as well as dolls, stuffed animals and other toys are on display. And the Dierenpark Planckendael is where animals past their prime or otherwise not fit from the Antwerp Zoo spend their twilight years.

Tourist information

(015 29 76 55/fax 015 29 76 53). Guided tours arranged every weekend.

Limburg & Liège

In Tongeren, the Flemish-speaking province of Limburg boasts the oldest town in Belgium, while neighbouring francophone Liège is the gateway to the Ardennes. The two provinces are linked by the Meuse river.

Limburg

Falling between the Meuse and the Scheldt rivers, this is a province that works: a gateway to the Rhine, eastern Europe and the Liège basin, Limburg has attracted a lot of investment from big business. Owing to its origins as a Dutch duchy, its historic leanings have been with the Dutch, which did not sit well with the very nationalistic Flemish.

Although this is a thoroughly Flemish province, there is an ethnic mix of Italians and Polish who came to work in the coal mines after World War II. Although the original immigrants and their offspring born here have retained the nationality of their heritage, they have in most cases become fully assimilated into Belgian life. Limburg is, above all, a province of balance: industry with the environment, culture with culture.

Hasselt

When the other Flemish talk about the people of Limburg, their tone is generally slightly mocking: the main comment is that they sing when they speak, sort of lilting like a hillbilly. But the accent is deceiving: the people of Hasselt are known for their love of fashion, which is evident in some of the most attractive luxury shops, trendiest cafés and chicest restaurants in Belgium.

Hasselt has all the expected sites (a *beguinage*, churches and so on) but more interesting is the National Museum of Genever, which offers a taste of this Belgian specialty to every visitor – making up for the fact that all the guides and information are in Dutch only. The history of this alcoholic beverage is presented, and there are flasks, antique bottles and demonstrations of how it's made.

Of special note also is the Dockside, one of the largest house clubs in Belgium attracting students and twentysomethings from all over the country.

Further information

Getting there *by train* from Gare du Nord, Gare Centrale or Gare du Midi; *by car* N2.
If you want to stay the *De Borgraaf Holiday Centre* (011 22 31 88) offers some of the cheapest accommodation for groups, couples and singles in a hostel-like setting. A little more upmarket is the *Hotel Century* (011 22 47 99), which has a tavern-restaurant as well.
Eating and drinking The *Martenshuys* (011 22 96 56) serves grilled dishes and salads for moderately high prices, which are almost justified by the listed building that houses the restaurant – it's also a museum. *La Belle Epoque* is a slightly pretentious tearoom which still manages to be charming, but if you feel like a genever, then 't Stokerijke is the place to stop by.

Tourist information

3 Lombardstraat, 3500 Hasselt (011 23 95 40). **Open** 10am-noon, 1-5pm, Mon-Fri.

Tongeren

The oldest town in Belgium, Tongeren was the capital of the Tungri, a pre-Roman tribe, and later a major Roman settlement, mentioned by Julius Caesar. Fragments of the old Roman wall can still be seen running through open meadows outside the city, but Tongeren exists today more as a gentle diversion than a major destination: springtime is especially lovely, when fruit trees and fields around town are in full bloom.

The Gothic Basilica has an old cloister that has stood the test of time, and well-preserved stretches of Roman wall are testament to Tongeren's past. Today the town plays host to one of the largest flea markets in Europe, and its Gallo-Roman Museum is well worth going out of your way for. Next to the basilica, the museum's exterior is a mix of glass walls and copper panels. Inside, a vast collection of Roman remains are displayed in a light and airy environment.

Don't miss the permanent exhibit in the cellar, 'The Secret of Dodecahedron,' which features the 12-sided bronze object with spheres attached to its corners – one of only 76 in the world. As to their purpose, your guess is as good as any art historian's.

Art deco typifies the rest of the town's architecture, a splendid exception being the *beguinage*, featuring sixteenth-century houses along cobblestoned lanes. On Sundays, take advantage of the flea market on Leopoldwal, near the Veemarkt: this is one of the biggest, if not the biggest (as locals allege) fleamarkets in Europe.

Further information

Getting there *by train* from Gare du Nord, Gare Centrale or Gare du Midi to Hasselt, switch for Tongeren; *by car* A3 to Waremme, switch to N69.

Tourist information

9 Stadhuisplein, 3700 Tongeren (012 39 02 55). **Open** 8am-noon, 1-4pm, Mon-Fri; 11am-4pm Sat, Sun.

The Meuse

The Meuse has been the source of some bad blood between the Dutch and the Flemish, as the environmentally friendly former accuse the latter of polluting this waterway, which flows from Belgium into Holland. Liège and Maastricht are two of the cities it winds its way through, making it the border between Belgium and the Dutch province of Limburg. If you're in the area, you might want to stop by the old town of Rekem, which has three lovely châteaux and a church museum. The town of Lanaken has medieval ruins and its own châteaux, interesting enough for a few hours' visit, but Maaseik is the most attractive tourist destination in the whole region, boasting boat tours, architectural attractions (25 seventeenth- and eighteenth-century houses, for a start) and the Museactron (a combination of three museums dedicated to archaeology, history and baking). Maaseik is pleasant enough, if not exactly worth going out of your way for. (*See also below* **Liège: Messing about in boats**.)

Getting there *by train* from Gare du Nord, Gare Centrale or Gare du Midi to Liège, then switch; *by car* E314 motorway.

Tourist information

45 Markt, 3680 Maaseik (089 56 63 72). **Open** 10am-noon, 2-4pm, Mon-Fri.

Liège

A very varied province, Liège bears the contradiction of being so close to Holland but so far away culturally: this is what France would be like if it didn't take itself so seriously. Hilly and flat, with lush greenery and sparkling (if not pristine) waterways, Liège offers something for everyone.

It is the gateway to the Ardennes, the lush, verdant area where every Belgian lusts to have a chalet or two (if they have not already been blessed). The city that gives the region its name is to Wallonia what Antwerp is to Flanders: the city everyone aspires to.

Liège

As Brussels is technically a bilingual city, it cannot truly claim to be the premier francophone city in Belgium: that honour belongs to Liège, a city only spitting distance away from Maastricht, but which maintains its unique Latin flavour nonetheless. From nightlife to daytime, Liège does merit your going out of your way to see it.

The history of Liège dates back to 705 AD, with the assassination of the Bishop of Tongeren-Maastricht Saint-Lambert in the region then called Legia. In tribute to him, his successor built a sanctuary on the same spot, attracting pilgrims traveling to homage. The Bishop eventually took his parish elsewhere, but he left behind the beginnings of what is today Liège.

PEOPLE POWER

Craftsmen, merchants and other professionals were drawn to the city in the first centuries of its existence; these were troublesome times until the clergy and the citizens found a tenuous means of sharing governance of the city in 1316. The charter signed then made Liège one of the first *slightly* democratic principalities in Belgium.

But, Belgium being Belgium, Liège did have its share of the same invading forces, upheavals and intrigue that faced other cities: Charles the Bold destroyed the city (save the churches) in 1468, the French Revolution took its toll, and both World Wars have left their lasting marks on the city.

There are four different parts to the city: the Quartier de l'Ile, an ancient island on the Meuse; the Quartier d'Outre-Meuse; the Quartier de la Pierreuse and l'Assaut du Mont Saint-Martin.

The real traditional and historic heart of the city is Saint-Lambert, the site of the Palais des Princes-Eveques, a stately building incorporating different architectural styles, each evocative of an era of the building's history. The Palais now serves as a government building. The outer court of the building is accessible to the public, but the more intimate second court is sealed off from outside visitors.

WAFFLE, WAFFLE

Waffles, the national pastry that has more of a reputation abroad than its consumption at home merits, are the speciality of Liège. Served either topped with chantilly and chocolate with tea, or bought hot from vendors on the street, they are more substantial snacks than their foreign imitations. If shopping is on your agenda, take advantage of the proximity of Maastricht to hop over and hit the stores: their clothing stores offer a trendier selection than Liège.

Liège, though, does have a wealth of museums, many worth a visit, but among the most outstanding is the Musée d'Armes, the second largest of its kind in Europe, which isn't surprising when you take into account that Belgium is a major arms producer. For both the curious and the connoisseur, the museum's collection includes several pieces from Napoleon's time. The Musée de l'Art Wallon offers over 3,000 works – paintings and sculpture – that give a sample of the best of Brussels and Wallonia. For lovers of Magritte and Delvaux, this is an essential stop.

The Musée Curtius has an impressive collection displayed in an equally impressive environment: decorative objects going back to the tenth century

Liège – *the premier francophone city in Belgium, since the capital is officially bilingual.*

and prehistoric artefacts going back even further, many with religious significance and in precious metals and stones, with a sumptuous seventeenth-century Renaissance *mosan* palace as its backdrop. The same building houses the Musée de Verre, where you can see thousands of glassworks from the craft's beginnings until the late 1800s – from Byzantine to baroque, the collection crosses cultures, featuring chalices, crystal and more.

In a similar vein, in Seraing, crystal lovers can peruse works at the Musée du Val Saint-Lambert (041 37 09 60/fax 041 37 67 81), housed in an eighteenth-century building that has been completely restored. Glass-blowers and -makers show how pieces are made in an adjacent studio, while vases, candlesticks and other objects from the present collection are on display and on sale. If all this works up an appetite, Val Saint-Lambert also has a restaurant.

Further information

Getting there *by train* from Gare du Nord, Gare Centrale or Gare du Midi; *by car* A3.

Eating and drinking Nightlife thrives in the Carré, a pedestrian area lined with cafés, discos and bars popular with teens and twentysomethings. At *Le Vaudrée* (041 23 18 80) you can choose from over a thousand beers, each with its own special character. The *Taverne Saint-Paul* (041 23 72 17), founded more than 100 years ago, has a good selection of beers on tap. In the centre of town, try *Casa Nicaragua* (041 77 37 36), popular for its poetry readings and themed parties. Profits from the bar go to Nicaraguan charities. *Les Caves de Porto* (041 23 23 25) has another take on Latin, this time Portuguese-Brazilian. *Le Pergola* (041 42 57 08) is a mom-and-pop affair that has one of the warmest, most intimate dining rooms in Liège. Pasta dishes, salads and chianti are served in a discreet setting. An old-time charm pervades *L'Annexe 13*, which has an authentic Liégeois ambience that makes you feel instantly at home. A favourite of artists, professionals and locals. The menu changes, depending on what's in season and on the market prices for the blood sausage; offal-based main courses and lots of pork

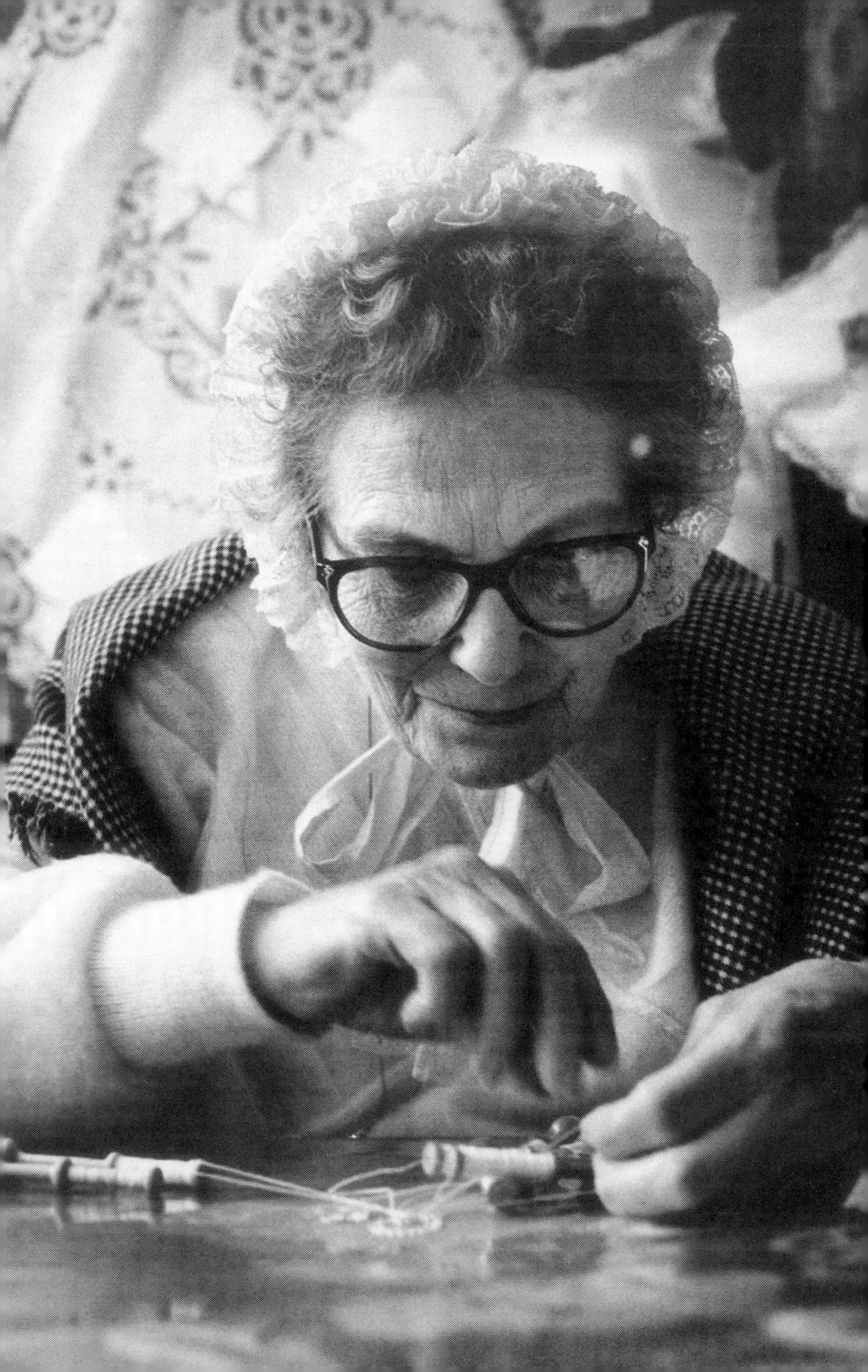

Messing about in boats

The compact city centre of Liège is situated on the west bank of the Meuse (*see also above* **Limburg: The Meuse**). Opportunities abound for seeing the city from the water, or for travelling further downstream.

Unlike the smaller boats, which offer little sitting room and only a cramped view of the surroundings, Cruises Along the Meuse (04 387 43 33/fax 04 387 58 50) gives you space to walk around and stretch out on two decks. The boats travel along the lower Meuse as well as along the Lanaye lock going to Maastricht. Trips run from July to November.

South of Liège on the River Amblève, Coo-Stavelot is worth a stop for two reasons. The Descente de l'Ambleve (080 68 42 65/fax 080 68 44 43), running through the Ambleve Valley, is a must for kayakers. It is open from March to 1 November. And Telecoo (080 68 42 65/fax 080 68 44 43), which sits on the Cascade of Coo, is an amusement park that takes full advantage of the lush woods and clean air. A sky tram travels from to the bottom of the Cascade, with a breathtaking aerial view, while go-kart racing, slalom rides and a rodeo complement the standard game park.

The Grottes de Remouchamps (041 84 46 82/fax 041 60 91 08) is the site of the world's longest subterranean passage. Open to the public since 1912, the grotto has two parts: the first is navigable by foot and was inhabited 8,000 years ago by paleolithic hunters. The second part must be visited by boat on a river that wanders underground for 600 metres.

– traditional, stick-to-your ribs fare. The fact there's no telephone makes it all the more exclusive. It's in the Outremeuse area and is cheap. But if you're looking to impress, try *Au Vieux Liège* (041 23 77 88). The sixteenth-century house that is the setting for this restaurant has dining rooms full of refined charm. The seafood dishes are especially delicious, but the menu features a wider range of sophisticated French cuisine.

If you want to stay the *Hotel le Simenon* (041 41 20 20) takes its name from the Liège-born novelist who is something of a national hero. The ornate exterior of the hotel gives way to a more subdued and elegant interior, with reasonable charges for what you're getting. Passable and practical, the *Hotel l'Univers* (041 54 55 55) opts for efficiency over elegance. More unique accommodation can be found on the Bateau-peniche *L'Embrun* (041 21 11 20), a boat hotel.

Tourist information

92 Feronstree, 4000 Liège (041 21 92 21). **Open** *Apr-Oct* 9am-6pm Mon-Fri; 10am-4pm Sat; 10am-2pm Sun. *Nov-Mar* 9am-5pm; 10am-4pm Sat; 10am-2pm Sun.

Tourist information

place de Guellimins, 4000 Liège (041 52 44 19). **Open** *Apr-Sept* 9am-noon, 12.30-5.30pm, Mon-Sat; *Oct-Mar* 10am-12.30pm, 1.30-4pm, Mon-Sat.

Province of Liège Tourism Federation

77 boulevard de la Sauviniere (041 22 42 10). **Open** 8.30am-5pm Mon-Fri; 9am-1pm Sat.

Spa

Spa, source of the world-famous mineral water, also gave its name to the word for a curative mineral spring. The town has charms that are every bit as relaxing as its name would have you believe.

'A remarkable spring that emerges in several places and tastes of iron,' is how Pliny the Elder summed it up in his *Natural History*.

Today the casino and the thermal establishment, as well as the theatres and concert halls built during the Belle Epoque (at the height of Spa's renown), look as though they've seen better days. But the Thermes de Spa (087 77 25 60/fax 087 77 50 66) still provides cures, and the town's peat-baths and mineral water treatments attract even Belgians – proof that its reputation is not all historical hype.

If taking a dip isn't your thing, you can take advantage of the free running springs (*pouhons*), whose high metallic content makes Spa (only 33 mg of salts per litre) seem feeble. These are accessible to anyone walking along the scenic Tour des Fontaines, a trail through a quiet patch of forest. Fishing on one of the town's lakes also provides a peaceful diversion.

Further information

Getting there *by train* from Gare du Nord, Gare Centrale or Gare du Midi to Liège, switch for Verviers, switch for Spa; *by car* A3 to A7 at Chaineux, then A27 to Sart and switch to N629 for Spa.

Eating and drinking If you feel like splurging, then the *Brasserie du Grand Maur* offers not only excellent traditional French cuisine but a gorgeous and elegant ambience as well. More down-home is the *Steak House* (087 77 15 05).

If you want to stay, the *Hotel Relais* (087 77 40 33/fax 77 25 93) has a pleasant ambience and a lovely flowered exterior. Moderately priced, it has the added advantage of being central. And if you want to sleep among some of the most beautiful countryside in Belgium, the *Parc des Sources* (087 77 23 11), open from mid-March to October, is the largest campground in Spa, with 171 lots.

Tourist information

41 place Royale, 4900 Spa (087 77 25 19/fax 087 77 07 00). **Open** 9am-12.30pm, 2-6pm, Mon-Fri; 10am-12.30pm, 2-6pm, Sat, Sun.

Luxembourg

Far – but never too far – from the bustle of Brussels, the province that shares a border with the Grand Duchy of the same name is not short on touristic attractions.

Much greener than this province you don't get. Lacking a major city to draw attention to it, it still attracts nature-lovers and ski enthusiasts, who flock to the Ardennes, which cover a good portion of Luxembourg. It has more animal reserves than any other province.

La Roche-en-Ardenne

World War II destroyed much of La Roche-en-Ardenne, which dates back to the Celts and the Romans and has seen the passage through it of Louis XIV, Philip II and Charles Quint. Today it has been largely rebuilt.

There are four attractions that together make La Roche a popular stop in this region. The Parc à Gibier (084 41 13 42) is a nature park featuring animals native to Belgium, of both farm and wild varieties. Children love it.

The Musée de la Bataille des Ardennes (084 41 17 25) is a more modest museum than the American Historical Center and Memorial (*see below* **Bastogne**), but it still merits a visit. It includes remnants of the era and the battle which took 114 Ardennais lives in 1944. Cars and motorcycles, photographs and mannequins dressed in period costume effectively bring the war home to you. The Ruins of Château Feodal (084 41 13 42) boast not only the big neolithic house of the former Kings of the Franks, but also its ancient Romanesque fort outside. And if you're feeling a little creative, do stop by Les Gres de la Roche pottery museum (084 41 18 78), where you can not only see some lovely ceramics, but aslo have a go at creating some.

Tourist information

15 place du Marché, 6980 La Roche-en-Ardenne (064 41 13 42). **Open** *Jul-Sept* 10am-noon, 2-5pm, Mon-Fri. *Oct-Jun* 10am-noon, 2-5pm, Mon, Tue, Thur, Fri.

Bastogne

The American Historical Center and Memorial in Bastogne (061 21 27 11) is dedicated to commemorating one event, the World War II Battle of Bastogne. The displays feature figures of all the principals as well as battle scenes. It makes for an educational visit.

Further information

Getting there *by train* from Gare Centrale or Schuman to Libramont, switch for Bastogne; *by car* N4 to Semonchamps, go east on secondary road.

St Hubert

The namesake of this small town set amid woods was a young prince who ended up becoming the patron saint of hunters, due to his passion for the sport. St Hubert the town, dating back to the seventh century, is nowheresville for nightlife and clubbing, but if you are in the mood for something a bit more cerebral, then it definitely merits a visit.

Among the buildings of note is the eleventh-century Basilique St-Pierre-St-Paul-St-Hubert – its architectural styles are even more diverse than its name: late Renaissance, Gothic, sixteenth- and seventeenth-century classical all figure from the crypt to the steeple. The result is more harmonious in style than you would think. The old abbeys next to the basilique are somewhat less ornate, with sturdy oak doors and sedate marble hearths.

Further information

Getting there *by train* from Gare Centrale or Schuman to Ciney, switch for Poix St Hubert; *by car* A4 to Forêt de Luchy, then north-west on N89.
Events *Concerts and recitals* are given throughout the town in July. The first Sunday in September is devoted to the *Cortège Historique des Chasseurs et des Veneurs*, a procession honouring hunters.

Redu

The Village du Livre du Redu claims to have been the first village devoted completely to books, although Redu has only been devoted to books since 1984. It's more for collectors than book-lovers and avid readers – the emphasis is on rare books, though there are some lower-priced books for sale as well. In addition there are art galleries, gift shops, jewellery stores and other outlets ready to take your cash.
Tourist information *(061 61 30 10).*

Transinne

Right in the middle of the Ardennes, Transinne is the location of the Euro Space Center (061 65 64 65), which is the largest attraction of its kind in

Bouillon – *educational and recreational.*

Belgium. Exhibits dedicated to the French *Ariane* and *Hermes* programmes, the *Mir* space station and the United States' Space Shuttle *Discovery,* available on video and in model form (sometimes two storeys high), make up the lion's share of the visit. Very impressive.

Bouillon

Bouillon is a tourists' bonanza as it offers both recreational and educational attractions for visitors. The Moulin de la Falize (061 46 62 00) has the kind of all-in-one sports facility impossible to find in major cities, because space there is at a premium. But here you can take advantage of a covered, heated swimming pool, bowling alleys, sauna, gym and camping grounds. There are mountain bikes for hire, and, in the winter, ski equipment for those who want to do some cross-country.

The nearby Rapides du Saty are run by Moulin de la Falize and offer kayaking from March to November. A smallish go-kart racing track has just been opened at Karting (061 46 78 07), which also has a children's playground.

The nature park La Crête des Cerfs (061 46 71 52) offers an up-close look at wildlife, with bison, lynx and ostriches just a few of the animals you can inspect. Château Fort (061 46 62 57) lays claim to being the oldest and most interesting remnant of feudalism in Belgium. A glorious view of the town is afforded from the top of the château.

Further information

Getting there *by car* A4 until Forêt de Luchy, then south-east on N89 until N828.
Tourist information *(061 46 62 57).*

Torgny

Belgium's only real vineyard is to be found here, courtesy of the Romans' tenure in Torgny. The southernmost village in the country, blessed with a microclimate, Torgny is unapologetically small.

Further information

Getting there *by car* A4 until Stockem, switch for N82 to Virton, take N811 to St Mard, switch to secondary road going south-east.

Durbury

Easy to miss on the map, Durbury has worked its quaintness overtime, claiming to be the smallest town in the world to get some tourist recognition back in the 1970s. The ploy worked: today, busloads of Dutch and Belgian tourists come year-round to see the medieval cobblestoned streets, ancient façades and almost Disney-like tweedom.

Further information

Getting there *by car* N4 until Marche-en-Famenne, then north on N63 until Baillonville, then go east on N929.
Tourist information *(086 21 24 28).*

Vielsalm

This village sits amid hills and woods, offering breathtaking views as well as the Musée Coticule (080 21 57 68), which is housed in an old workshop and shows the history of *coticule*, a raw metal used in the fabrication of straight razors that, being unique to Vielsalm, was this region's bread and butter. Disposable razors meant the end of *coticule*'s earning potential, so now the museum sits as the only testament to its former importance.
Tourist information *(080 21 50 52).*

Marche-en-Famenne

The oldest church in Belgium is located here, the eleventh-century Eglise Waha, as well as examples of Gothic and eighteenth-century architecture. Marche-en-Famenne also has a school for lace-making, but lay men and women can visit the Musée de la Dentelle (084 31 21 35), a private home that has been transformed into one of the few lace museums in the country. The work of more than 800 lace-makers from around Belgium, going back to the eighteenth century, as well as foreign pieces, and tools of the trade, are displayed here.

Tourist information

7 rue des Brasseurs, 6900 Marche-en-Famenne (084 31 21 35). **Open** *Oct-May* 9am-noon, 1.30-5.30pm, Mon-Sat. Jun-Sept 9am-noon, 1.30-5.30pm, Mon-Sat; 2-5pm Sun.

Namur

Pastoral and pleasing, Namur is a relaxed province where leisure is king. Bordering France, there is more than enough greenery to content those desiring to discover nature.

There is no shortage of châteaux and museums for those with a thirst for historical knowledge, and there are sports activities for visitors to the province who just want to kick back. Namur is very accessible from Brussels.

Once a fortress for the Gauls, Namur has had Caesar, Charlemagne, Vikings, Normans, France, Holland, Austria and Germany each have a go at ruling it. It has weathered all this, maintaining an ultra-unperturbable calm – at least to those on the outside. Defiant to change, Namur resisted the Industrial Revolution and, more recently, the attempts of speculators to develop it. Namur has survived both intact.

Namur

The Citadelle de Namur (081 22 68 29), in the town which shares its name with the province, is one of the largest forts still existing in Europe. Now a partly recreational, partly educational theme park, the Citadelle features rides, dioramas and museums dedicated to weaponry, both firearms and swords. It's good for children. Nearby Chevetogne has the Domaine Provincial Valery Cousin (083 68 88 21), a retreat of parks, woods and lawns. A slow train gives a guided tour of the grounds, which include an Olympic-sized swimming pool, a covered area for horseriding, fish ponds, sports fields, a miniature golf course, an amusement park, a garden of plants known for their medicinal properties, and too many other attractions to list. From châteaux to camping grounds, this is one of the best parks Belgium has to offer.

Further information

Getting there *by train* from Gare Centrale or Schuman; *by car* N4.

Eating & drinking Deep pockets should try out *La Petite Figue* (081 23 13 20), an intimate two-room establishment where French cuisine is re-fashioned and re-interpreted for a very appreciative clientèle: this is a name restaurant. But if your appetite is bigger than your finances (or if you'd just prefer to go to somewhere more typically Namurois), *Le Palmier* (081 22 07 39) serves a good selection of shellfish, game, meat and poultry dishes prepared as in traditional Belgian and French kitchens. More than decent portions. Although the name wouldn't make you think it, *L'Eblouissant* is actually an Irish pub. An eclectic selection of beers from around the world complements the expected Irish and British malts, ales etc on the drinks menu. But *Extérieure-Nuit* (081 23 09 09) is more spacious, but a touch alienating: metallic accents, videos and barebrick walls can leave you cold. Best visited with a large group of friends.

If you want to stay An old private hotel dressed up for contemporary tastes is the *Hôtel Saint-Loup* (081 23 04 05). Not ridiculously expensive, but no bargain, either. Swank restaurant. The *Hôtel Opéra-Le Parisien* (081 23 13 90) proves the maxim 'Beware of hotels with posh names invoking foreign cities'. While this is hardly Hades hotel-wise, the sterility of the rooms does annoy. Clean and cheaper than the Saint-Loup. If you are on a budget, the *Auberge de Jeunesse* (081 22 36 88) has over 100 beds with rooms accommodating four to six in a renovated townhouse overlooking the Meuse – 3 km from the centre.

Tourist information

18 rue Pieds d'Alouette, 5000 Namur (081 40 80 10).
Open 8am-5pm Mon-Fri.

Annevoie

A few kilometres south of Namur on the N96 are the Château and Gardens d'Annevoie (082 61 15 55) in the Meuse Valley. They offer a package deal – as châteaux go, this isn't really the most impressive – and a garden alone is rarely enough to go out of your way for. Still, the late-seventeenth- to early-eighteenth-century château *is* a château, complete with chapel. The garden, for which the original owners of the château devised special irrigation and a means of planting in the mid-1700s, is maintained pretty much as it was back then. This makes its delicate flower beds and well-arranged shrubbery, bubbling fountains and placid ponds all the more impressive.

Many Belgian beers were originally brewed in monasteries such as the Abbaye de Maredsous (082 69 93 96). This monastery dates back to 1872, and now has a brewery and terrace for guests. The neo-Gothic building makes for perfect snapshots. For more beer information, the Musée des Bières Belges (081 41 11 02) has a fine collection of beer memorabilia, doo-dads and objects of interests from all over the world.

Dinant

More than a speck on the map, Dinant has an easy way about it – which means it's easy to pass by. If you happen to be in the region, take advantage of the Cruises Along the Meuse (*see chapter* **Limburg & Liège: Messing about in boats**), to travel to Namur, Freyr and other nearby destinations taking in the valley, woods and attempts at urbanisation that dot the shores. Do tip the guide, as they have been known to turn nasty.

Four hundred and eight steps take you to the top of the Citadelle of Dinant (082 22 36 70). Besides providing a great view of the region, there's an arms museum, exhibits and a torture chambre in the in-house prison. It's slightly less carefree and jolly fun than the Citadelle of Namur.

Further information

Getting there *by train* from Gare Centrale or Schuman to Namur, switch for Dinant; *by car* A4 to N97 near Achene, switch to N94.

Tourism information

37 rue Grande, 5500 Dinant (082 22 70 31). **Open** *Sept-Jun* 8.30am-8pm daily; *Jul-Aug* 8.30am-5pm daily.

Mariembourg

In Mariembourg, the Karting des Fagnes (060 31 26 70) offers go-karting enthusiasts what is reputed to be the longest track in Europe. Showers are available for those who want to freshen up after a session, and the canteen offers a panoramic view.

The Chemin de Fer à Vapeur de Trois Vallées (tel/fax 060 31 24 40) translates as the Three Valleys Steam Railway, which is as accurate a description as you need. It runs at a leisurely pace from Mariembourg through lush, green countryside into Givet in France. Nostalgic and fun, it's highly recommended.

Han-sur-Lesse

A tourist attraction largely because of the river Styx, an imaginatively named waterway flowing 100 metres below sea-level. Stalactites and stalagmites, limestone bluffs, water rushing over jagged rocks are all illuminated during your ride through the Grotte de Han. An old steam train takes you to the site of the cave, slightly faster than a newborn's crawl – but all the more charming for it.

Further information

Getting there *by train* to Jemelle; *by car* N4 until between Hogne and Marche-en-Famenne, switch to N803.

Rochefort

The historical site of the battle between the Austrians and Lafayette, this is a hot spot for Belgian and Dutch tourists who have neither the time nor the money to make it to the Côte d'Azur but still want to bask in the sun. Best visited if you already happen to be in the area, because most of what would make the town stand out is in the past. This is evident at the Musée Archéologique du Château (084 21 25 06), in which the remains of the once-grand Château Comtal that houses the museum are actually more interesting than the artefacts on exhibit. The Grottes de Rochefort (084 21 20 80) also offers prehistoric appeal, with its tunnels, caverns, passages and streams running as deep as 60 metres underground.

Further information

Getting there *by train* from Gare Centrale or Schuman to Marloie; *by car* A4, then switch to N911 near Ciergnon.
Eating and drinking *Le Plateau du Gerny* (084 22 18 08) is about kilometres from Rochefort, in the fly-speck-sized village of Humain, but it's the best restaurant in the area. Possessing a gentle country charm that immediately relaxes the guest, the restaurant specialises in local cuisine, with ingredients fresh from outlying farms.
If you want to stay the *Hotel le Limbourg* (084 21 44 23) offers clean, quiet, affordable – if unspectacular – accommodation.

Tourist information

2 rue du Behogne, 5580 Rochefort (084 21 25 37). **Open** *Apr-Sept* 9am-12.30pm, 1-6pm, Mon-Fri; *Oct-Mar* 9am-12.30pm, 1-5pm, Mon-Fri.

Namur – *the province has resisted both the Industrial Revolution and property developers.*

Hainaut

From the coal mines of Charleroi to gold clocks and jewellery in a unique Mons museum, the province of Hainaut offers variety – and great chips.

On the French border, this is one of the most overlooked provinces of Belgium, largely due to its lacking a major city on the same level as Ghent, Antwerp or Brussels (Charleroi, for the reasons listed below, doesn't count). Also, being in the shadow of France hasn't helped. The most Latin of Belgium's ten provinces, Hainaut follows its own timeclock: don't expect to be in and out of a shop in a hurry, because Hainautiens have a habit (or charm, depending on your view) of taking their time. A large part of the Ardennes lies in Hainaut – on the whole, charming, if a bit slow.

Charleroi

This is the Black Country, so called because of the area's many coal mines. It may not be a popular tourist destination, but the city of Charleroi does hold some charms that, if you happen to be in the area, are worth a look.

Founded by the Romans, Charleroi is actually composed of two cities from the first conquests of Belgium and took on its present name in 1666. Louis XIV builth the city up in that period, only to have the Spanish seize control in 1679. A constantly changing list of occupiers (from Austria to Dutch to French to Spanish) wreaked havoc with Charleroi's development, until France took it under its wing for a relatively stable period of 20 years following the French Revolution. But Napoleon's defeat in Waterloo put an end to that.

The city flourished during the Industrial Revolution as its coal mines provided the raw resources and its people provided the manpower to sustain the economy. As social protection for workers was not yet considered important, many perished in the mines, with families being forced to work hellish hours and child labour was exploited. In 1886, a depression hit and the miners went on strike, followed by the foundries and glassworks. The owners of these businesses tried to supress the action militarily, but eventually lost out as grand social reforms began to be instituted.

When coal was king, everything was fine. But its decline devastated Charleroi, as the city was largely a one-industry town. As in most countries, the mines had provided work not only for the lower classes but also for the immigrant population: a look through Charleroi's telephone directories today reveals a wealth of Italian, Polish and Spanish surnames, the remnants of the influx of people from these countries coming to do the work that Belgians largely didn't want to do.

Charleroi still has yet to find its feet sense. Like Detroit or northern coal-mining towns in the UK there is a permanent air of desperation in the city: anyone who has the talent, luck and/or means to get out, flees. Those who stay behind are resigned, content with visits from or daytrips to the outside world. This dissatisfaction is most clearly evinced in Charleroi's nightlife scene which has a nationwide reputation as being one of the most violent and aggressive.

The city is divided into an uptown and a downtown section: downtown is tourist central, with the higher proportion of hotels, restaurants and clubs in the city. Of historical note is the tiny St Fiancre Chapel, a brick building from the seventeenth century that falls between uptown and downtown. More exceptional is Charleroi's city hall, which, built in 1936, is younger than its administrative counterparts elsewhere in Belgium. The columned building is a fine example of art deco architecture that can look a bit sinister in the wrong light. It also houses the Musée des Beaux Arts (071 23 02 94), whose paintings lean more to the politically aware than to the aesthetically pleasing.

A chronologically correct presentation of the history of glass and the process of making it are on display at the Musée de Verre and the Musée Archéologique (071 31 08 38). Glass pieces from the Middle Ages to art deco and art nouveau styles are exhibited. An archaeology section takes up a small space on the ground floor, showing remnants of a Roman city from 2 AD.

Further information

Getting there *by train* from Gare du Nord, Gare Centrale or Gare du Midi; *by car* N5.

Eating and drinking *Le Trou Normand* (071 32 51 34) gives you old-style Belgian and French cuisine in a charmingly rough-hewn interior. Not a vegeterian's paradise, a good selection of meats, fish, poultry and (when in season) game is served. *Moules de Zélande* (071 32 50 97) is a seafood alternative, with mussels arriving daily and prepared in more than 30 different ways. Kitsch baroque is the décor of *Cour de Miracles* (071 30 22 71): lots of gold and red, plaster statuettes and yellow lighting give the joint a B-movie feel. *Bubble Gum* (071 30 28 68) is a charming take on Americana: cowskin barstools, Budweiser and student-party music.

Social climbing in Antwerp – see page 228.

Events Charleroi has its annual carnival celebration right before Lent, while in nearby Jumet there is the Marché de la Madeleine parade on the Sunday closest to July 22, when more than 2,000 men participate in a recreation of a Napeoleonic army's descent on the city. For the acquisitive, there is the *Brocante des Quais*, a huge flea market that attracts bargain-hunters every June and there's the *Comics Fair* every November.
If you want to stay the *Grand Hotel Buisset* (071 31 34 14) offers a calm, modest-sized (25 rooms) accommodation that is modern and reasonably priced.

Tourist information

by Gare Sud (071 31 82 18). **Open** 8.30am-noon, 1-5pm, Mon-Fri.

Ath

Ath is another city whose renown came after it was destroyed by marauders in the Middle Ages – they left only its Tower of Burbant standing. Today, this smallish city features little of note to interest the visitor, save the charming cafés surrounding the Grand Place, which is also the site of the impressive seventeenth-century Hôtel de Ville.

The surrounding area boasts several fine attractions, including the following:

Archéosites d'Aubechies

15 rue d'Abbaye, 7972 Aubechie-Beloeil (069 67 11 16). **Open** Easter-1 Nov.
The neolithic age is on display here in houses that have been recreated from that period. During the summer months, craftsmen come to give demostrations on the different crafts of that period, such as metal work and tanning leather. Two museums exhibiting Gallo-roman artefacts round out the educational experience.

Château d'Attre

8 avenue du Château, 7941 Attre (068 45 44 60). **Open** Apr-late Oct.
The management of the Château has tried hard to avoid creating the mothballed atmosphere of most châteaux. Instead, they have succeeded in giving this eighteenth-century building a feeling of homeliness: fresh-cut flowers, framed photographs of children, newspapers left neatly behind on coffee tables, cars parked in the drive outside and desks set up in studies to look as though the person working there has just stepped away all make it seem so cosy and familial that you almost feel as if you are trespassing on someone else's hearth. Numerous lounges surround the Château's park, with the original décor, well-preserved furniture and original wall coverings evoking Regency and Louis XIV and Louis XV. The grounds include centuries-old oak trees, which provide wonderful shade on the odd occassion that Belgium actually has some sunshine.

Parc Paradisio

1 Domaine de Cambron, 7940 Cambron-Casteau (068 45 46 53). **Open** 10am-7pm daily.
Part nature reserve, part historic monument, this sanctuary for fowl from all over the world is housed in a thirteenth-century abbey. The abbey itself has an interesting history: it originally housed monks whose love of the finer things in life ran counter to the beliefs of most at the time – they were dubbed Cambron la Pervetie. The monks are long gone, and the area around the neo-classical tower, the crypt and the Grand Escalier bridge is now home to two large ponds of waterfowl: black swans, pelicans and geese swim under tulip trees and sycamores. Elsewhere on the grounds, a wide array of parrots, macaws, parakeets and cockatoos reside in cages. All birds were bred in captivity or taken in after sustaining injuries in the wild.
Falconry exhibits throughout the day.

Château de Beloeil

rue du Château, 7970 Beloeil (069 68 94 26). **Open** Apr-Nov.
Although the Château dates back to the seventeenth century, it wasn't until war hero Charles-Joseph, a descendant of the line of royalty who had made the Château their home, moved in that the Beloeil began to acquire some of the grandeur now associated with it. The park that gives on to the Château was his initiative – so impressed was he by the English-style garden that he duplicated one here. Today it is private, but can be seen from afar. More accessible is the courtyard, which is especially majestic, with four round towers encircling it. Tens of rooms, lounges and chambers are turned out in tapestries, furnishings and other home accessories reaching back over the Château's history. Unfortunately, as some of Charles-Joseph's heirs still live here, not all rooms are accessible to guests. The old library is especially worth a visit, with over 20,000 volumes spanning five centuries. There's a café housed in the Château's chapel.

Further information

Getting there *by train* from Gare du Nord, Gare Centrale or Gare du Midi to Ath; *by car* N6 to N7, then direct to Ath.

Soignies

This city known for its blue-stoned buildings has a heavily religious history. Its peak came in the fourteenth century courtesy of the textile industry, and since then its appeal has faded to an innocuous charm that is easy to miss if you're driving through too fast.

Although a cemetery might seem a macabre choice of tourist sites, Le Vieux Cimitière possesses a kind of faded beauty that is strangely comforting. In the centre of the grounds is an immense chapel which, according to local authorities in such matters, is the first parish church of the twelfth century.

The rage for English gardens in Belgium is evident in the Château de Louvignies, one of the châteaux near Soignies in Chaussée-Notre-Dame-Louvignies. The other castle of note in the area is the Château d'Ecaussinnes-Lalaing (067 44 24 90), open from April to October, which is complemented by the chic but far from cheap Pilori restaurant nearby. Originally it was finished in the twelfth century in grey stone, but renovations three centuries later employed the blue stone characteristic of this area. From the religious objects which dominate the first floor of the Château (which is also fitted with an infirmary) to to the chapel on the grounds, this Château is more impressive than intimate. In nearby Horrues, L'Eglise Saint-Martin is an austere twelfth-century church that is furnished in the comparatively contemporary sixteenth-century style.

Also worth a look is the Moulin du Moulinet, a water-powered mill, which has been functioning daily for almost a century.

Further information

Getting there *by train* from Gare du Nord, Gare Centrale or Gare du Midi; *by car* N6.
Events Soignies is the principal stop on the *Grand Tour*, an annual religious procession taking place on Whit Monday. A fair for singles is held on the Grand Place on the same day.

Tourist information

23 rue de la Regence, 7060 Soignies (tel/fax 067 33 46 93). **Open** 8am-noon, 1-4.35pm, Mon-Fri; 10am-noon, 2-5pm, Sat; 2-5pm Sun.

Tournai

Founded by Roman soldiers as a place to rest midway between Boulogne and Cologne, Tournai is the second oldest city in Belgium. Its long and complex history is fascinating. The capital of France, courtesy of Clovis (who preferred it to Paris), in the fifth century, an English cathedral city in the sixteenth century, and today again a little piece of France in Belgium.

The city still has remnants of its former occupiers: the English only left behind names such as Big Ben and the Grenadier Guards (which pubs bear as names) and an English rose gracing a fresco in the cathedral which Henry VIII had painted. The French have fared better, influencing much of the culture largely from old allegiances – Tournai had been part of France for longer than it has been part of Belgium. French flags still fly in many parts of the town, and it's hard to tell the French from the Belgians: in fact, the citizens of Tournai are among the few Walloons who aren't insulted to be taken for French.

CLEVER MONET

The city today is either quaint or banal, depending on your tastes. More impressive for its past than its present, which is evidenced in its seven museums. The most impressive are the Musée d'Histoire Naturelle, which has a large collection of dioramas and biotopes, and the Musée des Beaux Arts, which was built by Victor Horta in the 1920s and contains works by Rubens, Monet and Van Gogh, among other greats. Horta's trademark willowy, art nouveau style is not in evidence – instead, it's his later, streamlined art deco design of galleries giving off from the courtyard which is still arguably as beautiful as any of the works displayed there. And for grandmothers and interior decorators, the porcelain of Tournai is on display at the new Musée des Arts Decoratifs. The belfry of Tournai, the oldest in Europe and a major attraction, is currently being restored.

Much of the old quarter was lost to bombing in World War II, but Romanesque churches and stones houses going back to the thirteenth century still stand in some places. The cathedral dominating the town is considered one of the finest in Belgium. The huge, sober interior is supported by sturdy Roman pillars adorned at the top with carvings of medieval faces and mythological beasts.

Other major sites include the statue of Gabrielle Petit, a local heroine who was executed by the Germans on April Fool's Day in 1916. Her final words? 'I will show them that a Belgian woman knows how to die.'

Today, Tournai is the home of the prestigious St Luc School of Art and Architecture, attended by 4,000 students – which means that there is the possibility of finding someone with a pulse.

Further information

Getting there *by train* from Gare du Nord, Gare Centrale or Gare du Midi; *by car* N6, switching to N7 at Halle, then continue to Tournai.
Eating and drinking *Lapin Vert* (69 23 59 39) offers rabbit with prunes and other regional dishes in the setting of a converted pharmacy. If Italian and Belgian cuisine is more your palate, then *Les Trois Pommes d'Orange* (069 23 59 82) is a must as much for what's on the menu as for the warm ambience. And for drinks, try the *Latchodrom*, which will be worth writing home about: a candlelit prehistoric grotto decorated with animal skins is the backdrop for intimate conversation. *Le Purgatoire* offers live music with drinks in a convivial setting.
If you want to stay contact *Agritourisme* in Brussels (230 72 95) to find out about farmhouses for rent near the city by week or the weekend. *Le Panoramique* (069 23 31 11/fax 069 23 33 23) provides a gorgeous view of the city from Mont Saint-Aubert in from the large bay windows that are a feature of most rooms. The small pool is even open to take a dip, weather permitting. Ultra-charming.

There's no shortage of amusements for children in Hainaut – try **Parc Paradisio,** *see p243.*

Tourist information

14 rue Vieux Marché aux Poteries, 7500 Tournai (069 22 20 45/fax 069 21 62 21). **Open** 9am-7pm Mon-Fri; 10am-1pm, 3-6pm, Sat, Sun.

Mons

Mild, gentle and softly seductive are the best words to describe Mons (or Bergen in Flemish). This is the administrative capital of Hainaut, with a history that reaches back to the Romans. The city's existence began with a monastery founded by Waudru, a pious lady who went on to become the patron saint of the city. The city prospered in the Middle Ages as the centre of the region's textile activity. Religious wars and bombings courtesy of Louis XIV brought down the city by the end of the seventeenth century. Constantly being lost and regained by the French, only with Belgian independence did Mons regain some kind of social stability.

LEFT 'ERE

The Maison Van Gogh (065 35 56 11), where the Dutch master lived from 1879-80, features an audiovisual exhibit and a living space that the curators have tried to preserve as Vincent would have known it, but it impresses only because of the Van-Gogh-slept-here factor. The Collégiale Sainte-Waudru (065 33 55 80) is a splendid example of Brabant gothic architecture, built between the thirteenth and fifteenth centuries and strengthened from the fifteenth to the seventeenth. Religious artefacts and curios – paintings, icons, the whole lot – are displayed throughout. The Musée des Beaux-Arts (065 34 95 55) has a collection comprising engravings, paintings and sculpture from 1400 to the present day.

A seventeenth-century infirmary is the setting for the Musée du Folklore et de la Vie Montoise (065 31 43 57), which shows a curious assortment of everyday instruments and objects from the past – compasses, rulers, chairs and tables. What was considered banal in the past takes on ironic, tragic or amusing significance when looked at through modern eyes: one fascinating artefact is a window rescued from an orphanage, which served as the depository for unwanted children. The Musée François Duesberg (065 36 31 64) has an eclectic collection of French gold and bronze objects, including clocks, busts and jewellery, that ranks as unique in the world.

BON MONS

A new museum in town, the Musée du Château Comtal (065 33 55 80), is the former home of the Counts of Hainaut and has one of the best views of Mons and the region. Medieval icons and the like make up the majority of the collection, exhibited in the eleventh-century Chapelle Saint-Calixte, which has been recently been restored.

Outside of Mons, near the French border, is the industrial archaeological site of Grand Hornu (065 77 07 12). A notable example of the functional urbanism that in 1810 preceded the Indutrial Revolution. Founder Henri du Gorge built the neo-classical, self-contained workers' complex out of nothing. It is interesting for its aesthetic appeal as well as the function of its buildings.

A bicycle is your best bet in Bruges, tourist supermagnet of **West Flanders** *– see page 248.*

Further information

Getting there *by train* from Gare du Nord, Gare Centrale or Gare du Midi; *by car* N6.
Eating & drinking Chips – or frites – are served at *Friterie Bily*, the best friture in Mons. The queues can be long, but the portions are the definition of value for money. Fifty metres from the Grand Place – anyone in Mons will be able to point you directly to it, so well is it known. A tourist trap is what *No Maison* (065 34 74 74) unfortunately has become: its location on the Grand Place has done it in, in terms of being a magnet for busloads of visitors. The food is standard Belgian fare, which compares well with the cuisine of other countries. If the hustle and bustle of a brasserie setting doesn't deter you, the prices are actually okay. *Chez Henry* (065 35 23 06) has an attractive brick interior that, in its sensible style, reflects its clientèle: mostly city workers. The menu features grilled meat and fish and homemade soups and desserts. Intimacy is the key to the appeal of *Le Chinchin* (065 84 29 15), located in the cellar of the Saint-Georges hostel. A favourite of people to meet up in before a night on the town or to go to as the night winds down. The name is French for 'cheers'. *L'Arnaque* (065 36 40 16) has seen better days, but it is still a nightlife staple: you always end up there at some point in the evening. Loud and in the middle of the bar district, so there's always somewhere else to hop to if this doesn't strike your fancy.
If you want to stay The *Château de la Cense au Bois* (065 31 60 00) offers luxury accommodation in a newish château (nineteenth century). Large, comfortable beds, huge bathrooms and a breathtaking view of the surrounding wood. This ain't cheap, so save it for a special occasion. Less dear is the more centrally located *Hôtel Saint Georges* (065 31 16 29). The rooms are comfortable, if characterless – and the location makes it all worth it.

Tourist information

22 Grand Place, 7000 Mons (065 33 55 80). **Open** *Apr-Sept* 9am-6.30pm Mon-Sat; 10am-1.30pm Sun; *Oct-Mar* 9am-5pm Mon-Sat; 10.30am-1.30pm Sun.

Binche

The golden age of Binche came in the sixteenth century, when it was passed on to Marie of Hungary. She received emperors in the grand palace that she had constructed, becoming celebrated for her lavish parties and being the 'hostess with the mostest' until the French (as was their habit, back then) destroyed the city. Although its size would not lead you to believe it, every Belgian knows Binche. The reason? Its yearly carnival outshines others throughout the country.

Most ancient pagan rituals do possess an oddness about them when looked at through today's eyes, and Binche's carnival is no exception. This one-day event goes back to the time of Marie of Hungary and features the *gilles* de Binche, chosen participants who are supposed to be dressed like South American Indians – or at least a medieval European idea of what a South American Indian should look like. Why choose a South American Indian to be involved in a celebration to mark the beginning of Lent? South America had been discovered a few decades before, and evidently the powers-that-were decided it would be a cool idea to have participants dressing up as the latest found culture – not dissimilar to the way in which we sport ethnic tattoos and nose rings and turn saris and dashikis into Western fashion statements.

In the carnival each *gille* is masked and dressed in a tunic stuffed with a pillow in the belly, trousers emblazoned with lions, elaborate hats and belts with curled-toed shoes – in short, looking as much like an Inca as the Pope. They meet in front of the city hall, with spectators, clowns and harlequins all ready to start the procession. Everyone dances to folk music played on tambourines and mandolins, as the *gilles* do their *chapeaux* up in plumes and toss oranges to the crowd of spectators. A large tourist contingent is always on hand for this freaky event every year, which goes to show that controlled substances were very much a part of life way back when.

At the Musée International du Carnaval et du Masque (064 33 57 41) the bronze statue of the *gille* out front lets you know that you are entering a building dedicated to frivolity. Masks, costumes and other objects of interests from carnivals around the world are on display in this former college for monks. Some of the models are borderline scary – which means that children susceptible to nightmares should be guided very carfully. A special section is devoted to items and explanations of the carnivals of Wallonia, with displays of how the costumes are made.

ANCIENT REGIME

A short drive from Binche is the Musée Royal de Mariemont (064 21 21 93), which sits in a 50-hectare park that was once land owned by the ubiquitous Marie of Hungary. The park itself features ruins of the eighteenth-century château that once sat here, now overgrown with ivy; in addition there are centuries-old trees and relaxing promenades. The museum stands out against the aged environment: it's a modern cinder-block of a building that has used the remains of another château partly destroyed by fire to achieve its look, with mixed results. The collections are admirable, however: ancient Egyptian, Roman and Greek pieces all figure, as do funeral masks and items from the Far East. Not the largest museum you will ever have visited, but a decent one for its size.

The Eco-Musée du Bois-du-Luc (064 28 20 00) makes for an interesting visit, but make sure you have a tour guide – otherwise, it's easy to get lost in this old industrial area. Disused trains, miners' houses and other dormant buildings that were once important parts of town life in Bois-du-Luc.

Further information

Getting there *by train* from Gare du Nord, Gare Centrale or Gare du Midi; *by car* N27.

Tourist information

14 rue Saint-Paul, 7130 Binche (064 33 37 21). **Open** 8am-noon, 12.30-4.30pm, Mon-Thur; 8am-noon Fri.

West Flanders

With all the coastal attractions, and the added fact that tourist supermagnet Bruges falls into the territory, West Flanders is one of the most visited provinces in Belgium.

If you're going to have seafood while you're in Belgium, this is the best area for it: something about the sea air on the coast, combined with the freshness of the mussels, monkfish and other piscine species fished from the North Sea makes it better than what you might get even in the best restaurants in Brussels. But the province's pleasures are more than merely piscine.

Ostende

This city is the most popular coastal destination every summer, so attractive that even Queen Victoria took a dip here in 1834. The site in the early seventeenth century of battles between the Dutch and Spanish (who left behind many offspring from liaisons with local women, evident in the more Mediterranean complexions of some natives), Ostende was once Belgium's answer to Monte Carlo: beaches, museums and racetracks of international renown.

Alas, it is showing signs of decline. The racetrack has ceased racing horses. But locals and entrepreneurs are hoping that the same space will succeed as a rock venue, to complement the famed Casino, where many musicians that you may have thought were long dead (Percy Sledge, James Brown and Barry White) attract sell-out crowds.

Along the coast is where the best seafood, especially shellfish, is to be had. An age-old rule of thumb for mussels, which are to Belgium what herring is to Scandinavia, is never to eat them in months without an r – that is, only from September to April. The air here is among the best in Belgium, and the beaches amongst the cleanest, although you should avoid the water during jellyfish season. Also, the Kleine Strand is where all the sewage washes up, and as a result is not all that popular with bathers.

The Kappellestraat is Ostende's high street: Hennes & Mauritz, C&A, Leonidas and other older shops have locations here. Upscale shops that once dotted the Adolf Buylstraat have moved on to a glass-ceilinged gallery nearby. The Lulu Shop is just about the only place women can get Vivienne Westwood, Jean Paul Gaultier and up-and-coming Belgian designer Mieke Cosijn, and on the nearby Christinastraat, men on the look-out for Armani, Helmut Lang and Dutch designer So flock to the men's shop Jaeger. Alberdeen is the emporium for men's sportswear by such style titans as Gianni Versace and Calvin Klein, and those wanting something more alternative stop by Mandarijntje for Asian jewellery, piercings and henna tattoos.

On a more cultural note, PMMK – the Provinciaal Museum voor Moderne Kunst – specialises in collections of Belgian twentieth-century artists, with symbolism and expressionism as well as more contemporary movements well-represented. Panamarenko, Permeke, Tytgat and the Cobra movement are just a few of the delights in the permanent collection.

James Ensorhuis (17 Vlaanderenstraat) is a former souvenir and seashell store. Inherited from his aunt, James Ensor turned it into a salon to entertain visiting artists, critics and friends until his death. The store's stock of seashells and tortoise shells, stuffed swans and carnival masks remain on permanent exhibit.

The Maritime School of the Belgian Merchant Marine, which ran from the 1930s-60s, sits in the Port de Plaissance near the Vindictivelaan and makes for an interesting visit.

THEY LOVE LUCY

The Paulusfeest in mid-August is the high point of the summer: local and international musicians, dancers and acting troupes converge on the city, which becomes a big carnival for a week. If you want a real understanding of Ostende, then you have to be in the audience during a performance of Lucy Loes, an Ostende folk singer who has become legendary. This is no exaggeration: the current Lucy Loes is not the original one, who died many years ago. It's unclear whether the name passed directly from the original Lucy to the reigning Lucy, or if there were Lucys in between, but, in any event, she moves the crowd to tears with her renderings of traditional folk songs in the Ostende dialect.

The Langestraat is the site of the Long Street Happening, a rougher, low-rent version of the Paulusfeest – but is still worth a look.

Further information

Getting there *by train* from Gare du Nord, Gare Centrale or Gare du Midi; *by car* A10.
Eating and drinking TheLangestraat is lined with bars and smaller dance clubs that are popular with

Ostende's working class – lots of Johnnys and Marinas, the Flemish equivalent of Sharons, Traceys and Dwaynes – who have rather lenient door policies, except when it comes to the British. Unfortunately, some Englishmen (for some reason, they always seem to be English and they always seem to be men) have given the whole UK the reputation of being drunken sods who destroy the atmosphere of any club by brawling. So, if you really want to go to one of these clubs, either play down your Britishness or go accompanied by a Flemish friend. The *Visserplein* is trendier – that is, they dress as though they know what decade it is. This is where the city's concentration of gay bars is, as well as establishments for youngsters and yuppies. Within spitting distance is the Kaai (quay), which is renowned for its fish stands and, for those with more time, excellent fish restaurants. Among the best is *'t Vistrapje*. On a clear day, a walk along the boardwalk affords you a sea-view that stretches as far as France. At the end of the pier is *Beaufort*, a tavern with an interesting history. Its name is French for gale force, which is appropriate: the original café on this spot was blown away in a storm. The current tenants assure patrons that things won't get so carried away in the future.

If you want to stay there are over 5,000 beds available in Ostende, so you should be able to find somewhere suitable to lay your weary head. If you're travelling on the cheap, then the *De Ploate Jeugdherberg* (059 80 52 97/fax 059 80 92 74) is for you. A modern, comfortable hostel, it's also dead in the centre of town. The *Hotel Thevenet* (059 70 10 35/fax 059 80 94 19) has clean rooms with showers and is a short walk to the beach. And if you're in the position to spend a little more, try the *Hotel Flanders* (059 80 66 03/fax 059 80 16 95) across from the town's cathedral.

Tourist information

2 Monacoplein, 8400 Ostende (059 70 11 99). **Open** 9am-7pm Mon-Fri; 10am-7pm Sat, Sun.

De Panne

Possessing what are arguably the most beautiful dunes on the Belgian coast, De Panne also has the largest beach: over 500 hectares with more than half of that designated as a nature reserve. There is an ample amount of space on the beach set aside for recreation: fishing is allowed, as are windsurfing, surfing and of course swimming.

A truly touristic town that makes no bones about it, De Panne has a good range of three-star hotels, five camping grounds, and a wide selection of sports clubs where the activities range from badminton through body building to bowls. A short walk going north-east along the seafront, with the sea on your left, will bring you to St Idesbald and the Museum Paul Delvaux (*see below*), a gallery space dedicated to the late great Belgian surrealist painter. If you follow the strip along the beach in the other direction, with the sea on your right, France is just a brisk walk away.

Museum Paul Delvaux

42 Kabouterweg, 8670 St Idesbald (058 52 12 29). **Open** 10.30am-6.30 Tue-Sun. **Admission** 150BF; 100BF students, over-60s.

A large number of Delvaux's paintings and sketches are on permanent display here, and although some will be moved temporarily to Brussels for the retrospective to celebrate the artist's centenary from 21 March to 7 July 1997 (*see chapters* **Sightseeing: Eyes wide shut** *and* **Museums**), many will stay. Indeed, a new room is due to be opened here in March 1997, when admission prices will show a slight increase.

Further information

Getting there *by train* from Gare du Nord, Gare Centrale or Gare du Midi to Ghent, switch for De Panne; *by car* A10 to Ostende, then west on N34.

Tourist information

21 Zeelaan, 8660 De Panne (058 42 18 18). **Open** *Sept-Jun* 9am-noon, 1.30-5pm, Mon-Fri; 9am-noon Sat. *Jul, Aug* 9am-noon, 1.30-5pm, Mon-Fri; 9am-noon, 1.30-5.30pm Sat.

Blankenberghe

Three kilometres long and 3.5km wide, Blankenberghe's beach is another popular spot for sun-lovers and others on holiday. The dunes between Blankenberghe and Zeebrugge, a less popular spot, are called the Fonteintjes, and attract many hikers and strolling couples and families. Diversion for youngsters is also provided by the modest 'Nordic' amusement park.

Further information

Getting there *by train* from Gare du Nord, Gare Centrale or Gare du Midi; *by car* A10 to Ostende, then east on N34.

Bredene

Bredene has the largest camping grounds along the coastal area in Belgium. With Ostende and Bruges within spitting distance (you could even inline-skate from Bredene to the other two without breaking a sweat), it's an ideal place to pitch your tent if you're on a camping holiday. Nature- and sports-lovers enjoy Paelsteenveld, a ten-hectare recreational park that has a mix of spectacular gardens, flowering playgrounds for children and sports facilities.

Bredene also has other attractions for sporty types: several mini-golf courses, two stables, tennis courts, bowls courts, and even a covered swimming pool for those who can't be bothered with the sea. Fishing, windsurfing and sailing are also permitted, but in designated zones.

Ieper

Ieper has been much destroyed throughout the ages, but just as ingeniously rebuilt. Once as large and renowned as Ghent and Bruges, Ieper now has an off-the-beaten-path charm and is more like what real Belgium is than Brussels. Beyond the usual churches and ruins, what makes Ieper memorable is its Cat festival.

Taking place on the second Sunday in May, this feline celebration stems from a medieval ritual of throwing cats off the top of the belfry. Today's politically correct climate dictates that stuffed cats

For children of all ages

There are a variety of amusement parks on the coast for days when the weather fails you – which is all too often in Belgium. The Boudewijnpark (050 38 38 38) in Sint Michiels near Bruges is one of the best in Belgium, with one of the largest, most modern dolphin aquaria in Europe. Bambinoland caters to tots, while the main park has more than 30 different attractions and rides. The Dadipark in Dadizele (056 50 05 05) features the Pirate's Tower, the largest suspension bridge in Europe, petting zoos and other attractions, mostly for kiddies.

But kids of all ages from all around the country flock annually to Bellewaerde (057 46 86 86), which is as close as Belgium gets to EuroDisney. The park is divided into six different theme areas: Mexico City features an airborne carrousel and a pirate boat, as well as a double-loop backward rollercoaster; Frontier City has shooting galleries, river splash rides and a western ranch; Jungle is replete with wildlife, from capuchin monkeys to wildebeest, hippos and crocs; Pepinoland features elephants, an inflatable castle and games; India has shows and stunts, as well as a ride over the rapids; and Canada has a nature reserve, as well as the highest splash ride in Europe. The larger the group you're here with, the better.

be hurled instead. A cats' parade is held every three years, the next being in 1997.

Further information

Getting there *by train* from Gare du Nord, Gare Centrale or Gare du Midi to Ghent, switch for Ieper; *by car* N8 via Kortrijk.

Tourist information

34 Grote Markt, 8900 Ieper (057 20 07 24). **Open** 9am-5.30pm daily.

Bruges

Although Brussels dwarfs it in terms of size, Bruges is the number one destination for tourists in Belgium. Allegedly the site of Europe's first stock exchange, Bruges today has only one real business, and that's tourism. The Industrial Revolution passed it by, activity at its port is but a memory now compared to Antwerp and Ghent, and the charm of centuries gone by has been better preserved here than in most of Belgium, making it one of the best cities for chronicling the country's history and pre-history.

LET'S GO BRUGES

There are a few drawbacks to Bruges' current status. Firstly, because it is such a hit with tourists, be prepared for coachload after coachload to be descending on the city alongside you, choking the most popular areas and canal rides and restaurants, camera swinging around the neck, postcard shopping, elbowing each other for a better view. And if you get sick of manoeuvring your way through the herds and hordes, imagine how the locals feel, who live with it year in, year out.

The bridges, palaces and gabled houses overlooking the canals are being restored to keep the city alive economically, but the effect of making everything palatable and understandable to the tourist is almost turning the city into a theme park.

If you can get through the tourist bull, Bruges actually has a lot to offer someone seriously interested in history. Medieval art and architecture, picturesque canals, and overall an atmosphere best described as quaint – if not for the cars and people, you would be lost in time wandering around the city. It wouldn't even exist if the Count of Flanders hadn't chosen the area where it now stands as the site for a castle to protect himself from Viking raids. Eventually, Bruges became the capital of the Duchy of Flanders in 1093 and developed into a major textile centre over the next two centuries. Its majesty can still be seen in buildings such as the Onze Lieve Vrouwekerk, the tallest church in Belgium.

BARRIER METHOD

The network of canals was built between 1297 and 1300, and at the same time a moat, walls and ramparts were built around Bruges to protect it while making it more accessible to sea-faring traders exchanging Flemish cloth for produce, wool, wine and other goods.

Bruges' building of barriers between itself and the rest of the country was symbolic: the wealth that existed here was in stark contrast to the poverty and political unrest elsewhere in Belgium. The upper classes supported Flanders' status as a duchy of France, while the Flemish peasants wanted independence; the Flemish merchants wanted non-interference from the overlords. Flemish rebellion led to more suppression, which precipitated

Small, cute and completely charming – ***Bruges*** *isn't bad either.*

the Hundred Years War, with havoc and instability the result.

Bruges saw an economic revival in 1384 when the Duke of Burgundy inherited Flanders through marriage. The city's population had grown to over 200,000 by the fifteenth century, and Van Eyck, Memling and others had used the city as a base to create what was the Golden Age of Flemish Art. This period would not be long-lived, though: the textile trade would soon decline; Antwerp would become the dominant port of trade – draining Bruges of its most prominent merchant families; and Bruges became a battleground of rebels and Spanish overlords. A fling with recovery came with the construction of the Boudewijn Canal, which pumped trade into the city via a new port at Zeebrugge. But World Wars I and II destroyed the canal – and Bruges' reawakening.

Today, the link with the sea has been restored and outside of Bruges, industry thrives. The College of Europe is also located here, which has put it on the map academically.

Further information

Getting there *by train* from Gare du Nord, Gare Centrale or Gare du Midi; *by car* N9 via Ghent.
Eating and drinking *Taverne the Hobbit* (050 33 55 20) has a yuppie and student following, who come to take advantage of the reasonable prices on pasta, chicken and other standard fare, served at big round tables by candlelight. Despite its pretentious name, *Le Chagall* (050 33 61 12) serves delicious seafood in a relaxed environment. The shellfish come highly recommended. And if you are really in the mood to spend, *De Witte Poorte* (050 33 08 83) is the last word in fine dining in Bruges. This former wine warehouse has been done over in exquisite style (from the china to the ceiling, it is de luxe) and the menu measures up to the décor's promise. Although *waterzooi* (a chicken stew) is a Ghent speciality, the version served here ranks with the best.
Events Forty days after Easter each year, Bruges holds the *Procession of the Holy Blood* (*Heilig-Bloedprocessie*, for the linguistically adept) to celebrate Ascension Day (Jesus going up to Heaven, for the religiously inept). A tradition for more than eight centuries, the event is a pageant of biblically and medieval costumed participants carrying a holy relic through the streets. Not as heavy as it sounds. *See also chapter* **Brussels by Season**.
If you want to stay Splurge on a stay at the Hôtel Die Swaene (050 34 27 98), if you get the chance. In a fifteenth-century mansion overlooking a canal, this romantic hotel is as close to Venice as you can get in Belgium. More earthbound price-wise is the Hôtel Jacobs (050 33 56 94), which has comfortable, practical rooms that are good value for money. For bargain-hunters, the Snuffel Travellers' Inn (050 33 31 33) offers hostel-like accommodation in rooms of two to eight.

Tourist information

11 Burg, 8000 Bruges (050 44 86 86). **Open** *Apr-Sept* 9.30am-6.30pm Mon-Fri; 10am-noon, 2-6.30pm, Sat, Sun. *Oct-Mar* 9.30am-5pm Mon-Fri; 9.30am-12.45pm, 2-5pm, Sat, Sun.

The charm of centuries gone by has been better preserved in **Bruges** *than anywhere else.*

East Flanders

If you think Belgium as a whole has language problems, just wait until you visit Flanders. Don't even think of speaking French here, and come to that, Flemish might not get you very far – it's just as well most of the locals speak English.

This is one of the most interesting provinces, especially in relation to its neighbour, West Flanders. Just as George Bernard Shaw said of England and America, that they are two countries divided by a common language, so is the whole of Flanders divided along dialect lines that sometimes mean a person living in one village cannot understand a word spoken by someone living five kilometres away. So pronounced is the difference that it has been known for two Flemish speakers to opt for English whenever one couldn't get a grip on the dialect of the other.

Ghent

With a large student population, brown cafés and a generally laid-back feel, it's easy to think you're in Holland when walking around Ghent. This is one of the few major cities in Belgium where bicycling, along cobblestoned streets, is a major means of transportation, which means that it has a more human touch. Somewhere between Antwerp's attitude, Bruges' quaint cutesiness and Brussels' many different facets, Ghent falls comfortably into its own niche.

Its rich history is evident in its buildings: the Saint-Bavon cathedral, a mostly gothic structure that is part of a church dedicated to Saint John the Baptist; the majestic Belfort, the town's belfry, which dates back to the fifteenth century when it was a trading centre for fabric; and the Stadhuis, an edifice that took over 400 years to build, set out to be the largest town hall in Europe but, alas, only made it to about 20 per cent of its intended size. These are just a few monuments to what, along with Antwerp and Bruges, was a major centre of trade in what is now Belgium.

GHENT GENTRY

The 400 years it took to build the town hall is not a reflection on the city's inability to find good help those days: it says more about the volatile history of Ghent. The city sprang up circa 600 AD around two abbeys that later became the most powerful in Flanders. The Treaty of Verdun in 843 AD split Flanders, putting Ghent in the hands of the French – which helped the city prosper due to its access to the French market. But, as ever in Belgium, the city changed hands over and over throughout history – three times again by the French after Spain, Holland and England had their turns. The French influence, though, is still very much in evidence in Ghent, where – because much of the aristocracy and upper classes descend from the time when only the peasants spoke Flemish – the bourgeoisie and those above speak French. Despite the left-leaning sympathies of the city (which has been a socialist stronghold for more than a century), speaking French, the mark of a privileged life, is not frowned upon.

As with Antwerp, Ghent hit a historical dry spell. In the fourteenth century, Ghent was second only to Paris in size (according to population) when the 100 Years War broke out. Caught between England, a source of raw materials, and France, a

Ghent – *it's easy to think you're in Holland.*

market, Ghent, courtesy of the Count of Flanders, sided with France. Thus began its decline. Outside forces squabbled with Ghent being the venue for religious and nationalist disputes, and the blocking of the Scheldt river by Philip II (in an attempt to purge Flanders of protestants) killed off much of the city's vitality.

With the exception of German occupation during the world wars, the city's being tossed between foreign powers ended with the establishment of the Belgian state. The Industrial Revolution saw Ghent become a centre for Flemish socialism, and Flemish became the dominant cultural influence in education in the 1930s. Today, Ghent boasts the second largest port in Belgium and, as the capital of East Flanders, balances its war-torn history with a progressive present.

HEAVEN-SENT GHENT

Amongst the things to see in Ghent, do not miss Sint-Michielsbrug, from which bridge the towers of Sint-Baafskathedraal, the Belfort and Sint Niklaaskerk are all visible. The never-completed but two-centuries-in-the-building Sint-Michielskerk can also be viewed from the bridge. To get to the heart of old Ghent, the Graslei and the Korenlei provide the most scenic routes. Houses going back to 1100 AD and with mainly Flemish Renaissance-style façades and architecture are among the sites you can see from these two quays. Het Pand, an old Dominican monastery, is now a cultural centre of the University of Ghent – which means it is free to visit.

The Museum van Hedendaagse Kunst, the museum of contemporary arts, and the Museum voor Schone Kunsten, the museum of fine arts, are housed in the same building, and both boast works that make a visit worthwhile. The fine arts museum is more interesting for the lesser works of greater artists of the Flemish school. The contemporary arts museum shines, with works by Bacon, Warhol, Beuys and others.

Set in a sumptuous eighteenth-century townhouse built by the wealthy cloth merchant family De Coninck, the Museum voor Sierkunst is as interesting for its interior as it is for its contents: antique and period furniture and home accessories of the highest quality. Art deco and art nouveau as well post-rococo, modernist and Empire feature, and Horta, Lalique and Mies van der Rohe all figure in the collection, so be sure to reserve enough space on your schedule if this is up your alley.

The Kasteel of Ooidonk is a popular site in the city, a chateau with sixteenth-century Spanish-Flemish design (lots of spires, stepped gables and turrets) and exquisite tapestries, furniture and porcelain inside.

The major shopping areas are the Mageleinstraat and Volderstraat. Also check out the Lange Munt and Koestaraat.

Further information

Getting there *by train* from Gare du Nord, Gare Centrale or Gare du Midi; *by car* A10.
Eating and drinking The seafood served at *Guido Meerschaut* (09 223 53 49) is definitely worth the moderate to high prices, especially if you want to impress. But for more polished surroundings, try *Het Cooremeterhuys* (09 223 49 71) – the well-preserved old guildhouse provides the perfect setting for the fine French cuisine it serves. More moderate in price but a tad twee (if you're not a cat-lover) is *'t Kattenhuis* (09 224 31 88). Beware, though, if you're allergic to felines: a real live spicimen roams around the joint. And for those on a tight budget, *Diavolo* (09 223 10 05) is a good bet for pastas, salads and soups. The building it's housed in is hard to miss: it's the only electric-blue townhouse on the block. Also, *waterzooi*, a delicious chicken and vegetable stew-like dish, is a speciality of Ghent – so if you're going to have it anywhere in Belgium, have it here. More than 100 Belgian beers are served at *Het Waterhuis aan de Bierkant*, which has a terrace looking out to the Groenten Markt and is popular during the warmer months. Moodier is *Roccocco*, in the Paterhol area, where artists gather around candlelit tables and a piano sits in the corner, sometimes too tempting for the would-be chanteur who's had a few too many. And many people end up at the *Lazy River Jazz Club* to finish off the night with drinks and live music.
Events Like most university towns, Ghent begins to bustle as Spring school term closes. To mark the beginning of the summer season, city illuminations of monuments around town begin in May and continue nightly until October, after which they occur only on Friday and Saturday. *The Gentse Feesten* is where you see the alternative side of Flanders – hippies and punks, rastas and trendies all flock (along with your average Belgian) to the ten-day event featuring street theatre, concerts, folk processions and terraces all over town. Unlike most festivals of this kind, the Gentse Feesten remains on a human scale: it's a perfect time to wander the streets and discover the city, because there's something happening behind every corner but there's space enough not to feel crowded. The beginning of autumn marks the annual *Festival van Vlaanderen*, a major classical music event where concerts are held in many of Ghent's historical buildings. If you want to get about by bike you can rent one from *Ganesh & Co, 30 Zwartzustersstraat, 9000 Ghent.*
If you want to stay the *De Draecke Youth Hostel* (09 233 70 50) is the best bet for cheap digs, and it's been completely renovated. The *Hotel Adoma* (09 222 65 50) is also a bargain – and has the advantage of being two minutes by foot from the railway station.

Tourist information

Provincial office: 3 Woodrowwilsonplein 9000 Ghent (267 70 20). **Open** 8.30am-noon, 1.15-4.45pm, Mon-Fri.
City office: Stadhuis, Botermarkt, 9000 Ghent (224 15 55). **Open** 9.30am-6.30pm daily.

Sint Niklaas

Not exactly the most happening of towns, Sint Niklaas's major attraction is its Thursday market, which covers all 3.2 hectares of its Grote Markt every week.

The Saint-Bavon Cathedral in **Ghent** *– a mostly Gothic structure, part of a church dedicated to St John the Baptist.*

The city's mascot is a beet – which would sound silly until you remember that Brussels' symbol is a little boy pissing.

Worth seeing are the Mercator Museum, dedicated to the works of the sixteenth-century cartographer, and the Salon des Beaux-Arts, which features porcelain and furniture from the nineteenth and early twentieth centuries in a renovated townhouse setting.

Further information

Getting there *by train* from Gare Centrale; *by car* A12 to N16, N16 to N403.

Tourist information

45 Grote Markt, 9100 Sint Niklaas (03 777 26 81). **Open** 9.30am-noon, 2-4pm, Mon-Fri.

Oudenaarde

The capital of the Flemish Ardennes, this pastoral brewing and textile centre was once at the border between the French and German empires, which could hardly have been the most ideal of locations. The town's former wealth is evident in Oudenaarde's town hall, a gorgeous Gothic building finished in 1537. Its features include a golden statue of Hanske de Krijger, the town's protector. Other notable buildings in Oudenaarde include the Notre dame de Pamèle church and the Notre Dame hospital.

The ideal time to visit is the last wekend of June, for the beer festival. Taste some of the local specialities in the interests of historical research.

Further information

Getting there *by train* from Gare du Nord, Gare Centrale or Gare du Midi to Ghent, switch to Oudenaarde; *by car* A40 to Ghent, switch to N60.

Geraardsbergen

A strategically important military base in the Middle Ages, Geraardsbergen is now known to professional cyclists all over the world, sometimes by its French name Grammont. The Wall of Geraardsbergen (or Grammont) is one of the important points to pass on the yearly Tour of Flanders bicycle race.

The city also has Krakelingenstoet and Tonnekebrand, a historic festival that falls on the last Sunday of February featuring a cortège, followed by brioches being thrown into the crowd – a poor substitute for the gold coins originally employed way back when. The city also has its own version of the Manneken Pis.

Further information

Getting there *by car* N8 to Ninove, switch to N255 until Denderwindeke, go west on side road.

Tourist information

Stadhuis, 9500 Geraadsbergen (054 41 41 21). **Open** 10am-1pm, 2-4pm, Mon-Fri.

Aalst

Between Ghent and Brussels, Aalst was once the capital of Imperial Flanders, a status still evident in some of the well-preserved buildings of that era. But if you can choose a period to visit, try to do so during carnival: the Sunday before Lent kicks off the festivities, which includes onion tossing from the Belfry. This is not as bizarre as it sounds: many Belgian towns have some foodstuff that they traditionally hurl on such occasions, although the people of Aalst must be especially sadistic as surely a softer vegetable could have been chosen. Comic crossdressers also get into the act – some men are always looking for an excuse to get dolled up as women.

Further information

Getting there *by train* from Gare Centrale; *by car* N9.

Tourist information

3 Grote Markt (053 73 22 62) 9300 Aalst. **Open** *Oct-Apr* 8.45am-noon, 1.30-6pm, Mon, Tue, Thur, Fri; 8.45-11.45am,1.30-7pm, Wed. *Jun-Sept* 8.45am-noon, 1.30-6pm, Mon, Tue, Thur, Fri; 8.45-11.45am,1.30-7pm, Wed; 10-11.30am, 2-5pm, Sat, Sat.

Ghent – *falls comfortably into its own niche.*

Survival

Survival

Musts for life – from bodily health and financial fitness to phoning home and spiritual hotlines.

Invasion of the purse-snatchers – watch out.

Useful numbers

(Fr = French; Fl = Flemish)
Operator assistance/reverse charge calls 1324 *Fr*, 1224 *Fl.*
Police 101; **Fire** 100; **Ambulance** 100.
Directory enquiries (domestic) 1307 *Fr*, 1207 *Fl*; **(international)** 1304 *Fr*; 1204 *Fl (English also spoken).*
Telegrams 1325 *Fr*, 1225 *Fl.*
Time 1300 *Fr*, 1200 *Fl.*
Wake-up service 1348 *Fr*, 1248 *Fl* (or set the time yourself – eg to be woken at 6.15am, dial 1348 06 15 0).

Bureaucracy, living & working

All British visitors need a valid passport to enter Belgium. The same goes for Swiss citizens and EU nationals, who can also use a valid national ID card. Visitors from the USA, Australia, New Zealand and Japan need only a valid passport to stay for three months as a tourist (no visa is required).

If you wish to stay longer you must participate in a maddening paper chase. For EU nationals, the process is fairly simple. You don't need to apply for a work permit, but you must register with the police. This involves a trip to the town hall of the *commune* in which you are living. Provide three photos, pay a nominal fee, have your fingerprints taken (not all *communes* insist on this), and you'll receive a three-month residence card. This is renewable for another three months. You're then eligible to receive an ID card valid for five years, should you wish to stay. Don't lose this card – it's very valuable in Belgium!

Before starting work EU nationals should apply for forms Council Regulations 1408/71 and 574/72, which concern social security payments for those moving within the EU. For non-EU citizens the situation is more tricky. Due to high unemployment in Belgium, it's becoming more difficult to get work permits (*permis de travail/werkvergunning*). The applicant must prove that no Belgian or other EU national can do the job. Your employer must apply for the permit on your behalf. You'll also need three photos, a certificate of good health and a copy of your work contract. Processing can take up to 12 weeks.

The type of permit you receive depends on how long you are planning to stay in Belgium. Most people receive B permits which are valid for one year and then must be renewed; they are not transferable from one employer to another. After three or four years with a B permit, one can apply for an A permit which is valid indefinitely with any employer in any field.

Ministère de l'Emploi et du Travail

51 rue Belliard, 1040 (233 41 11/fax 233 44 88). Métro Maelbeek. **Open** 9am-noon, 2-4pm, Mon-Fri.
Contact them for a work permit application form.

Legal points

If you live or work in Belgium, you must carry your Belgian identity card (*carte d'identité/identiteitskaart*) with you at all times. If you don't have one, carry your passport. Belgian police have the right to stop you at any time to see proof of identity. If you can't produce it, they can hold you at a police station until your identity is proven, even if you haven't committed a crime.

Communications

Post

Post offices are generally open 9am-5pm Mon-Fri, but times can vary greatly according to branch. If you need to post something urgently, try the central post office next to Gare du Midi on 48a avenue Fosny, 1060. It's open 24 hours daily.

Letters mailed to the UK and other European countries usually take three days. Air mail to the States takes about a week.

Postal rates

A letter weighing up to 20g costs 16BF to any EU country, and 13BF if left unsealed. Mail to non-EU countries costs 30BF up to 20g. Due to the complexity of the postage system, it's best to buy stamps at a post office rather than from a vending machine. Price is determined by the size of the envelope. A word to the wise: stick to using Belgian envelopes as non-standard envelope sizes – even if different by only a fraction of an inch – can jack up the cost of postage. They *will* measure.

Sending packages

Packages up to 2kg can be mailed from any post office. Anything heavier should be taken to a post office at a railway station or the airport. All packages weighing more than 20kg must be shipped. The exception is if you use EMS Taxipost, an express delivery service offered by the Belgian postal system. Its limit is 27kg. Taxipost guarantees delivery within 24-72 hours. It's cheaper but also a bit slower than other express delivery companies. Call your local branch for prices.

DHL International

(715 50 50). **Open** 24 hours Mon-Sat.

It can express deliver to most parts of the world. In the downtown area, pick-ups can be made until 8.30pm; in other areas, packages must be picked up before 5pm or 6pm. Call a day in advance if you want to send something on Saturday.

Telephones

Using the Yellow and White Pages in Brussels is a cinch, as both include an English index.

Public telephones

Public telephone booths are found at stations, post offices and other usual locations. There are several close to the Grand Place, near place de Brouckère and the Bourse. Booths sporting European flags can be used for direct-dial international calls. Coin-operated public phones accept 5BF and 20BF coins. Local calls cost a minimum of 10BF. Many public phones accept only prepaid electronic telephone cards. You can buy these at post offices, stations, newsstands, and some banks and supermarkets (200BF for 20 units; 1000BF for 105 units).

Many ***public phones*** *now only take cards.*

Making calls

To call overseas, dial 00 then the country code and number (Australia 61; Canada 1; France 33; Germany 49; Holland 31; Ireland 353; New Zealand 64; UK 44; USA 1). To call other parts of Belgium, dial 0 plus the city code and number (Antwerp 3; Bruges 5; Ghent 91; Liège 41). To call Belgium from abroad, dial the international code then 32, and then 2 if you want Brussels.

International calls, especially transatlantic ones, are expensive. Rates are a little lower on Sundays, holidays and between 8pm-8am. However, if you plan to stay in Belgium for an extended period, the best way to save on calls is to sign on with a discount call service such as **Kallback** (call 00 1 206 216 1200 in the US for more information).

For a short-term stay, a calling card with **Sprint** or **AT&T** is recommended. Despite a surcharge for each call, rates are lower than Belgacom's.

Faxes

You can always find a working telephone, buy a telecard or send a fax, telex or telegram at TT (*Telephone-Telegraphe/Telefoon-Telegraaf*) centres. The one on 17 boulevard de l'Impératrice is open daily from 7am-10pm.

Mobile phones & pagers

Belgium is part of the growing European mobile telephone network called GSM. Telephones on this system work in most of Western Europe and even beyond. You can rent GSMs at the airport or from some car hire agencies. The rental fee is usually low but the cost per call is high. The price to buy ranges from 10000BF to 25000BF. The dialling prefix for mobile phones on Belgium's only network, Proximus, is 075.

Most pagers work simply: dial the pager number and after the recording punch in your phone number and end with the # key. Pagers usually cost a few thousand francs with a monthly charge of several hundred. Some work beyond Belgium, extending to Holland and Luxembourg.

Utilities

Belgian electricity operates on 220V AC, which is fine for British appliances that run on 240V; you only need a new plug or an adaptor with two prongs to use Belgian sockets. Americans need a transformer to use any 110V electrical appliances from home (*see chapter* **Essential Information**).

Belgian utilities are very expensive. On top of the usage fee, consumers are required to pay a whopping 20.5 per cent VAT. Be sure to pay bills within ten days otherwise you'll face a penalty, or worse, being cut off. You'll then have to fork out more money to get reconnected. To avoid such hassles it's wise to pay by standing order (*domiciliation des paiements/domiciliering van betalingen*) through your bank.

A number of electricity and gas companies service Brussels. Check your meter or ask your landlord which firm handles your area. See Electricité & Gaz (Sociétés d')/Elektriciteits & Gasmaatschappijen in the *Yellow Pages* for a breakdown of companies by area.

Gas leaks

If you smell gas, call *any* gas company. Two of the biggest ones are:
Sibelgaz *(244 34 54) 24 hours daily.*
Interga *(512 05 06) 24 hours daily.*

Water

All of Brussels is serviced by one water company. Call it if you have questions about your bill, or if there's leakage from a water main.
Compagnie Intercommunale Bruxelloise des Eaux/Brusselse Intercommunale Watermaatschappij *70 rue aux Laines, 1000 (518 81 11/emergencies 739 52 11). Métro Louise.* **Open** 8.30am-4pm Mon-Fri.

Left luggage

The airport and most railway stations in Brussels have adequate facilities for storing baggage. If you're coming from London with Eurostar, you'll arrive at Gare du Midi. There they charge 60BF per bag per day.

Driving in Brussels

While it may be an exaggeration to say they would rather crash than give up their place in a traffic queue, Belgians are truly aggressive drivers. To enter congested traffic, you need to be ruthless.

Beware of Belgium's right-of-way rules and drive on the right-hand side of the road (*see also chapter* **Getting Around**). Officially you need an international driver's licence, but police will usually accept a valid licence from your home country. If your car is towed, go to the nearest police station to get a document releasing it. Police may give you the document free of charge or demand up to 2000BF, depending on the area of town. They will then give the address of the garage holding your car. Present the police letter there and pay another 3000BF-4000BF to get the car back.

The cost of fuel is similar to that in the UK. If you have a Belgian bank account, you can get a Bancontact/Mister Cash card, which allows you to buy petrol 24 hours a day at hundreds of stations across Belgium.

Driving with no traffic (a rare occurrence) and no stops, it takes about 30 minutes to Antwerp, 45 minutes to Ghent, 90 minutes to Liège and Bruges. Calais and Amsterdam are about two-and-a-half hours away and Paris three hours.

Major roads have phones along them. Seat belts are compulsory. Drink-driving penalties are stiff. And immediate fines are common if you are caught speeding and are not Belgian.

Breakdown services

In the event of a breakdown, there are two national organisations to call:
Tourist Club Belgique (TCB) *44 rue de la Loi, 1040 (24-hour emergency service 070 344 777/enquiries 233 22 11 9am-5pm Mon-Fri).*
Royal Automobile Club de Belgique *53 rue d'Arlon, 1040 (24-hour emergency service 078 152 000/enquiries 287 09 11 9am-5pm Mon-Thur; 9am-4pm Fri).*

Repairs & services

Stranded? The agents listed below can get you back on the road again. For more options, check the *Yellow Pages* under Carrosseries (Reparations)-Autos/Carrossieriehersteilingen-Auto's.
Autocenter East NV 'Toyota' *438 chaussée de Louvain, 1930 (725 12 00). Métro Meiser.* **Open** 8am-7pm Mon-Fri; 9am-6pm Sat. **Credit** AmEx, DC, MC, V.
BMW Brussels *22-38 rue du Magistrat, 1050 (641 57 11). Métro Louise.* **Open** 7.30-5.30pm Mon-Thur; 7.30am-4.30pm Fri. **Credit** AmEx, DC, MC, V.
Durieux Nissan *24 rue des Trois Ponts, 1160 (672 15 72). Métro Hankar.* **Open** 8am-noon, 1-6pm Mon-Fri; 9am-noon Sat. **Credit** AmEx, MC, V.
Rover Grand Garage St Michel *35-43 rue de l'Escadron, 1040 (732 46 00/fax 736 51 31). Métro Thieffry.* **Open** 8am-6pm Mon-Fri; *showroom* 10am-5pm Mon-Fri. **Credit** AmEx, DC, V.

Embassies & consulates

It's advisable to telephone first to check opening hours. Some situations may require an appointment. In emergencies it's worth ringing after hours; staff may be on hand to deal with crises. For embassies or consulates not listed below, check the *Yellow Pages*.

American Embassy *27 boulevard du Regent, 1000 (508 21 11). Métro Arts-Loi.* **Open** 9am-noon Mon-Fri.

Australian Embassy *6 rue Guimard, 1040 (231 05 00). Métro Arts-Loi.* **Open** 9am-noon, 2-5pm, Mon-Fri (visas morning only).

British Embassy *85 rue Arlon, 1040 (287 62 11). Métro Maelbeek.* **Open** 9.30am-noon, 2.30-4.30pm, Mon-Fri (passports morning only).

Canadian Embassy *2 avenue de Tervuren, 1040 (741 06 11). Métro Merode.* **Open** 9am-noon, 2-4.30pm, Mon-Fri.

Irish Embassy *89 rue Froissart, 1040 (230 53 37). Métro Schuman.* **Open** 10am-1.30pm Mon-Fri.

New Zealand Embassy *47-48 boulevard de Regent, 1000 (512 10 40). Métro Arts-Loi or Madou.* **Open** 9am-1pm, 2-3.30pm, Mon-Fri. For other enquiries, call to make an appointment.

Health

Belgium has an excellent healthcare system. Most doctors are fluent in English.

Doctors

Most doctors with private practices don't have receptionists, preferring to handle the administration of payments and appointments themselves. You can walk in without an appointment during weekday office hours. If you are too sick to go in, some doctors will make house calls. After hours, you can often reach your physician (or another on call) through an answering service. Even if you're insured, expect to pay for your visit on the spot in cash or with a cheque. The same goes for pharmacies. Hang on to all receipts for reimbursement from your insurance company.

Hospitals

Outpatient clinics at private or university hospitals have an excellent reputation worldwide for their state-of-the-art technology, but often suffer from overcrowded waiting rooms and bureaucracy. Despite the drawbacks, they have a convenient concentration of specialists in one place, as well as laboratory and X-ray facilities on hand.

The following hospitals offer consultations and can provide 24-hour emergency assistance. Call first for consultation hours.

Hôpital Universitaire St Luc *10 avenue d'Hippocrate, 1200 (764 11 11/fax 764 3703). Métro Alma.*

Hôpital Erasme *808 route de Lennik, 1070 (555 31 11/fax 555 44 05). Métro Veeweyde.*

Hôpital St Pierre *322 rue Haute, 1000 (535 31 11/fax 535 40 06). Métro Porte de Hal.*

Hôpital Brugmann *2 place van Gehuchten, 1020 (477 21 11/fax 479 97 02). Métro Houba-Brugmann.*

Problem with security? Go straight to ZZ top.

Emergencies with children

Hôpital Universitaire des Enfants Reine Fabiola (paediatric emergency room) *15 avenue Jean Jacques Cocq, 1020 (477 31 00/477 31 01). Métro Heysel.* **Open** *emergencies* 24 hours daily; *consultations* 9-11.30am, 2-4.30pm, Mon-Fri; 9am-noon Sat.

Hôpital St Pierre *322 rue Haute, 1000 (535 43 60). Métro Porte de Hal.*

Ambulances

In an emergency, dial 100 and a medical crew will take the patient by ambulance to the nearest hospital. A doctor's approval is needed to transfer the patient to another hospital. If the situation is not so urgent, call Red Cross Ambulance Service on 105 to go to the hospital of your choice. General practitioners and dentists who are off duty usually have a tape recording of emergency information. Otherwise call 479 18 18 or 648 40 14 for 24-hour emergency medical assistance; and 426 10 26 for emergency dental help (evenings 9pm-7am; weekends 24 hours; holidays 7am-9pm).

Alternative medicine

Homeopathy is still considered alternative medicine in Belgium. Listed below are two practitioners in Brussels. Call the Federation of Medical Homeopathy on 511 05 49 for further information.

Dr Dany Dejonghe *2 De Robianostraat, Tervuren 3080 (767 56 57). Tram 44.* **Open** *appointments* 8-11am, 3-5pm, Mon-Fri; *medical information* 7-8pm Mon-Fri.
Dr Paul Taub *5 avenue de la Closière, 1410 (354 12 00). Métro Albert.* **Open** 9am-5pm Mon-Fri.

Pharmacies

Pharmacies (*pharmacies/apotheeks*) are marked with a green cross. Most are open 9am-6pm/7pm Mon-Fri. Some also open Saturday mornings or afternoons. When closed, each pharmacy displays a list of alternative pharmacies open after hours.

Dentists

Dental care in Belgium is of a high standard. The Community Liaison Office of the American Embassy (513 38 30 ext 2227) can provide a list of English-speaking dental practitioners, as can the Community Help Service Helpline (648 40 14).

Chiropractors

Belgian Chiropractors' Union

(091 221 76 58). **Open** 24 hours daily.
Contact this Ghent-based association for a list of about 20 chiropractors in the Brussels area.

Poison control centres

Centre Antipoisons/Antigifcentrum

(345 45 45). **Open** 24 hours daily.
A group of physicians man this free helpline. They will try to determine if someone has swallowed a poisonous substance and offer advice on what measures to take.

Support groups

Brussels' large foreign community has established an extensive network of support groups. Unless indicated, the groups below are for English speakers. More are listed at the back of the *Bulletin*.

Community Help Service (CHS) Helpline

(648 40 14). **Open** 24 hours daily.
A group of 42 trained English-speaking volunteers take turns manning the phones and can handle problems ranging from the critical to the mundane. They can also refer you to other specialists. There is no charge for callers. To make an appointment for a private face-to-face counselling session, call 647 67 80 (rates for this are determined by one's means).

AIDS

Act Together

(511 33 33/fax 512 09 09).
An HIV/AIDS support group that organises referrals, arranges buddying and runs a helpline on 512 05 05.

Alcoholism/eating disorders

Alcoholics Anonymous (537 82 24) offers daily meetings in English or counselling by phone. **Al-Anon English-speaking Group** (762 76 53/771 52 64) gives phone counselling to friends and relatives of alcoholics. It holds meetings every Tuesday at 8pm at the International Cultural Affairs Center, 8 rue Amédée Lynen, 1040 (Métro Madou). **Overeaters Anonymous** (502 47 71) is a self-help group for sufferers of anorexia or bulimia. Call for information on meetings.

Rape/battered women

Amazone

10 rue du Méridien, 1210 (229 38 00/fax 229 38 01). Métro Botanique or Madou/tram 92, 93, 94/bus 61, 65, 66. **Open** 9am-5pm Mon-Fri.
Various women's groups – including La Coordination des Groupes Contre la Violence Faite aux Femmes – and a restaurant are housed here. Amazone's emphasis is on sexual equality, but it is also a gay-friendly centre (*see also chapter* **Women's Brussels**).

Le Refuge (Collectif pour Femmes Battues)

29 rue Blanche, 1060 (647 00 12). Tram 93, 94. **Open** 9am-7pm Mon-Fri; 9.30am-5pm Sat, Sun.
The Collective for Battered Women can be of help if you speak French. Otherwise try the CHS Helpline.

SOS Viol

29 rue Blanche, 1060 (534 36 36). Tram 93, 94. **Open** 9.30am-5.30pm Mon-Fri.
This is mainly a French-speaking support group for rape victims. A few staff members speak basic English. For after-hours assistance try the CHS Helpline.

Gay & lesbian information

See also chapter **Gay & Lesbian**.

Artemys

galerie Bortier, 8-10 rue St Jean, 1000 (512 03 47). Métro Gare Centrale. **Open** noon-6pm Mon; 10am-6pm Tue-Thur; 10am-7pm Fri, Sat.
This feminist and lesbian bookstore near Grand Place stocks many books in English (*see chapter* **Women's Brussels**).

Shalhomo

127 avenue Besme, 1190 (no phone). Métro Albert.
If you're gay or lesbian and Jewish, this is the place to contact. Write or drop by for details on meetings.

Employment agencies

Job seekers can try recruitment agencies for help in finding employment. Usually there's no cost to the candidate as fees are paid by employers. For details of **Focus Career Services**, a non-profit careers counselling centre, *see chapters* **Business** *and* **Women's Brussels**. Check the *Yellow Pages*, and the *Bulletin* has a weekly listing of situations vacant at the back of the magazine. The Belgian national dailies also have jobs sections, usually in their weekend editions.

Social clubs

For the thousands of wives trailing after their Eurocrat or business-oriented husbands, there are several clubs designed to make the adjustment smoother. Besides those below there are several more listed at the back of the *Bulletin*.

American Women's Club *1 avenue des Erables, 1640 (358 47 53/fax 358 47 44).* **Open** 9.30am-3.30pm Mon-Fri.

This long-established group maintains a busy schedule of activities for members ranging from lectures to luncheons and newcomer courses. It also publishes *Hints for Living in Belgium* (440BF), which provides detailed information on how to deal with Belgian bureaucracy and tips for setting up a household abroad. Annual membership is 3500BF with a first-year registration fee of 500BF.

British & Commonwealth Women's Club of Brussels *509 rue au Bois, 1150 (772 53 13).* **Open** 10am-3pm Mon-Fri.

This club hosts several activities, from French courses to tennis lessons to outings around Belgium. It also runs newcomer classes at offices in Woluwe St Pierre. Membership costs 2000BF a year.

Canadian Women's Club *(354 22 66).*

An international bilingual group with about 120 members. It holds meetings at various members' homes and plans outings in Brussels and the countryside. Ask for Claudia van der Heyden, president of the club, for more details.

Contraception & abortion

Condoms are sold at supermarkets and pharmacies. Birth control pills can be bought at pharmacies with a doctor's prescription. In some instances, abortion is legal in Belgium: with a patient's written permission, a doctor can perform an abortion if the pregnancy hasn't advanced beyond the twelfth week and the mother is in a 'state of distress'; an abortion can be performed after the twelfth week if the pregnancy puts the mother's life at risk or if the foetus has an incurable disease.

Lost property

Report lost belongings to the nearest police inspector's office or police headquarters on rue du Marché au Charbon (517 96 11). Ask for a certificate of loss for insurance purposes. If you lose your passport, contact your local embassy or consulate (*see above*).

Air

If you've lost an item on a flight to Brussels, you need to contact your airline. Sabena and Belgavia are the handling agents that represent most of the major airlines.

Sabena Airlines *(723 60 11).* **Open** 24 hours daily.

Contact the Belgian airline for any items left on their flights. They also represent KLM, Air France, Swiss Air and Austrian Airlines.

Belgavia *(723 07 07).* **Open** 6am-11pm daily.

Belgavia is the handling agent for British Airways, Lufthansa, Alitalia and Iberia among others.

Airport

If you've misplaced something at the airport, try any of the lost and found numbers below. There's usually someone on duty who speaks English.

Belgian Police (Gendarmerie/Rijkswacht) *(715 62 11).* **Open** 24 hours daily.

The lost property office is in the new main terminal on the departure level near border control. Although there's no office number, directions are indicated by overhead signs.

Airport Police (Police Aeroportuaire/Luchthavenpolitie) *(753 70 00).* **Open** 24 hours daily.

They have their own building next to the Sheraton Hotel and opposite the departure hall.

Airport Authorities (Regie des Voies Aerienne/ Regie der Luchtwegen) *(753 68 20).* **Open** 8am-4pm Mon-Fri.

Anything not claimed at either of the police offices ends up here, in office 418 on the departure level, in the old part of the terminal building. Follow signs for F14 – just before the entrance you'll find steps leading to the office.

Rail

For articles left behind on a train, enquire at the nearest railway station or check with the main rail lost property office at Gare du Nord (224 61 12).

Métro, buses & trams

STIB/MIVB *Porte de Namur, 1050 (515 23 94).* **Open** 9.30am-5pm Mon-Sat.

The STIB/MIVB lost property office is inside Porte de Namur Métro station next to the newspaper and book store Press Shop.

Police & security

The number of violent crimes is low compared to London or New York, but one has to be on the lookout for petty theft. Pickpockets and purse-snatchers are part of the city's landscape, especially in cinema auditoria and particularly crowded areas such as Grand Place and around Gare du Midi.

Public toilets

Public toilets in Brussels, as is the case in most major cities, are not very clean. Most city centre restaurants don't mind you using their loos – though you are expected to cough up a few francs for the attendant.

Religious services

Many churches and synagogues hold services in English. There are several mosques in the city, but none with English services. For places away from the city centre, it is advisable to telephone for directions.

Anglican & Episcopal

All Saints' Church *services held at Centre Notre Dame d'Argenteuil, 563 chaussée de Louvain, 1380 (384 35 56). Bus 558.* **Services** *English* 11.15am Sun.

Holy Trinity Church *29 rue Capitaine Crespel, 1050 (511 71 83/fax 511 10 28). Métro Louise.*

The Holy Communion service in English is held at 8.30am and 10.30am on Sundays, and evening praise is at 7pm. The International Christian Fellowship is held by the church's African congregation at 8pm on Fridays.

Protestant

International Protestant Church *services held at International School of Brussels, 19 mont des Chats, 1170 (673 05 81). Bus 366.*
This church offers interdenominational services in English on Sundays at 10.45am (there is also a church school for children at 9.30am).

Presbyterian

St Andrew's Church of Scotland *181 chaussée de Vleurgat, 1050 (649 02 19). Métro Louise/tram 93, 94.* **Services** *English* 11am Sun.

Roman Catholic

Eglise St Nicolas *1 rue au Beurre, 1000 (contact Rev Phillip Sandstrom on 734 90 27 for details). Métro Bourse or De Brouckère.*
Roman Catholic Mass is held at 10am on Sundays (*see also chapter* **Sightseeing: Hidden churches**).
St Anne's Church *10 place de la Ste Alliance, 1180 (354 53 43/fax 351 23 14). Bus 43.*
Mass for the Our Lady of Mercy parish is held in English on Saturdays at 5pm, and Sundays at 10am and 1pm.

Quaker

Quaker House (Quaker Council for European Affairs) *50 square Ambiorix, 1000 (230 49 35/fax 230 63 70). Métro Schuman.* **Open** *office* 9am-5pm Mon-Fri.
Meetings for worship are held on Sundays at 11am and Wednesdays at 1-1.30pm.

Synagogues

Beth Hillel Liberal Synagogue of Brussels *96 avenue de Kersbeek, 1190 (332 25 28/fax 376 72 19). Tram 18, 52/bus 54.*
This liberal Jewish synagogue is led by an English-speaking rabbi, Abraham Dahan. Services are held on Friday evenings at 8pm and Saturdays at 10.30am. It's advisable to call for directions before setting off.

Libraries

American Cultural Center & Library

1c square du Bastion, 1050 (512 21 29). Métro Porte de Namur/bus 71. **Open** 2-6pm Mon-Thur.
Largely a research and reference library, this provides Belgian readers with information about the US. ID is required for entrance. A borrower's card is free.

ULB (Université Libre de Bruxelles)

50 avenue Franklin Roosevelt, 1050 (reception 650 47 00/audiovisual department 650 43 78). Tram 93, 94/bus 71. **Open** 8am-10pm Mon-Fri; 10am-5pm Sat; *English audiovisual section* 1.30-5.30pm Mon-Fri.
Although this library is mainly for students, it's also open to non-students for 1000BF a year. It holds a surprisingly large collection of materials in English in various media. ULB bought the materials from the British Council Resources Centre when it closed down.

VUB (Vrije Universiteit Brussel)

2 Pleinlaan (boulevard de la Plane), 1050 (629 21 11/library 629 25 05). Métro Petillon/tram 23, 90/bus 34, 95, 96,.
See chapter **Students**.

Children's Library

Centre Crousse, 11 rue au Bois, 1150 (672 48 76). **Open** 10am-noon Sat. Phone for directions.
Opening hours are limited, but this library is useful for kids' education. Run by a group of volunteers, it stocks over 7,000 books with a steady stream of new stock.

Foreign media

Newspapers & magazines

The English-language community of Brussels relies heavily on the weekly listings magazine, the *Bulletin*, which comes out every Thursday. Most of the UK papers appear on newsstands on the same day as publication. And a limited selection of American papers – including the *International Herald Tribune*, *USA Today* and the Brussels-based *Wall Street Journal Europe* – are available.

Try the following for your fix of home news:

Librairie de Rome *50b avenue Louise, 1050 (511 7937). Métro Louise.* **Open** 8.30am-9.30pm daily. **Credit** AmEx, DC, MC, V.
For a price you can find just about any foreign publication you need here, including the *Sunday New York Times*.
WH Smith *71-75 boulevard Adolphe Max, 1000 (219 27 08). Métro De Brouckère.* **Open** 9am-6.30pm Mon, Wed-Sat; 10am-6.30pm Tue. **Credit** MC.
The British chain's Brussels store stocks loads of English-language magazines and papers in addition to books.
Europair *14 rue de l'Enseignement, Nivelles 1400 (067 212 616).* **Open** 9am-noon, 2-5pm, daily.
If you'd rather stay in bed on a Sunday morning, Europair can bring the British Sunday papers to you.

TV & radio

Because of Belgium's position – nestled between Holland, Germany and France – one can receive TV programmes from those countries on cable or satellite. In addition, **BBC1**, **BBC2**, **CNN** and **MTV** are usually available. Some Dutch-speaking channels feature US shows in English with subtitles. You can tune into a few English-language radio stations, but reception isn't always great. The BBC's **World Service** is on 648khz, **Radio 4** is on 198khz and **Radio 5 Live** is on 693khz or 909khz. **American Forces Network** broadcasts 24 hours a day on 101.7 FM, but can only be picked up in some areas. (*See also chapter* **Media**.)

Tipping & VAT

Service and VAT are automatically included in hotel and restaurant prices. At lower-price restaurants you should round the bill up a few francs. At mid-priced restaurants customers usually kick in up to 5 per cent extra. At first-class restaurants, it's customary to add an extra 10 per cent as a tip. Tips are also included in metered taxi fares, which are very expensive. Brace yourself for additional charges for baggage, Sundays and night trips.

Vets

Check Vétérinaires/Dierenartzen in the Liberal Professions section of the *Yellow Pages*. Veterinarian surgeries are recognisable by a blue cross. For an English-speaking vet, try the CHS Helpline (648 40 14) for recommendations. In an emergency (weekends and evenings) call 538 1699.

Further Reading

Literature

Baudelaire, Charles *Amoenitates Belgicae*
Not Baudelaire's finest poems, but a scathing and often pertinent look at the Belgians and their culture. They are rarely published by themselves, but can be found in editions of Baudelaire's collected works.
Bertin, Eddy C
His collections are not available in English, but short stories by this Belgian writer do occasionally turn up in out-of-print horror anthologies.
Brontë, Charlotte *The Professor*
Brontë's first novel was set in Brussels, and she struggled to find a publisher for it even after the success of later works. Much of the material was re-used in *Villette*.
Brontë, Charlotte *Villette*
Brussels was the model for the town of Villette in Brontë's final novel based on her experience of teaching there.
Claus, Hugo *The Sorrow of Belgium*
Milestone novel set during the Nazi occupation by a foremost Dutch-language novelist.
Faulks, Sebastian *Birdsong*
Evocative novel set in World War I and although it is set in northern France rather than Belgium, conditions in the trenches of Flanders would have been comparable.
Freeling, Nicolas *Cold Iron*
Although Nicolas Freeling's most famous creation may be his Amsterdam-based detective Van Der Valk, many of his crime novels are also set in France and Belgium.
Gardner, Brian (ed) *Up the Line to Death*
A good collection of World War I poems, many of them written by troops fighting around Ypres and Mons.
Hergé *The Tintin books*
Belgium's most famous author needs no introduction, although a recent biography highlighting his willing collaboration with the Nazis has dented his reputation.
Hollinghurst, Alan *The Folding Star*
Fictional art history and sexual obsession in a dreary city in northern Belgium.
Martin, Stephen (ed) *Poetry of the First World War*
Another good poetry anthology, again with poems about the Flanders battlefields.
Royle, Nicholas *Saxophone Dreams*
Magical-realist adventures in the landscapes of Belgian surrealist Paul Delvaux, including a role for Delvaux himself. There are scenes set in Brussels and coastal town De Panne.
Simenon, Georges *Maigret's Revolver*
Or just about any other title by this celebrated master of the crime/detective fiction genre.
Thackeray, William Makepeace *Vanity Fair*
The middle section of the book describes the social scene in Brussels on the eve of Waterloo.
Yourcenar, Marguerite *Zeno of Bruges*
The wanderings of an alchemist in late medieval Europe.
Yourcenar, Marguerite *Anna, Soror*
The tragic love of a sister for her brother.
Yourcenar, Marguerite *Alexis*
The confession of a pianist, to his wife, as he declares his homosexuality.
Yourcenar, Marguerite *A Coin in Nine Hands*
The story of a Roman coin which passes from one hand to another and to another and so on. Marguerite Yourcenar – a Belgian-born French novelist and poet, born in Brussels in 1903 – was the first writer to give Mussolini a bloody nose, in the above title. Several of her books are religiously kept in print in the UK by the Harvill Press.

History & politics

Since Belgium did not exist until 1830, there are few books dealing specifically with its history. Instead, the keen reader will have to search for information in books about Spain, Austria, the Netherlands, Napoleon, World War I and so on. However, a few books are particularly relevant.
Parker, Geoffrey *The Dutch Revolt*
Excellent history of one of Belgium's most interesting periods, when the Spanish empire was crumbling in the sixteenth century.
Kossman, EH *The Low Countries*
Dull but informative history of Belgium from 1780-1940.
Leonard, Dick *The Economist Guide to the EU*
As it sounds.

Art & architecture

Rombout, Marc *Paul Delvaux*
Excellent selection of colour plates plus biographical text which is good in all respects except for the fact it gives Delvaux's date of birth as 1887 instead of 1897, which would have had him reach the age of 107 before his death in 1994 (*see also JG Ballard on Delvaux in chapter* **Sightseeing: Eyes wide shut**).
Schneede, Uwe M *Surrealism*
This 1973 surrealism primer contains colour plates and text covering the major figures of the movement (*see also George Melly on Magritte in chapter* **History: Altered images**).
Shinomura, Junichi *Art Nouveau Architecture, Residential Masterpieces 1892-1911*
The section of photographs of the Maison Horta would be a fine addition to anyone's coffee table.
White, Christopher *Pieter Paul Rubens: Man and Artist*
A lavishly illustrated look at the Antwerp-born artist's work.

Cookery

Gordon, Enid & Shirley, Midge *Belgian Cookbook*
Mussels, chips, waffles, waterzooi and more.
Hellon, John *Brussels Fare*
A journalist based in Belgium selects recipes from Belgian restaurants.
Hezelton, Nika *Belgian Cookbook*
Nika Hezelton presents her own cook's tour of the country.
Van Waerebeek, Ruth *Everybody Eats Well in Belgium*
Beautifully designed Belgian cookbook with a great title.
Pierre Wynants *Creative Belgian Cuisine*
Anyone who has eaten at Wynants' Comme Chez Soi (*see chapter* **Restaurants**) will need no further encouragement.

Miscellaneous

Bryson, Bill *Neither Here Nor There*
Belgium and Brussels do not figure hugely in travel literature, but they are the subject of two amusing, if predictable, chapters in Bryson's travels around Europe.
Glover, Michael *A New Guide to the Battlefields of Northern France and the Low Countries*
Covers Waterloo as well as the World War I battlefields.
Webb, Tim *Good Beer Guide to Belgium and Holland*
Just one of several books for beer hunters published by CAMRA Books.

Index

Page numbers in **bold** indicate section giving key information on topic; *italics* indicate illustrations.

a

Aalst 256
AB 184
Abbaye de la Cambre 40
Abbaye de Maredsous 240
abbeys *see* churches and abbeys
abortion 217, 264
Académie Royale des Beaux Arts de Bruxelles 213
accommodation **15–28**
  bed and breakfast 28, 223
  hotels 15–28, 232, 233, 237, 240, 241, 243, 244, 252, 254
  residence hotels 17
  student 216
  youth hostels 28, 254
accountants 200
aerobics 190
African Museum *see* Museum voor Midden-Afrika
AIDS/HIV 212, 263
air travel 9
  lost property 9, 264
airport 9
  lost property 9, 264
  transport to and from 9
Albert, Archduke of Austria 65
Albert I 76
alcoholism 263
Alfred Library 88
Alliance Française 214–215
Amazone 217, *217*, **218**, 263
Ambiorix, square 56, 97, 206
Amblève Valley 237
ambulances 262
American Cultural Center & Library 265
American Documentation Center 215
American Historical Center and Memorial, Batogne 238
amusement parks 206–207
Anderlecht 84, **94–95**, 192
  football club 95, 189–190
Animation Festival 32
Annevoie 240
Anspach Centre 87
antiques:
auctions 142
  shops 148
Antoine Dansaert, rue 117
Antwerp 56, 60, 61, 63, 64, 67, 68, 69, 70, *228*, **228–232**, *229*, *243*
  art galleries 164–165
  ballet 196
  Centraal Station 230
  clubs 171, 172
  DeSingel 181, 195
  Ethnographic Museum 231
  Jewish quarter 230
  Koninklijk Museum voor Schone Kunsten 164, 230
  markets 146
  Middelheim Open-air Sculpture Museum 164–165
  Miniature City 231
  MUHKA (Museum voor Hedendaagse Kunst) 230–231
  Onze Lieve Vrouwe Cathedral *231*
  Plantin-Moretus 231
  Provincaal Museum voor Fotografie 165
  Red Light District 231
  religious conflict 230
  rock venue 188
  Rubens' House *66*, 231
  shops 132, **144–145**, 230
  Sjacherbeurs 146
  Vlaamse Opera 182, 198
  in WWI 76
  Zoo 207, 230
Antwerp province 228–232
Aqualibi 44, 206, **227**
Arc de Triomphe 33, *33*, 48, 55, 98
Archéosites d'Aubechie 243
architecture **52–56**
  museums of 156–158
archives, women's 218
Ars Musica festival 180
art 61
  in Métro stations 165
  museums 156–158, 164–165
art galleries **162–165**
  commercial 164
  outside Brussels 164–165
  photography 163–164
Artois 67
L'Atelier 182
Atelier 340 162–163, *163*
Atelier St Anne 196
Ath 243
athletics 189
  Brussels 20-kilometre Run 30, 189, 192
Atomium 35–37, *40*, 50, 98, 207
Attre, Château d' 143
auctions 142
Audi Jazz Festival 32, 187
Auditorium 44 186
Autoworld 160
L'Autre Musée 163

b

babysitters 208
badminton 190
bakeries 142
Balat, Alphonse 55
banks 4, 200
  opening times 7
Basilique Nationale du Sacré Coeur 40
basketball 190–191
Bastogne 128
Battle of Golden Spurs 5, 60
Battle of Waterloo 30, 71
Baudouin, King 78, *79*, 217
bed and breakfast 28, 223
beer **120–121**, 160
  museum 160
béguinages 94, 224, 232, 233
Belgian Tourist Information Office 4
Beloeil, Château de 243
Benelux Customs Union 78
Berlaymont 39, *42*, **42**, 82, 96
Beursschouwburg 184–185
Bibliothèque Royale Albert I 215
bicycles *see* cycling
Binche **247**
  Carnival 32, 247
  Musée International du Carnaval et du Masque 247
Black Death 60
Blankenberghe 249
Blérot, Ernest 55, 56
Bobbejaanland, Lichtaart 232
Bois de la Cambre 48, *48*, 91, 92, 192, 206
Bois-du-Luc 247
Bois des Rêves 226
books:
  business reference 201
  shops 151, 216, 218, 238
Boston University Brussels 213
Botanique 45, 184, *184*
Boterhammen in het Park 187
Bouchers, rue des 102
Bouillon 239
La Bourse 45, 86, **200**
bowling 191
Brabançon Revolution 68
Brabant 59, 60, 63, **224–227**
Brabant Wallon 224, **226–227**
Brachot, Christine et Isy, gallery *162*, 164
Bredene 249
Brederode, rue 88, *88*
Breydel building 42, 82
Broodhuis 34–35
Brosella Jazz & Folk Festival 30, 187
De Brouckère 87
Bruegel, Pieter, the Elder 90–91, 163
Bruges 60, 61, 64, **250–252**, *251*, *252*
  art galleries 165
  canals 250, 252
  Groeninge Museum 165
  Hans Memling Museum 165
  Onze Lieve Vrouwekerk 250
  rock venue 188
  walls 250
Bruparck **107**, 205
Brussels Annual Fair 31
Brussels Film Festival 32, 177
Brussels Language Studies 215
Brussels 20-kilometre Run 30, 189, 192
Bruyn, Willem de 41
bureaucracy 259
Burgundy, Dukes of 60–62
buses 10–11
  lost property 264
business **200–204**
  equipment hire 203
  information 200–201
Butte de Lion 44, *47*

c

café-théâtre 196
cafés and bars 86, 87, 90, 93, 98, **117–128**
  Anglophone bars and pubs 126
  bars 118–119, 123–126
  in Brabant 225
  café-concerts 186–187
  cafés and tearooms 126–128
  folk venues 186–187
  gay and lesbian 86, **209–211**
  jazz venues 188

in Liège 235
opening times 118
in Ostende 248–249
rock venues 185, 186
student 216
Calvinism 63, 64, 65
Cambron-Casteau, Parc Paradiso 243, *245*
carnival 32, 247
Musée International du Carnaval et du Masque 247
cars:
airport parking 9
breakdown services 261
driving regulations 261
driving tips 13
fines 261
hire 13
repairs and services 261
speed limits 13
towing away 261
Cat festival, Ieper 249–250
Cathédrale des Sts Michel et Gudule 40–2, 52, *53*, 181
Cauchie, Paul 55, 56
Center for American Studies 215
Centre d'Art Contemporain 163
Centre Belge de la Bande Dessinée 49, 52, *155*, **156**
Centre Botanique 96
Centre de Danse Choreart 198, 207
Centre Feminin d'Education Permanente (CFEP) 218
Centre Sportif de Woluwe St Pierre 192, 208
CERAN Lingua 215
Chambers of Commerce 200–201
Chapelle des Brigittines 196–198
Chapelle Royale 181
Charleroi **242–243**
city hall 242
events 243
Musée Archéologique 242
Musée des Beaux Arts 242
Musée de Verre 242
St Fiancre Chapel 242
Charles II of Spain 67
Charles V, Emperor 63, 64
Charlier, Guillaume 157
Château d'Attre 243
Château de Beloeil 243
Château de Bouchout 225
Château Comtal 241
Château d'Ecaussinnes-Lalaing 244
Château Féodal, la Roche-en-Ardenne 238
Château Fort, Bouillon 239
Château de Louvignies 244
Château Malou 39–40
Chaubon, Alban 55
chess 191
Chevetogne 240
childminding 208
children **205–208**
emergencies 208, 262
museum 160
shopping 140, 208
Children's Library 265
chiropracters 263
churches and abbeys **40–43**
Abbaye de la Cambre 40
Abbey of Tongerlo, Diest 225–226
Basilique Nationale du Sacré Coeur 40
Basilique St-Pierre-St-Paul-St-Hubert, St Hubert 238
Cathédrale des Sts Michel et Gudule 40–42, 52, *53*, 181
Chapelle Royale 181
Collégiale Sainte-Gertrude, Nivelles 227
Collégiale des Sts Pierre et Guidon 42, 52, 94
Eglise de la Madeleine 41
Eglise Notre Dame de la Chapelle 41, 52
Eglise Notre Dame du Finistère 41
Eglise Notre-Dame de Laeken 42–43
Eglise Notre Dame aux Riches Claires 41, 54
Eglise St Boniface 93
Eglise St Jacques-sur-Coudenberg 43, 88
Eglise des St Jean et Ste Etienne aux Minimes 182
Eglise St Jean-Baptiste 43, 54, 87
Eglise St Josse 96
Eglise St Nicolas 41, *41*
Eglise St Servais 96
Eglise Ste Cathérine 43, *84*, 87
Eglise Ste Marie 96
Eglise de la Trinité 94
Eglise Waha, Marche-en-Famenne 239
Engelenconvent, Diest 226
Notre Dame du Bon Secours 41
Notre Dame du Sablon *37*, 39, 52, 88–90
Onze Lieve Vrouwe Cathedral, Antwerp *231*
Onze Lieve Vrouwekerk, Bruges 250
St Bavon Cathedral, Ghent 164, 253, *255*
St Fiancre Chapel, Charleroi 242
St Michael's, Leuven 224
St Peter's, Leuven 224
Saint-Sulpice Church 226
Sint-Michielskerk, Ghent 254
cinemas *see* film
Cirque Royal 184, 185, 198
climate 7
clinics for women 220
Clock 43
clothes shops 134–137
secondhand 137–138
shoes 138
underwear 138
clubs 91, **171–176**
doormen 171
dress 171
gay and lesbian 211
in Ostende 248–249
party series 176
private gay and lesbian 212
rock venues 185–186
social 263–264
South American 175
Cluysenaer, Jean-Pierre 55
coaches 10, 222–223
coal-mining 242
Colignon, place 96
Collégiale Sainte-Gertrude, Nivelles 227
Collégiale des Sts Pierre et Guidon 42, 52, 94
Colonne du Congrès 44, *45*, 96
comics (*bandes dessinées*) 49
Centre Belge de la Bande Dessinée 49
100 Years of Comic Strips 32
murals 49
shops 151
communications 260
Concours Musical International Reine Elisabeth de Belgique 30, 180
Confédérés, rue des 97
conference centres 201–203
hotel facilities 15–20
Congo 73
Congress of Vienna 69
Conrad Hotel 56
Conservatoire Royal de Musique 181, *183*
consulates 262
contraception 220, 264
Coo-Stavelot 237
Cortège Historique des Chasseurs et des Veneurs 238
Coudenburg Palace 68
Couleur Café 187
Council of Blood (of Troubles) 64
Council of Ministers 42, 56, 96
Counter-Reformation 65–67
couriers 203
crèches 208
credit cards 4
La Crête des Cerfs 239
cricket 191
crime 7, 264
currency 3–4
exchange 4
Customs regulations 3
cycling 13, 191
bike hire 13, 191
events 189

d

Damasquine 164
dance **196–198**
ballet 196
classes 198
festivals 198
information 198
outside Brussels 198
venues 196–198
day trips 223
delicatessens 142
Delvaux, Paul 34–35, 249
Vénus Endormie 35
demonstrations 80
dentists 263
department stores 134
DeSingel, Antwerp 181, 195
Diest 225–226
Abbey of Tongerlo 225–226
Engelenconvent 226
Saint-Sulpice Church 226
Dinant 240–241
disabled, travel facilities 11
discos 171–176
gay and lesbian 211
doctors 262
Domaine Provincial Valéry Cousin 240
Dour, rock venue 188
drink *see* food and drink
driving *see* cars
dry cleaners 152
Durbury 239
Dutch Revolt 64

e

eating disorders 263
Ecaussinnes-Lalaing, Château d' 244
Eco-Musée du Bois-du-Luc 247
Ecole Nationale Supérieure des Art Visuels de la Cambre 213
economy 67, 74–75, 77, 80
Edict of Toleration 68
education:
see also universities
exchange schemes 215–216
funding 213
international schools 208
language schools 214–215
Eglise de la Madeleine 41
Eglise Notre Dame de la Chapelle 41, 52
Eglise Notre Dame du Finistère 41
Eglise Notre-Dame de Laeken 42–43
Eglise Notre Dame aux Riches Claires 41, 54
Eglise St Boniface 93
Eglise St Jacques-sur-Coudenberg 43, 88
Eglise des St Jean et Ste Etienne

aux Minimes 182
Eglise St Jean-Baptiste 43, 54, 87
Eglise St Josse 96
Eglise St Nicolas 41, *41*
Eglise St Servais 96
Eglise Ste Cathérine 43, *84*, 87
Eglise Ste Marie 96
Eglise de la Trinité 94
Eglise Waha, Marche-en-Famenne 239
electricity 7, 261
electronic services 203
e-mail 203
embassies 262
emergencies, health 208
Emerson College 213
employment agencies 204, 263
Ensor, James 163
Erasmus, Desiderius 45
Maison d' 45, 94–95
Espace Moselle 203
Espagne, place d' *37*
estate agents 204
Ethnographic Museum, Antwerp 231
Euro Info Centre – Commerce Extérieur 201
Euro Space Center 238–239
Europalia 32, 155
European Christmas Market 32
European Commission buildings 42
European Parliament 42, 56, 96
European quarter 96–98
European Union (EU) **82**, 102
Ex-Voto 185

f

famine 60
farm 206
fashion shops 134–137
accessories 138–140
in Antwerp 144
for children 140
faxes 260
Fayd'herbe, Luc 43, 54
Ferme du Caillou 71
ferry crossings 10
Festival d'Eté de Bruxelles 31
Festival du Dessin Animé 32
Festival van Vlaanderen 254
festivals and events **29–32**, 177, 179, 180, 187, 198, 226, 232, 249–50, 252, 254
film **177–179**
Brussels Film Festival 32, 177, 179
children's 206
cinema specials 179
cinemas 50, 92, **177–179**
drive-in 177
Festival du Dessin Animé 32, 179
fitness centres 191
Flanders 59, 60, 63
Flanders, East **253–256**
Flanders, West **248–252**
Floral Carpet 32
flower shops 141
Focus Career Services 218–220
Foire du Midi 31, 205
Foire Internationale du Livre 30
Fondation 9 215
food and drink 102, 115, 234
beer **120–121**, 160
museums 160, 240
chips 112
drink shops 147
glossary 116
gueuze 121
health food shops 142, 147
shops 142, 146
wine 118
Fool Moon 185
football 189–190, 191
Forest National 184, **185**, 196
Forêt de Soignes 50, 98
Franks 230

g

Galeries St Hubert 55, 76, 86, **132–134**, *133*
gardens 48–50
Gare Centrale 56
Gare du Midi 9, 80
Gare du Nord 80, 96
gas leaks 261
gay and lesbian **209–212**
associations 212
cafés and bars 86, **209–211**
clubs 211
information 263
private clubs 212
restaurants 211
rights 209, 230
saunas 211–212
Geel 232
Gentse Feesten 254
Geraardsbergen (Grammont) 256
Ghent 56, 60, 61, 64, 69, *253*, **253–254**, *256*
Belfort 253
Kasteel of Ooidonk 254
Museum van Hedendaagse Kunst 254
Museum voor Schone Kunsten 254
Museum voor Sierkunst 254
(Het) Pand 254
rock venue 188
St Bavon Cathedral 164, 253, *255*
Sint-Michielsbrug 254
Sint-Michielskerk 254
Stadthuis 253
University 76, 77
Girault, Charles 33, 50, 55
glass and crystal:
museums 235, 242
shops 148
go-karting 239, 241
golf 191
government offices 204
Grand Hornu 245
Grand Sablon, place du 39, 90
Grand'Place/Grote Markt 33–34, *51*, 52, 67, 84, 117
guildhouses 34–5, 54, 61
market 143
Grimbergen 225
Groenendaal Arboretum 50
Groeninge Museum, Bruges 165
Grotte de Han 241
Grottes de Remouchamps 237
Grottes de Rochefort 241
guildhouses 34–35, 54, 61
guilds **61**
Guimard, Barnabé 45, 54, 88
gymnasia 191

h

Hainaut 59, 60, **242–247**
hairdressers, gay 212
Halle 225
Halles de Schaerbeek 45, *95*, 96
Han-sur-Lesse 241
Hankar, Paul 39, 55, 56, 88
Hans Memling Museum, Bruges 165
Hanswijk procession 232
Hapsburg empire 62
Hasselt 233
health **262–263**
alternative medicine 262–263
condom shop 152
emergencies 208, 262
health and beauty shops 144, 152
health food shops 142, 147
insurance 3
women's **220**
working out 191
Heilig-Bloedprocessie 30, 252
helplines:
support groups 263
for women 220
Heritage Days 32
Hervé 76
Heysel Stadium 98, 190, *190*
history **58–78**
Austrian rule 67–68
Burgundian rule 60–62
Catholic-liberal strife 72–76
Counter-Reformation 65 67
early 59–60, 228–30
French occupation 68–69
German occupation 76–67
independence 70–76
joint kingdom with Netherlands 69–70
key events 58
medieval 60
postwar 78, 80
regionalism 81
revolution **70**, 88
Spanish rule 62–67, 230
today 80–82
World War I 76–77
World War II 77–78
HIV *see* AIDS/HIV
hobbies shops 141–142
Hoegaarden 226
holidays, public 5–7, 29
homeopathy 262–263
Horrues 244
horse racing 190
horse riding 191
Horta, Victor 32, 55, 56, 94, 155–156, 158, 244
hospitals 262
hostels 28
Hotel Astoria 182
Hôtel Ciambarlani 94
Hôtel Communal, Schaerbeek 95–96
Hôtel Hannon 94
Hôtel Janssens 94
Hôtel Ravenstein 45
Hôtel Solvay 45, 92
Hôtel de Ville, St Gilles 94
Hôtel de Ville (Town Hall) 37, 52, 61, 67
hotels **15–28**
animals in 15
in Antwerp 232
in Bruges 252
in Charleroi 243
in Ghent 254
in Liège 237
in Limburg 233
in Mons 247
in Namur 240
in Ostende 249
residence 17
in Rochefort 241
in Spa 237
star ratings 15
in Tournai 244
100 Years of Comic Strips 32

i

ICHEC (Institut Catholique des Hautes Etudes Commerciales) 213–214
Iconoclastic Riots 64
identity cards 259
Ieper (Ypres) 60, 67, **249–250**
Ilôt Sacré 84, *86*, **86**
Industrial Revolution 242, 250, 254
industry 61, 69, 74–75, 78
Inquisition 64
insurance 3
International Book Fair 30
Internet:
access 203
library catalogues 215

interpreters 204
Ixelles 52, *91*, **91–92**, 102, 117
Ixelles, chaussée d' 93

j

James Ensorhuis, Ostende 248
Janneken Pis 44, *44*
Janssen, Rodolphe, gallery 164
Jazz Marathon 30, 187
Jesuits 65–67
Jeu de Balle, place du *89*, 91, *118*
Joseph II of Austria 68
Journées du Patrimoine 32, 33

k

kayaking 237, 239
Keersmaeker, Anna Teresa de 196, *196*
Kessel-Lo, Provincial Recreational Centre 224–225
Klinkende Munt 187
Koninklijk Museum voor Schone Kunsten, Antwerp 164, 230
Krakelingenstoet and Tonnekebrand 256
Kunstenfestivaldesarts 198

l

Laeken 50, **98**, 207
Lanaken 234
language 8, 72, 76, 77, 78, 81, 222, 253
  classes in 214–215
  food glossary 116
Lanzenburg, Fred, gallery 164
lawyers 204
League of Nobles 63
left luggage 261
legal requirements 259
Léopold I 70
Leopold II of Austria 68
Léopold II of Belgium 50, 55, **73**, 98, 158
Léopold III of Belgium 77, 78
Leuven (Louvain) 60, **224–225**
  Clothmaker's Hall 224
  Great Beguinage 224
  Grote Markt 224
  Municipal Museum Vander Kelen-Mertens 224
  Papal College 224
  Provincial Recreational Centre 224–225
  St Michael's Church 224
  St Peter's Church 224
  Tafelrond 224
  Town Hall 224, *225*
  University 68, 73, 224
  Van Dale College 224
libraries 215, 265
  children's 265
Lichtaart, Bobbejaanland 232
Liège 59, 60, 68, **234–237**, *235*
  Musée d'Armes 234
  Musée de l'Art Wallon 234
  Musée Curtius 234–235
  Musée du Val Saint-Lambert 235
  Musée de Verre 235
  Palais des Princes-Evêques 234
  rock venue 188
Liège province 234–237
Lier 232
Limburg 233–234
Lion Hill (Butte de Lion) 44, *47*
listings 169
lost property 9, 264
Louise, avenue 55, **91–92**, *92*, 132
Louvain *see* Leuven
Louvain, chaussée de 96
Louvain-la-Neuve **226**
  Théâtre Jean Vilar 195
  University 224, 226
Louvignies, Château de 244
Lower Town 84, **86–87**
luggage, storage 261
Lunatheater 182, 198
Lutherans 63–64
Luxembourg, place de 97
Luxembourg (province) 59, 60, **238–239**

m

Maaseik 234
magazines 168–169, 265
Magritte, René 75, 163
  L'Empire des Lumières (*The Dominion of Light*) *74*, 75
Maison de Bruegel 45
Maison Communale 93
Maison d'Erasmus 45, 94–95
Maison du Peuple 55, 158
Maison du Roi 34–35
Maison de St Cyr 56
Management Centre Europe 203
Manneken Pis 37, 54, 86
maps 4–5, 10
Marché au Charbon, rue du 117
Marché de Noël 32
Marché du Midi 143, *143*
Marché St Géry 47, 86
Marche-en-Famenne 239
Maria Theresa, Empress 68
Marie-Louise, square 97
Mariembourg 241
markets *89*, 91, **143**, 233, 243
Marolles 80, *89*, *90*, **90–91**, 143
martial arts 191
Martyrs, place des 87
maternity benefits 217
Matonge 84, **92–93**, *93*
  shops 132
Mechelen (Mechlin) 60, 228, **232**
  University 73
media 168–170
  foreign 265
medical treatment *see* health
Meiboom 31–32
Memling, Hans 163, 165, 252
Mercator Museum, Sint Niklaas 256
Métro 10–11
  lost property 264
  underground art scene 165
Meunier, Constantin 157
Meuse, River **234**, 237
Middelheim Open-air Sculpture Museum, Antwerp 164–165
Mini-Europe 43, 50, *97*, 98, 207
money 3–4
Mons **245–247**
  Maison Van Gogh 245
Musée du Château Comtal 245
  Musée du Folklore et de la Vie Montoise 245
  Musée François Duesberg 245
Mont des Arts 192
Montgomery 98
Monument aux Martyrs Juifs 44, *47*
Monument aux Martyrs de 1830 44
Monument du Pigeon Soldat *77*
Moulin de la Falize 239
Moulin de Lindekamaele 45
Moulin du Moulinet 244
MUHKA (Museum voor Hedendaagse Kunst), Antwerp 230–231
Musée d'Antoine Wiertz 97, **157**
Musée Archéologique, Charleroi 242
Musée d'Armes, Liège 234
Musée d'Art Ancien 155, *157*, **157**, 182
Musée d'Art Moderne 155, **157**
Musée de l'Art Wallon, Liège 234
Musée de la Bataille des Ardennes 238
Musée des Beaux Arts, Charleroi 242
Musée des Beaux Arts, Tournai 244
Musée des Bières Belges, Annevoie 240
Musée Charlier 157, 182
Musée du Château Comtal, Mons 245
Musée du Cinéma 177
Musée du Cire 205
Musée Communal 67
Musée Communal d'Ixelles 93, 156, *156*, **157**
Musée de Constantin Meunier 157
Musée du Costume et de la Dentelle 160
Musée Coticule, Vielsalm 239
Musée Curtius, Liège 234–235
Musée David et Alice van Buuren 156, **158**
Musée de la Dentelle, Marche-en-Famenne 239
Musée de la Dynastie 88, **160**
Musée des Enfants 160
Musée du Folklore et de la Vie Montoise, Mons 245
Musée François Duesberg, Mons 245
Musée de la Gueuze 95
Musée d'Historie Naturelle, Tournai 244
Musée Horta 94, **158**, *159*
Musée International du Carnaval et du Masque, Binche 247
Musée International des Marionettes 206
Musée du Jouet 205–206
Musée de la Résistance 95
Musée Royal de l'Armée et d'Histoire Militaire 55, **160**, *161*
Musée Royal de Mariemont 247
Musée de Transport Urbain Bruxellois 98, **160**
Musée du Val Saint-Lambert, Liège 235
Musée de Verre, Charleroi 242
Musée de Verre, Liège 235
Musée de la Ville de Bruxelles 37, **160**
Musée Wellington 71
Musées des Beaux Arts 88, 155
Musées Royaux d'Art et d'Histoire 55, 155, **158**
Museum voor Hedendaagse Kunst, Antwerp 230–231
Museum van Hedendaagse Kunst, Ghent 254
Muséum de l'Institut Royal des Sciences Naturelles de Belgique 97, **158**
Museum voor Midden-Afrika (African Museum) 50, 55, 73, *73*, 98, **158**
Museum Paul Delvaux, De Panne 249
Museum voor Schone Kunsten, Ghent 254
Museum voor Sierkunst, Ghent 254
Museum Vander Kelen-Mertens, Leuven 224
museums **155–160**
  opening times 7, 156
  specialist:
  archaeology 242
  art and architecture 156–158, 164–165, 230–231, 234, 244, 248, 249, 254
  beer 160, 240
  carnival 247
  for children 160, 205–206
  cinema 177
  comic strips 49, 52, *155*, **156**
  Congo 50
  costume 160
  genever 233
  glass 235, 242
  history 160
  lace 160, 239
  military 234, 238

natural history 244
puppet 206
science 158, 206
toys and games 205–206, 232
transport 98, **160**
wax 205
music, classical and opera **180–182**
Ars Musica 180
Children's Opera 205
church venues 181–182
Festival van Vlaanderen 254
opera venues 182
orchestras 180
Queen Elisabeth International Music Competition 30, 180
tickets 181
venues 181–182
music, rock, folk and jazz **184–188**
Audi Jazz Festival 32, 187
Brosella Jazz & Folk Festival 30
clubs 171–176
festivals 30, 187, 226
folk venues 188–189
Jazz Marathon 30, 187
jazz venues 187–188
out-of-town venues 188
rock groups 184
rock venues **184–186**

n

Namur 240
Namur (province) 59, 60, **240–241**, *241*
Napoleon 69, 71, 227, 230, 242
National Botanical Garden 225
National Day 31, 70
National Museum of Genever, Hasselt 233
NATO 82, 102
Neuve, rue 132
newspapers 168
foreign 265
Nivelles 227
Collégiale Sainte-Gertrude 227
Musée Communale 227
Notre Dame du Bon Secours 41
Notre Dame du Sablon *37*, 39, 52, 88–90
numbers 5

o

Océade 192, *205*, 207
Office de la Propriété Industrielle 201
offices:
equipment hire 203
opening times 7
Ommegang 30, *65*
Onze Lieve Vrouwe Cathedral, Antwerp *231*
Onze Lieve Vrouwekerk, Bruges 250
Open University 214
opening times 7, 33, 118, 156
opticians 152
Ostende 218–219
Oudenaarde 256

p

Paelsteenveld, Bredene 249
Palais des Beaux Arts 56, *56*, 88, 155, **163**, *164*, **181**, *197*, 198
Palais du Centenaire 47
Palais de Charles de Lorraine *39*, 40, 54
Palais des Congrès 88, 203
Palais d'Egmont 40
Palais de Justice 37–39, 55, 76, 90, *90*
Palais de la Nation 45, 54, 68, 88
Palais du Roi (Royal) 40, 68, 88
Open Days 31
Palais Stocklet *39*, 40, 98
De Panne 249
Parc Astrid 95
Parc de Bruxelles 48, 88
Parc du Cinquantenaire 33, **48–49**, *50*, 76, 97, 177, 205, 206
Parc Duden 49–50, 94
Parc de Forest 94
Parc à Gibier, La Roche-en-Ardennes 238
Parc Josaphat 50, 96
Parc de Laeken 50, 98
Parc Léopold 50, 97
Parc Paradiso 243, *245*
Parc de Tervuren 50, 206
Parc de Woluwe 50, 98, *192*, 206
Parc de Wolvendael 50
parking, airport 9
parks:
central **48–50**
for children 206
outside town 50
passports 259
Patent Office 201
pâtisseries 142
Paulusfeest 248
Pavillon Chinois 47
Petit Sablon, place du *37*, 39, 88
pharmacies 263
Philip II of Spain 63–65, 230, 254
photography, galleries 163–164
plague 60
Planétarium National 43
Plankendael Animal Park 206
Plantin-Moretus, Antwerp 231
playgrounds 206
Poelaert, Joseph 39, 42, 43
poison control centres 263
police 264
Porte de Hal 45
Poseidon 192, 208
post 60, 260
post offices 260
opening times 7
postcard shops 152
prison 94
Procession of the Holy Blood 30, 252
prostitution 231
Provincaal Museum voor Fotografie, Antwerp 165
Provincaal Museum voor Moderne Kunst (PMMK), Ostende 248
public holidays 5–7, 29
puppets 206

q

Queen Elisabeth International Music Competition 30, 180

r

racism 80–81
radio 169, 265
railways 9–10, 222
left luggage 261
lost property 264
Raising of the Maypole 31–32
rambling 191
rape and sexual violence 217, 220, 253
Rapides du Saty 239
Ravenstein, rue *87*
record shops 93, **148–151**
red-light district 92, 96
Redu 128
Reformation 63–64
Rekem 234
religion, conflicts 63–67, 68, 72–73, 230
religious services 264–265
Remouchamps, Grottes de 237
removals 204
Rencontres d'Octobre 198
residence card 259
Résidence Palace **47–48**, 56, 97
restaurants 98, **102–115**
in Antwerp 231–232
in Bruges 252
Caribbean 113
in Charleroi 242
for children 208
French and Belgian 102–106
gay and lesbian 211
in Ghent 254
Greek 112
in Hasselt 233
Indian 113
Italian 111
in Liège 235–237
Middle Eastern 112–113
in Mons 247
in Namur 240
in Rochefort 241
Russian and East European 111
South-East Asian 113
in Spa 237
Spanish 111
tipping 265
in Tournai 244
traditional 106–111
vegetarian 113–115
Rideau de Bruxelles 93
Rihoux, Meert, gallery 164
road system 81
Robbins, Tim 31
La Roche-en-Ardenne 238
Rochefort 241
Rollebeek, rue 90
rollerskating 192
Romans 59, 242
Royal Hothouses *29*, 30, *43*, 44, 55
Royal Quarter 52, **87–90**
Royale, place 68, 88
Rubens, Pieter Paul 66, 163
House, Antwerp *66*, 231
rugby 190, 192
running 30, 192

s

Sabine Wachters Fine Arts 164
Sablon/Zavel *37*, 39, 117, *117*
market 141
safety, women 217–218
St Bavon Cathedral, Ghent 164, 253, *255*
St Fiancre Chapel, Charleroi 242
St Géry, place 117
Saint Gilles 52, 54, 84, **93–94**
St Hubert 238
Saint Josse 84, **96**
Sainte Cathérine **86–87**
Sainte Cathérine, place *85*, 87, 102
Salle de la Madeleine 187
Salon des Beaux-Arts, Sint Niklaas 256
saunas 152
gay and lesbian 211–212
Schaerbeek 54–5, 84, **95–96**
Scherpenheuvel 226
schools, international 208
Schuman quarter 97
Schuman, Rond Point 102
Scientastic Museum 206, *207*
seasons 7
security 264
Senne, River 76
Serres Royales *29*, 30, *43*, 44, 55
sex shops 212
shoes:
repairers 152
shops 138
shops **132–152**
antiques 148
in Antwerp 132, **144–145**
arts and crafts 141–142
books 151, 216, 218, 238
children's 140, 208
collectibles 148

comics 151
crystal 148
department stores 134
entertaining 138
ethnic goods 152
fashion 134–138, 144
fashion accessories 138–140
flowers 141
gifts 140–141
health and beauty 144, 152
hobbies 141–142
home furnishings 147–148
interiors 145
jewellery and watches 144
leisure 145
magic 208
newsagents 151
opening times 7
in Ostende 248
pets' accessories 152
postcards 152
records 93, **148–151**
secondhand books 151
secondhand clothes 137–138
sex 212
shoes 138
shopping centres 87, 132–134
silverware 148
sporting goods 152
stationery 141
tailors 138
toys 140, 208
VAT 147
silverware, shops 148
Sint Niklaas 254–256
Sint-Michielskerk, Ghent 254
Sjacherbeurs, Antwerp 146
skateboarding 192
smoking 7
social clubs 263–264
social security 217, 259
Soignies 243–244
Solvay, Armand 55
Spa 237
Spanish Fury 64, 67
Spanish rule 62–64
speed limits 13
Speelgoed Museum (Mechelin) 232
sports **189–192**
for children 207–208
organisations 190
participating in 190–192
spectator 189–190
sports goods shops 152
squash courts 192
staff hire 204
Strauven, Gustave 56
street crime 7
street names 5
students **213–216**
accommodation 216
bookshops 216
exchanges 215–216
Styx, River 241
Suikkerock 226
support groups 263
swimming 192

t

tailors shops 138
Tapis des Fleurs 32
tattooists 152
taxis 11–13
airport 9
fares 171, 265
tipping 265
tearooms 126–128
Teleco 237
telecommunications 204
telephones 7, 260
emergency numbers 262
making calls 260
mobile 260–261
pagers 261
public 260, *260*
useful numbers 259
television 169–170, 206, 265
tennis 190, 192
Tervuren 98
Tervuren Arboretum (Forêt de Soignes) 50
Tervuren, avenue de 55, 98
theatre **193–196**
café-théâtre 196
for children 206
dance 196–198
English-language groups 196
listings 193
outside Brussels 195
puppet 206
Théâtre de la Balsamine 198
Théâtre 140 193
Théâtre Jean Vilar, Louvain-le-Neuve 195
Théâtre de la Monnaie 47, 52, *69*, 87, *181*, **182**, 198
Théâtre National 193
Théâtre de Poche 48, **195**
Théâtre Royal le Peruchet 206
Théâtre Royal du Parc 195
Théâtre de Toone 44, 193, 195, *195*, 206
Théâtre de Vaudeville 195
Thermes de Spa 237
TIB 4
tickets, public transport 11
Tienen 226
time 7
tipping 8, 265
toilets, public 264
Tongeren 233–234
Torgny 239
Tour Japonaise 48
Tour du Midi 56
tour organisers 50
tourist information 4
Tournai **244–245**
toy shops 140, 208
trams 10–11
lost property 264
Transinne 238–239
translators 204
transport **9–13**, 81
discount travel 3
public 10–11
tickets 11
travel passes 11
travel passes 11
TV Tower *170*

u

Uccle 52, 84
ULB (Université Libre de Bruxelles) 213, **214**
library 265
(De) Ultieme Hallucinatie 96
Union of Arras 64
Union of Utrecht 64
universities 68, 70, 72–3, 93, **213–214**
education system 213
Upper Town 84, **87–98**
shops 132
utilities 261

v

Van de Velde, Henri 55
Van der Weyden, Rogier 163
Van Eetvelde, Edmond 55
Van Eyck, Jan 163, 252
Van Ruysbroeck, Jan 37
Vandekeybus, Wim 196
VAT 147, 261, 265
Vesalius College 214
vets 265
Vielsalm 239
Vikings 230
visas 3
Viva Brazil 187
Vlaams Brabant 224–226
Vlaamse Opera 182, 198
vocabulary 8, 116
VUB (Vrije Universiteit Brussel) 213, **214**, 265

w

Walibi 44, 207, **227**
walking, tips 13
Wallonia 78
War of the Grand Alliance 67
War of Spanish Succession 67
water 8
water company 261
Waterloo **227**
Lion of Waterloo 227
Tourist Information Centre 4
Wellington Museum 227
Waterloo, boulevard de 132
Wavre 227
Wax Museum 205
weights and measures 7
Wellington Museum, Waterloo 227
Werchter, rock venue 188
Wiertz, Antoine 157, 163
William I 70
wines 118
women **217–220**
battered, support for 263
bookshops 218
centres 218–220
groups 218–220
health 220
helplines 220
lesbian cafés and bars 209–210
lesbian clubs 211
lesbian information 263
maternity benefits 217
private lesbian club 212
rights 217
safety 217–218
social clubs 263–264
woods 48–50
work:
employment agencies 204, 263
permits 259
World War I 76–77
World War II 77–78, 95
museums 238
Wouters, Rik 163

x

Xavier Hufkens gallery 164

y

youth hostels 28, 254
Ypres *see* Ieper
Ypres, boulevard d' 132

z

Zimmer, Joachim 48
Zoo, Antwerp 207

Advertisers' Index

Please refer to the relevant sections for addresses/telephone numbers

Amadeus **IFC**

Essential Information

W.H. Smith **2**
Eurolines **6**
Western Union **6**

Accommodation

New Continental Flat Hotel **16**
Hotel Galia **22**
Château du Lac **26**

Sightseeing

La Fonderie **46**

Eating & Drinking

Belgo **100**
Le Fils de Jules **108**
My-Tai **110**
La Sucrerie **114**

Shopping & Services

Tax Free Shopping **130**

Museums & Galleries

Royal Military History and Army Museum **154**
Royal Museum for Art and History **154**

Arts & Entertainment

Modern Painters **166**

Clubs

i-D **174**

Time Out
Film
Guide

Maps

Brussels	276
Street Index	284
Brussels Métro	285
Around Brussels	286
Trips Out of Town	287
Antwerp	288
Ghent	289
Bruges	290

Place of Interest and/or Entertainment . . .

Hospital or College . . . .

Pedestrianised Zone . . . .

Area Name . . . . LE SABLON

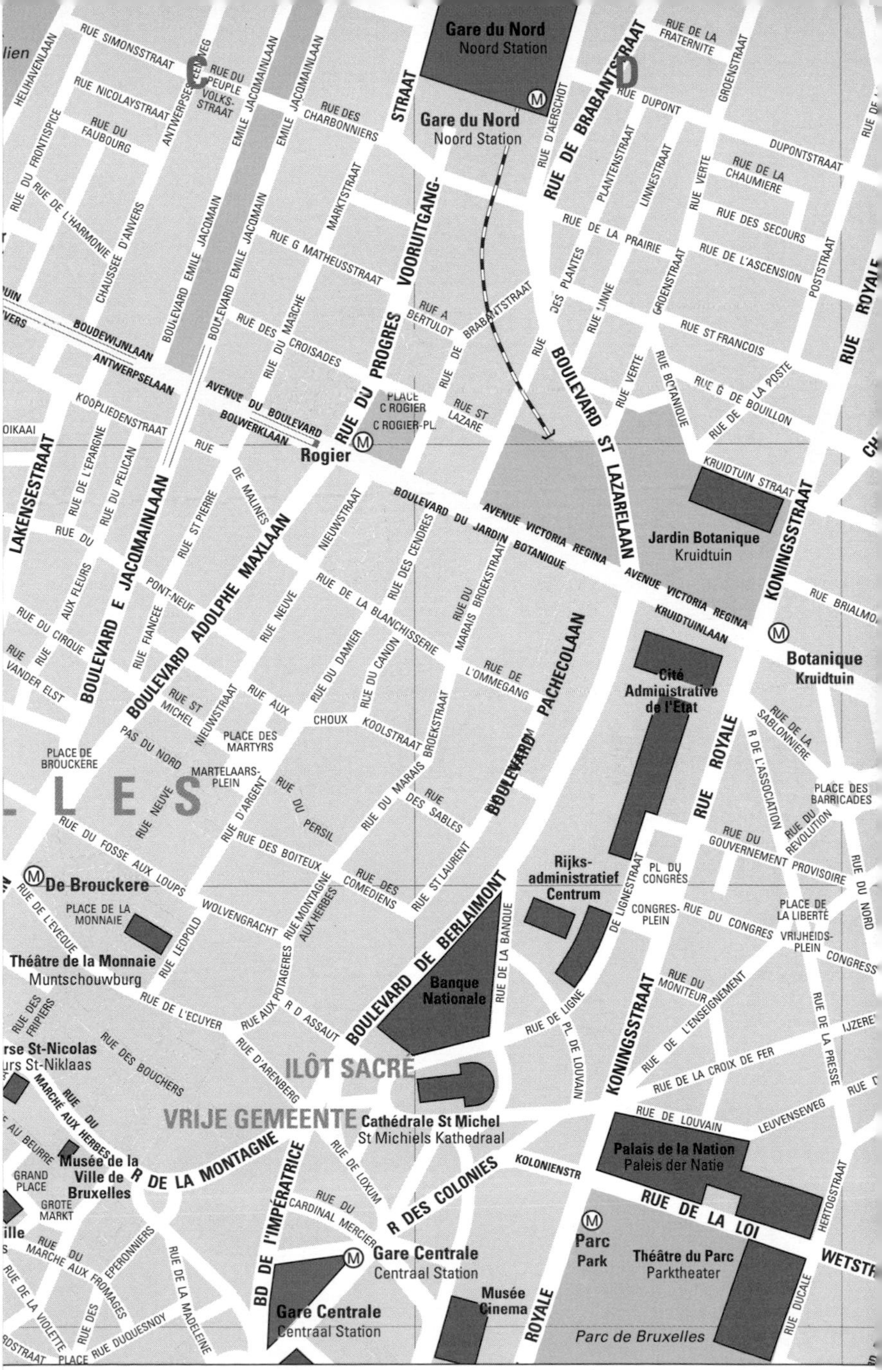

Railway Station ....

Métro Station .... Ⓜ

0 250 500 m

N

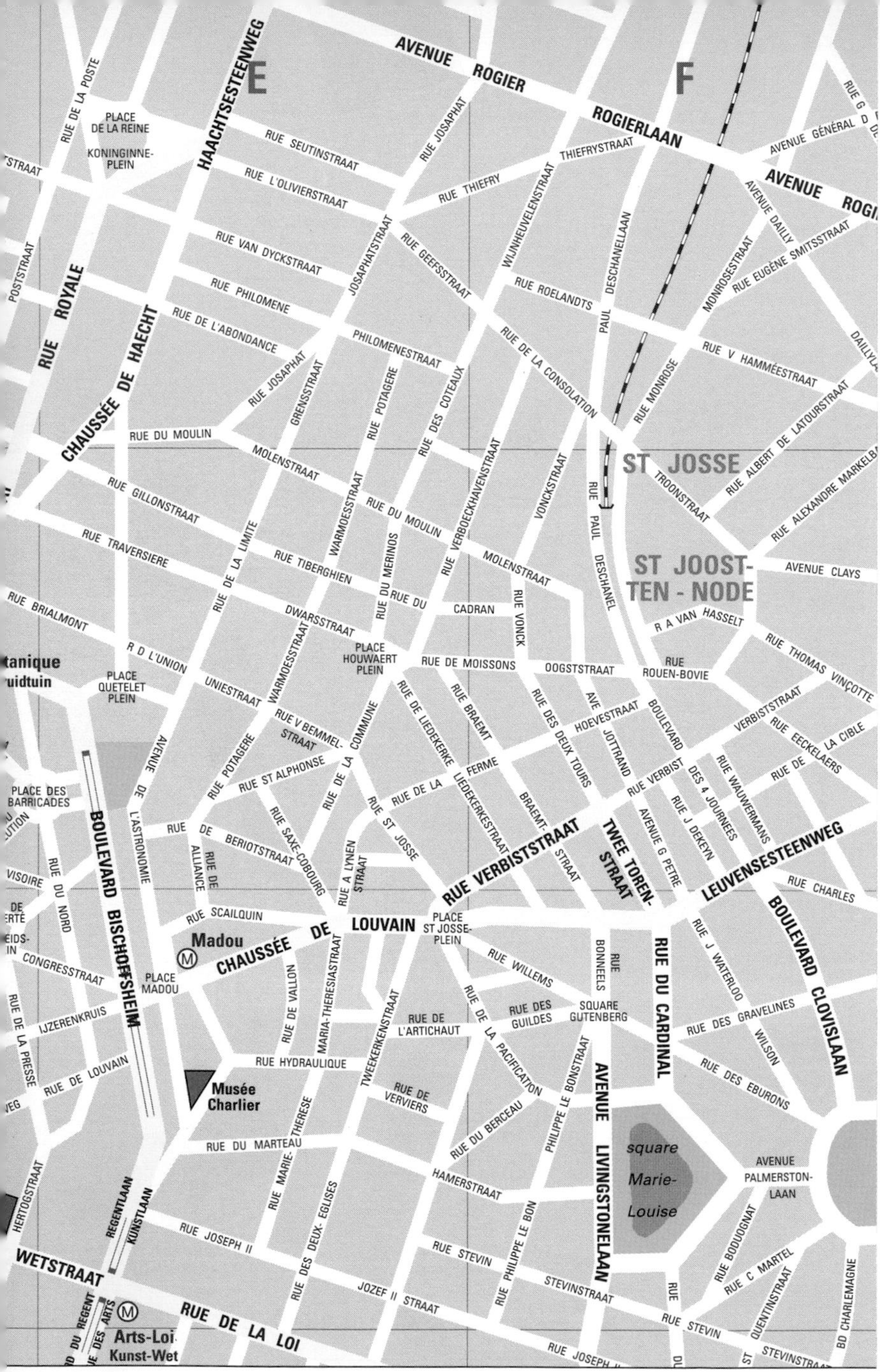

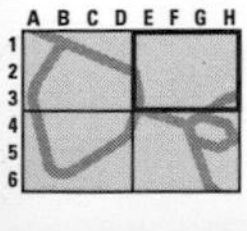

Place of Interest and/or Entertainment . . .

Hospital or College . . . .

Pedestrianised Zone . . . .

Area Name . . . . **LE SABLON**

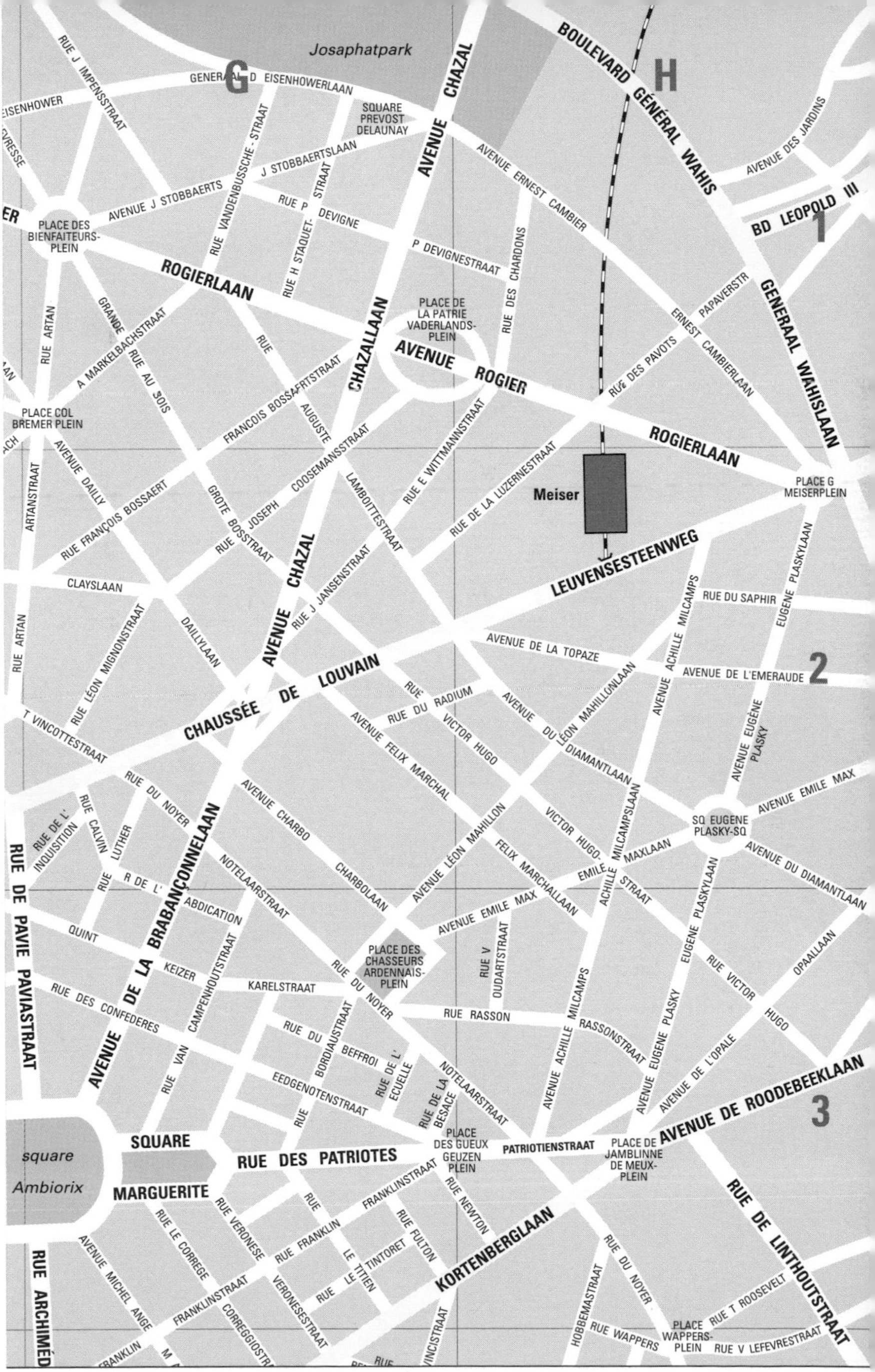

Railway Station ....

Métro Station .... Ⓜ

0 250 500 m

N

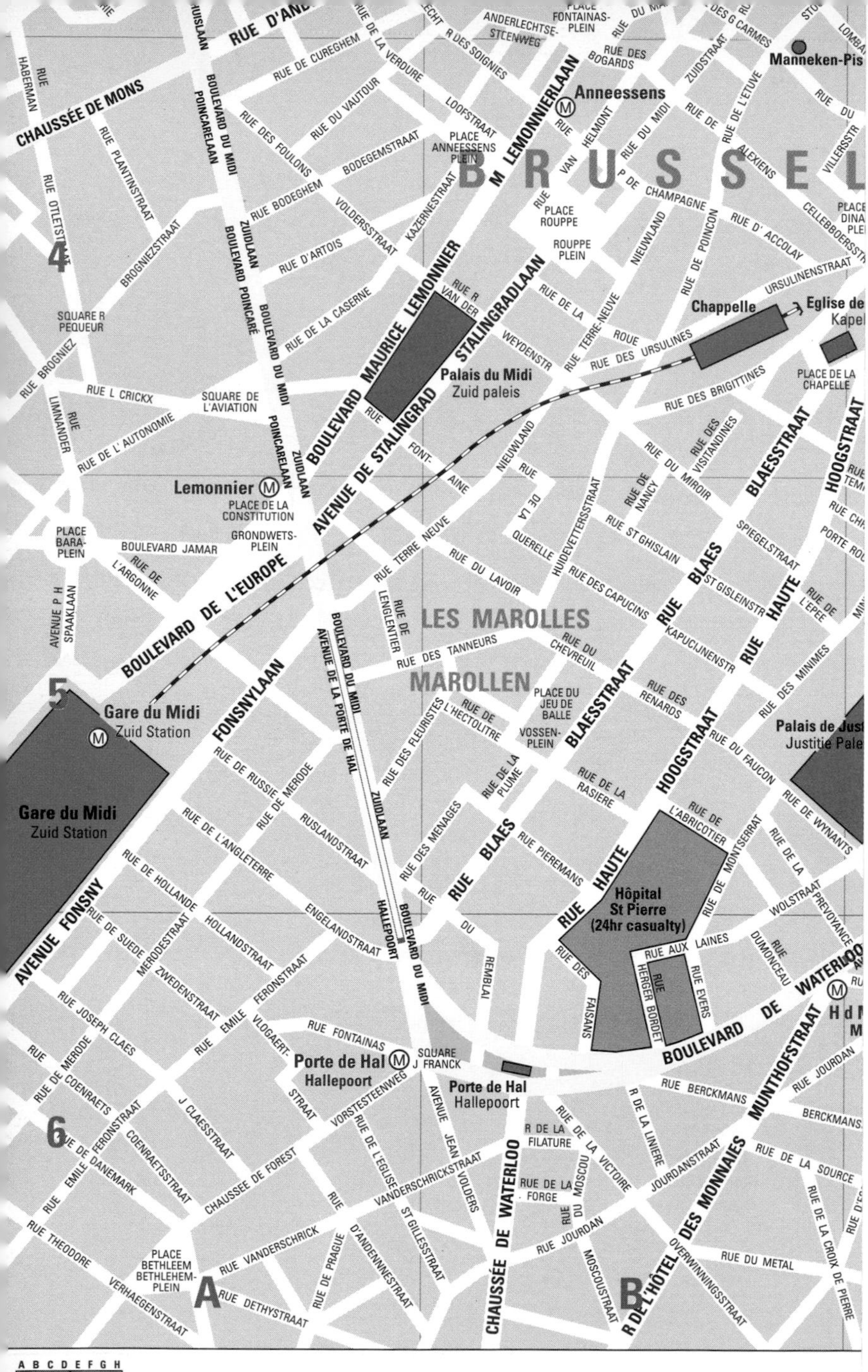

A B C D E F G H
1 2 3 4 5 6

Place of Interest and/or Entertainment . . .

Hospital or College . . . .

Pedestrianised Zone . . . .

Area Name . . . . LE SABLON

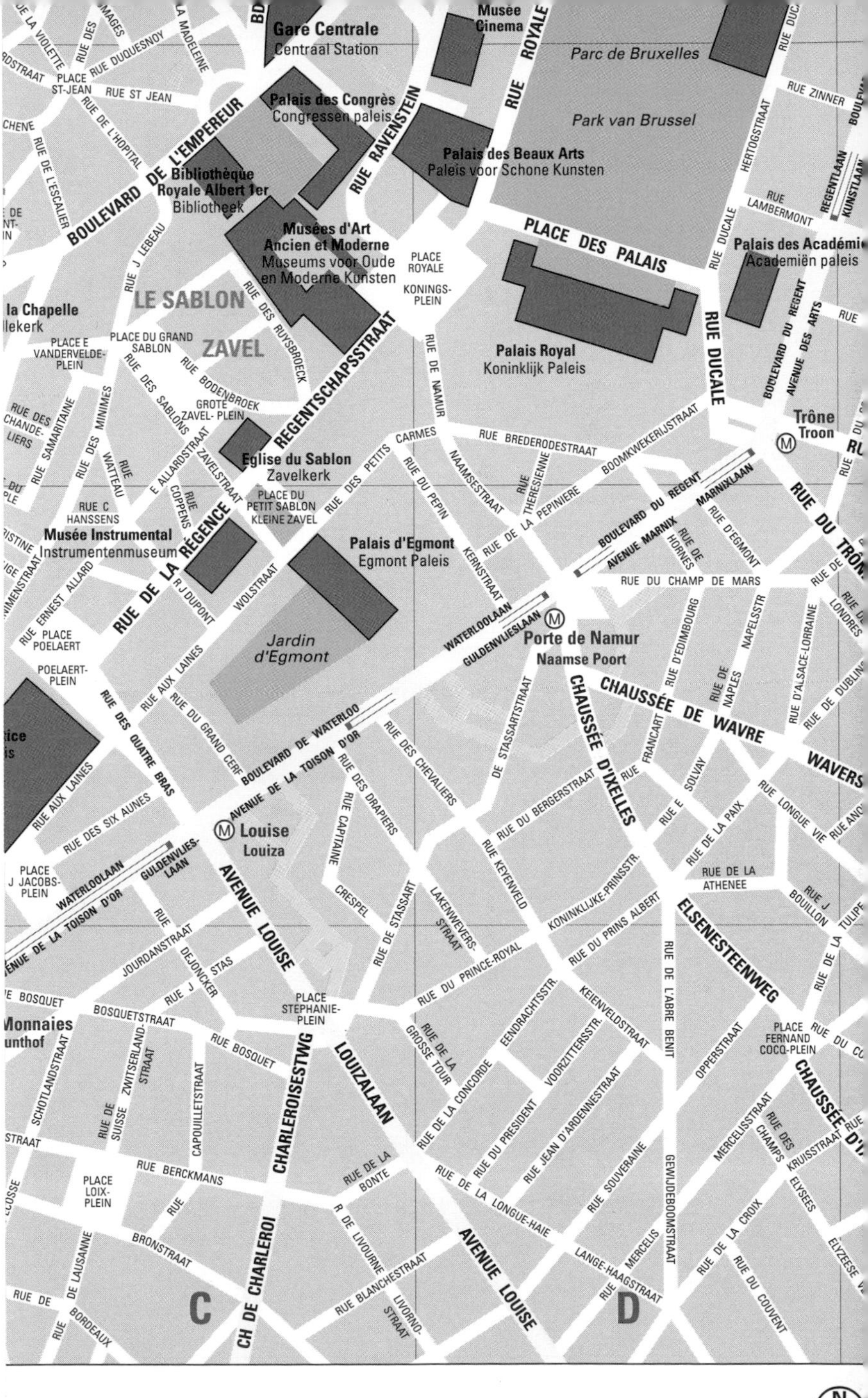

Railway Station

Métro Station Ⓜ

0 250 500 m

N

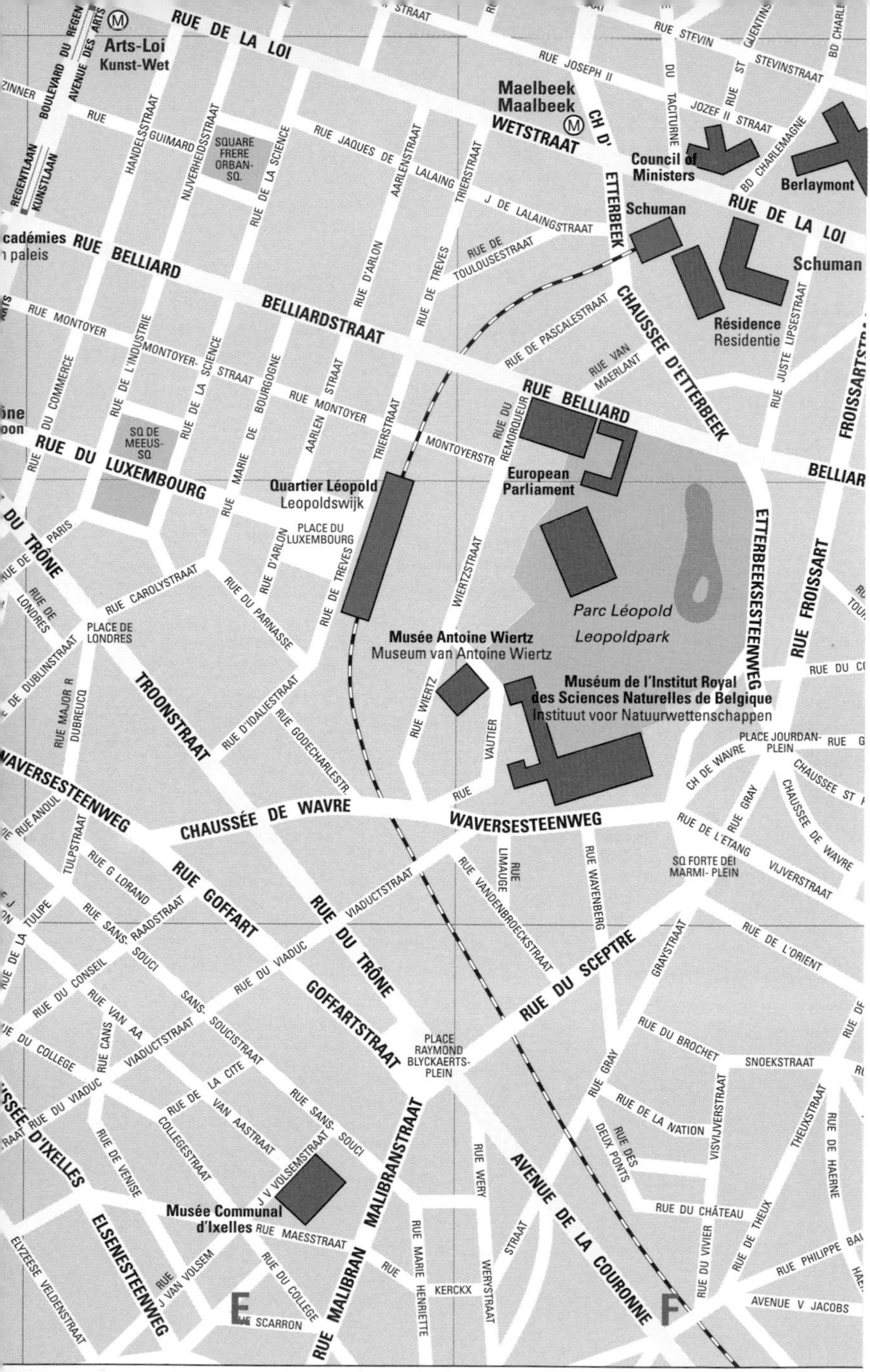

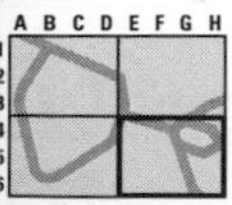

Place of Interest and/or Entertainment . . .

Hospital or College . . . .

Pedestrianised Zone . . . .

Area Name . . . . LE SABLON

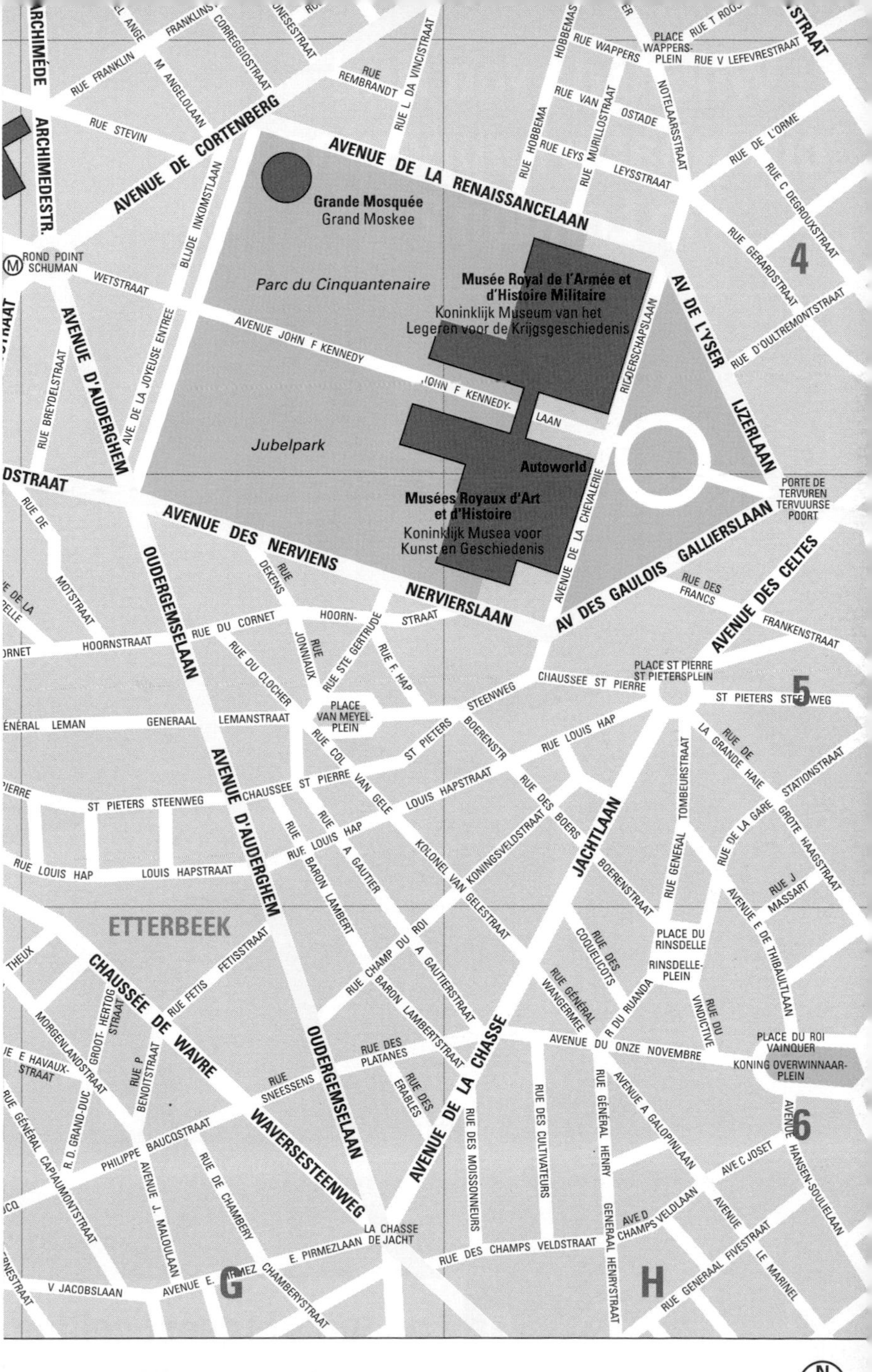

Railway Station ....

Métro Station .... Ⓜ

0 250 500 m

N

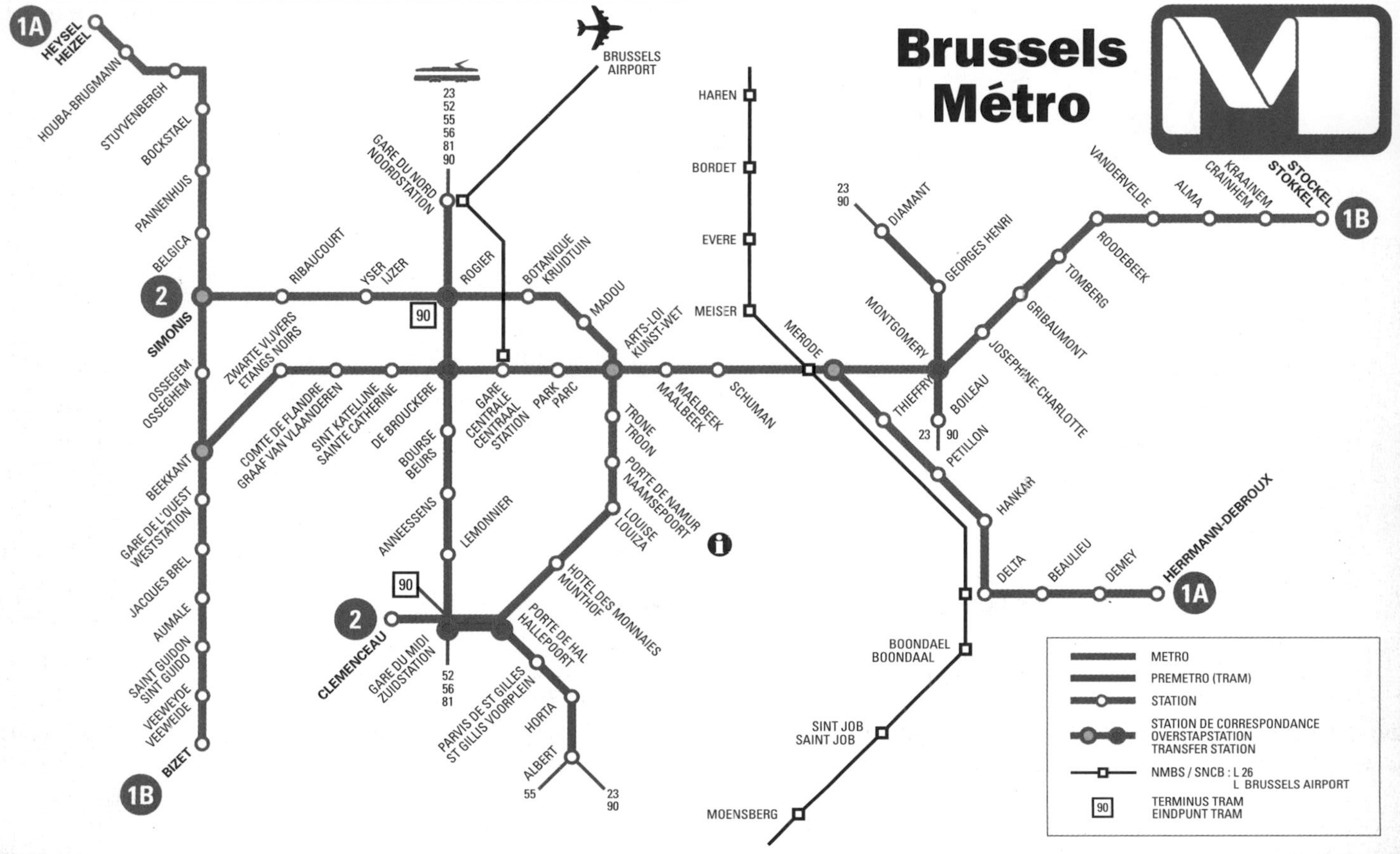

Brussels
Métro
1A
HEYSEL
HEIZEL
HOUBA-BRUGMANN
STUYVENBERGH
BOCKSTAEL
PANNENHUIS
BELGICA
2
SIMONIS
OSSEGEM
OSSEGHEM
BEEKKANT
GARE DE L'OUEST
WESTSTATION
JACQUES BREL
AUMALE
SAINT GUIDON
SINT GUIDO
VEEWEYDE
VEEWEIDE
BIZET
1B
RIBAUCOURT
YSER
IJZER
ZWARTE VIJVERS
ETANGS NOIRS
COMTE DE FLANDRE
GRAAF VAN VLAANDEREN
SINT KATELIJNE
SAINTE CATHERINE
DE BROUCKERE
GARE DU NORD
NOORDSTATION
23
52
55
56
81
90
BRUSSELS
AIRPORT
ROGIER
90
BOTANIQUE
KRUIDTUIN
MADOU
GARE
CENTRALE
CENTRAAL
STATION
PARK
PARC
ARTS-LOI
KUNST-WET
BOURSE
BEURS
ANNEESSENS
LEMONNIER
2
CLEMENCEAU
GARE DU MIDI
ZUIDSTATION
52
56
81
PARVIS DE ST GILLES
ST GILLIS VOORPLEIN
PORTE DE HAL
HALLEPOORT
HORTA
ALBERT
55
23
90
HOTEL DES MONNAIES
MUNTHOF
LOUISE
LOUIZA
PORTE DE NAMUR
NAAMSEPOORT
TRONE
TROON
MAELBEEK
MAALBEEK
SCHUMAN
HAREN
BORDET
EVERE
MEISER
MERODE
BOONDAEL
BOONDAAL
SINT JOB
SAINT JOB
MOENSBERG
23
90
DIAMANT
GEORGES HENRI
MONTGOMERY
THIEFFRY
BOILEAU
23
90
PETILLON
HANKAR
DELTA
BEAULIEU
DEMEY
HERRMANN-DEBROUX
1A
JOSEPHINE-CHARLOTTE
GRIBAUMONT
TOMBERG
ROODEBEEK
VANDERVELDE
ALMA
KRAAINEM
CRAINHEM
STOCKEL
STOKKEL
1B
METRO
PREMETRO (TRAM)
STATION
STATION DE CORRESPONDANCE
OVERSTAPSTATION
TRANSFER STATION
NMBS / SNCB : L 26
L BRUSSELS AIRPORT
90
TERMINUS TRAM
EINDPUNT TRAM

Around Brussels

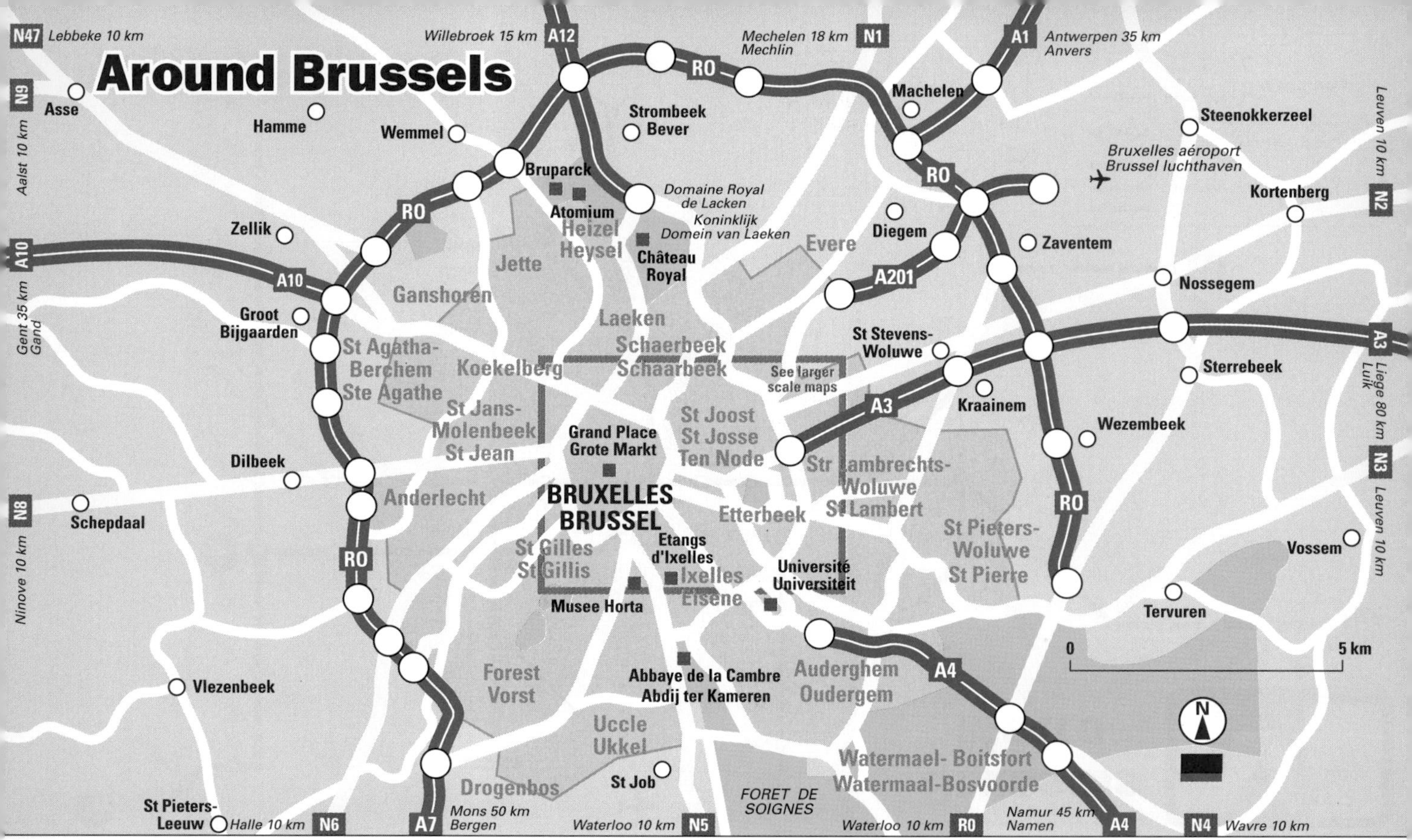

Trips Out of Town

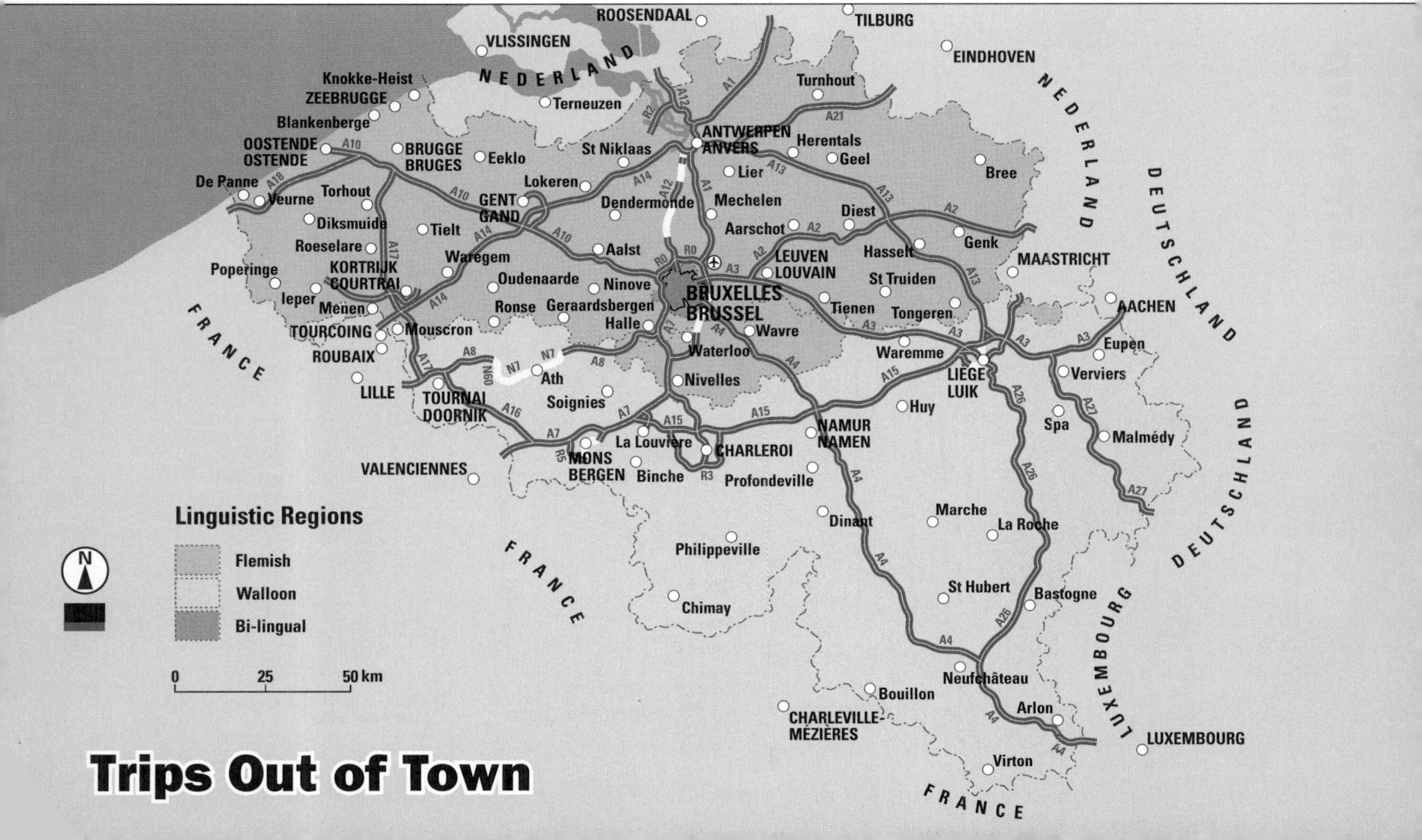

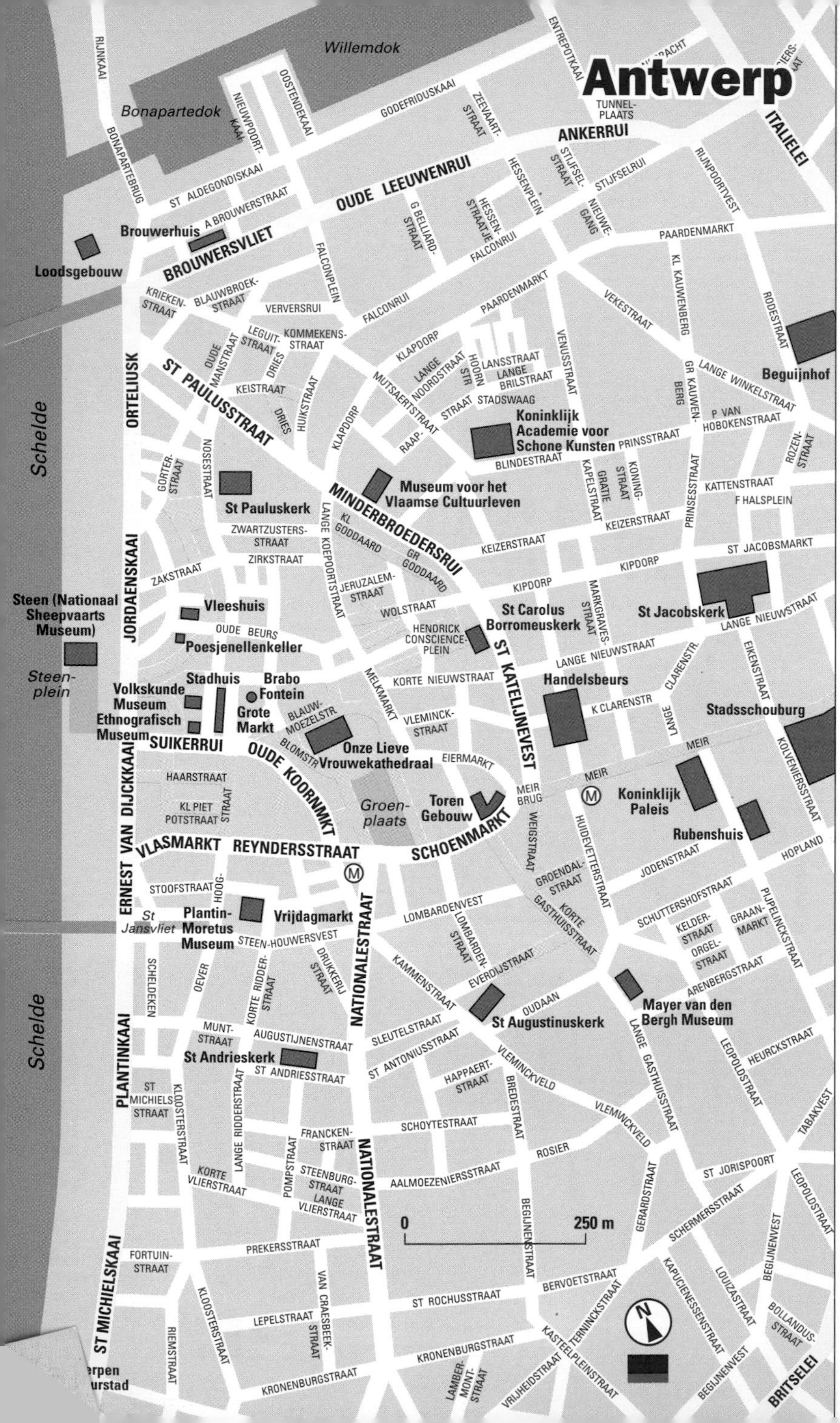
Antwerp
Willemdok
Bonapartedok
RIJNKAAI
BONAPARTEBRUG
NIEUWPOORT-KAAI
OOSTENDEKAAI
GODEFRIDUSKAAI
ZEEVAART-STRAAT
ENTREPOTKAAI
TUNNEL-PLAATS
ANKERRUI
ITALIELEI
ST ALDEGONDISKAAI
A BROUWERSTRAAT
OUDE LEEUWENRUI
G BELLIARD-STRAAT
HESSEN-STRAATJE
HESSENPLEIN
STIJFSEL-STRAAT
STIJFSELRUI
NIEUWE-GANG
RIJNPOORTVEST
PAARDENMARKT
Brouwerhuis
Loodsgebouw
BROUWERSVLIET
FALCONPLEIN
FALCONRUI
KRIEKEN-STRAAT
BLAUWBROEK-STRAAT
VERVERSRUI
KL KAUWENBERG
VEKESTRAAT
RODESTRAAT
Beguijnhof
LEGUIT-STRAAT
KOMMEKENS-STRAAT
OUDE MANSTRAAT
DRIES
KLAPDORP
LANGE NOORDSTRAAT
HOORN STR
LANSSTRAAT
LANGE BRILSTRAAT
VENUSSTRAAT
GR KAUWEN-BERG
LANGE WINKELSTRAAT
ORTELIUSK
ST PAULUSSTRAAT
KEISTRAAT
HUIKSTRAAT
MUTSAERTSTRAAT
STADSWAAG
Koninklijk Academie voor Schone Kunsten
P VAN HOBOKENSTRAAT
Schelde
NOSESTRAAT
GORTER-STRAAT
RAAP-STRAAT
BLINDESTRAAT
PRINSSTRAAT
ROZEN-STRAAT
St Pauluskerk
MINDERBROEDERSRUI
Museum voor het Vlaamse Cultuurleven
KAPELSTRAAT
GRATIE-STRAAT
KONING-STRAAT
PRINSESSTRAAT
KATTENSTRAAT
F HALSPLEIN
ZWARTZUSTERS-STRAAT
LANGE KOEPOORTSTRAAT
KL GODDAARD
GR GODDAARD
KEIZERSTRAAT
ST JACOBSMARKT
JORDAENSKAAI
ZIRKSTRAAT
ZAKSTRAAT
JERUZALEM-STRAAT
KIPDORP
MARKGRAVES-STRAAT
St Jacobskerk
Steen (Nationaal Sheepvaarts Museum)
Vleeshuis
WOLSTRAAT
St Carolus Borromeuskerk
LANGE NIEUWSTRAAT
OUDE BEURS
HENDRICK CONSCIENCE-PLEIN
Poesjenellenkeller
ST KATELIJNEVEST
Steen-plein
Stadhuis
Brabo Fontein
MELKMARKT
KORTE NIEUWSTRAAT
Handelsbeurs
CLARENSTR.
EIKENSTRAAT
Volkskunde Museum
Grote Markt
BLAUW-MOEZELSTR.
VLEMINCK-STRAAT
K CLARENSTR
LANGE
Stadsschouburg
Ethnografisch Museum
SUIKERRUI
BLOMSTR
Onze Lieve Vrouwekathedraal
EIERMARKT
MEIR
KOLVENIERSSTRAAT
OUDE KOORNMKT
HAARSTRAAT
KL PIET POTSTRAAT
STRAAT
Groen-plaats
Toren Gebouw
MEIR BRUG
Koninklijk Paleis
Rubenshuis
ERNEST VAN DIJCKKAAI
VLASMARKT
REYNDERSSTRAAT
SCHOENMARKT
WEIGSTRAAT
HUIDEVETTERSSTRAAT
HOPLAND
JODENSTRAAT
STOOFSTRAAT
HOOG-
Plantin-Moretus Museum
Vrijdagmarkt
GROENDAL-STRAAT
KORTE GASTHUISSTRAAT
SCHUTTERSHOFSTRAAT
KELDER-STRAAT
GRAAN-MARKT
ORGEL-STRAAT
PIJPELINCKSTRAAT
St Jansvliet
LOMBARDENVEST
LOMBARDEN-STRAAT
STEEN-HOUWERSVEST
NATIONALESTRAAT
SCHELDEKEN
OEVER
KORTE RIDDER-STRAAT
DRUKKERIJ-STRAAT
KAMMENSTRAAT
EVERDIJSTRAAT
ARENBERGSTRAAT
OUDAAN
Mayer van den Bergh Museum
St Augustinuskerk
PLANTINKAAI
MUNT-STRAAT
AUGUSTIJNENSTRAAT
SLEUTELSTRAAT
ST ANTONIUSSTRAAT
LANGE GASTHUISSTRAAT
LEOPOLDSTRAAT
HEURCKSTRAAT
St Andrieskerk
ST ANDRIESSTRAAT
HAPPAERT-STRAAT
VLEMINCKVELD
BREDESTRAAT
ST MICHIELS STRAAT
KLOOSTERSTRAAT
LANGE RIDDERSTRAAT
FRANCKEN-STRAAT
SCHOYTESTRAAT
TABAKVEST
ROSIER
KORTE VLIERSTRAAT
POMPSTRAAT
STEENBURG-STRAAT
LANGE VLIERSTRAAT
AALMOEZENIERSSTRAAT
GERARDSTRAAT
ST JORISPOORT
0
250 m
SCHERMERSSTRAAT
BEGIJNENSTRAAT
ST MICHIELSKAAI
FORTUIN-STRAAT
PREKERSSTRAAT
VAN CRAESBEEK-STRAAT
BERVOETSTRAAT
KAPUCIENESSENSTRAAT
LOUIZASTRAAT
BEGIJNENVEST
ST ROCHUSSTRAAT
TERNINCKSTRAAT
N
KLOOSTERSTRAAT
RIEMSTRAAT
LEPELSTRAAT
BOLLANDUS-STRAAT
KRONENBURGSTRAAT
KASTEELPLEINSTRAAT
LAMBER-MONT-STRAAT
VRIJHEIDSTRAAT
BRITSELEI
erpen
urstad

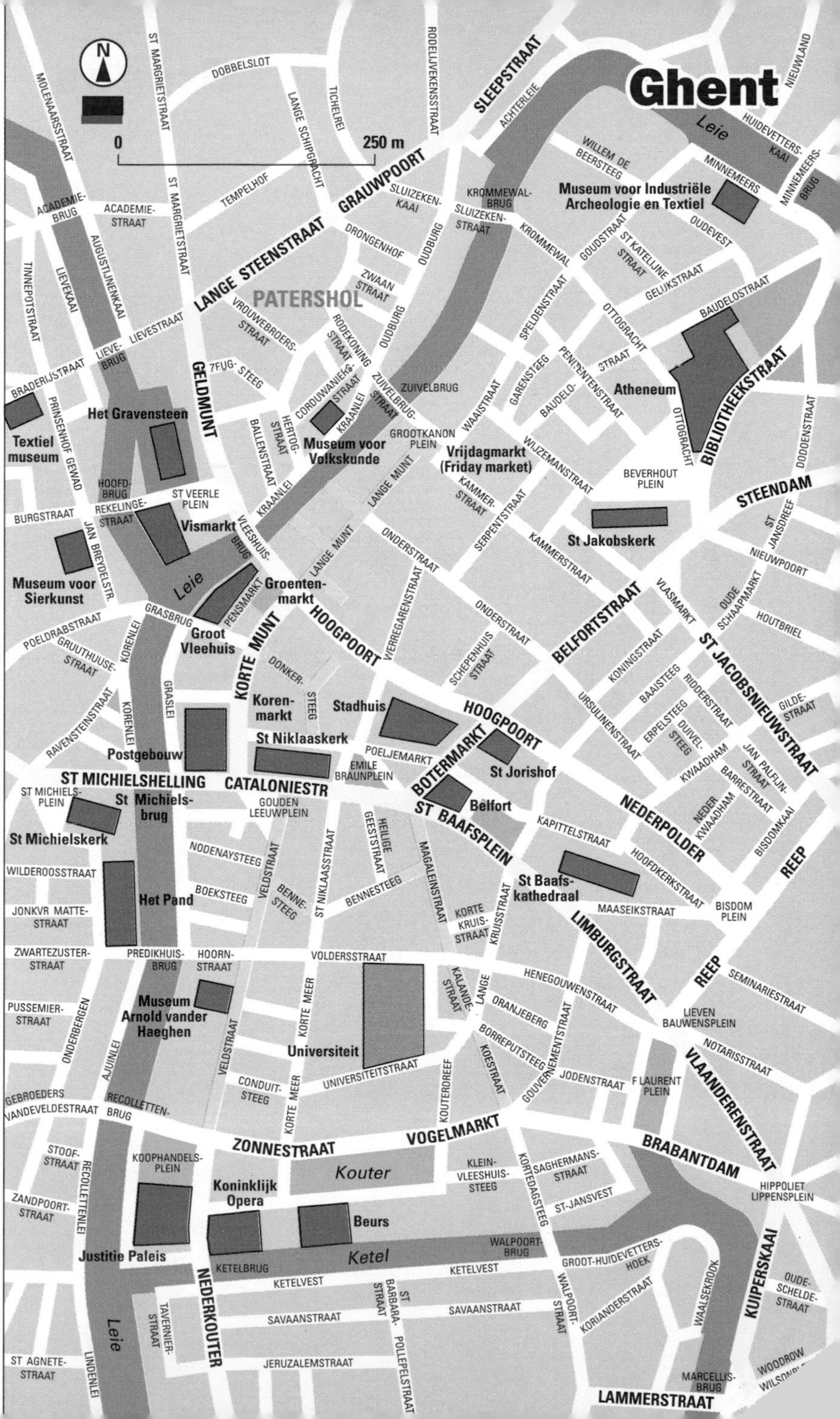

Ghent
N
0
250 m
Leie
Ketel
Kouter
PATERSHOL
Museum voor Industriële Archeologie en Textiel
Atheneum
Het Gravensteen
Textiel museum
Museum voor Volkskunde
Vrijdagmarkt (Friday market)
Vismarkt
Museum voor Sierkunst
Groot Vleehuis
Groentenmarkt
Korenmarkt
Stadhuis
St Niklaaskerk
Postgebouw
St Jorishof
Belfort
St Jakobskerk
St Michielskerk
St Michielsbrug
Het Pand
St Baafskathedraal
Museum Arnold vander Haeghen
Universiteit
Koninklijk Opera
Beurs
Justitie Paleis
SLEEPSTRAAT
GRAUWPOORT
LANGE STEENSTRAAT
GELDMUNT
KORTE MUNT
HOOGPOORT
BELFORTSTRAAT
ST JACOBSNIEUWSTRAAT
BIBLIOTHEEKSTRAAT
STEENDAM
NEDERPOLDER
BOTERMARKT
ST BAAFSPLEIN
ST MICHIELSHELLING
CATALONIESTR
LIMBURGSTRAAT
REEP
VLAANDERENSTRAAT
BRABANTDAM
ZONNESTRAAT
VOGELMARKT
NEDERKOUTER
KUIPERSKAAI
LAMMERSTRAAT
MOLENAARSSTRAAT
ST MARGRIETSTRAAT
DOBBELSLOT
LANGE SCHIPGRACHT
TICHELREI
RODELIJVEKENSSTRAAT
ACHTERLEIE
NIEUWLAND
HUIDEVETTERS-KAAI
MINNEMEERS
MINNEMEERS-BRUG
WILLEM DE BEERSTEEG
ACADEMIE-BRUG
ACADEMIE-STRAAT
TEMPELHOF
SLUIZEKEN-KAAI
KROMMEWAL-BRUG
SLUIZEKEN-STRAAT
KROMMEWAL
GOUDSTRAAT
ST KATELIJNE STRAAT
OUDEVEST
GELIJKSTRAAT
BAUDELOSTRAAT
OTTOGRACHT
DRONGENHOF
ZWAAN STRAAT
OUDBURG
AUGUSTIJNENKAAI
LIEVEKAAI
TINNEPOTSTRAAT
LIEVESTRAAT
LIEVE-BRUG
VROUWEBROERS-STRAAT
RODEKONING STRAAT
SPELDENSTRAAT
PENITENTENSTRAAT
GARENSTEEG
BRADERIJSTRAAT
ZUIVELBRUG
ZUIVELBRUG-STRAAT
CORDUWANIERS-STRAAT
KRAANLEI
WAAISTRAAT
BAUDELO-STRAAT
PRINSENHOF
GEWAD
HERTOG-STRAAT
BALLENSTRAAT
GROOTKANON PLEIN
WIJZEMANSTRAAT
OTTOGRACHT
DODOENSTRAAT
HOOFD-BRUG
ST VEERLE PLEIN
REKELINGE-STRAAT
BURGSTRAAT
LANGE MUNT
KAMMER-STRAAT
BEVERHOUT PLEIN
JAN BREYDELSTR.
VLEESHUIS-BRUG
ONDERSTRAAT
SERPENTSTRAAT
KAMMERSTRAAT
ST JANSDREEF
NIEUWPOORT
PENSMARKT
GRASBRUG
VLASMARKT
OUDE SCHAAPMARKT
HOUTBRIEL
POELDRABSTRAAT
GRUUTHUUSE-STRAAT
KORENLEI
VERREGARENSTRAAT
SCHEPENHUIS STRAAT
KONINGSTRAAT
DONKER-STEEG
GRASLEI
BAAISTEEG
RIDDERSTRAAT
URSULINENSTRAAT
ERPELSTEEG
DUIVEL-STEEG
GILDE-STRAAT
RAVENSTEINSTRAAT
POELJEMARKT
EMILE BRAUNPLEIN
KWAADHAM
JAN PALFIJN-STRAAT
BARRESTRAAT
ST MICHIELS-PLEIN
GOUDEN LEEUWPLEIN
KAPITTELSTRAAT
NEDER KWAADHAM
BISDOMKAAI
NODENAYSTEEG
HEILIGE GEESTSTRAAT
MAGALEINSTRAAT
HOOFDKERKSTRAAT
WILDEROOSSTRAAT
VELDSTRAAT
BOEKSTEEG
BENNE-STEEG
BENNESTEEG
ST NIKLAASSTRAAT
KRUISSTRAAT
MAASEIKSTRAAT
BISDOM PLEIN
JONKVR MATTE-STRAAT
KORTE KRUIS-STRAAT
ZWARTEZUSTER-STRAAT
PREDIKHUIS-BRUG
HOORN-STRAAT
VOLDERSSTRAAT
KALANDE-STRAAT
LANGE
HENEGOUWENSTRAAT
SEMINARIESTRAAT
PUSSEMIER-STRAAT
ONDERBERGEN
KORTE MEER
ORANJEBERG
LIEVEN BAUWENSPLEIN
BORREPUTSTEEG
GOUVERNEMENTSTRAAT
NOTARISSTRAAT
AJUINLEI
KOESTRAAT
JODENSTRAAT
F LAURENT PLEIN
UNIVERSITEITSTRAAT
CONDUIT-STEEG
KOUTERDREEF
GEBROEDERS VANDEVELDESTRAAT
RECOLLETTEN-BRUG
STOOF-STRAAT
RECOLLETTENLEI
KOOPHANDELS-PLEIN
KLEIN-VLEESHUIS-STEEG
SAGHERMANS-STRAAT
KORTEDAGSTEEG
HIPPOLIET LIPPENSPLEIN
ZANDPOORT-STRAAT
ST-JANSVEST
WALPOORT-BRUG
GROOT-HUIDEVETTERS-HOEK
KETELBRUG
KETELVEST
ST BARBARA-STRAAT
OUDE-SCHELDE-STRAAT
TAVERNIER-STRAAT
SAVAANSTRAAT
WALPOORT-STRAAT
KORIANDERSTRAAT
WAALSEKROOK
ST AGNETE-STRAAT
LINDENLEI
JERUZALEMSTRAAT
POLLEPELSTRAAT
MARCELLIS-BRUG
WOODROW WILSONPL

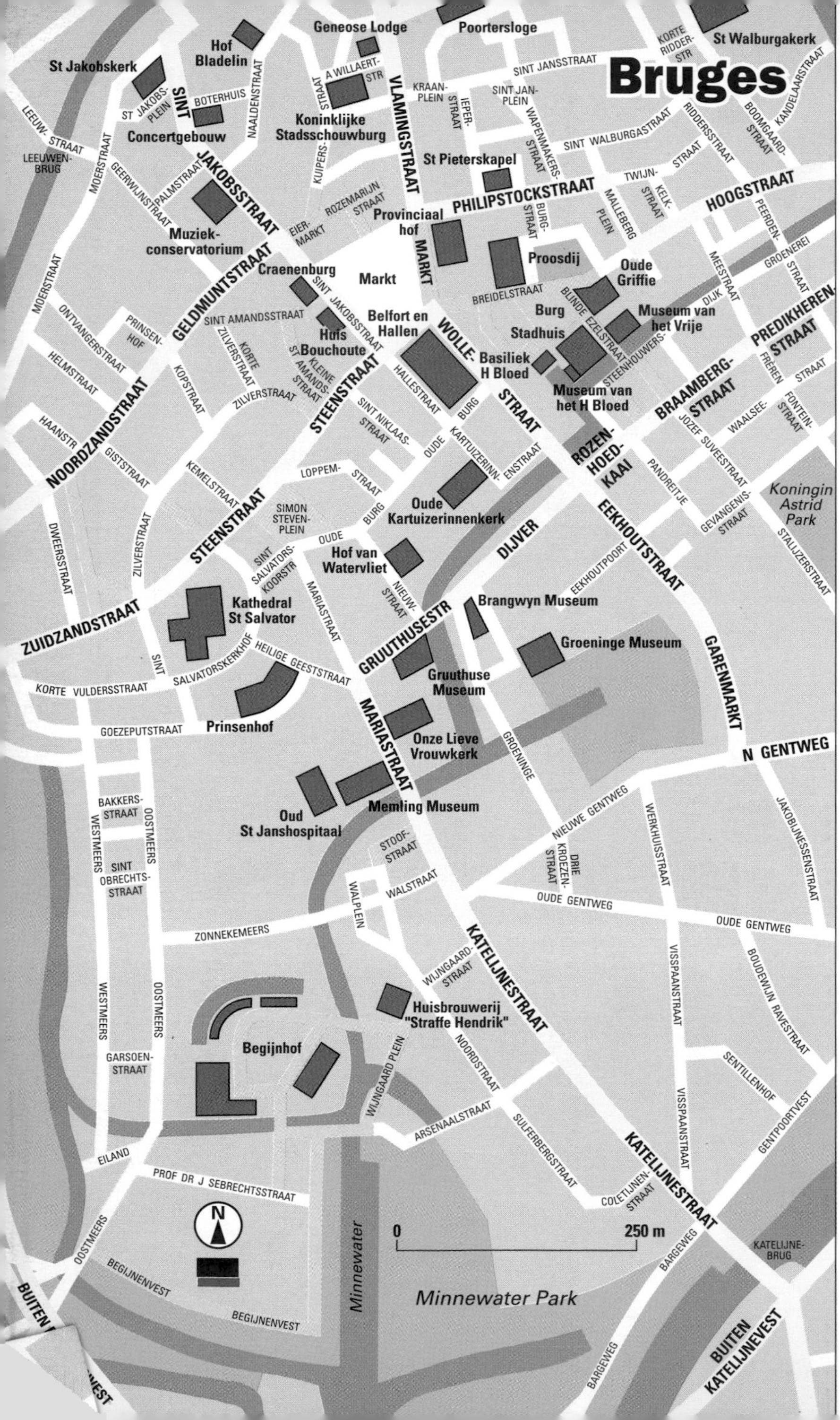

Bruges
St Jakobskerk
Hof Bladelin
Geneose Lodge
Poortersloge
St Walburgakerk
Koninklijke Stadsschouwburg
Concertgebouw
St Pieterskapel
Muziek-conservatorium
Provinciaal hof
Markt
Proosdij
Oude Griffie
Craenenburg
Belfort en Hallen
Burg
Museum van het Vrije
Huis Bouchoute
Stadhuis
Basiliek H Bloed
Museum van het H Bloed
Oude Kartuizerinnenkerk
Hof van Watervliet
Koningin Astrid Park
Kathedral St Salvator
Brangwyn Museum
Groeninge Museum
Gruuthuse Museum
Prinsenhof
Onze Lieve Vrouwkerk
Memling Museum
Oud St Janshospitaal
Huisbrouwerij "Straffe Hendrik"
Begijnhof
Minnewater
Minnewater Park
0
250 m
N
VLAMINGSTRAAT
PHILIPSTOCKSTRAAT
HOOGSTRAAT
JAKOBSSTRAAT
GELDMUNTSTRAAT
NOORDZANDSTRAAT
STEENSTRAAT
ZUIDZANDSTRAAT
WOLLESTRAAT
ROZENHOEDKAAI
EEKHOUTSTRAAT
DIJVER
GRUUTHUSESTR
MARIASTRAAT
GARENMARKT
N GENTWEG
KATELIJNESTRAAT
BRAAMBERGSTRAAT
PREDIKHERENSTRAAT
BUITEN KATELIJNEVEST
SINT JANSSTRAAT
SINT WALBURGASTRAAT
OUDE GENTWEG
NIEUWE GENTWEG
ZONNEKEMEERS
WESTMEERS
OOSTMEERS
GOEZEPUTSTRAAT
KORTE VULDERSSTRAAT
HEILIGE GEESTSTRAAT
BEGIJNENVEST
PROF DR J SEBRECHTSSTRAAT
ARSENAALSTRAAT
WIJNGAARD PLEIN
NOORDSTRAAT
SULFERBERGSTRAAT
COLETIJNENSTRAAT
BARGEWEG
KATELIJNEBRUG
VISSPAANSTRAAT
WERKHUISSTRAAT
JAKOBIJNESSENSTRAAT
BOUDEWIJN RAVESTRAAT
GENTPOORTVEST
SENTILLENHOF
STALIJZERSTRAAT
GROENINGE
WALSTRAAT
WALPLEIN
STOOFSTRAAT
LEEUWSTRAAT
LEEUWENBRUG
MOERSTRAAT
GEERWIJNSTRAAT
PALMSTRAAT
ONTVANGERSTRAAT
HELMSTRAAT
HAANSTR
GISTSTRAAT
KEMELSTRAAT
ZILVERSTRAAT
DWEERSSTRAAT
KOPSTRAAT
SINT AMANDSSTRAAT
LOPPEMSTRAAT
HALLESTRAAT
SINT NIKLAASSTRAAT
BREIDELSTRAAT
BLINDE EZELSTRAAT
STEENHOUWERSDIJK
MEESTRAAT
GROENEREI
PEERDENSTRAAT
WAALSESTRAAT
JOZEF SUVEESTRAAT
PANDREITJE
GEVANGENISSTRAAT
EEKHOUTPOORT
EILAND